A Resource Guide for Elementary School Teaching

Planning for Competence

THIRD EDITION

Richard D. Kellough
Patricia L. Roberts

California State University, Sacramento

MACMILLAN COLLEGE PUBLISHING COMPANY
NEW YORK

MAXWELL MACMILLAN CANADA
TORONTO

MAXWELL MACMILLAN INTERNATIONAL
NEW YORK   OXFORD   SINGAPORE   SYDNEY

Editor: Debbie Stollenwerk
Production Supervisor: Betsy Keefer
Production Manager: Francesca Drago
Text Designer: Jane Edelstein
Cover Designer: Viqui Maggio

Photograph on page 1 by Richard D. Kellough; all other photographs by Warren Hyde.

This book was set in 11/13 New Baskerville by Compset, Inc., and printed and bound by Semline. The cover was printed by Phoenix Color Corporation.

Macmillan College Publishing Company
866 Third Avenue, New York, New York 10022

Macmillan College Publishing Company is part of the Maxwell Communication Group of Companies.

Maxwell Macmillan Canada, Inc.
1200 Eglinton Avenue East
Suite 200
Don Mills, Ontario M3C 3N1

Library of Congress Cataloging-in-Publication Data

Kellough, Richard D. (Richard Dean)
    A resource guide for elementary school teaching : planning for
competence / Richard D. Kellough, Patricia L. Roberts.—3rd ed.
        p.   cm.
    Includes bibliographical references (p.) and index.
    ISBN 0–02–362581–3
    1. Elementary school teaching.   2. Competency based education.
I. Roberts, Patricia, 1936–   II. Title.
LB1555.K39   1994
372.11′02—dc20   93-28071
                                                  CIP

Printing: 1 2 3 4 5 6 7   Year: 4 5 6 7 8 9 0

Preface

The ascendancy of cognitive learning theory and its view of intelligence, of the constructivist approach to conceptual understanding, of the use of social-interactive learning as an important instructional practice; the revival of interest in discovery and inquiry learning and the concomitant involvement of children in metacognition and problem solving; a national economic depression accompanied by severe cutbacks in schools' budgets; developments in the reorganization and restructuring of schools; and continuing activities regarding student differences and diversity have prompted us to make major changes for this third edition of our resource guide. From a sound research base, revisions have been accurately infused throughout: In essence, the resource guide has been reorganized and rewritten. We continue in our desire to provide a resource guide that is as current, accurate, comprehensive, and practical as possible for college and university students who are in the process of becoming competent elementary school teachers.

In preparation for this resource guide, we saw our task not as that of making the teaching job easier for you—competent teaching is never easy—but as that of improving your competencies and providing resources from which you may select and build upon what works best for you. Your greatest resource is people, the children and adults with whom you work. We cannot tell you what will always succeed best with your students; you will know them better than we do. We are sharing what we believe to be the best of practice, the most useful of research findings, and the richest of experiences. Here is what we believe and how we have incorporated our beliefs into the third edition of this resource guide.

We continue in our belief that learning should be active, pleasant, fun, and productive. Consequently, with each edition of this resource guide, we have been persistent in our effort to prepare it in a positive, enthusiastic, and cognitive-humanistic way that is helpful to its users.

We believe teaching competencies can be learned. As in medicine, where there are skills and knowledge to be learned and developed before the student physician is licensed to practice with live patients; as in law, where there are knowledge and skills to be learned and developed before the law student is licensed to practice in an actual legal case; so it is in teacher education: *There are knowledge and skills to be learned and developed before the teacher candidate is licensed to practice the art and skills of teaching with active, responsive learners.* We would never consider allowing a person "off the street" to treat our own child's illness or to defend us in a legal case; the professional education of teachers is no less important! Receiving professional education in how to teach is absolutely necessary, and certain aspects of that education *must* precede any interaction with alert, lively children if teachers are to become truly competent professionals.

We believe there are developmental elements involved in becoming a competent, professional

iii

elementary school teacher. This resource guide is organized around four developmental elements: *what, why, how,* and *how well.* For each of those four developmental elements this edition of our resource guide now is divided into four parts.

Part I: Orientation to Elementary School Teaching and Learning

For this third edition, the four chapters of Part I have been rewritten to reflect the reality of elementary school teaching today. For example, Chapter 1 describes the characteristics of the various schools that come under the heading of "elementary school" and ways those schools are organized. Chapter 1 has been expanded with information about the differences and diversity among today's elementary school students and guidelines for teaching to that diversity. We conclude Chapter 1 with a presentation of critical issues and problems facing schools today in this final decade of the twentieth century.

Because of developments in cognitive learning theory, an emphasis on discovery learning, and teaching for and about thinking, we follow in Chapter 2 with relevant information about how children learn, think, and develop intellectually.

Chapter 3 has been reorganized and rewritten to reflect accurately the expectations and responsibilities of today's elementary school classroom teacher, and the teacher behaviors necessary to facilitate student learning.

Because the teacher must have the students' attention before he or she can effectively instruct, Chapter 4 concludes Part I with a presentation of guidelines for establishing and maintaining classroom procedures and an effective and safe classroom learning environment. Historically, authors of methods books have treated those topics *after* teacher candidates have learned how to prepare lessons and units. We are not sure why this has been so, because, for more than 2,000 years, it has been well known that student attention is a *prerequisite* to efficient learning. Indeed, there are programs of teacher preparation that cover those topics *after* their teacher candidates are already in the classroom trying to teach children. From our work with student teachers, we are convinced, as are our reviewers, that topics related to the establishment and maintenance of an effective and safe classroom learning environment should come early in the candidate's training, *before* learning how to prepare lessons and, most certainly, before they are given responsibility for teaching children.

Throughout Part I, users of previous editions of the resource guide will find much updated information and many new, relevant, and interesting exercises.

Part II: Planning for Instruction in an Elementary Classroom

Chapters 5 (rationale for planning and how to select content) and 6 (instructional objectives) have been updated and rewritten for clarity. For example, Chapter 5 now contains information about the status of the development of **national curriculum standards** in each area of the elementary school curriculum. The chapter on instructional planning (Chapter 7) includes a section on the planning of interdisciplinary thematic units. Sample units and lessons, in Chapters 7 and 8, have been updated, as have the guidelines for preparing daily lessons (Chapter 8).

Part III: Choosing and Implementing Instructional Strategies, Aids, and Resources

We continue in our belief that the *how* component of professional teacher preparation is essential to becoming a competent teacher. The *how* component continues to be reflected in a major portion of this resource guide, especially in Part III. Although it remains difficult to anticipate the twenty-first century, particularly to predict what specifically children of today will need to know when they are in the work force of that century, we do believe that they will need to know how to learn, how to read, how to reason and think critically, how to work cooperatively with others, and how to enjoy doing these things.

We continue to be adamant in our belief that elementary school children need to develop skills in acquiring knowledge, in processing information, and in learning experiences that will utilize their fullest potential for thinking; they need skills that foster effective communication and productive and cooperative behaviors. We want students to feel good about themselves, about others, about their learning, and about their schools. For reaching these goals we believe that the best teaching strategies are those that incorporate thoughtful planning, acceptance of all, honesty, trusting, sharing, risking, communicating, and cooperating. Furthermore, *we believe children best learn these skills and values from teachers who model the same.* This resource guide continues to be dedicated to that hope and to that end. In preparing this third edition we strove to improve the content and to design exercises that will effectively guide users in thinking about their own thinking (metacognition) and in analyzing and planning their own skill development.

Part III has been completely rewritten to reflect currency and accuracy, and our belief in the importance of an **eclectic style of instruction.** Part III begins with a brief but important presentation of the theoretical considerations for the selection of instructional strategies—Chapter 9. Because of its importance in teaching, questioning has been isolated, that is, presented in its own chapter—Chapter 10. Chapter 11, on the use of specific instructional strategies, has been updated to include a greater emphasis on ways of grouping students for instruction, such as for cooperative learning, for assuring equality in the classroom, and for helping children to develop their intellectual skills.

Chapter 12, on aids and resources, now contains guidelines on what to do when equipment breaks down and current and important information on the placement and use of computers in schools. This chapter also discusses field trips and contains many relevant new exercises.

The final chapter of Part III, Chapter 13, on guidelines, aids, and resources for specific content areas of the curriculum, has been completely rewritten and updated with relevant new information, guidelines, and specific resources for teaching elementary school language arts, mathematics, science, social science, art, music, physical education, and related curriculum areas. In Chapter 13, we believe we have provided an enormous number of resources that will be valuable to the teacher for years to come.

Part IV: Assessment and Professional Development

Part IV, the final part of this resource guide, focuses attention on the fourth and final element of competent teaching, that is, *how well* the teacher and the students are doing. It contains two chapters, the first (Chapter 14) deals with the assessment of student achievement, and, new to this edition, cooperative learning groups and evaluation, student portfolios and self-assessment, guidelines for parent-teacher collaboration, and an increased emphasis on alternative assessment strategies.

The final chapter, Chapter 15, focuses the reader's attention on the assessment of teaching effectiveness and on continued professional growth and development. This chapter has been completely rewritten and updated. The micro peer teaching exercise, popular with reviewers of the previous edition, has been made even more clear and useful. We continue to provide a guide for the student-teaching component of teacher preparation, as well as guidelines and resources for obtaining a teaching position. New to this chapter is the section on development of a professional employability portfolio, as are several sections suggesting ways for a teacher's continued professional development.

We continue to respond to the many reviewers and users of this resource guide and have made these changes as a result of their feedback. People who have provided in-depth suggestions and important contributions, for which we are deeply grateful, are as follows: V. Robert Agostino, Duquesne University; Anita S. Baker of Baylor University; Dolly S. Baldwin of Bluefield State College; Judith A. Bazler of Lehigh University; T. J. Betenbough, Western New Mexico University; Julie Black, fifth-grade teacher; Karen A. Bosch, Old Dominion University; Lorraine Brown, kindergarten teacher; José Cintron, California State University, Sacramento; Calvin Claus of the National College of Education; Arthur L. Costa, past president of the Association for Supervision and Curriculum Development; Karl Engeman, California administrative judge; Maxel J. Ferguson, Southern Utah University; Richard P. Finn, University of Massachusetts, Boston; Paula Frkovich, fourth-grade teacher; Gordon E. Fuchs, University of Dayton; Mary Gentry, second-grade teacher; Robert P. Green, Jr., of Clemson University; Will Hightower, middle school teacher; Edward W. Holmes, Towson State University; Lillian Norris Holmes, Morgan State University; Don Larson, former associate superintendent of the Elk Grove Unified School District; John Mattingly, principal, and the faculty of Foulks Ranch Elementary School; Frank Miller, Pittsburg State University, Kansas; Mary Jane Pearson, commissioner on California's Commission on Teacher Credentialing; Teri Schuddeboom, first-grade teacher; Doris A. Simonis, Kent State University; Dawn Thomas, American University; Richard Uhleman, Edinboro University of Pennsylvania; Mary Beth Waller, University of Wisconsin–Parkside; and Jon Wiles, University of South Florida.

We have reviewed and updated, where necessary, all exercises, and have added a number of new ones. Nearly all Questions for Class Discussion at the end of the chapters have been rewritten, and the lists of Suggested Readings are current and relevant. A glossary is included. The index and table of contents are thorough for ease of cross-reference. Preparation of this edition and its accompanying instructor's manual has involved the most major rewrite yet; we hope you find it useful now and throughout your professional career.

As always, we appreciate the help we receive from former students who forgave us our trespasses; teachers and colleagues who continue to share their ideas and successes and have permitted us to include their names in this book; authors and publishers who graciously granted their permissions to reprint materials; and manuscript reviewers who have helped us improve each edition—although, as always, we assume full responsibility for the book's shortcomings. The education of teachers is an ever-increasingly complex enterprise, and no single book can possibly tell you everything you will need to know. We hope that with this resource guide we have given you what you need to feel comfortable on the road to becoming a competent elementary school classroom teacher.

We express our admiration and appreciation to the many editorial, design, and production people at Macmillan with whom we have had a continuing productive and pleasant relationship for many years.

We are indeed indebted to and grateful for all the people in our lives, now and in the past, who have interacted with us and reinforced that which we have always known: Teaching is the most rewarding profession of all.

R. D. K.

P. L. R.

Contents

2 What Do I Need to Know About How Children Learn, Think, and Develop Intellectually?   50

3 What Are the Expectations, Responsibilities, and Facilitating Behaviors of an Elementary School Teacher?   86

4 What Do I Need to Know to Establish and Maintain an Effective and Safe Classroom Learning Environment?   119

PART II   PLANNING FOR INSTRUCTION IN AN ELEMENTARY CLASSROOM   173

5   Why Should I Plan and How Do I Select Content?   175

6   What Are Instructional Objectives and How Do I Use Them?   204

PART III CHOOSING AND IMPLEMENTING INSTRUCTIONAL STRATEGIES, AIDS, AND RESOURCES   295

12 What Aids and Resources Are Available to Me as an Elementary School Classroom Teacher?   389

13   What Additional Instructional Guidelines, Aids, and Resources Are Available to Me for Specific Content Areas of the Curriculum?   433

PART IV   ASSESSMENT AND PROFESSIONAL DEVELOPMENT   489

14   How Do I Assess and Report Student Achievement?   491

PART I

Orientation to Elementary School Teaching and Learning

Part I assists you with:

- An understanding of how children learn, think, and develop intellectually.
- An understanding of the expectations, responsibilities, and facilitating behaviors of an elementary school classroom teacher.
- An understanding of the importance of home, school, and community partnerships.
- An understanding of the realities of elementary school teaching.
- An understanding of the role of elementary school administrators.

- Guidelines for beginning the school year.
- Guidelines for establishing and maintaining a safe and effective classroom learning environment.
- Guidelines for making school visitations and observations.
- Guidelines for working with the differences and diversity among children.

Although as a classroom teacher you cannot solve all the ailments of society, you do have an opportunity and responsibility to make all children feel welcome, respected, and wanted.

To encourage the wonderment of learning is every teacher's challenge, and within each person's lifetime wonderment should never cease.

During one school year you will make literally thousands of decisions, many of which can and will affect the lives of children for years to come. You may see this as an awesome responsibility, which it is.

Being coldly consistent is not the same as being fair and professional. As a teacher you are a professional who deals in matters of human relations and who must use professional intuition and judgment. You are not a robot, nor is any of your students.

When teaching a group of children of mixed learning abilities, mixed modality strengths, mixed language proficiency, and mixed cultural backgrounds, the integration of learning modalities is a must. A teacher who, for all students, uses only one style of teaching in the same classroom setting, day-after-day, is short-changing the children who learn better another way.

1

What Do I Need to Know About Today's Elementary Schools?

You are probably reading this resource guide because you are interested in a career in elementary school teaching. Whether you are in your early twenties and starting your first career, or older and in the process of beginning a new career, this book is for you—it is written for any person interested in becoming a professional teacher of children in kindergarten through grade 6.

If you are in a program of teacher preparation, then it is possible that near the completion of the program you will be offered your first teaching contract. When that happens, you will be excited—eager to sign the contract and to begin your new career. After the initial excitement you will have time to reflect. Many questions will then begin to surface. You undoubtedly will ask: What grade(s) will I have? What preparations will I need to make? Will I be a member of a teaching team?

Regardless of the grade you are preparing to teach, you will want to know: What will the students be like? What will their parents or guardians be like? If in a multiple-school district, to which school will I be assigned? Will it be a magnet school (a school that specializes in a particular academic area)?[1] A fundamental school (one that specializes in teaching basic skills)? An alternative school (one that is usually small in size, with an informal atmosphere, and that provides each student with personal attention and guidance)? Or will it be an experimental school? How can I prepare for students I have never met? What are the school and district policies that I need to know about (see Figure 1.1)? What support services will I have? Will there be an orientation for new teachers? How do I get answers to all of my questions?

To guide you through this initial experience and to help answer some of the questions you might have in the future, the following information about schools, students, teachers, administrators, and parents or guardians offers a first glimpse into today's world of elementary school teaching. This ebullient, active, rapidly changing world is so complex that few authors can say everything that needs to be said to every teacher. However, because it is necessary to start somewhere, we begin with this overview.[2]

[1] Magnet schools occur at all levels: elementary school, middle school, and high school. North Dade Center for Modern Languages, for example, is a public elementary magnet school that focuses on international studies and provides students with the opportunity to become bilingual, biliterate, and multicultural. See Lois Lindahl and Rebecca Maquire, "Global Awareness Teaching Strategies," *Media and Methods* 28(1):32–34 (September–October 1991).

[2] Perhaps, during your teacher preparation program, the course you are now in has been preceded by certain other teacher preparation courses and the material in this and other chapters of Part I are a review. If that is the case, you will want to review this material and then move quickly to Part II. If the information in Part I is new to you, then you should study it and review the questions for discussion and suggestions for further reading at the end of each chapter.

Here is a partial list of things every classroom teacher should know before the students arrive. You and your classmates may want to add other questions to the list.

1. Do I collect lunch money?
2. Do I have recess duty? lunch duty? cafeteria duty? hall duty? bus duty?
3. What are the fire and emergency drill procedures?
4. Where are the entrances and exits for my students?
5. If I wish to contact parents for any reason, may I do so directly or should I contact the principal first?
6. Do my students sit as a group in the cafeteria, or is there open seating?
7. Am I expected to organize and supervise extracurricular activities?
8. Is there a test administrator for standardized tests or do I administer them?
9. Do I design my own pretests and posttests for each subject of the curriculum?
10. Do I design formal lesson plans for the principal to check?
11. Do I teach art, music, and physical education, or is there a special teacher for these subjects?
12. Do I teach science, or is it taught to my students by a science resource teacher?
13. What reading program is used? Must I use it? May I supplement it?
14. What mathematics program is used? Must I use it? May I supplement it?
15. If I am expected to teach science, what science program is used? Must I use it? May I supplement it?
16. What social studies program is used? Must I use it? May I supplement it?
17. Where and how do I obtain classroom supplies?
18. Where do I get films, and how far in advance must they be ordered?
19. What are the school discipline system and expectations?
20. Am I allowed to send disruptive students to the principal?
21. Is there a prep period?
22. What are my duty hours?
23. What is the school's dress code?
24. What instrument is used for teacher evaluation?
25. How many times a year will I be formally evaluated?

Figure 1.1 Things every classroom teacher should know before the students arrive.[3]

A. ORIENTATION MEETINGS

As a beginning teacher, you will be expected to participate in an orientation meeting for new and beginning teachers. Some school districts start the academic year with a districtwide orientation, and others schedule on-site orientations at each school. Many school districts do both, with perhaps a districtwide morning meeting followed by on-site meetings in the afternoon. Of course, the scheduling and planning of orientation meetings will vary, district by district and school by school. The objectives for

[3]Courtesy of Maxel J. Ferguson.

all orientation meetings, however, should be similar. As a beginning teacher, you will be encouraged by district personnel to do the following:

1. Become familiar with the district's (or school's) written statement of its beliefs and goals—its statement of mission or philosophy—and what that statement means to the people affiliated with the district or school. For example, the mission statement of the Snively Elementary School in Winter Haven, Florida, is as follows:

   > Snively Elementary School believes that the education of children is our reason for being. We expect each child to learn all skills needed for promotion to the next grade.[4]

2. Become familiar with the policies of the school and district. Such policies are many and often cover a wide range. There are policies for procedures relating to injuries of students at school; natural disasters, such as earthquakes or severe storms; allowing students to take their prescribed medications; finding nonprescribed drugs, other controlled substances, and weapons; playground use; parking on campus; class conduct; school programs, off-campus field trips, and parties in the classroom; grading, promotion, and retention; completing absentee and tardy forms; sending students to the office; and sponsoring student activities. And these examples are just the beginning!
3. Become familiar with the myriad forms that teachers must fill out. There are forms for injuries at school, for textbook loans, for key loans, for attendance and tardies, for student academic deficiencies, for sponsoring student activities, for field trips, and for referrals of students for their misbehavior, to name just a few.
4. Become familiar with the approved curriculum that defines what teachers are to teach and what students are to learn. This means that you must become familiar with the courses of study, curriculum guides, resource units, teacher's manuals, student textbooks, and supplementary materials—all of which should reflect the school's philosophy and approved curriculum.
5. Meet other teachers and establish the beginning of new collegial friendships and professional relationships.
6. Become familiar with the school or district plan for monitoring, assessing, and supervising implementation of the curriculum.
7. Study available resource materials and equipment, as well as procedures for reserving and using them on certain dates.
8. Become familiar with the school library/resource center, its personnel, and its procedures.
9. Meet district and school personnel and become familiar with the many services that support you in your classroom.
10. Prepare your classroom for instruction.

As a teacher candidate in a program for teacher preparation, you may be expected to participate in an orientation meeting at your college or university. The meeting may be held at the beginning of the program or just before the beginning of

---

[4]John A. Stewart, "Filling in the Gaps," *Phi Delta Kappan* 73(2):166–168 (October 1991). At the Snively Elementary School, high expectations are a vital part of learning, and they have paid off. That school's performance has won its district's Flag of Distinction Award for five consecutive years, and in 1991–92 the school was awarded a grant from the Next Century Schools program, sponsored by RJR Nabisco Corporation. With that award Snively received a grant of $750,000 to expand and document its activities and strategies. Snively Elementary School is in a rural area, and 25 percent of its children are from families of migrant workers. About half its student body is Hispanic. Eighty-five percent of all children at the school receive free or reduced-price lunches.

your field experience, or at both times. Perhaps this meeting will be a function of one of your college or university courses. You will receive your school assignment, the name of the school and the school district, the school's location, the date when you should report to that assignment, the name of your cooperating teacher(s),[5] the grade level(s), the subject(s), and perhaps the name of your college or university supervisor. You will probably be encouraged to follow many of the previously listed objectives and to meet other teacher candidates.

When you arrive at your assigned school and introductions have been made, you can begin to become familiar with the school campus and the way the school is organized. Walk around the campus, perhaps with a copy of the school map, and learn the location of your classroom, discover the playground area assigned for your class, and locate the nearest restrooms for girls, for boys, and for faculty men or women. Become familiar with such areas as the teacher's workroom, the faculty room, the faculty lunchroom (which may or may not be a single area). Determine where students eat their lunches and their snacks. Is there a multipurpose room—a room used for lunch as well as for educational purposes? Where is the nurse's room? The nearest first-aid and emergency equipment? How do you notify maintenance personnel quickly and efficiently? Where are the written procedures for fire drills and other emergencies? Where is information about the warning system? Is there a plan posted in a conspicuous place for all to see? Where are the various administrative offices? The office of student activities? Where is the library? The media center? The resources room? Where are textbooks stored? How are they checked out and distributed? Where is the attendance office? Are there offices for resource specialists?

At an orientation session, you may meet the grade-level chairperson, or interdisciplinary team leader and members of that team. How can you discover where those persons are to be found at various times during the school day? Where are teaching supplies kept, and how do you obtain them? Have you located your faculty mailbox and the place to check in or out when you arrive at or leave the school? What procedures do you follow if you are absent because of illness, or when you are going to be late? Do you have the necessary phone numbers? And, not least in importance, if you drive to school, where do you park? Otherwise, what is the best local transportation available to you for getting to school each day?

After you become familiar with the school site and obtain answers to some of your more urgent questions, you will want to focus your attention on the school schedule.

B. TEACHER SCHEDULES

Teacher schedules vary from state to state, from district to district, and from school to school. Most school years begin in late August or early September and continue through late May or mid-June. Some elementary schools operate on a year-round schedule. With a year-round schedule, a teacher might teach for three-quarters of the year and be off for the following one-quarter, or teach in a 45/15 program, which means nine weeks (45 days) of school followed by three weeks off, throughout

---

[5]The classroom teacher to whom you are assigned during your field experience is referred to variously as the "cooperating teacher," the "student-teaching supervising teacher," the "mentor teacher," or the "master teacher." Throughout this resource guide, the term "cooperating teacher" is used.

the year. The school year, lengthened only slightly in most states and districts in the 1980s, still approximates 180 days.

After being assigned to a school and having become familiar with the campus, you should turn your attention to all of the available school schedules: schedules for playground duty, lunch, bus duty, library, special programs and special days, and the different tracks (in year-round schools, teachers and students are on tracks—starting and ending times of academic instruction will vary depending on the track).

The school day usually begins at about 8:00 A.M. and lasts until about 3:00 P.M. In schools that are crowded, beginning and ending times of the school day may be staggered, and some students and teachers may start as early as 7:30 A.M. and end at 2:30 P.M. Others may begin at 9:00 A.M. and continue until 4:00 P.M. District and state laws vary, but generally require that teachers be in the classroom no less than 15 minutes prior to the start of school, and remain in their classrooms no less than 15 minutes after dismissal of the students.

The time spent daily on each subject taught in elementary schools will vary with grade level and may be dictated by state law or district policy, but for each grade the curriculum plans should include lessons for multiple subjects: reading, language arts, mathematics, physical education, music, art, science, and social sciences. In some schools and in some grades, not all of these subjects are taught every day. Unfortunately, in only a few elementary schools is foreign language a part of the curriculum. In some schools, particularly in intermediate and middle-level grades, there may be teams of teachers rather than the traditional self-contained pattern for a single grade. An interdisciplinary team will meet one group of children for a block of time, perhaps two hours, working with the children as a team. The teaching team is an integral part of the **school-within-a-school** concept, which is a major consideration in today's restructuring of existing schools.

Restructuring and the School-Within-a-School Concept

In reference to schools, the term *restructuring* has different but authentic meanings—such as site-based management, collaborative decision making, school choice, personalized learning, integrated curricula, and collegial staffing. No matter how restructuring is defined, the point is this: the design and functions of schools must reflect the needs of children who will be in the work force in the twenty-first century, rather than of the society of the nineteenth century.

As you might suspect, there is a tremendous variation from one school to the next in the amount of time spent on different subjects. Because many teachers today use a holistic approach to teaching and learning and emphasize interdisciplinary thematic teaching, it is difficult to generalize with any degree of accuracy about how much time is actually spent on any given discipline. For example, in many elementary schools teachers have greater autonomy today than they had in the past in making decisions about time allotments for the various subjects they must teach.

Elementary School Teacher Schedules

Figures 1.2 through 1.7 are sample teacher schedules. Complete Exercise 1.1 and compare your experience with these sample schedules.

Exercise 1.1: Reflecting on My Own Elementary School Experiences

Instructions: The purpose of this exercise is to help you recall, as much as possible, your own elementary school experiences. When you have completed the exercise, share your reflections with others in your class.

Name(s) of elementary school(s) attended _____

Public or private? _____ Dates _____

Location(s) _____

1. What do you remember most from your elementary school experiences? _____

_____

_____

_____

_____

_____

2. What do you remember about your teachers? _____

_____

_____

_____

_____

_____

3. What do you remember about other students? _____

_____

_____

_____

_____

4. What do you remember most about school life? _____

_____

_____

_____

_____

_____

5. What grade (or class) do you specifically recall with fondness? Why? _____

_____

_____

_____

_____

6. What grade (or class) would you particularly like to forget? Why? _____

_____

_____

_____

_____

7. What do you recall about peer and parental pressures? _____

_____

_____

_____

_____

8. What do you recall about your own feelings during those years? _____

_____

_____

_____

_____

9. Is there any other aspect of your life as an elementary school student you wish to share

   with others? _____

_____

_____

_____

_____

_____

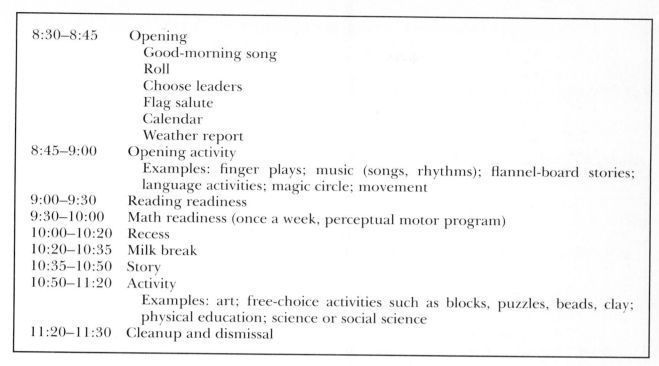

8:30–8:45	Opening
	Good-morning song
	Roll
	Choose leaders
	Flag salute
	Calendar
	Weather report
8:45–9:00	Opening activity
	Examples: finger plays; music (songs, rhythms); flannel-board stories; language activities; magic circle; movement
9:00–9:30	Reading readiness
9:30–10:00	Math readiness (once a week, perceptual motor program)
10:00–10:20	Recess
10:20–10:35	Milk break
10:35–10:50	Story
10:50–11:20	Activity
	Examples: art; free-choice activities such as blocks, puzzles, beads, clay; physical education; science or social science
11:20–11:30	Cleanup and dismissal

Figure 1.2 A kindergarten class schedule.[6]

8:25–8:55	Community circle
	Attendance
	Flag salute
	Patriotic song
	Community song
	Calendar process
	Weather graph
	Lost tooth chart
	Appreciations
	Share a sentence
8:55–9:15	Spelling activities
9:15–10:05	Reading activities
10:05–10:20	Recess and snack time
10:20–10:50	Reading continued
10:50–11:15	English/handwriting
11:15–12:00	Lunch/recess
12:00–12:10	Semisilent sustained reading
12:10–12:20	Read aloud to class
12:20–12:35	Community circle/math oriented
	Number line
	Make the date in cents

(continued)

Figure 1.3 A first-grade class schedule.[7]

[6]Courtesy of Lorraine Brown, kindergarten teacher, Prairie Elementary School, Elk Grove Unified School District, Elk Grove, California.
[7]Courtesy of Teri Schuddeboom, first-grade teacher, Hemlock Elementary School, Vacaville Unified School District, Vacaville, California.

	Add one straw each day to straw box and group into tens
	Clock work
12:35–1:05	Math (or library one day a week)
1:05–1:35	Social studies, science, or health
1:35–2:15	Art, music, physical education, or journal writing
2:15–2:25	Room cleanup
2:25	Dismissal

Figure 1.3   (*continued*).

8:20–9:20	Reading for morning readers (lower-level groups)[8]
9:20–9:30	Recess (afternoon readers arrive)
9:30–9:35	Opening role, lunch count, flag salute
9:35–10:00	Language (daily oral)
10:00–10:35	Math activities
10:35–10:45	Recess
10:45–11:45	Music, spelling, or art
11:45–12:30	Lunch
12:30–12:40	Silent reading, show and tell
12:40–1:10	Science, social studies, physical education, language arts
1:10–1:30	Library
1:30–1:40	Recess (dismissal of morning readers)
1:40–2:40	Reading for afternoon readers (higher-level groups)
2:40	Dismissal of afternoon readers

Figure 1.4   A second-grade class schedule.[9]

8:00–8:20	M–Th Boardwork
	F Correct and collect homework
8:20–8:50	M–Th Opening (Song, mental math, time line); whole class reading
	F Opening, speeches, math
8:50–9:55	M Explain homework, spelling pretest, math
	T–Th Math
	F Opening, speeches, math
9:55–10:10	Recess
10:10–10:45	M, W, Th, F Phonics, reading
	T Publishing
10:45–11:30	M Music
	T, Th, F Computers/science resource teacher
	W Art

(*continued*)

Figure 1.5   A third-grade class schedule.[10]

[8]By staggering the beginning and ending of the school day, allowing some students to arrive before or leave after others, student-teacher ratios are reduced, at least during parts of the school day, allowing the teacher more direct contact with students. For further information, see *Every Student Succeeds: A California Initiative to Ensure Success for Students at Risk* (Sacramento: California Department of Education, 1990).

[9]Courtesy of Mary E. Gentry, second-grade teacher, Cirby Elementary School, Roseville Unified School District, Roseville, California.

[10]Courtesy of Vickie Hillier, third-grade teacher, Foulks Ranch Elementary School, Elk Grove Unified School District, Elk Grove, California.

11:30–12:20	Lunch and recess
12:20–1:05	M, T Sustained silent reading; social studies
	W, Th, F Sustained silent reading, writer's workshop
1:05–1:15	Recess
1:15–1:55	M, F Physical education
	T, W, Th Read aloud, oral language, spelling
1:55	Dismissal
1:55–2:40	Success groups (optional)

Teacher note: Although this constitutes our basic schedule, it is sometimes altered due to special projects or presentations. Furthermore, since I use thematic and integrated teaching, certain areas may often overlap.

Figure 1.5 (*continued*).

9:00–9:15	Attendance, lunch count, write down assignments
9:15–9:30	Library (Tuesday)
9:15–9:45	Journal writing
	Math and language review (review math skills from previous day and daily oral language sentences)
9:45–10:22	Physical education (one-half class to P. E., one-half to English)
10:22–10:36	Recess
10:36–11:00	Read aloud to class; snack
11:00–11:45	Math
11:45–12:15	Current events and history (share local, state, national, world news and find geographic locations on map)
12:15–1:00	Lunch
1:00–1:56	Language arts/writing
	Computer lab (Wednesday only)
	(Every third week students participate in a one-half day visual and performing arts lesson, taught by visual and performing arts teachers)
1:56–2:10	Recess
2:10–2:30	Sustained silent reading
2:30–2:50	Spelling
2:50–3:25	Science
3:25–3:30	Cleanup
3:35	Dismissal

Figure 1.6 A fourth-grade class schedule[11]

8:35–9:10	Log-entry writing assignment
	Attendance
9:10–9:30	Correct homework and review skills involved

(*continued*)

Figure 1.7 A fifth-grade class schedule[12]

[11]Courtesy of Paula Frkovich, fourth-grade teacher, Rocklin School, Rocklin Unified School District, Rocklin, California.
[12]Courtesy of Julie Black, fifth-grade teacher, Pennycook School, Vallejo City Unified School District, Vallejo, California.

9:30–10:15	Language arts (reading, writing, speaking, listening)
10:15–10:25	Recess
10:25–10:35	Announcements; snack
10:35–12:00	Math activities
12:00–12:40	Lunch and recess
12:40–1:10	Teacher reads aloud (accompanied by discussion before, during, and after)
1:10–1:50	Science or social studies
1:50–2:00	Recess
2:00–2:45	Physical education, art, music, or *Weekly Reader*
2:45–3:00	Explain homework; review the day
3:00	Dismissal (Mondays at 1:45)

Figure 1.7   *(continued)*.

Inside your own busy classroom, you will be learning the names of your students, making decisions, following your detailed lesson plans, and keeping one eye on the clock for a day or two—a behavior that helps you keep to the schedule for recess, lunch, coordinating with other teachers, and dismissal at the end of the day.

Middle School Teacher Schedules

As an elementary school teacher, you may find your first job teaching at the middle school level. What should you know about this level of education? First, you need to know that there are two sometimes quite different types of schools, both of which are called middle schools. One is the former traditional junior high school, with perhaps a few minor changes, including a name change to "middle school." The second is the exemplary middle school, which, as shown in Figure 1.8, is quite different from the traditional junior high. To understand the significance of the schedules of middle school teachers, certain background information is necessary.

Exemplary middle schools are usually organized into some type of flexible or block scheduling—an alternative to the traditional method of assigning students to six or seven different classes of 45 to 60 minutes each, five days a week, for the entire school year.

Teaching Teams

Middle school teachers of exemplary middle schools are members of a professional team. Four or five teachers of different subjects work together to plan the curriculum for a common group of students. These **teaching teams**[13] include one teacher for each of the following: English/language arts, mathematics, science, and history/social studies. The four subject areas are known as the **core curriculum.** Other teachers may also be part of the team: teachers of physical education, art, music, and even those specializing in teaching students who are at risk or who have learning disabilities. Because a growing number of middle school students are identified as being "at risk" of dropping out of school, a school counselor or a community resource person

[13]A distinction must be made between teaching teams and team teaching. Team teaching refers to two or more teachers simultaneously providing instruction to students in the same classroom. Members of a teaching team may participate in team teaching.

	Junior High School	*Exemplary Middle School*
Most common grade-span organization	Grades 7–8 or 7–9	Grades 6–8
Scheduling	Traditional	Flexible, usually block
Subject organization	Departmentalized	Integrated and thematic Interdisciplinary, usually language arts, math, science, and social studies
Guidance/counseling	Separate advisement by counselor on individual or "as needed" basis Full-time counselors	Advisor-advisee Home base or homeroom
Exploratory curriculum	Electives by individual choice	Common "wheel" of experiences for all students
Teachers	Subject-centered Grades 7–12 certification	Interdisciplinary teams Student-centered Grades K–8 or 6–8 certification
Instruction	Traditional Lecture Skills and repetition	Thematic units Discovery techniques "Learning how to learn" (study skills)
Athletics	Interscholastic sports, emphasizing competition	Intramural programs, emphasizing participation

Figure 1.8 Summary of differences between junior high schools and middle schools.

may be asked to join the team. Core and specialty subjects cross different disciplines of study; therefore, such teams are commonly called **interdisciplinary teaching teams** or simply interdisciplinary teams.

School-Within-a-School

In a middle school, an interdisciplinary teaching team is sometimes referred to as a "house," as a school-within-a-school, where each team of teachers is assigned each day to the same group of about 125 students for a common block of time.[14] Within this block of time, teachers on the team are responsible for the many professional decisions necessary, such as how to make school meaningful to students' lives, the specific responsibilities of each teacher, the guidance activities to be implemented, the

[14]Russell Frank, "Linking School Reform to Empowerment: A Bottom-up Model for Middle School Reform," *California ASCD Journal for Supervision and Curriculum Development* 2(3):23–29 (Spring–Summer 1989), p. 27. See also Jerry Villars, *Restructuring Through School Redesign*, Fastback 322 (Bloomington, IN: Phi Delta Kappa Educational Foundation, 1991).

special attention needed by individual students, and how students will be grouped for instruction.

The school-within-a-school concept (also incorporated into some elementary schools) helps students make important and meaningful connections between disciplines and provides them with peer and adult group identification, giving an important and concomitant sense of belonging. The advantages of teaching in this collegial environment have been expressed as follows:[15]

1. The combined thinking of several teachers creates an expanded pool of ideas, enhances individual capacities for handling complex problems, and provides intellectual stimulation and emotional support. The synergism of talents produces an energy that impacts positively on the instructional program.
2. The beginning teacher who joins a team has the benefit of support from more experienced teammates.
3. Individual teachers tend to work harder on improving the overall instructional quality of their team.
4. When a team member is absent, other members of the team work closely with the substitute, resulting in less loss of instructional time for students.
5. More and better planning for students occurs as teachers discuss, argue, and reach agreement on behavioral expectations, curriculum emphasis, instructional approaches, and materials.

Common Planning Time

For an interdisciplinary team of teachers to plan a common curriculum, members must meet frequently. This is best accomplished by scheduling a common planning time. Instead of each teacher having a different preparation period, the four or five members of the team share the same preparation time to plan curriculum and discuss the progress and needs of individual students.

Lead Teachers

Each teaching team assigns a member to be the "lead teacher" or "teacher leader." The lead teacher facilitates discussions during the common planning time, organizes the meetings, and acts as liaison with the school principal and, sometimes, district office personnel to make sure the team has the necessary resources to put plans into action. The responsibility of being a lead teacher is usually accepted by each member of the team in rotation throughout the school year.

Flexible Scheduling

To accommodate common planning time for teachers and to allow for more instructional flexibility, most middle schools use some form of "block scheduling" in assigning students to teachers for instruction. Blocks of time ranging from 70 to 90 minutes replace the traditional structure of 45- to 60-minute-long classes. The sample

---

[15]Robert J. McCarthy, *Initiating Restructuring at the School Site,* Fastback 324 (Bloomington, IN: Phi Delta Kappa Educational Foundation, 1991), p. 11.

Teacher	Advisor-Advisee 7:45–8:10	Block 1 8:10–9:35 M W F	Block 1 T Th	Block 2 9:35–11:35 M W F	Block 2 T Th	Block 3 11:35–1:00 M W F	Block 3 T Th	Block 4 1:00–2:25 M W F	Block 4 T Th	T Th Exploratories	T Th Exploratories
A	yes	Sci-6	Sci-6	Planning time		Sci-6	Sci-6	Reading	Intramural	Keyboarding	Outdoor Life
B	yes	Eng-6	Eng-6	Planning time		Eng-6	Eng-6	Reading	Intramural	Speech	Study Skills
C	yes	SS-6	SS-6	Planning time		SS-6	SS-6	Reading	Intramural	Comparative Lit.	Lab
D	yes	Math-6	Math-6	Planning time		Math-6	Math-6	Reading	Intramural	Math pull-out	Math-6
E										Politics	Speech
F										Nature	Individual Technology
G										GEP	Study Skills
H										Computer	Home Economics
I				PE-6	Art-6	PE-6	PE-6				
J				Art-6	PE-6	Mus-6	PE-6				
K				Mus-6	Mus-6	PE-6	Mus-6				
L				Bd-6	Art-6	PE-6	Art-6				
M				PE-6	Art-6	Orch-6	PE-6				

Figure 1.9 Sample sixth-grade teaching team block schedule.[16]

block schedule in Figure 1.9 illustrates the assignment of sixth-grade teachers to different classes and blocks. Notice that at that school there are 13 teachers who provide some type of instruction to the sixth graders. Four teachers, identified as A through D, constitute the sixth-grade interdisciplinary teaching team. Their common planning time occurs in block 2, from 9:35 until 11:35 each day. The school day consists of four blocks of 85 minutes each, with a homeroom (advisor-advisee) each day from 7:45 until 8:10.

School Schedules and Students Who Are at Risk

In addition to school restructuring, other efforts at helping children who are at risk, which can effect the schedules of their teachers, include (1) special literacy programs before school, after school, or during school, in which students are placed in special classes, (2) teacher mentors and community or business mentors, to provide positive adult role models, (3) technology and work-study programs contributed by private business and industry, (4) and the appointment of at-risk program coordinators within school districts and at-risk counselors at the school campus.

Obviously, it is quite difficult to generalize about teachers' schedules, but perhaps you have been given sufficient information and examples to arouse your curiosity about the many variations that currently exist. Later, you will visit schools and learn firsthand more about teachers and their schedules.

[16]Adapted from Kellough, R. D., Kellough, N. G., and Hough, D. L. *Middle School Teaching: Methods and Resources* (New York: Macmillan, 1993), p. 73. By permission of Macmillan Publishing Company.

C. STUDENTS

The bell rings for class to begin and the students enter your classroom, "all unique, each a bundle of idiosyncrasies, different strengths, different attitudes and aptitudes, different needs."[17] What a challenge for you—to understand and to teach 30 or so unique individuals, all at once, and to do it five and a half to six hours a day, five days a week, 180 days a year!

To help you meet the challenge, there is a wealth of information available about teaching and working with children. As a credentialed teacher, you are expected to know, or at least to know where you can find, all necessary information, and to review it at an appropriate time. Certain information you have learned and stored in memory will surface and become useful at the most unexpected times. Coming to mind may be the fact that elementary school students first develop large-muscle control and then small-muscle control, or perhaps that students are eight years old before they gain vision accommodation. Then again, it may be the knowledge that there often is a growth spurt when a student reaches the fifth or sixth grade. While concerned about all students' safety and physical well-being, you will want to remain sensitive to each child's attitudes, values, social adjustment, emotional well-being, and cognitive development. You must be prepared not only to teach several subjects, but to do it effectively with students of different cultural backgrounds, of diverse linguistic abilities, of different learning styles, and with students who have been identified as having special needs. A challenge indeed!

Students with Special Needs

Increasing your need for background knowledge is the realization that students with special needs—that is, students who deviate from the average or norm in mental characteristics, sensory abilities, neuromotor or physical characteristics, social behavior, communication abilities, or who have multiple disabilities—must, to the extent possible, be educated with their peers in the regular classroom. Since 1975, **Public Law 94-142** and its amendments have mandated that all students have the right to a full and free public education, and to nonbiased testing. Emphasizing mainstreaming and normalizing the educational environment for "exceptional children," this legislation requires provision of the least restrictive environment for these students. A **least restrictive environment** is one that is as normal an environment as possible. Students who are identified as special may be placed in the regular classroom for the entire school day (**inclusion**), as is the trend today,[18] for the greater part of the school day (**partial inclusion**), or only for designated periods. This placement concept is known as **mainstreaming.** A student who is mainstreamed into the regular classroom for only part of the day is one who has more specialized needs than a child placed there for the entire day. You will need information and skills unique to teaching exceptional children in your classroom. In effect, this means that you must be, part of your time, a teacher of students with special needs.

---

[17]Mary Hatwood Futrell, *Education Week*, April 3, 1985, p. 10.
[18]See, for example, Anne Wheelock, "The Case for Untracking," *Educational Leadership* 50(2):6–10 (October 1992). See also Richard A. Villa and Jacqueline S. Thousand, "How One District Integrated Special and General Education," *Educational Leadership* 50(2):39–41 (October 1992).

Actually, teaching exceptional children is not so different from ordinary teaching, except that it requires more care, better diagnosis, greater skill, more attention to individual needs, and greater understanding of the students. Yet the challenges of teaching students with special needs in the regular classroom are great enough that to do it well, you need additional specialized training far beyond that which can be provided by this book. At some point in your teacher preparation you should, or may be required to, take one or more courses in working with the special child in the regular classroom.

As a regular classroom teacher, you should keep this important fact in mind: *When a student with special needs is placed in your classroom, your objective should not be to make the student normal, but, rather, to deal directly with the differences between this student and other students in your classroom.* To deal directly with these differences, you should:

1. Develop an understanding of the general characteristics of different types of special-needs students.
2. Identify the student's unique needs relative to your classroom.
3. Design lesson plans that teach to different needs at the same time.

When students with special needs have been identified, they are placed in a particular category, based on what is known as their **primary area of exceptionality.** These areas of exceptionality may include the following: gifted and talented; educable mentally retarded (EMR); behavior disordered (also known as emotionally handicapped, or EH); learning disabled (LD); hearing impaired; visually impaired; speech and language disordered; physically handicapped; and chronic health problems.

Having been categorized according to one of these specific areas does not necessarily mean that a student will not have strengths and weaknesses in another area. For example, a student identified as being gifted and talented might have some difficulties in speech, or could be visually impaired. A student identified as hearing impaired could be academically gifted—Beethoven was deaf. The category of exceptionality with which a student is identified is simply that which appears to be the primary area of special need, not necessarily the only one.

Because of its concern for problems of the special-needs child, Congress, in Public Law 94-142, has decreed that an **Individualized Educational Program** (IEP) be devised annually for each differently abled (exceptional) student. According to that law, for each student an IEP is drawn up each year by a team that includes special education teachers, the child's parents, and the classroom teachers. The IEP contains (1) a statement of the student's present educational levels, (2) the educational goals for the year, (3) specifications for the services to be provided and the extent to which the student should be expected to take part in the regular program, and (4) the evaluative criteria for the services to be provided. Consultation by special and skilled support personnel is essential in all mainstream IEP models. A consultant works directly with teachers or with students and parents. As an elementary school classroom teacher, you may have an active role in the preparation of the specifications for the exceptional students assigned to your classes, as well as major responsibility for implementing the program.

The effective teacher is aware of all that is happening in the classroom.

Guidelines for Working with Exceptional Children

General guidelines for working with special-needs children who are wholly or partially mainstreamed follow. Although these guidelines are important for teaching *all* children, they are especially necessary for teaching children with special needs in the regular classroom. Generally, you should:

- *Define the instructional objectives in behavioral terms.* (Discussed in Chapter 6).
- *Exercise your withitness.* That is, be aware of everything that is going on in the classroom, at all times, monitoring children for signs of restlessness, frustration, anxiety, and off-task behaviors. (Teacher withitness is discussed further in Chapter 3.) Be ready to reassign individual children to different activities as the situation warrants.
- *Maintain consistency in your expectations.* Special-needs children can become frustrated when they do not understand a teacher's expectations.
- *Maintain consistency in your responses.* Special-needs children can become frustrated when they cannot depend on a teacher's reactions.
- *Plan interesting learning activities that help the child connect what is being learned with his or her real world* (see Chapter 9).
- *Provide for and teach toward student success.* Offer children activities and experiences that ensure success and mastery at some level. Use of student portfolios (discussed

in Chapter 13) can give evidence of progress and help in building student confidence.

- *Teach students the procedures for routines.* Simply telling children how to do things is not enough. Explain and rehearse classroom rules and procedures, not only with special-needs students, but with all students (discussed further in Chapter 4).

Specifically, you should:

- *Adapt and modify materials, lessons, and procedures to the needs of the special student.* For example, a child who has extreme difficulty sitting still for more than a few minutes will need planned changes in learning activities. When assigning student seating, give preference to students according to their special needs. Be sure to incorporate into your lessons activities that engage relevant learning modalities—visual, auditory, tactile, and kinesthetic.
- *Break complex learning into simpler components, moving from the most concrete to the abstract* (see Chapter 9). Check frequently for student comprehension of content.
- *Plan your questions and questioning sequence* (discussed in Chapter 10). Plan the questions you will ask special-needs students, so that they are likely to answer with confidence. Use signals to let children know you are likely to call on them. After asking a question, give the child adequate time to think and to respond.
- *Provide help in the organization of students' learning.* For example, give instruction in the organization of their notes and notebooks. Have a three-hole punch available so that students can put papers into their notebooks immediately, thus avoiding disorganization and the loss of papers. During class presentations to older children, use an overhead projector with transparencies. Then children who need more time can copy material from the transparencies. Ask students to read their notes aloud to each other in small groups, thereby aiding their recall and encouraging them to take notes for meaning rather than for rote learning.
- *Reward approved and acceptable behavior.* Unacceptable behavior, if not too disruptive, can sometimes be ignored (discussed in Chapter 4).
- *Have students copy assignments for the week into a folder, which is kept in their notebooks.* Post assignments for the week in a special place on the bulletin board and remind students of deadlines.

Recognizing and Working with Crack-Affected Children

In a recent editorial, Ron Brandt, executive editor of *Educational Leadership*, said that "the problems that children bring with them to school these days are upsetting and overwhelming. Most of us, when we chose to become teachers and administrators, did not expect to be dealing with such matters. But many children are, in fact, at risk. Educators must not only recognize that but must do whatever they can to improve their chances."[19] A problem only now surfacing in the schools is the number of children affected by mothers who abused cocaine or its cheaper form, crack, while they were pregnant. Waller says that "approximately 400,000 children are born annually to mothers who used crack or cocaine during pregnancy. These drugs are chemically similar and have the same effects on fetuses."[20]

[19]Ron Brandt, "Yes, Children Are Still at Risk," *Educational Leadership* 50(4):4 (December 1992–January 1993).
[20]Mary Bellis Waller, "Helping Crack-Affected Children Succeed," *Educational Leadership* 50(4):57–60 (December 1992–January 1993), p. 57.

Characteristics of Crack-Affected Children

"Children affected by crack and cocaine look like other children: they show the full range of size, vigor, and intelligence. However, many of them also show a number of problems that do not simply resolve themselves, and unless those crack-affected children receive specially designed interventions, they will continue to experience the problems during each developmental stage."[21] Children affected by crack tend to:

1. Be impulsive and sometimes violent.
2. Be distractible, hyperactive, and disruptive; normal discipline procedures seem ineffective.
3. Exhibit learning and memory problems.
4. Remain isolated and appear to have difficulty in developing friendships.
5. Show inappropriate social behaviors and are likely to blurt out comments.
6. Be unable to understand nonverbal cues; for example, a smile or a frown.
7. Have difficulty understanding the relationship between cause and effect.[22]

Guidelines for Working with Crack-Affected Children[23]

1. Since it is affect that appears damaged, teachers must work with the child's intellect, which is undamaged. Words are the tools for teaching. Nonverbal cues and displays are not.
2. Encouragement and praise must be given verbally.
3. The teacher must use only one teaching modality. Teaching must be by direct instruction, by telling, reteaching, retelling, modeling, demonstrating, and then having the child demonstrate the lesson.
4. Teacher demonstrations must be explained while they are being done.
5. Play has no intrinsic value to these children; they tend to be disorganized and to make no sense out of their experiences. Play must also be taught, first by direct instruction; next, by guided play; and then, under supervision.
6. Transitions are difficult for the crack-affected child, such as the transition from a quiet activity to recess, or from one subject to another. The teacher must prepare the child for the transition by talking about it and reviewing the things that will happen with the change, for instance, questioning the child or by role-playing.
7. The crack-affected child may be overwhelmed by too many simultaneous stimuli, such as would result if while talking to the child the teacher also uses direct eye contact and touches the child on a shoulder. It is important to not overload the crack-affected child's sensory input mechanisms.

Diversity and Differences

There is another consideration that increases your need for background knowledge. Although a teaching credential authorizes you to teach in any public school throughout a state, and in some instances, in a region that consists of several states, in many states today that means teaching in a school that is ethnically, culturally, linguistically, and socioeconomically diverse. The United States is a country of a va-

---

[21]Ibid., p. 58.
[22]Ibid., p. 58. Adapted by permission of Mary Bellis Waller.
[23]Ibid., pp. 59–60. Adapted by permission of Mary Bellis Waller.

riety of families, many with different ethnic heritages—African American, Cambodian American, Chinese American, and Cuban American. We have families that are Filipino American, French Canadian American, Hungarian American, Iranian American, Italian American, Jewish American, Laotian American, Mexican American, Native American, Polish American, Puerto Rican American, Russian American, and Vietnamese American, to name but a few. California students, for example, represent more than 70 language groups and dozens of nations.[24] One out of every six of California's elementary school students was born in another country.[25] Some inner-city California school systems have student bodies that represent 40 to 50 different languages. It will be important for you to determine the language groups and nationalities represented by the students in your classroom.

A major problem for recent immigrants and some ethnic groups is learning a second language. In many cities, and even in smaller communities today, it is not uncommon for more than half the children in school to come from homes where the native language is not English. Yet standard English is a necessity in most communities of this country if a person is to become vocationally successful and to enjoy a full life. Learning to communicate reasonably well in English can take a child at least a year, probably more; some authorities say three to seven years.

Teaching students who have limited proficiency in English (LPE) includes hands-on, experiential, and cooperative learning—all effective ways to teach LPE students.

Some students with limited English proficiency may not be proficient in their native languages; therefore you may need a teaching aide to help such students make the transition to becoming truly bilingual. Federal grants are available for provision of such classroom assistance.

Many schools offer an instructional plan by which part of the student's school time is spent in special bilingual classes and the rest of the time in regular classrooms. As a teacher of a regular classroom, you need to know the extent to which your LPE students are in such a program. You may be expected to work in conjunction with the bilingual program teacher in developing an individualized educational program for such students. Specific guidelines for working with LPE students are as follows:

- Assist the LPE child in learning two vocabulary sets: the vocabulary needed to learn and the vocabulary needed for content.[26]
- Concentrate on the use of multisensory approaches, utilizing various learning modalities—visual, verbal, tactile, and kinesthetic. (These are discussed further in Chapter 3.)
- Parents of new immigrant children are usually truly concerned about the education of their children and may be quite interested in cooperating with their teachers in any way possible. If their help is solicited, they may do all they can to help, and perhaps can help you to facilitate their children's learning.
- Use small-group, mixed-ability, cooperative learning, with individual rewards for students according to group achievement (see Chapter 11).
- Use the most concrete (least abstract) forms of instruction (see Chapter 9).

---

[24]Laurie Olson, "Crossing the Schoolhouse Border: Immigrant Children in California," *Phi Delta Kappan* 70(3):211–18 (November 1988).
[25]California State Superintendent of Public Instruction, *Its Elementary!* (Sacramento: Elementary Grades Task Force Report, State Superintendent of Public Instruction, 1992, p. xi.
[26]See Daniel L. Watson, Linda Northcutt, and Laura Rydell, "Teaching Bilingual Students Successfully," *Educational Leadership* 46(5):59–61 (February 1989).

A teacher whose preparation occurs exclusively among students whose backgrounds are similar to his or her own may not be prepared well enough to teach in a classroom of such diversity. You will need to learn as much as you can about each child and to become aware of any child who has difficulties in adjusting or developing at school because of economic factors, racial insensitivity, home environment conditions, or limited proficiency in English.

Guidelines for Communicating with Children

To be compatible with, and able to teach, students who come from backgrounds different from yours, you need to develop special skills that include the following (each of which is discussed in detail in subsequent chapters):

- Build the learning around the child's individual learning style (see Chapter 3).
- Communicate positively with every child and with his or her parents or guardians, learning as much as you can about the child and the child's culture, and encouraging family members to participate in the child's learning.
- Establish a classroom environment where *each child* feels he or she can learn (see Chapter 4).
- Establish a classroom environment where *every child* feels welcome (see Chapter 4).
- Involve parents, guardians, and the community in the educational program so that all have a sense of ownership and responsibility and feel positive about the program.
- Involve the child in understanding and in making important decisions about her or his own learning, so that the child feels ownership of that learning.
- Personalize learning for each child. For example, at Saturn School, a magnet school for fourth- through eighth-grade students of all abilities and socioeconomic levels (St. Paul School District, St. Paul, Minnesota) a computer-based **Personal Growth Plan** (PGP) is established for each student.[27]
- Provide learning activities adapted to the child's skill level.
- Teach to a child's needs by using a variety of strategies to achieve an objective, or a number of different objectives at the same time (referred to as **multilevel** or **multitask** teaching).
- Use techniques that emphasize cooperative learning and that deemphasize competitive learning (see Chapter 11).

Students Who Are Gifted and Talented

Sometimes neglected in the elementary school classroom are those students who are intellectually gifted and who have special talents (see theory of multiple intelligences under "Learning Styles," Chapter 2), that is, students who have been fortunate enough to have already developed their special intellectual gift or talent. There is no one accepted method for identification of these students, although for placement in special classes or programs for the gifted and talented in elementary school and middle-level schools, most school districts have traditionally used standard intelligence quotient (IQ) testing. Many exemplary schools today plan their curriculum around

---

[27]D. Thomas King, "The Saturn School of Tomorrow: A Reality Today," *T.H.E. Journal* 19(9):66–68 (April, 1992). For additional information about Saturn School, write to St. Paul Schools, Saturn School of Tomorrow Project, 360 Colborne Street, St. Paul, MN 55102. See also Jo Anna Natale, "Is Saturn Coming Down to Earth?" *Executive Educator* 13(9):39–42 (September 1991).

the philosophical position that all students have the potential to be gifted and talented learners. Guidelines recommended for working with gifted and talented students, whether or not they are identified as such, are as follows:

- Become familiar with special programs (local, regional, and national) specifically designed for gifted and talented children, and encourage their parents or guardians to consider involving them in such programs. District specialists can help identify the programs. Scholarships are often available.
- Emphasize skills in critical thinking, problem solving, and inquiry.[28]
- Involve the child in inviting effective guest speakers to class.
- Involve the child in planning interesting field trips.
- Plan and provide optional and voluntary enrichment activities. Self-instructional packages, learning activity centers, special projects, and computer and multimedia programs are excellent tools for provision of enrichment activities.
- Plan assignments and activities that challenge each child to the fullest of his or her abilities. *This does not mean overloading a child with homework,* but rather carefully planning so that the time spent on assignments and activities is *quality time,* rather than simply quantity time.
- Provide in-class seminars for a child to discuss topics and problems he or she is pursuing individually or in a learning team.
- Provide independent and dyad learning opportunities. A child who is intellectually gifted sometimes prefers to work alone or with one other gifted student.
- Use preassessments for reading level and subject achievement so that you are better able to prescribe objectives and activities for the student.
- Work with the gifted child in some planning of his or her own objectives and activities for learning.

Working with Young Adolescents

Historically, many teachers have found children of ages 10–14 to be at a particularly troublesome stage with which to cope. This is the age of students in middle school and junior high school. An understanding of the general characteristics of children in this age range provides not only a further understanding of these children, but also, by inference, increased understanding of the differences between them and children in the earlier grades. (Chapter 2 will further your understanding of these differences.) Furthermore, in some states an elementary school teaching credential qualifies the holder to teach in grades kindergarten through eight.

Characteristics of Middle-Level Students

Through experience and research, experts have come to accept certain precepts about middle-level students. These are presented here in five developmental categories: intellectual, physical, psychological, social, and moral and ethical development.[29]

---

[28]For example, in English and language arts the critical thinking skills of gifted students can be challenged with the use of mystery literature. See Jerry Flack, "Sherlock Holmes Meets the 21st Century," *Gifted Child Today* 14(4):15–21 (July–August 1991).

[29]*Caught in the Middle: Educational Reform for Young Adolescents in California Public Schools* (Sacramento, CA: California State Department of Education, 1987), pp. 144–48.

Intellectual Development

Middle-level students tend to:

1. Be egocentric; argue to convince others; exhibit independent, critical thought.
2. Be intellectually at risk; that is, they face decisions that have the potential to affect major academic values with lifelong consequences.
3. Be intensely curious.
4. Consider academic goals as a secondary level of priority, whereas personal-social concerns dominate thoughts and activities.
5. Display a wide range of individual intellectual development as their minds experience change from the concrete-manipulatory stage to the capacity for abstract thought. This change makes possible:

   • Ability to project thought into the future, to expect, and to formulate goals.
   • Analysis of the power of a political ideology.
   • Appreciation for the elegance of mathematical logic expressed in symbols.
   • Consideration of ideas contrary to fact.
   • Insight into the nuances of poetic metaphor and musical notation.
   • Insight into the sources of previously unquestioned attitudes, behaviors, and values.
   • Interpretation of larger concepts and generalizations of traditional wisdom expressed through sayings, axioms, and aphorisms.
   • Propositional thought.
   • Reasoning with hypotheses involving two or more variables.

6. Experience the phenomenon of metacognition—that is, the ability to think about one's thinking, and to know what one knows and does not know.
7. Exhibit strong willingness to learn what they consider to be useful, and enjoy using skills to solve real-life problems.
8. Prefer active over passive learning experiences; favor interaction with peers during learning activities.

Physical Development

Middle-level students tend to:

1. Be concerned about their physical appearance.
2. Be physically at risk; major causes of death are homicide, suicide, accident, and leukemia.
3. Experience accelerated physical development marked by increases in weight, height, heart size, lung capacity, and muscular strength.
4. Experience biological development five years sooner than adolescents of the nineteenth century; since then, the average age of menarche has dropped from 17 to 12 years of age.
5. Experience bone growth faster than muscle development; uneven muscle/bone development results in lack of coordination and awkwardness; bones may lack protection of covering muscles and supporting tendons.
6. Experience fluctuations in basal metabolism, which at times can cause either extreme restlessness or listlessness.

7. Face responsibility for sexual behavior before full emotional and social maturity have occurred.
8. Have ravenous appetites and peculiar tastes; may overtax digestive system with large quantities of improper foods.
9. Lack physical health; have poor levels of endurance, strength, and flexibility; as a group are fatter and less healthy.
10. Mature at varying rates of speed. Girls are often taller than boys for the first two years of early adolescence and are ordinarily more physically developed than boys.
11. Reflect a wide range of individual differences, which begin to appear in prepubertal and pubertal stages of development. Boys tend to lag behind girls at this stage, and there are marked individual differences in physical development for both boys and girls. The greatest variation in physiological development and size occurs at about age 13.
12. Show changes in body contour, including temporarily large noses, protruding ears, long arms; have posture problems.

Psychological Development

Middle-level students tend to:

1. Be easily offended and are sensitive to criticism of personal shortcomings.
2. Be erratic and inconsistent in their behavior; anxiety and fear are contrasted with periods of bravado; feelings shift between superiority and inferiority.
3. Be moody, restless; often feel self-conscious and alienated; lack self-esteem; are introspective.
4. Be optimistic, hopeful.
5. Be psychologically at risk; at no other point in human development is an individual likely to meet so much diversity in relation to self and others.
6. Be searching for adult identity and acceptance even in the midst of intense peer group relationships.
7. Be searching to form a conscious sense of individual uniqueness—"Who am I?"
8. Be vulnerable to naive opinions, one-sided arguments.
9. Exaggerate simple occurrences and believe that personal problems, experiences, and feelings are unique to themselves.
10. Have an emerging sense of humor based on increased intellectual ability to see abstract relationships; appreciate the double entendre.
11. Have chemical and hormonal imbalances which often trigger emotions that are frightening and poorly understood; may regress to more childish behavior patterns at this point.

Social Development

Middle-level students tend to:

1. Act out unusual or drastic behavior at times; may be aggressive, daring, boisterous, argumentative.
2. Be confused and frightened by new school settings that are large and impersonal.

3. Be fiercely loyal to peer group values; sometimes cruel or insensitive to those outside the peer group.
4. Be impacted by the high level of mobility in society; may become anxious and disoriented when peer group ties are broken because of family relocation.
5. Be rebellious toward parents but still strongly dependent on parental values; want to make their own choices, but the authority of the family is a critical factor in final decisions.
6. Be socially at risk; adult values are largely shaped conceptually during adolescence; negative interactions with peers, parents, and teachers may compromise ideals and commitments.
7. Challenge authority figures; test limits of acceptable behavior.
8. Experience low-risk trust relationships with adults who show lack of sensitivity to adolescent characteristics and needs.
9. Experience often traumatic conflicts because of conflicting loyalties to peer group and family.
10. Refer to peers as sources for standards and models of behavior; media heroes and heroines are also singularly important in shaping both behavior and fashion.
11. Sense the negative impact of adolescent behaviors on parents and teachers; realize the thin edge between tolerance and rejection; feelings of adult rejection can drive the adolescent into the relatively secure social environment of the peer group.
12. Strive to define sex role characteristics; search to set up positive social relationships with members of the same and opposite sex.
13. Want to know and feel that significant adults, including parents and teachers, love and accept them; need frequent affirmation.

Moral and Ethical Development

Middle-level students tend to:

1. Ask broad, unanswerable questions about the meaning of life; do not expect absolute answers but are turned off by trivial adult responses.
2. Be at risk in the development of moral and ethical choices and behaviors; depend on the influences of home and church for moral and ethical development; explore the moral and ethical issues that are met in the curriculum, in the media, and in the daily interactions with their families and peer groups.
3. Be idealistic; have a strong sense of fairness in human relationships.
4. Be reflective, introspective, and analytical about their thoughts and feelings.
5. Experience thoughts and feelings of awe and wonder related to their expanding intellectual and emotional awareness.
6. Face hard moral and ethical questions for which they are unprepared to cope.

D. TEACHERS

Teachers represent myriad individual personalities—perhaps impossible to capture in generalizations. Effective elementary school teachers exhibit much individuality. Let us imagine that a teaching colleague mentions that Linda Hall, in room 17, is a "fantastic teacher," "one of the best teachers in the district," "super," and "magnificent." What might be some of the characteristics you would expect to see in Linda's teaching behaviors?

We can expect Linda to know the curriculum she is employed to teach and how best to teach it; to be enthusiastic, motivated, well organized; to show effective interpersonal skills; and to be warm and caring about all children at whatever age and grade level she is teaching.

Children need teachers who are well organized and who know how to establish and manage an active and supportive learning environment, even with its multiple instructional demands. Students want teachers who provide leadership and who enjoy their function as role models, advisers, and mentors. They want and need warm, caring relationships with their teachers. These bonds of understanding and friendship have special significance during the critical, formative elementary school years.

The topic of teacher behavior begins again in Chapter 2, but for now let us look at the chief administrator in charge of everything at the school site—the principal.

E. THE PRINCIPAL

One person significantly responsible for the success of any school is its principal. What are the characteristics of an effective elementary school principal? Perhaps foremost is that the principal has a vision of what a good school is, and strives to bring that vision to life—school improvement is the effective principal's constant theme.[30] In addition, the school principal establishes a climate where teachers and students share ownership of the responsibility for determining the appropriate use of time and facilities.

An effective principal:

- Admonishes behaviors, rather than personalities.
- Encourages people, when they have made a mistake, to say "I'm sorry," rather than making them feel compelled to cover their mistakes.
- Follows up promptly on recommendations, concerns, or complaints.
- Fosters professional growth and development for faculty, with opportunities for visitations, demonstrations, conferences, workshops, and projects.
- Is an advocate for teachers and students.
- Is positive in her or his outlook.
- Keeps everyone well informed of events.
- Makes sure staff and students receive proper recognition for their accomplishments.
- Makes sure that basic school policies are closely defined and clearly communicated.
- Stresses the importance of making everyone feel like a winner.
- Runs a school of problem-solvers, not one of blamers and faultfinders.
- Spends time each day with students.
- Tries to catch teachers and students doing right, rather than wrong.
- Makes sure that teachers' administrative chores and classroom interruptions are limited to only those that are critically important to student learning and effective functioning of the school.

[30]*What Works: Research About Teaching and Learning* (Washington, DC: United States Department of Education, 1986), p. 50.

- Tries to develop a community support base for the school, its faculty, and its mission.
- Involves teachers, parents, and students in decision making.
- Models the very thinking skills expected of students and staff.

In addition to the school principal, there may be vice principals, persons with responsibilities in specific program areas. Sometimes teachers who are designated team leaders, or grade-level coordinators, may also serve administrative functions. However, the principal is the person with the final responsibility for everything that happens at the school. As a new teacher, or as a student teacher, one of your tasks is to become familiar with the administrative organization in your school and district.

F. HOME, SCHOOL, AND COMMUNITY PARTNERSHIPS

The final decade of the twentieth century has seen educators begin partnerships between the home, school, and community to promote the success of students. Although, traditionally, many teachers do effectively involve parents and guardians in their children's schoolwork, many families still have little positive interaction with the schools their children attend. Later, especially in Chapter 14, specific suggestions are offered about ways teachers can communicate with parents or guardians. Among these are the following: make time for parent conferences; write positive notes home about a child's learning or behavior; see that the student portfolio is shared with parents or guardians; and send communications home to parents about specific ways they can help with their child's learning.

Some states, districts, and local schools have adopted formal policies about home and community partnerships. According to Zelma P. Solomon, "Any school can be more successful if parents are productively involved in their children's education. Any student can be more successful if schools link comprehensive parent involvement programs to curricula."[31] School and administrative efforts to foster parent and community involvement include student-teacher-parent contracts, weekly assignment calendars, and folders that include the student's work and are sent home each week. Further, there are home visitor programs, involvement of community leaders in the classroom as aides and role models, and workshops for parents. Some schools have homework hotline programs through which students and parents can, by phone, get help with homework.[32]

G. THE OVERALL PICTURE

Certainly, no feature of education receives more attention from the media or causes more concern among parents and teachers than a decline (factual or otherwise) in students' achievement in the public schools. Reports are issued, polls taken, debates

---

[31]Zelma P. Solomon, "California's Policy on Parent Involvement," *Phi Delta Kappan* 72(5):359–62 (January 1991), p. 362.
[32]For a description of partnership programs, see the special section "Parent Involvement," *Phi Delta Kappan* 72(5):344–88 (January 1991).

organized, and blue-ribbon panels formed. Community members write letters to local editors, news editors devote extra space, television anchors comment, and documentaries and specials focus on the situation. Such attention, beginning about two decades ago, has never been matched in the political interest and participation generated, and it has affected the public schools and the programs for teacher preparation. This attention has led to several major reports.

Key National Reports

Never were so many reports about education published in such a short time as there were in 1983 and 1984. More than 120 national studies were published during just those two years, and the interest continues. Consider this brief sample list:

Adler, M. J. *We Hold These Truths.* New York: Macmillan, 1987.

America 2000. Washington, DC: United States Department of Education, 1991.

A Nation at Risk: The Imperative for Educational Reform. National Commission on Excellence in Education. Washington, DC: United States Department of Education, 1983.

A Nation Prepared: Teachers for the 21st Century. Washington, DC: Carnegie Forum on Education and the Economy, 1986.

Applebee, A. N., et al. *The Writing Report Card: Writing Achievement in American Schools.* Princeton, NJ: National Assessment of Educational Progress at Educational Testing Service, 1986.

Applebee, A. N., et al. *Who Reads Best?* Princeton, NJ: National Assessment of Educational Progress at Educational Testing Service, 1988.

Becoming a Nation of Readers: The Report of the Commission on Reading. Prepared by R. Anderson et al. Washington, DC: National Institute of Education, United States Department of Education, 1984.

Educating Americans for the 21st Century. Washington, DC: National Science Board, 1983.

Feistritzer, E. *The Conditions of Teaching: A State-by-State Analysis.* Princeton, NJ: Princeton University Press.

Glasser, W. *The Quality School.* New York: Harper & Row, 1990.

Goodlad, J. I. *A Place Called School.* New York: McGraw-Hill, 1984.

Goodlad, J. I. *Teachers for Our Nation's Schools.* San Francisco: Jossey-Bass, 1990.

Goodlad, J. I., Soder, R., and Sirotnik, K. A., eds. *Places Where Teachers Are Taught.* San Francisco: Jossey-Bass, 1990.

Herbst, J. *And Sadly Teaching: Teacher Education and Professionalization in American Culture.* Madison: University of Wisconsin Press, 1989.

Kozol, J. *Savage Inequalities.* New York: Crown, 1991.

Ravitch, D., and Finn, C., Jr. *What Do Our 17-Year-Olds Know?* New York: Harper & Row, 1987.

Tomorrow's Teachers: A Report of the Holmes Group. East Lansing, MI: Holmes Group, 1986.

What Works: Research About Teaching and Learning. Washington, DC: United States Department of Education, 1986.

Key Actions Resulting from the National Reports

In response to the reports, educators and politicians acted. Around the country, their actions resulted in:

- Changes in standards for teacher certification.
- Commitments to upgrade the teaching force.
- Emphases on helping students to make connections between what is being learned and real life and connections between disciplines.

- Emphases on test scores rising, dropout rates dropping, class time increasing, and curricula changing.[33]
- Emphasis on education for cultural diversity.
- Financial recognition and new roles for teachers as mentors.
- Financial rewards for schools that show significant increases on standardized tests.
- Formation of school-home-community partnerships to enhance the education of children.
- Improvement of school quality.[34]
- Increased involvement of parents and guardians in their children's education.
- Increased standards for a high school diploma.
- Longer school day and school year.
- Merit pay plans for teachers (salary tied to performance).
- New ways for teaching children whose primary language is not English.[35]
- Statewide competency testing programs for students.
- Stringent homework requirements.
- Teacher-competency testing.

Key Practices Today

For school improvement, most educators would agree that key practices include:

- Community and parental involvement.[36]
- Cooperative learning as a significantly useful instructional approach.
- Flexible and block scheduling.
- Sensitivity to the special needs of students from diverse backgrounds.[37]
- Interdisciplinary teams of teachers with a common planning time.
- Peer and cross-age tutoring as instructional strategies.
- Assignment of students to the same group of teachers and peers for the years spent at a particular school (school-within-a-school program).
- Taking advantage of new instructional technology to restructure the school effectively.[38]
- Teacher-student adviser programs.

By 1985 it appeared that a crisis was developing in education, as too few college students were showing a desire to assume teaching as a career, and, in 1986, the United States Office of Education projected that by 1993 there would be a serious

---

[33]Student scores on standardized tests began rising in the mid-1970s. By 1986 some stood at a 30-year high and scores have continued to rise. See Gerald W. Bracey, "Why Can't They Be Like We Were?" *Phi Delta Kappan* 73(2):104–117 (October 1991).

[34]See, for example, the 18 articles on "Improving School Quality" in the November 1992 issue of *Educational Leadership* 50(3).

[35]See, for example, Charles L. Glenn, "Educating the Children of Immigrants," *Phi Delta Kappan* 73(5):404–408 (January 1992).

[36]See Joyce L. Epstein, "What Matters in the Middle Grades—Grade Span or Practices?" *Phi Delta Kappan* 71(6):438–444 (February 1990).

[37]See, for example, Lee Little Soldier, "Cooperative Learning and the Native American Student," *Phi Delta Kappan* 71(2):161–163 (October 1989).

[38]For an overview of ten major school restructuring initiatives, see *Restructuring the Education System: A Consumer's Guide, Volume 1* (Denver, CO: Education Commission of the States, 1991), available for a charge from the ECS Distribution Center, 707 17th Street, Suite 2700, Denver, CO 80202.

shortfall of new teachers. However, when 1993 arrived the nation was in a serious economic depression. Consequently, veteran teachers delayed their retirements, more college students showed an interest in teaching as a career, and states and school districts did not have funds to build needed new classrooms and hire as many new teachers as needed. Nevertheless, we predict that the shortfall of teachers will become increasingly serious during the remaining years of this century as the nation gradually recovers from the economic depression.

The problems are further compounded: While the number of minority students increases, the relative number of minority teachers does not. And as the number of potentially at-risk students increases, the number of qualified teachers may also be at risk, especially if the predicted shortfall becomes a reality during the next few years.

On the other hand, there are signs of optimism, in that school improvements are paying dividends, as fewer students are dropping out of school,[39] SAT scores are on the rise, and more high school graduates are meeting college entrance requirements. For example, in California, from 1983 to 1990 the percentage of African American students meeting California State University entrance requirements more than doubled, increasing from 9.1 to 18.6 percent; the percentage of Latino students meeting those requirements increased from 15.3 to 17.3 percent; the number of Asian American students increased from 49.0 to 61.5 percent; and the number of Caucasian students increased from 33.5 to 38.2 percent.

Critical Problems and Issues Facing Our Nation's Schools

Today, major issues in education include:

- A decline in the percentage of male teachers in the elementary grades. In 1991, while approximately 28 percent of all public school teachers were male, only 12 percent of all elementary teachers were male, the lowest percentage of male elementary school teachers in a quarter of a century.
- A movement away from standardized testing of young children.
- A national system of uniform educational standards[40] and assessment.[41]
- Children at risk of dropping out of school. For example, in 1991 the Austin (Texas) Independent School District reported that of its children in prekindergarten through grade 6, 33.2 percent were at risk. It is also reported that most children become at risk while in elementary school.[42] Despite the national tendency toward improved mean performance of students on standardized tests, and the national decrease in dropouts, the dropout rate in some urban areas remains close to 45 percent, or may be even higher.[43] These figures include students who drop out during late elementary and middle school years and recent immigrant children who have not enrolled in school since coming to this country.

[39]Nationally, according to the 1990 U.S. Census figures, the percentage of 16- to 19-year-olds not in school and without a high school diploma fell from 13 percent in 1980 to 11 percent in 1990.
[40]See Chapter 5, Section D.
[41]For several articles dealing with the issue of national educational standards and national exams, see the entire November 1991 issue of *Phi Delta Kappan* 73(3).
[42]Linda Frazer and Todd Nichols, *At-Risk Report: 1990–91: Executive Summary* (Austin, TX: Office of Research and Evaluation, Austin Independent School District, 1991).
[43]For example, according to 1990 census figures, in one urban area of Sacramento County, Sacramento, California, 58 percent of the children between ages 16 and 19 were not in school and did not have a high school diploma. Sixty percent of those children were also unemployed.

- Controversy over the content of school textbooks.[44]
- Crime and drugs on school campuses and in school neighborhoods.
- The need to help cocaine- or crack-affected children succeed in school.
- Inadequate finances for purchasing textbooks and other basic teaching materials.
- Lack of funds for transportation for field trips.
- Lack of money to provide transportation for children to and from school.
- Overcrowded classrooms.
- Teaching and evaluating for higher-order thinking skills.
- The education of teachers to work effectively with children who may be too overwhelmed by family problems (or other problems) to succeed in school.[45]
- The education of teachers to work effectively with students who are culturally different from themselves.[46]
- Scarcity of funds needed to provide safe and effective schools.
- Scarcity of minority teachers to serve as effective role models for minority students. In 1991, 86.8 percent of the nation's public school teachers of grades K–12 were white. In California, for example, 82 percent of teachers were white, while only 45 percent of students were white.
- The specifics of how, where, and when to teach about acquired immune deficiency syndrome (AIDS);[47] the acceptance of a student with acquired immune deficiency syndrome in the classroom.[48]

Perhaps you and your classmates can identify additional issues and problems that face our nation's schools. Exercises 1.2 through 1.7 will aid your understanding of the reality of teaching today.

---

[44]See, for example, the debate over the Houghton Mifflin social studies textbooks for grades K–8: Edward Berenson, "Getting the Story Straight," *Phi Delta Kappan* 74(2):160–162 (October 1992); and William F. Ellis and Kitty Kelly Epstein, "Who Needs Defending—Textbook Publishers or Students?" *Phi Delta Kappan* 74(2):163–165 (October 1992).

[45]For example, in California, as of 1992, 20 percent of children live in poverty.

[46]For example, in California, as of 1992, one of every six children is an immigrant.

[47]See David L. Kirp and Steven Epstein, "AIDS in America's Schoolhouses: Learning the Hard Lessons," *Phi Delta Kappan* 70(8):585–593 (April 1989).

[48]For informative articles about AIDS, see Douglas Tonks, "Can You Save Your Students' Lives? Educating to Prevent AIDS," and Paul Sheckler, "When a Student Is HIV Positive," *Educational Leadership* 50(4):48–54 and 55–56, respectively (December 1992–January 1993).

Exercise 1.2: Interviewing an Elementary School Student

Instructions: The purpose of this exercise is to gain insight into an elementary student's perceptions of his or her own school experiences. Visit an elementary school and interview one or more students from the grade level(s) of your choice. Use the question format that follows. You may duplicate this blank form for each student interviewed. It is suggested that you privately interview one student at a time. Share with others in your class the results of your interviews.

Name and location of school _____

Date of visit _____ Name of interviewee _____

1. How old are you (interviewee)? _____

2. What grade are you in? _____

3. What other schools have you attended? _____

_____

4. With whom do you live? (parent or guardian, and how many adults are at home) _____

_____

_____

5. What do you like most about this school? _____

_____

_____

_____

_____

6. Is there anything you dislike about this school? _____

_____

_____

_____

_____

7. What do you like most about your teachers this year? _____

_____

_____

_____

8. Is there anything you dislike about your teachers at this school? _____

_____

_____

_____

9. What do you like about the other students at this school? _____

_____

_____

_____

_____

10. Is there anything you dislike about the students? _____

_____

_____

_____

_____

11. What has been your favorite class at this school? Why? _____

_____

_____

_____

_____

12. What has been your least favorite class? Why? _____

_____

_____

_____

_____

13. What do you hope to do when your schooling is finished? _____

_____

_____

_____

_____

14. Is there anything else you can tell me that will help me understand your experiences and feelings about being a student at this school? _____

_____

_____

_____

_____

Exercise 1.3: Interviewing an Elementary School Principal

Instructions: The purpose of this exercise is to gain information about an elementary school from its principal. Visit an elementary (or middle) school and interview the principal, using the question format that follows. Appointments should be arranged in advance. Follow-up thank-you letters are recommended. (*Note:* Because principals are very busy, an alternative to conducting individual interviews at various schools, is to invite one or more principals to your class.) Share with others in your class the results of your interview.

Name and location of the school _____

Grade span of school _____

Date of interview _____

Name of principal _____

1. What is your official title? _____

2. What are your official functions? _____

   _____

3. How did you get this job? _____

   _____

4. What other administrators are there on your school staff? _____

   _____

5. What are your teachers' administrative functions? _____

   _____

6. What is the philosophy or mission of your school? _____

   _____

   _____

7. Is this your first administrative experience? How many years have you been working in schools, and in what capacities? _____

   _____

   _____

   _____

   _____

8. Do you believe you were adequately prepared to administer? _____

   _____

   _____

9. Do you intend to remain at this school for the rest of your career? _____
_____
_____

10. What do you like most about your job? _____
_____
_____

11. What do you like least about your job? _____
_____
_____

12. What are some of your school's most recent accomplishments? _____
_____
_____

13. What are some of your school's most pressing problems? _____
_____
_____

14. What would you like to tell me (us) about your school's home-school-community partnership activities? _____
_____
_____

15. What can you tell me (us) about your school's curriculum? _____
_____
_____

16. What do you see for the future of schools such as yours? _____
_____
_____

17. What advice can you give me (us) about my own (our) preparation to teach at this level?
_____
_____
_____

18. Is there anything else you would like me (us) to know about schools, teaching, or students? _____
_____
_____

Exercise 1.4: Attending an Open House or Back-to-School Night

As part of your experiences in a teacher education program, you may be expected to participate in an open house (usually in the spring) or back-to-school night (usually in the fall) at a school. The purpose of this exercise is to provide an opportunity for you to observe the educational and community-related activities planned for this special event.

Instructions: Schedule an observational visit to an elementary school and attend an open house or back-to-school night. If you want to visit more than one school, you may duplicate this form. Record your observations and share them with others in your class.

Name of school _____

Grade span _____

Date _____

1. What exhibits did you see? _____

   _____

   _____

   _____

2. What presentations did you hear? By whom? Effectiveness? Response by audience? ___

   _____

   _____

   _____

3. What displays of student work did you see? _____

   _____

   _____

   _____

4. Whom did you meet (principal, teachers, parents or guardians, grandparents, students, clerical staff)? _____

   _____

   _____

   _____

   _____

5. What questions were asked by parents? Of whom? _____

   _____

   _____

   _____

   _____

6. What comments were made? By whom? _____

_____

_____

_____

7. How did parents and teachers respond to one another? _____

_____

_____

_____

8. What evidence was there that teachers and students worked together to prepare for the

event? _____

_____

_____

9. Did the educators show self-confidence, optimism, enthusiasm, and clarity in expecta-

tions for their school? Did they describe their programs and goals clearly so that visitors

understood? _____

_____

_____

10. Would you like to have been a student in this school? Why? _____

_____

_____

_____

11. Would you like to be a teacher in this school? Why? _____

_____

_____

_____

12. Would you be satisfied if your own child were a student in this school? Why? _____

_____

_____

_____

13. What other observations about this visit would you like to share? _____

_____

_____

_____

Exercise 1.5: Attending a Parent-Teacher or Parent-Teacher-Student Organization Meeting

The purpose of this exercise is to gain an understanding of how a parent-teacher organization serves a school and its students. Parents and teachers, linked together by common interests in their children, are usually supportive of one another in the academic achievement of the students and in the total development—social, physical, psychological, intellectual, moral, and ethical—of each child. To show this support and interest, teachers and parents join together in a parent-teacher organization (PTO), association (PTA), parents' club, or perhaps a parent-teacher-student organization (PTS).

Instructions: Attend one meeting as an interested teacher candidate, observe and record your observations as follows, then share your observations with others in your class.

Name of school _____

Grade span _____

Date of visit _____

1. Membership of the organization _____

2. Number of parents in attendance _____

3. Number of teachers in attendance _____

4. Number of administrators in attendance _____

5. Agenda of the meeting _____

   _____

   _____

   _____

   _____

   _____

6. Interests as related to the school _____

   _____

   _____

   _____

   _____

   _____

7. Educational issues raised _____

   _____

   _____

8. Attitudes of members _____

9. Fund-raising projects _____

10. Other observations (your own) _____

Exercise 1.6: Interviewing a Teacher Candidate

Instructions: The purpose of this exercise is to identify reasons why other teacher candidates have selected teaching as a career goal. Select one teacher candidate (preferably one who is not in your class), record that person's responses to the following questions, and share these with other members of your class. (*Note to instructor:* This exercise could be used during the first week of your school term as an icebreaker.)

Date of interview _____

Name of interviewee _____

1. What motivated you to select elementary school teaching as a career? _____

   _____

   _____

   _____

2. Do you look forward to being free from teaching during the summer months? If so, what

   do you plan to do during that time? _____

   _____

   _____

   _____

3. Would you like to teach in a year-round school? Why? _____

   _____

   _____

   _____

4. Do you plan a lifetime career as a classroom teacher? Why? _____

   _____

   _____

   _____

5. Are there any other teachers in your family? _____

   _____

   _____

   _____

6. At this time, do you have a favorite grade level? a favorite subject? _____

   _____

   _____

   _____

7. How and when did you decide on teaching as a career? _____

_____

_____

_____

_____

8. Do you plan a career as a classroom teacher, or do you plan eventually to move into a specialty or administrative position? _____

_____

_____

_____

_____

9. How would you describe your current feelings about being a teacher? _____

_____

_____

_____

_____

10. What, specifically, are you looking forward to most during this program of teacher preparation? _____

_____

_____

_____

_____

11. What personal and professional characteristics do you feel you have that would make you an effective teacher? _____

_____

_____

_____

_____

12. What else would you like us to know about you and your feelings concerning the program so far? _____

_____

_____

_____

Exercise 1.7: Interviewing an Elementary School Teacher

Instructions: The purpose of this exercise is to gain insight into the experiences of elementary school teachers. For this exercise you are to interview one or more teachers, perhaps one who is relatively new to the classroom and one who has been teaching for ten years or more, or a teacher of primary grades and a teacher of older children. Use a separate questionnaire for each interview; for this purpose, you may duplicate this form. Share the results with your classmates.

Name of school _____

Grade span _____

Date of interview _____

Name of teacher _____

Grade level and/or subject _____

1. Why did you select teaching as a career? _____

_____

_____

_____

_____

_____

2. Why are you teaching at this grade level? _____

_____

_____

_____

_____

_____

3. What preparation or training did you have? _____

_____

_____

_____

_____

_____

4. What advice about preparation can you offer me? _____

_____

_____

_____

5. What do you like most about teaching? _____

6. What do you like least about teaching? _____

7. What is most important for me to know to be an effective classroom teacher? _____

8. What specific advice do you have for those of us entering teaching at this level? _____

SUMMARY

In beginning to plan for developing your teaching competencies, you have read an overview of today's schools, reflected on your own school experiences, visited a school, and talked with teachers, administrators, and other teacher candidates. Such knowledge and experiences will provide a background as you read the subsequent chapters of this book.

QUESTIONS FOR CLASS DISCUSSION

1. From your point of view, what societal influences most affect today's students? Explain the effects to someone in your group.
2. Consider an elementary school class with which you are familiar. Are the students involved in making decisions about school activities? Describe the evidence leading to your conclusion.
3. When students are regularly dismissed from school between 2:00 and 3:00 P.M., where do they go? Is a parent or other adult guardian likely to be present when they arrive home from school? What is the problem that needs to be addressed in this situation?
4. The Independence, Missouri, school district has "21st Century Schools," offering extended hours (7:00 A.M. to 6:00 P.M.) for child care to eliminate the problem of unsupervised latchkey children. Preschoolers receive home visits from parent educators or attend day-care centers in the schools. There are day-care referrals for families, training for providers of home day care, half-day care for kindergartners, school-based day care for preschoolers, and before- and after-school care for elementary students. What schools in your area have extended hours?
5. In various states, schools have started "empowerment programs" (school-based management plans) in which a school organizes a local school council to be run by elected parents, community members, teachers, and principals. Critics say that this plan is suspect because it may shift the responsibility for school improvements (as well as the blame for failing to make a difference) from the school district to volunteer and untrained parents and community members. What is your opinion about this kind of program? Discuss this and other types of empowerment programs with your class.
6. What is the dress code, if any, for elementary schools in your area? Officials in one school district in southern California recently contemplated a ban on Los Angeles Raider's hats, T-shirts, and jackets. School officials thought that the clothing had an outlaw image—an intimidating silver and black logo showing crossed swords and a helmet-clad player with an eye patch. The purpose of the proposed ban was to stop gang activity from spreading in the area. Some students and parents argued that clothes do not necessarily make the student. Discuss your view on this subject with others in your class.
7. Investigate the history and outcomes of recent experimental programs that were designed to help in the academic success of African American males, such as those at Monnier (after-school program), Malcolm X, Marcus Garvey, and Paul Robeson elementary schools (predominately all-male academies) in Detroit, Michigan; Dr. Martin Luther King Jr. African American Immersion Elementary

School and Robert L. Fulton Middle School in Milwaukee, Wisconsin; Matthew A. Henson elementary school in Baltimore, Maryland (special all-male classes); the special-class programs of the San Diego, California, public schools; the health-oriented program of Tampa, Florida, sponsored by the Greater Tampa Urban League; and the Helping Hands mentoring program of Wake County (Raleigh, North Carolina) public schools.

8. In some elementary schools, ungraded classrooms (continuous promotion), that is, mixed-age classes, are making a comeback as an alternative to retention of students in the same grade for another year. Research the literature on the pros and cons of this approach and report your findings to your class.

9. What is the evidence of educational benefit of a year-round school? Discuss the following with your colleagues: Year-round schools are praised and decried. Those who praise such a plan believe that it provides continuity for the students, that the shorter time off helps the child to retain information, that family vacations so scheduled are more enjoyable, and that teachers do not have to review as much when students return from vacation.

   Critics say that with this plan students have two months twice a year to forget what was learned, that because neighborhood children are on different cycles some playmates are in school when others are on vacation. They further argue that since there are fewer days of instruction, the school day is longer—too long for first- and second-graders' attention spans. Curriculum is limited by the length of the track, and a child does not get to grow physically and mentally between tracks. Some cycles provide the least desirable vacation schedules for families. The state does not save any money by giving school districts financial incentives to establish year-round schedules. Such schedules, opponents state, are intended simply to reduce the demand and expense of building new schools. Although some studies indicate that migrant and disadvantaged children seem to learn more on a year-round schedule, for other children there was no significant difference as determined by achievement testing.[49]

10. What questions do you have about the content of this chapter? How might answers be found?

SUGGESTED READINGS FOR CHAPTER 1

Ascher, C. "School Programs for African-American Males . . . and Females." *Phi Delta Kappan* 73(10):777–782 (June 1992).

Boutte, G. S. "Frustrations of an African-American Parent: A Personal and Professional Account." *Phi Delta Kappan* 73(10):786–788 (June 1992).

Bracey, G. W. "Why Can't They Be Like We Were?" *Phi Delta Kappan* 73(2):105–117 (October 1991).

Brobeck, J. K. "Teachers Do Make a Difference." *Journal of Learning Disabilities* 23(1):11 (January 1990).

Calfee, R. C., and Wadleigh, C. "How Project READ Builds Inquiring Schools." *Educational Leadership* 50(1):28–32 (September 1992).

[49]See Marjie Lambert, "Year-round Schools Praised, Decried," *The Sacramento Bee*, Metro Section (July 29, 1990), pp. 1 and 4.

Carnegie Council on Adolescent Development. *Turning Points: Preparing American Youth for the 21st Century.* Report of the Task Force on Education of Young Adolescents. New York: Carnegie Corporation, 1989.

Cawelti, G. *Challenges and Achievements of American Education.* 1993 ASCD Yearbook. Alexandria, VA: Association for Supervision and Curriculum Development, 1993.

Clinchy, E. "Helping Parents Make the School System Work for Them: Buffalo Public Schools' Parent Center." *Equity and Choice* 7(2–3):83–88 (Spring 1991).

Darling-Hammond, L. "Reframing the School Reform Agenda." *Phi Delta Kappan* 74(10):753–761 (June 1993).

Dayton, C., et al. "The California Partnership Academies: Remembering the Forgotten Half." *Phi Delta Kappan* 73(7):539–545 (March 1992).

Eitzen, D. S. "Problem Students: The Sociocultural Roots." *Phi Delta Kappan* 73(8):584–590 (April 1992).

Frymier, J. "Children Who Hurt, Children Who Fail." *Phi Delta Kappan* 74(3):257–259 (November 1992).

Fullan, M. G., and Miles, M. B. "Getting Reform Right: What Works and What Doesn't." *Phi Delta Kappan* 73(10):745–752 (June 1992).

George, P., et al. *The Middle School—And Beyond.* Alexandria, VA: Association for Supervision and Curriculum Development, 1992.

Glasser, W. "The Quality School." *Phi Delta Kappan* 71(6):424–435 (February 1990).

Goodlad, J. I., and Lovitt, T. C. *Integrating General and Special Education.* New York: Macmillan, 1993.

Kellough, R. D., Kellough, N. G., and Hough, D. L. *Middle School Teaching: Methods and Resources.* New York: Macmillan, 1993.

Leake, D., and Leake, B. "African-American Immersion Schools in Milwaukee: A View from the Inside." *Phi Delta Kappan* 73(10):783–785 (June 1992).

Males, M. "Top School Problems' Are Myths." *Phi Delta Kappan* 74(1):54–56 (September 1992).

Oakes, J., and Lipton, M. "Detracking Schools: Early Lessons from the Field." *Phi Delta Kappan* 73(6):448–454 (February 1992).

Slavin, R. E., and Madden, N. A., eds. *Effective Programs for Students at Risk.* Boston: Allyn & Bacon, 1989.

Slavin, R. E., Karweit, N. L., and Waskik, B. A. "Preventing Early School Failure: What Works?" *Educational Leadership* 50(4):10–18 (December 1992–January 1993).

Stevens, L. J., and Price, M. "Meeting the Challenge of Educating Children at Risk." *Phi Delta Kappan* 74(1):18–23 (September 1992).

Stevenson, C. *Teaching Ten- to Fourteen-Year-Olds.* New York: Longman, 1992.

Tye, K. A. "Restructuring Our Schools: Beyond the Rhetoric." *Phi Delta Kappan* 74(1):8–14 (September 1992).

Vandergrift, J. A., and Greene, A. L. "Rethinking Parent Involvement." *Educational Leadership* 50(1):57–59 (September 1992).

Walling, D. R. *English as a Second Language: 25 Questions and Answers,* Fastback 347. Bloomington, IN: Phi Delta Kappa Educational Foundation, 1993.

2

What Do I Need to Know About How Children Learn, Think, and Develop Intellectually?

An understanding of children—how they develop intellectually, how they think, what they think about, and how they learn—is essential to becoming an effective classroom teacher. As you continue toward your goal of becoming a competent elementary school teacher, you bring to this chapter your own personal knowledge and opinions about its content. Your knowledge and opinions come from your previous experiences and your perceptions about those experiences. This chapter constructs and presents a framework of theoretical and practical knowledge designed to cause you to examine your own perceptions and deepen your understanding about the way children learn and develop intellectually.

Your task as a teacher is essentially the same, to cause children to examine their perceptions and build deeper and broader frameworks for understanding. Because no child comes to your classroom directly from his or her mother's womb, each has had a wealth of prior personal experiences, and so will come to school with perceptions about most everything. To cause children to examine and change some of their mental precepts is not a simple task. No one ever said that to become an effective teacher is easy. If they did, they didn't know what they were talking about.

In this chapter you are presented with a review of important historical and recent work of cognitive psychologists. This work has led to a modern view of teaching and the learning of children. *This modern view stresses the importance of learning as a personal process, by which each learner builds on his or her personal knowledge and experiences.* Like the construction of a skyscraper, learning is a gradual and sometimes tedious process. This modern view of teaching is in opposition to the traditional view, which sees teaching as "covering the material." Today's concept of correct pedagogy is to start where the children are, and then build upon and connect their understandings and experiences. The methodology uses what is often referred to as a "hands-on" and "minds-on" approach to constructing, and often reconstructing, the child's perceptions. As stated by Watson and Konicek, teaching in this **constructivist** mode

> is slower and involves discussion, debate, and the re-creation of ideas. Rather than following previously set steps, the curriculum . . . evolves, depends heavily on materials, and is determined by the children's questions. Less "stuff" will be

covered, fewer "facts" will be remembered for the test, and progress will some-times be exceedingly slow.[1]

Be cautioned: this chapter does not provide everything you might need or want to know about children's development and learning. Indeed, entire books and university courses are devoted to topics that are discussed in this chapter. Furthermore, although some information may be too close to the vanguard to be immediately useful to you, you should be knowledgeable about today's research on intellectual development, as well as that of the historical and recent past.

Expanding on information presented in Chapter 1, this chapter aims to help you build on your prior knowledge and translate those understandings into perceptions necessary to be the best teacher you can be. Be assured, however, that although researchers have learned much about children's intellectual development, thinking, and learning, there is still much more to be learned.

As you study this chapter your task is twofold: (1) to comprehend the theories, their relationships, and interrelationships and (2) to synthesize the information into both the individual and social learning contexts you will be providing for your students through planning and instruction.

Chapter 1 discussed the characteristics of children in the middle grades; we begin here with a review of the general characteristics of all children.

A. GENERAL CHARACTERISTICS OF CHILDREN

If you are to be effective as a teacher, you must be aware of and use what is known about the general traits of children. Knowing and understanding these characteristics can make the teaching and learning an enjoyable and rewarding experience for both you and your students. The following are general characteristics of children, regardless of their individual genetic or cultural differences.

Egocentric. Most children, to some degree or another, are egocentric. This is certainly true of preschool and primary-grade children. To egocentric children, everything is important to them insofar as it relates to themselves. In young children, this egocentricity is quite natural, because they find themselves in a strange yet wonderful world, filled with phenomena that are constantly affecting them. They tend to interpret the phenomena in relation to how the phenomena affect them, and to use everything they learn for the express purpose of adjusting to the world in which they live, whether for better or for worse. As a teacher, you can help young children to understand this world and to adjust to it in positive ways. As they develop psychologically, emotionally, and intellectually, children tend to overcome this egocentricity. But to do that requires the important skill of **listening** to others with understanding and empathy. Teachers must help children to develop that skill.

Interpreting. Children are constantly interpreting their environment. Very often their interpretations of the environmental phenomena that affect them are incomplete or even incorrect. However, children will continue to arrive at interpretations that satisfy them and allow them to function adequately in their daily lives. In so doing, they show evidence of their imaginations in developing hypotheses and devis-

[1]Bruce Watson and Richard Konicek, "Teaching for Conceptual Change: Confronting Children's Experience," *Phi Delta Kappan* 71(9):680–685 (May 1990), p. 685.

ing ways of verifying their hypotheses. A child tries to construct meaning to his or her experiences by referring to what is termed a **schema,** that is, a body of related information stored in long-term memory from prior experiences. Learning continues by fitting new information into a schema (**assimilation**) and modifying or forming a new schema (**accommodation**), thus allowing the child to function adequately. Children's interpretations of phenomena change with their increasing maturity. Consequently, they are engaged in a constant process of revising interpretations as they grow in ability to understand and to think abstractly.

Children come to your classroom with existing schemata, which from an adult's point of view may or may not be sound (that is, that may be at variance with accepted views) but, nevertheless, are valid. These schemata are sometimes called **naive theories** (also called **conceptual misunderstandings** and **misconceptions**), and a teaching task is to correct children's naive theories. Because children are naturally resistant to alterations in their interpretations, changing their misconceptions is no easy task. Research has shown a persistence of misconceptions even after children have had corrective instruction.[2] However, "Whenever students are asked to think about an idea in a way that questions common sense or a widely accepted assumption, that relates new ideas to ones previously learned, or that applies an idea to the problems of living, then there is a chance that good teaching is going on."[3]

Regardless of the grade level you are teaching, children do come to your class with misconceptions. Your understanding, patience, and creative instruction will be needed in the often long and arduous task of correcting such misconceptions. Children are much more likely to modify data from their experiences to accommodate their schemata than to change their beliefs as a result of new experiences.[4] This reluctance is not difficult to understand. There are stories of reputable scientists who have been tempted to modify data to support their own hypotheses. Stubborn persistence and openness to change, virtuous although conflicting human attributes, are characteristic of children as well.

Children are persistent. They like to achieve their objectives, and will spend unusual lengths of time and effort at activities that are important and interesting to them. With those efforts comes a sense of accomplishment and personal satisfaction. We know of a young man who, at age ten, spent hours at a time playing his electronic *Game Boy,* yet was unwilling to spend more than five minutes a day practicing his piano lesson. The teacher must take advantage of children's persistence and desire to achieve by presenting learning in the form of interesting and meaningful activities.

Children are naturally curious. For them, the world is filled with wonder and excitement. Their curiosity will vary, depending on what catches their interest. Generally, they are more interested in things that move than things that don't. They are more interested in an object that makes things happen than in one to which things are happening. Their curiosity reaches a peak with things that appear mysterious and magical. To initiate effective learning in the classroom, good instruction takes advantage of this natural curiosity.

Children love to explore. When given an object to play with, younger children try to take it apart and then put it together again. They love to touch and feel objects. They are always wondering "what will happen if? . . ." and suggesting ideas for finding out. Children are natural questioners. The words *what, why,* and *how* are common

[2]See, for example, Edward L. Smith and Charles W. Anderson, "Plants as Producers: A Case Study of Elementary Science Teaching," *Journal of Research in Science Teaching* 21(7):685–698 (October 1984).
[3]Martin Haberman, "The Pedagogy of Poverty Versus Good Teaching," *Phi Delta Kappan* 73(4):290–294 (December 1991), p. 294.
[4]Watson and Konicek, p. 683.

in their vocabulary. While investigating, children work and learn best when they experience firsthand. Therefore, a teacher should provide a wide variety of experiences that involves **hands-on doing.** Hands-on learning engages the child's mind, causing questioning. The teacher should encourage rather than discourage a child's questions. Hands-on and **minds-on learning** encourages students to question and then to devise ways of investigating tentative but satisfactory answers to their questions.

Children are energetic. They would rather not sit for a long time. For some, it is near impossible. They would rather do than listen, and even while listening, they move their bodies restlessly. This difficulty in sitting still has a direct bearing on children's attention spans. As a result, teaching should provide for many activities that give children the opportunity to be physically active.

Children are social beings. They like to be with and to be accepted by their peers. They like to work together in planning and carrying out their activities. Children work very well together when given proper encouragement, clear direction, and worthwhile opportunity. Furthermore, each child forms a self-concept through early social experiences in school. The child will develop satisfactory self-esteem when given an opportunity to work with others, to offer ideas, and to work out peer relationships. Your teaching can help foster not only the learning but also the develop-

Children are social beings. They like to be with and accepted by their peers. A child will develop a satisfactory self-esteem when given an opportunity to work with others, offer ideas, and work out peer relationships. A teacher can help foster not only learning but also development of each child's self-esteem.

ment of each child's self-esteem through such teaching strategies as cooperative learning, peer tutoring, and cross-age teaching.

Children have a variety of needs. Abraham Maslow presented a continuum, beginning with the most basic—**physiological** need (provision of food, clothing, and shelter), then a need for **security** (feeling of safety), **social** need (sense of love and belonging), a need for **self-esteem,** and the highest—a need for **self-actualization** (full use of talents, capacities, abilities, acceptance of self and others).[5] When children become frustrated because of lack of satisfaction of one or more of these needs, their classroom behavior becomes affected and their learning is stifled.[6] Some children become aggressive and disrupt normal classroom procedures, acting this way to satisfy a basic need for recognition. Others become apathetic, and fail to participate in class activities. Perhaps such behavior is best explained by D. S. Eitzen, professor of sociology at Colorado State University:

> Everyone needs a dream. Without a dream, we become apathetic. Without a dream, we become fatalistic. Without a dream and the hope of attaining it, society becomes our enemy. We educators must realize that some young people act in antisocial ways because they have lost their dreams. And we must realize that we as a society are partly responsible for that loss. Teaching is a noble profession whose goal is to increase the success rate for *all* children. We must do everything we can to achieve this goal. If not, we—society, schools, teachers, and students—will all fail.[7]

The wise teacher is alert to any child whose needs are not being satisfied. Perhaps it is the child who comes to school hungry. Perhaps it is the child who comes to school feeling insecure because of problems at home. Although the classroom teacher cannot solve all the ailments of society, the teacher does have an opportunity and responsibility to make all children feel welcome, respected, and wanted, at least while in the classroom.

With the understanding of the general characteristics of children and the importance of their basic needs, we can next consider what we know about how children learn and think, and how that knowledge can be used.

B. LEARNING: CONTRIBUTIONS OF LEARNING THEORISTS

Jean Piaget, Robert Gagné, Jerome Bruner, and David Ausubel are four learning theorists who have had significant historical influence on pedagogy. Of the several psychologists whose theories of learning made an impact during the last half of the twentieth century, perhaps no other had such a wide-ranging influence on education than did the Swiss psychologist Jean Piaget. Although Piaget began to publish his insights in the 1920s, his work was not popularized in this country until the 1960s.

---

[5]See Abraham H. Maslow, *Motivation and Personality* (New York: Harper & Row, 1970).
[6]See, for example, Sally Reed and R. Craig Sautter, "Children of Poverty: The Status of 12 Million Young Americans," *Phi Delta Kappan* 71(10):K1–K12 (June 1990).
[7]D. Stanley Eitzen, "Problem Students: The Sociocultural Roots," *Phi Delta Kappan* 73(8):584–590 (April 1992), p. 590.

Piaget's Theory of Cognitive Development

Piaget postulated four stages of mental development that occur from birth to post-adolescence. Even though you will not have children in your classroom in all stages, you must understand that mental development is a continuing process and that children must begin with the first stage and progress developmentally through each succeeding stage. A child cannot skip a stage. Furthermore, because children in your classroom might be at different stages of mental development, it is imperative that you attend to each child's developmental stage. This means that, when possible, you should individualize the instruction. Consider the following review of Piaget's stages of cognitive development.

Sensorimotor Stage (Birth to Two Years)

At this stage children are bound to the present and to their immediate environment. Learning and behaviors at this stage result from direct interaction with stimuli that the child can see or feel. Objects that are not seen are found only by random searching. Through direct interaction the child begins to build mental concepts, associating actions and reactions, and later in the stage will begin to label people and objects and to show imagination. The child, then, is developing a practical base of knowledge that forms the foundation for learning in the next stage.

Preoperational Stage (Two to Seven Years)

Children at this stage can imagine and think before acting, rather than only respond to external stimuli.

You must be cautious about placing too much reliance on the age ranges assigned to Piaget's stages of cognitive development. For example, about 5 percent of middle school children, that is, children ages 10–14, operate at the preoperational level. Furthermore, when confronted with perplexing situations, evidence indicates that for many learners there is a tendency to revert to an earlier developmental stage. What this means is that many elementary school students are in some phase of this concrete-preoperational stage of cognitive development. As their teacher, your task is to facilitate their readiness for the next stage.

This stage is called "preoperational" because a child at this point does not yet use logical operations in thinking. At this stage the child is **egocentric.** The child's world-view is subjective rather than objective. Because of this egocentrism, it is difficult for the child to consider and accept another person's point of view. The child is perceptually oriented; that is, judgments are made by how things look to him or her. The child does not think logically and therefore cannot reason by implication. Instead, an intuitive approach is used, and judgments are made according to how things seem to the child. At this stage, when confronted with new and discrepant information about a phenomenon, the child adjusts the new information to accommodate his or her existing beliefs. Children at this stage of development often make humorous comments, ask many *why* questions, and are quite serious about their play.

At this stage the child can observe and describe variables (properties of an object or aspects of a phenomenon), but concentrates on just one variable at a time, usually one that is visually conspicuous. The child cannot coordinate variables, so has difficulty in realizing that an object has several properties. Consequently, it is difficult for the child to combine parts into a whole. The child can make simple classifications according to one or two properties, but finds it difficult to realize that multiple classifications are possible. The child can also arrange objects in simple series, but has trouble arranging them in a long series or inserting a new object in its proper place within a series. To the child, space is restricted to the child's neighborhood, and time is restricted to hours, days, and seasons.

The child in this stage has not yet developed the concept of conservation. This means the child does not understand that if several objects are rearranged, the number of the objects remains unchanged; that if the size, shape, or volume of a solid or liquid is changed, the amount of solid or liquid will be unchanged, or conserved. For example, if two rows of ten objects are arranged so they take up the same area, the child will state that the two rows are the same and that there are the same number of objects in each row. If the objects in one row are spread out so that the row is longer, the child is likely to maintain that the longer row now has more objects in it. Similarly, if the child is shown two identical balls of clay, the child will agree that both balls contain the same amount of material. When, in full view of the child, one of the balls is stretched out into the shape of a sausage, the child is likely to say the sausage has more clay because it is larger, or less clay because it is thinner. Either way, the child at this stage is "centering" his or her attention on just one particular property (here, length or thickness) to the neglect of other properties.

In both of the preceding examples the reason for the child's thinking is that the child does not yet understand **reversibility.** The child's thinking cannot yet reverse itself back to the point of origin. As a result, the child does not understand that since nothing has been removed or added, the extended row of objects can be rearranged to its original length, and the clay sausage can be made back into the original ball. The child does not yet comprehend that action and thought processes are reversible. Not yet able to use abstract reasoning, and only beginning to think conceptually, students at this stage of development learn best by manipulating objects in concrete situations, rather than by verbal learning alone. For children at this stage of development, conceptual change comes very gradually.

The Three-Phase Learning Cycle

For conceptual development and change, Piaget developed a theory of learning that involves children in a three-phase **learning cycle.** The three phases are (1) an **exploratory** hands-on phase, (2) a **concept development** phase, and (3) a **concept application** phase. When a learner is applying a concept (the third phase), he or she is involved in a hands-on activity. During application of a concept the learner may discover new information that causes a change in his or her understanding of the concept being applied. Thus the process of learning is cyclic.

Concrete Operations Stage (7–11 Years)

Although the age span of this stage is approximately 7–11, there seem to be several substages, and a task of the school program is to foster the development of children's thinking through this stage.

At this stage the child can now perform **logical operations.** The child can observe, judge, and evaluate in less egocentric terms than in the preoperational stage, and can formulate more objective explanations. As a result, the child knows how to solve physical problems. Because the child's thinking is still concrete and not abstract, the child is limited to problems dealing with actual concrete experiments. Early in this stage the child cannot generalize, deal with hypothetical situations, or weigh possibilities.

The child can make multiple classifications, and can arrange objects in long series and place new objects in their proper places in a series. The child can begin to comprehend geographical space and historical time. The child develops the concepts of conservation according to their ease of learning: first, number of objects (ages 6–7), then matter, length, area (age 7), weight (ages 9–12), and volume (age 11 or older). The child also develops the concept of reversibility and can now reverse the physical and mental processes when numbers of objects are rearranged or when the size and shape of matter are changed.

Later in this stage children can hypothesize and do higher-level thinking. Not yet able to use abstract reasoning, and only beginning to be able to think conceptually, students at this stage of development still learn best by manipulating objects in concrete situations, rather than by verbal learning alone.

Formal Operations Stage (11–15 Years)

Piaget initially believed that most adolescents reached formal operational thinking by age 15, but now it is quite clear that many high school students, and even some adults, do not yet function at this level.

Essentially, students who are quick to understand abstract ideas are formal thinkers. However, most elementary school and middle school students are not at this stage. For them, **metacognition** (planning, monitoring, and evaluating one's own thinking) may be very difficult. In essence, metacognition is today's term for what Piaget referred to as **reflective abstraction,** or the reflection upon one's own thinking, without which continued development cannot occur.[8]

At this stage the individual's method of thinking shifts from the concrete to the more formal and abstract. The learner can now relate one abstraction to another and grows in ability to think conceptually. At this stage too, the learner can develop hypotheses, deduce possible consequences from them, then test the hypotheses with controlled experiments in which all variables are identical except the one being tested. When approaching a new problem, the learner begins by formulating all the possibilities and then determines which ones are substantiated through experimentation and logical analysis. After solving a problem, the learner can reflect upon or rethink the thought processes that were used.

Brain Growth Patterns and Piaget's Stages of Cognitive Development

According to Herman Epstein, the human brain grows in spurts, times of rapid increase in the mass of the brain, followed by a period of stabilization or less growth.[9] He calls this phenomenon **phrenoblysis.** There may be a relationship between Piaget's stages of cognitive development and these brain growth patterns.

[8]For attempts to clarify today's concept of "metacognition," see I. Braten, "Vygotsky as Precursor to Metacognitive Theory: I. The Concept of Metacognition and Its Roots," *Scandinavian Journal of Educational Research* 35(3):179–192 (1991).

[9]Herman T. Epstein, "Brain Growth and Cognitive Functions." In D. Steer, ed., *The Emerging Adolescent: Characteristics and Educational Implications* (Columbus, OH: National Middle School Association, 1980).

According to Epstein, the brain develops in five sets of growth (plateau) stages. The first four parallel the cognitive stages of development as defined by Piaget. Brain weight increases from 5 to 10 percent during each of the last four stages, resulting in a 30 percent increase overall. The rapid increase in the mass of a body organ always signals the appearance of important new functions.

Researchers have found that in approximately 85 percent of all people, the brain grows in weight and volume mainly during five age periods: 3–10 months; 2–4 years; 6–8 years; 10–12+ years; and 14–16+ years. Brain cell replication ceases at or about 18 months; therefore, the final four brain growth stages occur without any increase in the number of brain cells.

If intellectual development is directly related to periods of brain growth, it is possible that a fifth Piagetian stage exists. However, the jury is still out on the validity of Epstein's position. As stated by Wadsworth, "While there are undoubtedly links between what goes on inside the brain and intellectual development, it does not yet seem clear what those links are or what educational conclusions can be reasonably drawn from them."[10]

Female brain growth tends to occur earlier than that of males during all two-year growth stages. The normal growth at any particular stage seems to occur more rapidly in more intelligent children. During the (two-year) ages 10–12 and ages 14–16 growth stages, data show an average mental growth of 38 months. During the two-year plateau, mental age growth averages 7 months.

Implications for Teaching

If the human brain is more receptive to new learning during growth spurts, and less able to cope with new learning during plateaus, this would have important implications for instruction. For example, it would imply that during growth spurts is the time to introduce new skills and concepts. During plateaus is the time to challenge the mind with intensive study, to work on reinforcing existing knowledge and skills, and to provide additional exposure to life experiences that broaden the experiential base of knowledge.

New principles are emerging from current brain research that may have profound effects on teaching and on how schools are organized. For example, as stated by Caine and Caine, "Because there can be a five-year difference in maturation between any two 'average' children, gauging achievement on the basis of chronological age is inappropriate."[11] As stated in Chapter 1, research indicates brain growth spurts for students in grades 1, 2, 5, 6, 9, and 10. If schools were organized solely according to this criterion, they would be configured in grade clusters K, 1–4, 5–8, and 9–12.[12] The emergence of the exemplary middle school may be an indicator of a movement in that direction.

Many advances are expected in knowledge about neurological processing during the next few years, and it is important to understand the complexity and ramifications of the continuing quest to learn more about how children learn and process information. It is quite clear that if we define learning as only the accumulation of bits and

[10]Barry J. Wadsworth, *Piaget's Theory of Cognitive and Affective Development*, 3rd ed. (White Plains, NY: Longman, 1984), p. 222.
[11]Renate Nummela Caine and Geoffrey Caine, "Understanding a Brain-Based Approach to Learning and Teaching," *Educational Leadership* 48(2):66–70 (October 1990), p. 66.
[12]R. Sylwester, J. S. Chall, M. C. Wittrock, and L. A. Hart, "The Educational Implications of Brain Research," *Educational Leadership* 39(1):6–17 (October 1991).

TABLE 2.1   GAGNÉ'S GENERAL LEARNING HIERARCHY

Type 8	Problem Solving
Type 7	Principle Learning
Type 6	Concept Learning
Type 5	Multiple Discrimination
Type 4	Verbal Association
Type 3	Chaining
Type 2	Stimulus-Response Learning
Type 1	Signal Learning

pieces of information, then we already know how that is learned and how to teach it. However, accumulation of pieces of information is at the lowest end of a wide spectrum of types of learning. We are still learning about learning, about teaching for understanding, and about the reflective use of that understanding. For higher levels of thinking and learning, recent brain research supports current methods of teaching such as the **whole language** approach to reading, **thematic teaching,** and connecting life experiences with the curriculum.[13] *To be most effective in teaching important understandings to the diversity of children in today's schools, learning must be integrated with the whole curriculum, and made meaningful to the lives of the children, rather than taught as unrelated and separate disciplines at the same time each day.*

Robert Gagné and the General Learning Hierarchy

Robert Gagné is well known for his hierarchy of learning levels. According to Gagné, *learning is the establishing of a capability to do something that the learner was not capable of doing previously.* Gagné postulates a hierarchy of learning capabilities. Learning one particular capability usually depends on having previously learned one or more simpler capabilities.

For Gagné, observable changes in behavior constitute the only criteria for inferring that learning has occurred. It follows, then, that the beginning, or lowest, level of a learning hierarchy would include very simple behaviors. These behaviors would form the basis for learning more complex behaviors in the next level of the hierarchy. At each higher level, learning would require that the appropriate simpler, or less complex, behaviors have been acquired in the lower learning levels.

Gagné identifies eight levels of learning in this hierarchy. Beginning with the simplest and progressing to the most complex, these levels are shown in Table 2.1 and described briefly as follows.

Signal Learning

The child learns to make a general conditioned response to a given signal. Examples are a child's pleasure at the sight of a pet, or an expression of fright at the sound of a loud noise.

---

[13]Caine and Caine, p. 67. See also Patricia L. Roberts, *A Green Dinosaur Day: A Guide for Developing Thematic Units in Literature-Based Instruction, K–6* (Boston: Allyn and Bacon, 1992).

Stimulus-Response Learning

The child acquires a precise physical or vocal response to a discriminated stimulus. An example is a child's initial learning of words by repeating the sounds and words of adults.

Chaining

Sometimes called **skill learning,** chaining involves the linking together of two or more units of simple stimulus-response learning. Chaining is limited to physical, nonverbal sequences. Examples include winding up a toy, writing, running, and opening a door. The accuracy of the learning at this level depends on practice, prior experience, and reinforcement.

Verbal Association

This is a form of chaining, but the links are verbal units. Naming an object is the simplest verbal association. In this case, the first stimulus-response link is involved in observing the object, and the second is involved in enabling the child to name the object. A more complex example of verbal chaining would be the rote memorization of a sequence of numbers, a formula, or the letters of the alphabet in sequence. Considered alone, these learned behaviors are not usually seen as important goals of teaching. However, viewed as a level in a hierarchy, they may be significant first steps in certain higher levels of learning.

Multiple Discrimination

Individual learned chains are linked to form multiple discriminations. Examples of learning at this level include the identification of the names of children in a classroom, the learner associating each child with his or her distinctive appearance and correct name; and learning the distinction between solids, liquids, and gases.

Concept Learning

Learning a concept means learning to respond to stimuli by their abstract characteristics (such as position, shape, color, and number), as opposed to concrete physical properties. A child may learn to call a two-inch cube a "block," and to apply this name to other objects that differ from it in size and shape. Later, the child learns the concept "cube," and by so doing can identify a class of objects that differ physically in many ways (e.g., by material, color, texture, and size). Rather than learning concepts in a trial-and-error fashion, under the careful guidance of the teacher, a child's learning is sequenced in such a way as to lead to improved conceptual understanding.

Principle Learning

In simplest terms, a principle is a chain of two or more concepts. In principle learning the individual must relate two or more concepts. An example is the relation of a circle's circumference to its diameter. Three separate concepts (circumference, pi, and diameter) are linked or chained together.

Problem Solving

According to Gagné, problem solving is the most sophisticated type of learning. In problem solving, the individual applies principles learned, to achieve a goal. While achieving this goal, however, the learner becomes capable of new performances by using the new knowledge. When a problem is solved, new knowledge has been acquired, and the individual's capacity moves forward. The individual is now able to handle a wide class of problems similar to the one solved. What has been learned, according to Gagné, is a higher-order principle, which is the combined product of two or more lower-order principles.

Thus, when a child has acquired the capabilities and behaviors of a certain level of learning, we assume that the child has also acquired the capabilities and behaviors of all the learning levels below this level. Furthermore, if a child is having difficulty in demonstrating the capabilities and behaviors for a certain level, the teacher can simply test the child on the capabilities and behaviors of the lower levels to determine which one or ones were causing the difficulty.

Benjamin Bloom and Mastery Learning

Benjamin Bloom has made numerable significant contributions to our understanding of learning. Bloom and his colleagues developed a *Taxonomy of Educational Objectives,* which divides cognitive goals of instruction into a hierarchy of levels of thinking and doing (presented in Chapter 6), similar to Gagné's simple-to-complex hierarchy of types of learning. Like Gagné, Bloom stresses the importance of prior experiences and learning and their effect on current learning.

Research has shown that student achievement in learning is related to time and to the quality of attention given to the learning task. In 1968, Bloom developed a concept of individualized instruction called **mastery learning,** based on the premise that students need sufficient time-on-task to master content before moving on to new content. Although Bloom is usually given credit for the concept of mastery learning, the idea did not originate with him. He reinforced and popularized a model developed earlier by John Carroll.

In 1968, Fred Keller developed a similar model called the Keller Plan, or the Personalized System of Instruction (PSI). The Keller Plan quickly became a popular teaching technique, particularly in higher education. In about 1972, Rita and Stuart Johnson developed their model of mastery learning and called it the **Self-Instructional Package** (SIP). The SIP concept has been popular ever since, as a way of individualizing and assuring learning for any student, regardless of subject, grade level, or the child's ability. (See Chapter 11, Section J, for a sample SIP and instructions on the development of an SIP.)

Although a Self-Instructional Package takes time to develop, teachers report that it is time well spent. It is reported that students taught by mastery learning do better than 85 percent of students taught in a traditional fashion, and 70 percent of them attain levels reached by only the top 20 percent of students taught in traditional ways.[14]

Jerome Bruner and Discovery Learning

Although a leading interpreter and promoter of Piaget's ideas in the United States, Jerome Bruner made his own significant contributions to the understanding of how children learn.[15]

Like Piaget, Bruner maintains that each child passes through stages that are age-related and biologically determined, and that learning depends primarily on the developmental level the child has attained. Bruner's theory also encompasses three major sequential stages called representations. These are **enactive representation** (knowing that is related to movement, i.e., from direct experiencing), **ikonic representation** (knowing that is related to visual and spatial representations, e.g., pictures and films), and **symbolic representation** (knowing that is related to reason and logic, i.e., from use of words). These correspond to Piaget's sensorimotor, concrete operations, and formal operations. Bruner's general description of what happens during these three representations also corresponds to that of Piaget's stages, but he differs from Piaget in his interpretation of the role of language in intellectual development. Piaget believes that although thought and language are related, they are different systems. He posits that the child's thinking is based on a system of inner logic that evolves as the child organizes and adapts to experiences. Bruner, however, maintains that thought is internalized language, that the child translates experience into language, and then uses language as an instrument of thinking.

Bruner and Piaget differ in their attitudes toward a child's readiness for learning. Piaget's experiments led him to conclude that a child's readiness for learning depends on maturation and intellectual development. Bruner, however, believes that a child is always ready to learn a concept at some level of sophistication. He states that any subject can be taught effectively in some intellectually honest form to any child in any stage of development. He supports this concept, for example, by noting that the basic ideas of science and mathematics are simple, and only when these ideas are out of context with the child's life experiences, and formalized by equations and complex verbal statements, do they become incomprehensible to young children (and to adults).

Concept Attainment

According to Bruner, a child can learn concepts only within the framework of whichever stage of intellectual development the child is in at the time. In teaching children, then, it is essential that each child be helped to pass progressively from one stage of intellectual development to the next. The teacher can do this by providing challenging but usable opportunities and problems that tempt the child to forge

[14]Arthur A. Carin and Robert B. Sund, *Teaching Science Through Discovery*, 6th ed. (New York: Macmillan, 1989), p. 41.
[15]See, for example, Jerome S. Bruner, *The Process of Education* (Cambridge, MA: Harvard University Press, 1960).

ahead into the next stages of development. As a result, the child acquires a higher level of understanding.

Bruner states that the act of learning involves three almost simultaneous processes: (1) the process of **acquiring** new knowledge, (2) the process of **manipulating** this knowledge to make it fit new tasks or situations, and (3) the process of **evaluating** the acquisition and manipulation of this knowledge. A major objective of learning is to introduce the child at an early age to the ideas and styles that will help him or her to become literate. Consequently, the curriculum should be built around major conceptual schemes, skills, and values that society considers to be important. These should be taught as early as possible in a manner that is consistent with the child's stages of development and forms of thought.

Benefits of Discovery Learning

Bruner has been an articulate spokesperson for **discovery learning.** He advocates that, whenever possible, teaching and learning should be conducted in such a manner that children are given the opportunity to discover concepts for themselves. He claims that four major benefits are derived from learning by discovery. First, there is an increase in intellectual potency. Discovery learning helps children learn how to

The best teaching allows for, provides for, and encourages coincidental learning.

learn. It helps children to develop skills in problem solving, enabling them to arrange and apply what has been learned to new situations, and thus learn new concepts. Second, there is a shift from extrinsic to intrinsic rewards. Discovery learning shifts motives for learning, away from satisfying others and toward internal self-rewarding satisfaction, that is, satisfying oneself. Third, there is an opportunity to learn the working **heuristics of discovery.** By heuristics Bruner means the methods by which a person is educated to find out things independently. Only through the exercise of problem solving and the effort of discovery can the child find out things independently. The more adept the child becomes in the working heuristics of discovery, the more effective the decisions the child will make in problem solving, the decisions leading to a quicker solution than any trial-and-error approach would achieve. Fourth, there is an aid to memory processing. Knowledge resulting from discovery learning is more easily remembered, and is more easily recalled when needed.

Bruner's work, strongly supported by recent brain research, provides a rationale for using discovery and hands-on activities. However, Gagné and Bruner differ in their emphases on learning. Gagné emphasizes primarily the product of learning, whereas Bruner emphasizes the process of learning. For Gagné the key question is, "*What* do you want the child to know?" For Bruner it is, "*How* do you want the child to know?" Gagné's emphasis is on learning itself, whether by discovery, review, or practice. For Bruner, the emphasis is on learning by discovery; it is the method of learning that is important.

Gagné stresses problem solving as the highest level of learning, with the lower learning levels prerequisite to this highest level. For Gagné, the appropriate sequence in learning (and teaching) is from these lower levels toward problem solving. The teacher begins with simple ideas, relates all of them, builds on them, and works toward the more complex levels of learning. Bruner, however, begins with problem solving, which in turn leads to the development of necessary skills. The teacher poses a question to be solved and then uses it as a catalyst to motivate children to develop the necessary skills.

Piaget, Bruner, and Gagné also differ in their attitudes toward the child's readiness for learning. As stated earlier, Piaget believes that readiness depends on the child's maturation and intellectual development. Bruner believes that the child is always ready to learn a concept at some level of sophistication. Gagné, however, feels that readiness is related to the successful development of lower-level skills and prior understandings.

David Ausubel and Meaningful Verbal Learning

David Ausubel is an advocate of **reception learning,** the receipt of ideas through transmission. He agrees with other psychologists that the development of problem-solving skills is a primary objective in teaching. However, like Gagné, he feels that effective problem solving and discovery are more likely to take place after children have learned key and supporting concepts.

Ausubel strongly urges teachers to use learning situations and examples that are familiar to their students. This helps children to assimilate what is being learned with what they already know, making their learning more meaningful. Ausubel believes that discovery learning is too time-consuming to enable children to learn all they should know within the short time allotted to learning in the elementary grades. Like

Bruner and Gagné, he suggests that children in the primary grades should work on as many "hands-on" learning activities as possible, but for children beyond the primary grades, he recommends the increased use of learning by transmission, using teacher explanations, concept mapping, demonstrations, diagrams, and illustrations. Ausubel cautions against learning by rote.

To avoid rote memorization, Ausubel encourages teachers to make learning meaningful and longer lasting by using **advance organizers,** ideas that are presented to students before new material and that mentally prepare them to integrate the new material into previously built cognitive structures.[16] Many textbook programs today are designed in this way.

There is no doubt that the most effective teaching occurs when the students see meaning to what is being taught. A danger in expository teaching (listening, reading, and memorizing), however, is that there may be a tendency to rely too heavily on spoken communication, which means for many children it is highly abstract and thus unlikely to be very effective. (See the "Learning Experiences Ladder" in Chapter 9.)

Concept Mapping

Based on Ausubel's theory of meaningful learning, concept mapping is a technique that has been found useful for helping children in changing their misconceptions. As defined by Novak, "Concepts are regularities in events or objects designated by some arbitrary label."[17] A concept map typically refers to a visual or graphic representation of concepts and their relationships (see Figure 2.1, a concept map drawn by children during a social studies lesson about growing farm crops). The general procedure for concept mapping is to have the children (1) identify important concepts in materials being studied, often by circling those concepts, (2) rank order the concepts from the most general to the most specific, and then (3) arrange the concepts on a sheet of paper, connect related ideas with lines, and define the connections between the related ideas. Concept mapping has been found to help children in their ability to organize and to represent their thoughts,[18] and to help them to connect new knowledge to their past experiences and precepts.[19]

Teaching for Thinking

Synthesizing what has been learned about learning and brain functioning, Arthur Costa encourages teachers to integrate explicit thinking instruction into daily lessons and help students develop their thinking skills. As stated by Costa,

In teaching for thinking, we are interested not only in what students know but also in how students behave when they don't know. . . . Gathering evidence of the performance and growth of intelligent behavior is difficult through stan-

[16]In this resource guide, the terms *advance organizer, orientation set,* and *anticipatory set* are considered as synonymous; that is, they represent different educational jargon for the same idea.
[17]Joseph D. Novak, "Application of Advances in Learning Theory and Philosophy of Science to the Improvement of Chemistry Teaching," *Journal of Chemistry Education* 61(7):607–612 (July 1984), p. 607.
[18]Carole F. Stice and Marino C. Alvarez, "Hierarchical Concept Mapping in the Early Grades," *Childhood Education* 64(2):86–96 (December 1987).
[19]For details of concept mapping, see Joseph D. Novak, "Concept Maps and Vee Diagrams: Two Metacognitive Tools to Facilitate Meaningful Learning," *Instructional Science* 19(1):29–52 (1990).

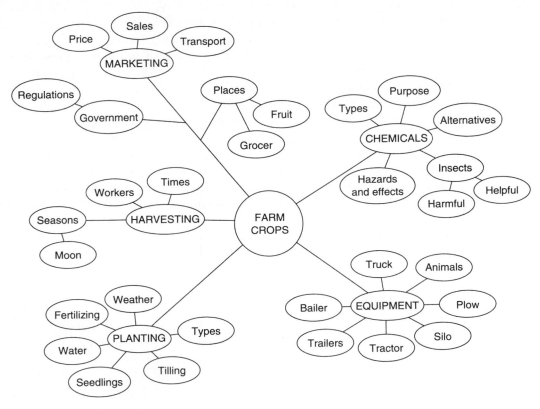

Figure 2.1   A sample concept map.

dardized testing. It really requires "kid-watching": observing students as they try to solve the day-to-day academic and real-life problems they encounter in school, at home, on the playground, alone, and with friends. By collecting anecdotes and examples of written, oral, and visual expressions, we can see students' increasingly voluntary and spontaneous performance of these intelligent behaviors.[20]

Identified and articulated by Costa are 14 characteristics of intelligent behavior that teachers can teach for and observe developing in children. These are:

1. *Cooperative thinking—Social intelligence.* Humans are social beings. Real-world problem solving has become so complex that seldom can any person go it alone. Not all children come to school knowing how to work effectively in groups. They may exhibit competitiveness, narrow-mindedness, egocentrism, ethnocentrism, or criticism of others' values, emotions, and beliefs. Listening, consensus seeking, giving up an idea to work on someone else's, empathy, compassion, group leadership, cooperative learning, knowing how to support group efforts, altruism— these are behaviors indicative of intelligent human beings, behaviors that should be learned in the classroom.

[20]Arthur L. Costa, *The School as a Home for the Mind* (Palatine, IL: Skylight Publishing, 1991), p. 19. From original in Arthur L. Costa, ed., *Developing Minds,* 2nd ed. (Washington, DC: Association for Supervision and Curriculum Development, 1991).

2. *Decreasing impulsivity.* When students develop this behavior they think more before acting. Children can be taught to think before shouting out an answer, before beginning a project or task, before arriving at conclusions with only limited data.

3. *Drawing on past knowledge and applying it to new situations.* The ultimate goal of education is that students apply school-learned knowledge to real-life situations.

4. *Flexibility in thinking.* Intelligent people can approach a problem from a new angle. De Bono refers to this as **lateral thinking.**[21] Students can learn to consider alternative points of view and to deal with several sources of information simultaneously.

5. *Ingenuity, originality, insightfulness: Creativity.* Students should be encouraged to do, and discouraged from saying "I can't." Students should be taught in such a way to encourage intrinsic motivation, rather than to rely on extrinsic sources. Teachers should be able to offer criticism in such a way that the child understands that it is not a criticism of self. Students learn the value of feedback. They learn the value of their own intuition, of guessing.

6. *Listening to others—With understanding and empathy.* Some psychologists believe that the ability to listen to others, to empathize with and understand their point of view, is one of the highest forms of intelligent behavior. Piaget refers to this behavior as **overcoming egocentrism.** Children can be taught to listen to, and build upon, the ideas of others. In think tanks and in legislative bodies, people from various walks of life convene to share their thinking, explore their ideas, and broaden their perspectives by listening to the ideas and reactions of others.

7. *Metacognition.* Awareness of one's own thinking. Students can learn to be aware of their own thinking processes while they are thinking.

8. *Persistence.* Sticking to a task until it is completed. Consider these examples of persistence:

Failed in business	1831
Defeated for legislature	1832
Again failed in business	1833
Elected to legislature	1834
Defeated for Speaker	1838
Defeated for Elector	1840
Defeated for Congress	1843
Elected to Congress	1846
Defeated for Congress	1848
Defeated for Senate	1855
Defeated for Vice-President	1858
Defeated for Senate	1858
Elected President of the United States	1860
The person? Abraham Lincoln.	

Thomas Edison tried approximately 3,000 filaments before finding one that worked. For years Babe Ruth held not only the record for the most home runs, but also for the highest number of strikeouts.

[21]E. de Bono, *Lateral Thinking: Creativity Step by Step* (New York: Harper & Row, 1970).

9. *Questioning and problem posing.* As said before, young children are full of questions, and they ask them. We want students to be alert to, and to recognize, phenomena and discrepancies in their environment and to inquire about their causes.

10. *Risk taking.* We should encourage students to venture forth and explore their ideas. Teachers can provide this opportunity with techniques such as brainstorming, experimenting, and cooperative learning.

11. *A sense of humor.* The positive effects of humor on the body's physiological functions are well established: a drop in the pulse rate; the secretion of endorphins; an increase of oxygen in the blood. Humor liberates creativity and provides high-level thinking skills, such as anticipation, discovery of novel relationships, and visual imagery.

    The acquisition of a sense of humor follows a developmental sequence similar to that described by Piaget[22] and Kohlberg.[23] Initially, children may find humor in all the wrong things—human frailty, ethnic traits, sacrilegious riddles, ribald profanities. Later, creative children thrive on finding incongruity and will demonstrate a whimsical frame of mind during problem solving.

12. *Striving for accuracy and precision.* Teachers can observe growth in this behavior when students (a) take time to check their work, (b) review the procedures, and (c) use more concise language.

13. *Using all the senses.* When appropriate, teachers should encourage students to use all their senses to learn, rather than to depend on only one or two.

14. *Wonderment, inquisitiveness, curiosity, and the enjoyment of problem solving—A sense of efficacy as a thinker.* Young children express wonderment. Through classroom learning they should be able to develop the feeling "I can" and express the sense "I enjoy." This expression should always be encouraged, supported, and accepted.

Costa has given us 14 characteristics of intelligent behavior which we should help our students develop. Chapter 3 discusses specific teacher behaviors that facilitate this development.

Teaching for Resiliency

Additional research findings that are important considerations in facilitating the learning of children include the identification of traits of resiliency that help kids "make it" when they face the most dire circumstances in their lives.[24] The following traits have been associated with children who are resilient:

- Developing a sense of control over one's life.
- Developing a sense of humor.
- Gaining people's attention in a positive way.
- Having a feeling of autonomy.
- Maintaining a positive vision of life.
- Persisting in the face of failure.
- Planning ahead and solving problems.
- Relating to a caring "other" person.

[22]Jean Piaget, *The Psychology of Intelligence* (Totowa, NJ: Littlefield Adams, 1972).
[23]I. Kohlberg, *The Meaning and Measurement of Moral Development* (Worcester, MA: Clark University Press, 1981).
[24]Nancy L. Cecil and Patricia L. Roberts, *Developing Resiliency Through Children's Literature* (Jefferson, NC: MacFarland, 1991).

These traits can be actively developed and reinforced by a teacher who shows his or her conviction that life is good and worthwhile. You can foster awareness of these traits by introducing children to children's books that have main characters who are overcoming adversity and demonstrating traits of resiliency. A helpful resource that will allow you to use children's literature for fostering resiliency is *Developing Resiliency Through Children's Literature* (Cecil and Roberts, 1991). This book contains summaries of books that feature main characters who are resilient survivors, and it provides accompanying activities.

C. BRAIN HEMISPHERICITY, LEARNING MODALITIES, LEARNING STYLES, AND TEACHING STYLES

As mentioned earlier, students differ in many ways, including their abilities to learn, readiness to learn, and learning skills. They also vary in methods of learning, and it is expected that you will attempt to match your style of teaching to your own students' styles of learning.

Brain Hemisphericity

Research has shown that how a person learns is related to differences in the left and right hemispheres of the brain. This theory is sometimes referred to as **brain laterality.** Verbal learning, logical and convergent thinking, and the academic cognitive processes are dominated by the left cerebral hemisphere, while affective, intuitive, spatial, emotional, divergent thinking, and visual elements are dominated by the right cerebral hemisphere. Some students are oriented toward right cerebral hemisphere learning, and others toward the left. This means that some students learn better through verbal interactions, and others learn through visual, kinesthetic, and tactile involvement. However, "in a healthy person the two hemispheres are inextricably interactive, irrespective of whether a person is dealing with words, mathematics, music, or art."[25]

In providing a variety of instructional options, a teacher is more likely to teach to more of the children more of the time. When integrating disciplines in the school curriculum and connecting what is being learned with real-life situations, the teacher is most likely to be teaching to both hemispheres (see Section B in Chapter 13).

Learning Modalities

Learning modality refers to the way students prefer to receive sensory reception (**modality preference**), or the actual way a student learns best (**modality adeptness**). Some students prefer learning by seeing, a **visual modality**; others prefer learning through instruction from others or self, an **auditory modality**; while still others prefer learning by doing and being physically involved, referred to as a **kinesthetic modality,** and by touching objects, the **tactile modality.** Sometimes a student's modality preference is not that student's modality strength. While primary modality strength can be determined by observing students, it can also be mixed and can change as the result

[25]Caine and Caine, p. 67.

of experience and intellectual maturity. The research of Barbe and Milone on modality strengths and learning include these findings:[26]

- Young children enter school with stronger auditory strengths. However, once they are in school the situation changes drastically. For much of their waking day, they are expected to use the visual modality (through reading) and the kinesthetic modality (through writing). Teachers sometimes even tend to suppress audition, sometimes actively, to maintain an orderly classroom.
- Children with auditory-oriented strengths do better with the spoken word than with the printed word, and probably do less well on standardized tests, which tend to favor children of mixed or visual modality strengths.
- Children between kindergarten and sixth grade experience a shift in modality strength, when the visual becomes the dominant modality, and kinesthesia overtakes audition.
- Between late middle-level grades and adulthood another shift takes place as audition becomes more important than kinesthesia, but vision remains dominant.
- Modality integration (using all modalities) has been found to contribute to success in developing reading skills.
- Teachers who are not well trained in pedagogy tend to teach the way they learn best (modality strength), but students may have modality strengths different from their teacher's. This difference can affect achievement.
- Supervisors (i.e., university supervisors of student teachers, or building principals) need to be aware that their perceptions of a teacher's effectiveness may be clouded by their own modality strengths.
- There seems to be no relationship between a child's ethnicity, gender, and modality strength.

Instruction that uses a singular approach, such as auditory (e.g., teacher talk), will affect students who learn better another way. This difference can affect student achievement. Sometimes, when a teacher's verbal communication conflicts with his or her nonverbal messages, the children can become confused, and this too can affect their learning. Further, when there is discrepancy between the verbal and the nonverbal, the nonverbal will win every time.[27] Actions do speak louder than words. For example, a teacher who has just finished a lesson on the conservation of energy and who, upon leaving the classroom with the children for recess, does not turn off the lights, has, by inappropriate modeling behavior, created a "discrepant event" and defeated the purpose of the lesson. A teacher who verbally asks, "Richard, don't you see the quiet signal?" while using a hand signal (teacher's hand raised until all are quiet) to obtain quiet in the classroom, is intruding on that very behavior he or she is trying to encourage.

You are advised to use strategies that integrate modalities. The use of reception learning and cognitive mapping is an example of modality integration. When well designed, integrated thematic units incorporate modality integration too. *When teaching a group of children of mixed learning abilities, mixed modality strengths, mixed language proficiency, and mixed cultural backgrounds, the integration of learning modalities is a must.*

---

[26]Walter B. Barbe and Michael N. Milone, Jr., "What We Know About Modality Strengths," *Educational Leadership* 38(5):378–380 (February 1981).
[27]Patrick W. Miller, *Nonverbal Communication* (Washington, DC: National Education Association, 1986), pp. 6 and 7.

Learning Styles

Learning style is a person's style of learning, "a gestalt combining internal and external operations derived from the individual's neurobiology, personality, and development and reflected in learner behavior."[28] Although there are probably as many types of learning styles as there are individuals, most learning style classifications center on four general types, based on the earlier work of Carl Jung.[29] Later, David Kolb described two major differences in how people learn: how they **perceive** situations and how they **process** information.[30] For example, in their perception of a new situation, some people probe (sense and feel) their way through, while others think and analyze. In processing information about the situation, some people are watchers, while others are doers. It is important to note that learning style is not an indicator of intelligence, but an indicator of how a person learns.

Bernice McCarthy describes four major learning styles, briefly described here as follows:[31]

1. *The imaginative learner.* Imaginative learners perceive information concretely and process it reflectively. They learn well by listening and sharing with others, integrating the ideas of others with their own experiences. Imaginative learners often have difficulty adjusting to traditional teaching.
2. *The analytic learner.* Analytic learners perceive information abstractly and process it reflectively. They prefer sequential thinking, need details, and value what experts have to offer. Analytic learners do well in traditional classrooms.
3. *The common sense learner.* Common sense learners perceive information abstractly and process it actively. This type of learner is pragmatic and enjoys hands-on learning. Common sense learners sometimes find school frustrating unless they can see immediate use for what is being learned.
4. *The dynamic learner.* Dynamic learners perceive information concretely and process it actively. They also prefer hands-on learning, and are excited by anything new. Dynamic learners are risk takers and are frustrated by learning if they see it as being tedious and sequential.

With the 4MAT System developed by McCarthy, teachers employ a learning cycle of instructional strategies that reach each student's learning style. As stated by McCarthy, in the cycle, learners "sense and feel, they experience, then they watch, they reflect, then they think, they develop theories, then they try out theories, they experiment. Finally, they evaluate and synthesize what they have learned in order to apply it to their next similar experience. They get smarter. They apply experience to experiences."[32]

In contrast to Jung's four learning styles, Howard Gardner's **Theory of Multiple Intelligences,** which grew from his work with gifted children and those with learning

[28]James W. Keefe and Barbara G. Ferrell, "Developing a Defensible Learning Style Paradigm," *Educational Leadership* 48(2):57–61 (October 1990), p. 59.
[29]See Carl G. Jung, *Psychological Types* (New York: Harcourt Brace, 1923). See also Anthony Gregorc, *Gregorc Style Delineator* (Maynard, MA: Gabriel Systems, 1985); and Rita Dunn and Kenneth Dunn, *Teaching Students Through Their Individual Learning Styles* (Reston, VA: Reston Publications, 1978).
[30]See David Kolb, *The Learning Style Inventory* (Boston, MA: McBer and Co., 1985).
[31]Bernice McCarthy, "Using the 4MAT System to Bring Learning Styles to Schools," *Educational Leadership* 48(2):31–37 (October 1990), p. 32.
[32]Ibid., p. 33.

problems, introduces *seven* learning styles (independent forms of knowing and processing information) that individuals exhibit in differing ways: verbal-linguistic, logical-mathematical, intrapersonal, visual-spatial, musical-rhythmic, body-kinesthetic, and interpersonal.[33] Some educators indicate that students who are at risk may be dominant in a cognitive learning style that is not in synchronization with traditional teaching methods. Traditional methods are largely of the first three Gardner types: verbal-linguistic, logical-mathematical, and intrapersonal.[34] Consequently, some teachers[35] and schools[36] have restructured their goals around Gardner's seven ways of learning.

Implications for Teaching

The importance of this presentation about learning styles is that it can enable you to realize two facts:

1. *Intelligence is not a fixed or static reality, but can be learned, taught, and developed.*[37] This concept is important for children to understand too. When students understand that intelligence is incremental, something that is developed through use over time, they are more motivated to work at learning than when they believe intelligence is a fixed entity.[38]
2. *Not all children learn and respond to learning situations in the same way.* A child may learn differently according to the situation or according to the student's ethnicity or socioeconomic status. A teacher who, for all children, uses only one style of teaching, or who teaches to only one or a few styles of learning, day-after-day, is short changing those children who learn better another way.

Teaching Styles

Teaching style is the way teachers teach, their distinctive mannerisms complemented by their choices of teaching behaviors and strategies. A teacher's style affects the way that teacher presents information and interacts with students. It clearly is the manner and pattern of those interactions with students that determines a teacher's effectiveness in promoting students' learning, positive attitudes about learning, and self-esteem.

A teacher's style is determined by the teacher's (1) personal characteristics, (2) experiences, and (3) knowledge of research findings. Teaching style can change, intentionally or unintentionally, as a result of changes that occur to the teacher in these three areas.

[33]See Howard Gardner and Thomas Hatch, "Multiple Intelligences Go to School: Educational Implications of the Theory of Multiple Intelligence," *Educational Researcher* 18(8):4–9 (November 1989); Tina Blythe and Howard Gardner, "A School for All Intelligences," *Educational Leadership* 47(7):33–37 (April 1990); or Howard Gardner, "The Theory of Multiple Intelligences," *Annals of Dyslexia* 37:19–35 (1987).
[34]See, for example, Thomas Armstrong, "Learning Differences—Not Disabilities," *Principal* 68(1):34–36 (September 1988).
[35]See, for example, L. Ellison, "Using Multiple Intelligences to Set Goals," *Educational Leadership* 50(2):69–72 (October 1992).
[36]See, for example, Thomas R. Hoerr, "How Our School Applied Multiple Intelligences Theory," *Educational Leadership* 50(2):67–68 (October 1992).
[37]David G. Lazear, *Teaching for Multiple Intelligences*, Fastback 342 (Bloomington, IN: Phi Delta Kappa, 1992), p. 8. See also Gerald W. Bracey, "Getting Smart(er) in School," *Phi Delta Kappan* 73(5):414–416 (January 1992).
[38]Lauren B. Resnick and Leopold E. Klopfer, *Toward the Thinking Curriculum: Current Cognitive Research*, 1989 ASCD Yearbook (Alexandria, VA: Association for Supervision and Curriculum Development, 1989), p. 8.

TABLE 2.2   A CONTRAST OF TWO TEACHING STYLES

	Traditional Style	*Facilitating Style*
Teacher is	autocratic	democratic
	curriculum-centered	student-centered
	direct	indirect
	dominative	interactive
	formal	informal
	informative	inquiring
	prescriptive	reflective
Classroom is	teacher-centered	student-centered
	linear (seats facing front of room)	grouped or circular
Instructional modes	abstract learning	concrete learning
	teacher-centered discussion	discussions
	lectures	peer and cross-age coaching
	competitive learning	cooperative learning
	some problem solving	problem solving
	demonstrations by teacher from simple to complex	student inquiries start with complex tasks and use instructional scaffolding and dialogue
	transmission of information from teacher to students	reciprocal teaching, using dialogue, between teacher and a small group of students, then among students

While there are other ways to label and describe teaching styles,[39] here we will consider two contrasting teaching styles—the **traditional** and the **facilitating** styles (see Table 2.2), emphasizing that although *today's teacher must be eclectic, that is, must use aspects of each, there must be a strong leaning toward a facilitating style.*

Multilevel Teaching

As stated earlier in Chapter 1, **multilevel** (or **multitasking**) **teaching** happens when several levels of teaching and learning are occurring simultaneously in the classroom. In many classrooms, individual and small groups of students will be doing different activities at the same time to accomplish the same or different objectives. While some students may be working independently of the teacher (within the facilitating mode), others may be receiving direct instruction (within the traditional mode).

Rather than reacting differently to students according to their ethnicity, gender, or some other personal characteristic, the teacher must interact with each student gauging the interactions in a way the teacher believes will best facilitate student development and learning.

[39]For example, see M. Ramirez and A. Castañeda, *Cultural Democracy, Bicognitive Development and Education* (New York: Academic Press, Inc., 1974), pp. 177–178; or Donna M. Gollnick and Philip C. Chinn, *Multicultural Education in a Pluralistic Society,* 3rd ed. (New York: Macmillan, 1990), pp. 286–287. Their descriptions of "field-independent" and "field-sensitive" teaching styles are similar to the "traditional" and "facilitating" teaching styles described here. Joyce and Weil describe four categories of teaching models or styles: social interaction, informational processing, personal source, and behavior modification. See B. Joyce and M. Weil, *Models of Teaching* (Englewood Cliffs, NJ: Prentice-Hall, 1972).

The Theoretical Origins of Teaching Styles

Teaching styles are deeply rooted in certain theoretical assumptions about children and their development. Although it is beyond the scope of intent for this resource guide to explore deeply into those assumptions, there are three major theoretical positions and research findings that may help you understand the basis of your own emerging teaching style. Each of the three positions is based on certain philosophical and psychological assumptions that suggest different ways of working with children. These theoretical positions are:

1. The child's mind is neutral-passive to good-active, and the main focus in teaching should be the addition of new ideas to a subconscious store of old ones (tied to the theoretical positions of *Romanticism-Maturationism*). Key persons include Jean J. Rousseau and Sigmund Freud. Key instructional strategies include classic lecturing with rote memorization.
2. The child's mind is neutral-passive with innate reflexes and needs, and the main focus in teaching should be on successive, systematic changes in the learner's environment to increase the possibilities of desired behavioral responses (tied to the theoretical position of *Behaviorism*). Key persons include John Locke, B. F. Skinner, A. H. Thorndike, and John Watson. Key instructional strategies include practice and reinforcement, as epitomized in programmed instruction.
3. The child is a neutral-interactive, purposive individual in simultaneous interaction with the physical and biological environments, and the main focus in teaching should be on facilitating the child's gain of new perceptions that lead to desired behavioral changes and, ultimately, to a more fully functioning individual (tied to the theoretical position of *Cognitive-Experimentalism*). Key persons are John Dewey, Jerome Bruner, Jean Piaget, and Arthur W. Combs. Key instructional strategies include discovery, inquiry, and cooperative learning.

We continue to hold the hypothesis that a competent teacher assumes a combination of thoughts from these three theoretical positions, which, then, makes that teacher's style an eclectic one. As in previous editions of this resource guide, we also continue in our belief that, with a diversity of students, to be competent a teacher must be eclectic, utilizing at appropriate times the best of strategies and knowledgeable instructor behaviors, regardless of whether individually they can be classified within any style dichotomy, such as "traditional or facilitating," "direct or indirect," "formal or informal," or "didactic or progressive." Our own bias as we have taught and as we have prepared this resource guide is to provide an eclectic approach with a strong bent toward Cognitive-Experimentalism, because of its emphasis on divergence in learning and the importance given to learning as a change in perceptions.

Although there are several ways to determine the nature of your interactions with students, hence your teaching style, the techniques essentially center on the collection and analysis of two types of data: (1) the amount of talking done by you and individual students, and (2) the quality of your interactions with students (for instance, giving praise or criticism, asking questions, and initiating discussion). Several devices are available for data collecting, such as the Spaulding Teacher Activity Rating Schedule (STARS),[40] or the Flanders' Verbal Interaction Category System (VICS).[41]

Now you are asked to consider teaching styles as you complete Exercises 2.1 and 2.2.

[40]See G. R. Guerin and A. S. Maier, *Informal Assessment in Education* (Palo Alto, CA: Mayfield, 1983).
[41]See Edmund Amidon and Elizabeth Hunter, *Improving Teaching: The Analysis of Classroom Verbal Interaction* (New York: Holt, Rinehart and Winston, 1966).

Exercise 2.1: Developing a Statement About My Own Emerging Teaching Style

Instructions: The purpose of this exercise is to help you clarify and articulate your own assumptions about teaching and learning. You will develop a profile of your emerging teaching style, and from that, a statement representative of your current thinking about teaching and learning. Proceed with the following four steps.

Step 1. Read each of the 50 statements and rate your feelings about each, giving a *1* to those with which you strongly agree, a *2* to those to which you are neutral, and, a *3* to those with which you strongly disagree.[42]

Remember: *1* = agree; *2* = neutral; *3* = disagree

_____ 1. Most of what children learn, they learn on their own.

_____ 2. Children should be concerned about other students' reactions to their work in the classroom.

_____ 3. An important part of schooling is learning to work with others.

_____ 4. Children learn more by working on their own than by working with others.

_____ 5. Children should be given opportunities to participate actively in class planning and implementation of lessons.

_____ 6. In an effective learning environment, grades are inappropriate.

_____ 7. Children enjoy working in a classroom that has clearly defined learning objectives and assessment criteria.

_____ 8. I favor teaching methods and classroom procedures that maximize student independence to learn from their own experiences.

_____ 9. Most of what children learn is learned from other children.

_____ 10. Children should be concerned with getting good grades.

_____ 11. An important part of teaching and learning should be to learn how to work independently.

_____ 12. A teacher should not be contradicted or challenged by a student.

_____ 13. Interchanges between children and a teacher can provide better ideas about content than those found in a textbook.

_____ 14. For children to get the most out of a class, they must be aware of the primary concerns and biases of the teacher.

_____ 15. Children should not be given high grades unless clearly earned.

_____ 16. Learning should help a child to become an independent thinker.

_____ 17. Most of what children learn is learned from their teachers.

[42]Adapted with permission from William H. Berquist and Steven R. Phillips, *A Handbook for Faculty Development* (Washington, DC: The Council for Independent Colleges, June 1975), pp. 25–27.

_____ 18. A teacher who makes children do things they don't want to do is an ineffective teacher.

_____ 19. Learning takes place most effectively under conditions in which children are in competition with one another.

_____ 20. A teacher should try to convince students that particular ideas are valid and exciting.

_____ 21. To do well in school children must be assertive.

_____ 22. Facts in textbooks are usually accurate.

_____ 23. I favor the use of teaching methods and classroom procedures that maximize student and teacher interaction.

_____ 24. Most of what children learn is learned from books.

_____ 25. A teacher who lets children do whatever they want is incompetent.

_____ 26. Children can learn more by working with an enthusiastic teacher than by working alone.

_____ 27. I favor the use of teaching methods and classroom procedures that maximize student learning of basic subject-matter content.

_____ 28. Ideas of other children are useful in helping a child understand the content of lessons.

_____ 29. A child should study what the teacher says is important and not necessarily what is important to that child.

_____ 30. A teacher who does not motivate student interest in subject content is incompetent.

_____ 31. An important part of education is learning how to perform under testing and evaluation conditions.

_____ 32. Children can learn more by sharing their ideas than by keeping their ideas to themselves.

_____ 33. Teachers tend to give students too many trivial assignments.

_____ 34. Ideas contained in the textbook should be the primary source of the content taught.

_____ 35. Children should be given high grades as a means of motivating them and increasing their self-esteem.

_____ 36. The ideas a student brings into a class are useful for helping the child to understand subject content.

_____ 37. Students should study what is important to them and not necessarily what the teacher claims is important.

_____ 38. Learning takes place most effectively under conditions in which children are working independently of one another.

_____ 39. Teachers often give students too much freedom of choice in content, methods, and procedures.

_____ 40. Teachers should clearly explain what it is they expect from students.

_____ 41. Childrens' ideas about content are often better than the ideas found in textbooks.

_____ 42. Classroom discussions are beneficial learning experiences.

_____ 43. A student's education should help the student to become a successful and contributing member of society.

_____ 44. Learning takes place most effectively under conditions in which students are working cooperatively with one another.

_____ 45. Teachers often are too personal with their students.

_____ 46. A teacher should encourage children to disagree with or challenge that teacher in the classroom.

_____ 47. Children have to be able to work effectively with other people to do well in school.

_____ 48. For children to get the most out of school, they must assume at least part of the responsibility for their learning.

_____ 49. Students seem to enjoy discussing their ideas about learning with the teacher and other students.

_____ 50. A child's education should help the child to become a sensitive human being.

Step 2. From the list of 50 items, write the items (by their number) in two columns; those with which you strongly agreed in one column, those with which you strongly disagreed in the other column. Ignore those items to which you gave a *2* (were neutral).

Strongly Agreed   **Strongly Disagreed**

Step 3. In groups of three or four, discuss your lists (in Step 2) with your classmates. From the discussion, you may rerank any items you wish.

Step 4. You now have a finalized list of those items with which you are in agreement, and those with which you disagree. On the basis of those two lists, write a paragraph that summarizes your philosophy about teaching and learning. It should be no longer than one-half page in length. This statement is a theoretical representation of your present teaching philosophy.

_____

_____

_____

_____

_____

_____

_____

_____

_____

_____

_____

Step 5. Compare your philosophical statement with the three theoretical positions as discussed earlier in this chapter. Can you clearly identify your position? Name it:

_____

_____

_____

_____

_____

Explain your rationale: _____

_____

_____

_____

_____

_____

At the completion of this text, you may wish to revisit your philosophical statement, perhaps even to make revisions to it. It will be useful to have your educational philosophy firmly in mind for teaching job interviews at a later date.

Exercise 2.2: Analyzing One Teacher's Style[43]

Instructions: The purpose of this exercise is to analyze a teacher's instructional style. Obtain permission to visit one teacher and explain to the teacher being observed that you are observing, not evaluating, for teaching style. The host teacher may be interested in discussing with you the results of your observation. A follow-up thank-you letter is appropriate.

Observe the teacher's behavior at one-minute intervals for a period of ten minutes and tabulate the appropriate items on the following chart. Continue for the entire class meeting.

School visited _____

Class and grade level _____

	Minute										
	1	2	3	4	5	6	7	8	9	10	Total
Traditional Teacher Behaviors *Prescribing:* Giving advice, directions; being critical, evaluative; offering judgments *Informing:* Giving information, lecturing, interpreting *Confronting:* Directly challenging students											

Traditional behaviors total _____

	1	2	3	4	5	6	7	8	9	10	Total
Facilitating Teacher Behaviors *Relaxing:* Releasing tension, using humor *Mediating:* Asking for information, being reflective, encouraging self-directed problem solving *Supporting:* Approving, confirming, validating, listening											

Facilitating behaviors total _____

Total traditional behaviors divided by total facilitating behaviors (T/F Ratio): _____

Conclusions about the host teacher's style on this day: _____

_____

_____

_____

_____

[43]Adapted from J. Heron, *Six Category Intervention Analysis* (Mimeo, Guildford: Centre of Adult Education, University of Surrey, England, 1975).

_____

_____

_____

_____

_____

_____

_____

_____

_____

_____

_____

_____

_____

_____

_____

_____

_____

_____

Did you discuss your observations with the host teacher? _____

_____

_____

_____

_____

_____

_____

_____

_____

_____

_____

_____

SUMMARY

In recent years many variables have been shown to have a relationship between instruction and learning. Categorically, these are the *learning environment; lesson planning; teacher instructional behaviors*; and the *nature of the learner and learning*. Within each of these categories, there are teacher decisions and actions that have positive effects on student learning. While the nature of the learner has already been discussed, and other variables are discussed in later chapters, here is a synopsis of what is known about the learning environment, lesson planning, and instructional behaviors.

Learning Environment. The classroom environment in which learning takes place is crucial. Optimum learning takes place when the learner:

- Can maintain some control over the pace of the learning.
- Develops a better understanding of his or her own learning style and thinking processes.
- Feels accepted by the teacher.
- Feels that although the learning is demanding, the rewards are within reach.
- Feels welcomed in the classroom.
- Is personally involved in the learning activities.
- Perceives the teacher as being approachable.
- Perceives the teacher as being friendly, understanding, sympathetic, and nurturing.
- Understands class expectations.

Lesson Planning. Within the category of lesson planning, the following teacher actions contribute positively to student learning. The teacher:

- Implements lessons of student-perceived content relevancy, that is, learning that is meaningful to the students.
- Provides lessons that are thoughtfully prepared (and students can tell).
- Provides content links between what the students already know and what they are going to learn, as is done in concept mapping.
- Provides frequent learning practice and comprehension checks.
- Provides interesting and motivating lesson introductions, such as with the use of anticipatory sets (advance organizers).
- Provides specific and clearly stated learning expectations (that are understood by the students).

Instructional Behaviors. Discussed more fully in Chapter 3, the following teacher behaviors are contributors to student learning. The teacher:

- Adjusts his or her teaching style according to student learning styles and activities.
- Appreciates the importance of and allows for student "think time."
- Can function effectively as a decision maker; is in control of classroom events.
- Demonstrates enthusiasm for teaching and learning.
- Gives sincere but low-keyed praise for individual student achievement.
- Is able, in class, to attend to more than one thing at a time; this is called overlapping behavior.
- Is approachable.

- Is businesslike, but with a sense of humor.
- Is constantly monitoring student activity.
- Poses thoughtfully prepared, and carefully worded, questions that are clearly understood by the children.
- Uses a variety of teaching-learning strategies.
- Uses a variety of types of questions and that are designed to lead students to higher levels of cognition.
- Uses meaningful gestures and body language.
- Uses questioning frequently, and allows for student response time.
- Uses variations in voice inflection.

In this chapter, teaching style is defined as the way teachers teach, their distinctive mannerisms complemented by their choices of teaching behaviors and strategies. Style develops from tradition, from one's beliefs and experiences, and from research findings. In this chapter you analyzed your own beliefs, observed one teacher and that teacher's style, and have begun the development of your own philosophy about teaching and learning, a philosophical statement that should be useful to you later during job interviews.

As stated earlier, exciting educational research is emerging from several, and related, areas: cognitive research about student learning, conceptual development, and thinking styles, and research in neurophysiology. The research seems to support the hypothesis that a teacher's best teaching style choice is eclectic with a bent toward the facilitating, at least until the day arrives when students of certain thinking styles are matched to teachers with particular teaching styles. Future research will undoubtedly shed additional light on the relationships between pedagogy, pedagogical styles, and student thinking and learning.

Today there seems to be much agreement that the essence of the learning process is a combined self-awareness, self-monitoring, and active reflection. The most effective teaching and learning is an interactive process, and involves both learning and learning how to learn. The exploration of specific teacher behaviors that facilitate student learning and learning how to learn continues in the next chapter.

QUESTIONS FOR CLASS DISCUSSION

1. Identify a teacher whom you consider to be very competent, and compare what you recall about that teacher's classroom with the variables of learning environment, lesson planning, and instructional behaviors discussed in this chapter.
2. How important are a child's prior experiences to learning in primary grades? In intermediate grades? In middle-level grades?
3. For a specific age or grade level and subject that is taught in elementary school, research the library and describe common, specific misconceptions of students about that subject. Share your findings with your colleagues. Describe how you would go about helping students change their misconceptions.
4. In small groups, discuss this question; then share a summary of your group's discussion with the entire class. Two teachers were asked the question, "What do you teach?" One teacher responded, "Children." The other answered, "English." From their responses, what tentative conclusions might be drawn about these two teachers?

5. It has been reported that approximately 20 percent of children ages 6–11 are living in poverty (*Phi Delta Kappan* 71[10], June 1990). Explain any relevance that this finding may have for you as a future teacher.

6. With a friend, discuss the advantages in learning by doing as opposed to learning by teacher explanation. Should/could the two be combined?

7. Explain the concepts of "hands-on" and "minds-on" learning. Explain how they are related; how they are different.

8. Select one of Costa's 14 characteristics of intelligent behavior and describe how you would encourage the development of that characteristic while teaching a specific topic to a specified group of children.

9. Read the 1962 ASCD Yearbook, *Perceiving, Behaving, and Becoming: A New Focus for Education*. After reading the book, compare the theory of learning as described by its authors with that of today's cognitive theorists. Share your comparison with others in your class.

10. Do you have questions about the content of this chapter? How might answers be found?

SUGGESTED READINGS FOR CHAPTER 2

Banks, C. B. "Harmonizing Student-Teacher Interactions: A Case for Learning Styles." *Synthesis* 2(2):1–5 (May 1991).

Beilin, H. "Piaget's Enduring Contribution to Developmental Psychology." *Developmental Psychology* 28(2):191–204 (March 1992).

Bransford, J. D., and Vye, N. J. "A Perspective on Cognitive Research and Its Implications for Instruction." In L. B. Resnick and L. E. Klopfer, eds. *Toward the Thinking Curriculum: Current Cognitive Research.* 1989 ASCD Yearbook. Reston, VA: Association for Supervision and Curriculum Development, 1989.

Browne, D. B., and Bordeau, L. "How South Dakota Teachers See Learning Style Differences." *Tribal College* 2(4):24–26 (Spring 1991).

Bruner, J. S. *Acts of Meaning.* Cambridge, MA: Harvard University Press, 1990.

Caine, R. N., and Caine, G. *Making Connections: Teaching and the Human Brain.* Alexandria, VA: Association for Supervision and Curriculum Development, 1991.

Carns, A. W., and Carns, M. R. "Teaching Study Skills, Cognitive Strategies, and Metacognitive Skills Through Self-Diagnosed Learning Styles." *School Counselor* 38(5):341–346 (May 1991).

Cecil, N. L., and Roberts, P. L. *Developing Resiliency Through Children's Literature.* Jefferson, MO: MacFarland, 1991.

Costa, A. L. *The School as a Home for the Mind.* Palatine, IL: Skylight Publishing, 1991.

Curry, L. "A Critique of the Research on Learning Styles." *Educational Leadership* 48(2):50–56 (October 1990).

DeBello, T. C. "Comparison of Eleven Major Learning Styles Models: Variables; Appropriate Populations; Validity of Instrumentation; and the Research Behind Them." Paper presented at the National Conference of the Association for Supervision and Curriculum Development, Orlando, FL, March 10–13, 1989.

DeVries, R., et al. "Sociomoral Atmosphere in Direct Instruction, Eclectic, and Constructivist Kindergartens: A Study of Teachers' Enacted Interpersonal Understanding." *Early Childhood Research Quarterly* (6)4:449–471 (December 1991).

Di-Gennaro, M., et al. "Incidental Science Knowledge in Fifth Grade Children: A Study of Its Relationship with Cognitive Development and Cognitive Style." *Research in Science and Technological Education* 10(1):117–126 (1992).

Dreyfus, A., et al. "Applying the 'Cognitive Conflict' Strategy for Conceptual Change—Some Implications, Difficulties, and Problems." *Science Education* 74(5): 555–569 (September 1990).

Ennis, C. D. "Discrete Thinking Skills in Two Teachers' Physical Education Classes." *Elementary School Journal* 91(5):473–487 (May 1991).

Fourgurean, J. M., et al. "The Link Between Learning Style and Jungian Psychological Type: A Finding of Two Bipolar Preference Dimensions." *Journal of Experimental Education* 58(3):225–237 (Spring 1990).

Fowler, C. "Recognizing the Role of Artistic Intelligence." *Music Educators Journal* 77(1):24–27 (September 1990).

Gardner, H. "Assessing Intelligences: A Comment on Testing Intelligence Without I.Q. Tests." *Phi Delta Kappan* 65(10):699–700 (June 1984).

———. *Art, Mind and Brain.* New York: Basic Books, 1982.

———. *Frames of Mind.* New York: Basic Books, 1985.

———. *The Unschooled Mind: How Children Think and How Schools Should Teach.* New York: Basic Books, 1991.

Gardner, H., and Hatch, T. "Multiple Intelligences Go to School: Educational Implications of the Theory of Multiple Intelligences." *Educational Researcher* 18(8):4–8 (November 1989).

Grady, M. P. *Whole Brain Education.* Fastback 301. Bloomington, IN: Phi Delta Kappa Educational Foundation, 1990.

Henderson, J. G. *Reflective Teaching: Becoming an Inquiring Educator.* New York: Macmillan, 1992.

Jenkins, J. M. "Learning Styles: Recognizing Individuality." *Schools in the Middle* 1(12):3–6 (Winter 1991).

Jones, B. F., and Fennimore, T. F. *The New Definition of Learning: The First Step to School Reform.* Chicago: North Central Regional Educational Laboratory, 1990.

Keefe, J. W. "Learning Style: Where Are We Going?" *Momentum* 21(1):44–48 (February 1990).

Krechevsky, M. "Project Spectrum: An Innovative Assessment Alternative." *Educational Leadership* 48(5):43–48 (February 1991).

Lazear, D. G. *Teaching for Multiple Intelligences.* Fastback 342. Bloomington, IN: Phi Delta Kappa Educational Foundation, 1992.

Lombardi, T. P. *Learning Strategies for Problem Learners.* Fastback 345. Bloomington, IN: Phi Delta Kappa Educational Foundation, 1992.

Neale, D. C., et al. "Implementing Conceptual Change Teaching in Primary Science." *Elementary School Science* 91(2):109–132 (November 1990).

Peterson, P. L., and Knapp, N. F. "Inventing and Reinventing Ideas: Constructivist Teaching and Learning in Mathematics." In Gordon Cawelti, ed. 1992 ASCD Yearbook. *Challenges and Achievements of American Education.* Alexandria, VA: Association for Supervision and Curriculum Development, 1993.

Piaget, J. *The Development of Thought: Elaboration of Cognitive Structures.* New York: Viking, 1977.

Prawat, R. S. *The Value of Ideas II: Problems versus Possibilities in Learning.* Elementary Subjects Center Series 51. East Lansing, MI: Center for the Learning and Teaching of Elementary Subjects, Michigan State University, 1992.

Resnick, L. B., and Klopfer, L. E., eds. *Toward the Thinking Curriculum: Current Cognitive Research.* 1989 ASCD Yearbook. Alexandria, VA: Association for Supervision and Curriculum Development, 1989.

Rollins, T. J. "Analysis of Theoretical Relationships Between Learning Styles of Students and Their Preferences for Learning Activities." *Journal of Agricultural Education* 31(1):64–70 (Spring 1990).

Samples, B. "Using Learning Modalities to Celebrate Intelligence." *Educational Leadership* 50(2):62–66 (October 1992).

Shaughnessy, M. F. "Cognitive Structures of the Gifted: Theoretical Perspectives, Factor Analysis, Triarchic Theories of Intelligence, and Insight Issues." *Gifted Education International* 6(3):149–151 (1990).

Strommen, E. F., and Lincoln, B. "Constructivism, Technology, and the Future of Classroom Learning." *Education and Urban Society* 24(4):466–476 (August 1992).

Sylwester, R., and Cho, J. "What Brain Research Says About Paying Attention." *Educational Leadership* 50(4):71–75 (December 1992–January 1993).

Titus, T. G., et al. "Adolescent Learning Styles." *Journal of Research and Development in Education* 23(3):165–171 (Spring 1990).

Watson, B., and Konicek, R. "Teaching for Conceptual Change: Confronting Children's Experience." *Phi Delta Kappan* 71(9):680–685 (May 1990).

Whalen, S. P., and Csikszentmihalyi, M. *Putting Flow Theory into Educational Practice: The Key School's Flow Activities Room.* Chicago, IL: Report to the Benton Center for Curriculum and Instruction, University of Chicago, 1991.

Wilson, V. L. "Performance Assessment, Psychometric Theory and Cognitive Learning Theory: Ships Crossing in the Night." *Contemporary Education* 62(4):250–254 (Summer 1991).

Yarusso, L. "Constructivism versus Objectivism." *Performance and Instruction* 31(4):7–9 (April 1992).

3

What Are the Expectations, Responsibilities, and Facilitating Behaviors of an Elementary School Teacher?

A major expectation of students, parents, guardians, administrators, and the general public, is that as a teacher, you will be effective in helping *all* children to learn. Although you will see this as a primary goal, there are other expectations and responsibilities as well.

Your professional responsibilities will extend well beyond those of working effectively in a classroom from approximately 8:00 A.M. until mid- or late afternoon. This chapter discusses the many professional responsibilities you will assume as a classroom teacher and the competencies and behaviors necessary for accomplishing them. Twenty-two competencies and four categories of responsibilities are identified. The categories of responsibilities are (1) your responsibility as a reflective decision maker, (2) your commitment to children and to the profession, (3) your instructional responsibilities and fundamental teaching behaviors, and (4) your noninstructional responsibilities. As these competencies and categories of responsibilities are presented and discussed, you are guided through the reality of these expectations as they exist for today's elementary school teacher.

A. THE TEACHER AS A REFLECTIVE DECISION MAKER

During any school day you will make hundreds of decisions, sometimes instantaneously. In addition, to prepare for the teaching day you will have already made many decisions. During one school year a teacher makes literally thousands of decisions, many of which can and will affect the lives of children for years to come. This may seem to be an awesome responsibility—and indeed it is.

To be an effective teacher, you must become adept at decision making. Some decisions will be carefully reasoned over time, and others must be made on the spot. To be adept in making decisions that affect students in the most positive kinds of ways you will need (1) common sense, (2) intelligence, (3) a background of theory in cur-

Today's elementary school teachers assume significant roles and responsibilities in collaborative decision making about the school and its programs. The trust built through shared decision making results in an enriched and challenging curriculum for the children.

riculum and instruction, along with extended practical experience in working with children, and (4) the willingness to reflect on your teaching and to continue learning all that is necessary to become an exemplary teacher.

Initially, of course, you may make errors in judgment, but you will also learn that (1) children are resilient and that (2) there are experts who will guide you, aid you, and help you to assure that the children are not damaged severely by any errors in your judgment. You can learn from your errors. Keep in mind that the sheer number of decisions you make each day will mean that not all of them will be the best decisions that could have been made had you had more time to think and/or better resources for planning.

Although pedagogy is based on scientific principles, good classroom teaching is as much an art as it is a science, and few rules apply to *every* teaching situation. In fact, decisions about the selection of content, the selection of instructional objectives, the selection of materials for instruction, the selection of teaching strategies, your response to misbehavior, and the selection of techniques for assessment of learning experiences are all results of subjective judgments. Although many decisions are made at a somewhat unhurried pace when you are planning your instruction, many others will be made intuitively and *tout de suite*. Once the school day has begun, you may lack time for making carefully thought-out judgments. At your best, you will base decisions on your knowledge of school policies, your teaching style, pedagogical research, the curriculum, and the nature of the children in your classroom. You will also base your decisions on instinct, common sense, and reflective judgment. The better your understanding and experience with schools, the content of the curriculum, and children, and the more time you give to careful reflection, the more likely it will be that your decisions will result in the learning you had planned. You will reflect upon, conceptualize, and apply understandings from one teaching experience to the next. As your understandings about your classroom experiences accumulate, your teaching will become more routinized, predictable, and refined.

Decision-Making Phases of Instruction

Costa divides instruction into four decision-making and thought-processing phases.[1] These are the planning or preactive phase, the teaching or interactive phase, the analyzing and evaluating or reflective phase, and the application or projection phase. The *preactive phase* consists of all those intellectual functions and decisions you make prior to actual instruction. The *interactive phase* includes all the decisions made during the immediacy and spontaneity of teaching itself. As stated earlier, decisions made during this phase are likely to be more intuitive, unconscious, and routine than those made during the planning phase. The *reflective phase* is the time you will take to reflect on, analyze, and judge the decisions and behaviors that occurred during the interactive phase. As a result of this reflection, decisions are made about how to use what was learned in subsequent teaching actions. At this point, you are in the *projective phase,* abstracting from your reflection and projecting your analysis into subsequent teaching actions.

Reflection and the Locus of Control

It is during the reflective phase that teachers have a choice of whether to assume full responsibility for the instructional outcomes, or whether to assume responsibility for only the positive outcomes of the planned instruction, while placing blame for the negative outcomes on outside forces (e.g., parents and guardians, children, other teachers, administrators, textbooks). Where the responsibility for outcomes is placed is referred to as *locus of control.* Competent teachers tend to assume responsibility for instructional outcomes, regardless of whether they are as intended in the planning phase.[2]

B. CHARACTERISTICS OF THE COMPETENT TEACHER

The overall purpose of this resource guide is to assist you in identifying and building on your instructional competencies. This section of this chapter is our starting place, beginning with the presentation of 22 specific competencies. You will continue to build on these competencies through your study of the rest of this resource guide and throughout your professional career as a teacher.

No teacher expertly models all the characteristics that follow; they represent an ideal to strive for:

1. *The teacher is knowledgeable about subject content taught in the elementary school.* This means that you have both historical understanding and current knowledge of the structure of those subjects you are expected to teach, and of the facts, principles,

---

[1]Arthur L. Costa, *The School as a Home for the Mind* (Palatine, IL: Skylight Publishing, 1991), pp. 97–106.
[2]Ibid., p. 105.

concepts, and skills needed for those subjects. This means that you need not know everything about a subject, but more than you are likely to teach. Chapter 13 can assist you in developing this competency.

2. *The teacher is an active member of professional organizations, reads professional journals, and dialogues with colleagues, maintaining currency in methodology and knowledge about the children and the subject he or she is expected to teach.* While this resource guide offers valuable information about teaching and learning, it is much closer to the start of your professional career than it is to the end. As a teacher you are a learner among learners. "Throughout your professional career, through workshops, advanced course work, coaching and training; through further knowledge acquisition by reading and study; and in collaboration with and through role modeling of significant and more experienced colleagues, you will be in a continual learning mode."[3] Chapter 15 offers further guidance for your continued professional development.

3. *The teacher understands the processes of learning.* As teacher, you will assure that students understand the lesson objectives, your expectations, and classroom procedures; that they feel welcomed to your classroom and involved in the learning activities; and that they have some control over the pacing of their own learning. Furthermore, your lessons will include consideration of children's levels of development (as presented in Chapter 2), present content in reasonably small doses—and in a logical and coherent sequence—use visual, verbal, tactile, and kinesthetic learning activities, and provide opportunities for guided practice and reinforcement, with frequent comprehension checks to assure that the students are learning.

4. *The teacher is an "educational broker."* You will learn where and how to discover information about the subject(s) you are expected to teach. You cannot know everything there is to know about each subject, but you are willing to become knowledgeable about where and how to best research it, and how to assist children in developing some of these same skills. Among other things, this means that you should be computer literate.

5. *The teacher uses effective modeling behaviors.* Your own behaviors must be consistent with those expected of your students. If, for example, you want your students to demonstrate regular and punctual attendance, to have inquiring minds, to behave cooperatively, to be attentive to recitations of others, to suspend judgments until sufficient data are in, to demonstrate critical thinking, and to use proper communication skills, then you will do likewise, modeling these same behaviors and attitudes for the children.

6. *The teacher is open to change, willing to take risks and to be held accountable.* If there were no difference between what is and what can be, then formal education would be of little value. A competent teacher is aware not only of historical and traditional values and knowledge, but also of the value of change, and is willing to plan carefully and to experiment, to move between that which is known and that which is not. Realizing that little of value is ever achieved without a certain amount of risk, the competent teacher, because of personal strength of conviction, stands ready to be held accountable, as he or she undoubtedly will be, for assuming such risks.

7. *The teacher is unbiased and nonprejudiced against any individual because of gender, sexual preference, ethnicity, skin color, religion, physical handicap, learning disability, or national origin.* In practice, this means no sexual innuendoes, religious jokes, or racial slurs. It means being cognizant of how teachers, male and female, knowingly or unknowingly, historically have mistreated female students, and of how to avoid these

[3]Arthur L. Costa, Foreword to *A Resource Guide for Teaching: K–12*, by Richard D. Kellough (New York: Macmillan, 1993), p. vii.

errors in your own teaching (Chapters 11 and 13 offer specific guidelines). It also means, as discussed in Chapter 1, learning about and attending to the special needs of individual students in your classroom.

8. *The teacher organizes the classroom and plans lessons carefully.* Long-range plans and lessons are prepared thoughtfully and well in advance, reflected on, revised, and competently implemented with creative, motivating, and effective strategies and skill. Much of this resource guide is devoted to assisting you in the development of this competency.

9. *The teacher is an effective communicator.* The competent teacher uses thoughtfully selected words, carefully planned questions, expressive voice inflections, useful pauses, meaningful gestures, and productive and expressive body language. Throughout this resource guide we provide useful suggestions for your development of this competency.

10. *The teacher can function effectively as a decision maker.* The elementary classroom is a complex place, busy with fast-paced activities. In a single day you may engage in a thousand or more interpersonal exchanges with students, and possibly many more with the adults whom you encounter. The competent teacher initiates, rather than merely reacts, and is proactive and in control of her or his classroom, having learned about how to manage time, to analyze, and to develop her or his interpersonal behaviors. (For this purpose many teachers have found it valuable to videotape a portion of a day, or an entire day's class, for later analysis of student and teacher interactions. This technique is discussed in Chapter 15, in regard to the development of your teaching behaviors.)

11. *The teacher is constantly striving to further develop a repertoire of teaching strategies.* As discussed earlier (competency 2), competent teachers are good students, continuing their learning by assessing their own work, attending workshops, studying the work of others, and talking with children, parents and guardians, and colleagues.

12. *The teacher demonstrates concern for the safety and health of the children.* The teacher strives to maintain a comfortable room temperature with adequate ventilation, and to prevent hazards to children's safety in the classroom (see Chapter 13) and on the playground. Students who are ill are encouraged to stay home to get well. If a teacher suspects that a child may be ill or may be suffering from abuse at home (see Chapter 4), the teacher appropriately and promptly acts on that suspicion by reporting it to the school nurse or an appropriate administrator. Teachers consistently model safety procedures, assuring precautions necessary to protect the health and safety of the children.

13. *The teacher demonstrates optimism for the learning of every child, while providing a constructive and positive environment for learning.* Much of this resource guide is devoted to the provision of specific guidelines and resources for developing this competency. Both common sense and research tell us clearly that students enjoy and learn better with a teacher who is positive, encouraging, nurturing, happy, and optimistic, than with one who is pessimistic, discouraging, uninterested, and grumpy.

14. *The teacher demonstrates confidence in each student's ability to learn.* For a student, nothing at school is any more satisfying than to be taught by a teacher who demonstrates confidence in that child's abilities. Unfortunately for some children, a teacher's show of confidence may be the only positive indicator that child ever receives. Each of us can recall with admiration a teacher (or other significant person) who showed confidence in our ability to accomplish seemingly formidable tasks. A competent elementary school teacher demonstrates this confidence with each child.

15. *The teacher is skillful and fair in the assessment of student learning.* One hears the statement, "A teacher should be firm, fair, and friendly." To be such a person, the competent teacher knows the importance of providing immediate, intensive intervention when learning problems occur, is knowledgeable about the implementation of learning assessment tools, and avoids abusing the power afforded by the assessment process (see Chapter 14).

16. *The teacher is skillful in working with parents and guardians, colleagues, administrators, and the clerical and custodial staff, and maintains and nurtures friendly and ethical professional relationships.* Teachers, parents and guardians, administrators, and classified staff all share one purpose—to serve the education of the children, which is best accomplished when they function cooperatively. A skillful teacher assures that parents or guardians are involved in their children's learning. Later chapters of this resource guide provide guidelines and resources for developing this competency.

17. *The teacher demonstrates continuing interest in professional responsibilities and opportunities.* Knowing that ultimately every school activity has an effect on the classroom, the competent teacher assumes an active interest in total school life. The purpose of the school is to serve the education of the children, and the classroom is the primary, but not only, place where this occurs. Every committee meeting, every school event, every faculty meeting, every school board meeting, every office, program, and planned function that is related to school life shares in the ultimate purpose of better serving the education of the school's children.

18. *The teacher demonstrates a wide range of interests.* This includes interest in the activities of the children and the many aspects of the school and its surrounding community. The competent teacher is interesting because of his or her interests; a teacher with varied interests more often motivates and captures the attention of more students.

19. *The teacher shares a healthy and enjoyable sense of humor.* Because humor releases tension and anxiety, girls and boys appreciate and learn more from a teacher who shares a sense of humor. Competent teachers ensure that the humor is not self-deprecating or disrespectful of others.

20. *The teacher is quick to recognize a student who may be in need of special attention.* A competent teacher is alert to recognize a child who demonstrates behaviors indicating a need for special attention, such as counseling. The teacher knows how and where to refer the student, doing so with minimal class disruption or embarrassment to the child. For example, a pattern of increasingly poor attendance is one of the more obvious early signals of the potential at-risk or dropout student.[4] Teacher or office staff contact with an adult in the child's home should be made immediately whenever a child is absent.

21. *The teacher makes special and frequent efforts to demonstrate how the subject content may be related to the lives of the children.* A potentially dry and boring topic is made significant and "alive" when taught by a competent teacher. Somewhere, a topic considered to be uninteresting is being taught by competent teachers, and one of the significant characteristics of their effectiveness is that they make that topic alive and relevant to their students, helping the children to make connections. Obtaining ideas from professional journals, attending workshops, and talking with colleagues are effective ways of discovering how to make a dry topic interesting and alive for your students.

[4]See John V. Hamby, "How to Get an 'A' on Your Dropout Prevention Report Card," *Educational Leadership* 46(5):14–18 (February 1989).

22. *The teacher is reliable.* The competent teacher can be relied on to fulfill promises and commitments. A teacher who cannot be relied on is quick to lose credibility with students. An unreliable teacher is an incompetent teacher. A teacher who is chronically absent from his or her teaching duties is an "at-risk teacher."

Specific teacher behaviors are discussed later in this chapter, and guidelines and resources to assist you in your development of these competencies can be found throughout this resource guide.

C. COMMITMENT AND PROFESSIONALISM

A teacher is expected to show commitment to the school's philosophy and mission statement, and to facilitate the personal as well as intellectual development of children. Not only do effective teachers expect, demand, and accomplish achievement of their students' learning in the classroom, but they are also involved in the activities of the students outside the classroom. To do this, they willingly sacrifice personal time to be accessible to students to give them personal attention and guidance. Thus, you are expected to be truly committed to the academic and personal development of the children.

Exemplifying a commitment to students is the following statement from the Code of Ethics of the Education Profession.[5] (This code is often printed on the reverse side of a teaching credential.) The two sections of the code guide your pledge of commitment to the students and the profession.

Principle I—Commitment to the Student

The educator strives to help each student realize his or her potential as a worthy and effective member of society. The educator therefore works to stimulate the spirit of inquiry, the acquisition of knowledge and understanding, and the thoughtful formulation of worthy goals. In fulfillment of the obligation to the student, the educator—

1. Shall not unreasonably restrain the student from independent action in the pursuit of learning.
2. Shall not unreasonably deny the student access to varying points of view.
3. Shall not deliberately suppress or distort subject matter relevant to the student's progress.
4. Shall make reasonable effort to protect the student from conditions harmful to learning or to health and safety.
5. Shall not intentionally expose the student to embarrassment or disparagement.
6. Shall not on the basis of race, color, creed, sex, national origin, marital status, political or religious beliefs, family, social or cultural background, or sexual orientation, unfairly:
    a. Exclude any student from participation in any program.
    b. Deny benefits to any student.
    c. Grant any advantage to any student.

---

[5]"Principle I—Commitment to the Student," *Code of Ethics of the Education Profession* (Washington, DC: National Education Association, 1975).

7. Shall not use professional relationships with students for private advantage.
8. Shall not disclose information about students obtained in the course of professional service, unless disclosure serves a compelling professional purpose or is required by law.

Exemplifying the teacher's commitment to professionalism is the following statement from the Code.[6]

The education profession is vested by the public with a trust and responsibility requiring the highest ideals of professional service. . . . In fulfillment of the obligation to the profession, the educator—

1. Shall not in an application for a professional position deliberately make a false statement or fail to disclose a material fact related to competency and qualifications.
2. Shall not misrepresent his or her professional qualification.
3. Shall not assist entry into the profession of a person known to be unqualified in respect to character, education, or other relevant attributes.
4. Shall not knowingly make a false statement concerning the qualifications of a candidate for a professional position.
5. Shall not assist a noneducator in the unathorized practice of teaching.
6. Shall not disclose information about colleagues obtained in the course of professional service unless disclosure serves a compelling professional purpose or is required by law.
7. Shall not knowingly make false or malicious statements about a colleague.
8. Shall not accept any gratuity, gift, or favor that might impair or appear to influence professional decisions or actions.

D. NONINSTRUCTIONAL RESPONSIBILITIES

The aspects of a teacher as a decision maker, and one who has professional commitments, assume substance when you consider the specific noninstruction-related and instruction-related responsibilities of the classroom teacher.

Often underestimated by the beginning teacher, as to importance and the amount of time necessary, the following items should focus your attention on the many noninstructional responsibilities you will undertake, especially during your first year of teaching.

1. I need time to become knowledgeable about activities of interest to the students.
2. I need time to become familiar with the school buildings and grounds.
3. I need time to become acquainted with members of the faculty and with the nonteaching staff.
4. I need time to become familiar with school and district policies on everything of relevance to the classroom teacher.

[6]"Principle II—Commitment to the Profession," *Code of Ethics of the Education Profession* (Washington, DC: National Education Association, 1975).

5. I need time to become knowledgeable about the backgrounds of my students.
6. I need time to become familiar with the community that is served by the school.
7. I need time to become knowledgeable about such routine matters as:
   a. Procedures for planning before- and after-school activities and events.
   b. Rest room regulations.
   c. Procedures for the distribution and collection of school materials.
   d. Procedures for daily dismissal.
   e. Procedures for ordering supplies.
   f. Procedures for the collection of lunch tickets or money.
   g. Established fire-drill routine.
   h. What to do in case of severe weather conditions.
   i. Policy for recording daily attendance and tardies.
   j. Procedures for student assemblies.
   k. School and district expectations and policies for classroom and on-campus conduct.
   l. How to share instructional space with other teachers.
   m. Procedures for arranging for and preparing displays for common areas of the school, such as hall display cases.
8. I need time to become knowledgeable about and to prepare for my expected role in teaching common elements of the school curriculum, such as writing.
9. I need time to think about classroom duties, such as the following:
   a. Maintaining a cheerful, pleasant overall classroom environment.
   b. Opening and closing classroom windows as needed.
   c. Preparing or locating needed materials and supplies for each lesson for each day.
   d. Keeping the teaching supplies in order.
   e. Cleaning the writing board each day, as needed.
   f. Supervising the children who are my helpers.
   g. Maintaining constant vigilance over the safety of children who are under my direct supervision.
10. I need to become knowledgeable about my expected role in attending and in participating in parent-teacher and community meetings.
11. I need time to anticipate and prepare for the many conferences that will be needed, such as between:
    a. Teacher and teacher.
    b. Teacher and student.
    c. Teacher and parent or guardian.
    d. Teacher and administrator.
    e. Teacher and community representative.
12. I need time for professional meetings, such as:
    a. Meetings of the interdisciplinary teaching team.
    b. Faculty meetings.
    c. Other school and district committee meetings.
    d. Parent-teacher organizations and other meetings involving members of the community.
    e. Meetings, conferences, and workshops sponsored by local, regional, state, and national professional organizations.
13. I need time to relax and to enjoy my family and hobbies.

E. INSTRUCTIONAL RESPONSIBILITIES

The following list introduces you to your instructional responsibilities.

1. I need time for planning the daily lessons.
2. I need time to learn of activities of interest to the students so I can connect my lessons to those interests.
3. In planning daily lessons, I need time to incorporate ways to address the individual learning styles of my students.
4. I need time each day for reading student papers.
5. I need time each day for assessing and recording student progress.
6. I need time each day to record evaluative marks in my record book.
7. I need time each day to prepare my classroom.
8. I will spend five or six hours each day on classroom instruction.
9. I need time for thinking and for my own professional growth and development.
   a. I may attend college or university courses.
   b. I will attend workshops and presentations offered by the school district or professional organizations.
   c. I will read professional journals, magazines, and newsletters.
10. I need time each day for preparing materials needed for my lessons.
11. I will take time to think about and develop my classroom management policies and incorporate a "firm but fair" management system.
12. I need time to prepare long-range teaching plans.
13. I will take time to reacquaint myself with the developmental characteristics of the age level of my students.
14. I will take time to become familiar with the background of students with special problems, and who might cause concerns in the learning environment of my classroom.
15. I will take time to further develop my techniques and plans for the use of cross-age tutoring, peer coaching, cooperative learning, and other specific and useful teaching strategies.
16. I will take the time necessary to give careful attention to ensuring the safety of children for whom I have direct responsibility.
17. As a member of a teaching team, I will need to reserve time necessary for team planning.
18. I need time to think about, assess, and continue development of my basic instructional skills.

Now that you have reviewed these lists, turn your attention to the total role of a first-year teacher. Do Exercise 3.1, which is also a model exercise in cooperative learning.

Exercise 3.1:   Reviewing the Professional Responsibilities of an Elementary School Teacher During the First Year of Teaching—An Exercise in Cooperative Learning

Instructions: The purposes of this exercise are (1) to review the responsibilities of a first-year teacher and (2) to experience, firsthand, a cooperative learning strategy. To prepare for this exercise, have your class of teacher candidates divide into groups of four. (If your class has an uneven number of members, one group could have three or five members; members may assume more than one role, or share a role.) Within each group, members should decide who will play each of the following roles: group facilitator, recorder, materials manager, and reporter. Each group is to concentrate on one of these six categories of responsibilities:

1. Audiovisual responsibilities.
2. Classroom environment responsibilities.
3. Clerical responsibilities.
4. Instructional responsibilities.
5. Professional activities responsibilities.
6. Supervision responsibilities.

Each group should then read the selected responsibilities for its category and prioritize them, beginning with the responsibility considered by the group as most important. The *group facilitator* will lead this discussion. With the leadership of the *materials manager,* groups may cut apart the cards listing the responsibilities so that the responsibilities can be physically manipulated as priorities are discussed. The *group recorder* should take notes of the group's work; the notes can then be discussed by the group and will lead to the development of a report that will be made to the whole class.

After a prearranged discussion time, recall the entire class to order and ask each group's *reporter* to provide leadership for a whole-class discussion and to share their group's (1) prioritized order of responsibilities and (2) estimate of the amount of time each week that a beginning teacher might devote to these responsibilities.

As each group reports, all members of the class should record the priority on the Recap Sheet and also note the time estimate for each group of responsibilities.

At completion of this exercise your class may wish to discuss the group dynamics of this in-class model of cooperative learning (for which you may wish to refer to Section C of Chapter 11). For discussion in either large or small groups, key questions might be:

1. What did you think of this form of discussion for use in your own teaching? _____
   _____
   _____

2. Identify ways that you could divide a class into groups of four. _____
   _____
   _____

3. Other discussion questions or items as generated by the group work. _____
   _____
   _____
   _____

FOR YOUR NOTES

Cards for Exercise 3.1
Audiovisual Group

Audiovisual responsibilities to be considered by your group:

Selecting, ordering, and returning filmstrips, cassettes, films, videodiscs, and other materials.

Preparing and operating equipment.	Taking time to review selected audiovisual materials.
After preview, planning class introduction to the audiovisual materials that will be shared.	Other audiovisual responsibilities as determined by the group.

Group's estimate of the time each week that a beginning teacher will devote to audiovisual responsibilities = _____ hours.

Cards for Exercise 3.1
Classroom Environment Group

Classroom environment responsibilities to be considered by your group:

Planning and constructing displays.	Preparing bulletin board displays.
Reading, announcing, and posting class notices.	Managing a classroom library collection.
Opening and closing windows, as needed; arrangement of furniture; cleaning the writing board.	Other responsibilities relating to the classroom environment, as determined by the group.

Group's estimate of the time each week that a beginning teacher will devote to creating and maintaining an effective classroom environment = _____ hours.

Cards for Exercise 3.1
Clerical Responsibilities Group

Classroom clerical responsibilities to be considered by your group:

Maintaining attendance and tardy records.	Entering grades, scores, or marks into a record or grade book.
Preparing progress reports and grade reports.	Typing, drawing, and duplicating instructional materials (including collating and stapling, when needed).
Locating resource ideas and materials to support teaching units and lessons.	Other clerical tasks as determined by the group.

Group's estimate of the time each week that a beginning teacher will devote to clerical responsibilities = _____ hours.

Cards for Exercise 3.1
Instructional Responsibilities Group

Classroom instructional responsibilities to be considered by your group:

Additional teaching, e.g., teaching individuals who need one-to-one instruction, students who have been absent, small groups for review.	Correcting papers; e.g., homework, workbooks, and so on.
Preparing special learning materials.	Preparing, reading, and scoring tests; helping students to self-evaluate.
Writing information on the board for students.	Preparing long-range and daily lesson plans.
Grouping for instruction.	Other instruction-related responsibilities as determined by the group.

Group's estimate of the time each week that a beginning teacher will devote to responsibilities that bear directly on instruction = _____ hours.

Cards for Exercise 3.1
Professional Activities Group

Professional activities responsibilities to be considered by your group:

Collecting information for and writing teacher reports.	Attending teachers' meetings and school district committee meetings.
Planning, attending, and participating in parent-teacher meetings.	Attending and participating in local teachers' organization meetings.
Attending and participating in state, regional, and national professional organizations; attending university classes.	Other professional activities as determined by this group.

Group's estimate of the time each week that a beginning teacher will devote to professional activities = _____ hours.

Cards for Exercise 3.1
Supervision Responsibilities Group

Supervision responsibilities to be considered by your group:

Supervising before- or after-school activities.	Supervising hallways, lunchrooms, and bathrooms.
Supervising student assemblies.	Supervising field trips.
Supervising classroom laboratory activities.	Settling disputes and quarrels between students.

Other supervision responsibilities as determined by this group.

Group's estimate of the time each week that a beginning teacher will devote to supervising students outside the classroom = _____ hours.

Exercise 3.1: Recap Sheet

How did the audiovisual group prioritize its responsibilities?

1. _____
2. _____
3. _____
4. _____
5. _____

How did the classroom environment group prioritize its responsibilities?

1. _____
2. _____
3. _____
4. _____
5. _____
6. _____

How did the clerical group prioritize its responsibilities?

1. _____
2. _____
3. _____
4. _____
5. _____
6. _____

How did the instructional group prioritize its responsibilities?

1. _____
2. _____
3. _____
4. _____
5. _____
6. _____
7. _____
8. _____

How did the professional activities group prioritize its responsibilities?

1. _____
2. _____

3. _____

4. _____

5. _____

6. _____

How did the supervision group prioritize its responsibilities?

1. _____

2. _____

3. _____

4. _____

5. _____

6. _____

7. _____

F. TEACHER BEHAVIORS NECESSARY TO FACILITATE STUDENT LEARNING

Your ability to carry out your instructional responsibilities effectively is directly dependent on your knowledge of and the quality of your teaching skills. Throughout your teaching career you will be developing your strategy repertoire along with your skills in using specific strategies. To be most effective, you need a large repertoire from which to select a specific strategy for a particular goal with a distinctive group of students. In addition, you need to develop skill in using that strategy. This section of this chapter is designed to help you to consider and begin the building of your strategy repertoire and the development of your skill in the use of specific strategies important for teaching children of any age.

First, you must know why you have selected a particular strategy. An unknowing teacher is likely to use the strategy most common in teaching college classes—the lecture. The traditional lecture is seldom, if ever, an effective way to instruct elementary school students. As a rule, by preference and by adeptness, most elementary school children are not strong auditory learners. For most of them, learning by sitting and listening is difficult. By preference and by ability, they learn best when physically and intellectually active—that is, through tactile and kinesthetic experiences, by touching objects, feeling shapes and textures, moving objects around, and by talking about and sharing what they are learning. (We return to the selection of strategies in Part III.)

Second, there are basic teacher behaviors that create the conditions needed to enable children to think and to learn. The behaviors are those that produce the following results:

- Students are physically and mentally engaged in the learning activities.
- Instructional time is efficiently used.
- Classroom distractions and interruptions are kept to a minimum.

Third, the effectiveness with which a teacher carries out the basic behaviors can be measured by *how well the children learn.*

Basic teacher behaviors that facilitate student learning are:

1. Structuring the learning environment.
2. Demonstrating instructional accountability.
3. Demonstrating withitness and overlapping.
4. Providing a variety of motivating and challenging lessons.
5. Modeling.
6. Facilitating student acquisition of data.
7. Accepting.
8. Clarifying.
9. Maintaining silence.
10. Questioning.

Later in this chapter there are exercises that will help you in evaluating your current level of competency for each of these behaviors and that will facilitate improvement in areas where you need help. It is necessary, first, to identify each facilitating behavior and consider some examples.

Fundamental behaviors of the effective elementary school teacher are those that create conditions needed to enable children to learn, whether the learning is a further understanding of concepts, the internalization of attitudes and values, the development of cognitive processes, or the actuating of the most complex psychomotor behaviors. To further your understanding, we suggest that for each of these teacher behaviors, the examples be discussed in your class. Additional examples can be found throughout this book; use the index to locate them.

1. **Structuring.** The effective teacher establishes an intellectual, psychological, and physical environment that enables students to productively act and to react. Specifically, the teacher does the following:

   1.1. Plans detailed lessons that begin each class meeting promptly and end when the class is officially ended.
   1.2. Learns and uses student names beginning with the first class meeting.
   1.3. Delineates tasks, responsibilities, and expectations.
   1.4. Communicates using an instructive vocabulary.
   1.5. Establishes, clearly communicates, and maintains classroom rules and procedures.
   1.6. Organizes the students.
   1.7. Provides clear definitions and instructions.
   1.8. Identifies time and resource constraints.
   1.9. Communicates the objectives for each lesson.
   1.10. Provides summary reviews.
   1.11. Attends to the organization of the classroom so that it is a positive, safe, and efficient learning environment.
   1.12. Helps students organize their learning. Provides instructional scaffolds, such as by building bridges to student learning, helping students connect what is being learned with what they already know and have experienced.
   1.13. Plans and implements techniques for schema building, such as by providing content and process outlines, visual diagrams, and concept mapping.
   1.14. Plans and implements techniques for student metacognitive development, such as with "think-pair share" (students are given a concept or idea and asked to think about it and to share with each other in pairs what they already think they know about it, and then with the entire class) or by the use of a technique sometimes known as "jigsaw" (individuals or small groups of students are given responsibilities for separate tasks which lead to a larger task or understanding, thereby putting together parts to make a whole, as was done in Exercise 3.1 of this chapter).

2. **Accountability.** While holding students accountable for their learning, the effective teacher is willing to be held accountable for the effectiveness of the instruction. The teacher shares responsibility for decision making and risk taking with the students and does the following:

   2.1. Attends to student questions and recitations.
   2.2. Requires students to demonstrate their learning.
   2.3. Calls upon students to share their thinking.
   2.4. Signals to students that they may be called upon to demonstrate their learning.
   2.5. Plans activities that engage students in the learning.
   2.6. Provides continuous cues for desired learning behaviors.

2.7. Provides incentives contingent upon acceptable performance, such as grades, points, rewards, and privileges.

2.8. Communicates to students that accomplishment of course objectives is a responsibility they share with the teacher.

2.9. Makes active and cooperative efforts to improve the effectiveness of the instruction.

2.10. Communicates clearly to parents, administrators, and colleagues.

2.11. Sets up an understood program of monitoring and feedback.

Thus the teacher assumes responsibility for professional decision making, as well as the risks associated with that responsibility.

3. **Withitness and Overlapping.** Two separate but closely related behaviors are withitness and overlapping. The teacher demonstrates withitness by being able to intervene and redirect potential misbehavior, and overlapping by being able to attend to several matters at the same time. To do this, the effective teacher:

3.1. Attends to the entire class while working with one student or with a small group of students, communicating this awareness with hand gestures, body language, and verbal cues.

3.2. Refocuses or shifts activities when student attention begins to fade.

3.3. Dwells on one topic only as long as necessary for the students' understanding.

3.4. Continually monitors classroom activities to keep students on task.

3.5. Immediately attends to an incessantly disruptuve student by following the school and district policy, which may mean asking the student to report to the principal's or vice principal's office and to meet privately later with the teacher.

3.6. Demonstrates an understanding of when comprehension checks are needed.

3.7. Continues to monitor the class during any distraction, such as a visitor entering the classroom.

4. **Variation, Motivation, and Challenges.** The effective teacher uses a *variety of activities* that *motivate* and *challenge* students to work to the best of their abilities and that engage and challenge the preferred learning styles of more of the students more of the time. Specifically, the teacher:

4.1. Shows pride in learning, thinking, and teaching.

4.2. Demonstrates the expectation that each student will work to the best of his or her ability.

4.3. Shows enthusiasm for teaching and learning.

4.4. Demonstrates optimism about each student's ability.

4.5. Plans and uses periodic shifts in activities and intellectual challenges.

4.6. Plans and effectively implements transition shifts that boost student interest.

4.7. Plans exciting and interesting lessons.

4.8. Paces the lessons so they move along smoothly and briskly.

5. **Modeling.** The teacher's behaviors are consistent with those expected of the students. The teacher:

5.1. Demonstrates rational problem-solving skills.

5.2. Models higher-order intellectual processes.

5.3. Shows respect for students.

5.4. Avoids the royal "we" (uses "I" when "I" is meant, "we" when "we" is meant).

5.5. Readily admits and corrects his or her mistakes.

5.6. Spells correctly.

5.7. Uses proper grammar.

5.8. Writes clearly and legibly.

5.9. Arrives promptly to class and demonstrates on-task behaviors for the entire class meeting.

5.10. Communicates clearly and concisely.

5.11. Is prompt to return homework with comments that provide instructive and encouraging feedback to the student.

5.12. Does not interrupt a student when the student is showing rational thinking.

5.13. Uses mental modeling, such as thinking aloud while reading a text to the students or while solving a problem.

6. **Facilitating the Acquisition of Data.** The teacher makes data accessible to students as input that they can process. To achieve this, the teacher:

6.1. Provides clear and specific instructions.

6.2. Emphasizes major ideas.

6.3. Creates a responsive classroom environment.

6.4. Provides direct-learning experiences.

6.5. Serves as a resource person.

6.6. Uses cooperative learning, thus regarding students as potential resources.

6.7. Uses older students as resource persons.

6.8. Uses other faculty as resource persons.

6.9. Uses the community as a resource.

6.10. Assures that sources of information are readily available.

6.11. Selects books and materials that facilitate student learning.

6.12. Provides feedback about each student's performance.

6.13. Ensures that equipment and materials are readily available.

7. **Acceptance.** The teacher offers appropriate nonevaluative and nonjudgmental responses that provide a psychologically safe learning environment. With students, the teacher:

7.1. Avoids the use of criticism. Criticism is a negative value judgment, and "when a teacher responds to a student's ideas or actions with such negative words as 'poor,' 'incorrect,' or 'wrong,' the response tends to signal inadequacy or disapproval and ends the student's thinking about the task."[7] Some evidence does indicate that mild (and only occasional) criticism, such as the nonacceptance of a student's absolutely wrong answer, does have some positive effect on the achievement of students at the upper end of the spectrum of socioeconomic status and academic ability. Students achieve less well when taught by teachers who criticize them frequently.

7.2. Is cautious with the use of strong praise.[8] For young children, teacher praise, a positive value judgment and the opposite of criticism, has value as a form of positive reinforcement. When praise is used for older children (middle school age), it should be mild, private, sincere, and for specific accomplishment, rather than for effort; for each student, the use of praise should be gradually decreased. In other words, as well as giving praise, the teacher should communicate to the student specifically *what* the student did that was worthy of praise. As emphasized by Good and Brophy, praise

---

[7]Costa, 1991, p. 54.

[8]See Herbert J. Wahlberg, "Productive Teaching and Instruction: Assessing the Knowledge Base," *Phi Delta Kappan* 71(6):470–478 (February 1990). See also Mary B. Rowe, "Wait Time and Rewards as Instructional Variables: Their Influence on Language, Logic and Fate Control," *Journal of Research in Science Teaching* (11):81–94 (1974).

Statement of Praise	**Statement of Encouragement**
1. Your painting is excellent.	1. It is obvious that you enjoy painting.
2. I am delighted that you behaved so well on our class field trip.	2. I am so delighted that we all enjoyed the class field trip.
3. You did a good job on those word problems.	3. I can tell that you have been working hard on your math and are now enjoying it more.
4. Your oral report was very good.	4. I can tell that you got really interested in your topic for your oral report.
5. Great answer, John!	5. John, your answer shows that you gave a lot of thought to the question.

Figure 3.1 Examples of statements of praise versus encouragement.

should be simple and direct, delivered in a natural voice (such as, "That's interesting, I never thought of that before," without gushing ("Wow!") or dramatizing ("Isn't that wonderful?"). Gushing and dramatized statements of praise are condescending and more likely to embarrass than reward. Even very young children see theatrics as insincere and phony.[9]

Let us pause to consider this point.[10] There is probably nothing in this book that raises more eyebrows than the statement that praise for *older* children has little or no value as a form of positive reinforcement. Indeed, praise from others may well motivate some people. Yet at what cost? Praise and encouragement are often confused and considered as one and the same, but they are not the same (see Figure 3.1), nor do they have the same long-term results. The idea is best explained by Jane Nelsen, a marriage, family, and child therapist:[11]

For many years there has been a great campaign for the virtues of praise in helping children gain a positive self-concept and improve their behavior. This is another time when we must "beware of what works." Praise may inspire some children to improve their behavior. The problem is that they become pleasers and approval "junkies." These children (and later these adults) develop self-concepts that are totally dependent on the opinions of others. Other children resent and rebel against praise, either because they don't want to live up to the expectations of others or because they fear they can't compete with those who seem to get praise so easily. Even though praise may seem to "work," we must consider the long-range effects. The alternative that considers long-range effects is encouragement. The long-range effect of encouragement is self-confidence. The long-range effect of praise is dependence on others.

   7.3. Frequently uses minimal reinforcement (i.e., nonjudgmental acceptance behaviors, such as a nod of the head, writing the student's response on the board, or saying, "I understand"). Whereas elaborate praise is generally

[9]From Thomas L. Good and Jere E. Brophy, *Looking in Classrooms*, 4th ed. (New York: Harper & Row, 1987), pp. 239–240.
[10]This important topic is discussed further in Chapter 10, Section C. For a further analysis of "encouragement versus praise," see Len A. Froyen, *Classroom Management: The Reflective Teacher-Leader*, 2nd ed. (New York: Macmillan, 1993), pp. 294–298.
[11]Jane Nelsen, *Positive Discipline* (New York: Ballantine Books, 1987), p. 103.

unrelated to student achievement, minimal reinforcement does correlate with achievement. Words such as "right," "okay," "good," "uh-huh," and "thank you" correlate with achievement gains for elementary school children. Whereas minimal reinforcement and mild praise seem to enhance the achievement of students of low socioeconomic levels and academic ability, mild (and only occasional) criticism seems more effective with students at the other end of the spectrum of socioeconomic status and academic ability.[12]

7.4.   Uses paraphrasing and reflective listening.

7.5.   Uses empathic acceptance of a student's mood or expression of feelings.

7.6.   Plans within the lessons positive actions that show respect for the experiences and ideas of individual students.

7.7.   Uses nonverbal cues (e.g., a friendly smile) to show awareness and acceptance of individual students.

7.8.   Writes reinforcing personalized comments on student papers.

7.9.   Provides positive individual student attention as often as possible.

7.10. Provides incentives and rewards for student accomplishments.

8. **Clarifying.** The teacher's responding behavior seeks further elaboration from a student about his or her idea or comprehension. The teacher therefore does the following:

8.1.   Provides step-by-step sequential learning experiences.

8.2.   Proceeds with the next step after the preceding step has been learned.

8.3.   Provides frequent summary reviews.

8.4.   Invites a student to be more specific.

8.5.   Asks a student to elaborate on or rephrase an idea.

8.6.   Asks a student to provide a concrete illustration of an idea.

8.7.   Ensures adequate practice for the content being learned.

8.8.   Repeats student responses, allowing the student to correct any teacher misinterpretation.

8.9.   Provides frequent comprehension checks to see whether the students understood (on the average of once every 10 minutes).

8.10. Relates new content to that previously learned.

8.11. Relates content to student experiences.

8.12. Helps students make learning connections between disciplines.

9. **Silence.** The teacher effectively uses periods of silence in the classroom. To achieve this, the teacher:

9.1.   Provides pauses for thinking and reflection.

9.2.   Uses pauses of longer than two seconds after asking a question or posing a problem.

9.3.   Uses teacher silence to stimulate group discussion.

9.4.   Uses teacher silence when students are working quietly.

9.5.   Uses teacher silence and active listening when a student is talking.

9.6.   Uses teacher silence when students are attending to a visual display that demands their concentration.

9.7.   Uses nonverbal signals and cues to maintain classroom control.

---

[12]For a discussion of research studies on the use of praise and criticism, see David L. Silvernail, *Teaching Styles as Related to Student Achievement*, 2nd ed. (Washington, DC: National Education Association, 1987), pp. 17–21.

10. **Questioning.** The teacher uses thoughtfully worded questions to induce cognitive learning and to stimulate thinking and the development of students' thinking skills. Specifically, the teacher:

    10.1. Uses a variety of questions, including those that stimulate both divergent and convergent thinking.

    10.2. Helps students develop their own questioning skills.

    10.3. Plans questioning sequences that elicit a variety of thinking skills, and that maneuver students to higher levels of cognition.

    10.4. Encourages student questioning, without judging the quality or relevancy of a student's question.

    10.5. Attends to students' questions and responds, often by building on the content of their questions.

The use of questioning is also the topic of Chapter 10. Direct your attention now to Exercises 3.2a and 3.2b.

Exercise 3.2a: Facilitating Behaviors: My First Self-Assessment

Instructions: The purpose of this exercise is for you to evaluate your perceived ability to perform each of the ten facilitating behaviors described in the preceding section. Upon completion of your self-evaluation, share it your colleagues and make appropriate revisions to your self-analysis. Then proceed to Exercise 3.2b. Later in the term, and again during student teaching, you may want to do follow-up assessments to determine progress in the development of your skills in using these behaviors. Use the extra space for comments, evidence, and resources.

Facilitating Behavior	**Competent**	**Need Practice**
1. Structuring	_____	_____
2. Accountability	_____	_____
3a. Withitness	_____	_____
3b. Overlapping	_____	_____
4a. Variation	_____	_____
4b. Motivating	_____	_____

4c. Challenging   _____   _____

5. Modeling   _____   _____

6. Facilitating the acquisition of data   _____   _____

7. Acceptance   _____   _____

8. Clarifying   _____   _____

9. Silence   _____   _____

10. Questioning   _____   _____

Exercise 3.2b: Facilitating Behaviors: My Plan for Skill Development

Instructions: The purpose of this exercise, following completion of Exercise 3.2a, is to develop a personal plan for strengthening your skills in those behaviors you identified as needing improvement. Use the following format.

1. Behaviors needing improvement (identify them by name):

    _____

    _____

    _____

    _____

    _____

    _____

    _____

    _____

2. Specific actions I will take to facilitate improvement (separate for each behavior):

    Behavior   **Actions I will take**

    _____   _____

    _____   _____

    _____   _____

    _____   _____

    _____   _____

    _____   _____

    _____   _____

    _____   _____

    _____   _____

    _____   _____

3. Identification of resources to facilitate my improvement (separate for each behavior):

    Behavior   **Resources**

    _____   _____

    _____   _____

    _____   _____

    _____   _____

    _____   _____

_____   _____
_____   _____
_____   _____
_____   _____
_____   _____
_____   _____

4. Time line for improvements (separate for each behavior):

   Behavior   **Time line for improvement**

_____   _____
_____   _____
_____   _____
_____   _____
_____   _____
_____   _____
_____   _____
_____   _____
_____   _____
_____   _____

5. How I will know improvement has been made (separate for each behavior):

   Behavior   **Evidence of improvement**

_____   _____
_____   _____
_____   _____
_____   _____
_____   _____
_____   _____
_____   _____
_____   _____
_____   _____
_____   _____

SUMMARY

In this chapter you reviewed the realities of the responsibilities of today's classroom teacher. You should now clearly understand that to be an exemplary classroom teacher demands more than teaching language arts, or science, or mathematics, or physical education, or whatever your special fields of interest might be. Although it is personally rewarding, to be a good teacher takes time, concentrated effort, and just plain hard work.

A major expectation is that you will be effective in helping students to learn and, perhaps, to do well on a state-mandated test. To achieve this goal requires that you individualize instruction to the fullest extent possible. Individualizing instruction begins with recognizing and attending to the worth and dignity of each child in your class.

Throughout these first three chapters it has been emphasized that children learn differently; they do not all learn and respond to learning situations in the same way. Children also learn differently according to a number of factors: whether it is morning or afternoon, the brightness of the classroom lighting, the amount of mobility allowed during learning, whether the child is allowed to chew gum, eat, or drink while learning, the amount of peer interaction allowed during the learning experience, and the student's ethnicity or socioeconomic status. *A teacher who, for all students, uses only one style of teaching, in the same classroom setting, day-after-day, is short-changing those children who learn better another way.*

As a teacher your professional responsibilities extend well beyond the four walls of the classroom, the five to six hours of the school day, the five days of the school week, and the 180 days of the school year. This chapter has presented the many expectations of the classroom teacher: (1) to be an effective decision maker; (2) to be committed to children, to the school's mission, and to the profession; (3) to be an effective teacher of particular disciplines and grade levels; and (4) to carry out the many noninstructional responsibilities. As you have read and discussed these expectations, you have probably begun to comprehend the reality of being an elementary school classroom teacher. In the next and final chapter of Part I, you will consider ways to establish the safe and effective learning environment needed to carry out these responsibilities.

QUESTIONS FOR CLASS DISCUSSION

1. Explain how you now feel about being a classroom teacher—for instance, motivated, enthusiastic, befuddled. Explain and discuss your feelings with a classmate. Sort out common concerns and design avenues for correcting any negative feelings you might have.
2. Which instructional responsibilities interest you most? Which concern you most? Why? Discuss those feelings with others in your class.
3. Which noninstructional responsibilities interest you most? Which concern you most? Why? Discuss your feelings with others in the class.
4. Approximately 30 years ago, a publication entitled *Six Areas of Teacher Competencies* (Burlingame, CA: California Teachers Association, 1964), identified six roles of the classroom teacher: director of learning, counselor and guidance worker, me-

diator of the culture, link with the community, member of the school staff, and member of the profession. Are those six roles of importance for the elementary school classroom teacher today as well? Explain.

5. Some schools have a minimum day as often as every few weeks—a day when children are dismissed early or perhaps do not come to school at all. What do teachers do on those days? What do the students do? Find answers to these questions and report to your class.

6. Describe the differences between the two teaching behaviors called "withitness" and "overlapping." Give examples of each.

7. Do you understand the difference between active, passive, and empathic acceptance? Give examples of each.

8. Explain the difference between giving a student reinforcement and praising the student. Is it possible to do one without the other? Explain. Explain when each is appropriate for a teacher to use.

9. Explain when, if ever, a teacher should use planned or unplanned silence in the classroom.

10. Do you have questions about the content of this chapter? How might answers be found?

SUGGESTED READINGS FOR CHAPTER 3

Aleman, M. P. "Redefining 'Teacher'." *Educational Leadership* 50(3):97 (November 1992).

Borich, G. D. *Effective Teaching Methods*. 2nd ed. New York: Macmillan, 1992.

Brookfield, S. D. *The Skillful Teacher*. San Francisco: Jossey-Bass, 1990.

Brophy, J. "Teacher Praise: A Functional Analysis." *Review of Educational Research* 51(1):5–32 (Spring 1981).

Costa, A. L., ed. *Developing Minds: Programs for Teaching Thinking*. Rev. ed. Alexandria, VA: Association for Supervision and Curriculum Development, 1991.

———. *The School as a Home for the Mind*. Palatine, IL: Skylight Publishing, 1991.

Good, T. L., and Brophy, J. E. *Looking in Classrooms*. 5th ed. New York: Harper & Row, 1991.

Henderson, J. G. *Reflective Teaching: Becoming an Inquiring Educator*. New York: Macmillan, 1992.

Lombardi, T. P. *Learning Strategies for Problem Learners*. Fastback 345. Bloomington, IN: Phi Delta Kappa Educational Foundation, 1992.

Silvernail, D. L. *Teaching Styles as Related to Student Achievement*. 2nd ed. Washington, DC: National Education Association, 1986.

Tobin, K. "Effects of Extended Wait Time on Discourse Characteristics and Achievement in Middle School Grades." *Journal of Research in Science Teaching* 21(8):779–791 (1984).

Watts, M., and Bentley, D. "Constructivism in the Classroom: Enabling Conceptual Change by Words and Deeds." *British Educational Research Journal* 13(2):121–135 (1987).

4

What Do I Need to Know to Establish and Maintain an Effective and Safe Classroom Learning Environment?

To be effective and to have a minimum of disruptions in the classroom, you must remember and apply what you remember about the developmental needs and characteristics of children. Your effective techniques of classroom management derive from your knowledge, careful thought, and planning and should not be learned on the job. To be most effective as a teacher, you will find it necessary to establish a classroom environment conducive to student learning, to help the children perceive the importance of what is being taught, and to help them realize that they can successfully learn it. You will find that students are more willing to spend time on a learning task when they perceive a *value* or *reward* in doing it, when they have some *ownership* in planning and carrying it out, and when each feels that he or she *can* do it.

This chapter supports your understanding by presenting guidelines to help you set up and maintain a classroom environment that is favorable to student learning. You will also be guided in establishing procedures for efficiently managing and effectively controlling the behavior of your students day by day and throughout the school year.

A. BEGINNING THE SCHOOL YEAR

Effective teaching and classroom management throughout the school year begins with the way you start the year; a good beginning is very important to having a good year. To effectively start the school year, consider the following guidelines:

1. *Students must feel that the classroom environment is supportive.* Before school begins, spend time thinking about how you can provide a supportive classroom environment. Plan how you will:
   - *Emphasize students' positive efforts and minimize the negative.* The key here is to remember this phrase: "Catch the students being good."

The effective teacher develops a classroom management plan *before* meeting the children for the first time. The plan includes procedures that children follow for everything. Children understand the procedures. The teacher is consistent about everyone following the procedures. When procedures are understood by the children and enforced by the teacher, there are fewer problems and students learn, and learning is fun.

- *Get to know students as individuals.* Many experienced teachers learn as much as possible about each child *before* the children arrive the first day. Of course, having the same students for several consecutive years, as in the school-within-a-school program, is helpful. Other ways of getting to know your students before they arrive is to talk with their former teachers and to read their cumulative folders. Otherwise, during the first week of school you will want to plan activities that will help you to get to know your students quickly. Monitoring group activities and talking with individual students are key ways of doing this.
- *Physically arrange the classroom to be the most supportive environment.* See the discussion in Section B of this chapter.
- *Let the students know your expectations for classroom behavior, and the consequences for their not meeting those expectations.*
- *Make students' learning seem worthwhile.*
2. *Plan your lessons and be ready to begin immediately the learning process.* Long before you first meet your students you must have your curriculum and lessons organized and ready to go from the first day of school. In addition, before that first day you will want to spend time at school getting your room organized, talking and planning with teachers, finding out where equipment and materials are kept, and putting the final touches to your lesson plans for that first week, which may include making copies of student handouts.

The First Day of School

On the first day you will want to cover certain major points of common interest to you and the children.

1. *Greeting the students.* Welcome your students with a smile as they arrive, and then the entire class with a friendly but businesslike demeanor.
2. *Student seating.* Tell children (grades 3 and above) that by the end of the week each should be in a permanent seat, from which you will make a seating chart so that you can quickly learn their names and efficiently take attendance each day (see Section B).
3. *Information about the class.* Explain to students what the class is about, what they will be learning, and how they will learn it. Many elementary school teachers (grades 4 and above) make a list of expectations, give each child a copy, and review it with them, specifically discussing the teacher's expectations about how books will be used, about their notebooks, portfolios, and homework, and about the location of resources in the classroom.
4. *Classroom procedures.* In a positive way, explain your expectations regarding classroom behavior (see Figure 4.1). Children work best when teacher expectations are

---

When establishing your rules for classroom behavior, remember this: Learning time should run efficiently (i.e., with no "dead spots"), smoothly (i.e., with established routines and transitions between activities occurring with fluidity), and with minimum disruption. When stating your expectation for students' classroom behavior, try to do so in a positive manner, emphasizing desired behaviors, stressing what children should *do*, rather than what they should *not do*. Then rehearse these behaviors with the children.

As you prepare your rules and procedures, consider what the children need to know from the start, such as:

- *How to obtain your attention and help.* Most teachers who are effective classroom managers expect their students to raise their hands—and for only as long as necessary; that is, until the teacher acknowledges (usually by a nod) that the child's hand has been seen. With that acknowledgment, the student should lower his or her hand. To prevent the student from becoming bored and restless in waiting, you must attend to the student as quickly as possible.
- *How to enter and leave the classroom.* From the time the class is scheduled to begin and until it officially ends (many schools do not ring bells at passing time), teachers who are effective classroom managers expect students to be in their assigned seats, or at their assigned learning stations, and to be attentive to the teacher or learning activity.
- *How to maintain, obtain, and use learning materials and items of personal use.* Students need to know where, when, and how to store, retrieve, and care for items such as their coats, books, pencils, and medicines, how to get papers and other materials, and when to use the pencil sharpener and wastebasket. Classroom control is easiest to maintain when items students need for class activities and for their personal use are neatly arranged and located in places that require minimum foot traffic, when there are established routines that students clearly expect and understand, when there is the least amount of student off-task time, and when

(continued)

Figure 4.1   Establishing classroom behavior rules and procedures.

students do not have to stand in line for anything. Therefore, you will want to plan the room arrangement, equipment and materials storage, preparation of equipment and materials, and transitions between activities so as to avoid needless delays and confusion.[1]

- *When they can go to the drinking fountain and the bathroom.* Normally, children should be able to take care of these matters between classes or (in the instance of kindergarten and primary grades) at regular intervals; however sometimes they do not, or, for medical reasons, cannot. Reinforce the idea that they should do those things before coming into your classroom, but be flexible enough for the occasional child who has an immediate need.

  For reasons of safety, when a kindergarten or primary-grade child must be excused from class to go to the bathroom, the child is accompanied by another child or a teacher's aide.

- *How to behave during a class interruption.* Unfortunately, class interruptions do occur. The principal or another person from the school's office may need to interrupt the class with an important message for the teacher or a child, or to make an announcement of importance to the entire class. Students need to know the behavior that is expected of them during such interruptions. Expectations are that they remain polite, quiet, and studious.

- *What to do when they are late to your class, or when they will be leaving early.* You need to understand and reinforce school policies on early dismissals and tardies. Plan and routinize your own procedures so students clearly understand what they are to do if they must leave your class early (e.g., for a medical appointment) or arrive late.

- *What the consequences are for inappropriate behavior.* Most teachers who are effective classroom managers routinize their procedure for handling inappropriate behavior, and make sure that the students understand the consequences.

  For older students (grades 4 and above), the consequences are discussed and posted in the classroom and may be similar to the following:

  First offense results in a reminder (verbal or nonverbal).
  Second offense results in a warning and a note to parent or guardian.
  Third offense results in detention and phone call home.
  Fourth offense results in a three-day suspension from class, a note sent home, and a conference including parent or guardian, student, teacher, and principal.
  Fifth offense results in permanent suspension from school.

- *Rules for behavior and procedures to follow during emergency drills, real or practice.* Students need to know what to do, where to go, and how to behave during an emergency such as a fire, storm, earthquake, or disruption by an intruder.

Figure 4.1   (*continued*).

well understood, with clearly established routines. In the beginning it is important that there be no more rules than necessary to get the class moving effectively for daily operation. A maximum of five rules may be enough. Too many can be restricting and confusing to students. You will want to explain and rehearse expected behavior and procedures for daily classroom routines. Later you may add, drop, or modify rules as necessary, perhaps during a class meeting when students discuss situations where rules may be changed. After reading the guidelines in Figure 4.1 on establishing rules and procedures, do Exercises 4.1 and 4.2 to begin thinking about and writing your own classroom management system.

[1]Thomas L. Good and Jere E. Brophy, *Looking in Classrooms*, 4th ed. (New York: Harper & Row, 1987), p. 232.

Exercise 4.1: Teachers' Behavior Management Systems

Instructions: The purpose of this exercise is to discover how one teacher manages the classroom. Interview a teacher, using the following format. Share the results with your classmates, perhaps in small groups.

Teacher interviewed _____

Date _____

Grade level _____

1. Please describe your classroom management system. Specifically, I would like to know your procedures for the following:

   a. How children are to signal that they want your attention and help. _____

   _____

   _____

   _____

   b. How you call on students during question and discussion sessions. _____

   _____

   _____

   _____

   c. How and when children are to enter and exit the classroom. _____

   _____

   _____

   _____

   d. How children are to obtain the materials for instruction. _____

   _____

   _____

   _____

   e. How children are to store their personal items. _____

   _____

   _____

   _____

   f. How children are to go to the drinking fountain or bathroom. _____

   _____

   _____

   _____

g. How children are to respond during class interruptions. _____
_____
_____
_____

h. Late arrival or early dismissal. _____
_____
_____
_____

i. Turning in homework. _____
_____
_____
_____

2. Describe your expectations for classroom behavior and the consequences for misbehavior.
_____
_____
_____
_____
_____
_____
_____
_____
_____

Discussion of Results

Today many teachers advocate a highly structured classroom management system and, as appropriate over time during the school year, sharing more of the responsibility with the students. Did you find this to be the case with the majority of teachers interviewed? _____
_____
_____
_____
_____
_____
_____

Exercise 4.2: My Classroom Management System

Instructions: The purpose of this exercise is to begin preparation of the management system that you will explain to your students (and their parents or guardians) during the first day or first week of school. Answer the questions that follow. Share the answers with your peers for their feedback, then make changes as appropriate.

My anticipated grade level _____

1. Attention to procedures. Write a statement to explain your procedural expectation for each of the following:

   a. How children are to signal that they want your attention or help. _____
   _____
   _____

   b. How you call on students during question and discussion sessions. _____
   _____
   _____

   c. How and when children are to enter and exit the classroom. _____
   _____
   _____

   d. How children are to obtain materials for instruction. _____
   _____
   _____

   e. How children are to store their personal items. _____
   _____
   _____

   f. Procedures for going to the drinking fountain or bathroom. _____
   _____
   _____

   g. Procedures during class interruptions. _____
   _____
   _____

   h. Procedures for late arrival or early dismissal. _____
   _____
   _____

   i. Procedures for turning in homework. _____

_____

_____

2. List of student behavior expectations that I will present to my class of children (no more than five):

Rule 1 _____

_____

_____

Rule 2 _____

_____

Rule 3 _____

_____

Rule 4 _____

_____

Rule 5 _____

_____

3. Explanation of consequences for broken rules. _____

_____

_____

_____

_____

_____

_____

4. How my procedures, rules, or consequences may vary (if at all) according to the grade level taught, or according to any other criteria, such as in team teaching. _____

_____

_____

_____

_____

Routines and Interruptions of Routines

As stated earlier, children must understand the procedures for daily routines, such as the start of class, attendance taking, or sharpening pencils. It is possible, however, that classroom routines may be interrupted, especially on certain days and at certain times during the school year. For instance, students' energy levels are not equal on all days. Your anticipation of and careful planning for days of high energy levels will help preserve your own mental health. Times when children's energy level may be high include the following:

- At the beginning of each school day.
- Before a field trip.
- Before a holiday.
- Before a school event, e.g., picture day, or a school assembly.
- Grade report day.
- Immediately before lunch.
- On a minimum day.
- School newspaper day.
- The day a substitute teacher is present.
- Toward the end of each school day.
- Toward the end of school each Friday.

From the very first day of the school year you will want to steadily monitor student behavior in your classroom and respond quickly and appropriately to both "good" and "bad" student behaviors, establishing early your expectations and the consequences students may expect.

Responding to Appropriate Student Behaviors

Behaviors that are reinforced are those most likely to recur. Knowing that, then, emphasizes the importance of reinforcing appropriate student behaviors, and of *not* reinforcing those that are inappropriate. Teacher reinforcement of appropriate student behaviors usually comes in some form of praise. For positive reinforcement of student behaviors, the form of that praise is important. As discussed in the preceding chapter, praise from the teacher that is effective is:

- Private, low-keyed, and specific to the child's behavior.
- Spontaneous, sincere, verbal *and* nonverbal, and individualized.

Responding to Inappropriate Student Behaviors

Although you follow the guidelines as established in this resource guide, there still will be occasional misbehaviors of students. As stated by Borich, "For most teachers, confronting some sort of behavior problem is a daily occurrence. These problems may include simple infractions of school or classroom rules, or they can involve far more serious events, including disrespect, cheating, obscene words and gestures, and open display of hostility."[2] Infrequent and minor disruptions resulting from the behaviors of students can and sometimes should be ignored by the teacher (for example, when a child is slow to close his workbook after the teacher has asked the class to put their workbooks away and get ready for another activity). Too-frequent interventions by a teacher can cause more problems than they cure. Sometimes you and a child will have a better relationship when you ignore minor infractions by that child. When to ignore, and the importance of being consistent and fair, is something of a dichotomy that involves your professional judgment and intuition. *Being coldly consistent is not the same as being fair and professional.* As a teacher, you are a professional who deals in matters of human relations and who must use professional intuition and judgment. You are not a robot, nor is any of the students. Human beings differ from one another, and seemingly similar situations can vary substantially, because the people involved are different. Consequently, a teacher's response, or lack of response, to each of two separate but quite similar situations may differ.

Too often teachers respond to misbehaviors with verbal commands (**direct intervention**), when nonverbal gestures (**indirect intervention**) such as eye contact, touch, and body language are less disruptive and more effective in quieting a misbehaving student. For an identical offense, the teacher's intervention for one student may have to be direct, while for another indirect intervention is adequate. To redirect a student's attention, your usual first effort can be indirect intervention.

Direct intervention should be reserved for the most serious misbehaviors. When using direct intervention, you should give a direct statement either reminding the child of what he or she is supposed to be doing, or telling the child what to do. We suggest that you do not question (for instance, "Josephine, why are you doing that?"). When giving students directions about what they are supposed to be doing, you may be asked, "Why do we have to do this?" Give a brief academic reason, but do not become defensive or make threats. And rather than spending an inordinate amount of time on the misbehavior, try to focus the child's attention on a desired behavior.

Most classroom problems will be prevented or resolved by following the guidelines that are presented in this resource guide. However, by the time the students reach the upper elementary grades, peer pressure and resentment of authority by some students can result in classroom management becoming a major concern of their teachers. Major problems in classroom control may call for extra effort on the part of the teacher in understanding and in dealing with them (discussed later in this chapter). There are no short-term solutions for a teacher who is trying to resolve a conflict with a child who causes major problems. Although punishment (e.g., suspension) may offer short-term relief, long-term counseling is often called for. Good and Brophy point to the lack of success by psychotherapists in this area:

> There has been much debate, but little research and certainly no conclusive evidence, about how to handle the most serious problems: racial and other group tensions; severe withdrawal and refusal to communicate; hostile, antisocial acting-out; truancy; refusal to work or obey; vandalism; and severe behavioral disorders or criminality. Psychotherapists have not achieved much success in dealing with behavior disorders, and neither they nor correctional institutions have achieved even modest success in dealing with severe delinquency and criminality. Yet teachers typically are asked to cope with such problems.[3]

[2]Gary D. Borich, *Effective Teaching Methods*, 2nd ed. (New York: Macmillan, 1992), p. 344.
[3]Good and Brophy, p. 274.

However, there *are* success stories. A recommendation for helping difficult students make the proper connection with school is to ask teachers to identify students with particular difficulty in establishing a sense of connection with the purpose of schooling, and to counsel the students to take part in extracurricular activities. Schools have experienced success in establishing this connection by encouraging *all* students to participate in school activities, regardless of their skills or academic grades.

Another successful effort at helping students make a connection with the value and goals of school has been through school and business partnerships. A special form of partnership—**mentoring**—has had great success with at-risk students as they become more receptive to schooling. The mentoring component of the partnership movement is a one-on-one commitment by community volunteers to improve the self-esteem, attitudes, and attendance of youngsters, beginning as early as kindergarten. For example, in the Norwalk Public Schools in Connecticut, mentors and students are matched in a one-on-one relationship that may begin as early as kindergarten, where at-risk children are first identified. The mentoring may continue throughout the school years until high school graduation.[4] Building self-esteem and preventing school dropout are the primary goals of the Norwalk program. In selecting students for the program, priority is given to those children who exhibit one or more of the following characteristics:[5]

- Frequent trips to the principal's office.
- Inability to take risks.
- Increased detentions.
- Increasing hostility.
- Intact family with history of drug or alcohol abuse.
- Lack of self-esteem.
- No parents, being raised by someone else with little or no support.
- One-parent family with little or no support.
- Poor attitude.
- Poor eye contact.
- Poor school attendance.

Around the country there are a number of other successful mentoring programs, and many different forms are being established at a rapid pace.[6]

B. ESTABLISHING AND MAINTAINING A SUPPORTIVE CLASSROOM ENVIRONMENT

Effective teachers strive to provide a classroom atmosphere that is supportive of students and their efforts, where all children feel welcome and accepted by the teacher. Teachers whose classes are friendly and positive find that their students learn and behave better than students of teachers whose classes are restrictive, repressive,

---

[4]Susan G. Weinberger, *How to Start a Student Mentor Program*, Fastback 333 (Bloomington, IN: Phi Delta Kappan Educational Foundation, 1992), p. 8.
[5]Ibid., p. 16.
[6]Ibid., pp. 27–28.

and gloomy. One step you can take toward providing a supportive classroom environment is to consider the physical arrangement of student seating.

Physical Arrangement of the Classroom

If student desks or chairs are fixed, as they are in some older classrooms, there is less flexibility for arranging student seating. If desks and chairs are moveable, however, consider a circular seating arrangement, as opposed to linear. In the traditional linear arrangement the seats are arranged in rows and all students face the front of the room. Such an arrangement is suitable for presentations by guest speakers, audiovisual presentations, or demonstrations to the entire class, but does not encourage the most productive interactive learning or a feeling of "we-ness." It may be better to arrange students in a hollow square or a circle (favored by many teachers for whole-class discussions, demonstrations, and audiovisual presentations), or in groups (small circles). Small groups are most effective for **cooperative learning** activities. Many teachers prefer to arrange student seating variously, according to the type of activity for the moment.

Depending on the physical layout and space available, you may have several types of arrangements concurrently. Since some students learn better in a body position other than sitting at a desk or in a chair, many teachers have effectively arranged their classrooms to accommodate varying learning modalities. For example, a carpet in one area accommodates students who prefer sitting on the floor in a more relaxed posi-

Many teachers vary the seating arrangement of their classrooms to accomodate specific types of learning activities and the varying learning modalities of the children.

tion, while in another location a learning center accommodates those students who learn best alone or in dyads. In other areas of the room, there are tables and chairs to accommodate small learning groups.

Getting to Know the Children

There are several ways that the busy teacher can learn more about individual students:

- *Classroom sharing during the first week of school.* Many teachers take time during the first week of school to have each child present information about him- or herself. For instance, each child answers questions such as:

  What name would you like to be called by?
  Where did you attend school last year?
  Tell us about your hobbies and other interests.

  You might have children share information of this sort with each other in small groups, while you visit each group in turn. Yet another approach is to include everyone in a game, having children answer the questions on paper and then, as you read their answers, asking them to guess which student wrote each.
- *Observations of children in the classroom.* During classroom learning activities the effective teacher is constantly alert to the individual behavior (nonverbal as well as verbal) of each child in the class, whether the student is on-task or gazing off and perhaps thinking about other things. Be cautious, however; just because a child is gazing out the window does not mean that the student is not thinking about the learning task. During group work, such as in cooperative learning groups, is a particularly good time to observe students and get to know more about each one's skills and interests.
- *Observations of students outside the classroom.* Another method of learning more about students is to observe them outside class, for example, at lunchtime, during intramural activities, on the playground, and during other school functions.
- *Conversation with students.* You will want to spend time casually talking with individual or small groups of students during lunchtime, on the playground, and during other out-of-class occasions.
- *Conferences and interviews with students.* Conferences with students, and sometimes with their parents or guardians as well, afford yet another opportunity to show that you are genuinely interested in each child as a person as well as a student. Some teachers, perhaps within the block schedule time (if there is one), plan a series of conferences during the first few weeks in which, in small groups of three or four students, each student is interviewed by the teacher. Such conferences and interviews are managed by the use of open-ended questions. The teacher indicates by the questions, and by nonjudgmental and empathic responses, a genuine interest in the students.
- *Student writing.* Much can be learned about students by what they write. It is important to encourage writing in your classroom, and you will want to read everything that students write and to ask for clarification when needed.
- *Open-ended questionnaires.* Many teachers of older students (grades 4 and above) use open-ended questionnaires to learn more about them. Students are asked questions such as the following:

  When at lunch with your friends, what do you usually talk about?

> When you read for fun, what do you usually read?
> What are your favorite movies (or TV shows)?
> Who are your favorite music video performers?
> What do you like to do when you just hang around?
> Where do you like to hang around?
> What do you plan to do when you graduate from high school?

- *Cumulative record.* Held in the school office is the cumulative record for each child in the school, containing information recorded every year by teachers and other school personnel. Although you must use discretion before arriving at any conclusions about such information (the history of the student as someone has recorded it to be), the file may afford information for getting to know a particular student better.
- *Discussions with other professionals.* To better understand an individual student, it is often helpful to talk with that child's other teachers or counselor, to learn of their perceptions and experiences with the student.

Creating a Positive Classroom Atmosphere

The classroom should be a pleasant place for each child to come to and learn in. All children should feel welcome in your classroom and accepted by you as individuals with dignity. Although these feelings and behaviors should be reciprocal, that is, expected of the students as well, they begin with the teacher modeling the behaviors expected of the students. You must help students learn that your denial of a child's specific behavior is *not* a denial of that child as a worthwhile person. Specific ways to create a positive classroom environment are as follows:

- Admonishing behavior, not persons.
- Attending to the classroom's physical appearance and comfort.
- Being an interesting person and an optimistic and enthusiastic teacher.
- Encouraging children to set high yet realistic standards for themselves, and then showing them how to work, in increments, toward these standards.
- Encouraging high aspirations from each student, letting each child know that you are confident in her or his ability to achieve.
- Helping students develop their skills in cooperative learning (see Chapter 11).
- Involving children in every aspect of their learning, including the planning of learning activities, thereby giving them part ownership in their learning. One elementary teacher, for example, achieves this by running her classroom as a technology-based token economy. The children hold classroom jobs and use computer software to track money earned, manage checking accounts, and disburse classroom cash.[7]
- Making sure there is no prejudice displayed against any child (see Chapter 11, Section C).
- Making the classroom an attractive place to be.
- Making the learning fun, using humor as a medium for learning.
- Phoning or sending positive notes home to parents or guardians (see Exercise 4.3).
- Rewarding individual successes, no matter how small the accomplishment.
- Rewarding positive behaviors.
- Using interesting teaching strategies that increase student motivation for learning.

[7]See Leni Donlan, "Curriculum Connection: Create a Classroom Community," *Instructor* 101(1):77–78 (August 1991).

Two items in the preceding list are statements about giving encouragement. When using encouragement to motivate student learning, there are a few important behaviors that you should *avoid* because they discourage learning:

- Avoid comparing one child with others.
- Avoid encouraging competition among children. Instead, encourage cooperation.
- Avoid giving up or appearing to give up at any time on any child.
- Avoid telling a child how much better he or she could be.
- Avoid using qualifying statements, such as "I like what you did, but . . ." or "It's about time."

Proceed now by doing Exercise 4.3.

Exercise 4.3: Writing a Positive Note to a Student's Home

Instructions: The purpose of this exercise is to practice writing a positive note to a student's home. For too many parents and guardians, the only communications ever received from their child's teachers are negative messages about the child's academic or social behavior. Communication to a parent can convey a positive message as well. (After writing a positive message, rather than sending it to the child's home, some teachers choose to phone the parent). First, think of a situation you might want to tell about, then practice writing one positive message. Ask another teacher candidate to read and react to your message. Does your message convey what you intend it to say?

Situation _____

_____

_____

_____

Practice note to parent or guardian _____

_____

_____

_____

_____

_____

_____

_____

Reaction comments _____

_____

_____

_____

_____

_____

_____

_____

_____

Review the comments. What areas do you want to focus on for class discussion? Talk about them with others in your class.

FOR YOUR NOTES

C. CONDUCTING DAILY CLASS SESSIONS

Once the school day or class period begins (as noted, some schools do not use a bell system for the beginning and ending of class periods), begin the class activities in an organized manner. At the start of each day, greet the children and give the students an assignment to work on (sometimes called a "bell activity"). While the children are working on that assignment, you can take attendance and attend to other routine administrative matters.

When there are no announcements or other administrative matters to attend to, some teachers prefer to begin the day's lesson immediately and then, within a few minutes after the students have begun their lesson activities, take attendance. Still other teachers begin the day's lesson immediately, giving a reliable classroom teaching aide the responsibility of taking attendance and dealing with other routine administrative tasks. The teaching aide might be a paid or volunteer adult, a responsible upper-class student assistant, or a reliable and responsible student periodically selected from your own class of students. Whichever the case, when another person performs the daily attendance routines, it is still the legal responsibility of the credentialed classroom teacher to check and sign the relevant attendance forms.

Once the class period has begun, routines and lesson activities should move forward briskly and steadily until the official end of the class period or school day.

Principles of Movement Management

The pace of learning activities should be lively enough to keep children alert and busy, without dead time, but not so fast as to discourage or to lose students. The effective teacher runs a businesslike classroom, where at no time does any student sit or stand around with nothing to do. To maintain a smooth and brisk pace, to lessen distractions, and to allow no dead time, the teacher uses the principles of effective movement management.[8]

- The **first principle of effective movement management** is that by beginning the lesson efficiently and in an organized manner, you are discouraging the kind of fooling around and time wasting that might otherwise occur. As a beginning teacher, you must practice this principle and adhere to it from the very beginning of your teaching, to minimize problems with classroom control.
- The **second principle of effective movement management** is that student movement about the classroom should be routinized, controlled, restricted, and purposeful to the lesson activities. As a beginning teacher, it is also important that you practice this principle and adhere to it from the very first day you begin teaching— again, to minimize problems with classroom control.

As will be understood by your cooperating teacher and college or university supervisor during your student teaching, it will take some time for you to develop the skills necessary for the most successful application of this second principle. At the beginning of your student teaching you will want to follow the movement procedures already established by your cooperating teacher, assuming, of course, that the procedures exemplify this second principle.

[8]The principles of movement management were adapted from Jacob S. Kounin, *Discipline and Group Management in the Classroom* (New York: Holt, Rinehart and Winston, 1977), pp. 102–108.

- The **third principle of effective movement management** is that the lesson should move forward briskly and purposefully, with natural transitions from one lesson activity to the next, and with each activity starting and ending conclusively. As a beginning teacher, it may take time to develop finesse in your application of this third principle. During your student teaching experience, your cooperating teacher and college supervisor will understand that it takes time, and will help you develop and hone your skill in the application of this principle.

Smooth Application of the Principles of Movement Management

Teachers who are less effective in the application of the principles of movement management are often those who themselves fail to adhere to these principles. To be sure that your movement management is most effective, it is important to adhere to the following guidelines:

- When giving verbal directions to children, do so quickly and succinctly, without talking too much or giving so much detail that children begin to get restless and bored.
- Once your children are busy and on task, avoid interrupting them with additional verbal instructions, statements, or announcements, particularly if those additional instructions can be written on the writing board or overhead transparency.
- Before starting a new activity, be sure that the present one is satisfactorily completed by most children. End each activity conclusively before beginning a new one, and bridge the new activity with the previous one with a relevant and carefully prepared transition.
- Carefully and continuously monitor all children at all times in the classroom.
- If one or two children become inattentive and begin to misbehave, quietly (indirect intervention) redirect their attention without interrupting the rest of the students.

Additional specific guidelines for establishing and maintaining an effective learning environment are given in a later section, following a consideration of the legal rights of the teacher and students.

D. LEGAL GUIDELINES FOR THE CLASSROOM TEACHER

As a beginning teacher, you need to be knowledgeable about basic legal matters regarding the teaching and supervision of children. This knowledge can minimize the possibility of making errors that abuse the rights of children and result in litigation. For example, you should know that (by **Federal Law Title IX**) you are prohibited from discriminating among students on the basis of their gender. In all aspects of school, girls and boys must be treated the same. This means, for example, that a teacher must *not* pit boys against girls in a subject content quiz game, or for any other activity or reason.

Further, no teacher, student, administrator, or other school employee may make sexual advances toward a student (touching or speaking in a sexual manner). Students should be informed of their rights under Title IX and should be encouraged to report any suspected violations of their rights to the school principal. Since mid-1992, female students have exercised their rights under Title IX to be free from sexual harassment by their male peers. Each district or school should have a clearly delineated statement of steps to follow in the process of protecting students' rights.

Among teachers and teacher candidates, the topic of teacher and student rights generates many questions of concern. You are, or will be, interested in teacher tenure laws, retirement laws, and professional organizations. And you will be concerned about the collective bargaining framework, legal requirements concerning student discipline, teacher negligence, and teacher liability and insurance—topics that are covered in many readily available resources.

Most teacher candidates want to know about their legal status during the field experiences of their teacher preparation program. Such information should be available from your college or university office of field experience or student teacher placement.

The following section offers guidelines that will alert you to situations that can be faced by a classroom teacher. It is not intended as a definitive treatment of legal issues in education. In addition to federal laws, specific guidelines may be affected by state laws, local school board policies, and building regulations. Upon completion of this chapter, you may want to turn to the suggested readings at the end of the chapter and to documents available from schools in your area to learn more about specific school-related legal matters.

Legal Guidelines Regarding Teacher and Student Rights

First, consider the rights of the classroom teacher and the rights of students by completing Exercise 4.4.

Exercise 4.4: A Self-Check on Legal Guidelines Regarding Teachers' and Students' Rights

Instructions: The purpose of this exercise is to check your knowledge of the legal rights of teachers and students. Consider and respond to the questions that follow. When difficult to respond with a clear yes or no, you may add a note of explanation in the margin. Check your responses with the answer key, then discuss them with your classmates and instructor. During your discussion, you should become familiar with the education laws and other legal documents for your state. Perhaps your instructor can provide those documents. If not, they can be found in your university library or at a local school district office.

Teachers' Rights	*Yes*	*No*
1. Do I have the right to expect my classroom to be free from disruptions by students, parents, and others?	_____	_____
2. Do I have the right to expect students to come to class with the basic materials (books, pencil, paper) necessary to accomplish the educational activities?	_____	_____
3. Do I have the right to pertinent information about any child placed in my classroom?	_____	_____

4. For specified reasons, do I have the right to request that a particular student be transferred out of my classroom? _____ _____

5. As a teacher responsible for an extracurricular activity, do I have the right to exclude a particular student from that activity because of the student's misbehavior? _____ _____

6. Do I have the right to suspend a student from my class? _____ _____

7. Do I have the right to use reasonable physical restraint to protect myself or a student from bodily harm? _____ _____

8. Do I have the right to expect educational support from the school principal? _____ _____

9. Do I have the right to expect the same general rules for student behavior during after-school activities as during regular classes? _____ _____

10. Do I have the right to expect that students will obey my instructions during class activities? _____ _____

Students' Rights

11. Do students have the right to due process of law? _____ _____

12. Does due process of law include knowledge of the charges, a hearing, and the student's opportunity to defend? _____ _____

13. Do students have the right to understand the behavior that is expected of them while they are in my class? _____ _____

14. Do students have rights under the federal Family Rights and Privacy Act? _____ _____

15. Do students in my classes have the right to know what consequences will occur for noncompliance with classroom rules of expected behavior? _____ _____

16. Do students whom I supervise during extracurricular activities have the right to know what consequences will occur for misbehavior? _____ _____

17. Do students have the right to be treated courteously and respectfully while in my classes and under my direct supervision? _____ _____

18. Do students have the right to expect that their constitutional rights will not be violated while in my classes and under my direct supervision? _____ _____

19. Providing that they meet the qualifications of a sponsoring organization, do students have the right to participate in extracurricular activities? _____ _____

20. Does a student who is innocent of any wrongdoing have the right to be free of punishment for acts done by others? _____ _____

Answer Key to Exercise 4.4: Although education law varies from state to state, we predict that for your state, all answers to the preceding questions will be yes. It is important that you understand the general principle involved for each item. For that understanding, you and your colleagues should have a thorough discussion about any of the 20 items about which there may be confusion or ambiguity about the intent.

Legal Basics and Guidelines for the Classroom Teacher

It is important to reiterate that this section does not offer a comprehensive treatment of legal matters of importance to the classroom teacher. Indeed, entire books could (and may) be devoted to any item in this section. The intention is to provide the basic understanding necessary to teach students fairly, with minimum disruption and fear of litigation.

Teacher Liability and Insurance

Credentialed teachers and student teachers, of public schools, are usually protected by their districts against personal injury litigation (i.e., a negligence suit filed as the result of a student being injured at school or at a school-sponsored activity). *Student teachers* and *credentialed teachers* should investigate carefully the extent of their tort liability coverage in districts where they work. You may decide that the coverage provided by the district is insufficient. Additional liability coverage can be obtained through private insurance agents and through national teachers' organizations. Talk with or write to teachers' association representatives about teacher liability protection that may be available through professional organizations (e.g., National Education Association, American Federation of Teachers, National Reading Association, National Science Teachers Association), and with insurance agents, before deciding what is best for your particular situation.

Teachers sometimes find themselves in situations where they are tempted to transport children in their own private automobiles, such as for field trips (see Chapter 12, Section E). Before transporting schoolchildren in your automobile or in private automobiles driven by volunteer parents or guardians, you and the volunteers should inquire from your insurance agents whether you have adequate automobile insurance liability coverage to do so.

It is inevitable that teachers will take personal items to school—purses, audio or video recorders, videotapes and discs, for example. It is unlikely that the school's insurance policy covers your personal items if stolen or damaged. A homeowner's or apartment renter's policy might. The recommendation is *not* to take a purse to school, and be sure that all personal items of value are covered by your homeowner's or apartment renter's insurance policy when taken to your classroom.

Child Abuse

Since child abuse has become a grave matter of pressing national concern, teachers in *all* states now are legally *mandated* to report *any suspicion* of child abuse (e.g., physical abuse, emotional maltreatment, physical neglect, sexual abuse, malnutrition, improper clothing, and inadequate dental care). Proof of abuse is not necessary. If you suspect child abuse but do not report it, you may be in violation of your state law. If you do report your suspicion, you are probably immune from a libel suit. Check your own state or local school district for details about (1) what is designated as child abuse, (2) to whom to report your suspicion, (3) how to report and (4) what immunity or protection is provided to a teacher who does report suspected child abuse.[9,10]

Administering First Aid and Medication

Accidents do occur to children at school. While doing a science experiment, a student is cut by glass. Another is injured by a falling windowpane when the teacher is trying to open a window that is stuck. Another has an eye injury resulting from falling and landing on a sprinkler head during physical education. Each of these incidents has occurred. What should *you* do when a student is injured?

You should give first aid only when necessary to save a child's limb or life. When life or limb is not at risk, then you should follow school policy in referring the student to immediate professional care. When immediate care is unavailable, and you believe that immediate first aid is necessary, then you can take prudent action, as if you were that child's parent or legal guardian. However, you must be cautious and knowledgeable about what you are doing so that you do not cause further harm.

Unless you are a licensed medical professional, you should *never* give medication to students, whether prescription or over-the-counter. A student who needs to take medication should bring from home a written parental statement of permission and instructions. Under your supervision, or that of the school nurse (if there is one), the student can then take his or her own medicine.

Teacher Contract and Tenure

What will it mean when you sign your first teaching contract? Consider the following:

1. The teaching contract is a legal agreement between you and the governing board of the district.
2. The contract guarantees you employment, a teaching assignment, a salary, and an expected length of service, except when there is a decline in enrollment and no longer a need for your service.
3. Your length of service is identified in the contract, that is, service for one year, or for continuing service to the district.
4. You are legally required to perform your assigned duties as specified in your teaching contract.

[9]For an informative article for teachers about child abuse, see Thelma Bear et al., "Supporting Victims of Child Abuse," *Educational Leadership* 50(4):42–47 (December 1992–January 1993).
[10]To report a suspicion of child abuse, you can telephone toll free 1-800-4-A-CHILD.

5. Before a tenure contract is offered, there is a probationary period of continued employment within the district (this period varies from state to state, but usually is one to three years).

6. "Tenure is a creation of state statute designed to maintain adequate, permanent and qualified teaching staffs free from political and personal arbitrary interference. Tenure laws cannot be circumvented by local school board regulations or policies. Although there is no constitutional right to tenure, once tenure is granted a constitutional 'property' right arises and due process is required before dismissal."[11] Tenure is not a safeguard against reduction-in-force policies or a protection against job loss. Tenure is not a guarantee that your job will continue regardless of events or financial situations that arise in the district.

7. No reasons need to be given for noncontract renewal of a probationary (nontenured) teacher.

Now do Exercise 4.5, an analysis of what you know, and what you need to know, about legal guidelines in your state.

[11]*Deskbook Encyclopedia of American School Law* (Rosemount, MN: Data Research, Inc., 1987), p. 390.

Exercise 4.5: A Self-Check on What I Know About Legal Guidelines in My State

Instructions: The purpose of this exercise is to analyze what you know, and what you should know, about your state's legal guidelines for teachers. Respond to each of the following questions with a yes or a no. Then research the correct answers according to the education code of your state. Compare those answers with the answer key that follows this exercise.

	Yes	*No*
1. As a credentialed female teacher, can I expect less salary than a credentialed male teacher when we perform similar teaching services, have similar years of experience, and similar college degrees and credits?	_____	_____
2. Has teacher tenure been abolished in my state?	_____	_____
3. Will my substitute teaching and summer school teaching be included in the computation toward my permanent teaching status?	_____	_____
4. Can I be assigned supervision duties outside my regular teaching assignment?	_____	_____
5. Once tenured, can I be dismissed for not following the prescribed course of study?	_____	_____
6. Must I maintain records of student attendance?	_____	_____
7. May I discipline a student who refuses to stand and salute the flag of the United States of America?	_____	_____

8. May I require that my students purchase a weekly news supplement if I provide free copies to those who cannot afford it?   _____   _____

9. Can I receive royalties for a state-adopted textbook of which I am co-author?   _____   _____

10. May I administer a survey, a questionnaire, or a test asking about a student's sexual beliefs, practices, or preferences without parental (or legal guardian's) written permission?   _____   _____

11. May I search a student or a student's locker at random?   _____   _____

12. Can I be considered negligent if I am present in the classroom when a physical injury occurs to one of my students?   _____   _____

13. Is a student guilty of a felony if the student places glue in the lock of a classroom door?   _____   _____

14. Can I suspend a student from my class?   _____   _____

15. Can I arrest a student?   _____   _____

16. Can I arrest a student for taunting and challenging another student to fight?   _____   _____

17. If I am attacked, assaulted, or menaced by a student, is someone in the administration obligated to report the incident to local law enforcement authorities?   _____   _____

18. If a student resists my arrest with force, can the local authorities charge the student with assault and battery?   _____   _____

19. Can one student arrest another?   _____   _____

20. Do I have a professional obligation to break up a seemingly friendly altercation?   _____   _____

21. Do I have the professional and legal obligation to administer consequences for misbehavior?   _____   _____

22. Can I suspend a student from school for a week or longer?   _____   _____

23. While in the faculty lounge and arguing over school policy, can I call the school principal or another teacher an abusive name?   _____   _____

24. Am I obligated to give students the right to be heard so long as that process does not substantially disrupt the orderly operation of the school?   _____   _____

25. Must I tolerate student statements or actions that degrade others?   _____   _____

26. Can a student be expelled for selling or furnishing narcotics or other controlled substances? _____ _____

27. Can a student be expelled for causing or attempting to cause physical injury to me or to other school personnel? _____ _____

28. Can a student be expelled for the use of weapons or instruments or substances for or capable of doing bodily harm to me? _____ _____

29. Must I report a suspected instance of child abuse? _____ _____

30. Must a student be given a *Miranda* warning before being questioned by school authorities? _____ _____

31. Can I administer corporal punishment[12] to a student for that student's misbehavior? _____ _____

32. Can public school officials unilaterally expel students with exceptional needs when they are violent or disruptive? _____ _____

33. Do public school officials have the right to censor student newspapers? _____ _____

34. Should I administer first aid by putting burn ointment on a student who has burned a hand while in my classroom? _____ _____

35. If physically abused by a student, should I file legal charges against the student? _____ _____

36. Should a serious threat by a student to a teacher be reported? _____ _____

37. Should I give aspirin to a student who is complaining of a headache? _____ _____

38. Should I give cough drops to a student who is coughing? _____ _____

39. While on a field trip off campus, should I allow a student to go to a public rest room unescorted? _____ _____

40. Title IX prohibits discrimination against females. Does it also prohibit discrimination against males? _____ _____

Answer Key to Exercise 4.5: Many of the items in this key are based on the Education Code, the Health and Safety Code, and the Penal Code, of California. Others are based on common sense, and still others on legal decisions that have affected public schools. You are urged to become familiar with the laws of your own state and local district.

---

[12]Corporal punishment, forbidden in many school districts, as it should be in all schools, "can be interpreted as other actions besides spanking, slapping, or paddling. Putting a student in a dark closet, making a student do an excessive number of push-ups in a gym class for forgetting his gym clothes, or making a student stand on his tip-toes with his nose in a circle drawn on a blackboard could cause physical or emotional harm to a student and may be interpreted as forms of corporal punishment." From Robert L. Monks and Ernest I. Proulx, *Legal Basics for Teachers*, Fastback 235 (Bloomington, IN: Phi Delta Kappan Foundation, 1986), p. 28.

1. No   Title VII of the Civil Rights Act of 1964; California Fair Employment Act Government Code sections 12900 *et seq.*

2. No

3. No   California Education Code sections 44913 and 44914.

4. Yes   California Education Code section 44807.

5. Yes   California Education Code section 44805.

6. Yes   California Education Code section 46000.

7. No   *West Virginia State Board of Education v. Barnette* 319 U.S. 624.

8. No   California Education Code section 60070.

9. Yes   California Education Code section 60076.

10. No   California Education Code section 60650.

11. No   This would probably violate the student's Fourth Amendment right against unreasonable search and seizure. You should leave this to school security and administrators. *In re Donaldson* 269 Cal. App. 2d 509.

12. Yes   *Biggers v. Sacramento City Unified School Dist.* 25 Cal. App. 3d 269.

13. No

14. Yes   California Education Code sections 48900 and 48910.

15. Yes   California Penal Code section 837.

16. Yes   California Penal Code section 415.

17. Yes   California Education Code section 44014.

18. Yes   *People v. Garcia* 274 Cal. App. 2d 100.

19. Yes   California Penal Code section 837.

20. Yes   *Daily v. Los Angeles Unified School District* 2 Cal. 3d 741.

21. Yes   California Education Code section 44807.

22. No   California Education Code section 48910. A teacher may suspend a student from class for that day and the day following and must immediately report the suspension to the principal.

23. No   You should be careful. *Connick v. Myers* 461 U.S. 138 (1983) held that a public employee's critical or antagonistic speech is protected only if it addresses public concerns that outweigh the public employer's interest in workplace efficiency and discipline.

24. Yes   California Education Code section 48907.

25. No   California Education Code section 32051.

26. Yes   California Education Code section 48900 and California Health and Safety Code sections 11351 through 11368.

27. Yes   California Education Code section 48900.

28. Yes   California Education Code section 48909.

29. Yes   California Penal Code sections 1165.7, 11166, and 11172.

30. No   *In re Christopher W.* 29 Cal. App. 3d 777.

31. Not in California.   California Education Code section 49001.

32. No   Federal law requires that the states provide special procedural safeguards relating to the expulsion of students with exceptional needs. See, for example, California Education Code section 48915.5.

33. Yes   In 1988, the United States Supreme Court in *Hazelwood School Dist. v. Kuhlmeier* 484 U.S. 260, gave broad powers to school officials to edit the style and content of student newspapers as long as their actions are related to legitimate pedagogical concerns. However, a teacher should know his or her state's laws governing this subject. For example, California Education Code section 48907 forbids educators from censoring student speech unless the material is obscene, libelous, slanderous; or incites others to create a clear and present danger, or to commit unlawful acts

on school premises, or to violate lawful school regulation, or to substantially disrupt the orderly operation of the school.

34. No
35. Yes
36. Yes
37. No   The student might be allergic to aspirin.
38. No
39. No
40. Yes   Title IX of Federal Law.

So far, in this chapter, you have learned about coping with the daily challenges of teaching, about your legal rights and responsibilities, and about those of your students. We turn now to the ever-important topic of classroom control, offering additional guidelines for maintaining a positive classroom environment.

E. THE MEANING OF "CLASSROOM CONTROL"

Classroom control has always been a topic of concern to teachers and especially to beginning teachers. There is good cause for their concern. In one respect, being a classroom teacher is much like being a driver of a truck who must remain alert while going down a steep and winding grade, knowing that otherwise the truck most assuredly will get out of control, veer off the highway, and crash. You will be happy to know that to help you with your concerns about control, and to help you avoid a crash, there are, in addition to this chapter, volumes of literature with sound advice. Some are listed in the suggested readings at the end of this chapter.

To set the stage for your understanding, we begin by contrasting what the term *classroom control* has meant historically with what it means today.

In the 1800s, instead of classroom control, educators spoke of "classroom discipline," and that meant "punishment." That interpretation was consistent with the then-popular learning theory that assumed children were innately bad and that inappropriate behavior could be prevented by strictness or treated with punishment.[13] In the middle of that century schools were described as being "wild and unruly places," and "full of idleness and disorder."[14]

By the early 1900s, educators were asking, "Why are the children still misbehaving?" The accepted answer was that the children were misbehaving *because* of the rigid punitive system.[15] At this point, the era of progressive education began, which provided students more freedom to decide for themselves what they would learn. The teacher's job then became one of providing a classroom rich in resources and materials to stimulate the students' natural curiosity. And since the system no longer would be *causing* misbehavior, punishment would no longer be necessary. However, classes that were highly permissive turned out to cause more anxiety than the restrictive classes of the 1800s.

[13]Robert R. Reilly and Ernest L. Lewis, *Educational Psychology* (New York: Macmillan, 1983), p. 557.
[14]Irwin A. Hyman and John D'Allessandro, "Oversimplifying the Discipline Problem," *Education Week* 3(29):24 (April 1984).
[15]Reilly and Lewis, p. 558.

Today, rather than classroom "discipline," educators talk of classroom "control," referring to *the process of controlling student behavior in the classroom.* Classroom control is an important aspect of the broader area of classroom "management." Classroom control involves (1) steps in *preventing inappropriate student behaviors* and (2) procedures for *dealing with inappropriate student behaviors.* Up to now, this chapter has dealt primarily with the prevention of inappropriate behaviors. In the remaining pages it focuses more on procedures for handling inappropriate student behaviors.

Although eclectic in their approaches to classroom control, today's teachers share a concern for selecting techniques that (1) enhance student self-esteem and (2) help children learn how to assume control and ownership of their own learning. A teacher's classroom control procedures reflect the teacher's philosophy about how children learn and the teacher's interpretation and commitment to the school's stated mission. In sum, those behaviors represent the teacher's concept of effective management.

F. TODAY'S EFFECTIVE CLASSROOM MANAGEMENT SYSTEMS

The intent of this chapter is to provide background information that will guide you toward the development of your own successful classroom management system, one that is consistent with your beliefs, with the needs of elementary school children, and with the philosophy of your school. Although some elementary schools subscribe heavily to one approach, such as Canter's Assertive Discipline system, many other effective classroom management systems are more eclectic, having evolved from the historical works of several leading authorities. The contributions of these authorities follow.

Lee Canter and **Marlene Canter** emphasize that (1) as a teacher, you have professional rights in your classroom and should expect appropriate student behavior; (2) your students have rights to choose how to behave in your classroom, and you should plan limits for inappropriate student behavior; (3) your assertive discipline approach means you clearly state your expectations in a firm voice and explain the boundaries for behavior; and (4) you establish consequences for student misbehavior and follow through in a consistent manner.[16] These four points are included in the guidelines presented earlier in this chapter.

Rudolf Dreikurs emphasized six points to consider in determining your effectiveness as a teacher. You are effective if you (1) are a democratic teacher, fair, firm, and friendly, and involve your students in developing and implementing class rules; (2) arrange your classroom so the children know and understand the rules and consequences for misbehavior; (3) allow the students to be responsible not only for their own actions but for influencing others to maintain appropriate behavior in your classroom; (4) encourage children to show respect for themselves and for others, and you provide each child with a sense of belonging to the class; (5) recognize and encourage student goals of belonging, gaining status, and recognition; and (6) recognize but do not reinforce correlated student goals of getting attention, seeking power, and taking revenge.[17]

---

[16]For an informative critique of Canter's Assertive Discipline system, see David Hill, "Order in the Classroom," *Teacher Magazine* 1(7):70–77 (April 1990).
[17]See Rudolf Dreikurs, *Discipline Without Tears* (New York: Harper & Row, 1972).

William Glasser developed his concept of "reality therapy" (i.e., the condition of the present contributes to inappropriate behavior) for the classroom. Glasser emphasizes that (1) students have a responsibility to learn at school and to maintain appropriate behavior while there; (2) with the teacher's help, the children can make appropriate choices about their behavior in school; and (3) classroom meetings can be devoted to establishing class rules, student behavior, matters of misbehavior, and the consequences.[18]

Haim G. Ginott emphasizes ways for you and a student to communicate: (1) by sending a clear message (or messages) regarding a *situation* instead of the student's character; and (2) by modeling the behavior you expect from your students.[19] These two guidelines have been stressed in this and the preceding chapter. Ginott's suggested messages are those that express feelings appropriately, acknowledge student's feelings, give appropriate direction, and invite cooperation.

Jacob S. Kounin is well known for his identification of the "ripple effect" (i.e., the effect of your response to one student's misbehavior on students whose behavior was appropriate), and of "withitness" (i.e., the teacher's ability to remain alert in the class, to spot quickly and prevent, by redirecting, potential student misbehavior—analogous to having "eyes in the back of your head").[20] In addition to being alert to everything that is going on in the classroom, there is another characteristic of a teacher's withitness, and that is the teacher's ability to attend to the right student.

To develop your skills of withitness, you should do the following:

- Maintain constant surveillance of the entire class. Look around the room frequently. Move around the room. Be on top of potential misbehavior and redirect student attention before the misbehavior occurs or gets out of control.
- Keep students alert by calling on them randomly, asking questions and then calling on an answerer, circulating from group to group during team learning activities, and frequently checking on the progress being made by individual students.
- Keep all students in the act. Avoid becoming too involved with any one student or group. Avoid concentrating your attention on only those students who appear most interested or responsive.
- Quietly redirect the behavior of a child who is beginning to go off-task and to misbehave.
- If two or more errant behaviors are occurring simultaneously but in different locations in the classroom, attend to the most serious first while giving the other a nonverbal gesture showing your awareness and displeasure.
- Above all, maintain a high level of student interest by adding variety and sparkle to your teaching.

Kounin challenges you to (1) realize the influence of the ripple effect on students; (2) exhibit "withitness" by remaining alert to all students in your classroom always; (3) keep the teaching-learning momentum going during classroom activities (i.e., avoid "dead spots"); (4) plan smooth transitions from one activity to the next, and (5) hold each child responsible for learning the lesson.

A prerequisite to being withit is having the skill to attend to more than one matter at a time. This skill is referred to as "overlapping" ability. The teacher with overlap-

---

[18]A useful reference is William Glasser's *Control Therapy in the Classroom* (New York: Harper & Row, 1986).
[19]See Haim G. Ginott, *Teacher and Child* (New York: Macmillan, 1971).
[20]See Jacob S. Kounin, *Discipline and Group Management in Classrooms* (New York: Holt, Rinehart and Winston, 1970).

ping skill uses body language, body position, and hand signals to communicate with students. Consider the following examples of overlapping:

- Rather than being seated at the teacher's desk and allowing students to come to the desk with their papers and problems, the teacher expects students to remain seated and to raise their hands, while the teacher moves around the room monitoring and attending to individual students.
- While attending to a messenger who has walked into the room with a note from the office, and while reading the message, the teacher demonstrates verbally or by gestures to the class that he expects the students to continue their work.
- While the teacher is working with a small group of students, a student in another part of the room has raised his hand, wanting the teacher's attention. Continuing to work with the group of students, the teacher signals with her hand to the student, an acknowledgment that she is aware that he wants her attention and will get to him quickly—and she does.
- Without missing a beat in her talk, by gesture, eye contact, and moving closer to the student, the teacher aborts the behavior of a potentially disruptive student.

In addition to the preceding approaches to classroom management presented by the Canters, Dreikurs, Glasser, Ginott, and Kounin there is another of importance to today's teacher. You are probably familiar with the term "behavior modification"— several popular techniques effective in changing the behavior of others in an observable and predictable way—and with B. F. Skinner's ideas about how students learn, how behavior can be modified by reinforcements (rewards), and how his principles of behavior shaping have been extended by others.[21]

Behavior modification begins with four steps: (1) identifying the problem behavior that you wish to modify; (2) recording how often and under what conditions that particular behavior occurs; (3) arranging for a change to occur by reinforcing a behavior you want repeated, by following the behavior with a rewarding consequence (a positive reinforcer); and (4) considering the different types of positive reinforcers to award—auditory (music), edibles (food and drink), manipulatives (games), social (attention, praise), tactile (artwork time), and visual (pictures).

As you review these classic contributions to today's approaches to effective classroom management, you read of expert opinion as well as research evidence that reminds you of the importance of your doing the following:

- Concentrate your attention on desirable student behaviors.
- Involve children by providing challenges, class meetings, ways of establishing rules and consequences, opportunities to receive and return compliments and to build self-esteem.
- Keep all students on task.
- Maintain alertness to all that is happening in your classroom.
- Prevent "dead" time.
- Provide smooth transitions.
- Quickly attend to any student beginning to demonstrate inappropriate behavior.

Figure 4.2 illustrates the main ideas of each authority and allows you to compare the recommended approaches.

[21]See B. F. Skinner, *The Technology of Teaching* (New York: Appleton-Century-Crofts, 1968).

Authority	To Know What Is Going On	To Provide Smooth Transitions	To Maintain Group Alertness	To Involve Students	To Attend to Misbehavior
Canter and Canter	Realize that the student has the right to choose how to behave in your class, with the understanding of the consequences that will follow his or her choice.	Insist on decent, responsible behavior.	Set clear limits and consequences; follow through consistently; state what you expect; state the consequences, and why the limits are needed.	Use firm tone of voice; keep eye contact; use nonverbal gestures as well as verbal statements; use hints, questions, and direct messages about requesting student behavior; give and receive compliments.	Follow through with your promises and the reasonable, previously stated consequences that have been established in your class.
Dreikurs	Realize that the student wants status, recognition, and a feeling of belonging. Misbehavior is associated with mistaken goals of getting attention, seeking power, getting revenge, and wanting to be let alone.	Identify a mistaken student goal; act in ways that do not reinforce these goals.	Provide firm guidance and leadership.	Allow students to have a say in establishing rules and consequences in your class.	Make it clear that unpleasant consequences will follow inappropriate behavior.
Ginott	Communicate with the student's feelings about a situation and about him- or herself.	Invite student cooperation.	Model the behavior you expect to see in your students.	Build student's self-esteem.	Give a message that addresses the situation and does not attack the student's character.
Glasser	Realize that the student is a rational being; that the student can control his or her behavior.	Help the student make good choices; good choices produce good behavior, and bad choices produce bad behavior.	Understand that class rules are essential.	Realize that classroom meetings are effective means for attending to rules, behavior, and discipline.	Accept no excuses for inappropriate behavior; see that reasonable consequences always follow.
Kounin	Develop "withitness," a skill enabling you to see what is hap-	Avoid jerkiness which consists of thrusts (giving directions before your group is	Avoid slowdowns (delays and time wasting) that can be caused by overdwelling (too	Avoid boredom by providing a feeling of progress for the students, by offering challenges,	Understand that teacher correction influences the behavior of other nearby stu-

(continued)

Figure 4.2 Comparing approaches to classroom management.

	pening in all parts of the classroom at all times.	ready); of dangles (leaving one activity dangling in the verbal air, starting another one, and then returning to the first activity); of flip-flops (terminating one activity, beginning another one, and then returning to the first activity).	much time spent on explanations) and by fragmentation (breaking down an activity into several unneccessary steps). Develop a group focus through format (active participation by all students in the group); through accountability (holding all students accountable for the concept of the lesson), and by attention (seeing all the students and using unison responses as well as individual responses).	varying class activities, changing the level of intellectual challenge, varying lesson presentations, and using many different learning materials and aids.	dents (the ripple effect).
Skinner	Realize value of nonverbal interaction, i.e., smiles, pats, and handshakes to communicate to students that you know what is going on.	Realize that smooth transitions may be part of your procedures for awarding reinforcers, i.e., points and tokens, to reward appropriate behavior.	Set rules, rewards, and consequences; emphasize that responsibility for good behavior rests with each student.	Involve students in "token economies," in contracts, and in graphing their own behavior and performance.	Provide tangibles to students who follow the class rules; represent tangibles as "points" for the whole class to use to "purchase" a special activity.

Figure 4.2   (*continued*)

Using the criteria of your own philosophy, your feelings, your values, your knowledge gained from the research studies of others, and your perceptions, you are encouraged to devise a classroom environment and management system that is positive and effective for both you and your students. Remember: you must have their attention before you can teach them.

You must also be aware of your own moods, your personal high-stress or low-energy days, and anticipate that your own tolerance levels on those days may be lower than normal for you. Students, too, are susceptible to being stressed by personal problems. As you get to know your students well, you will be able to tell when certain children are experiencing stress and anxiety. For many children, for example, one source of stress is the breakup of the family—a divorce. Teachers interested in learning more about how to help these children cope may be interested in resources designed to do just that, such as those listed in Figure 4.3.

> *Banana Splits: A School-Based Program for the Survivors of the Divorce Wars*, Interact Publishers, Box 997, Lakeside, CA 92040 (800) 359-0961.
>
> *Rainbows for All God's Children, Inc.*, 1111 Tower Road, Schaumburg, IL 60173 (708) 310-1880.
>
> Stepfamily Association of America, Inc., 215 Centennial Mall South, Suite 212, Lincoln, NE 68508 (402) 477-STEP.
>
> The Pittsburgh Centre for Stepfamilies, Dr. Judith L. Bauersfeld, 4815 Liberty Avenue, Suite 422, Pittsburgh, PA 15224 (412) 362-7837.

Figure 4.3   Resources to help children cope.

Types of Student Misbehavior

Sometimes elementary school teachers are confronted with major problems of misbehavior that have ramifications beyond the classroom or that begin elsewhere and spill over into the classroom. If this happens, you may need to ask for help and should not hesitate to do so.

Charles describes the following types of student misbehavior that teachers may have to contend with, listed here in order of decreasing seriousness:[22]

- **Aggression.** Occasionally, aggressive students, and campus intruders, physically or verbally attack teachers or other students. As you learned earlier, this can be a punishable offense by law, and you are best advised to find out what your own state and local laws are about physical and verbal attacks on teachers and students. A teacher should never have to contend with this type of serious misbehavior. Whenever you are in doubt about what action to take, you should discuss your concern about a student's aggressive behavior with a school counselor or administrator. In some instances you may need to send for help immediately. Never hesitate when you feel that immediate help is needed. Many teachers are fearful about the increase in violence by young people, partly attributed to drug trafficking and easy access to violent weapons.[23] As a teacher, you must stay alert.
- **Immorality.** This type of misbehavior includes cheating, lying, and stealing. A child who habitually exhibits any of these behaviors may need to be referred to a specialist. Whenever you have good reason to suspect immoral behavior of a student, you should discuss your concerns with the school counselor or principal.
- **Defiance of authority.** When a child refuses, perhaps hostilely, to do what you tell the student to do, this defiance is worthy of temporary or permanent removal from the classroom—at least until there has been a conference about the situation, a conference that involves perhaps the student, the teacher, the student's parent or guardian, and a school official.
- **Class disruptions.** This type of misbehavior includes talking loudly or out of turn, walking about the room without permission, clowning, and tossing objects, all of which every child who has reached the intermediate grades knows are unacceptable behaviors in the classroom. In dealing with these kinds of misbehaviors, it is impor-

---

[22]C. M. Charles, *Building Classroom Discipline: From Models to Practice*, 3rd ed. (New York: Longman, 1989), p. 2.
[23]For an informative account of aggression on school campuses, see Denise Foley, "Danger: School Zone," *Teacher Magazine* 1(8):57–63 (May 1990).

tant that you have communicated to the children the consequences of such inappropriate behaviors. Then, following your stated rules for misbehavior, deal promptly and consistently with the misbehavior. You must *not* ignore minor infractions of this type, for if you do they will escalate beyond your worst expectations.

- **Goofing off.** This least serious type includes those misbehaviors that are most common to the classroom: fooling around, not doing assigned tasks, daydreaming, and just generally being off-task. Fortunately, in most instances, this type of misbehavior is momentary and might sometimes be best ignored by you for a moment or so. If it persists, all it may take to get the child back on task is a quiet redirection from you (indirect intervention). It is important that you not make "mountains out of molehills," otherwise you could cause more problems than you would resolve.

Examples of trivial "misbehaviors" that you need not worry about, unless they become too disruptive, are occasional calling out during discussions, brief whispering among students during a lesson, or brief periods of inattentiveness, perhaps accompanied by visual wandering or daydreaming. For you to react to these kinds of student behavior would "consume too much of your energy, interrupt your lessons constantly, and detract from your classroom's climate."[24]

Teacher-Caused Student Misbehavior

As implied in the preceding section, some student misbehaviors and problems in classroom control are teacher- or school-caused. One of your major responsibilities is to model appropriate behavior, and not to be a cause or contributor to student misbehavior and problems in the classroom.

In addition to the necessity of sometimes ignoring minor infractions of your classroom behavior rules and procedures, you should also *avoid* the use of negative methods of rule enforcement and ineffective forms of punishment, such as exemplified by the following situations.

- **Nagging.** A fourth-grade teacher's continual and unnecessary scolding and criticizing upsets the recipient students and arouses resentment from student peers. Nagging by the teacher resolves nothing, and creates for him even more problems in the classroom.
- **Assigning extra schoolwork.** When students in a third-grade reading class misbehave, the teacher habitually assigns extra reading and written work as punishment, even for the most minor offenses. This behavior has simply reinforced the view of many of her students that school is drudgery, so they no longer look forward to her classes, and behavior problems for the teacher have steadily increased since the beginning of the school year.
- **Punishing the group.** Because a sixth-grade teacher has not developed his withitness and overlapping skills, he has developed the unfortunate habit of punishing the entire class for every instance of misbehavior. Yesterday, for example, some students were noisy during the showing of a film, and he gave the entire class an unannounced quiz on the content of that film. He has lost the respect of the students,

[24]Edmund T. Emmer et al., *Classroom Management for Secondary Teachers,* 2nd ed. (Englewood Cliffs, NJ: Prentice-Hall, 1989), p. 105.

the students are hostile toward him, and his problems with classroom control are getting worse.

- **Lowering academic marks.** A second-grade teacher has a policy of writing the student's name on the board each time a student is reprimanded for misbehavior. When a student has accumulated five marks on the board, she lowers that student's academic grade by one letter. As a result of her not separating their academic and social behaviors, students in her class are now achieving less well than at the start of the year. Parents and students have complained about this policy to the administration, arguing that the academic grades students are getting from the teacher are contradictory to their academic progress or abilities.

- **Physical punishment.** A sixth-grade social studies teacher punishes students by making them go outside and do push-ups or run around the school grounds when they misbehave in his class. Last week, one of the students whom he told to go out and run four laps, for "mouthing off in class," collapsed and died while running. The teacher has been placed on paid leave and is being sued for negligence by the parents of the child who died.

- **Writing as punishment.** Because "the students were too noisy," a fifth-grade health teacher punished his class of 28 students by making them hand-copy ten pages from encyclopedias. When the students had finished this writing and turned their pages in to the teacher, he tore them up in front of the class and said, "Now, I hope you have learned your lesson and will, from now on, be quiet." Upon hearing about this, all six of the school's language arts teachers filed a complaint with the principal about this teacher's use of writing as punishment.

- **Threats and ultimatums.** Threats and ultimatums from a third-grade teacher are like empty promises—once made, the teacher is stuck when the students call for the payoff. But because of not following through, this teacher's credibility with the students has been lost forever. The word has spread through the school like wildfire— "kids get away with murder in this teacher's class."

- **Premature judgments and actions.** Because of a teacher's impulsiveness, not thinking clearly before acting, more than once she has reprimanded the wrong student. Because of her hasty and faulty judgments, students have lost respect for her as a teacher; for many of them, coming to her classroom has become pure drudgery.

- **Inconsistency.** Because of her arbitrary and inconsistent enforcement of classroom rules, a fifth-grade teacher has lost the respect and trust of her students, as well as control of her classes. Students are constantly testing her to see what they can get away with.

- **Loud talk.** The noisiest person in this sixth-grade teacher's language arts classes is the teacher himself. His constant and mistaken efforts to talk over the classes have led to his yelling and screaming, to complaints from neighbor teachers about how noisy his classes are, and to a reprimand from the principal.

- **Harsh and humiliating punishment.** A middle school physical education teacher has lost control of his classes and the respect of his students. His thrashing, whipping, tongue-lashings and use of humiliation are ineffective and indicative of his loss of control. Parents have complained, and one has sued this teacher; the district has given the teacher official notice of the termination of his contract.

Your attention is now directed to other specific instances of teacher behaviors, some of which reinforce or cause student misbehavior. Do Exercises 4.6 through 4.10.

Exercise 4.6: A Self-Check on Identifying Teacher Behaviors That Cause Student Misbehavior

Instructions: The purpose of this exercise is to practice your awareness of the kinds of teacher behaviors to avoid, namely those that tend to reinforce or cause student misbehavior. Place a check next to each of the following paragraphs that you believe describe such teacher behaviors. Then describe what the teacher should do instead. Share your responses with your classmates. An answer key follows.

_____ 1. Ms. Chung is nearly always late in arriving at her sixth-grade language arts class that meets immediately after lunch, seldom beginning class until at least five minutes past the time it is supposed to start.

_____

_____

_____

_____

_____

_____

_____

_____ 2. Mr. Jones ignores brief whispering between two students during a quiet activity in his third-grade classroom.

_____

_____

_____

_____

_____

_____

_____

_____ 3. While lecturing to her students during a science lesson, Ms. Whyte ignores brief talking between two students.

_____

_____

_____

_____

_____

_____

——— 4. During a class discussion in Mr. Stephen's social studies lesson, one student appears to be daydreaming and just staring out the window.

_____

_____

_____

_____

_____

_____

——— 5. During quiet study time in his sixth-grade reading class, Mr. Daniels asks for everyone's attention. He then verbally reprimands two students for horsing around, and writes out a referral for each of the two students.

_____

_____

_____

_____

_____

_____

_____

——— 6. Ms. Gomez advises her students to pay attention during the viewing of the film; if they do not, she will give them a quiz on the film's content.

_____

_____

_____

_____

_____

_____

——— 7. Ms. Lee tells a sixth-grade student that because of his behavior in class today he must come in after school and be detained with her for ten minutes, the same amount of time that he disturbed the class.

_____

_____

_____

_____

_____

_____

_____

_____

_____

8. Mr. Stefani sees a student cheating on a science test, so walks over to the student, picks up the student's test paper, and tears it up in front of the student and the rest of the class.

_____

_____

_____

_____

_____

_____

_____

_____

9. While Ms. Wong is talking to her second-grade class, the building principal walks into the room. Ms. Wong stops her talking and walks over to greet the principal and to find out what the principal wants.

_____

_____

_____

_____

_____

_____

_____

10. While a student learning team is giving its oral report to the third-grade class, Mr. Durken, the teacher, begins a conversation with several students in the back of the room.

_____

_____

_____

_____

_____

_____

_____

_____

_____

Answer Key to Exercise 4.6: For reasons explained below, you should have checked situations 1, 3, 5, 6, 7, 8, 9 and 10 as teacher behaviors that reinforce or cause student misbehavior. In some instances, because situations can vary, there may be some disagreement, but you should talk about these with your classmates and arrive at common understandings.

1. Ms. Chung's behavior is poor modeling for her students. She must model her expectations, as well as the school's expectations of students—in this instance, arriving and starting on time.

2. Minor infractions such as this are often best ignored if, as in this instance, the whispering is brief and not disturbing.

3. This behavior should not be ignored. Students are expected to give their attention to the teacher or whomever has the floor at the moment—that is common courtesy. By not attending to these students (perhaps by eye contact, proximity, mentioning a student's name, or some other form of indirect intervention) Ms. Whyte is saying that it is okay for students to be discourteous and to talk during the teacher's lecture. In this instance, Ms. Whyte is not following through with classroom behavioral expectations. Her lack of follow-through will cause further and increasingly disturbing management problems.

4. Minor infractions are sometimes best ignored. Perhaps the student is really thinking about ideas presented in the discussion.

5. By his disruption of the class learning activity, Mr. Daniels is reinforcing the very behavior he considers inappropriate from his students. This lack of consistency will cause continued problems in management for Mr. Daniels.

6. Threats are unacceptable behaviors, from students or from teachers. Moreover, tests should never be administered as punishment. Ms. Gomez could recommend that students take notes (mental or written) during the film, as these notes will serve as a focus for discussion after the film's showing, and there *will* be a follow-up quiz later.

7. By giving the student even more individual attention after school, Ms. Lee is reinforcing and rewarding the student's misbehavior that caused the problem in the first place. Besides, this may not be safe for Ms. Lee to do. Detention, supervised by someone other than this teacher, is usually a better alternative.

8. Mr. Stefani, who has taken no time to diagnose and to prescribe, is reacting too hastily and with hostility. This sort of teacher behavior reinforces the notion that the student is guilty until proven innocent and that process is of greater importance than the individual student. In addition, Mr. Stefani has violated this student's right to due process.

9. The error here is that by stopping her lesson, Ms. Wong and the principal are reinforcing the notion that classroom disruptions are acceptable—that the act of teaching is of less importance than other school business.

10. This is disrespectful and poor modeling. Mr. Durken and his class should be giving their full attention to the students' report. Mr. Durken is not modeling the very behavior he undoubtedly expects from his students when he is leading the class.

FOR YOUR NOTES

Exercise 4.7: Resolving a Student Behavior Problem: Brainstorming Ideas

Instructions: The purpose of this exercise is to assist in your continuing development of a repertoire of ideas about what you might do when a student is misbehaving. You can complete this exercise in a small group or alone, whenever you have a student who is causing a problem in your classroom. Completion of this exercise will generate ideas. Follow each step closely.

1. *State the problem.* Identify a specific problem you have with a particular child. State the situation as clearly as you can, for example: "The child's steady verbal outbursts are disruptive to classroom learning"; "The child just sits and does nothing from day to day"; or "The child is steadily ridiculed by others in the class and seems to be withdrawing."

2. *Describe what you know and have observed about this student.* List all you know about this child, whether or not you believe it to be relevant. Include student behaviors, appearance, grade level, subject, grades, attendance, parents, hobbies, skills, disabilities, peer relationships, and so on.

3. *List strategies that have been tried.* List everything you have tried with this child and their results, such as isolation, referral, conferences, rewards, and so forth.

4. *Share steps 1 through 3 with your colleagues.* During discussion you may get new ideas about the student, the student's behavior, and how you might try to work more positively with the student.

5. *Record new strategies to try.* As you complete the previous step, you will most certainly gain new ideas about ways of working with this child. As ideas are generated, write them down.

6. *Report on the new strategy.* At some later date, perhaps in a week or so, list here (and perhaps report to your group) what you tried and describe the results.

1. Statement of the problem. _____

   _____

   _____

   _____

   _____

   _____

   _____

   _____

2. Observations about the child. _____

   _____

   _____

   _____

   _____

   _____

   _____

   _____

3. What I originally tried and the results. _____
_____
_____
_____
_____
_____
_____

4. Notes on sharing. _____
_____
_____
_____
_____
_____

5. New ideas. _____
_____
_____
_____
_____
_____
_____

6. New strategy tried and its results. _____
_____
_____
_____
_____
_____
_____

Exercise 4.8: Applying Measures of Control

Instructions: The purpose of this exercise is to provide practice in deciding your various options when there is a behavior problem in your classroom. For each of the following, as specifically as possible, identify a situation in which you *would* and a situation in which you *would not* use that measure. Share and discuss your responses with your classmates.

1. Eye contact and hand signal to a student.

    Yes: _____

    _____

    _____

    _____

    No: _____

    _____

    _____

    _____

    _____

2. Immediately send student to the office.

    Yes: _____

    _____

    _____

    _____

    _____

    No: _____

    _____

    _____

    _____

3. Ignore the student behavior.

    Yes: _____

    _____

_____
_____
_____
_____

No: _____
_____
_____
_____
_____

4. Assign the child to detention.

   Yes: _____
   _____
   _____
   _____
   _____

   No: _____
   _____
   _____
   _____
   _____

5. Send a note home to parent or guardian about the child's misbehavior.

   Yes: _____
   _____
   _____
   _____
   _____

   No: _____
   _____
   _____

6. Touch the child on the shoulder.

Yes: _____

_____

_____

_____

_____

No: _____

_____

_____

_____

_____

7. Provide candy as a reward.

Yes: _____

_____

_____

_____

_____

No: _____

_____

_____

_____

_____

8. Provide an academic time-out.

Yes: _____

_____

_____

_____

No: _____

9. Verbally redirect a child's attention.

Yes: _____

No: _____

10. Use a strong verbal reprimand.

Yes: _____

No: _____

Exercise 4.9: Selecting Measures of Control

Instructions: The purpose of this exercise is to help you in determining which measures of control you would apply in some selected situations. For each of the following, state the first thing you would do in the situation described. Then share and discuss your responses with your colleagues.

1. A sixth-grade student reveals a long knife and seriously threatens to cut you. _____

   _____
   _____
   _____
   _____
   _____

2. During a test, a student appears to be copying answers from a neighboring student's answer sheet. _____

   _____
   _____
   _____
   _____

3. Although you have asked a sixth-grade student to take his seat, he refuses. _____

   _____
   _____
   _____
   _____

4. While talking with a small group of students, you observe two students on the opposite side of the room tossing paper airplanes. (The lesson has not been about airplanes.)

   _____
   _____
   _____
   _____

5. During small-group work one fourth-grader is aimlessly wandering around the room.

   _____
   _____
   _____
   _____

6. Although chewing gum is not permitted at the school, at the start of class you observe a student chewing what you suspect to be gum. _____
_____
_____
_____

7. During band rehearsal you (as band director) see a student about to stuff a scarf into another student's saxophone. _____
_____
_____
_____

8. During the viewing of a film two students on the opposite side of the room from you are quietly whispering. _____
_____
_____
_____

9. At the start of the class period, when a student is about to take her seat, a boy pulls the chair from beneath her. She falls to the floor. _____
_____
_____
_____

10. Suddenly, and for no clear reason, a student in your fourth-grade class gets up and leaves the room. _____
_____
_____
_____
_____

Exercise 4.10: Becoming Aware of a Complex Social Phenomenon That Affects Schools

Instructions: The purpose of this exercise is to help you to become aware of a complex social phenomenon: factors associated with rates of violence. In groups, discuss with your colleagues one or more of the following six research findings.[25] Within your group, arrive at a conclusion about how a community (of which schools are a part) can foster the welcoming of newcomers in a way that prevents violence. Share your group's conclusion with the rest of your class. Arrive at a class consensus about how a community can foster nonviolence as it welcomes newcomers. Record your group's ideas below.

Research Findings

1. National, regional, or local economic downturns increase ethnic violence and protests.

   _____

   _____

   _____

   _____

   _____

2. Ethnic violence is contagious. When an event of violence takes place, the likelihood of another event immediately arises. _____

   _____

   _____

   _____

   _____

3. Immigrant groups often meet violence upon arriving in this country. For example, southern, eastern, and central European groups all were targeted in the late nineteenth and early twentieth centuries. Asian immigrants were even more victimized. _____

   _____

   _____

   _____

   _____

[25]From the findings of researcher Susan Olzak, as reported in "Researcher Compares Violence Patterns," *CTA Action* 30(7):10 (April 1992).

4. Immigration-promoted violence was even more persistent against a nonimmigrant group—native-born African Americans. More than half of 263 violent events in the period of intense immigration, 1877 to 1914, were aimed at American-born blacks. A similar pattern is evident in other periods of high immigration, for instance, 1965 to 1985.

_____

_____

_____

_____

_____

_____

5. Regardless of their literacy rates, white immigrants were able to move up from lower-status jobs more quickly in cities with large black populations than in those without, lending credibility to the hypothesis that the presence of lower-status blacks enabled some caucasians to move up, out of segregated occupations.

_____

_____

_____

_____

_____

6. Most ethnic violence occurs where competing groups are in close proximity. In other cases, ethnic violence also has occurred against Asian Americans and African Americans in places where very few lived, indicating a complex social phenomenon. _____

_____

_____

_____

_____

_____

Class conclusions _____

_____

_____

_____

_____

_____

SUMMARY

In this chapter you learned about ways of coping with the daily challenges of teaching, about guidelines for effectively managing students in the classroom, and about your legal rights and responsibilities. Within that framework, your attention was then focused on specific approaches and additional guidelines for effective classroom management and control. This chapter has provided important guidelines for helping you set up and maintain a classroom environment that is favorable to student learning, and to establish procedures for efficiently managing and effectively controlling the behavior of your students from day-to-day, throughout the school year.

You are now ready for Part II of this book, which guides you in planning for instruction.

QUESTIONS FOR CLASS DISCUSSION

1. Explain the difference between a teacher's use of praise and the use of positive reinforcement. Which, if either, should be used more often? Why?
2. Could punishment ever be mistaken as a reward by a student? Explain.
3. Explain what you would do if there were two errant behaviors by students occurring simultaneously but in different locations in your classroom.
4. Have you ever seen teachers making "mountains out of molehills"? If so, describe and discuss those observations. Does that behavior create more problems than it solves? Explain.
5. How do you feel about assigning student seating? Will you do it? If so, how? Will you change the seating assignment periodically? If so, how often? On what basis?
6. Should a teacher allow students to leave their seats and move toward the exit of the classroom before the time class is officially over? Explain.
7. Is an educational choice plan that includes private schools legal? Interestingly enough, the Wisconsin Supreme Court has refused to block such a plan enacted by the Wisconsin legislature (1990). The plan permits up to 100 low-income Milwaukee students to attend nonsectarian private schools. Up to $2,500 in state aid, which would have gone to the public schools, will follow each student to his or her school of choice. Wisconsin's state school superintendent, the state teachers' union, and the NAACP have joined in a lawsuit to have the program declared unconstitutional because it allegedly violates a state constitutional provision that requires schooling to be "nearly as uniform as possible" for all students. What is your view about such a program?
8. Emergency planning and crisis drills are becoming more prevalent throughout the country and have heightened since the spread of violence. Some schools are adapting "duck and cover" drills (the new generation of bomb-shelter drills held in the 1950s) to protect students from the threat of neighborhood shootings on school grounds. Children are asked to drop flat to the floor, to keep away from the windows, and to slither like a snake if shots are fired on the playground. Teachers are asked to, when notified, lock their classrooms, keeping the children inside, and to pull the audiovisual curtains across the windows to prevent being viewed by intruders on the school campus. Other security measures include metal detectors, campus security patrols, and parent patrols. Inquire to determine the security measures taken by your school.

9. In the schools you have visited, are there detention or quiet rooms in use after, during, or before school? If so, how are they managed? By whom? Do you think they are worthwhile? Explain.
10. How quickly during the first day of the school year should a teacher get into the academic lessons? Explain.
11. Do you have questions about the content of this chapter? How might answers be found?

SUGGESTED READINGS FOR CHAPTER 4

Baron, E. B. *Discipline Strategies for Teachers*. Fastback 344. Bloomington, IN: Phi Delta Kappan Educational Foundation, 1992.

Blendinger, J., et al. *Win-Win Discipline*. Fastback 353. Bloomington, IN: Phi Delta Kappan Educational Foundation, 1993.

Charney, R. S. *Teaching Children to Care: Management in the Responsive Classroom*. Greenfield, MA: Northeast Foundation for Children, 1992.

Dreikurs, R., Grunwald, B., and, Pepper, F. *Maintaining Sanity in the Classroom*. New York: Harper & Row, 1982.

Evertson, C. M., et al. *Classroom Management for Elementary Teachers*. 2nd ed. Englewood Cliffs, NJ: Prentice-Hall, 1989.

Fisher, B. "Starting the Year in a First Grade Classroom." *Teaching PreK–8* 23(1):56–58 (August–September 1992).

Froyen, L. A. *Classroom Management: The Reflective Teacher-Leader*. 2nd ed. New York: Macmillan, 1993.

Imber, M. *Education Law*. New York: McGraw-Hill, 1993.

Johnson, D. W., et al. "Teaching Students to Be Peer Mediators." *Educational Leadership* 50(1):10–13 (September 1992).

Jones, F. *Positive Classroom Discipline*. New York: McGraw-Hill, 1987.

Kounin, J. *Discipline and Group Management in Classrooms*. New York: Holt, Rinehart and Winston, 1970.

Lee, V. E., and Smith, J. B. "Gender Equity in Teachers' Salaries: A Multilevel Approach." *Educational Evaluation and Policy Analysis* 12(1):57–81 (Spring 1990).

McIntyre, T. "The Teacher's Role in Cases of Suspected Child Abuse." *Education and the Urban Society* 22(3):300–306 (May 1990).

Mills, C. D. "Important Education-Related U.S. Supreme Court Decisions (1943–1993)." In Gordon Cawelti, ed. 1993 ASCD Yearbook. *Challenges and Achievements of American Education*. Alexandria, VA: Association for Supervision and Curriculum Development, 1993.

Pinsker, S. "Teaching in a Litigious Time." *Change* 21(4):50–54 (July–August 1989).

Stead, T. "Setting the Scene as Head of the Family." *Teaching PreK–8* 23(1):59–62 (August–September 1992).

Sylwester, R., and Cho, J. "What Brain Research Says About Paying Attention." *Educational Leadership* 50(4):71–75 (December 1992–January 1993).

Tingley, S. "Negative Rewards." *Educational Leadership* 50(1):80 (September 1992).

PART II

Planning for Instruction in an Elementary Classroom

Part II provides guidelines and resources for:

- Planning your instruction.
- Preparing daily lessons.
- Preparing interdisciplinary thematic units.
- Preparing instructional objectives.
- Preparing units of instruction.
- Selecting and using textbooks.

You are responsible for planning at three levels; there are critical decisions to be made at each level. These three levels are planning the school year, planning the units, and planning the lessons.

Two important goals of a teacher should be (1) not to waste anyone's time and (2) to select strategies that assure student learning.

Your challenge is to use performance-based criteria, yet simultaneously with a teaching style that encourages the development of intrinsic sources of student motivation, and that provides for and encourages coincidental learning—learning beyond what might be considered as predictable, immediately measurable, and minimal expectations.

Of special interest to elementary school teachers are units built around interdisciplinary themes, rather than content topics that are single-subject specific. Thematic teaching helps children to bridge the disciplines and to connect school learning with real-life experiences.

Every lesson or unit of instruction should begin with some type of preassessment of what the children already know, or think they know about the topic of the ensuing study.

5

Why Should I Plan and How Do I Select Content?

To teach effectively, you must prepare for every minute of time that children are in your classroom. Although careful and thoughtful planning does not automatically assure success in teaching, lack of adequate attention to planning most assuredly will create major problems and will perhaps result in failure. Like a good map, a good plan facilitates reaching a destination with greater confidence and fewer wrong turns.

Effective teaching does not just happen; it is brought about by carefully planning each phase of the learning process. Effective teachers begin their planning months before meeting their students for the first time. Their daily lessons are part of the larger picture of their long-range goals for the year. Any teacher who ignores this broader context, or who does not take into account where the students have been or where they are going, is doing them a disservice. The children deserve better. Administrators and parents and guardians expect better. The rationale for careful planning and the components of that planning are the topics of this chapter.

The chapters in this part discuss the planning processes and how to prepare written plans for instruction. Then, correlated with your plans, chapters in Part III guide you through the development of your strategy repertoire for implementing your plans.

A. RATIONALE FOR PLANNING

The primary reason for careful planning is *to provide program coherence*. Periodic lesson plans are an integral part of a larger plan represented by course goals and objectives. Students' learning experiences are thoughtfully planned in sequence, and then orchestrated by the teacher, who understands the rationale for their respective positions in the curriculum—not precluding, of course, an occasional diversion from planned activities.

There are other reasons teachers must plan. These are:

• *To provide a mechanism for scope and sequence in the curriculum.* Unless your course or class stands alone, following nothing and leading to nothing (which is unlikely),

Books can provide children with important content organization and resources for learning.

there are prerequisites to what you want your students to learn, and there are learning objectives that follow and build on this learning.

- *To teach to individual differences.* The diversity of students demands that, in planning, you give consideration to individual differences—these are students' cultural experiences, learning styles, varying reading abilities, special needs, or any other concerns.
- *To assure efficient and effective teaching with a minimum of classroom-control problems.* Following the decision on *what* content to teach is the difficult and important task of deciding *how* to teach it. To assure efficient use of instructional time, two important goals of a teacher should be (1) not to waste anyone's time and (2) to select effective strategies that assure student learning.
- *To ensure program continuation.* In your absence, your plans can enable a substitute teacher to continue the program.
- *To serve as a criterion for teacher self-assessment.* After an activity and at the end of a school year, your plans can help you to assess what was done and its effect on student achievement.

- *To evaluate your teaching.* Your plans represent a criterion recognized and evaluated by administrators. To those experienced in such matters, it is clear that inadequate attention to planning is usually a precursor to incompetent teaching.

B.   LEVELS OF INSTRUCTIONAL PLANNING

As previously indicated, planning for instruction is a major part of your job. You will be responsible for planning at three levels: planning the school year, the units, and the lessons. At each level you will need to make critical decisions.

The heart of good planning is good decision making. For every plan, and at any of the three levels, you must decide on the goals, the objectives, the specific subject matter to be introduced, the materials available and appropriate, the methods to be used to accomplish the objectives, and the methods that will be used to assess student achievement toward these objectives. Making such decisions is complicated, because there are so many options available. Decisions made at all three levels result in a complete instructional plan.

C.   COMPONENTS OF A COMPLETE INSTRUCTIONAL PLAN

A complete instructional plan has eight components:

1. *Statement of philosophy.* This is a general statement about *why* the plan is important and about *how* the children will learn its content.
2. *Needs assessment.* By its wording, the statement of philosophy should demonstrate an *appreciation for the cultural plurality of the nation and of the school, with a corresponding perception of the needs of society, its children, and of the functions served by the school.* The statement of philosophy and needs of the learners should be consistent with the school's statement of philosophy or mission statement.
3. *Aims, goals, and objectives.* The plan's stated aims, goals, and objectives should be consistent with the statement of philosophy.
4. *Sequence.* This component refers to the plan's relationship to preceding curriculum and to subsequent curriculum. Vertical articulation represents a plan's relationship to the learning that preceded and the learning that follows, in the prekindergarten through grade-12 curriculum.
5. *Integration.* The plan is integrated with other curriculum and co-curriculum activities across a particular grade level. This is horizontal articulation.
6. *Sequentially planned learning activities.* This is the presentation of organized and sequential units and lessons appropriate for the subject or grade level, and for the age and diversity of the learners.
7. *Resources needed.* This is a list of resources, such as books, speakers, field trip locales, and audiovisual materials.
8. *Assessment strategy.* This component is the planned procedure for evaluating student achievement in learning.

D. PLANNING THE YEAR

When planning the school year, you must decide *what* is to be accomplished in that time period. For help in deciding what is to be accomplished, you will

- Review school and other public resource documents for mandates and guidelines.
- Talk with other teachers and learn of common expectations.
- Probe, analyze, and translate your own convictions, knowledge, and skills into behaviors that foster the intellectual development of your students.

Documents That Provide Guidance for Content Selection

State department of education curriculum publications, district courses of study, and school-adopted printed or nonprinted materials are the sources you will examine, with the guidance of Exercises 5.1, 5.2, and 5.3. Your college or university library and local school districts can be a source for the documents called for in these exercises. At this time you may also want to refer to Chapter 13 which presents guidelines for instruction in the content areas of the elementary school curriculum.

National Curriculum Standards

The National Council on Education Standards and Testing has recommended that national standards for subject content be developed for all core subjects—the arts, civics/social studies, English/language arts/reading, geography, history, mathematics, and science. For the subjects and grade level of interest to you, you will need to follow the development of national curriculum standards. For example, the National Council of Teachers of Mathematics issued standards for mathematics for grades K–12 (see Chapter 13). By 1992 more than 40 states, usually through state curriculum frameworks, were following those standards to guide what and how mathematics is taught and how student progress is assessed.

At the time of preparation of this resource guide, there are a number of other projects in various stages of development:[1]

Arts

With a grant from the U.S. Department of Education, standards for the visual and performing arts are being developed jointly by the American Alliance for Theater and Education, the National Art Education Association, the National Dance Association, and the Music Educators National Conference. Standards for the arts are expected to be completed by 1994. For information, contact the Music Educators National Conference (MENC), 1902 Association Drive, Reston, VA 22091.

---

[1]For additional information about national standards, see the entire issue of *Educational Leadership* 50(5), February 1993.

Civics/Social Studies

With grants from the U.S. Department of Education and the Pew Charitable Trust, the Center for Civic Education and the National Center for Social Studies are in the process of developing standards for civics and for social studies. The standards for social studies are expected to be completed in late 1993. For information contact the National Council for the Social Studies (NCSS), 3501 Newark Street NW, Washington, DC 20016. The standards for civics, centered on the values and principles of the U.S. Constitution, are expected to be completed in 1994. For information, contact the Center for Civic Education, 5146 Douglas Fir Road, Calabasas, CA 91302.

English/Reading/Language Arts

With a grant from the U.S. Department of Education, standards for English are being developed jointly by the International Reading Association, the National Council of Teachers of English, and the University of Illinois Center for the Study of Reading. Completion of these standards is expected in 1994 or 1995. For information, contact the Center for the Study of Reading, 174 Children's Research Center, 51 Gerty Drive, Champaign, IL 61820.

Foreign Languages

The American Council on the Teaching of Foreign Languages is developing outlines for three levels of language proficiency based on the number of years a language is taken. For information contact ACTFL, Six Executive Plaza, Yonkers, NY 10701.

Geography

The Association of American Geographers, the National Council for Geographic Education, and the National Geographic Society, with a grant from the U.S. Department of Education, are developing standards for geographic education, expected to be completed in 1993. For information, contact Geography Standards Project, 1600 M Street NW, Washington, DC 20036.

History

The U.S. Department of Education and the National Endowment for the Humanities provided funding to the National Center for History in the Schools to develop standards for history education, expected to be completed in 1994. For information, contact the National Center for History in the Schools, UCLA, 231 Moore Hall, 405 Hilgard Avenue, Los Angeles, CA 90024.

Physical Education

Defining the characteristics of physically educated students and desirable outcomes of a physical education program, *Outcomes of Quality Physical Education Programs,* was published in 1992 by the National Association of Sports and Physical

Education (NASPE). For information, contact NASPE, 1900 Association Drive, Reston, VA 22091.

Science

Through a grant from the U.S. Department of Education, the National Research Council's National Committee on Science Education Standards and Assessment, with input from the American Association for the Advancement of Science and the National Science Teachers Association, is developing standards for science education, expected to be completed in late 1994. For information, contact the National Science Education Standards, 2101 Constitution Avenue NW, HA 486, Washington, DC 20418.

Once the new standards have been completed, they will be used (along with the mathematics standards) by state and local school districts for the revision of their curriculum documents. Guided by these standards and the content of state frameworks, especially those of larger states such as Texas and California, publishers of student textbooks and other instructional materials will then develop their new or revised printed and nonprinted instructional materials. It is likely that by the year 2000 these new standards will be in place and will have a positive effect on student achievement.

Now do Exercises 5.1–5.3.

Exercise 5.1: Examining State Curriculum Documents

Instructions: The purpose of this exercise is to become familiar with state curriculum documents. Determine whether your state department of education publishes a curriculum framework for various subjects taught in elementary schools. State frameworks provide valuable information pertaining to content and process, and teachers need to be aware of these documents. You may duplicate this form to use in evaluation of several documents. After examining documents that interest you, use the following questions as a guide for small- or large-group class discussion.

Are there state curriculum documents available to teachers in your state? If so, describe them, and how they are obtained.

Title of document _____

Source _____

Most recent year of publication _____

Other pertinent information _____

_____

_____

1. Examine how closely the document follows the eight components (listed in Section C). Are any components omitted? Are there any additional components? Does the document contain the following components? (Check yes or no.)

	Yes	*No*
a. Statement of philosophy.	_____	_____
b. Evidence of a needs recognition or assessment.	_____	_____
c. Goals and objectives.	_____	_____
d. Schemes for vertical articulation.	_____	_____
e. Schemes for horizontal articulation.	_____	_____
f. Recommended instructional procedures.	_____	_____
g. Recommended resources.	_____	_____
h. Assessment strategies.	_____	_____

Other _____

_____

2. Are the documents specific as to subject content for each grade level? Describe evidence of both vertical and horizontal articulation schemes. _____

_____

_____

_____

3. Do the documents offer specific strategies for instruction? If yes, describe. _____
   _____
   _____
   _____
   _____

4. Do the documents offer suggestions for dealing with students of diverse backgrounds and for students with special needs? Describe. _____
   _____
   _____
   _____

5. Do the documents offer suggestions or guidelines for dealing with controversial topics? If so, describe. _____
   _____
   _____
   _____

6. Do the documents distinguish between what *shall* be taught (mandated) and what *can* be taught (permissible)? _____
   _____
   _____
   _____

7. Do the documents offer suggestions for specific resources? _____
   _____
   _____
   _____

8. Do the documents refer to assessment strategies? Describe. _____
   _____
   _____
   _____

9. Is there anything else about the documents you would like to discuss in your group?
   _____
   _____
   _____

Exercise 5.2: Examining Local Curriculum Documents

Instructions: The purpose of this exercise is to become familiar with local curriculum documents. A primary resource outlining what is to be taught is referred to as a *curriculum guide,* or *course of study,* that has been developed by teachers of a school or district. Samples may be available at your university library or at a local school district resource center, or they may be borrowed from teachers whom you visited earlier (see Chapter 1). Obtain samples from a variety of sources and examine them, using the format that follows. (You may duplicate this form for each document examined.) An analysis of several documents will give you a good picture of expectations. If possible, compare documents from several school districts and states.

Title of document _____

District or school _____

Date of document _____

1. Examine how closely each document follows the eight components (listed in Section C). Does the document contain the following components?

	Yes	*No*
a. Statement of philosophy.	_____	_____
b. Evidence of a needs recognition or assessment.	_____	_____
c. Goals and objectives.	_____	_____
d. Schemes for vertical articulation.	_____	_____
e. Schemes for horizontal articulation.	_____	_____
f. Recommended instructional procedures.	_____	_____
g. Recommended resources.	_____	_____
h. Assessment strategies.	_____	_____

2. Does the document list expected learning outcomes? If so, describe them. _____

    _____

    _____

    _____

    _____

    _____

3. Does the document contain detailed unit plans? If so, describe them by answering the following.

    a. Do they contain initiating activities (how to begin a unit)? _____

        _____

        _____

b. Do they contain specific learning activities? _____

_____

_____

c. Do they contain suggested enrichment activities (as for gifted and talented children)?

_____

_____

d. Do they contain culminating activities (activities that bring a unit to a climax)? _____

_____

_____

e. Do they contain assessment procedures (for determining student achievement)? _____

_____

_____

f. Do they contain activities for learners with special needs? Or for learners who are different in other respects? _____

_____

_____

4. Does the document provide bibliographic entries for:

The teacher? _____

The children? _____

5. Does the document list audiovisual and other materials needed? _____

_____

_____

_____

6. Does the document clearly help you understand what you are expected to teach? _____

_____

_____

_____

_____

7. Do you have questions that are not answered by your examination of this document? If so, list them for class discussion. _____

_____

_____

_____

Exercise 5.3: Examining National Curriculum Standards

Instructions: The purpose of this exercise is to become familiar with the status of national curriculum standards being developed for various subjects of the curriculum. Using sources provided earlier in this section under "National Curriculum Standards" and other sources, such as professional journals, discover the status of the development of standards and their implementation for a subject area of interest to you. Use the following questions as a guide for small- or large-group class discussions. Following small subject-area group discussions, share the development in each field with the rest of the class. Duplicate this form for each subject area investigated.

Subject Area _____

1. Status of the National Curriculum Standards _____

_____

_____

_____

_____

2. Developed by _____

3. Specific K–12 goals as specified by the new standards. _____

_____

_____

_____

_____

_____

_____

4. Are the standards specific as to subject-matter content for each grade level? Explain.

_____

_____

_____

5. Do the standards offer specific strategies for instruction? Describe. _____

_____

_____

_____

6. Do the standards offer suggestions for teaching children of diverse backgrounds and for

   children with special needs? Describe. _____

_____

_____

7. Do the standards offer suggestions or guidelines for dealing with controversial topics? Describe. _____

_____

_____

_____

_____

8. Do the standards offer suggestions for specific resources? Describe. _____

_____

_____

_____

_____

9. Do the standards refer to assessment? Describe. _____

_____

_____

_____

_____

10. In summary, compared with what and how it has been taught in this field, do the standards contain anything new? _____

_____

_____

_____

_____

_____

11. Is there anything else about the standards you would like to discuss in your group?

_____

_____

_____

_____

_____

E. STUDENT TEXTBOOKS

School districts have periodic textbook adoptions (usually every five years or so). The books are then used for several years, until the next adoption cycle. If you are a student teacher or a first-year teacher, this most likely means that someone will tell you, "Here are the books you will be using." Starting now, you should become familiar with books you are likely to be using and how you are likely to use them.

For several reasons—the recognition of students' individual learning styles, the increasing costs of school textbooks and the decreasing availability of funds, and the availability of nonprint learning materials—textbook appearance, content, and use has changed considerably in recent years. Still, "90 percent of all classroom activity is regulated by textbooks."[2]

How Textbooks Can Help

Textbooks can be of help because they can provide:

- A base for building higher-order thinking activities (i.e., inquiry discussions and student research) that enable the development of critical-thinking skills.
- A basis for selecting subject matter that can be used for content emphasis.
- An organization of basic or important content for students.
- Information about other readings and resources to enhance the learning experiences of students.
- Several previously tested activities and suggestions for learning experiences.

Problems with Reliance on a Textbook

A student textbook should not be the "be all and end all" of the instructional experience. The textbook is one of many teaching tools, and should not be cherished as the ultimate word. Among the many ways in which you may use a student textbook, perhaps the *least* acceptable is to rely completely on a single book and require students simply to memorize its content. This exemplifies the lowest level of learning; furthermore, it implies that you are unaware of other significant printed and nonprinted instructional materials and that you have nothing more to contribute to student learning.

Reliance on a single textbook may cause yet another problem. Because textbook publishers prepare books for use in a larger market, that is, for national or statewide use, your state and district-adopted textbook[3] may not, in the view of your school community, adequately address issues of special interest and importance to your own community of children and their parents or guardians. This is another reason that some teachers and schools provide supplementary printed and nonprinted instructional materials.[4]

---

[2]J. Starr, "The Great Textbook War." In H. Holtz, I. Marcus, J. Dougherty, J. Michaels, and R. Peduzzi (Eds.), *Education and the American Dream: Conservatives, Liberals and Radicals Debate the Future of Education* (Grandy, MA: Bergin and Garvey, 1989), p. 106.

[3]Twenty-four states use statewide textbook-adoption review committees to review books and to then provide lists of recommended books. A public school district may select its books from the list and purchase them with funds provided by the state.

[4]For a case in point, read the interesting account of the issues involved in California's adoption of the Houghton Mifflin social studies series for grades 1–8 in Robert Reinhold, "Class Struggle," *The New York Times Magazine,* September 29, 1991, pp. 26–29, 46–47, 52.

Still another problem caused by reliance on a single source is that the reading level of the adopted textbook may not be appropriate for many children. In today's heterogeneous (mixed ability grouping) classrooms the reading range can vary by as much as two-thirds of the chronological age of the students. This means that if the chronological age is 9 years (typical for fourth-grade students), then the reading-level range would be 6 years; that is, the class may have some students who cannot read at all, as well as others who have a middle school (seventh-grade) reading ability. That is why many teacher-education programs today require a teaching-of-reading course for all credential candidates: teachers of most subjects and grade levels will need to devote time to helping their students develop their reading skills. All teachers need to know about the various kinds of reading problems and to share the responsibility of seeing that students with such problems receive help in developing their skills. As an elementary school teacher, above all else, you are a teacher of language arts.

Guidelines for Using a Textbook

The following guidelines can assist you in using the textbook as a learning tool:

1. For most grades and courses taught in elementary schools, it is beneficial for each student to have his or her own copy of a textbook, especially when that textbook is the current edition. However, because of budget constraints experienced by many school districts, the textbook may *not* be the current edition, and in some schools there may be only classroom sets, to be used only in the classroom. When that is the situation, students may not be allowed to take the books home or can only occasionally check them out. In other classrooms, because of such budget restrictions, there may be no textbook at all.

2. Maintain supplementary reading materials for student use in the classroom. School and community librarians are usually delighted to cooperate with teachers in the selection and provision of reading materials.

3. Some students benefit from drill, practice, and reinforcement afforded by accompanying workbooks, but this does not mean that all students necessarily benefit from such activities, nor do all benefit from doing the same activity. As a matter of fact, the traditional workbook, now nearly extinct at upper-grade levels and in some disciplines, is being replaced by a modern alternative afforded by computer software, compact discs, and interactive videodiscs (see Chapter 12). As the costs of hardware and software programs become more realistic for schools, their use is also becoming more common. Computers provide students with a psychologically safer learning environment. With computer programs and interactive media, the student has greater control over the pace of instruction, can repeat instruction if necessary, or ask for further clarification without the fear of having to publicly ask for help or admit that help is needed.

4. Provide vocabulary lists to help students learn meanings of important words and phrases.

5. Teach students how to study from their textbook, perhaps by using the **SQ4R** method: *survey* the chapter, ask *questions* about what was read, *read* to answer the questions, *recite* the answers, *record* important items from the chapter into their notebooks, then *review* it all. Or they may use the **SQ3R** method: *survey, question, read, recite,* and *review.*

6. Encourage students to search other sources for content that will update the textbook. This is especially important in certain disciplines—such as science and social

studies, where there is such a growth in the amount of new information—and when the student textbook is several years old.

7. Encourage students to be alert for errors in the textbook, both in content errors and in printing, perhaps giving them some sort of credit reward, such as points, when they bring an error to your attention. Urging students to be alert for errors in the textbook encourages critical reading, critical thinking, and healthy skepticism. For example, a social studies book is recently reported to have stated that the first person to lead a group through the length of the Grand Canyon was John Wesley Powell. Critically thinking students quickly made the point that perhaps Powell was only the first *white* person to do this. After all, Native Americans had traveled the length of the Grand Canyon for centuries.[5]

8. Progressing from one cover of the textbook to the other in one school term is not necessarily an indicator of good teaching. The textbook is one resource; to enhance their learning children should be encouraged to use a variety of resources.

9. Individualize the learning for students of varying reading and learning abilities. Consider differentiated reading and workbook assignments, both in the textbook and in supplementary materials. When using supplementary materials, consider using several rather than just one. Except to make life a bit simpler for the teacher, there is no advantage in all students working in the same workbook or doing the same workbook exercises. However, when students are to use workbooks not designed to accompany their text, you should cut and edit the exercises so they do relate well to your course objectives.

10. Encourage students to respect their books by covering and protecting them, and by not marking in them. In many schools this is a rule, and at the end of the term students who have damaged or lost their books are charged a fee.

Future of Textbooks

Within the span of your teaching career you may witness and be a part of a revolution in the design of school textbooks. Some school districts already allow teachers in certain disciplines to choose between traditional student textbooks and interactive videodisc programs. It is predicted that with the revolution in microcomputer chip technology, student textbooks soon will take on a completely new appearance. There will also be dramatic changes in the importance and use of student texts, as well as new problems for the teacher, some of which are predictable. Student "texts" may become credit-card size, increasing the chance of students "losing" their books. On the positive side, it is probable that the classroom teacher will have available a larger variety of "textbooks" to better address the reading levels, interests, learning styles, and abilities of individual students. Distribution and maintenance of reading materials could create an additional demand on the teacher's time. Yet, dramatic and exciting changes have begun to happen to a teaching tool that had remained essentially the same throughout the history of education in this country. As an electronic, multimedia tool, the textbook of the twenty-first century may be "an interactive device that offers text, sound, and video."[6]

Proceed now to Exercise 5.4 to examine student textbooks and accompanying teacher's editions.

[5]Ibid., p. 46.
[6]Bernard R. Gifford, "The Textbook of the 21st Century," *Syllabus* 19 (October–November 1991), pp. 15–16.

Exercise 5.4: Examining Student Textbooks and Teacher's Editions

Instructions: The purpose of this exercise is to become familiar with elementary school textbooks. Student textbooks are usually accompanied by a teacher's edition, which contains specific objectives, teaching techniques, learning activities, assessment instruments, test items, and suggested resources. Your university library, local schools, or cooperating teachers are sources for locating these books. Select a textbook that is accompanied by a teacher's edition and examine its contents, using the following format. After completion of this exercise, share your book and your analysis with your colleagues.

Title of book _____

Author(s) _____

Publisher _____

Date of most recent publication _____

	Yes	*No*
1. Does the teacher's edition contain the following elements?		
a. Goals that are consistent with those of local guides and/or state guides.	_____	_____
b. Specific objectives for each lesson.	_____	_____
c. Scope and sequence charts for teacher reference.	_____	_____
d. Units and lessons sequentially developed with suggested time allotments.	_____	_____
e. Suggested provisions for individual differences.	_____	_____
For reading levels.	_____	_____
For children with special needs.	_____	_____
For children who are gifted and talented.	_____	_____
f. Specific techniques and strategies.	_____	_____
g. Listings of suggested aids, materials, and resources.	_____	_____
h. Suggestions for extension activities (to extend the lessons beyond the usual topic or time).	_____	_____
i. Specific guidelines for assessment of student learning.	_____	_____
2. Analyze the student textbook for the following elements.		
a. Does it treat the content in adequate depth?	_____	_____
b. Does it treat ethnic minorities and women fairly?	_____	_____
c. Is the format attractive?	_____	_____
d. Does the book have a good quality binding and a suitable type size?	_____	_____

    e. Are illustrations and visuals attractive and useful?   _____   _____

    f. Is the writing clear and understandable to the students?   _____   _____

3. Would you like to use this textbook? Give reasons. _____

_____

_____

_____

_____

_____

_____

_____

_____

_____

_____

_____

_____

_____

_____

Students and the Textbook Reading Level

A frequent concern of teachers in the selection of books is the reading level of their students, and the availability of books that are neither too easy nor too difficult for their students. To determine a textbook's reading level, you can use any of several techniques, such as the Fry[7] or the Forecast[8] readability formulas. Since readability formulas give only the technical reading level of a book, you have to interpret the results by subjectively estimating the conceptual reading level of the work. To do so, you must consider your students' experience with the content, the number of new ideas introduced, and the level of abstraction of the ideas.

To tell how well students can read a text, many teachers use the **Cloze** technique. This technique, first described by Bormuth in 1968 and since then appearing in a number of versions,[9] is as follows: From the book that is being analyzed, select several typical passages so that you have a total of 400 to 415 words. Delete every eighth word in the passage except for those in the first and last sentences, proper names, numbers, and initial words in sentences. It is helpful to have deleted about 50 words. Duplicate the passages with 10 to 15 blank spaces replacing each deleted word. Pass out these duplicated passages to the students. Ask them to fill in the blanks with the most appropriate words they can think of. Collect the papers. To score them, count all the words that are the exact words of the original text and divide the number of correct responses by the numbers of possibles.[10] (Fifty blanks makes this division easier.)

$$\text{Score} = \frac{\text{Number of responses}}{\text{Number of possibles}}$$

You can assume that students who score better than 50 percent can read the book quite well, those who score between 40 and 50 percent can read the book at the level of instruction, and those who score below 40 percent will probably find the reading difficult and frustrating.[11]

To conduct a **silent and informal reading inventory,** have students read four or five pages of the text and then give them a 10-item quiz on what was read. Consider the text as too difficult for a student who scores less than 70 percent on the quiz. Or you might conduct an **oral and informal reading inventory** by having a student read a 100-word passage. The text may be too difficult if the student stumbles over or misses more than 5 percent of the words.[12]

F. BEGINNING PREPARATION FOR THE YEAR

You have reviewed the rationale and components for instructional planning, state and local curriculum documents, and student reading materials. While doing so, undoubtedly you have reflected on your own biases regarding content that you believe

---

[7]See Edward Fry, "A Readability Formula That Saves Time," *Journal of Reading* 11:587 (April 1968).

[8]See Novella M. Ross, "Assessing Readability of Instructional Materials," *VocEd*, 54:10–11 (February 1979).

[9]See J. Bormuth, "The Cloze Readability Procedure," *Elementary English* 45:429–436 (April 1968).

[10]Some persons recommend that only exact words be counted; others would allow exact synonyms. Perhaps you should not count synonyms or verbs of different tense. See N. McKenna, "Synonymic Versus Verbatim Scoring of the Cloze Procedure," *Journal of Reading* 20:141–143 (November 1976).

[11]From Joseph F. Callahan, Leonard H. Clark, and Richard D. Kellough, *Teaching in the Middle and Secondary Schools,* 4th ed. (New York: Macmillan, 1992), p. 349.

[12]See M. S. Johnson and R. A. Kress, *Informal Reading Inventories* (Newark, DE: International Reading Association, 1965).

should be included in a subject at a particular grade level. Now it is time to gain practical experience in long-range planning.

Although some authors believe that the first step in preparing to teach is to write the objectives, it is our contention that a more logical first step is to prepare a sequential topic outline. Then, following that outline, you write the instructional objectives—the focus of the next chapter.

Most beginning teachers will be presented with topic outlines and instructional objectives, with the expectation that they will teach from them. This may be the case for you as well, and of course someone—either one or several teachers—will have written them. As a teacher candidate, you must know how an outline is prepared, for someday you will be concentrating on this task in earnest.

Therefore, the next step is for you to experience preparing a year-long content outline for a subject and grade you intend to teach. Do Exercise 5.5.

Exercise 5.5: Preparing a Content Outline

Instructions: The purpose of this exercise is to organize your ideas about subject content and the sequencing of that content. Unless instructed otherwise by your course instructor, you may select the subject (e.g., science, social studies, mathematics, language arts, and so on) and the grade level.

With *three levels of headings,* prepare a sequential topic outline for a subject and grade level you intend to teach. (Do this on separate paper, as space for the outline is not included here.) Identify the subject by title, and clearly state the grade level. This is an outline of topic content only, and does *not* need to include student activities associated with the learning of that content (i.e., do not include experiments, assignments, assessment strategies, and so on).

Share your completed outline to obtain comments from your colleagues or university instructor (see evaluation guidelines that follow). As content outlines are never to be set in concrete, make adjustments to your outline as appropriate.

Content outline evaluation guidelines include:

• Does the outline follow a logical sequence, with each topic logically leading to the next?
• Does the content assume prerequisite knowledge or skills that the children are likely to have?
• Is the content inclusive and at an appropriate depth?
• Are there serious content omissions?
• Is there content of questionable value for this level of instruction?

G. DEALING WITH CONTROVERSIAL CONTENT ISSUES

Content issues that are controversial (usually involving matters of religion, ethnicity, politics, gender, and sex) abound in certain disciplines, particularly in language arts (e.g., controversial books), social studies (e.g., political issues), and science (e.g., biological evolution). Within your teaching career, you undoubtedly will have to make decisions regarding what you will do in your teaching with respect to content and issues that are controversial.

When selecting content that might be controversial, consider the following guidelines.

For the Student Teacher

Maintain perspective with respect to your own personal objective, which is to complete your credential so you can then seek your first paid teaching assignment. Student teaching is *not* the time to "make waves," to become involved in a situation that could lead to embitterment. If you maintain close communication with your cooperating teacher and your college or university supervisor, you should be able to prevent any major problems in dealing with controversial issues. Sometimes during normal discussion in the classroom, a controversial subject will emerge spontaneously, catching you off guard. When this happens, *think before saying anything.* You may wish to postpone discussion of the issue until you have had a chance to talk it over with your supervisors. Controversial issues can seem to come from nowhere for *any* teacher, and that is perfectly normal. Children are in the process of developing their moral and value systems and they *need* and want to know how adults feel about issues important to them, particularly those adults they hold in esteem—their teachers.

For All Teachers

Students need discussions about issues that are important to society, especially children of middle grades and above, and there is absolutely nothing wrong with dealing with those issues so long as the following guidelines have been established.

1. Students should learn about all sides of an issue. Controversial issues are open-ended questions and should be treated as such. They do not have "right" answers or "correct" solutions. If they did, there would be no controversy.[13] Therefore, the focus should be on process as well as on content. A major goal is to show children how to deal with controversial issues so as to make wise decisions on the basis of carefully considered information. Another goal is to help children learn how to disagree without being disagreeable. A third goal, of course, is to help students learn about the issues.
2. Like all lesson plans, one dealing with a topic that could lead to an area of controversy should be well thought out ahead of time. Problems for the teacher are most likely to occur when the plan has been poorly prepared. Potential problem areas, as well as instructional resources, must be carefully considered in advance.

---

[13]As used in this resource guide, an *issue* differs from a *problem* in that a problem generally has a solution, whereas an issue may elicit many opinions and several alternative solutions.

3. All persons involved have a right to offer their views—students, parents and guardians, community representatives, and other teachers. Moreover, parents or guardians, and students, should have the right to not participate, and without penalty.
4. Can there be anything wrong with students knowing a teacher's opinion about an issue *as long as it is made clear to them that they may certainly disagree without reprisal or academic penalty?* However, it is probably best that the teacher's opinion be reserved until after students have had full opportunity to study and report on opinions from other sources.

One characteristic that makes this country great is the freedom of its people to speak out on issues, to express their opinions. That freedom should not be excluded from school classrooms. Teachers and students should be encouraged to express their feelings, attitudes, and opinions about the great issues of today, encouraged to *study* the issues, to suspend judgment while collecting data, and then to form reasoned opinions. We must understand the difference between teaching truth, values, and morals, and teaching *about* truth, values, and morals.

To the teacher candidate who may still be taking college or university courses, it is not unusual to experience a professor who *pontificates* on an issue—perhaps on the right to life, on the liberation of a specific group of individuals in society, on the use of animals or the human fetus for medical research, or on any other of a long list of issues important to society today—*but as a public elementary school teacher you will not necessarily have the same so-called academic freedom.* It is important that you understand this. The children with whom you will be working are not adults, and they must be protected from dogma and allowed the freedom to learn and to develop their values and opinions, free from coercion from those adults who have power over their learning.

On this topic that should be of importance to you as a beginning teacher, what is your view? What do you think about the opinion and guidelines offered here? For development and expression of your opinion, proceed to Exercise 5.6.

Exercise 5.6: Dealing with Controversial Issues

Instructions: The educational purpose of this exercise is for you to discover, *before* teaching, some of the possibilities for controversial issues, and for you to consider what you can and will do with those issues. First complete this exercise, then share it with members of your class.

1. Spend time in your library studying current periodicals and talk with colleagues in the schools you visit to discover two or three controversial topics that are likely to come up during your teaching.

Issue	*Source*
Example: Use of chimpanzees for medical research.	*National Geographic*, March 1992

2. Select one of these issues and identify opposing arguments, naming current resources.

3. Identify your own position on this issue, and give a statement of your rationale.

_____

_____

_____

_____

_____

_____

4. How accepting can you be of students (and parents or guardians) who assume an opposing position? _____

_____

_____

_____

_____

_____

_____

_____

_____

_____

_____

5. Share your preceding answers with other teacher candidates. Note any of their comments that you find helpful or enlightening. _____

_____

_____

_____

_____

_____

_____

_____

_____

_____

_____

_____

SUMMARY

As you reviewed curriculum documents and student textbooks, you undoubtedly found most of them well organized and useful. In your comparison and analysis of courses of study and the teacher's editions of student textbooks you probably discovered that many are accompanied by sequentially designed *resource units* from which the teacher can select and build specific *teaching units*. A resource unit usually consists of an extensive list of objectives, a large number and variety of activities, suggested materials, and extensive bibliographies for teacher and students, from which the teacher will select those that best suit his or her needs to build an actual teaching unit.

As you may also have discovered, some courses of study contain actual teaching units that have been prepared by teachers of the particular school district. An important question often asked by beginning teachers, and by student teachers, is: How closely must I follow the school's curriculum guide or course of study? This is a question to which you need an answer *before* you begin teaching. To obtain the answer, you talk with teachers and administrators of that particular school.

Your final decisions about what content to teach are guided by all of the following:

• Articles in professional journals.
• Discussions with other teachers.
• Local courses of study.
• State curriculum documents.
• The differences, interests, and abilities of your students.
• Your own personal convictions, knowledge, and skills.

After discovering what you will teach comes the process of preparing the plans. The remaining chapters in Part II of this book will guide you through the planning process. Although teacher's textbook editions and other curriculum documents make the process easier, they *should never substitute for your own specific planning*.

QUESTIONS FOR CLASS DISCUSSION

1. Are the psychologies and theories of Ausubel, Bloom, Bruner, Costa, Gagné, Gardner, Maslow, Piaget, and others discussed in Chapter 2 evident in the curriculum documents you have examined? If so, which ones and how?
2. Reading seems to be more effective when it utilizes modality integration. Describe evidence of implementation of this concept that you found in your examination of curriculum documents.
3. Explain how you will decide what to teach. How will you know whether what you choose is the proper content to be taught?
4. Inquire of experienced teachers, of a grade and subject of most interest to you, as to whether they like the textbooks they are using. Share their replies with others in your class. Are the majority of teachers happy with their textbooks? Are there books in any particular area (e.g., social studies, science, language arts) with which the majority of teachers seem more pleased? Less pleased?

5. Historically, American schools have focused on broadly stated aims (in your university library, see reports of committees of the National Education Association in 1893, 1899, and 1913; and the Educational Policies Commission in 1938 and in 1961), but today the focus appears to be more on student achievement of specific competencies. Do you agree with this statement? What is the evidence to support or to reject the statement? If you agree, how is the shift explained?

6. Describe factors that distinguish a good student textbook from a bad one.

7. Jack W. Humphrey asks, "Why should students choose to read when a majority of the books in their school library media centers are obsolete and unattractive?"[14] Explore local school libraries and media centers. Are the student books obsolete and unattractive? For example, examine a book on the topic of space travel. Is it current or is its latest reference only to Sputnik? What are schools doing to maintain attractive and current reading materials for their students?

8. Have you observed any classes using nonprinted material as substitution for student textbooks? If so, describe your observations for others in your class.

9. It has been said that "while once a teacher might have been able to expect a relatively homogeneous classroom filled with average middle-class children, [today's teacher] can . . . look forward to the challenge of a heterogeneous group of children with a diverse set of individual backgrounds."[15] From what you have learned so far, describe ways a classroom teacher can attend to these individual differences.

10. Do you have questions about the content of this chapter? How might answers be found?

SUGGESTED READINGS FOR CHAPTER 5

Aldridge, B. G. "Project on Scope, Sequence, and Coordination: A New Synthesis for Improving Science Education." *Journal of Science Education and Technology* 1(1):13–21 (March 1992).

Brandt, R. S., ed. *Content of the Curriculum.* 1988 ASCD Yearbook. Alexandria, VA: Association for Supervision and Curriculum Development, 1988.

Bybee, R., et al. *Science and Technology Education for the Elementary Years: Framework for Curriculum and Instruction.* Andover, MA: The National Center for Improving Science Education, 1989.

Dempster, F. N. "Exposing Our Students to Less Should Help Them Learn More." *Phi Delta Kappan* 74(6):433–437 (February 1993).

Down, A. G., and Mitchell, R. "Shooting for the Moon: Standards for the Arts." *Educational Leadership* 50(5):32–35 (February 1993).

Eisner, E. "Why Standards May Not Improve Schools." *Educational Leadership* 50(5): 22–23 (February 1993).

English-Language Arts Model Curriculum Guide. Sacramento: California Department of Education, 1988.

Gagnon, P., ed. *Historical Literacy.* New York: Macmillan, 1989.

---

[14]Jack W. Humphrey, "The Glitzy Labyrinth of Nonprint Media Is Winning the Battle with Books," *Phi Delta Kappan* 73(7):538, p. 538.

[15]Nancy L. Cecil and Patricia L. Roberts, *Developing Resiliency Through Children's Literature: A Guide for Teachers and Librarians, K–8* (Jefferson, NC: McFarland, 1992), p. x.

Haynes, C. *Religion in American History: What to Teach and How.* Alexandria, VA: Association for Supervision and Curriculum Development, 1990.

Hoffman, K. M., and Stage, E. "Science for All: Getting It Right for the 21st Century." *Educational Leadership* 50(5):27–31 (February 1993).

Jacobs, H. H. *Interdisciplinary Curriculum: Design and Implementation.* Alexandria, VA: Association for Supervision and Curriculum Development, 1989.

Loucks-Horsley, S., et al. *Elementary School Science for the 90s.* Alexandria, VA: The Curriculum/Technology Resource Center, Association for Supervision and Curriculum Development, 1990.

O'Neil, J. "Can National Standards Make a Difference?" *Educational Leadership* 50(5): 4–8 (February 1993).

Parker, W. C. *Renewing the Social Studies Curriculum.* Alexandria, VA: Association for Supervision and Curriculum Development, 1991.

Physical Best: The AAHPERD Guide to Physical Fitness Education and Assessment. Reston, VA: The American Alliance for Health, Physical Education, Recreation, and Dance, 1989.

Resnick, L. B., and Klopfer, L. E., eds. *Toward the Thinking Curriculum: Current Cognitive Research.* 1989 ASCD Yearbook. Alexandria, VA: Association for Supervision and Curriculum Development, 1989.

Romberg, T. A. "NCTM's Standards: A Rallying Flag for Mathematics Teachers." *Educational Leadership* 50(5):36–41 (February 1993).

Singer, H., and Donlan, D. *Reading and Learning from Text.* Hillsdale, NJ: Lawrence Erlbaum, 1990.

Tchudi, S. *Planning and Assessing the Curriculum in English and Language Arts.* Alexandria, VA: Association for Supervision and Curriculum Development, 1991.

Toward Civilization: A Report on Arts Education. Washington, DC: National Endowment for the Arts, 1988.

Tyson-Bernstein, H. A. *Conspiracy of Good Intention: America's Textbook Fiasco.* Washington, DC: Council for Basic Education, 1988.

Victor, E., and Kellough, R. D. *Science for the Elementary School.* 7th ed. New York: Macmillan, 1993.

Walstad, W. B., and Soper, J. C., eds. *Effective Economic Education in the Schools. Reference and Resource Series.* Washington, DC: Joint Council on Economic Education, 1991.

Willoughby, S. S. *Mathematics Education for a Changing World.* Alexandria, VA: Association for Supervision and Curriculum Development, 1990.

With History—Social Science for All: Access for Every Student. Sacramento: California Department of Education, 1992.

Zabaluk, B. L., and Samuels, S. J. *Readability: Its Past, Present, and Future.* Newark, DE: International Reading Association, 1988.

6

What Are Instructional Objectives and How Do I Use Them?

Now that you have prepared a content outline (Exercise 5.5), you are ready to write specific instructional objectives, known also as **behavioral** or **performance objectives.**[1] Instructional objectives are *statements that describe what the student will be able to do upon completion of the instructional experience.*

A. AIMS, GOALS, AND OBJECTIVES

As a teacher, you will encounter the compound structure "goals and objectives." A distinction must be understood. The easiest way to understand the difference between the two words, "goals" and "objectives," is to look at your *intent.*

Goals are ideals that you intend to reach, that is, ideals that you would like to have accomplished. Goals may be stated as *teacher goals,* as *student goals,* or as *course goals.* Ideally, in all three, the goal is the same. If, for example, the goal is to improve students' reading skills, it could be stated as follows:

"To help students improve
  their reading skills"   *Teacher or course goal*

or

"To improve my reading skills"   *Student goal*

Goals are general statements of intent,[2] and are prepared early in course planning. Goals are useful when shared with students as advance mental organizers. The students then know what to expect and begin to prepare mentally to learn the appropriate material. Based on the goals, specific objectives are prepared and should be written in behavioral terms.[3] Objectives are *not* intentions. They are the actual behaviors teachers intend to cause students to demonstrate. In short, objectives are what students *do.*

---

[1] The terms "performance objective" and "behavioral objective" are synonymous.
[2] Some writers use the phrase "general goals and objectives," but that is incorrect usage. Goals *are* general; objectives are specific.
[3] The value of stating learning objectives in behavioral terms and in providing advance organizers is well documented by recent research. See Thomas L. Good and Jere E. Brophy, *Looking in Classrooms,* 4th ed. (New York: Harper & Row, 1987), p. 334.

Educational authorities have not standardized the terminology used for designating the various types of objectives. In the literature, the most general educational objectives are often called **aims**; the general objectives of schools, curricula, and courses are called **goals**; the objectives of units and lessons are called **instructional objectives**. Aims are more general than goals, goals are more general than objectives. Instructional objectives are quite specific.

As implied in the preceding paragraphs, goals *guide* the instructional methods; objectives *drive* student performance. Goals are general statements, usually not even complete sentences and often begin with the infinitive "to," which identify what the teacher intends the class of students to learn. Objectives, stated in performance (behavioral) terms, are specific actions. Objectives stated in behavioral terms are complete sentences that include the verb "will" to indicate what each student is expected to be able to do as the result of the instructional experience.

While instructional goals may not always be quantifiable, that is, readily measurable, behavioral objectives *must always be measurable*. Consider the following examples of goals and objectives.

Goals
1. To develop an appreciation for music.
2. To provide reading opportunities for students.
3. To demonstrate the relationship between mathematics and the natural environment.

Objectives
1. Each student will correctly identify ten different musical instruments by listening to a tape recording of the Boston Pops Symphony Orchestra and tell the class which instrument is being played at different times, as specified by the teacher.
2. The student will read two books, three short stories, and five newspaper articles at home, within a two-month period. The student will maintain a daily written log of these activities.
3. Using a sheet of graph paper, the student will plot the diagonals formed by Fibonacci numbers, forming an Archimedian spiral. The student will list at least three different forms in nature that resemble the Archimedian spiral formed by the drawing on the graph paper.

B. BEHAVIORAL OBJECTIVES: THEIR RELATION TO INSTRUCTION AND ASSESSMENT

One purpose of writing objectives in specific, behavioral terms is to enable the teacher to evaluate with precision whether the instruction has resulted in the desired terminal behavior. In many school districts the educational goals are established as competencies (i.e., **competency-based, or outcome-based education**) that the students are expected to achieve. These goals are then divided into specific performance objectives, sometimes referred to as **goal indicators**. When students perform the competencies called for by these objectives, their education is considered successful. The success of school curricula, teacher performance, and student achievement may each be assessed according to these criteria.

Assessment is not difficult when the desired performance is **overt**, that is, when it can be observed directly. Each of the three sample objectives listed in the preceding section is an example of an overt objective.

Assessment is difficult when the desired terminal behavior is **covert**, that is, when it is not directly observable. Behaviors that call for terminal behaviors of "understanding" or "appreciation," for example, are not directly observable, because they occur within a person and so are covert behaviors. Since covert behavior cannot be observed directly, the one way to tell whether an objective has been achieved is to observe behavior that may be indicative of such achievement. The objective, then, must be written in overt language, and evaluators can only assume or trust that the observed behavior is, in fact, indicative of the expected learning outcome.

While behaviorists (behaviorism) assume a definition of learning that deals only with changes in observable behavior (overt), constructivists (cognitivism), as discussed in Chapter 2, hold that learning entails the construction or reshaping of mental schemata and that mental processes mediate learning, and so are concerned with both overt and covert behaviors.

Furthermore, when assessing whether an objective has been achieved, the assessment device must be consistent with the desired learning outcome. When the measuring device and the learning objective are compatible, the assessment is referred to as being authentic. For example, a person's competency to teach children is best measured by directly observing that person *doing* that very thing—teaching children. That is **authentic assessment**. Using a standardized paper-and-pencil test to determine a person's ability to teach first-graders is not. (For further discussion of assessment, see Chapter 14.)

The point to remember is that when preparing instructional objectives, you should write them in overt terms.

C. WRITING BEHAVIORAL OBJECTIVES

When writing behavioral objectives you must ask yourself, "How is the student to demonstrate that the objective has been reached?" The objective must include an *action* that demonstrates that the objective has been achieved. This portion of the objective is sometimes referred to as the **terminal behavior**, and sometimes as the **anticipated measurable performance**.

The ABCDs of Writing Objectives

When completely written, a behavioral objective has four key parts. To aid in your understanding and remembering, you can refer to this as the ABCDs of writing behavioral objectives. One of these key parts is the **audience**—the A of the ABCDs, that is, the student for whom the objective is intended. To address this component, teachers sometimes begin their objectives with the phrase "The student will be able to . . . ." or, to personalize the objective, "You will be able to . . .".

The second key part of a behavioral objective is the expected **behavior**—the B of the ABCDs. The expected performance must be written with verbs that are measurable, that is, with action verbs (see Figure 6.1). The reason for this is to ensure that it is measurable (directly observable) that an objective has been reached. As discussed in the previous section, some verbs (covert behaviors) are too vague, ambiguous, and not clearly measurable. When writing behavioral objectives, you should avoid verbs that are not clearly measurable, such as *appreciate, believe, comprehend, enjoy, know, learn,*

1. "Creative" Behaviors

Alter	Generalize	Question	Regroup	Rephrase	Rewrite
Ask	Modify	Rearrange	Rename	Restate	Simplify
Change	Paraphrase	Recombine	Reorder	Restructure	Synthesize
Design	Predict	Reconstruct	Reorganize	Retell	Systematize

2. Complex, Logical, Judgmental Behaviors

Analyze	Compare	Deduce	Discover	Induce	Structure
Appraise	Conclude	Defend	Evaluate	Infer	Substitute
Assess	Contrast	Designate	Formulate	Plan	Suggest
Combine	Criticize	Determine	Generate		

3. General Discriminating Behaviors

Choose	Detect	Identify	List	Order	Point
Collect	Differentiate	Indicate	Match	Pick	Select
Define	Discriminate	Isolate	Omit	Place	Separate
Describe	Distinguish				

4. Social Behaviors

Accept	Argue	Disagree	Interact	Participate	Smile
Admit	Communicate	Discuss	Invite	Permit	Talk
Agree	Compliment	Excuse	Join	Praise	Thank
Aid	Contribute	Forgive	Laugh	React	Visit
Allow	Cooperate	Greet	Meet	Reply	Volunteer
Answer	Dance	Help			

5. Language Behaviors

Abbreviate	Capitalize	Print	Say	State	Translate
Accent	Edit	Pronounce	Sign	Summarize	Verbalize
Alphabetize	Hyphenate	Punctuate	Speak	Syllabicate	Whisper
Articulate	Indent	Read	Spell	Tell	Write
Call	Outline	Recite			

6. Music Behaviors

Blow	Compose	Hum	Pluck	Sing	Tap
Bow	Finger	Mute	Practice	Strum	Whistle
Clap	Harmonize	Play			

7. Physical Behaviors

Arch	Climb	Hit	March	Ski	Swim
Bat	Face	Hop	Pitch	Skip	Swing
Bend	Float	Jump	Pull	Somersault	Throw
Carry	Grab	Kick	Push	Stand	Toss
Catch	Grasp	Knock	Run	Step	Walk
Chase	Grip	Lift	Skate	Stretch	*(continued)*

Figure 6.1   Performance verbs for use in stating specific learning objectives.[4]

[4]Calvin K. Claus, National College of Education, Evanston, IL. By permission of Calvin K. Claus.

8. Arts Behaviors

Assemble	Dab	Handle	Paste	Saw	Stick
Blend	Dot	Heat	Pat	Sculpt	Stir
Brush	Draw	Illustrate	Polish	Send	Trace
Build	Drill	Melt	Pour	Shake	Trim
Carve	Fold	Mix	Press	Sketch	Varnish
Color	Form	Mold	Roll	Smooth	Wipe
Construct	Frame	Nail	Rub	Stamp	Wrap
Cut	Hammer	Paint			

9. Drama Behaviors

Act	Display	Express	Move	Perform	Show
Clasp	Emit	Imitate	Pantomime	Proceed	Sit
Cross	Enter	Leave	Pass	Respond	Turn
Direct	Exit				

10. Mathematical Behaviors

Add	Compute	Estimate	Integrate	Plot	Subtract
Bisect	Count	Extract	Interpolate	Prove	Sum
Calculate	Cumulate	Extrapolate	Measure	Reduce	Tabulate
Check	Derive	Graph	Multiply	Solve	Tally
Circumscribe	Divide	Group	Number	Square	Verify

11. Science Behaviors

Align	Connect	Grow	Limit	Remove	Specify
Apply	Convert	Increase	Manipulate	Replace	Straighten
Attach	Decrease	Insert	Operate	Report	Time
Balance	Demonstrate	Keep	Plant	Reset	Transfer
Calibrate	Dissect	Lengthen	Prepare	Set	Weigh
Conduct	Feed				

12. General Appearance, Health, and Safety Behaviors

Button	Cover	Empty	Stack	Unbutton	Wait
Clean	Dress	Fasten	Stop	Uncover	Wash
Clear	Drink	Fill	Taste	Untie	Wear
Close	Eat	Go	Tie	Unzip	Zip
Comb	Eliminate	Lace			

13. Miscellaneous Behaviors

Aim	Erase	Hunt	Peel	Scratch	Store
Attempt	Expand	Include	Pin	Send	Strike
Attend	Extend	Inform	Position	Serve	Supply
Begin	Feel	Kneel	Present	Sew	Support
Bring	Finish	Lay	Produce	Share	Switch
Buy	Fit	Lead	Propose	Sharpen	Take
Come	Fix	Lend	Provide	Shoot	Tear
Complete	Flip	Let	Put	Shorten	Touch
Correct	Get	Light	Raise	Shovel	Try
Crease	Give	Make	Relate	Shut	Twist
Crush	Grind	Mend	Repair	Signify	Type
Develop	Guide	Miss	Repeat	Slide	Use
Distribute	Hand	Offer	Return	Slip	Vote
Do	Hang	Open	Ride	Spread	Watch
Drop	Hold	Pack	Rip	Stake	Weave
End	Hook	Pay	Save	Start	Work

Figure 6.1 Performance verbs for use in stating specific learning objectives.[4]

like, and *understand* (see box below). In the three examples given earlier, the behaviors (actually two for each objective) are "will identify and tell," "will read and maintain," and "will plot and list."

Verbs to Avoid When Writing Instructional Objectives

Appreciate	Familiarize	Learn
Believe	Grasp	Like
Comprehend	Indicate	Realize
Enjoy	Know	Understand

The third ingredient is the **conditions**—the C of the ABCDs—the setting in which the behavior will be demonstrated by the student and observed by the teacher. In the first sample objective, for students to be able to "correctly identify ten different musical instruments," the condition is "by listening to a tape recording of the Boston Pops Symphony Orchestra." And for "tell the class which instrument is playing," the conditions are "at different times, as specified by the teacher." In the second sample, for "the student will read . . .," the conditions are "at home, within a two-month period." In the third sample objective, the conditions are "using a sheet of graph paper."

The fourth ingredient, not always included in objectives written by teachers, is the **level (or degree) of expected performance**—the D of the ABCDs. This is the ingredient that allows for the assessment of student learning. When mastery learning (achievement of 85 to 100 percent) is expected, then in writing behavioral objectives the level of performance is usually omitted (as it is understood).[5]

Performance level is used to evaluate student achievement, and sometimes to evaluate the effectiveness of the teaching. Student grades may be based on performance levels; evaluation of teacher effectiveness may be based on the level of student performance. In the 1990s interest in **performance-based assessment** has been rekindled.

Now, in Exercise 6.1, try your skill at recognizing measurable objectives.

---

[5]In teaching for mastery learning, the performance-level expectation is 100 percent. In reality, however, the performance level will most likely be between 85 and 95 percent, particularly when one is working with a group of students, rather than with an individual student. The 5 to 15 percent difference allows for human error, as can occur with written and oral communication.

Exercise 6.1: A Self-Check on Recognizing Instructional Objectives That Are Measurable

Instructions: The purpose of this exercise is to check for your understanding and recognition of instructional objectives that are stated in measurable terms. Place an *X* before each of the following that is an overt, student-centered behavioral objective, that is, a learning objective that is clearly measurable. Although "audience," "conditions," or "performance levels" may be absent, ask yourself, "As stated, is this a student-centered and measurable objective?" If so, place an *X* in the blank. An answer key follows. After checking your answers, discuss any problems with your classmates and instructor.

_____ 1. To develop an appreciation for art.

_____ 2. To identify numbers that are whole numbers.

_____ 3. To provide meaningful experiences for the students.

_____ 4. To recognize nouns in sentences.

_____ 5. To boot up the program on the computer.

_____ 6. To write a summary of the factors that led to the Persian Gulf War.

_____ 7. To develop inquiry skills.

_____ 8. To prepare a critical comparison of any two religions.

_____ 9. To illustrate an awareness of the importance of the hole in the ozone layer by supplying relevant newspaper articles.

_____ 10. To know all the rules of grammar usage.

Answer Key to Exercise 6.1: 2, 4, 5, 6, 8, 9.

Items 1, 3, 7, and 10 of the exercise are inadequate because of their ambiguity. Item 3 is not even a student objective; it is a teacher goal. "To develop" and "to know" can have too many interpretations.

Although the conditions are not given, items 2, 4, 5, 6, and 8 are clearly measurable. The teacher would have no difficulty recognizing when a learner had reached those objectives. However, in item 9, which is in the affective domain (see Section D), the teacher can only trust (and assume) that student awareness *is* demonstrated when the student brings in the newspaper articles.

D. CLASSIFYING BEHAVIORAL OBJECTIVES

Useful for planning are three domains used to classify learning objectives:

• **Cognitive domain.** This is the domain of learning that involves mental operations ranging from the lowest level of simple recall of information to high-level and complex evaluative processes.
• **Psychomotor domain.** This is the domain of learning that involves functions ranging from the low-level, simple manipulation of materials, to the higher level of communication of ideas, and finally to the highest level of creative performance.
• **Affective domain.** This domain of learning involves feelings, attitudes, and values, from lower levels of acquisition to the highest level of internalization and action.

The Domains of Learning and the Needs of Children

Elementary schools attempt to provide learning experiences designed to meet the needs of the total child. Specifically, as presented in Chapter 2, five areas of developmental needs are identified: (1) intellectual, (2) physical, (3) psychological, (4) social, and (5) moral and ethical. As an elementary school teacher, you should include learning objectives that address these developmental needs. In the classification of learning objectives, while the intellectual is primarily within the cognitive domain, and the physical is within the psychomotor, the other needs (i.e., psychological, social, moral and ethical) are mostly within the affective.

Too frequently, a teacher may direct attention to the cognitive, assuming that the psychomotor and affective will take care of themselves. Effective teachers direct their planning and teaching so that students are guided from the lowest to the highest levels of operation within *each* of the three domains.

Following are three developmental hierarchies to guide your understanding, so that you can address each of the five areas of needs. Notice the illustrative verbs within each hierarchy of each domain. These verbs can help you fashion your behavioral objectives for the lesson plans you will soon be developing.

Cognitive Domain Hierarchies

In a taxonomy of objectives that is widely accepted, Bloom and his associates arranged cognitive objectives into classifications according to the complexity of the skills and abilities they embody.[6] The resulting taxonomy portrays a ladder ranging from the simplest to the most complex intellectual processes.[7] (Note: *Regardless of the domain and within each, prerequisite to a child's ability to function at one level of the hierarchy is his or her ability to function at the preceding level or levels. In other words, when a child is functioning at the third level of the cognitive domain, then that child is automatically also functioning at the first and second levels.*)

The six major categories (or levels) in Bloom's taxonomy of cognitive objectives are:

1. **Knowledge.** Recognizing and recalling information.
2. **Comprehension.** Understanding the meaning of information.
3. **Application.** Using information.
4. **Analysis.** Ability to dissect information into component parts and see relationships.
5. **Synthesis.** Putting components together to form new ideas.
6. **Evaluation.** Judging the worth of an idea, notion, theory, thesis, proposition, information, or opinion.

Although space does not allow elaboration here, Bloom's taxonomy includes various subcategories within each of these six major categories. It is less important for an objective to be absolutely classified than for you to be cognizant of hierarchies of levels of thinking and doing, and to understand the importance of attending to student intellectual behavior from lower to higher levels of operation in all three domains.

A discussion of each of Bloom's six categories follows.

---

[6]Benjamin S. Bloom, ed. *Taxonomy of Educational Objectives, Book I: Cognitive Domain* (White Plains, NY: Longman, 1984).

[7]Rather than an orderly progression from simple to complex mental operations, as illustrated by Bloom's taxonomy, other researchers prefer an identification of cognitive abilities that range from simple information storage and retrieval, through a higher level of discrimination and concept attainment, to the highest cognitive ability to recognize and solve problems, as organized by Robert M. Gagné, Leslie Briggs, and Walter Wager, *Principles of Instructional Design*, 3rd ed. (New York: Holt, Rinehart and Winston, 1988).

Knowledge

The basic element in Bloom's taxonomy concerns the acquisition of knowledge—that is, the ability to recognize and recall information. (As discussed later in Chapter 10, this is similar to the **input level** of thinking and questioning.) Although this is the lowest level of the six categories, the information to be learned may not itself be of a low level. In fact, the information may be of an extremely high level. Bloom includes at this level knowledge of principles, generalizations, theories, structures, and methodology, as well as knowledge of facts and ways of dealing with facts.

Action verbs appropriate for this category include *choose, complete, define, describe, identify, indicate, list, locate, match, name, outline, recall, recognize, select,* and *state.* (Note that some verbs may be appropriately used at more than one cognitive level.)

The following are examples of objectives at this cognitive level. Note especially the verb used in each example.

- From memory the student will recall the letters from the English alphabet that are vowels.
- The student will list the organelles found in animal cell cytoplasm.
- The student will identify the major parts of speech in the sentence.
- The student will name the positions of players on a baseball team.

Beyond the first category, knowledge, the remaining five categories of Bloom's taxonomy of the cognitive domain deal with the *use* of knowledge. They encompass the educational objectives aimed at developing cognitive skills and abilities, including comprehension, application, analysis, synthesis, and evaluation of knowledge.

Comprehension

Comprehension includes the ability to translate or explain knowledge, to interpret that knowledge, and to extrapolate from it to address new situations.

Action verbs appropriate for this category include *change, classify, convert, defend, describe, estimate, expand, explain, generalize, infer, interpret, paraphrase, predict, recognize, summarize,* and *translate.*

The following are examples of objectives in this category:

- From a sentence, the student will recognize the letters that are vowels in the English alphabet.
- The student will describe each of the organelles found in animal cell cytoplasm.
- The student will recognize the major parts of speech in the sentence.
- The student will recognize the positions of players on a baseball team.

Application

Once students understand information, they should be able to apply it. This is the category of operation above comprehension.

Action verbs include *apply, compute, demonstrate, develop, discover, modify, operate, participate, perform, plan, predict, relate, show,* and *use.*

The following are examples of objectives in this category:

- The student will use in a sentence a word that contains at least two vowels.
- The student will discover the organelles found in animal cell cytoplasm.
- The student will demonstrate in a complete sentence each of the major parts of speech.
- The student will relate how the positions of players on a baseball team depend on each other.

Analysis

This category includes objectives that require students to use the skills of analysis.

Action verbs appropriate for this category include *analyze, break down, categorize, classify, compare, contrast, debate, deduce, diagram, differentiate, discriminate, identify, illustrate, infer, outline, relate, separate,* and *subdivide.*

The following are examples of objectives in this category:

- In a list of words, the student will differentiate those that contain vowels from those that do not.
- The student will differentiate under the microscope the organelles found in animal cell cytoplasm.
- The student will analyze a paragraph for misuse of major parts of speech.
- The student will illustrate on the chalkboard the different positions of players on a baseball team.

Synthesis

This category includes objectives that involve such skills as designing a plan, proposing a set of operations, and deriving a series of abstract relations.

Action verbs appropriate for this category include *arrange, categorize, classify, combine, compile, constitute, create, design, develop, devise, document, explain, formulate, generate, modify, organize, originate, plan, produce, rearrange, reconstruct, revise, rewrite, summarize, synthesize, tell, transmit,* and *write.*

The following are examples of objectives in this category:

- The student will rearrange a list of words into several lists according to the vowels contained in each.
- The student will devise a classification scheme of the organelles found in animal cell cytoplasm according to their functions.
- The student will write a paragraph that correctly uses each of the major parts of speech.
- The student will illustrate on the chalkboard an offensive plan that uses the different positions of players on a baseball team.

Evaluation

The highest cognitive category of Bloom's taxonomy is evaluation. This includes offering opinions and making value judgments.

Action verbs appropriate for this category include *appraise, argue, assess, compare, conclude, consider, contrast, criticize, decide, discriminate, evaluate, explain, interpret, judge, justify, rank, rate, relate, standardize, support,* and *validate.*

The following are examples of objectives in this category:

- The student will listen to and evaluate other students' identification of vowels in sentences written on the board.
- While observing living animal cell cytoplasm under the microscope, the student will justify his or her interpretation that certain structures are specific organelles.
- The student will evaluate a paragraph written by another student for proper use of the major parts of speech.
- The student will interpret the reasons for an opposing team's offensive use of the different positions of players on a baseball team.

Now, in Exercise 6.2, try your skill in recognizing the level of objectives within the cognitive domain.

Exercise 6.2: A Self-Check on Classifying Cognitive Objectives

Instructions: The purpose of this exercise is to check your ability to recognize instructional objectives according to their classification within the cognitive domain. For each of the following cognitive objectives, identify by appropriate letter the *highest* level of operation that is called for: (K) knowledge; (C) comprehension; (AP) application; (AN) analysis; (S) synthesis; (E) evaluation. Check your answers with the answer key, and discuss the results with your classmates and instructor. Your understanding of the concept involved is more important than whether you score 100 percent against the answer key.

_____ 1. When given a poem, the student will recognize the style as being that of Shelly.

_____ 2. In a given list, the student will recognize those words that are misspelled.

_____ 3. The student will read the pattern instructions and select the correct amount of material necessary to make a hand puppet.

_____ 4. The student will create a verse using a four-line stanza.

_____ 5. The student will write a critical appraisal of an essay on civil rights.

_____ 6. The student will correctly identify by name the colors shown.

_____ 7. The student will detect faulty logic in campaign advertising.

_____ 8. Given the facts of the political and economic situation, the student will draw a reasonable hypothesis concerning the causes of the 1992 riots in Los Angeles.

_____ 9. The student will devise a method to prove a ray to be the bisector of an angle.

_____ 10. Given a list of five solids, five liquids, and five gases, the student will describe the physical and chemical properties of each.

Answer Key to Exercise 6.2: 1 = C; 2 = K; 3 = AP; 4 = S; 5 = E; 6 = K; 7 = E; 8 = AN; 9 = S; 10 = K.

Affective Domain Hierarchies

Krathwohl, Bloom, and Masia developed a useful taxonomy for the affective domain.[8] The following are their major levels (or categories), from least internalized to most internalized:

1. **Receiving.** Awareness of the affective stimulus and the beginning of favorable feelings toward it.
2. **Responding.** Taking an interest in the stimulus and viewing it favorably.
3. **Valuing.** Showing a tentative belief in the value of the affective stimulus and becoming committed to it.
4. **Organizing.** Organization of values into a system of dominant and supporting values.
5. **Internalization of values.** Beliefs and behavior are consistent, and become a way of life.

The following paragraphs describe more fully the types of objectives that fit these categories of the affective domain. Although there is considerable overlap from one category to another, they do give a basis by which to judge the quality of objectives and the nature of learning within this domain.

Receiving

At this level, which is the least internalized, the student exhibits willingness to give attention to particular phenomena or stimuli, and the teacher is able to arouse, sustain, and direct that attention.

Action verbs appropriate for this category include *ask, choose, describe, differentiate, distinguish, demonstrate, hold, identify, listen, locate, name, point to, recall, recognize, reply, select,* and *use.*

Examples of objectives in this category are:

• The student will pay close attention to the directions for enrichment activities.
• The student will listen attentively to the ideas of others.
• The student will demonstrate sensitivity to the concerns of others.

[8]David R. Krathwohl, Benjamin S. Bloom, and Bertram B. Masia, *Taxonomy of Educational Goals, Handbook II: Affective Domain* (New York: David McKay, 1964).

Responding

Students respond to the stimulus they have received. They may do so because of some external pressure, or they may do so voluntarily because they find it interesting or because responding gives them satisfaction.

Action verbs appropriate for this category include *answer, applaud, approve, assist, comply, command, cooperate, discuss, greet, help, label, perform, play, practice, present, read, recite, report, select, spend (leisure time in), tell,* and *write.*

Examples of objectives at this level are:

- The student will read for enrichment.
- The student will discuss what others have said.
- The student will cooperate with others during group activities.

Valuing

Objectives at the valuing level have to do with students' beliefs, attitudes, and appreciations. The simplest objectives concern a student's acceptance of beliefs and values. Higher objectives concern a student's learning to prefer certain values and finally becoming committed to them.

Action verbs appropriate for this level include *argue, assist, complete, describe, differentiate, explain, follow, form, initiate, invite, join, justify, propose, protest, read, report, select, share, study, support,* and *work.*

Examples of objectives in this category include:

- The student will protest against racial discrimination.
- The student will support actions against gender discrimination.
- The student will argue in favor of or against the pro-choice position.

Organizing

This fourth level in the affective domain concerns building a personal value system. At this level the student is conceptualizing values and arranging them in a system that recognizes priorities and the relative importance of various values encountered in life.

Action verbs appropriate for this level include *adhere, alter, arrange, balance, combine, compare, defend, define, discuss, explain, form, generalize, identify, integrate, modify, order, organize, prepare, relate,* and *synthesize.*

Examples of objectives at this level are:

- The student will form judgments concerning proper behavior in the classroom, school, and community.
- The student will form and adhere to a personal standard of work ethics.
- The student will defend the important values of his or her own culture.

Personal Value System

This is the highest level within the affective domain. At this level the student's behaviors are consistent with his or her beliefs.

Action verbs appropriate for this level include *act, behave, complete, display, influence, listen, modify, perform, practice, propose, qualify, question, revise, serve, solve, verify,* and *work.*

Examples of objectives appropriate for this level are:

- The student will behave according to a well-defined and ethical code of behavior.
- The student will practice accuracy in his or her verbal communication with others.
- The student will work independently and diligently.

Psychomotor Domain Hierarchies

Whereas identification and classification within the cognitive and affective domains are generally agreed upon, there is less agreement on classification within the psychomotor domain. Originally, the goal of this domain was simply that of developing and categorizing proficiency in skills, particularly those dealing with gross and fine muscle control. Today's classification of that domain, as presented here, follows that lead but includes at its highest level the most creative and inventive behaviors, thus coordinating skills and knowledge from all three domains. Consequently, the objectives are arranged in a hierarchy from simple gross locomotor control to the most creative and complex, requiring originality and fine locomotor control—for example, from simply threading a needle to designing and making a piece of clothing. Harrow has developed the following taxonomy of the psychomotor domain.[9] Included with it are sample objectives, as well as a list of possible action verbs for each level of the psychomotor domain. The levels are as follows:

1. **Movement.** This level involves gross motor coordination.

    Action verbs appropriate for this level include *adjust, carry, clean, grasp, jump, locate, obtain,* and *walk.*

    Sample objectives for this level:
    - The student will demonstrate jumping a rope ten times without missing.
    - The student will correctly grasp the driving club used in golf.
    - The student will correctly grasp and carry the microscope to the desk.
2. **Manipulating.** This level involves fine motor coordination.

    Action verbs appropriate for this level include *assemble, build, calibrate, connect, focus, play,* and *thread.*

    Sample objectives for this level:
    - The student will build and fly a kite.
    - The student will play the C-scale on the clarinet.
    - The student will focus the microscope correctly.
3. **Communicating.** This level involves the communication of ideas and feelings.

    Action verbs appropriate for this level include *analyze, ask, describe, draw, explain, write,* and *listen.*

[9]A. J. Harrow, *Taxonomy of the Psychomotor Domain* (New York: Longman, 1977).

Sample objectives for this level:
- The student will demonstrate active listening skills.
- The student will describe his or her own feelings about the use of animals for medical research.
- The student will accurately draw what is depicted while observing a slide through the microscope.

4. **Creating.** This is the highest level of this domain, and of all domains, and represents the student's coordination of thinking, learning, and behaving in all three domains.

Action verbs appropriate for this level include *choreograph, create, design, invent, perform,* and *write*.

Sample objectives for this level:
- The student will write and perform a musical composition.
- The student will choreograph and perform new dance patterns.
- From materials that have been discarded in the environment, the student will create an environment for an imaginary animal that he or she has created.

E. USING THE TAXONOMIES

Theoretically, as noted earlier, the taxonomies are constructed so that students achieve each lower level before being ready to move to the higher levels. But because categories overlap, this theory does not always hold in practice. The taxonomies are important in that they emphasize the various levels to which instruction must aspire. For learning to be worthwhile, you must formulate and teach to objectives at the higher levels of the taxonomies as well as at the lower ones. Student thinking and behaving must be moved from the lowest to the highest levels of operation.

In using the taxonomies, remember that the point is to formulate the best objectives for the job to be done. The taxonomies provide a mechanism for assuring that you do not spend a disproportionate amount of time on learning that is relatively trivial. Writing objectives is essential to the preparation of good items for the evaluation of student learning. As mentioned many times previously in this book, clearly communicating your behavioral expectations to students and then assessing student learning against those expectations makes teaching most efficient and effective.

F. CHARACTER EDUCATION

Related especially to the affective domain, although not exclusive of the cognitive and psychomotor domains,[10] is a resurgence in a national interest in the development of students' values, especially those of honesty, kindness, respect, and responsibility,

---

[10]For example, Wynne and Ryan state that "transmitting character, academics, and discipline—essentially, 'traditional' moral values—to pupils is a vital educational responsibility." Thus, if one agrees with that interpretation, then the teaching of moral values is the transmission of character, academics, and discipline and clearly implies learning that crosses the three domains of learning presented in this chapter. (Edward A. Wynne and Kevin Ryan, *Reclaiming Our Schools: A Handbook on Teaching Character, Academics, and Discipline* [New York: Macmillan, 1993], p. 3.)

a growing interest in what is called **character education.**[11] Whether defined as ethics, citizenship, moral values, or personal development, character education has long been part of public education in this country.[12] Today, stimulated by a perceived need to reduce student antisocial behaviors (such as drug abuse and violence) and to produce more respectful and responsible citizens, with a primary focus on the affective domain, many schools and districts are developing curricula in character education, with the ultimate goal of "developing mature adults capable of responsible citizenship and moral action."[13] Repeated in later chapters of this resource guide, some specific techniques are: sensitize students to value issues through role play and creative drama, have students take the opposite point of view in discussions, promote higher-order thinking about value issues through appropriate questioning techniques, arrange action-oriented projects that relate to curriculum themes, involve students in planning and organizing the projects, use parents and community members to assist in projects, highlight examples of class and individual cooperation in serving the school and community, and make student service projects visible in the school and community.[14]

Resources on Character Education

Resources on character education include:

Character Education Institute, 8918 Tesoro Drive, San Antonio, TX 78217 (800) 284-0499.
Developmental Studies Center, Child Development Project, 111 Deerwood Place, Suite 165, San Ramon, CA 94583 (415) 838-7633.
Ethics Resource Center, 1120 G Street NW, Suite 200, Washington, DC 20005 (202) 434-8465.
Jefferson Center for Character Education, 202 S. Lake Avenue, Suite 240, Pasadena, CA 91101 (818) 792-8130.
Josephson Institute of Ethics, 310 Washington Boulevard, Suite 104, Marina Del Rey, CA 90292 (310) 306-1868.

Now, with Exercise 6.3, assess your skill at recognizing objectives according to which domain they are in, and then with Exercise 6.4, at writing your own objectives.

---

[11]Mary Massey, "Interest in Character Education Seen Growing," *ASCD Update* 35(4):1, 4–5 (May 1993).
[12]Kenneth Burrett and Timothy Rusnak, *Integrated Character Education,* Fastback 351 (Bloomington, IN: Phi Delta Kappan Education Foundation, 1993), p. 10.
[13]Ibid., p. 15.
[14]Ibid., p. 29.

Exercise 6.3: A Self-Check on Recognizing Cognitive, Affective, and Psychomotor Objectives

Instructions: The purpose of this exercise is to check your ability to recognize instructional objectives according to domain-cognitive, affective, and psychomotor. Classify each of the following instructional objectives by writing in the blank space the appropriate letter according to its domain: (C) cognitive; (A) affective; (P) psychomotor. Check your answers with the key at the end; discuss the results with your classmates and instructor.

_____ 1. The student will continue shooting free throws until she can successfully complete 80 percent of the attempts.

_____   2. The student will identify on a map the Appalachian mountain range of the eastern United States.

_____   3. The student will summarize the historical development of the Democratic party of the United States.

_____   4. The student will demonstrate a continuing desire to learn more about using the classroom computer for word processing by volunteering to work at it during free time.

_____   5. The student will volunteer to tidy-up the storage room.

_____   6. After listening to several recordings, the student will identify the respective composers.

_____   7. The student will translate a favorite Laotian poem into English.

_____   8. The student will accurately calculate the length of the hypotenuse.

_____   9. The student will indicate an interest in the subject by voluntarily reading additional library books about earthquakes.

_____   10. The student will successfully stack five blocks.

Answer Key to Exercise 6.3: (C) = 2, 3, 6, 7, 8; (A) = 4, 5, 9; (P) = 1, 10.

Exercise 6.4: Preparing My Own Behavioral Objectives

Instructions: The purpose of this exeercise is to practice your skill in writing behavioral objectives. For a subject content area and grade level of your choice, prepare ten specific behavioral objectives. It is not necessary to include audience, conditions, or performance level unless requested by your course instructor. Exchange completed exercises with your classmates; discuss them and make changes where necessary.

Subject _____ Grade Level _____

1. Cognitive knowledge _____

   _____

   _____

   _____

   _____

   _____

2. Cognitive comprehension _____

   _____

   _____

   _____

   _____

   _____

3. Cognitive application _____

   _____

   _____

   _____

   _____

   _____

4. Cognitive analysis _____

   _____

   _____

   _____

   _____

5. Cognitive synthesis _____

   _____

   _____

   _____

6. Cognitive evaluation _____

7. Psychomotor (low level) _____

8. Psychomotor (high level) _____

9. Affective (low level) _____

10. Affective (highest level) _____

SUMMARY

Many teachers do not bother to write specific objectives for all the learning activities in their teaching plans. However, it is clear that when teachers do prepare specific objectives (by writing them themselves, or by borrowing them for other sources) and teach toward those objectives, student learning is better. Most school districts require teachers to use objectives that are specifically stated. There is no question that clearly written instructional objectives are worth the time they take, especially when the teacher teaches toward those objectives and evaluates students' progress and learning against them—that is called **performance-based teaching** and **criterion-referenced measurement.** It is not imperative that you write all the instructional objectives that you will need. As a matter of fact, they are usually readily available in textbooks and other curriculum documents.

It is expected that, as a teacher, you will plan well and specifically that which you intend your students to learn; to convey your expectations to your students; and to *assess their learning against that specificity.* However, there is a danger inherent in such performance-based teaching: because it tends toward high objectivity, it could become too objective, and this can have negative consequences. The danger is that if students are treated as objects, then the relationship between teacher and student becomes impersonal and counterproductive to real learning. Highly specific and impersonal teaching can be discouraging to serendipity, creativity, and the excitement for real discovery, to say nothing of its possible negative impact on the development of students' self-esteem.

Performance-based instruction (known also as **outcome-based** and as **competency-based** instruction) works well in teaching toward mastery of basic skills, but mastery learning is inclined to imply that there is some foreseeable end point to learning, an assumption that is obviously erroneous. With performance-based instruction, the source of student motivation tends to be mostly extrinsic. Teacher expectations, grades, society, and peer pressures are examples of extrinsic sources that drive student performance. The challenge, in becoming an effective teacher, is to use performance-based criteria, but simultaneously with a teaching style that encourages the development of intrinsic sources of student motivation and that allows for, provides for, and encourages coincidental learning—learning that goes beyond that considered to be predictable and immediately measurable, and that represents minimal expectations. Part III is designed to assist you in meeting that challenge.

With your topic outline and instructional objectives in hand, you are now ready for preparation of detailed instructional plans, discussed in the next two chapters.

QUESTIONS FOR CLASS DISCUSSION

1. Describe observable behaviors that would enable you to tell whether a child is learning to think critically.
2. In your own teaching, do you believe you will place more emphasis on any one domain? If so, which? Explain.
3. Is performance-based (competency-based) instruction of equal value at all grade levels and in all subject areas? Explain.

4. Some people argue that it is easier to write behavioral objectives for a lesson after the lesson has been taught. What is the significance of that idea?

5. Clearly distinguish between the following terms: behavioral objectives, course goals, instructional objectives, learning objectives, instructional aims, performance objectives, teacher goals, teacher intentions, and terminal objectives. Some of the terms are synonymous. Which?

6. Describe ways in which a teacher can encourage serendipitous (coincidental) learning. Should a teacher do that? Explain.

7. Explain the difference between competency-based instruction and mastery learning. Critically analyze the advantages and disadvantages of each.

8. A complete behavioral objective statement contains four parts. Identify each part.

9. Describe the relationship between goals and objectives.

10. Describe the relationship between scope and sequence, and between instructional goals and objectives.

11. Do you have questions about the content of this chapter? How might answers be found?

SUGGESTED READINGS FOR CHAPTER 6

Alvino, J., et al. "Building Better Thinkers." *Learning 90* 18(6):40–55 (February 1990).

Gronlund, N. E. *How to Write and Use Instructional Objectives.* 4th ed. New York: Macmillan, 1991.

Lickona, T., and Ryan, K., eds. *Character Development in Schools and Beyond.* Washington, DC: Council for Research in Values and Philosophy, 1992.

Martin, B. L., and Briggs, L. J. *The Affective and Cognitive Domains.* Englewood Cliffs, NJ: Educational Technology Publications, 1986.

Ryan, K., and Wynne, E. A. *Reclaiming Our Schools: A Handbook on Teaching Character, Academics and Discipline.* New York: Macmillan, 1993.

7

How Do I Prepare
an Instructional Plan?

The teacher's edition of the student textbook and other resource materials will expedite your planning but should not substitute for it. You must know how to create an effective instructional plan. Having prepared a topic content outline (Exercise 5.5) and related instructional objectives (Exercise 6.4), you have initiated the development of an instructional plan. Using that outline and those objectives, in this chapter you will develop a complete instructional plan.

A. INSTRUCTIONAL PLANNING: A SEVEN-STEP PROCESS

Some of the guidelines that follow have previously been addressed, but are included here so you will understand where they fit in the "seven-step" planning procedure.

Step 1. *Course, grade level, and school goals.* Consider and understand your curriculum goals and their relationship to the goals and mission of the school. Your course or class is not isolated, as if it were being taught on Mars, but is an integral part of the total school curriculum.

Step 2. *Expectations.* Consider topics, attitudes, and skills that you are "expected" to teach, such as those that may be found in the course of study (Chapter 5).

Step 3. *Academic year-long calendar plan.* You must consider where you want your students to "be" months from now. Working from your tentative topic outline, and with the school calendar in hand, begin by deciding how much class time should be devoted to each topic, penciling those times into the subject outline. For teachers of self-contained or block classes, this must be done for each subject taught.

Step 4. *Class schedule.* For upper grades and middle school, this schedule becomes a part of the course syllabus (see Section B) presented to students during the first week of school. However, the schedule must remain flexible to allow for the unexpected, such as a cancellation or interruption of a class meeting, or an unpredictable extended study of a particular topic.

Step 5. *Class meeting lessons.* Working from the calendar plan or the class schedule you are now ready to prepare lessons for each class meeting, keeping in mind the abilities and interests of your students while making decisions about appropriate strat-

To a great degree, student achievement in learning is determined by two factors: (1) How well children understand and follow procedures, and (2) the method of instruction. Both of these factors are under the control of the teacher and must be carefully planned.

egies and learning experiences (strategies are the focus of Part III of this text). Preparation of daily lessons takes considerable time and continues throughout the year as you prepare instructional notes, demonstrations, discussion topics questions, and classroom exercises; arrange for guest speakers, the use of audiovisual equipment and materials, and field trips; and assemble tools for assessment of student achievement in learning.

Moreover, because one class meeting is often determined by accomplishments of the preceding meeting, your lessons are never "carved in stone," but need your continuing revision and evaluation.

Step 6. *Instructional objectives.* With the finalized course or subject schedule, and as you prepare the daily lessons, you will complete your preparation of the instructional objectives (begun in Exercise 6.4). These instructional objectives are critical for the proper development of step 7.

Step 7. *Assessment.* The final step is to decide how assessment of student achievement is to be accomplished. Included in this component are your decisions about assignments, diagnostic tools such as tests, and the procedure by which grades will be determined (see Chapter 14).

These are the steps in planning through which you will be guided step-by-step toward the development of your first instructional plan. Let us first consider the nature of the course syllabus.

B. THE SYLLABUS

You probably know that a course syllabus is a written statement about the workings of a particular course. As a college or university student, you have seen a variety of syllabi written by professors with their own ideas about what general and specific logistic information is most important for students to know about a course.

Related to the development and use of a course syllabus are the following three issues: (1) *Why?* What value is it? What use can be made of it? What purpose does it fulfill? (2) *How?* How do I develop a course or class syllabus? When do I begin? Where do I start? (3) *What?* What information should a syllabus include? When should the syllabus be distributed to students? How rigidly should the syllabus be followed?

Reasons for a Syllabus

A syllabus is written information about a course or class that is presented to students (or in the case of pre-K through lower primary grades, to parents or guardians), usually on the first day or during the first week of school.

A syllabus should:

- Help students feel at ease by providing an understanding of what is expected of them.
- Help students organize, conceptualize, and synthesize their learning experiences.
- Establish a rapport between students, parents (or guardians), and the teacher.
- Eliminate misunderstandings and misconceptions about the nature of the class—its rules, expectations, requirements, and other policies.
- Provide students with a sense of connectedness (often by allowing students to work in cooperative groups and actually participate in fashioning the syllabus).
- Stand as documentation, as to what is taking place in the classroom, for those outside the classroom (i.e., parents or guardians, administrators, other teachers and students).
- Serve as a resource for members of a teaching team. Each team member should have a copy of every other member's syllabus.
- Serve as a plan to be followed by the teacher and the students.

Development of a Syllabus

Sometimes a syllabus is prepared by the classroom teacher long before the first class meeting. On the other hand, some teachers have found that it is better when students participate in the development of the syllabus, thereby having ownership and commitment to it.

The steps shown in Figure 7.1 are suggested as a cooperative learning experience in which students spend approximately 30 minutes during the first, or an early, class meeting brainstorming the content of their syllabus.

1. Sometime during the first few days of school, arrange students in heterogeneous groups (mixed abilities) of three to five members to brainstorm the development of their course or class syllabus.
2. Instruct each group to spend five minutes listing everything they can think of that they would like to know. Tell the class that each group must chose a group *recorder* to write its list of ideas on paper and, when directed to do so, transfer the list to the writing board, to a large sheet of paper (to be hung in the classroom for all to see), or to an overhead transparency (a transparency sheet and pen are made available to each group). Ask them to select a group *spokesperson* who will address the class, explaining the group's list. Each group could also appoint a *materials manager,* whose job it is to see that the group has the necessary materials (e.g., pen, paper, transparency, chalk) and a *leader,* whose job is to keep the group on task and to report to the teacher when each task is completed.
3. After five minutes, have the recorders prepare their lists. When using a transparency or large sheets of paper, the lists can be prepared simultaneously while recorders remain with their groups. If using the writing board, the recorders, one at a time, write their lists on areas of the board that you have designated.
4. Have the spokesperson of each group explain the group's list. As this is being done, you should make a master list. If transparencies or large sheets of paper are being used, rather than the writing board, you can ask for them as backup to your master list.
5. After all spokespersons have explained their lists, ask the class collectively for additional input: "Can anyone think of anything else that should be added?"
6. You now use the master list to design a course syllabus, being careful to address each question and to include any items of importance that students may have omitted. However, your guidance during the preceding five steps should assure that all bases have been covered.
7. At the next class meeting, give each student a copy of the final syllabus. Discuss its content. (Duplicate copies to distribute to colleagues on your teaching team, interested administrators, and to parents at back-to-school night.)

Figure 7.1 Steps for Involving Students in the Development of Their Course or Class Syllabus.

Content of a Course or Class Syllabus

A syllabus should be concise, matter-of-fact, uncomplicated, and brief—no more than two pages. It should include the following:

1. *Descriptive information about the course or class.* This includes the teacher's name, course title, grade level, class, beginning and ending times, and room number.
2. *Explanation of the importance of the course or class.* This information should describe the course or class, tell how students will profit from it, and, in the case of middle-level teaching, state whether the course is a required course, a part of an accelerated program, a core curriculum course, a co-curriculum course, an exploratory or elective, or designated in some other way.
3. *Materials required.* Explain what materials are needed, such as a textbook, notebook, portfolio, supplementary readings, safety goggles, and so on. Indicate which items are supplied by the school, which must be supplied by each child, and what materials must be brought to class each day.

4. *Statement of goals and objectives.* These can be general, with a few specifics included.
5. *Types of assignments that will be given.* These should be clearly explained in as much detail as possible this early in the course.
6. *Assessment criteria.* Explain the grading procedures. Will there be quizzes, tests, homework, projects, group work? What will be their formats, coverage, and their weights in the grading procedure?
7. *Special information specific to the class.* Will there be field trips? Special privileges? Class projects? Classroom behavior rules should be included here.

Proceed now to Exercises 7.1 and 7.2.

Exercise 7.1: Content of a Syllabus

Instructions: The purpose of this exercise is to provide practice in developing a syllabus for a particular class. From the following list of items that might appear in a syllabus, identify (by circling) all those you would include in your own syllabus and, for each, explain why (in space provided after each item). After doing that, share it with those of your classmates. After sharing, you might want to make revisions to your own.

Subject and/or grade level for which I am preparing this exercise _____

_____

For parents (and guardians) only or for both parents and children (state which) _____

_____

1. Name of teacher (my name) _____

2. Course title (and/or grade level) _____

3. Room number _____

4. Beginning and ending times _____

_____

5. Time when students will confer with teacher _____

_____

_____

6. Course or class description _____

_____

_____

7. Statement of philosophy or rationale (underline which) _____

_____

_____

_____

8. Instructional format (such as lecture-discussion, student-centered learning groups, laboratory-centered) _____

_____

_____

9. Absence policy _____

_____

10. Tardy policy _____

_____

_____

11. Classroom behavior rules _____

   _____

   _____

12. Goals _____

   _____

   _____

13. Objectives _____

   _____

   _____

   _____

14. Policy about plagiarism _____

   _____

   _____

15. Name of textbook and other supplementary materials _____

   _____

   _____

16. Policy about use and care of textbook and other reading materials _____

   _____

   _____

   _____

17. Materials that student is to supply _____

   _____

   _____

   _____

18. Assignments _____

   _____

   _____

   _____

19. Policy about homework assignments (due dates, format, late assignments, weights for
   grades) _____

   _____

   _____

   _____

   _____

20. Class relationship to advisor-advisee program, core, co-curricular, exploratories, or some other aspect of the school curriculum _____

_____

_____

_____

21. Grading procedure _____

_____

_____

_____

22. Study skills _____

_____

_____

_____

23. Themes to be studied _____

_____

_____

_____

24. Field trips and other special activities _____

_____

_____

_____

25. Group-work policies and types _____

_____

_____

_____

26. Other members of the teaching team and their roles _____

_____

_____

_____

27. Tentative daily schedule _____

_____

_____

_____

28. Other (specify) _____
_____
_____
_____
_____
_____

29. Other (specify) _____
_____
_____
_____
_____
_____
_____

30. Other (specify) _____
_____
_____
_____
_____
_____
_____

Exercise 7.2: Preparing a Syllabus: A Collaborative Thinking Task

Instructions: The purpose of this exercise is to prepare (in a group) a syllabus for a course, subject, or grade level that you intend to teach. Using your results from Exercise 7.1, working in groups of three to five members, develop one syllabus for a specific class or grade level that you and other members of your group may someday teach. Grouping can be determined by subject or area content specialties, by elementary grade level interest, or in whatever way is decided by your class. Each group is to produce one syllabus that represents its members' collaborative thinking, which should then be duplicated and shared with the entire class. State whether your syllabus is for distribution to parents and guardians only, or for both parents and students. Discuss within your group the pros and cons of having students contribute to their course syllabus (see Figure 7.1). Share the results of that discussion also with the entire class.

C. UNIT PLANNING

Organizing an entire year's content into units makes the teaching process more manageable than when no plan or only random choices are made by a teacher. Whether in a self-contained primary-level classroom or in a course taught in middle school, the content you intend to present to children must be organized and carefully planned well in advance. A **course** is a complete and planned sequence of instruction that presents a major division of subject matter or a discipline. The teaching (or instructional) **unit**[1] is a major subdivision of a course (for one course or self-contained classroom there are several or many units of instruction), and is comprised of instruction *planned* around a central theme, topic, issue, or problem.

The teaching unit, whether an interdisciplinary thematic unit or a stand-alone subject unit, is not unlike a chapter in a book, an act or scene in a play, or a phase of work in a project such as building a house. Breaking down information or actions into component parts and then grouping the related parts makes sense out of learning and doing. The unit gives a sense of cohesiveness and structure to student learning and avoids the piecemeal approach that might otherwise unfold. You can learn to articulate lessons within, between, and among unit plans and to focus on important elements while not ignoring tangential but significant information. Students remember "chunks" of information, especially when those chunks are related to specific units.

Procedure for Planning and Developing Any Unit of Instruction

There are several types of unit plans: a standard unit, a contract unit, a learning package or module unit, and an interdisciplinary thematic unit. Steps in planning and developing *any* type of instructional unit, however, are as follows:

Step 1. *Select a suitable topic or theme.* Themes or topics may already be laid out in your course of study or textbook, or have been agreed upon by the teaching team.

Step 2. *Select the goals of the unit.* The goals are written as an overview or rationale, covering what the unit is about and what the students are to learn. In planning the goals, you should:

a. Become as familiar as possible with the topic and materials used.
b. Consult curriculum documents, such as courses of study, state frameworks, and resource units for ideas.
c. Decide what the children should learn about the topic and how.
d. Write a rationale or overview, in which you summarize what you hope the students will learn about the topic.
e. Be sure your goals are congruent with those of the course or grade level.

Step 3. *Select suitable specific learning objectives.* In doing this, you should:

a. Include understandings, skills, attitudes, appreciations, and ideals.
b. Be specific, avoiding vagueness and generalizations.
c. Write the objectives in behavioral terms.
d. Be as certain as possible that the objectives will contribute to the major learning described in the overview.

---

[1]*Teaching unit* as opposed to a *resource unit*. A resource unit is a general plan for a unit or a particular topic, and is designed to be used as a basis for building a teaching unit. Resource units, often found in curriculum centers and curriculum libraries, although often rich in resources, are not composed of sequentially planned lessons, as are teaching units.

Step 4. *Detail the instructional procedures.* These procedures include the subject content and the learning activities, established as a series of lessons. Proceed with the following steps in your initial planning of the instructional procedures:

a. Gather ideas for learning activities that might be suitable for the unit. Refer to curriculum documents and other teachers as resources.
b. Check the learning activities to make sure that they will actually contribute to the learning designated in your objectives, discarding those that do not.
c. Make sure that the learning activities are feasible. Can you afford the time, effort, or expense? Do you have the necessary materials and equipment? If not, can they be obtained? Are the activities suited to the maturity level of your students?
d. Check resources available to be certain they support the content and learning activities.
e. Decide how to introduce the unit. Provide **introductory activities** that:
   1. Arouse student interest.
   2. Inform students of what the unit is about.
   3. Help you learn about your students—their interests, abilities, experiences, and present knowledge of the topic.
   4. Provide transitions that connect this topic to things the children have already learned.
   5. Involve the students in the planning.
f. Plan **developmental activities** that:
   1. Sustain student interest.
   2. Provide for individual student differences.
   3. Promote the learning as cited in the specific objectives.
g. Plan **culminating activities** that:
   1. Summarize what has been learned.
   2. Bring together loose ends.
   3. Apply what has been learned to new and meaningful situations.
   4. Provide transition to the unit that follows.

Step 5. *Plan for assessment of student learning.* Evaluating student progress (**formative evaluation**) should permeate the entire unit. Plan to gather information in several ways, including informal observations, observation of student performance, and paper and pencil evaluations. It is the specific learning objectives that must be evaluated.

Step 6. *Provide for the materials of instruction.* The unit cannot function without materials. Long before the unit begins you must plan for audiovisual equipment and materials, references, reading materials, reproduced materials, and community resources. For example, assigned reading material that is not available to the students is not much help to them.

These six steps should be followed in developing any type of unit.

Preparing a Standard Teaching Unit

In addition to the preceding six steps to be followed in developing a teaching unit, there are two general points of importance:

1. There is no single format for a teaching unit that works best for all grades and all subjects. Particular formats may be best for specific disciplines or topics or grade levels. During your student teaching your college or university program for teacher preparation will probably have a form that you will be expected to follow. Regardless of specific format, the unit plan should include the seven items outlined in Exercise 7.4.

When planning, it is important to select content that lends itself to manageable learning activities. An activity-based program of study benefits all children.

2. There is no set time duration for a unit plan, although for specific units curriculum guides will indicate suggested time durations. Units may extend for a minimum of several days or, as in the case of interdisciplinary thematic units, for several weeks. The exact time duration will depend on the topic or theme, the grade level, and the interests and abilities of the students. As a very general rule, teaching units tend to lose their effectiveness as recognizable units of learning when they last much longer than three weeks. For Exercise 7.4 it is recommended that your unit plan be written for a two-week duration; that is, it should include lessons for ten consecutive school days.

Sample Unit Plan with Daily Lessons

The following is a sample unit plan with daily lessons, which can be adjusted for use for specific grade levels. As you read through this sample unit you will notice the use of an abbreviated format for presenting the eleven daily lessons, but with an extended narrative presentation of how the teacher might actually conduct each lesson. Notice also how the students' reading responses are varied from day to day throughout the unit. At the end of the unit are suggestions for unit extension and additional resources. These can provide ideas for daily variation to meet individual student needs, as well as assist you in the preparation of a similar unit. Your course instructor may provide additional samples of unit and lesson plans. After reviewing this sample, do Exercises 7.3 and 7.4.

SAMPLE UNIT PLAN

Grade _____   **Topic** *Early English Settlers in North America*

Teacher _____   **Duration** *10–11 days*

Introduction to Unit

This unit can be an adventurous one. It is a multidisciplinary unit and can readily be developed into an interdisciplinary thematic unit for use by a teaching team at any grade level. As presented here, it is designed for a fifth-grade class. Specifically addressed by this unit are the students'

1. Learning about early English settlers in North America.
2. Developing skills in reading.
3. Developing skills in studying.
4. Developing skills in thinking.

These are assessed during and at completion of this unit by use of a behavioral checklist.

This unit can present sailing ships, English and Spanish sea battles, golden treasures, hearty seadogs (captains), brave women and men, stockades at riverbank settlements, and trading with the Indians for food. Bulletin boards should be designed to interest students in this exciting part of North America's history. They could feature colorful illustrations of early explorers, captured treasure from Spanish ships, maps showing routes of explorations, pictures of early settlements and their leaders, and selected focus questions to develop students' understanding of the early settlers' adjustments to their new environment.

Goals of the Unit

This unit is part of the social studies program about the development of the United States of America. Through selected learning materials, students will develop a better comprehension of the United States as they study about people with different backgrounds, different ideas, and different ways of life. In this unit the students become acquainted with the study of the early settlement of the colonies, the people who lived there, and some of the reasons that they came to North America from England. As students learn about this historical period of United States history, with the teacher's guidance, they should compare that time with present-day events, thereby developing new insights about life in the United States today.

Day 1

Objective: Given assigned reading and student discussion about how English activity first began in North America, students will identify some of the explorers who first traveled from England to North America, their reasons for exploring, and some of their initial contributions to the development of the colonies.

Materials to begin unit: An attractive bulletin board is arranged to display pictures of early English explorers with a caption such as "Why Did Settlers and Explorers Travel to North America?" Illustrations for display might include John Cabot (Italian sea captain of the *Matthew* who sailed for North America from Bristol, England, in 1497), Sir Francis Drake (first English person to sail around the world), Sir Humphrey Gilbert (who attempted to begin a colony in Newfoundland), and Sir Walter Raleigh (who started a colony on Roanoke Island). Nearby on a learning resource table are books to accommodate a variety of reading interests and levels, maps, and supplementary materials that include information about the early settling of the colonies. In the front of the classroom there is a world globe and a large pull-down map that can be marked with chalk.

Activities: Discussing and locating information.

The teacher begins (anticipatory set; transition from previous unit of study): "Yesterday some of you mentioned reasons that the leaders of France sent explorers to North America. What were some of the reasons you mentioned? (Discussion.) "The leaders of another country, England, also had reasons for sending explorers to North America. As we read about the early English explorers, we'll be introduced to some new words." (Teacher turns to chart and draws attention to terms under pictures illustrating the meaning of each term.)

Vocabulary (Chart 1)

Newfoundland	colony
Nova Scotia	settlement
treasure	colonist
seadog	stockade

The teacher continues: "Let's turn to the table of contents to find the chapter we need, the one entitled 'Early English in North America.' Let's skim the contents to find the page information it contains about the chapter we need." (The teacher turns again to the chart stand and displays a second chart with the headline "WE READ AT DIFFERENT SPEEDS.")

We Read at Different Speeds (Chart 2)

When we want to find out if a page or book has
information we can use, WE READ RAPIDLY.
When we want to find an answer to a question,
We Read at a Moderate Speed.
When we are studying to understand information,
We Read Slowly.

The teacher questions: "When we want to find out whether the table of contents has information we can use, what is our reading speed?" (Students respond; the chapter page number is identified; and the students locate the beginning of the chapter in their textbooks.) "Let's read silently for the first three paragraphs on page _____ to find out the name of one of England's first explorers and his reason for exploring near North America. Since we will be studying to understand information, what reading speed should we use?" (Students respond.) After the silent reading, a discussion about John Cabot begins. "In reading these paragraphs, we've seen that John Cabot wanted to find a short, northern, all-water route to Asia." (One student is asked to trace the route with a chalk mark on the globe. Another is asked to identify Cabot's reason for exploration. Still another is asked to record Cabot's reason on a strip of construction paper and to attach the strip under the illustration of Cabot on the classroom bulletin board.) Giving reasons for silent and oral reading, the teacher guides additional reading about other early English explorers. To emphasize the importance of the students' reading slowly when they are studying for information, the teacher again turns to the chart stand and reviews these study skills from a third chart, entitled "WHEN WE STUDY TO UNDERSTAND INFORMATION."

When We Study to Understand Information (Chart 3)

We concentrate.
We have a question in mind.
We look at the pictures and read captioned information.
We read maps, charts, tables, and graphs.
We discuss and review what we have learned.

The teacher brings closure to this day's lesson and unit introduction, encouraging student thinking by asking higher-order questions: "Having completed our reading today about some of the early English explorers, you know some interesting information about them. Why do you think John Cabot wanted to travel a northern route across the Atlantic Ocean? What might have changed if Cabot had found a short, all-water route to Asia? What can we say about Raleigh and how he tried to help the English acquire land in North America? What might have changed if these early attempts to start colonies had been successful?"

Day 2

Objective: Given a class discussion about early English explorers, the students will identify reasons these explorers traveled to North America and will evaluate the success or lack of success of the explorers in starting colonies.

Activities: Discussing, defining, and evaluating.

The teacher provides a transition review statement: "Yesterday we were talking about early English explorers, and I want to pick up where we left off. Remember that we said several English explorers came to North America during the 1400s and 1500s. Let's name some of these explorers again." (Student responses.) "Fine, you remembered some of the people we talked about yesterday. Now let's use these explorers as examples of reasons that people travel and explore." (Connecting with what students already know.) "What can we say are reasons these explorers traveled to North America?" (Student discussion.) "Good thinking. Now, let's move away from this topic for a minute. Gretchen, you mentioned that Sir Francis Drake was a seadog. How does your textbook define *seadog*?" (Gretchen responds with definition.) "We can always define a term by reading a definition from a dictionary, a glossary, or a textbook. But there are other ways of defining a term. We can define a word or term by demonstrating something about it. Who will define a *seadog* by demonstrating something?" (Student response.) "We can also define by describing. Who can define *seadog* by describing something about the term?" (Student response.) "And then, we can define by displaying an illustration. Who will find a picture to help us define *seadog*?" (Student response.)

"Good. We have several definitions of *seadog*. Now, let's return to our main topic for today. We were talking about the reasons that early explorers came to North America. Considering their reasons and the rest of our reading about the explorers, would you say the early explorers were successful or unsuccessful in starting colonies in North America?" (Discussion continues as students respond and are asked to clarify and to support their opinions with evidence. The lesson is ended with a summary closure.)

Day 3

Objective: Given selected reading and a class discussion, the students will give the name of the first permanent settlement, identify the settlers' reasons for traveling to North America, and record some of the problems the settlers encountered.

Activities: Discussing, classifying, categorizing, and evaluating.

The teacher begins with a review transition: "In contrast to the unsuccessful attempts we talked about yesterday, there were some early English settlements that were successful. We want to discover the name of the first permanent settlement, the reason or reasons the settlers traveled to North America, and some of the problems they encountered." (Student reading and discussion.) The teacher records students' contributions of settlers' problems on the writing board. Then the teacher and the students review the list and group similar problems together under student-selected headings, such as "Shelter problems," "Food problems," and so on. The teacher then asks the students to evaluate the problems by ranking them in order, with the greatest hardship as number one and so on. Students are asked to justify their choices for these rankings. When the rank ordering and the discussion of the rank ordering is completed, the lesson is closed with an introduction to tomorrow's study of the settlement at Plymouth.

Day 4

Objective: Given an audio-filmstrip cassette presentation entitled "Thanksgiving Day" (produced by Westport Communication Group, No. 394-062264, and available from Random House School Division), the students will become familiar with the Pilgrims' settlement at Plymouth, their reason for settling, and the problems they encountered.

Activities: Gathering information.

After viewing and listening to "Thanksgiving Day," the students turn to the activity page at the end of the chapter and identify all of the questions they can respond to after gaining information from the filmstrip. If there is a textbook question for which they have no information, the text will be used as a reference source from which to locate the required information. Focus questions for review are "What do we know about the Pilgrims' settlement at Plymouth?" "What was their main reason for traveling to North America?" "What were some of the problems they encountered?" and "How do those problems compare with our lists from yesterday?"

Day 5

Objective: Given information about dissatisfaction in the colonies, the students will recognize how additional English colonies developed.

Activities: Cooperative learning groups.

As an opening to this lesson, the teacher says, "Yesterday some of you mentioned religious freedom as a reason that the English started colonies along the eastern coast of North America. After the colonies began, some of the people in the colonies became dissatisfied with their way of life. For today, Anthony's group will find out why one person, Roger Williams, was unhappy with his life-style and left the colony of Massachusetts. Anne Hutchinson was also dissatisfied with the leaders of the Massachusetts Bay Colony. Robyn's group will discover Hutchinson's reason for leaving the colony. Now, during the period of dissatisfaction, additional settlers came to North America. Merribeth's group will investigate who settled in New Amsterdam, the land now known as New York City." (Students form cooperative learning groups, select group leaders, managers, recorders, and so on, and make their assignments to collect the needed information for reports to the entire class.) This work continues for days 6 and 7, if needed.

Days 6 and 7 (as needed)

Cooperative learning group work continues.

Day 8

Objective: Given the group assignments, the students will become familiar with the beginnings of selected colonies.

Activities: Organizing and summarizing.

The groups report to the entire class. The teacher helps to summarize: "This week we've been discussing early English settlers. Now I want to find how we can pull our reports together. Using the information you have from the groups' reports, from the filmstrip, and from our readings and discussion, I would like you now to identify the colony with which a selected settler or group is associated and to identify the main reason the settler (or group) traveled to North America."

A worksheet to help them organize and summarize information about early settlers is distributed to the students for completion.

Can you organize and summarize? (a worksheet)

Scan your reading material, review your notes about the filmstrip entitled "Thanksgiving Day," and recall what you learned from the group reports to organize the material on this worksheet. Write the missing information in the blanks provided.

Date	Settler	Colony	Reason for Settling
1583	Sir Humphrey Gilbert	_____	_____
1585	Sir Walter Raleigh	_____	_____
1607	John Smith	_____	_____
1620	Pilgrims	_____	_____
1630	Puritans	_____	_____
1681	William Penn	_____	_____
1733	James Oglethorpe	_____	_____

To help you summarize, consider the following: Give a reason that the colonies of Rhode Island, Connecticut, and New Hampshire were started. Were the Middle colonies started for the same reason? Different reasons? How were the Southern colonies started? What is the main idea or statement you can make from this information?

_____

_____

_____

_____

Day 9

Objective: Given a map skills worksheet, the students will demonstrate their skills in locating places, determining distance, identifying latitude, and reading map symbols and color codes.

Activities: Map skills.

To introduce the lesson, the teacher says, "Yesterday you summarized the main idea you developed after organizing the information about the different reasons the colonies were started." (Take time to review those summaries.) "Today we want to gather additional information about the colonies from reading our maps correctly. We will locate some major places. We will use our rulers to measure selected distances. We'll review map symbols to locate latitude lines and match a color code to locate specific colonies." To review these map skills, the teacher distributes a worksheet similar to the one that follows. While students individually work on their map skills, the teacher roams the room and guides students who need assistance.

Map Skills (A Worksheet—Individual Student Activity)

Map I

   Find the map on page _____ of your text. Complete the following items:

1. Locate the English colony on Roanoke Island. Write the name of the ocean that surrounds the

   island. _____

2. Calculate the miles to inch with your ruler and measure the distance from the colony on Roanoke

   Island across the ocean to Raleigh Bay. _____

Map II

   Find the map on page _____ of your text. Complete the following items:

3. Locate the colony on Roanoke Island. Between which two lines of latitude was this colony located?

   _____ and _____

4. Study your map symbols to find out which group had the rights to the land where this colony

   started. _____

Map III

   Find the map on page _____ of your text. Complete the following items:

5. Review the color code on the map and write the names of the colonies that were known as the New

   England colonies.

   _____ _____ _____ _____

6. Which colonies were known as the Middle colonies?

   _____ _____ _____

7. Which colonies were known as the Southern colonies?

_____   _____   _____   _____

CONGRATULATIONS! You have completed your map skills work for today. Now it is time to talk about what you learned.

Day 10

Objective: Given a quiz show format, the students will describe an activity in a colony, identify the name of a settlement leader, and give a reason that this colony's settlers traveled to North America.

Activities: Concluding.

The students, with the teacher's guidance, will use their notes from the worksheet entitled "Can You Organize and Summarize?" to provide information for a quiz show about the early English settlers. One student describes an activity or gives other clues about a particular colony. A second student tries to identify the prominent leader of the colony. A third student identifies the main reason for the settlers of that colony traveling to North America. Points may be awarded for appropriate responses. Highest number of points determines the winner of the quiz review.

Day 11

Objective: Given a worksheet on which names of prominent colony leaders and descriptions of colony activities are mismatched, the students will match leaders with descriptions and then identify each leader with a reason for settling in North America.

Activities: Evaluating.

The students receive a worksheet on which the names of colony leaders and descriptions of certain colony activities are mismatched. The students are asked to match the leaders with the descriptions. After the matching, the students will identify each leader with a reason for settling in North America.

Unit Extension and Resource Ideas

Reading Assignments (including provisions for individual differences)

Gifted students: extensive reading from a unit bibliography that leads to class reports, independent inquiry, and biographical research about the following:

Sir George Carteret
Pocahontas
Squanto
Peter Stuyvesant
John Winthrop

Regular education students: reading from text and selected trade books to respond to questions in the unit study guide.

Less able students: reading from easy-to-read books, viewing filmstrips, working with peers in cooperating learning groups, accomplishing short assignments.

Language minority students: reading from bilingual materials as needed; emphasis on bicultural materials.

Blind and visually impaired students: brailled materials, talking books, raised relief maps, projection magnifiers and large-type printed materials.

Deaf and hearing impaired students: assistance from interpreter as needed; use of visuals and overhead projector to write questions and responses.

Physically impaired students: a buddy system to assist in use of reference materials and other equipment and resources.

Teaching Resources

BOOKS

Harness, C. *Three Young Pilgrims.* New York: Bradbury Press, 1992. (primary grades)

Hays, Wilma Pitchford. *Christmas on the Mayflower.* Illustrated by Roger Duvoisin. New York: Coward-McCann, 1965. (primary grades)

———. *Pilgrim Thanksgiving.* Illustrated by Leonard Weisgard. New York: Coward-McCann, 1965. (primary grades)

Knight, James E. *Blue Feather's Vision, the Dawn of Colonial America.* Mahwah, NJ: Troll Associates, 1982. (grades 4–6)

Lenski, Lois. *Puritan Adventure.* Illustrated by the author. New York: Lippincott, 1944. (middle grades)

Lobel, Arnold. *On the Day Peter Stuyvesant Sailed into Town.* Illustrated by the author. New York: Harper, 1971. (middle and upper grades)

Luhrmann, Winifred Bruce. *Only Brave Tomorrows.* Boston: Houghton Mifflin, 1989. (grades 4–8)

Meadowcroft, Enid. *The First Year.* Illustrated by Grace Paull. New York: Crowell, 1946 (primary grades)

Monjo, F. *The Secret of Sachem's Tree.* Illustrated by Margot Tomes. New York: Dell, 1973. (grades 2–4)

Penner, Lucille Recht. *Eating the Plates: A Pilgrim Book of Food and Manners.* Illustrated. New York: Macmillan, 1991. (grades 1–4)

Petry, Ann. *Tituba of Salem Village.* New York: HarperCollins, 1991. (upper grades)

Pilkington, Roger. *I Sailed on the Mayflower: The True Story of a Pilgrim Youngster.* Illustrated by Douglas Bisset. New York: Vintage, 1990. (middle grades)

San Souci, Robert. *N. C. Wyeth's Pilgrims.* Illustrated. San Francisco: Chronicle Books, 1990. (grades 3 and up)

Spear, Elizabeth George. *The Witch of Blackbird Pond.* New York: Dell, 1978. (upper grades)

Spier, Peter. *The Legend of New Amsterdam.* New York: Doubleday, 1979. (grades 2–4)

Waters, Kate. *Sarah Morton's Day: A Day in the Life of a Pilgrim Girl.* Illustrated by Russ Kendall. New York: Scholastic, 1989. (all grades)

FILMS AND FILMSTRIPS

Random House School Division, Department 9036, 400 Hahn Road, Westminister, MD 21157
  Obadiah the Bold by Brinton Turkle (primary grades)
  Thanksgiving Day, produced by Westport Communications Group (middle grades)
  Thuy Friend, Obadiah by Brinton Turkle (primary grades)

ORGANIZATIONS FOR STUDENTS WITH SPECIAL NEEDS

American Foundation for the Blind, Consumer Products Department, 15 West 16th Street, New York, NY 10011 (products, reports, films, and publications).

C.C. Publications, Inc., P.O. Box 23699, Tigard, OR 97223 (materials for learning disabled and educable mentally retarded persons).

Gryphon House, 3706 Otis House, P.O. Box 217, Mount Rainier, MD 20822 (multiethnic books).

National Clearinghouse for Bilingual Education, 1300 Wilson Boulevard, Suite B2-11, Rosslyn, VA 22209 (materials for teachers of bilingual students).

National Library Service for the Blind and Physically Handicapped, Library of Congress, Washington, DC 20542 (free reading program for persons who are blind or physically disabled that includes brailled materials).

Telesensory Systems, Inc., 3408 Hillview Avenue, P.O. Box 10099, Palo Alto, CA 94304 (equipment for disabled students).

SUPPLIERS OF READING AIDS FOR THE SPECIAL STUDENT

Magnifiers Best Visual Products Ltd., 65 Earle Avenue, Lynbrook, NY 11563.

Print to braille Curzweil Computer Products, Inc., 185 Albany Street, Cambridge, MA 02139.

Talking books
  Books on Tape, Inc., P.O. Box 7900, Newport Beach, CA 92660.
  Hendershot Individualized Instruction, 4114 Ridgewood, Bay City, MI 48706.
  Lexicon, Inc., 60 Turner St., Waltham, MA 20154.

Cassettes
  Cassette House, Inc., 530 W. Northwest Highway, Mount Prospect, IL 60056.
  Listen for Pleasure, Ltd., 417 Center Street, Lewistown, NY 14092.

Live Oak Media, P.O. Box 34, Ancramdale, NY 12503.

Mind's Eye, 4 Commercial Boulevard, Novato, CA 94947.

Recorded books

Listening Library Inc., 1 Park Avenue, Greenwich, CT 06970.

Recorded Books, P.O. Box 79, Charlotte Hall, MD 20622.

Spoken Arts, Inc., 310 North Avenue, New Rochelle, NY 10801.

Supplies: Selected sources

Alabama: Walker Restaurant and School Supply Company, 2112 University Boulevard East, Tuscaloosa, AL 35404.

Arizona: Western School Supply, 3154 N. 34th Drive, Phoenix, AZ 85017.

California: A+ Educational Supplies, 709 Jackson Street, Fairfield, CA 94533.

Bennetts Educational Materials, 4572 Telephone Road, Ventura, CA 93003.

Educational Supplies Plus, 248 Third Avenue, Chula Vista, CA 92010.

Oakland Parent Teacher Store, 3721 Macarthur Boulevard, Oakland, CA 94619.

Teachers Supplies, 6561-6571 Beach Boulevard, Buena Park, CA 90621.

The Learning Stop, 3220 New Stine Road, Bakersfield, CA 93309.

Colorado: Colburn's School Supply, P.O. Box 9348, Denver, CO 80209-0348.

Connecticut: Teacher-Parent Store, 181 Main Street, Danbury, CT 06810.

Florida: ACE Educational Supplies, 1255 S. State Road 7, Plantation, FL 33317.

All Florida School Supply Company, 939 University Boulevard N., Jacksonville, FL 32216.

Central Florida School Supply Inc., 1331 W. Church Street, Orlando, FL 32805.

Willis School Supply, 4101 N.W. 6th Terrace Street, Gainesville, FL 32601.

Georgia: ABC School Supply, 3312 N. Berkeley Lake Road, Duluth, GA 30136-9419.

Gwinett School Supplies Inc., 2429-B E. Main Street, Snellville, GA 30278.

School Days Supply Center, 3141 Washington Boulevard, Augusta, GA 30907.

Iowa: Metropolitan Supply Company, 602-616 Third Street SE, Cedar Falls, IA 52406.

Illinois: Swenson Scholastic Supply, 5138 W. Greenwood, Skokie, IL 60077.

Indiana: Hoosier School Supply, 929 East 23rd Street, Indianapolis, IN 46205.

School Stuff, 2321 Wicker Avenue, Schererville, IN 46375.

The Teacher's Aid, Inc., 223 N. Green River Road, Evansville, IN 47715.

Kansas: School Specialty Supply Inc., 3525 South Ninth, Salina, KS 67402.

Superior School Supply Center, 241 North Hydraulic, Wichita, KS 67214.

Kentucky: Central School Supply Company, 4100 Eastmoor Drive, Louisville, KY 40232.

Southern School Supply Company, 949 Pedigo Way, Bowling Green, KY 42101.

Louisiana: Louisiana Teachers Supply Inc., 101 N. 4th Street, West Monroe, LA 71291.

Massachusetts: New England School Supply, 609 Silver Street, Agawam, MA 01001.

Teaching Tools Inc., 321 Walnut Street, Newtonville, MA 02160.

Maryland: School and Pre-School, 5501 Edmondson Avenue, Baltimore, MD 21229.

Maine: Rhyme and Reason, 155 Center Street, Auburn, ME 04210.

Michigan: Teacher's Central/Learning Depot, 125 Dalla, Kalamazoo, MI 49002.

Minnesota: Triarco Arts and Crafts, 14650 28th Avenue North, Plymouth, MN 55441.

Missouri: Bradburn School Supply Inc., 2166 Hampton, St. Louis, MO 63139.

IPA Educational Supply, 2258 South Campbell, Springfield, MO 65807.

Montana: Colborn School Supply Co., 2702 Montana Avenue, Billings, MT 59103.

Northern School Supply Co., P.O. Box 431, Great Falls, MT 59401.

North Carolina: Bender-Burkot School Supply Inc., Route 17 North, Pollocksville, NC 28573.

Morgan Brothers School Supply Inc., P.O. Box 2279, Asheville, NC 28802.

North Dakota: Northern School Supply Company, 17 N. 8th Street, Box 2627, Fargo, ND 58102.

New Hampshire: The Teach and Learn Shop, 474 S. Main Street, Manchester, NH 03102.

New Jersey: The Teaching Room, 148 South Street, Morristown, NJ 07960.

New Mexico: Allied School and Office Products, 4900 Menaul Boulevard, Albuquerque, NM 87125.

Nevada: Learning Is Fun, 290 S. Decatur Boulevard, Las Vegas, NV 89107.

New York: Bardeens School Supply Inc., Fisher Road, East Syracuse, NY 13057.

Finger Lakes School Supply, 808 Mitchell Street, Ithaca, NY 14850.

Paul's Teacher Pet, Transitown Plaza, Buffalo, NY 14221.

Ohio: J R Holcomb and Co., P.O. Box 94636, Cleveland, OH 44101.

Oklahoma: The Apple Tree, 7204 E. 41st, Tulsa, OK 74145.

Oregon: Western School Supply, 5800 N.E. Hassalo Street, Portland, OR 97213.

Pennsylvania: Classroom Connection, 200 Howard Street, Montoursville, PA 17754.
    School Store, 3650 Nazareth Pike, Bethlehem, PA 18017.

South Carolina: Anderson Educational Center, 2718 North Main Street, Anderson, SC 29621.
    The Learning Center, 67 S. Windermere Center, Charleston, SC 29407.

South Dakota: Teachers Helper, 221 Petro Avenue, Sioux Falls, SD 57107.

Tennessee: P & S Paper & School Supply Co., 146 N. Peters Road, Knoxville, TN 37980.

Texas: Diamond School Supply, 901 E. Plano Parkway, Suite 101, Plano, TX 75074.
    Educational Products Inc., 11425 Mathis, Suite 402, Dallas, TX 75234.
    Southwest Teacher Supply, 7497 Southwest Freeway, Houston, TX 77074.

Utah: Utah-Idaho School Supply, 6550 South State Street, Murray, UT 84107.

Virginia: Teachers' Edition, 1723 Concord Drive, Charlottesville, VA 22901.

Vermont: M.D.P. School Supply, 21 Essex Way, Essex Junction, VT 05452-3385.

Washington: Learning World, Inc., 500 Westlake Avenue North, Seattle, WA 98109.
    School Daze, 400 Cooper Point Road, Olympia, WA 98502.

Wisconsin: Madison School Supply, 2219 Atwood Avenue, Madison, WI 53704.

West Virginia: Latta's, P.O. Box 2668, Huntington, WV 25726.

Wyoming: Baily School Supply Inc., 520 South Walnut, Casper, WY 82601.

ASSESSMENT STRATEGIES FOR UNIT

Checklist for assessment

A unit checklist can be developed from information gained from the unit. It can be a record of a student's participation, skills, and knowledge. If a checklist is used from unit to unit, the teacher may observe different behaviors and skills contributed by a student and will have a record of each student's individual differences.

Unit checklist: Date _____ Student _____

Objectives	*Achieved*
1. Identifies explorers, reasons for exploration, and initial contributions to colony development.	_____
2. Identifies settlements and problems.	_____
3. Recognizes how early English colonies developed.	_____
4. Develops skills:	
Discussing	_____
Locating information	_____
Reading at different speeds	_____
Studying	_____
Evaluating	_____
Making decisions and justifying choices	_____
Independent work	_____
Group work	_____

Classifying and categorizing   _____

Gathering information   _____

Reporting to class   _____

Organizing information   _____

Summarizing   _____

Reading and understanding maps   _____

Applying information   _____

Testing situations   _____

Other   _____

Additional teacher comments _____

_____

_____

_____

_____

_____

_____

_____

_____

_____

_____

_____

_____

_____

_____

_____

_____

_____

_____

_____

_____

Exercise 7.3: Studying the Sample Unit Plan

Instructions: The purpose of this exercise is to study the sample unit plan for its inclusions. Use the following questions as a guide to that study. Share and compare your responses with those of your classmates.

1. What is the central theme of this unit? _____
   _____
   _____
   _____

2. What is the intended duration of this unit? _____
   _____
   _____
   _____

3. What are the educational goals of this unit? _____
   _____
   _____
   _____

4. Are the learning objectives for this unit clearly stated? _____
   _____
   _____
   _____

5. Do the objectives appear to contribute to the learning goals of the unit? Explain. _____
   _____
   _____
   _____

6. Are the instructional procedures clearly spelled out? _____
   _____
   _____
   _____
   _____

7. Do the learning activities appear feasible? Explain. _____
   _____
   _____
   _____
   _____

8. Does the unit have an introductory activity that will accomplish the purposes as spelled out in the earlier discussion of the six steps for unit planning? Explain. _____

_____

_____

_____

9. Does the plan include developmental activities? If so, identify them. _____

_____

_____

_____

10. Does the plan include culminating activities? If so, identify them. _____

_____

_____

_____

11. Describe the unit's learning assessment strategies. _____

_____

_____

_____

12. Does the unit clearly identify the materials needed for implementation of the unit? And does it appear that the materials are readily available? _____

_____

_____

_____

13. Could this unit plan be adaptable and used as an interdisciplinary unit? If so, explain several changes that could be made to make it an interdisciplinary thematic unit. _____

_____

_____

_____

_____

14. Are there multiethnic components to this unit plan? If so, identify them. _____

_____

_____

_____

_____

15. Does this plan take into account student differences in learning styles and learning modalities? If so, explain how. _____

_____

_____

_____

_____

16. Identify by day the various teaching strategies used in the narrative discussion of implementation of this unit. For example: Day 1—teacher–led discussion; visuals; silent reading; teacher use of questioning (and so on). _____

_____

_____

_____

_____

_____

_____

_____

_____

_____

_____

17. Specifically how does this unit plan address student
    Reading skills? _____

_____

_____

_____

_____

Study skills? _____

_____

_____

_____

_____

Thinking skills? _____

_____

_____

_____

_____

18. Consider the questions used by the teacher in the sample unit plan (see Chapter 10 for help) and identify several that are at the

Recall (input) level _____

_____

_____

_____

_____

_____

Processing level _____

_____

_____

_____

_____

Application (output) level _____

_____

_____

_____

_____

19. Does this unit make any attempt at helping students make connections in their learning? If so, explain where and how. _____

_____

_____

_____

20. Would you label the suggested assessment procedures for this unit "authentic"? (See Chapter 14 if you need help on this question.) Explain. _____

_____

_____

_____

_____

_____

_____

21. Prepare an activity web for this unit. In the boxes for each of the content areas of the elementary school curriculum, place content-related activities that are studied in this unit.

Activity Web

Language Arts	Mathematics	Science

Central Theme
Early English Settlers
in North America

Art		Music

Social Science	Physical Education

22. Analysis of the activity web: How many content areas were touched upon in this unit? Which ones were? Which were not? _____

    _____

    _____

    _____

    _____

    _____

Exercise 7.4: Preparing a Standard Teaching Unit

Instructions: The purpose of this exercise is to prepare a two-week unit plan for a grade level, subject, and topic you are likely to teach. Prepare your plan on separate paper. Use a format that is practical, comfortable, and appropriate to your subject or grade level, but be sure to include each of the items that follow; then have your plan critiqued by your colleagues and course instructor. (To do an effective job with this exercise, you will need either to look ahead, particularly to Chapter 8 for lesson planning, Chapters 11 and 13 for strategy planning within lessons, and Chapter 14 for assessment strategies, or to do this exercise later.)

1. Identify the

   a. Grade level and subject

   b. Topic

   c. Time duration
2. State the rationale and general goals.
3. List the instructional objectives (these will be listed separately for each daily lesson). A two-week unit should include objectives from all three domains—cognitive, affective, and psychomotor.
4. List the materials and resources needed for the unit (and where thay can be obtained). These will also be listed for each daily lesson plan.
5. Include each daily lesson, a total of ten (see Chapter 8).
6. Identify assessment tools. Include all items that will be used for assessing student achievement during and at completion of the unit. For each item of assessment, code it to its related instructional objective.
7. Include provisions for individual student differences. Show how the unit will attend to variations in student reading levels, socioethnic backgrounds, special needs, and so on.

Of special interest to curriculum developers and teachers today are units built around interdisciplinary themes, rather than content topics that are single-subject specific. Thematic teaching helps children to bridge the disciplines and to connect school learning with real-life experiences.

Procedure for Planning and Developing an Interdisciplinary Thematic Unit[2]

The six steps outlined in the beginning of this section are essential in planning any type of teaching unit and, as mentioned, there are several types. The type of instructional unit of increasing interest to many teachers, and which is the topic now, is the interdisciplinary thematic unit. As you will learn, the interdisciplinary thematic unit is made of smaller subject-specific units, developed according to the preceding guidelines.

Primary responsibility for the development of interdisciplinary thematic units often depends upon the cooperation of several teachers, who, especially in the case of middle schools, represent several disciplines. As discussed in Chapter 1, this interdisciplinary team of teachers may meet daily during a common planning time. Flexible scheduling, providing instructional blocks of time, allows team members to have a common planning time and unit lessons, likewise, to be more flexible and less constrained by time.

Some teaching teams develop one interdisciplinary thematic unit each year, semester, trimester, or quarter; that is, from one to four a year. Over time, then, the team will have developed several units that are available for implementation. However, the most effective units are often the most current or those that are most meaningful to students. This means that ever-changing global, national, and local topics provide a veritable smorgasbord from which to choose, and teaching teams must constantly be aware of the changes in the world and society to update old units and develop new and exciting ones.

One teaching team's unit should not conflict with another's at the same or another grade level. Consider the following examples: If a school has two or more third-grade teams, the teams may want to develop units on different themes and share their products; a sixth-grade team must be cautious against developing a unit quite similar to one that the students will have in the seventh grade; and a middle school team may want to share its units with a high school team. The lines of communication within, between, and among teams and schools is critical to the success of thematic teaching.

Because developing interdisciplinary thematic units is an essential task for many elementary and middle school teachers, it is important for you to learn now the process that you will be practicing later as an employed teacher (as well as when student teaching). One other point should be noted: an interdisciplinary thematic unit can be prepared and taught by one teacher, but is more often prepared by and taught by a team. In the latter case, the instructional strategy is referred to as **interdisciplinary thematic team teaching.** Most often, the team is composed of teachers from at least four areas: social studies or history, language arts or English, mathematics, and sci-

[2]Adapted from Richard D. Kellough, Noreen G. Kellough, and David L. Hough, *Middle School Teaching: Methods and Resources* (New York: Macmillan, 1993), pp. 97–99, by permission of Macmillan Publishing Company.

ence. However, a thematic unit and teaching team might also consist of fewer than four—language arts and social studies, for example.

Following are nine steps to guide you in the process of developing interdisciplinary thematic units. A sample interdisciplinary thematic unit is shown in the Appendix.

Step 1. *Agree on the nature or source of origin for the interdisciplinary thematic unit.* Team members should view the interdisciplinary approach as a collective effort in which all team members (and other faculty) participate somewhat equally. Discuss how the team wants students to profit from interdisciplinary instruction. Trouble-shoot possible stumbling blocks.

Step 2. *Discuss subject-specific frameworks, goals and objectives, curriculum guidelines, textbooks and supplemental materials, and units already in place for the school year.* This discussion should focus on what each teacher must teach, and the scope and sequence should be explained so that all team members share an understanding of constraints and limitations.

Step 3. *Choose a topic and develop a time line.* From the information provided by each subject specialist teacher in step 2, start listing possible topics that can be drawn from the existing course outlines. Give-and-take is essential at this step, as some topics will fit certain subjects better than others. The chief goal here is to find a workable topic, that is, one that can be adapted to each subject without detracting from the educational plan already in place. This may require choosing and merging content from two or more previously planned units. The theme is then drawn from the topic. When considering a theme, the team should focus on these questions:

- Can this theme lead to a unit of proper duration, not too short and not too long?
- Do we have sufficient materials and resources to supply information we might need?
- Does the theme lend itself to active learning experiences?
- Is the theme topic helpful, worthwhile, and pertinent to the course objectives?
- Is the theme topic one with which teachers are not already too familiar so they can share in the excitement of the learning?
- Is the theme within the realm of understanding and experience of the teachers involved?
- Will the theme be of interest to all members of the teaching team?
- Will this theme be of interest to students? Will it motivate them to do their best?[3]

Step 4. *Set two time lines.* The first time line is for the team only and is to ensure that given dates for specific work required in developing the unit will be met by each member. The second time line is for students and teachers; it shows how long the unit will be, when it will start, and in which classes.

Step 5. *Develop the scope and sequence for content and instruction.* Refer to the six steps listed in "Procedure for Planning and Developing Any Unit of Instruction" (in a preceding section). Follow those steps for developing the unit. This should be done by team members individually, and as a group during common planning time so that they can coordinate dates and activities in logical sequence and depth. This is an organic process that will generate ideas but also produce some anxiety. Members of the team, under the guidance of the team leader, should strive to keep anxiety at a level conducive to learning, experimenting, and arriving at group consensus.

---

[3]For additional guidelines for selecting a theme for an interdisciplinary unit, see Scott Willis, "Choosing a Theme," *Curriculum Update* (Alexandria, VA: Association for Supervision and Curriculum Development, November, 1992), pp. 4–5.

Step 6. *Share goals and objectives.* Each team member should have a copy of the goals and objectives of every other member. This helps to refine the unit and lesson plans and to prevent unnecessary overlap and confusion.

Step 7. *Give the unit its name.* The unit has been developed from a common topic and is held together by the theme you have chosen. Giving the theme a name and using that name lets the students know that this unit of study is integrated, important, and meaningful to school and to life.

Step 8. *Share subject-specific units, lesson plans, and print and nonprint materials.* After teachers have finalized their units, exchange them for review comments and suggestions. Keep a copy of each teacher's unit(s) and consider whether you could present a lesson from it for your own subject area. If you can, the plans are probably workable. If you cannot, some modification may be necessary.

Step 9. *Check the thematic unit by field testing.* Beginning on the agreed-upon time, date, and class(es), present the lessons. Team members may trade classes from time to time. Team teaching may take place when two or more classes can be combined for instruction, such as can be done with flexible and block scheduling. After field testing, there is, of course, one final step. This is when the thematic unit is evaluated and, perhaps, adjusted and revised. Team members discuss successes and failures during their common planning time and determine what needs to be changed, how, and when to make the unit successful. Adjustments can be made along the way (formative evaluation), and revisions for future use can be made at the end of the unit (summative evaluation).

The preceding steps are not absolutes and should be viewed only as guides. Differing compositions of teaching teams and levels of teacher experience and knowledge make strict adherence to any modus operandi less productive than group-generated plans. For instance, many teachers have found that the fifth point under step 3 could be exactly the opposite—recommending that the topic for an interdisciplinary thematic unit be one that the team already knows well. In practice, the process that works for the team—one that results in meaningful learning and in students feeling good about themselves, about learning, and about school—is the appropriate process.

Now do Exercise 7.5 and Exercise 7.6.

Exercise 7.5: Themes for Interdisciplinary Units: Generating Ideas

Instructions: The purpose of this exercise is to use brainstorming to generate a list of potential theme topics suitable as interdisciplinary units. Divide your class into groups of three to five. Each group is to decide the grade level for which its unit ideas are generated. If the group chooses, cooperative learning can be used; group members are assigned roles (such as *facilitator, recorder, reporter, monitor of thinking processes, on-task monitor,* and so on). Within each group, list as many potential topics as possible. One member of each group should record all ideas. Reserve discussion until no further ideas are generated. Lists can be shared in the large group.

Grade level interest of group _____

1. Existing subject area content units (as the group knows them to be or as they are predicted

    to exist). _____

    _____

    _____

    _____

    _____

    _____

    _____

    _____

2. Current interest topics

    Of global interest _____

    _____

    _____

    _____

    _____

    _____

    _____

    _____

    Of national interest _____

    _____

    _____

    _____

    _____

    _____

    _____

Of state-wide interest _____

_____

_____

_____

_____

_____

Of local interest _____

_____

_____

_____

_____

_____

Of interest to the school _____

_____

_____

_____

_____

_____

Of interest to children of this age _____

_____

_____

_____

_____

_____

Exercise 7.6: Integrating the Topic

Instructions: The purpose of this exercise is to practice weaving interdisciplinary themes into curricula. In groups of three to five, choose one idea that was generated in Exercise 7.5 and derive a list of suggestions about how that theme could be woven into the curricula of various school classes, programs, and activities, as indicated below. It is possible that not all areas listed are relevant to the grade level to which your group is addressing its work in this exercise. Cooperative learning can be used, with roles assigned to group members. One person in the group should be the recorder. Upon completion, share the product of your group's work (the process and product of which will be much like that of an actual interdisciplinary teaching team) with the rest of your class. Make copies of the work of each group for those who want them.

Unit/Topic/Theme _____

1. Explain how the theme could be incorporated in core classes.

English/language arts _____

_____

_____

_____

_____

_____

Social studies/history _____

_____

_____

_____

_____

_____

_____

Mathematics _____

_____

_____

_____

_____

_____

_____

Science _____

_____

_____

_____

_____

_____

_____

_____

_____

Physical education _____

_____

_____

_____

_____

_____

_____

_____

_____

_____

_____

Art _____

_____

_____

_____

_____

_____

_____

_____

_____

_____

Music _____

_____

_____

_____

_____

_____

_____

_____

_____

2. Explain how the theme could be incorporated in co-curricular programs and activities:

Electives _____

_____

_____

_____

_____

_____

_____

_____

_____

_____

Clubs _____

_____

_____

_____

_____

_____

_____

_____

_____

_____

School functions _____

_____

_____

_____

_____

_____

_____

_____

Assemblies _____

_____

_____

_____

_____

_____

_____

_____

_____

Intramurals _____

_____

_____

_____

_____

_____

_____

_____

Study skills _____

_____

_____

_____

_____

_____

_____

_____

_____

_____

_____

3. Explain how the theme could be incorporated in exploratories (special nongraded courses designed to aid students in discovering areas of interest, usually found in exemplary middle schools). _____

_____

_____

_____

_____

_____

_____

_____

_____

_____

4. Explain how the theme could be incorporated in the homeroom program. _____

_____

_____

_____

_____

_____

_____

_____

_____

_____

_____

_____

5. Explain how multicultural components could be incorporated. _____

_____

_____

_____

_____

_____

_____

_____

_____

_____

_____

6. As individuals, and as a group, how productive was this exercise? Why? _____

_____

_____

_____

_____

_____

_____

_____

_____

_____

_____

SUMMARY

Developing units of instruction that integrate student learning and provide a sense of meaning for the children requires coordination throughout the curriculum—which is defined here as all the experiences students encounter while at school. Hence, learning for students is a process of discovering how information, knowledge, and ideas are interrelated, helping children make sense of self, of school, and of life. Forming chunks of information into units, and units into daily lessons, helps students to process and to make sense of knowledge. Having developed your first unit of instruction, you are well on your way to becoming a competent planner of instruction.

Chapter 8 will focus your attention on the preparation of lesson plans.

QUESTIONS FOR CLASS DISCUSSION

1. About which of the seven guidelines for planning (Section A of this chapter) do you feel most confident? Least confident? Share those concerns with your colleagues.
2. Describe at least three sources of ideas for interdisciplinary themes.
3. Describe a course syllabus, why it is important, and where or how you would use one.
4. Explain the value of organizing instruction into units.
5. Describe the steps of unit planning.
6. Describe each of the nine steps in interdisciplinary thematic unit development.
7. Identify and describe criteria for selecting a topic for a unit of study.
8. Describe the types of activities that could be used in the introductory phase of a unit, and those that could be used in the culminating phase.
9. Describe the concept of "integrative curriculum." Give an example.
10. Explain the importance of the idea that all teachers are teachers of reading, writing, studying, and thinking. Do you agree or disagree with the concept? Explain.
11. Do you have questions about the content of this chapter? How might answers be found?

SUGGESTED READINGS FOR CHAPTER 7

Boling, A. N. "They Don't Like Math? Well, Let's Do Something." *Arithmetic Teacher* 38(7):17–19 (March 1991).

Bomeli, C. L. "Mathematics and Meteorology: Perfect Partners." *School Science and Mathematics* 91(1):31–33 (January 1991).

Brutlag, D., and Maples, C. "Making Connections: Beyond the Surface." *Mathematics Teacher* 85(3):230–235 (March 1992).

Erb, T. O., and Doda, N. M. *Team Organization: Promise—Practices & Possibilities.* Washington, DC: National Education Association, 1989.

Gehrke, N. J. "Explorations of Teachers' Development of Integrative Curriculum." *Journal of Curriculum and Supervision* 6(2):107–117 (Winter 1991).

Jacobs, H. H., et al. *Interdisciplinary Curriculum: Design and Implementation.* Alexandria, VA: Association for Supervision and Curriculum Development, 1989.

Palmer, J., et al. "Teaching Location and Some Characteristics of Place: Using South Africa." *Social Education* 55(1):58–60 (January 1991).

Roberts, P. L. *A Green Dinosaur Day: A Guide for Developing Thematic Units in Literature-Based Instruction, K–6.* Boston: Allyn & Bacon, 1993.

Young, S. L. "Ideas." *Arithmetic Teacher* 38(7):24–33 (March 1991).

8

How Do I Prepare Lesson Plans?

As described in Section A of the preceding chapter, step 5 of the seven-step plan is the preparation for class meetings. The process of designing a lesson is important in getting you to think the lesson through so that the result is the most effective learning experience for the students. Next, we consider the guidelines for detailed lesson planning.

A. GUIDELINES FOR LESSON PLANNING

All teachers construct some type of lesson plans, whether they are formally written or informally thought out. Because of the diversity of teacher personalities, teaching styles, and methods of planning, a few assumptions about lesson plans and lesson planning are in order. Consider the following:

Assumption 1. All teachers need to understand the importance of the major elements of an effective lesson plan. The major elements are presented in Section B of this chapter.

Assumption 2. Student teachers and beginning teachers require more detailed, formal, written lesson plans than do experienced teachers who are more familiar with the school, the children's abilities and prior learning experiences, and the content of the subject. For a beginning teacher, a detailed plan of a lesson never before taught by that teacher helps the teacher stay on track.

Assumption 3. Some topics and lessons require more detailed planning than others. However, for reasons stated in Assumption 2, during student teaching you should detail all of your lesson plans. This helps to ensure that you plan carefully and thoroughly; your cooperating teacher and your college or university supervisor will expect it, and they will want to see and to assess your written plans.

Assumption 4. Lesson plans constructed from an interdisciplinary thematic unit should be formally written and require even more detail than those derived from standard units, because other members of the teaching team need to understand the plan, and perhaps even teach from it.

Assumption 5. Although they may not always write them out, experienced teachers have in mind clear goals and objectives (as well as justifiable rationales) for their lessons.

Assumption 6. Teachers are more apt to teach "to the lesson" when it is written, and more apt to teach the same lesson again in the same way when it is written formally.

Assumption 7. Although all contain major components, there is a variety of different, but acceptable, lesson plan formats. Some formats are more appropriate for certain types of lessons. For example, a lesson plan centered on the use of class discussions may be different from one that is principally a hands-on investigation.

Assumption 8. The lesson plan format that works is that which the teacher can most effectively implement. This is learned from experience. To gain that experience, a beginning teacher needs to try various formats.

Assumption 9. Most college or university programs of teacher preparation have preferred lesson plan formats for their student teachers. Although these may vary somewhat from one institution to the next, major components will be nearly identical.

Assumption 10. For student teachers, the lesson plan books used by some experienced teachers, which are nothing more than loose-leaf pages with small boxed spaces representing days of the week (see Figure 8.1), are inadequate for thorough and competent planning.

As illustrated, the lesson plan book may be fine for experienced teachers, but it does not allow adequate space for the detailed planning that must be done by beginning teachers. It certainly does not provide the space needed for detailing the lessons for **integrated programs,** that is, lessons that simultaneously include more than one subject, such as reading and social studies, or science and mathematics.

Rationale for Written Lesson Planning

The discussion in this chapter is about written lesson plans used by the classroom teacher as tools in the teaching and learning process. Therefore, consider the following eight reasons that beginning teachers must write detailed lesson plans.

Reason 1. Written and detailed lesson plans provide an important sense of security, especially useful to a beginning teacher. Like a rudder of a ship, it helps keep you on course. Without it you are likely to drift aimlessly. Sometimes a disturbance in the classroom can interrupt the lesson, causing the teacher to get "off track" or forget

DAILY LESSON PLAN BOOK

Grade _____   Lesson _____   Teacher _____

Date	*Content*	*Materials*	*Procedure*	*Evaluation*
Monday				
Tuesday				
Wednesday				
Thursday				
Friday				

Figure 8.1 Daily lesson plan book.

a part of the lesson. A written and detailed lesson plan helps the teacher get back on track.

Reason 2. Written lesson plans cause teachers to be or become reflective decision makers. Without a written plan, it is difficult or impossible to reflect after the lesson has been taught, to analyze how something might have been planned or implemented differently.

Reason 3. Written lesson plans help you organize material and search for "loopholes," "loose ends," or incomplete content.

Reason 4. Written lesson plans serve as resources for future use.

Reason 5. Written lesson plans are helpful in teacher self-evaluation, assessment of student achievement, and evaluation of the curriculum.

Reason 6. Written lesson plans provide substitute teachers and members of a teaching team with a specific guide to follow if you are absent.

Reason 7. Written lesson plans help other members of the teaching team understand what you are doing and how you are doing it. This is especially important when implementing an interdisciplinary thematic unit.

Reason 8. Preparing and writing your plans carefully shows everyone—your students, your colleagues, your administrator, and your college or university supervisor, if you are a student teacher—that you care.

These eight reasons clearly justify the need to write detailed lesson plans. The list is not exhaustive, however, and you may discover additional reasons that written lesson plans are crucial to effective teaching. Master teachers are experts in the art of lesson planning. They can construct exemplary lesson plans that are workable and validated in applied research. Two points of reality must be noted: (1) lesson planning is an ongoing process, even for competent veteran teachers, and (2) teachers must take time to plan, reflect, write, test, evaluate, and rewrite their plans to reach optimal performance. In short, writing lesson plans is important work.

B. LESSON PLAN FORMAT: COMMON ELEMENTS

There are a variety of lesson plan formats. Most, however, contain six common elements: (1) descriptive course or class data, (2) resources and materials, (3) goals and objectives, (4) rationale, (5) instructional components, and (6) plans for evaluation and revision.

As presented here, the six elements are not ordered sequentially. For example, you might want to place "resources and materials" after "instructional components." Nor are the listed elements inclusive or exclusive. You might choose to include additional elements or subsections. You may not want to spend time developing a formal rationale, although you probably should. Figure 8.2 illustrates a generic format that includes the six elements and sample subsections of each.

Descriptions of the Six Common Elements

Following are descriptions of the six common elements of lesson plan formats with explanations of why each is essential.

1. *Descriptive Course Data*

   Teacher _____ Class _____ Date _____

   Grade level _____ Room number _____ Period _____

   Unit _____ Topic _____

2. *Lesson Goals and Objectives*

   Goals:

   Objectives:
      Cognitive:

      Psychomotor:

      Affective:

3. *Rationale*

4. *Instructional Components*

   Content:

   Procedure with time plan:
      Set:

      Modeling reminders:

      Guided (Coached) Practice:

      Assignments:

      Closure:

5. *Materials Needed*

   Audiovisual:

   Other:

6. *Evaluation and Revision*

   Evaluation of lesson:

   Plan for revision:

Figure 8.2 Sample lesson plan format with the six common elements.

Descriptive Course Data

This is the demographic and logistic information that identifies details about the class of students. Anyone reading this information should be able to tell when and where the class meets, who is teaching it, and what is being taught. Although you, as the teacher, know this information, someone else may not. Administrators, members of the teaching team, and substitute teachers—and, if you are a student teacher, your supervisor—appreciate this information, especially when asked to "fill in" for you, even if only for a few minutes during a class session. Most teachers determine which items of descriptive data are most beneficial for them, and select or develop their own identifiers.

Remember this: *The mark of a well-prepared, clearly written lesson plan is the ease with which someone else (e.g., a member of your teaching team or a substitute teacher) could implement it.*

Goals and Objectives

In a lesson plan, the goals are general statements, taken from the unit plan and stated here in concise language, of what students will learn from that lesson. Teachers and students need to know what the lesson is designed to accomplish. The goal statement provides that information.

The objectives of the lesson are included as specific statements detailing precisely what students will be able to do as a result of the lesson. Teachers and students need to know that. Behavioral objectives provide clear statements of what learning is to occur. In addition, from clearly written behavioral objectives, assessment items can be derived and written to measure how well students have accomplished the objectives.

Rationale

A rationale is an explanation of why the lesson is important, and why the instructional methods chosen will achieve the objectives. Parents, students, teachers, administrators, and others have the right to know why specific content is being taught and why the methods employed are being used. Teachers become reflective decision makers when they challenge themselves to think about what they are teaching, how they are teaching it, and why it must be taught.

Body of the Lesson Plan

The plan includes all instructional components of the lesson. For reasons discussed earlier, teachers must plan their lessons and plan them carefully. As you prepare each lesson, attend to each of the instructional components as carefully as if you were a surgeon preparing for the operating room, or as if an administrator or your university supervisor were going to be visiting that day. To help you with preparation, each component of the body of the lesson is presented here in detail. The body of the lesson plan consists of the following:

• **Content,** the substance of the lesson, the information to be presented, obtained, and learned. Appropriate information is selected to meet the learning objectives, the level of competence of the students, and the requirements of the class.

• **Instruction,** the procedure(s) to be used. Appropriate instructional methods are chosen to meet the objectives, to match the students' learning styles, to attend to student modality strengths, and to ensure that all students have equal opportunity to learn.

• **Set,** to prepare the students mentally for the lesson. It is important for you to realize that students come to your classroom from other places, and to be mentally ready for your lesson they need to disassociate their minds from immediately preceding mental occupations. You must have their attention before you can teach; your lesson plan can be designed to establish a desired mind set, capturing student attention, readying students for your instruction. There are several ways to do this. Consider the following:

1. An **orientation set** (also known as an **anticipatory set** or **advance organizer;** see Chapter 2) that provides a framework for the ensuing lesson, capturing student interest and attention for that lesson. As examples, an orientation set might be as long as an entire class meeting, with students role-playing a situation that they are going to be studying for the next several meetings, or as brief as only a few minutes when a teacher clarifies for students the objectives for the lesson. An effective orientation set might even be noncontent related, as when a teacher captures students' attention with a friendly greeting as they arrive, or who begins the lesson with humor, a personal story, or a recent experience related to the lesson topic. (Incidentally, a set that is noncontent related would not, then, be an advance organizer.)
2. A **transition set** that provides a smooth transition from what the students have learned to what is to be covered in this lesson, relying on teacher use of examples and analogies. An effective transition set is also an orientation set.
3. An **assessment set** that evaluates student learning prior to the introduction of new material. Teachers are using an assessment set when they review material from a previous lesson through questioning. An effective assessment set can contain ingredients of all three set types—that is, it can orient student thinking, assess student comprehension, and provide transition.
4. The use of **metacognitive strategies.** That is, at the beginning of the lesson, involve students in planning, monitoring, and evaluating the progress of their thinking and learning of the lesson.

• **Modeling,** which means that by your actions and words, you demonstrate directly and indirectly those behaviors expected of your students. Children need adults who model those very behaviors expected of them. By effective modeling, you give examples of the anticipated learning outcomes.

• **Guided (or coached) practice.** With the guidance of their teacher, as a resident expert, students practice what they are learning. Students need to be guided through the learning process by a competent helper.

• **Transitions,** the planned procedures for moving children's thinking from one idea to the next, and their actions from one activity to the next. Transitions are best when smooth and meaningful, as opposed to rough or irrelevant.

- **Stimulus variation,** the variety of ways in which you stimulate the various student learning modalities, such as with use of body language and movements, gestures, voice inflections, pauses, and interaction strategies.
- **Assignment,** what students are instructed to do, including in-class work and homework. Whether accomplished during class or after class, homework and other assignments provide children opportunities to learn and to practice what is being learned.
- **Closure,** bringing the lesson to an end. Complementary to the way you initiate a lesson is the manner in which you bring the lesson to a close. A lesson may be closed with a summary review **(summary closure),** an opportunity for students to practice the new material **(reinforcement closure),** or by a natural crescendo **(climax closure).** Whichever the case, in planning a lesson you must attend to the manner in which the lesson is to be brought to a close. For many beginning teachers, closures and transitions are the most difficult aspects of a daily lesson. To master the necessary skills takes your concentrated effort in planning, practice, and reflection.

Unit planning should include activities that allow children to work alone, in dyads, and in small groups. Grouping children and assigning roles facilitates their learning. When children have specific and understood tasks and responsibilities, they have more direction and will demonstrate a greater interest in learning.

You must effectively plan your lessons so that the entire class time is used for student learning. In particular, the beginning and the last few minutes of a class period should not be wasted time (dead time, as discussed in Chapter 4), nor should students ever be allowed to meander toward the exit in anticipation of the end of class or the end of the school day. When students are actually engaged in learning activities, this is referred to as **on-task** behavior, but even more important is for students to be engaged in **quality on-task behaviors.** As a teacher, it is your job to see that instructional time is not wasted. An effective closure provides students with a sense of completeness and, with effective teaching, accomplishment and comprehension. Closure helps students to synthesize the information learned from the lesson.

Resources and Materials

Resources and materials include the textbook, supplementary reading, audiovisual equipment, and other supplies necessary to accomplish the lesson objectives. Teachers must be sure that the proper and necessary materials are available for the lesson. To do that takes planning. Students cannot use what they do not have available.

Evaluation and Plans for Revision

Evaluation refers to the methods and criteria used to determine the quality and quantity of learning that took place, and that includes how effective the lesson was. This allows the teacher to check for student comprehension and to make revisions in the lesson before its next implementation.

Sample Unit Plan with One Complete Daily Lesson

Chapter 7 discussed the details of unit planning and presented one complete unit plan with lessons outlined in a narrative format. In this chapter we are concerned with the details of lesson planning. Study the following sample unit plan with one complete daily lesson, followed by a second sample lesson from a different unit, and then proceed to Exercises 8.1, 8.2a, and 8.2b.

SAMPLE UNIT PLAN WITH ONE COMPLETE DAILY LESSON

Subject *Science (intermediate to middle grades)*

Teacher _____ **Duration of Unit** *ten days*

Title of Unit[1] *What's the Matter?*

Purpose of Unit: This unit is designed to develop students' understanding of the concept of matter. At the completion of the unit, students should have a clearer understanding of matter and its properties, of the basic units of matter, and of where matter comes from.

Rationale of Unit: This unit topic is important in building a foundation of knowledge for subsequent courses in science. This foundation can increase students' chances of success in those courses, thereby increasing their self-confidence and self-esteem. A basic understanding of matter and its properties is important because of daily decisions that affect the manipulation of matter. It is more likely that students will make correct and safe decisions when they understand what matter is, how it changes form, and how its properties determine its use.

Goals of Unit: The goals of this unit are for students to:
1. Understand that all matter is made of atoms.
2. Understand that matter stays constant and that it is neither created nor destroyed.
3. Develop certain science laboratory skills.
4. Develop a positive attitude about physical science.
5. Look forward to studying more science.
6. Understand how science is relevant to their daily lives.

Instructional Objectives of Unit: Upon completion of this unit of study, students should be able to:
1. List at least ten examples of matter.
2. List the four states of matter with one example of each.
3. Calculate the density of an object when given mass and volume.
4. Describe the properties of solids, liquids, and gases.
5. Demonstrate an understanding that matter is made of elements, and elements are made of atoms.
6. Identify and explain one way that knowledge of matter is important to their daily lives.

Unit Overview

Throughout this unit of study, students will be developing a concept map of matter. Information for the map will be derived from laboratory work, class discussions, lectures, and student readings and research. The overall instructional model is that of concept attainment. Important to that is an assessment of students' concepts about matter at the beginning of the unit of study. The preassessment and the continuing assessment of their concepts will center on the following:

1. What is matter and what are its properties? Students will develop the concept of matter by discovering the properties common to all matter (that is, it has mass and takes up space).
2. Students will continue to build on their understanding of the concept of matter by organizing matter into its four major states (solid, liquid, gas, and plasma). The concept development will be used to define the attributes of each state of matter, and students will gather information by participating in laboratory activities and class discussions.
3. What are some of the physical properties of matter that make certain kinds of matter unique? Students will experiment with properties of matter such as elasticity, brittleness, and density. Laboratory activities will allow students to contribute their observations and information to the further development of their concept of matter. Density activities enable students to practice their lab and math skills.

[1]Adapted with permission from unpublished material by William Hightower.

4. What are the basic units of matter, and where did matter come from? Students will continue to develop their concept of matter by increasing their understanding of mixtures, compounds, elements, and atoms.

Assessment of Student Achievement

For this unit, assessment of student achievement will be both formative and summative. Formative evaluation will be done daily through the use of checklists of student behavior, knowledge, and skills. Summative evaluation will be based on the following criteria:

1. Student participation as evidenced by completion of daily homework, class work, laboratory activities, and class discussions and as evidenced by the information afforded by the student behavior checklist.
2. Weekly quizzes on content.
3. Unit test.

Lesson Number _____   **Time Duration** *1–2 hours*

Unit Title *What's the Matter?*   **Teacher** _____

Lesson Title *Mission Impossible*   **Lesson Topic** *Density of Solids*

Objectives of Lesson: Upon completion of this lesson, students should be able to:
1. Determine the density of a solid cube.
2. Based on data gathered in class, develop their own definition of density.
3. Communicate the results of their experiments to others in the class.

Materials Needed
1. Two large boxes of cereal and two snack-size boxes of the same cereal.
2. Four brownies (2 whole and 2 cut in halves).
3. Four sandboxes (2 large plastic boxes and 2 small boxes, each filled with sand).
4. Two balances.
5. Several rulers.
6. Six handheld calculators.
7. Eighteen colored pencils (six sets with three different colors per set).
8. Copies of lab instructions (one for each student).
9. Graph paper.

Instructional Procedure with Approximate Time Line:
1. Anticipatory Set (10–15 minutes)
Begin class by brainstorming what students already know about density. Place the word *density* on the board or overhead, and ask students whether they have heard the word before. Write down their definitions and examples. Hold up the large box of cereal in one hand and the snack-size box in the other. Ask students which is more dense. Allow them time to explain their responses. Then tell them that by the end of this lesson they will know the answer to the question and that they will develop their own definition of density.
2. Laboratory Investigation (30–60 minutes)
The class is divided into teams, each with four students of mixed abilities. Each member of a team has a role:

Measure master: in charge of group's ruler and ruler measurements.
Mass master: responsible for all weighings.
Engineer: in charge of the group's calculator and calculations.
Graph master: in charge of plotting data on the graph paper.

Each team has eight minutes before switching stations. Each team completes three stations and then meets to make its graphs and to discuss results.

STATION 1: CEREAL BOX DENSITY

Students calculate the density of a large and a small box of cereal to determine whether a larger and heavier object is more dense. The masses versus the volumes of the two boxes are plotted on graph paper with one of the pencil colors.

Station 1 instructions:

a. The density of any object is determined by dividing its mass by its volume. Density in grams is divided by volume in cubic centimeters. Example: $20 \text{ g}/10 \text{ cm}^3 = 2 \text{ g/cm}^3$.

b. Measure the volume of the small cereal box (length × width × height), and use the balance to determine its mass in grams. The engineer can do the calculations on the calculator. The graph master graphs the results of each trial and connects two points with a straight line.

c. Repeat the procedure using the large box of cereal.

d. The engineer computes the density of both cereal boxes with the calculator. Record the density of each item in the spaces below the graph.

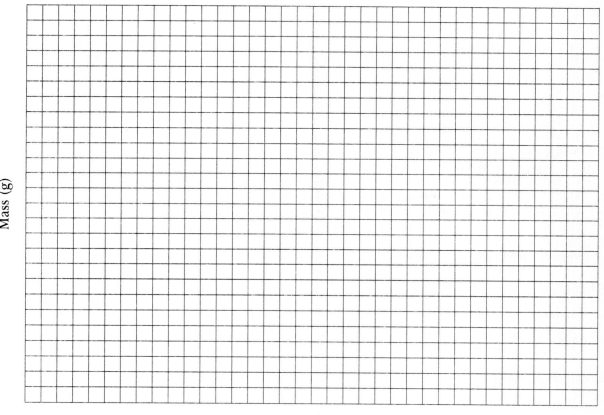

Mass (g)

Volume (cm³)

1. Large box of cereal _____

2. Small box of cereal _____

3. Large brownie _____

4. Small brownie _____

5. Large sandbox _____

6. Small sandbox _____

STATION 2: BROWNIE DENSITY

Students calculate the density of a full-sized brownie and a half-sized brownie. Results are plotted on the same graph used in Station 1, with a second color.

Station 2 instructions:

a. The density of any object is determined by dividing its mass by its volume. Density in grams is divided by volume in cubic centimeters. Example: $20 \text{ g}/10 \text{ cm}^3 = 2 \text{ g/cm}^3$.

b. Measure the volume of a small brownie (length $\times$ width $\times$ height), and use the balance to determine its mass in grams. The engineer can do the calculations on the calculator. The graph master graphs the results of each trial and connects two points with a straight line.

c. Repeat the procedure using the large brownie.

d. The engineer computes the density of both brownies. Record the density of each item in the spaces below the graph.

STATION 3: SANDBOX DENSITY

Students calculate the density of a large and a small box of sand, each filled. Results are plotted on the same graph (with the third color).

Station 3 instructions:

a. The density of any object is determined by dividing its mass by its volume. Density in grams is divided by volume in cubic centimeters. Example: $20 \text{ g}/10 \text{ cm}^3 = 2 \text{ g/cm}^3$.

b. Measure the volume of the small sandbox (length $\times$ width $\times$ height), and use the balance to determine its mass in grams. The engineer can do the calculations on the calculator. The graph master graphs the results of each trial and connects two points with a straight line.

c. Repeat the procedure using the large sandbox.

d. The engineer computes the density of both boxes. Record the density of each item in the spaces below the graph.

Lab worksheet. Teams return to their seats to do the graphing, analyze the results, and answer the following questions from their lab worksheets.

1. Is a larger, heavier object more dense than its smaller counterpart? Explain your evidence.
2. What is your definition of density?
3. Which is more dense, a pound of feathers or a pound of gold? Explain your answer.

3. Lesson Closure (10 minutes or more)

When all are finished, teams should display their graphs, then share and discuss the results.

Concepts

Density is one of the properties of matter.
Mass and volume are related.
Density is determined by dividing mass by volume.

Extension Activities

Use a density graph to calculate the mass and volume of a smaller piece of brownie.
Explore the story of Archimedes and the king's crown.

Evaluation and Revision of Lesson

Upon completion of this lesson and of the unit, on the basis of teacher observations and student achievement, this lesson may be revised.

Lesson Plan: Sample 2

SAMPLE LESSON PLAN[2]

Grade Level <u>6</u>   **Teacher** <u>*Ms. Arnold*</u>
Date _____   **Unit** <u>*Newspaper Reading*</u>
Lesson Number and Topic <u>*Lesson 1: Newspaper Reading*</u>

1. Instructional Objectives:
   Given copies of newspapers and individual copies of the worksheet "Read All About It," students will correctly identify sections and subsections of a newspaper, such as the editorials, sports, and classified.
2. Content: comprehension, content area reading, and locational skills.
3. Procedure:

Orientation Set (5–8 minutes)

TN[3]   Ask for a show of hands; TQ "How many of you have a newspaper delivered to your home?"
TQ   "Does anyone know what news was on the front page this morning?"
TN   (Allow think time; call upon several who have hands raised.)
T   "Starting today, we are going to see how a newspaper is put together and what types of articles are in the paper."

Lesson Body

3.1. (10 minutes) T separates a copy of a newspaper into sections and displays them for the class (use a student assistant). T explains and discusses the basic setup of a newspaper.
   a. World and national news—A section, headlines index
      TQ "What is the main headline?" (comprehension)
      TQ "Why is the index important?" (analysis)
   b. Metro—B section
      TQ "What do you think 'Metro' means?" (comprehension)
      TQ "What kinds of news articles might you find in this section?" (analysis)
   c. Classified—C section
      TQ "What does the classified section consist of?" (comprehension)
      TQ "Who do you think pays for the ads in the classifieds?" (synthesis)
   d. Sports—D section
      TQ "What sports might be in the news now?" (application)
      TQ "Do you think this is a popular section of the newspaper?" "Why?" (evaluation)
3.2. (2 minutes) T and S assistant distribute copies of the newspaper and Macmillan worksheet to individual students.
3.3. (30 minutes) Students work individually on the Macmillan worksheet.
      Remind them to use the index on the front page to find different sections.
      TN: Reinforce on-task behaviors and compliment good workers. Students may need individual help locating different parts of the newspaper to answer the questions on the worksheet.

Closure   (2 minutes)

This is the first in a series of three lessons on the newspaper. Eventually, the students can write their own class newspaper.
4. Materials and resources:
   Newspapers which have been arranged to be donated by two local newspaper companies; teacher

---

[2]Adapted from Missy Arnold, unpublished material. Reprinted by permission.
[3]For teacher use, codes recommended by us and as used in this lesson plan are as follows: "S" = students; "T" = teacher; "TQ" = question asked by teacher; "TN" = a note or reminder for the teacher.

is to pick them up (class set for each) before school this morning. Worksheet "Read All About It": class set

5. Assessment:
   Students will complete questions on worksheet with 80 percent accuracy.

Read All About It[4]
(Student Worksheet)

_____

Student Name

Use a newspaper in your classroom or school library to answer the following questions.

1. Does your newspaper have more than one headline on the front page? _____ If so, what headline did you find most interesting?

2. Write the name of a famous person found on page one. _____
   Why was this person in the news?

3. Look for each of the following sections in your paper. Are they all there? _____
   List your favorite item in each of the following sections.
   Cartoon strip:
   Movie that is advertised:
   TV program that is listed:
   Job advertised in the classified section:
   Car for sale:
   Special event taking place:
4. On what page can the editorials be found? _____
5. Give the final score of a game listed in the sports section _____
6. Tell about one article you found very interesting.

7. Compare two different newspapers. Answer these questions:
   a. Are they the same size? _____
   b. Do they have the same sections? _____
   c. List three things you found that were different.
   _____   _____   _____

Before proceeding with development of your first lesson plan, consider a sixth-grade "lesson that failed"—Exercise 8.1.

[4]From *Macmillan Instant Activities Program* by Macmillan Publishing Company. Copyright © 1981 by Macmillan Publishing Company. Reprinted by permission.

Exercise 8.1: Analysis of a Lesson That Failed

Instructions: The purpose of this exercise is to show that the planning and structure of a lesson are often predictors of the success of its implementation. Read the following synopsis of implementation of a lesson, answer the discussion questions individually, and use your responses as a basis for class discussion (in small groups) about the lesson. Questions for discussion follow the synopsis.

The Setting Sixth-grade science class; 1:12–2:07 P.M., spring.

Synopsis of events

1:12	Bell rings.
1:12–1:21	Teacher directs students to read from their text, while he takes attendance.
1:21–1:31	Teacher distributes to each student a ditto; students are now to "label the parts of a flower" shown on the handout.
1:31–1:37	Students reading ditto and labeling the parts of a flower.
1:37–1:39	Teacher verbally gives instructions for working on a real flower; e.g., compare with the flower drawing on the ditto; students can use the microscopes if they want.
1:39–1:45	Teacher walks around room distributing to each student a real flower.
1:45–2:07	Chaos erupts. Much confusion, students wandering around room, throwing flower parts at each other. Teacher begins writing referrals and sends two students to the office for their misbehavior. Teacher is flustered, directs students to spend remainder of period quietly reading from their texts. Two more referrals written.
2:05–2:07	A few students begin meandering toward the exit.
2:07	End of period (much to the delight of the teacher).

Questions for Class Discussion

1. Do you think the teacher had a lesson plan? If so, what (if any) were its good points? Its

    problems? _____

    _____

    _____

    _____

    _____

    _____

    _____

    _____

    _____

    _____

2. If you believe that the teacher had a lesson plan, do you believe the teacher had a written and detailed lesson plan? Explain your yes or no response. What is your evidence? _____

_____

_____

_____

_____

_____

_____

3. Explain how the lesson might have been prepared and implemented to avoid the chaos.

_____

_____

_____

_____

_____

_____

4. Was the format of the lesson "traditional"? Explain. _____

_____

_____

_____

_____

_____

_____

5. Have you ever experienced a class like this one? Explain. _____

_____

_____

_____

_____

_____

_____

6. What were this teacher's behaviors that were probable causes of much of the chaos? (Hint: see Chapter 4.) _____

_____

_____

_____

_____

_____

_____

7. What teacher behaviors could have prevented the chaos and made the lesson more effective? _____

_____

_____

_____

_____

_____

_____

8. Within the 55-minute period, students of this class were expected to operate rather high on the Learning Experiences Ladder (see Figure 9.3 of Chapter 9). Consider this analysis: 9 minutes of silent reading; 10 minutes of listening; 6 minutes of silent reading and labeling; 2 minutes of listening; 6 minutes of action (the only direct experience); and an additional 22 minutes of silent reading. In all, approximately 49 minutes (89 percent of the class time) of abstract verbal and visual symbolization. Is that a problem? _____

_____

_____

_____

_____

_____

_____

_____

_____

9. Explain what you have learned from this exercise. _____

_____

_____

_____

_____

_____

_____

_____

_____

_____

_____

_____

_____

_____

_____

_____

_____

_____

_____

_____

_____

_____

_____

Exercise 8.2a: Preparing a Lesson Plan

Instructions: The purpose of this exercise is to prepare your own lesson plan. Use the model lesson format (Figure 8.2), or an alternative format that is approved by your instructor, to prepare a _____ minute (length of lesson to be decided in your class) lesson for a grade and subject of your choice. After completing your lesson plan, evaluate it yourself, modify it, and then have your modified version evaluated by at least three peers, using Exercise 8.2b.

Exercise 8.2b: Evaluating a Lesson Plan

Instructions: The purpose of this exercise is to compare your own evaluation of your lesson plan with evaluations by others. You may duplicate blank copies of this form for evaluation of your lesson developed in Exercise 8.2a. Have your plan evaluated by at least three of your peers, colleagues, and instructor, and, if presently in a field component of your teacher preparation, by your cooperating teacher. Compare the results of your self-evaluation with those of others who evaluated your plan. After the evaluations, change your plan as necessary. For each of the 21 items, evaluators should check a box and write instructive comments.

	No	*Yes*	*Comments*
1. Are adequate descriptive data provided in a form that is clear, distinguishing the subject, grade level, lesson topic, and so on?	_____	_____	
2. Are instructional objectives clear and practical?	_____	_____	
3. Are goals clearly stated?	_____	_____	
4. Is the rationale clear and justifiable?	_____	_____	
5. Is the plan's content appropriate for children at this grade level?	_____	_____	
6. Does the plan's content contribute to achievement of the objectives?	_____	_____	
7. Is the instructional plan workable, given the time frame and other logistical considerations impacting the class?	_____	_____	
8. Does the set engage students, motivating them to want to learn?	_____	_____	
9. Does the plan indicate how guided (or coached) practice will be provided for each child?	_____	_____	
10. Are assignments clear, manageable, and related to the lesson objectives?	_____	_____	
11. Is adequate closure provided to reinforce learning, convey a sense of completeness, and synthesize the content of the lesson?	_____	_____	

12. Are materials appropriate for the grade level, adequate to meet the needs of all students, and do they contribute to the lesson? _____   _____

13. Do evaluative criteria provide informal data to determine how much students have learned from the lesson? _____   _____

14. Do evaluative criteria provide formal data to determine how much students have learned from the lesson? _____   _____

15. Do evaluative criteria provide informal data to determine how well the teacher accomplished the objectives? _____   _____

16. Do evaluative criteria provide formal data to determine how well the teacher accomplished the objectives? _____   _____

17. Is the lesson plan in any way coordinated with other aspects of the school program to provide for integration of subject matter? _____   _____

18. Does the lesson fit the needs of the children by attending to the total child—emotionally, physically, mentally, socially, morally, and ethically? _____   _____

19. Does the lesson provide a sense of meaning for the students? _____   _____

20. Is an adequate amount of time allotted to address the information presented? _____   _____

21. Could another teacher or a substitute teacher follow this plan? _____   _____

Comments

_____

_____

_____

FOR YOUR NOTES

C. TURNING THEORY INTO PRACTICE

While reviewing lesson plans and in preparing your own lesson plans, you may be introduced to a particular model of planning. When you are introduced to a particular model, ask questions about it, e.g., Does it work? Do students taught by this method of planning learn? Do they learn more? Or, do they learn faster?

As an example, consider Madeline Hunter's model of planning. Hunter's advocates claim that while Hunter's model has not been extensively evaluated, the principles on which it is based are supported by research.[5,6] Hunter's model includes these elements in a lesson plan: anticipatory set, objectives, checking for understanding, guided practice, independent practice, and closure. Her model also features activating a student's prior knowledge, teaching for transfer, and using cognitive strategies. This model, backed by educational and psychological theory, is called Instructional Theory into Practice (ITIP) and is discussed in Hunter's book *Teach More—Faster* (El Segundo, CA: TIP Publications, 1980).[7]

Hunter's critics ask: "Does it work?" "Do students taught by teachers who use Hunter's model learn more and learn faster?" "Does this model affect students' scores on standardized or criterion-referenced tests?" "Has the ITIP model been evaluated?"

To this last question the answer is yes, the model has been evaluated. In a three-year experimental-control study by Stallings,[8] the ITIP model was evaluated. Subjects were from a school in Napa, California. Results indicated some slight achievement gains by both the experimental and control groups in the first two years but no gains in the third year. Certainly, other questions could be asked about these results: "Was the model implemented as rigorously the third year as in the first two years?" "Were the teachers the same ones or new to the staff?" "If new to the staff, were the teachers appropriately trained?"

A second and larger-scale study also evaluated the model. In South Carolina, the model was incorporated into the Program for Effective Teaching (PET), and teachers were trained in Hunter's methods in 87 percent of that state's school districts.[9] An evaluation of the achievement effects of the program over a three-year period indicated that:

- After controlling for prior achievement and for social-economic status (SES), there were *no* differences in achievement between students of PET-trained teachers and students of the other teachers.
- In classes where teachers had been trained in PET, two to three years before the posttesting their students scored slightly *worse* than the students of untrained teachers.
- Achievement scores of students of PET-trained teachers were not significantly related to any of the following: (1) the amount or quality of the coaching, (2) their

[5]Robert E. Slavin, "PET and the Pendulum: Faddism in Education and How to Stop It," *Phi Delta Kappan* 70(10):753–758 (June 1989).

[6]See also Daniel Gursky, "Madeline," *Teacher Magazine* 3(2):28–34 (October 1991).

[7]There are several additional articles about Madeline Hunter and her Program for Effective Teaching, in *Educational Leadership* 46(4), December–January 1988–89, and in *Educational Leadership* 48(4), December–January 1990–91. See also Noreen B. Garman and Helen M. Hazi, "Teachers Ask: Is There Life After Madeline Hunter?" *Phi Delta Kappan* 69(9):669–672 (May 1988).

[8]Jane Stallings, "A Study of Implementation of Madeline Hunter's Model and Its Effect on Students," *Journal of Educational Research* 78(6):325–337 (July–August 1985).

[9]John D. Tudor, "Background for the South Carolina Implementation of the PET Inservice Teacher Training Program." Paper presented at the annual meeting of the American Educational Research Association, New Orleans (April 1988).

attitude toward PET, (3) self-reported teacher use of PET concepts and lesson plans, and (4) motivation for training.

A series of related follow-up studies of the South Carolina implementation showed that student achievement was not affected; although the training was well received by the teachers, the follow-up coaching was limited in quantity and not always consistent with Hunter's recommendations.[10]

Donovan, Sousa, and Walberg[11] reported an evaluation of programs for grades 3, 6, 9, and 11. In West Orange, New Jersey, ITIP-trained (35) and untrained (29) teachers participated in the study. Results indicated that adjusted achievement scores for the students of both groups of teachers were nearly identical. Although marketed with claims of improved instruction, increased student achievement, and an all-purpose lesson plan, considered together, the findings of these discussed studies indicate that the Hunter model has *not* resulted in significant improvement in student achievement.

SUMMARY

In this chapter you learned why lesson planning is important and how lessons are useful, pedagogical tools. Beginning with the course syllabus and progressing to specific daily plans, Part II of this book has provided you with guided practice in the processes necessary to prepare to teach in a classroom.

Part III will acquaint you with specific information about the selection and use of specific strategies, aids, and resources for effective instruction in the elementary school. When you have completed your study of Part III, you may wish to revisit this chapter and revise the lesson plan you have completed, or you may choose to develop new plans.

QUESTIONS FOR CLASS DISCUSSION

1. Do all effective teachers plan lessons for instruction? Explain.
2. Do all teachers prepare formal, written lesson plans for each class meeting? Explain.
3. List three characteristics of instructional goals.
4. Is there one best format for lesson planning? Explain.
5. In lesson planning, describe how the teacher can attend to student learning styles and to student modality strengths.
6. Research and describe your findings on the relationship between detailed lesson planning and student achievement.
7. Give several reasons that explain why both a student teacher and a first-year teacher need to prepare detailed lesson plans.

[10]Garrett K. Mandeville and Janelle L. Rivers, "The South Carolina PET Study: Teachers' Perceptions and Student Achievement," *Elementary School Journal* 91(4):377–401 (March 1991).

[11]James F. Donovan, David A. Sousa, and Herbert J. Walberg, "The Impact of Staff Development on Implementation and Student Achievement," *Journal of Educational Research* 80(6):348–351 (July–August 1987).

8. Explain why you need to know how to prepare detailed unit and lesson plans even if the textbook you are using provides them in a teacher's guide.
9. When preparing unit and lesson plans, will you need to consider student safety? Explain.
10. Do you have questions about the content of this chapter? How might answers be found?

SUGGESTED READINGS FOR CHAPTER 8

Bennett, W. J. "First Lessons." *Phi Delta Kappan* 68(2):125–129 (October 1986).

Goldberg, M. F. "Portrait of Madeline Hunter." *Educational Leadership* 47(5):141–143 (February 1990).

Hunter, M. "Madeline Hunter in the English Classroom." *English Journal* 78(5):16–18 (September 1989).

———. *Mastery Teaching.* El Segundo, CA: Instructional Dynamics, Inc., 1982.

Wresch, W., ed. *The English Classroom in the Computer Age: Thirty Lesson Plans.* Urbana, IL: National Council of Teachers of English, 1991.

PART III

Choosing and Implementing Instructional Strategies, Aids, and Resources

Part III helps you choose and implement strategies, aids, and resources by providing

- A listing of professional periodicals and copyrighted materials.
- Descriptions and guidelines for the use of inquiry and discovery.
- Guidelines and resources for the use of educational games, projected and nonprojected media aids and equipment, videodisc programs, and the classroom computer.
- Guidelines and skill development exercises for the use of questioning.

- Guidelines for teaching specific subjects of the elementary school curriculum, starting a resource file, and developing a self-instructional package.
- Guidelines for the use of the classroom writing board, learning activity center, and classroom bulletin board and other visual displays.
- Guidelines for the use of cooperative learning, teaching toward mastery learning, and assuring equality in the classroom.
- Guidelines for the use of demonstrations and discussions and the selection of instructional strategies.
- Guidelines for the use of student presentations and projects, papers, and oral reports.
- Guidelines for the use of textbooks, field trips, formal and informal teacher talk, and assignments and homework.
- Practice in recognizing selected teacher behaviors in classroom interaction.
- Resources for free and inexpensive materials.
- Strategies for teaching thinking skills.
- Resources for writing across the curriculum.

Students involved in direct experiences are using more of their sensory modalities, and when all the senses are engaged, learning is most effective and longest lasting. This is "learning by doing"—"hands-on, minds-on learning."

An effective teacher structures questions so as to guide students to higher levels of thinking.

Your goals are to help students learn how to solve problems, to make decisions, to think creatively and critically, and to feel good about themselves and their learning—rather than to simply fill their minds with bits and pieces of information.

Every lesson should begin with some sort of preassessment of what the children already know, or think they know, about the topic of the ensuing lesson.

9

What Theoretical Considerations Are Important for the Selection of Teaching Strategies?

In Chapter 3 you learned about specific teacher behaviors that must be demonstrated to enable children to learn. Those behaviors are fundamental and nondiscretionary teacher behaviors. By nondiscretionary we mean that the teacher has no choice but to use them and to use them well. As presented in Chapter 3, the nondiscretionary behaviors are (1) structuring, (2) accountability, (3) withitness and overlapping, (4) variety, motivating, and challenging, (5) modeling, (6) facilitating data acquisition, (7) accepting, (8) clarifying, (9) silence, and (10) questioning. In this part of the book you will learn not only more about how to implement certain of those fundamental behaviors, but also about how to select from and implement the large repertoire of other strategies, aids, and resources available for your use.

To properly select and effectively implement a particular strategy to teach specific content to a distinctive group of students, there are myriad decisions you must make along the way. Selection of a particular strategy depends in part on your decision either to deliver information directly (**direct, expository,** or **didactic teaching**) or to provide students with access to information (**indirect** or **facilitative teaching**). Direct teaching tends to be **teacher-centered,** while indirect teaching is more **student-centered.**

Note: Professional education is rampant with its own special jargon, which can be confusing to the neophyte. The use of the terms "direct teaching" or its synonym, "direct instruction," and the converse, "direct experiences," is an example of how confusing the jargon can be. "Direct teaching" (or "direct instruction," "expository teaching," or "teacher-centered instruction") can also have a variety of definitions, depending on who is doing the defining. Whereas specific strategies are discussed in Chapter 11, it is important now that you not confuse **direct instruction** with **direct experiences,** discussed in Section C of this brief but important chapter. The two terms indicate two separate (although not entirely incompatible) instructional modes.

A. PRINCIPLES OF INSTRUCTION AND LEARNING

To decide on a mode of instruction, you must bear in mind certain principles of instruction and learning. Several important principles that have evolved from studies of recent years are as follows:

- By the end of grade 8, students should have experienced and be able to engage in independent study and cooperative learning, and able to give and receive tutorial instruction.
- Children must be actively involved in their own learning and in the assessment of their learning.
- Regardless of anything else, you are a teacher of reading, writing, thinking, and study skills.
- To a great degree, the mode of instruction determines what is learned.
- You must hold high expectations for the learning of each child, and not waiver from those expectations.
- You must provide constant, steady, understandable, and reliable feedback to students about their learning.

As first emphasized in Part I, a student does not learn to write by learning to recognize grammatical constructs of sentences. Neither does a person learn to play soccer solely by listening to a lecture on soccer. School learning is superficial unless the instructional methods are appropriate for the understanding, skills, and attitudes desired. Memorizing, for instance, is not the same as understanding. Yet far too often, memorization seems all that is expected of students. The result is mere verbalism, the mouthing of poorly-understood words and sentences. That is *not* teaching, but merely the orchestration of short-term memory exercises. To make learning real to students, you should use direct and real experiences as often as possible. Vicarious experiences are sometimes necessary to provide students with otherwise unattainable knowledge; however, direct experiences that engage all the student's senses and all their learning modalities are more powerful. Students learn to write by writing and receiving coaching and feedback about their progress in writing. They learn to play soccer by playing soccer and receiving coaching and feedback about their developing skills and knowledge in playing the game. They learn these things best when they are actively (hands-on) and mentally (minds-on) engaged in doing them.

B. DELIVERY VERSUS ACCESS MODES

When selecting an instructional strategy there are two distinct choices: you must decide whether to deliver information to the students, or to provide students with access to information. The traditional mode (sometimes called the didactic style) is to deliver information; that is, knowledge is passed on from those who know (the teacher and the textbook) to those who do not (the students). Within the **delivery mode,** traditional and time-honored strategies are textbook reading, the lecture (teacher talk), questioning, and discussions. For the elementary school classroom teacher, teacher talk is an important and nearly unavoidable teaching tool, and it can be valuable when used judiciously.

Within the **access mode,** instead of direct delivery of information and direct control over what is learned, you provide access to information by working with the children in designing experiences that facilitate their obtaining new knowledge and skills. Learning often is better when children are taught by this mode, especially at higher levels of the learning domains.

An important instructional strategy within the access mode is **inquiry.** Inquiry most certainly will include questioning, although the questions more likely will come from the children, rather than from the teacher or the textbook. Discussions and lectures on particular topics, too, may be involved in a broader student inquiry. When used in the access mode, discussions and lectures follow or occur during, rather than precede, direct, hands-on learning by the children.

It is likely that you are more experienced with the delivery mode. (Chapter 11 provides guidelines for the use of strategies within this mode.) Yet to be most effective, you must also become knowledgeable and skillful in the use of access strategies. Although the intent here is *not* to imply that one mode is unquestionably more favorable, strategies within the access mode do facilitate the positive learning of students. *Regardless of your intended grade level or subject, to be most effective you should be eclectic in selecting strategies; that is, you should appropriately select and effectively use strategies within both modes, but with emphasis on access strategies.* The chapters that follow present techniques within each mode so that you can become knowledgeable and can make intelligent decisions for choosing the best strategy for particular goals and objectives for your own discipline or grade level and unique group of students. Figures 9.1 and 9.2 provide a review of specific strengths and weaknesses of each mode.

From a comparison of Figures 9.1 and 9.2, you can see that the strengths and weaknesses of one mode are nearly mirror opposites of the other. Although you should be skillful in the use of strategies within both modes, to be most effective *you should concentrate more on the use of strategies from the access mode.* Strategies within that mode are more child-centered, hands-on, and concrete, with students actually doing that which they are learning to do. Learning that occurs within this mode is longer lasting, and, as the learner develops a sense of "can do," more likely to serve adequately the learner's developing self-esteem.

C. A RULE FOR PLANNING AND SELECTING LEARNING ACTIVITIES

Can you imagine a teacher telling students how to read a barometer without ever letting them do it? Can you imagine having children learn the letters of the alphabet without ever having them put letters together to make words? Unfortunately, too

---

Strengths of the Delivery Mode
- Much content can be covered within a short span of time, usually by formal teacher talk, which then may be followed by an experiential activity.
- The teacher is in control of what content is covered.
- The teacher is in control of time allotted to specific content coverage.
- Strategies within the delivery mode are consistent with competency-based instruction.
- Student achievement of specific content is predictable and manageable.

Potential Weaknesses of Delivery Strategies
- The sources of student motivation are mostly extrinsic.
- Students have little control over the pacing of their learning.
- Students make few important decisions about their learning.
- There may be little opportunity for divergent or creative thinking.
- Student self-esteem may be inadequately served.

Figure 9.1   Delivery mode: its strengths and weaknesses.

Strengths of Access Strategies
- Students learn content in greater depth.
- The sources of student motivation are more likely intrinsic.
- Students make important decisions about their own learning.
- Students have more control over the pacing of their learning.
- Students develop a sense of personal self-worth.

Potential Weaknesses of Access Strategies
- Content coverage may be more limited.
- They are time-consuming.
- The teacher has less control over content and time.
- The specific results of student learning are less predictable.
- The teacher may have less control over class procedures.

Figure 9.2 Access mode: its strengths and weaknesses.

many teachers do just that. In planning and selecting learning activities, an important rule to remember is to select activities that are as direct as possible. *When students are involved in direct experiences, they are using more of their sensory modalities (auditory, visual, tactile, kinesthetic); and when all the senses are engaged, learning is most effective and longest lasting.* This is referred to as "learning by doing," or, as discussed in Chapter 2, "hands-on, minds-on learning"—one end of the spectrum on the Learning Experiences Ladder (Figure 9.3).[1]

Conversely, at the other end of the spectrum are abstract experiences, where the children are exposed only to symbols (that is, words and numbers), using only one or two senses (auditory or visual). The teacher lectures while the children sit and watch and listen. Visual and verbal symbolic experiences, although impossible to avoid when teaching, are less effective in ensuring that planned learning occurs. This is especially so in teaching younger children, children with special needs, slower learners, learners with limited proficiency in English, and intellectually immature learners. It is even true in teaching many adult learners. So, as stated earlier, when planning you should select activities and materials that engage the learners in the most direct experiences possible and appropriate for your specific group of children.

The Learning Experiences Ladder (Figure 9.3) depicts this range of experiences from most direct (bottom of ladder) to most abstract (top of ladder).

As can be inferred from the Learning Experiences Ladder, when teaching about tide pools (*Example 1* on the ladder), the most effective mode is to take the students to a tide pool (bottom of ladder; the most direct experience) where students can see, hear, touch, smell, and perhaps even taste (if it is not toxic) the water in the tide pool. The least effective mode is for the teacher merely to talk about the tide pool (top of ladder; the most abstract symbolic experience), engaging only one sense—auditory.

Of course, for various reasons—such as matters of safety, lack of resources for a field trip, location of your school, or a beach posted with No Trespassing signs because

---

[1]Earlier versions of this concept can be seen in Charles F. Hoban, Sr., et al., *Visualizing the Curriculum* (New York: Dryden, 1937), p. 39; Edgar Dale, *Audio-Visual Methods in Teaching* (New York: Holt, Rinehart & Winston, 1969), p. 108; Jerome S. Bruner, *Toward a Theory of Instruction* (Cambridge: Harvard University Press, 1966), p. 49.

Verbal Experiences
Teacher talk, written words; engaging one sense; using the most abstract symbolization; students are physically inactive.

Example 1: Listening to the teacher talk about tide pools.
Example 2: Listening to a student report about the Grand Canyon in Arizona.
Example 3: Listening to a guest speaker talk about how the state legislature functions.

Visual Experiences
Still pictures, diagrams, charts; engaging one sense; typically symbolic; students are physically inactive.

Example 1: Viewing slide photographs of tide pools.
Example 2: Viewing drawings and photographs of the Grand Canyon.
Example 3: Listening to a guest speaker talk about the state legislature while showing slides of it in action.

Vicarious Experiences
Laser videodisc programs; computer programs; video programs; engaging more than one sense; learner is indirectly "doing"; may be some limited physical activity.

Example 1: Interacting with a computer program about wave action and life in tide pools.
Example 2: Viewing and listening to a video program about the Grand Canyon.
Example 3: Taking a field trip to observe the state legislature in action.

Simulated Experiences
Role playing; experimenting; simulations; mock-up; working models; all or nearly all senses are engaged; activity often integrates disciplines; closest to the real thing.

Example 1: Building a classroom working model of a tide pool.
Example 2: Building a classroom working model of the Grand Canyon.
Example 3: Designing a classroom role-play simulation patterned after the operating procedure of the state legislature.

Direct Experiences
Learner is actually doing what is being learned; true inquiry; all senses are engaged; usually integrates disciplines; the real thing.

Example 1: Visiting and experiencing a tide pool.
Example 2: Visiting and experiencing the Grand Canyon.
Example 3: Designing an elected representative body to oversee the operation of the school-within-the-school program, one that is patterned after the state legislative assembly.

Figure 9.3 The Learning Experiences Ladder.

of toxic waste pollution—you may not be able to take the students to a tide pool. Sometimes it may not be possible, or appropriate, to use the most direct experience, and you must therefore select an experience higher on the ladder. Self-discovery teaching is not always appropriate. At times it is more appropriate to build on what others have discovered and learned. Although children do not need to "reinvent the wheel," the most effective and longest lasting learning *is* that which engages most or all of their senses, and on the Learning Experiences Ladder, these are the experiences that fall within the bottom three rungs—direct, simulated, and vicarious. This is true for adult learners, primary-grade children, and children of any age group in between.

Another value of direct, simulated, and vicarious experiences is that they tend to be interdisciplinary; that is, they tend to cross subject-content boundaries. That makes such experiences especially useful for teachers who want to help students connect the learning of one discipline with that of others, and with their own life experiences. Direct, simulated, and vicarious experiences are more like real life.

Now, recalling and analyzing your own learning experiences, do Exercise 9.1.

Exercise 9.1: Recalling My Own Learning Experiences in School

Instructions: The purpose of this exercise is to recall and share learning experiences from your own school days, and to reflect on them in relationship to the Learning Experiences Ladder and the preceding discussion about the access and delivery modes of instruction.

1. Recall one vivid learning experience from each level of your schooling and identify its position on the Learning Experiences Ladder.

Level of Experience	*Position on Ladder*

Elementary school experience _____   _____

_____

_____

_____

_____

_____

Middle grades experience _____   _____

_____

_____

_____

_____

_____

_____

High school experience _____   _____

_____

_____

_____

_____

_____

College experience _____   _____

_____

_____

_____

_____

_____

2. Share with classmates in small groups.

After sharing your experiences with others of your group, what conclusions, if any, can your group arrive at? Write them here and then share them with the entire class.

_____

_____

_____

_____

_____

_____

_____

_____

_____

_____

_____

_____

_____

_____

_____

_____

_____

_____

_____

_____

_____

_____

_____

_____

_____

_____

_____

SUMMARY

You have learned of the importance of learning modalities and about instructional modes; about children and their needs, and the importance of providing an accepting and supportive learning environment; about teacher behaviors necessary to facilitate student learning; and about long-range and daily planning. In the remaining chapters of Part III of this resource guide your attention is directed to the selection and implementation of specific strategies, aids, and resources to facilitate students learning of particular skills and content.

One strategy of fundamental importance to both the access and delivery modes, a strategy that is nondiscretionary—that is, one you cannot do without (first presented in Chapter 3)—is the use of questioning. Because of its importance, and because it is so often used and abused, Chapter 10 is devoted to this strategy.

QUESTIONS FOR CLASS DISCUSSION

1. Should you always respond to every student comment or query? Why? If not, on what basis do you decide when and how to respond?
2. To what extent can teachers assist students in identifying and resolving real-life conflicts?
3. Explain the difference between the following sets of terms: direct and indirect instruction; access and delivery modes of instruction; didactic and facilitating teaching styles.
4. While our emphasis for the elementary school teacher is on development of an eclectic model of teaching, some authors of methods books talk of "teaching models," such as discovery, inquiry, expository, social interaction, and so on. Explain the correlation and the difference between a teaching style and the teacher's choice of strategies. Explain how a teacher can be both eclectic and consistent.
5. Do girls learn differently from boys, or is it even fair to ask this question? Explain.
6. Explain the difference between nondiscretionary and discretionary teaching strategies. Give examples of each.
7. Identify six important principles of learning and tell how you would use each principle in your own teaching.
8. Explain why, when taught by strategies within the access mode, students may learn less content but learn it better. Given today's emphasis on mastery of content rather than on coverage of content, should a teacher rely more on use of strategies within the access or the delivery mode? Explain.
9. Explain what makes learning activities at the bottom of the Learning Experiences Ladder less abstract than those at the top of the ladder.
10. Explain the importance of the concept of the Learning Experiences Ladder.
11. Do you have questions about the content of this chapter? How might answers be found?

SUGGESTED READINGS FOR CHAPTER 9

Alvino, J., ed. "Building Better Thinkers." *Learning 90* 18(6):40–55 (February 1990).
Brookfield, S. D. *The Skillful Teacher.* San Francisco: Jossey-Bass, 1990.

Costa, A. L. *The School as a Home for the Mind.* Palatine, IL: Skylight Publishing, 1991.

———, ed. *Developing Minds: A Resource Book for Teaching Thinking.* Rev. ed. Alexandria, VA: Association for Supervision and Curriculum Development, 1991.

———. *Developing Minds: Programs for Teaching Thinking.* Rev. ed. Alexandria, VA: Association for Supervision and Curriculum Development, 1991.

DeVries, R., et al., "Sociomoral Development in Direct Instruction, Eclectic, and Constructivist Kindergartens: A Study of Children's Enacted Interpersonal Understanding." *Early Childhood Research Quarterly* 6(4):473–517 (December 1991).

Joyce, B. R. *Selecting Learning Experiences: Linking Theory and Practice.* Alexandria, VA: Association for Supervision and Curriculum Development, 1978.

Resnick, L. *Education and Learning to Think.* Washington, DC: National Academy Press, 1987.

Resnick, L. and Klopfer, L., eds. *Toward the Thinking Curriculum: Current Cognitive Research.* 1989 Yearbook of the Association for Supervision and Curriculum Development. Alexandria, VA: Association for Supervision and Curriculum Development, 1989.

10

What Do I Need to Know About the Use of Questioning?

A nondiscretionary strategy of fundamental importance to both the access and delivery modes is, as introduced in Chapter 3, that of questioning. Because it is so important, and because it is so frequently used and abused, this entire chapter is devoted to helping you develop skills in the use of questioning.

You will use questioning for so many purposes that there is no way you can achieve effectiveness in teaching unless skilled in its use. You will adapt the type and form of each question to the purpose for which it is asked.

A. PURPOSES FOR USING QUESTIONS

The purposes for which you might use questions can be separated into five categories:

1. *To politely give instructions.* For example, "Anthony, would you please turn out the lights so we can show the slides?" You can also use questions to regain student attention and maintain classroom control; for example, "Juanita, would you please attend to your reading?"
2. *To review and remind students of classroom procedures.* For example, if students continue to talk without first raising their hands and being recognized by you, you can stop the lesson and say, "Class, I think we need to review the procedure for answering my questions. What is the procedure for talking?"
3. *To gather information.* For example, "How many of you have finished the exercise?" or to find out whether a student knows something: "Rachael, can you please tell us the meaning of the word *homeostasis?*"
4. *To discover student interests.* For example, "How many of you would be interested in going on a field trip to the water treatment plant?"
5. *To guide student thinking and learning.* It is this category of questioning that is the focus of this chapter. Questions in this category are used to:
   * Develop appreciation.
   * Develop student thinking.
   * Diagnose learning difficulty.
   * Emphasize major points.

- Encourage students.
- Establish rapport.
- Evaluate learning.
- Give practice in expression.
- Help students in their own metacognition.
- Help students interpret materials.
- Help students organize materials.
- Provide drill and practice.
- Provide review.
- Show agreement or disagreement.
- Show relationships, such as cause and effect.

B. A GLOSSARY OF TYPES OF COGNITIVE QUESTIONS

Before we go further let us define, describe, and provide examples for each of the types of cognitive questions that you will use in teaching. Then, in the section that follows, we focus your attention on the levels of cognitive questions.

Clarifying Question

The clarifying question is used to gain more information from a student to help the teacher better understand a student's ideas, feelings, and thought processes. Examples of clarifying questions are: "Would you please explain to us what you mean by your statement 'the author was a nerd'?" Or, "What I hear you saying is that you would rather work alone than in your group. Is that correct?" Research has shown there to be a strong and positive correlation between student learning and development of metacognitive skills and the teacher's use of questions that ask students for clarification.[1] In addition, by seeking clarification, the teacher is likely to be demonstrating an interest in the student and his thinking.

Convergent Thinking Question

Convergent questions (also called "narrow" questions) are low-order thinking questions that have a singular answer (such as recall questions discussed and exemplified in the next section). Examples of convergent questions are: "If the radius of a circle is 20 feet, what is the circle's circumference?" "What is the subject of this sentence?"

Cuing Question

If you ask a question to which, after sufficient wait-time, no students respond or where their inadequate responses indicate they need more information, then you can ask a question that cues the answer or response you are seeking. In essence, you are going backward in your questioning sequence, to cue the students. For example, if a teacher asks her students, "How many legs do crayfish, lobsters, and shrimp have?"

---

[1]Arthur L. Costa, *The School as a Home for the Mind* (Palatine, IL: Skylight Publishing, 1991), p. 63.

and there is no accurate response, then she might cue the answer with the following information and question, "The class to which those animals belong is class Decapoda. Does that give you a clue about the number of legs they have?" If that clue is not enough, then she might ask, "What is a decathalon?" and so on.

Divergent Thinking Question

Divergent questions (also known as "broad," "reflective," or "thought" questions) are open-ended (i.e., usually having no singularly correct answer), high-order thinking questions, requiring students to think creatively, to leave the comfortable confines of the known and reach out into the unknown. Examples of questions that require divergent thinking are: "What measures could be taken to improve the trash problem after lunch at our school?" Or, "In view of the arguments presented by Senator Merlino and the National Rifle Association, do you think that the government should ban Saturday night specials?"

Evaluative Question

Some types of questions, whether convergent or divergent, require students to place a value on something, and these are sometimes referred to as evaluative questions. If the teacher and the students all agree on certain premises, then the evaluative question would also be a convergent question. If original assumptions differ, then the response to the evaluative question would be more subjective, and therefore divergent. Examples of evaluative questions are: "Should the United States send ground forces to former Yugoslavia?" "Should women be allowed to choose to have abortions?"

Focus Question

A focus question is any question that is designed to focus a student's thinking. For example, the last question of the preceding paragraph is a focus question when the teacher asking it is trying to focus student attention on the social issue involved.

Probing Question

Similar to a clarifying question, the probing question requires student thinking to go beyond superficial first-answer or single-word responses. Examples of probing questions are: "Why, John, do you think that to be the case—that every citizen has the right to say what he or she believes?" Or, "Could you give us an example?"

C. COGNITIVE LEVELS OF QUESTIONS

Questions posed by the teacher cue the students to the level of thinking expected by the teacher, ranging from the lowest level of mental operation, requiring simple recall of knowledge **(convergent thinking),** to the highest, requiring **divergent thought** and **application** of that thought. It is important that you (1) are aware of the levels of thinking, (2) understand the importance of attending to student thinking from low to higher levels of operation, and (3) understand that for one student what may be a matter of simple recall of information, for another may require a higher-order mental activity, such as figuring something out by deduction.

You should structure questions in a way that is designed to guide students to higher levels of thinking. To help your understanding, three levels of questioning and thinking are described as follows:[2]

1. *Lowest level (the data-input phase): gathering and recalling information.* At this level questions are designed to solicit from students' concepts, information, feelings, or experiences that were gained in the past and stored in memory. Sample key words and desired behaviors are:

complete, count, define, describe, identify, list, match, name, observe, recall, recite, select.

2. *Intermediate level (the data-processing phase): processing information.* At this level questions are designed to draw relationships of cause and effect, to synthesize, analyze, summarize, compare, contrast, or to classify data. Sample key words and desired behaviors are:

analyze, classify, compare, contrast, distinguish, explain, group, infer, make an analogy, organize, plan, synthesize.

3. *Highest level (the data-output phase): applying and evaluating in new situations.* Questions at this level encourage students to think intuitively, creatively, and hypothetically, to use their imaginations, to expose a value system, or to make a judgment. Sample key words and desired behaviors are:

apply a principle, build a model. evaluate, extrapolate, forecast, generalize, hypothesize, imagine, judge, predict, speculate.

You should use the type of question that is best suited for the purpose, use a variety of levels of questions, and structure questions in a way intended to move student thinking to higher levels (for an example, see Exercise 10.7). When teachers use higher-level questions, their students tend to score higher on tests of critical thinking and on standardized tests of achievement.[3]

Developing your skill in the use of questioning requires attention to detail. The following guidelines and exercises will be useful as you develop your skill in using this important instructional strategy.

D. GUIDELINES FOR QUESTIONING

Your goals are to help your students learn how to solve problems, to make decisions, to think creatively and critically, and to feel good about themselves and their learning—rather than to simply fill their minds with bits and pieces of information.

---

[2]Arthur L. Costa, *The Enabling Behaviors* (Orangevale, CA: Search Models Unlimited, 1989). This three-tiered model of thinking has been described variously by others. For example, in Elliot Eisner's *The Educational Imagination* (New York: Macmillan, 1979), the levels are referred to as "descriptive," "interpretive," and "evaluative." For a comparison of thinking models, see Costa, *The School as a Home*, p. 44. You probably recognize the similarity between these three levels of questions and the five levels of thinking in Bloom's taxonomy of cognitive objectives. For your daily use of questioning, it is probably more practical to think and behave in terms of these three levels, rather than of five.

[3]See, for example, B. Newton, "Theoretical Basis for Higher Cognitive Questioning—An Avenue to Critical Thinking," *Education* 98(3):286–290 (March–April 1978). See also D. Redfield and E. Rousseau, "A Meta-analysis of Experimental Research on Teacher Questioning Behavior," *Review of Educational Research* 51(2):237–245 (Summer 1981).

How you construct your questions and how you carry out your questioning strategy is important to the realization of these goals.

Preparing Questions

Use the following guidelines in preparing questions.

1. *Cognitive questions should be planned, thoughtfully worded, and written into your lesson plan.* Thoughtful preparation of questions helps to ensure that they are clear and specific, not ambiguous, that the vocabulary is appropriate, and that each question matches its purpose. Incorporate questions into all of your lessons as instructional devices, welcomed pauses, attention grabbers, and checks for student comprehension.

2. *Match questions with their purposes.* Carefully planning questions allows them to be sequenced and worded to match the levels of cognitive thinking expected of students. *Sequencing* is reviewed in the exercises that follow, but first we will consider the *wording* of questions.

To help children develop their thinking skills, you need to demonstrate (effectively model) how to do this. To demonstrate, you should use terminology that is specific and that provides students with examples of experiences consonant with the meanings of the cognitive words. You need to demonstrate this every day so that students learn the *cognitive terminology.*[4] Here are three examples:

Instead of	Say
"How else might you do it?"	"How could you *apply* . . .?"
"Are you going to get quiet?	"If we are going to hear what Mark has to say, what do you need to do?"
"How do you know that is the case?"	"What *evidence* do you have . . .?"

Implementing Questions

Careful preparation of questions is one part of the skill in questioning. Implementation is the other part. Here are guidelines for effective implementation of this strategy:

3. *Avoid bombarding students with too much teacher talk.* Sometimes teachers talk too much. This can be especially true of teachers who are nervous, as might be the case for many during the initial weeks of their student teaching. Knowledge of the guidelines presented here will be helpful in avoiding that behavior. Remind yourself to be quiet after you ask a question that you have carefully formulated. Sometimes, especially when a question has not been carefully planned by the teacher, the teacher asks the question, then, with a slight change in wording, asks it again, or asks several questions one after another. That is "shotgun" questioning—too much verbiage, which only confuses students and allows too little time for them to think.

4. *After asking a question, provide students with adequate time to think.* Knowing the subject better than the students know it, and having given prior thought to the subject, too many teachers fail to allow students sufficient time to think after asking a question. By the time they have reached middle grades (or sooner), students have learned pretty well how to play the "game"; that is, they know that if they remain

[4]Costa, 1991, p. 110.

silent long enough the teacher will probably answer his or her own question. After asking a well-worded question you should remain quiet for a while, allowing students time to think and to respond. If you wait long enough, they usually will.

Some students think and respond faster than others. Some respond faster than others whether or not they have thought about their response. You will want to instruct your students in the importance of **wait-time,** of giving all students time to think about the question before you begin to accept responses.

After asking a question, how long should you wait before you do something? You should wait at least two seconds, and as long as nine. Stop reading now, and look at your watch or a clock to get a sense of how long two seconds is. Then observe how long nine seconds is. Did it seem a long time? Because most of us are not used to silence in the classroom, only two seconds of silence can seem eternal. If for some reason students have not responded after a period of two to nine seconds of wait-time, then you can ask the question again (but do not reword an already carefully worded question, or students are likely to think it is a new question). Pause for several seconds; then, if you still have not received a response, you can call on a student, then another, if necessary, after sufficient wait-time. Soon you will get a response that can be built upon. *Seldom to never should you answer your own question!*

5. *Practice calling on all students, not just the bright or the slow, not just the boys or the girls, not only those in the front of the room, but all of them.* To do this takes concentrated effort on your part, but *it is important.* To ensure that students are called on equally, some teachers have in hand their seating chart on a bright neon-colored clipboard and make a mark next to the name of the student each time he or she is called on. (For additional suggestions, see Chapter 11, Section C, "Equality in the Classroom.")

6. *Give equal wait-time to all students.* This too will require concentrated effort on your part, but is also important. A teacher who waits for less time when calling on a slow student, or students of one gender more than the other, is showing a bias or a lack of confidence in certain students, both of which are detrimental to the effort to establish for all students a positive, equal, and safe environment for classroom learning. Show confidence in all students, and never discriminate by expecting less or more from some than from others.

We know of one teacher who, when using questioning, practices giving equal wait-time by placing one hand behind her back and slowly folding her fingers, one at a time, with each finger fold representing one second.

7. *When you ask questions, do not let students randomly shout out their answers; instead, require them to raise their hands and to be called on before they respond.* This helps to ensure that you call on all students equally, that you distribute your interactions equally, and that girls do not experience less interaction just because boys tend to be more vociferous (see Exercise 11.3). Even in college, male students tend to be more vocal than female students, and when allowed by the professor, tend to outtalk and to interrupt their female peers. Every teacher has the responsibility to guarantee an equal distribution of interaction time in the classroom.

8. *Use strong praise sparingly.* As discussed in Chapter 3, the use of strong praise is sometimes appropriate, especially when working with kindergarten and primary-grade children and with children who have special needs, and when asking questions of simple low-level recall, such as "Susan, which color is this?" But when you want students to think divergently and creatively, you should be stingy with your use of strong praise to student responses. Strong praise from a teacher tends to terminate divergent and creative thinking.

One of your goals is to help children find intrinsic sources for motivation. Strong praise tends to build conformity, causing students to depend on the giver of praise for their worth, rather than on themselves.[5] A strong praise (active acceptance) response is exemplified by a teacher who responds to a student answer with, "That's right! Very good." On the other hand, passive acceptance responses, such as "Okay, that seems to be one possibility," keep the window open for further thinking, particularly for higher-level, divergent thinking.

Another example of a passive acceptance response is one used in brainstorming sessions, when the teacher says, "After asking the question and giving you some time to think about it, I will hear your ideas and record them on the chalkboard." Only after *all* student responses have been heard and recorded does the class begin its consideration of each. In the classroom, that kind of nonjudgmental acceptance of all ideas will generate a great deal of high-level thought.[6]

9. *Encourage students to ask questions about content and process.* There is no such thing as a "dumb" question from a student. Sometimes students, like everyone else, ask questions that could just have easily been looked up. Those questions can consume precious class time. For a teacher, this can be frustrating. A teacher's initial reaction might be to quickly and mistakenly brush off that type of question with sarcasm, assuming that the student is too lazy to look up an answer. In such instances, you are advised to think before responding and to respond kindly and professionally, even though, in the busy life of a classroom teacher, that may not always be easy to do. However, be assured, there is a reason for a student's question. Perhaps the youngster is signaling a need for recognition.

In large schools it is sometimes easy for a child to feel alone and insignificant (although this seems less the case in schools that use a "school-within-a-school" plan, discussed in Chapter 1), and when a student makes an effort to interact with you, that can be a positive sign. Therefore, gauge carefully your responses to such efforts. If a child's question is really off track, off the wall, out of order, and out of context in relation to the content of the lesson, as a possible response, consider this: "That is an interesting question (or comment) and I would very much like to talk with you more about it. Could we meet at lunchtime, or before or after school?" (*Note:* Some teachers conduct a brown bag lunch session each day when students are welcome to come to their classrooms to share lunch and talk with them about anything.)

Student questions can and should be used as springboards for further questions, discussion, and investigations. Students should be encouraged to ask questions that challenge the textbook, the process, or other persons' statements, and to seek the facts or evidence behind a statement.

10. *Being able to ask questions may be more important than having right answers.* Knowledge is derived from asking questions. Being able to recognize problems and to formulate questions is a skill and the key to problem solving and the development of critical thinking skills. You have a responsibility to encourage students to formulate questions and to help them word their questions in such a way that tentative answers can be sought. This is the process necessary to build a base of knowledge that can be called upon again and again as a way to link, interpret, and explain new information in new situations.[7]

---

[5]Ibid., p. 55.
[6]For further discussion of research findings about the use of praise and rewards in teaching, see B. Joyce and B. Showers, *Student Achievement Through Staff Development* (New York: Longman, 1988).
[7]Lauren B. Resnick and Leopold E. Klopfer, eds., *Toward the Thinking Curriculum: Current Cognitive Research*, 1989 ASCD Yearbook (Alexandria, VA: Association for Supervision and Curriculum Development, 1989), p. 5.

11. *Questioning is the cornerstone to critical thinking and real-world problem solving.* In real-world problem solving, there are usually no absolute right answers. Some answers are better than others, rather than "correct" or "incorrect." The person with a problem (a) recognizes the problem, (b) formulates a question about that problem (e.g., Should I buy a house or rent? Should I date this person or not? Should I take this job or not? Which car should I buy? Should I abuse drugs or not?), (c) collects data, and (d) arrives at a temporarily acceptable answer to the problem, while realizing that at some later time new data may dictate a review of this conclusion. For example, if a biochemist believes she has discovered a new enzyme, there is no textbook (or teacher) to which she may refer to find out if she is right. On the basis of her self-confidence in problem identification, asking questions, collecting enough data, and arriving at a tentative conclusion based on those data, she assumes that for now her conclusion is safe. (This point is discussed further in Chapter 11, Section D.)

12. *Avoid bluffing an answer to a question for which you do not have an answer.* Nothing will diminish your credibility with your students more quickly than your faking an answer. There is nothing wrong with admitting that you do not know. It helps students realize that you are human. It helps them maintain adequate self-esteem, realizing that if they sometimes do not know answers, they still are okay. What *is* important is that you know where and how to find possible answers, and that you help students develop these same skills.

Exercises 10.1 through 10.6 are designed to aid your understanding and to build your skills in the use of questioning. Do these exercises now.

Exercise 10.1: A Self-Check on Identifying the Cognitive Levels of Questions

Instructions: The purpose of this exercise is to test your understanding and recognition of the levels of questions. Mark each of the following questions as follows:

1 = Lowest level—gathering and recalling data.
2 = Requires the student to process data.
3 = Highest level of mental operation; requires the student to apply or to evaluate data in a new situation.

Check your answers against the key that follows. Resolve problems by discussing them with your classmates and instructor.

_____ 1. Do you recall the differences between an Asian elephant and an African elephant?

_____ 2. Explain how the natural habitats of the two elephants are similar. How are they different?

_____ 3. Which of the elephants do you think is the most interesting?

_____ 4. What do you think the elephant uses its tusks for?

_____ 5. Do all elephants have tusks?

_____ 6. Did the trick ending make the story more interesting for you?

_____ 7. How might these conifer needles be grouped?

_____ 8. Could you explain how these two types of pine needles differ?

_____ 9. For how many years was the Soviet Union a communist-dominated nation?

_____ 10. What do you think the life expectancy of persons in this country will be by the year 2025?

_____ 11. What do you think caused the city to change the location of the zoo?

_____ 12. How would the park be different today had the zoo been left there?

_____ 13. How do zoos today differ from those of the mid-nineteenth century?

_____ 14. Should a teacher who earns $35,000 a year be entitled to unemployment benefits during the summer months or when school is not in session?

_____ 15. When $4X + 40 = 44$, what does X equal?

_____ 16. What happens when I spin this egg?

_____ 17. How does this poem make you feel?

_____ 18. What do you think will happen when we mix equal amounts of the red solution and the yellow solution?

_____ 19. What is the capital of Arkansas?

_____ 20. What do you think will be the long-term global effects if the trees of rain forests continue to be removed at the present rate?

Answer Key to Exercise 10.1: 1 = 1 (recall); 2 = 2 (compare); 3 = 3 (judge); 4 = 3 (imagine); 5 = 3 (extrapolate); 6 = 3 (evaluate); 7 = 2 (classify); 8 = 2 (contrast); 9 = 1 (recall); 10 = 3 (predict); 11 = 2 (explain cause and effect); 12 = 3 (speculate); 13 = 2 (contrast); 14 = 3 (judge); 15 = 1 (recall how to work the problem); 16 = 1 (observe); 17 = 1 (describe); 18 = 3 (hypothesize); 19 = 1 (recall); 20 = 3 (speculate or generalize).

FOR YOUR NOTES

Exercise 10.2: Observing the Cognitive Levels of Classroom Verbal Interaction

Instructions: The purpose of this exercise is to develop your skill in recognizing the levels of classroom questions. Arrange to visit an elementary school classroom and, in the spaces provided, tally each time you hear a question (or statement) from the teacher that causes students to gather or recall information, to process information, or to apply or evaluate data. In the left-hand column you may want to write in additional key words to assist your memory. After your observation, compare and discuss the results of this exercise with your colleagues.

School and class visited _____

Date of observation _____

	Question or Statement
Recall level Key words: *complete, count, define, describe,* and so on.	
Processing level Key words: *analyze, classify, compare,* and so on.	
Application level Key words: *apply, build, evaluate,* and so on.	

FOR YOUR NOTES

Exercise 10.3: Raising Questions to Higher Levels

Instructions: The purpose of this exercise is to further develop your skill in raising questions from one level to the next higher level. Complete the blank spaces with questions at the appropriate levels, then share and discuss your responses with your classmates.

Recall Level	*Processing Level*	*Application Level*
1. How many of you read a newspaper today?	Why did you read a newspaper today?	What do you think would happen if nobody ever read a newspaper again?
2. What was today's newspaper headline?	Why was that topic important enough to be a headline?	Do you think that news item will be in tomorrow's paper?
3. Who is the vice president of the United States today?	How does the work she has done compare with that done by the previous vice president?	
4. Has United States had a woman president?		
5. (Create your own questions.)		

FOR YOUR NOTES

Exercise 10.4: CREATING COGNITIVE QUESTIONS

Instructions: The purpose of this exercise is to provide practice in writing cognitive questions. Read the following passage. From the passage, compose three questions about it that cause students to identify, list, and recall; three that cause students to analyze, compare, and explain; and three that cause students to predict, apply, and hypothesize. Share and evaluate questions with your peers.

We Are One[8]
Truth, love, peace, and beauty,
We have sought apart
    but will find within, as our
Moods—explored, shared,
    questioned, and accepted—
Together become one and all.

Through life my friends
We can travel together,
    for we now know
Each could go it alone.

To assimilate our efforts into one,
While growing in accepting,
    and trusting, and sharing the
    individuality of the other,
Is truly to enjoy God's greatest gift—
Feeling—knowing love and compassion.

Throughout life my friends
We are together,
    for we must know
We are one.
                            —*R. D. Kellough*

Recall Questions

1. To identify _____

_____

_____

2. To list _____

_____

_____

---

3. To recall _____

_____

_____

Processing Questions

1. To analyze _____

_____

_____

2. To compare _____

_____

_____

3. To explain _____

_____

_____

Application Questions

1. To predict _____

_____

_____

2. To apply _____

_____

_____

3. To hypothesize _____

_____

_____

Exercise 10.5: Analyzing the Level of Questions in Course Materials

Instructions: The purpose of this exercise is to examine course materials for the levels of questions presented to students. Examine a student textbook (or other written or software program material) for a subject and grade level you intend to teach, specifically examining questions posed to the students, perhaps found at the ends of sections of instruction. Also examine workbooks, examinations, instructional packages, and any other written materials used by students in the course. Complete the exercise as follows, then share your findings with other members of your class.

1. Materials examined (include date of publication and target students)

   _____

   _____

   _____

   _____

   _____

   _____

2. Examples of level 1 (input recall level) questions found

   _____

   _____

   _____

   _____

   _____

   _____

3. Examples of level 2 (processing level) questions found

   _____

   _____

   _____

   _____

   _____

   _____

4. Examples of level 3 (application level) questions found

   _____

   _____

   _____

   _____

   _____

   _____

5. Approximate percentages of questions at each level:

   Level 1 = _____%   Level 2 = _____%   Level 3 = _____%

6. In *Caught in the Middle*, it is reported that "of more than 61,000 questions found in teacher guides, student workbooks, and tests for nine history textbooks, more than 95 percent were devoted to factual recall."[9] In a recent analysis of eight middle-grade science textbooks and their end-of-chapter questions, 87.5 percent of those questions were at the input level, and 78.8 percent of all textbook questions were at the input level.[10] How does your data from this exercise compare with those results?

   _____

   _____

   _____

   _____

   _____

   _____

   _____

7. Did you find evidence of question-level sequencing? If so, describe it.

   _____

   _____

   _____

   _____

   _____

   _____

   _____

8. After sharing and discussing with your classmates, what do you conclude as a result of this exercise? For example, was there any difference in the nature and quality of questions depending on the type of material analyzed, e.g., textbooks versus software programs?

   _____

   _____

   _____

   _____

   _____

[9]*Caught in the Middle*, (Sacramento, CA: California State Department of Education, 1987), p. 13.
[10]Edward L. Pizzini, et al., "The Questioning Level of Select Middle School Science Textbooks," *School Science and Mathematics* 92(2):74–78 (February 1992).

Exercise 10.6: Cooperative Learning Micro Peer Teaching: The Use of Questioning

Instructions: The purpose of this exercise is to practice preparing and asking questions that are designed to lead student thinking from the lowest level to the highest level. Before class, prepare a five-minute lesson that poses questions that will guide the learner (one of your peers) from the lowest levels to the highest levels of thinking. Teaching will be one-on-one, in groups of four, with each member of the group assuming a particular role—teacher, student, judge, or recorder. Each of the four members of your group will assume each of those roles once, five minutes each time. (If there are only three members in a group, the roles of judge and recorder can be combined, or if there are five members in the group, one member can sit out each round or two can work together as judge.)

  Suggested lesson topics:

- A particular teaching strategy, such as inquiry.
- A skill or hobby.
- Assessment of learning.
- Characteristics of youngsters of a particular age.
- Finding a teaching job.
- Learning styles.
- Student teaching and what it will really be like.
- Teaching competencies.
- Teaching styles.

Divide the class into groups of four and assign the following roles:

Teacher (sender): Pose recall (input), processing, and application (output) questions related to one of the listed topics, or to any topic you choose.

Student (receiver): Respond to the questions of the teacher.

Judge: Identify the level of each question or statement used by the teacher *and* the level of the student's response.

Recorder: Tally the number of each level of question or statement used by the teacher (S = sender) as indicated by the judge; also tally the level of the student's responses (R = receiver). Record any problems encountered by your group.

  You may duplicate the tally sheet to provide a separate sheet for each sender.

Tally Sheet for Exercise 10.6

Sender _____

Receiver _____

Minute		Input	Processing	Output
1	S			
	R			
2	S			
	R			
3	S			
	R			
4	S			
	R			
5	S			
	R			

FOR YOUR NOTES

E. STUDENT TEXTBOOK QUESTIONS

When using a textbook that you believe has a disproportionate percentage of questions at the input level, the following instructional suggestions are offered to incorporate higher-order questions and hence, higher-order thinking.[11]

1. Develop and present higher-level cognitive questions to students prior to textbook reading, requiring them to link prior textual information and their experiences with current textual information.
2. Prior to current text reading, develop and present higher-level cognitive statements and require students to prove or disprove each through the application of the current textual information.
3. Have students scan chapter subheadings and develop higher-level cognitive questions based on the subheadings, which they may answer through reading.
4. Progressively increase the number of higher-level cognitive questions inserted into the text from the first chapter to the last chapter. This enables students to become more experienced in responding to higher-level cognitive questions.
5. Where appropriate, have students develop higher-level cognitive questions from prior textual information that relates to the current textual information.
6. Integrate higher-level cognitive questions into chapter activities that require students to think about the information derived from the activity.
7. Require students to defend their answers to low-level cognitive chapter review and end-of-chapter questions with textual information and experience.

As stated earlier, the nature and quality of your interactions with students is a major key to effective teaching and learning. Thus far you have learned about the fundamental teacher behaviors necessary for learning to occur, including the use of questioning (in this chapter and in Chapter 3). You have also learned the importance of your consideration of modes of instruction and modalities of learning (Chapters 9 and 3, respectively). Now, related to those things you have learned, do Exercise 10.7.

[11]Pizzini, p. 78.

Exercise 10.7: A Self-Check on Identifying Teaching Behaviors in Classroom Interaction[12]

Instructions: The purpose of this exercise is to assess how well you can identify various types of teaching behavior. The following is a sample elementary school classroom interaction. It includes examples of various levels of questions and structuring and responsive behaviors. (You may want to refer to Chapter 3.) See whether you can identify them. Your answers should be taken from the following: *structuring, facilitating, active acceptance, passive acceptance, clarifying, input questioning, process questioning, and application questioning.* (There is an answer key at the end of the interaction.) See also the questions that follow the answer key.

---

[12]Adapted from Costa, 1989, pp. 75–78. By permission of Arthur L. Costa.

Interaction	*Teacher's Behavior*

Landon: Ms. Clarion, here's a picture that shows how a magnet works.

Teacher: Okay, Landon. Would you please share this with the rest of the group? Tell us what you think is happening.

1. _____

Landon: Well, this girl is in the garage using a magnet to pick up things, and over here it shows all the things a magnet will pick up.

Teacher: What kind of things are they, Landon?

2. _____

Landon: Nails, paper clips, spoons, screws, screwdr—

Molly: It will not pick up spoons, Landon. I've tried it.

Landon: It will too. It shows right here.

Olivia: I picked up a spoon with a magnet that my uncle gave me.

Landon: Sure it will!

Sarah: No it won't, 'cause—

Teacher: Just a minute. We'd like to hear everyone's idea, but we can't if we all talk at once. If you'll raise your hand, then I'll know whom to call on next.

3. _____

Teacher: Now, Landon says a magnet will pick up spoons. Sarah says that a magnet can't pick them up.

4. _____

Teacher: Yes, Sarah, what do you think?

5. _____

Sarah: I'm not sure, but I think it has to be metal.

Linda: I think it depends on the kind of spoon. Some spoons have metal and some are plastic and other stuff.

Teacher: That's another possibility.

6. _____

Teacher: How can we solve this problem as to whether a magnet will pick up spoons?

7. _____

Molly: We can get some spoons and try it with our magnet.

Teacher: All right. Anybody know where we can get some spoons?

8. _____

José: There's a spoon in my lunch bag.

Olivia: There are some spoons in the lunchroom. Can we go get them?

Teacher: Yes. José, would you get yours? Olivia, would you get some from the lunchroom? Be sure you ask the cook. Landon, would you get the magnet?

9. _____

Later

Teacher: Now, because this is José's spoon, what do you think would be the fair thing to do?

10. _____

David: Let him try the magnet on his own spoon.

Teacher: All right, José, what do you think will happen when we touch the magnet to your spoon?

11. _____

José: It probably won't pick it up because it's not the right kind of stuff for a magnet to pick up.

Teacher: What do you mean, "the right kind of stuff"?

12. _____

Sarah: He means the right kind of metal.

Teacher:	José, would you try it? Let's all watch.	13. _____
Molly:	See, I told you a magnet wouldn't pick up a spoon.	
Raul:	But it does pick up some spoons.	
Landon:	I don't mean all spoons, only those made of metal. The spoon in the book is made of metal.	
Linda:	Is this pin made out of steel?	
Teacher:	No, Linda, it isn't.	14. _____
Linda:	I thought it was steel or stuff like that—like a piece of car.	
Teacher:	I don't understand what you mean, Linda. What do you mean, "a piece of car"?	15. _____
Linda:	When Dad banged up our car, you could see the shining metal under the paint. He said it was steel.	
Sarah:	I think the most powerful magnet in the world might be able to pick it up.	
David:	An electromagnet, I think, is the strongest magnet that was ever invented.	
Teacher:	Are you saying, David, that you think a stronger magnet would pick up the spoon?	16. _____
David:	Um-hm. I think so.	
Teacher:	What would you want to do to find out?	17. _____
David:	We could set up our electromagnet and try it.	18. _____
Teacher:	Okay.	

Answer Key for Exercise 10.7: 1. Structuring; 2. input questioning (listing); 3. structuring; 4. active acceptance; 5. process questioning (explaining); 6. passive acceptance; 7. process questioning (problem solving); 8. input questioning (locating); 9. data acquisition (this might also be interpreted as a structuring behavior since the teacher directs the students to perform a task); 10. application questioning (evaluation); 11. application questioning (predicting); 12. clarifying; 13. data acquisition; 14. data acquisition; 15. clarifying; 16. clarifying; 17. process questioning (planning); and 18. passive acceptance.

How did you do? If you have any questions about this exercise, you may want to review this chapter and Chapter 3. In this interaction, can you tell if Ms. Clarion called on children equally, without regard to their gender? Circle one of the following: (Yes, she did; no, she did not; not sure). Discuss your answer to that question with your colleagues. Discuss and resolve any problems with this exercise with your classmates and instructor.

SUMMARY

Having learned of the importance of learning modalities and about instructional modes; about children and their needs, and the importance of the teacher's providing an accepting and supportive learning environment; and about teacher behaviors that are necessary to facilitate student learning, in the next chapter your attention is directed to the selection and implementation of specific strategies to facilitate students' learning of particular skills and content.

QUESTIONS FOR CLASS DISCUSSION

1. Have you ever observed that some teachers seem to anticipate a lower-level response to their questions from particular students? Explain.
2. Should a teacher always verbally respond to every student comment or inquiry? Why? If not, on what basis does the teacher decide when and how to respond?
3. When questioning students, does a teacher need to be concerned about how children from different cultures might respond to certain types of questions or to the teacher's questioning technique? Explain.
4. Explain the difference between a convergent question and a divergent question. Give an example of each. When would you use each type?
5. On average, how many questions a day do you suppose a teacher asks? How could you find out?
6. Describe and give examples of the different types of acceptance responses a teacher can make.
7. Explain why there is a caution about the teacher's use of strong praise. Describe when, if ever, and how, strong praise could be used by a teacher.
8. Explain why it is important to wait after asking the class a content question.
9. Explain the importance of the statement, "Give equal wait-time to all students."
10. Explain why questioning is such an important strategy for teaching and learning.
11. Do you have questions about the content of this chapter? How might answers be found?

SUGGESTED READINGS FOR CHAPTER 10

Carlsen, W. S. "Questions in Classrooms: A Sociolinguistic Perspective." *Review of Educational Research* 61(2):157–178 (Summer 1991).

Gilbert, S. W. "Systematic Questioning." *The Science Teacher* 59(9):41–46 (December 1992).

Wassermann, S. *Asking the Right Questions: The Essence of Teaching.* Fastback 343. Bloomington, IN: Phi Delta Kappa Educational Foundation, 1992.

Wiederhold, C. *Cooperative Learning and Critical Thinking: The Question Matrix.* San Juan Capistrano, CA: Resources for Teachers, 1990.

Wilen, W. W. *Questioning Skills for Teachers.* 3rd ed. Washington, DC: National Education Association, 1991.

11

What Guidelines Are Available for My Selection and Use of Specific Instructional Strategies?

Specific teacher behaviors that must be in place to enable children to learn have been discussed previously. In this chapter your attention is focused on a variety of specific instructional strategies among which you may select to teach toward particular goals. Regardless of strategies and of subject or grade level, all teachers share the responsibility for teaching reading, writing, thinking, and study skills. That responsibility is reflected throughout this chapter.

A. TEACHER TALK

Teacher talk is used for both talking *to* your students (formal lecture) and for talking *with* your students (informal discussion). Whether formal or informal, teacher talk has several risks associated with it.

Risks Associated with Using Teacher Talk

Perhaps the most important risk is that of talking too much. If you talk too much, the significance of your words may be lost, because some students, especially those of intermediate and higher grades, will tune you out.

Another danger is talking too fast. Students can hear faster than they can understand what is heard. It is a good idea to remind yourself to slow down and check for student comprehension frequently.

A third danger is not being heard or understood. Sometimes teachers talk at too low a pitch, or use words that are not understood by many of the children, or both. Vary the pitch of your voice, and, as discussed in an earlier chapter, stop and help children with their understanding of vocabulary words that are likely to be new to them.

Teaching with literature promotes the enjoyment of reading for a reader's lifetime, stimulates discussions, motivates writing, and reinforces literacy concepts.

A fourth danger is believing that students have learned something just because you told them about it. You may recall from the Learning Experiences Ladder (Chapter 9, Figure 9.3) that although it is an important form of communication, verbal communication is the least effective form because of its reliance on abstract symbolization—in this case, words—and on listening, at which many children are not very skilled.

Related to the previous danger is yet another: believing that children have attained a skill or learned something that was taught previously by you or by another teacher. During any discussion (formal or informal), rather than assuming that your students know something, it is a good idea to make sure. For example, if the discussion and a student activity that follows involve a thinking skill, then you will want to make sure that students know how to use that skill (see Section B). Every lesson should begin with a preassessment of what the children already know, or think they know, about the topic of the ensuing lesson.

Still another danger is a teacher's voice that is a humdrum monotone. Elementary school children need teachers whose voices exude enthusiasm and excitement about the subject and about teaching and learning. Enthusiasm is contagious. With a voice that demonstrates such excitement, you will do better at motivating your students.

Keeping these dangers in mind, proceed with the following general and specific guidelines for productive and effective use of teacher-talk strategies.

Teacher Talk: General Principles

There are certain principles that should be followed whether your teacher talk is formal or informal:

1. Begin a talk with an **advance mental organizer.** Advance mental organizers (see David Ausubel, Chapter 2) are introductions that mentally prepare students for a study by helping them make connections with material already learned (a **comparative organizer**), or by providing students with a conceptual arrangement of what is to be learned (an **expository organizer**).[1] For example, an advance organizer can be a brief introduction or statement about the main idea you intend to get across and how it is related to other aspects of the students' learning; it can be a conceptual map of the topic; or it might be a presentation of a discrepancy. Preparing an organizer helps you plan and organize the sequence of ideas, and its presentation can motivate children, help them to organize their own learning, and render their learning more meaningful by making important connections.

2. Your talk should be planned so it is replete with a beginning and an end and a logical order between. During the process of your talk you should reinforce it with visuals. These visuals may be the explaining and writing of unfamiliar terms on the board, still visuals such as graphs, charts, and photographs, or audiovisuals.

3. The *pacing* of your talk is important. It should move briskly, but not too fast. The ability to pace your instruction will improve with experience. Until you have perfected your skill in pacing lessons, and because many beginning teachers talk too fast and too much, it is sound practice to constantly remind yourself during lessons to slow down and to provide silent pauses and frequent checks for student understanding. Your talk should:
    a. Be brisk, but with occasional slowdowns to change the pace and to check for student comprehension.
    b. Be adequately paced to allow students time to make notes and to ask questions.
    c. Have a time plan. Remember, a talk planned for ten minutes, if interesting to students, will probably take longer.

4. Encourage *student participation* during your talk. Students' active participation enhances their learning. Such encouragement can be planned in the form of questions that you ask the class, time allowed for students to comment and ask questions, or a conceptual outline that students fill in during the talk.

5. Just as your talk should have a clear beginning, it should also have a clear ending, followed by another activity (during the same or next class period) that will help secure the learning. As in planning all lessons, *your aim is to have a clear and mesmerizing beginning, an involving lesson body, and a firm and meaningful closure.*

Teacher Talk: Specific Guidelines

Specific guidelines for the use of teacher talk are as follows:

1. *Purposes for teacher talk.* Teacher talk, formal or informal, can serve for any one, or a combination, of the following:
    • Discuss the progress of a unit of study.
    • Explain an inquiry.

---

[1]David P. Ausubel, *The Psychology of Meaningful Verbal Learning* (New York: Grune & Stratton, 1963), especially Chapter 2.

- Introduce a unit of study.
- Present a problem.
- Promote student inquiry or critical thinking.
- Provide a transition from one unit of study to the next.
- Provide information otherwise unobtainable to students.
- Share the teacher's experiences.
- Summarize a problem.
- Summarize a unit of study.
- Teach a thinking skill.

2. *Objectives of the talk.* Your talk should center on one idea, and the learning objectives—not too many for one talk—should be made clear to the students; otherwise, they may never know what you were talking about.

3. *Informal versus formal talk.* Although an occasional formal "cutting edge" lecture may be appropriate for some high school classes, spontaneous interactive informal talks of five to ten minutes duration are preferable when teaching elementary school children. *No teacher should ever give long lectures with no teacher-student interaction.* Remember too, today's students are of the "light generation" and are used to "commercial breaks," so that about ten minutes into most lessons, student attention is likely to begin to drift. This is when you need to have elements planned that will recapture their attention.

   Elements planned to recapture student attention can be verbal cues, such as voice inflections, planned pauses to allow information to sink in, and humor; visual cues, such as the use of slides, realia, or body gestures; or sensory cues, such as moving around the room or casually and gently touching a student on the shoulder without interrupting your talk. Perhaps most useful for recapturing student attention is to change to an entirely different strategy or modality. To change to a strategy or modality that is *entirely* different means that you would change from teacher talk to a student activity, rather than to a teacher-led discussion (mostly more teacher talk).

   Within a given time period, you may have as many as three or four separate learning activities, each led by you (teacher-centered), or with several concurrently being performed by small groups of students (which, as discussed earlier in previous chapters, is **multitasking** or **multilevel instruction**).

4. *Use notes as guide for your talk.* Planning your talk and preparing notes to be used during teacher talk is just as important as implementing the talk. There is nothing wrong with using notes during your teaching. You can carry them with you on a clipboard (perhaps an attractive neon-colored one) as you move around the room. Your notes for a talk can be prepared first in narrative form and then, for class use, reduced to an outline form. *Talks to students should always be spoken from an outline, never read from your narrative.*

5. *Rehearse the talk.* Rehearsing your planned talk is important whether you are a kindergarten teacher preparing a flannel-board story to tell to the children or a middle school teacher of gifted and talented science students preparing a talk about the density of matter. Rehearse your talk using a camera and video recorder, or an audio recorder, and remember to allow more time for implementation then it takes for rehearsal. Include a time plan for each subtopic so you can gauge your timing during implementation of the talk.

6. *Do not race through your talk solely to complete it by class dismissal time.* It is more important that students understand some of your talk than that you cover it all and they understand none of it. If you do not finish, continue later.

7. *Augment your talk with multisensory stimulation.* Your presentation should not rely exclusively on verbal communication. When using visuals, such as slides, overhead transparencies, or a flannel board, do not think that you must be constantly talking; after clearly explaining the purpose of a visual, give the children enough time to look at it, to think about it, and to ask questions about it.

8. *Content of your talk.* For upper-grade teachers, rather than simply rehashing content from the textbook, the subject matter of your talk should supplement and enhance that found in the student textbook. Students may never read their book if you tell them everything that is in it.

9. *Your voice.* Your voice should be pleasant and interesting to listen to, rather than a steady, boring, monotone or a constantly shrieking, high pitched irritant. On the other hand, it is good to show enthusiasm for what you are talking about. Use dramatic voice inflections to emphasize important points and meaningful body language to give students a visual focus.

10. *Vocabulary of the talk and opportunity to help children with their word morphology.* The words you use should be easily understood by the students, while still modeling professionalism and helping children to increase their vocabulary. When you are about to use a word that is likely to be new to most students, stop and ask a student to help explain its meaning and perhaps to demonstrate its derivation. Help students with word meaning. This helps students with their remembering. As previously mentioned, all teachers are language arts teachers. Knowledge of word morphology, an important component of skilled reading, includes the ability to gain information about a word's meaning, its pronunciation, and parts of speech of new words from their prefixes, roots, and suffixes. For some students every subject is like a foreign language. Every teacher has the responsibility of helping students learn how to learn, which includes helping children with their reading skills and with their thinking skills.

11. *Provide older students (grades 4 and above) with a conceptual outline or a study guide.* An outline of major ideas of the talk, with some lines connecting them (the beginning of a concept map, which students can complete), or a study guide (an expository organizer) can facilitate students' understanding and organization of the content of a teacher's talk. However, we emphasize here the importance of this aid being a skeletal outline, and not a complete copy of the talk.

12. *Use familiar examples and help students make relevant connections.* Connect the talk to ideas and events with which the students are already familiar. The most effective talk is that which makes frequent and meaningful connections between what students already know and what they are learning.

13. *Consider children who are different.* While preparing your talk, consider students who are disabled, who are culturally or linguistically different, and who have special needs. Personalize the talk for them by using analogies, examples, and audiovisuals.

14. *Establish eye contact frequently.* When teaching, you should consistently make eye contact with your students. Only momentarily should you look at your notes, visuals, writing board, and other objects in the classroom. With practice you can learn to scan a class of 30 students and *establish* eye contact with each student about once each minute. To "establish" eye contact means that the student is aware that you are looking at him or her. Frequent eye contact can have two major benefits. First, as you "read" student body posture and facial gestures, you gain clues about student attentiveness and comprehension. Second, eye contact helps to establish rapport between you and your students. Be alert, however, for

students in your class who are from cultures where eye contact is infrequent or unwanted and may have negative consequences.

Frequent eye contact is easier when using an overhead projector then when using the writing board. When using a writing board, you have to turn at least partially away from your audience, and you may have to pace back and forth from writing on the board and maintaining close proximity to students.

15. *Use meaningful and effective body language.* An effective teacher is one who is interesting to watch and who effectively communicates with her or his hands, body position and movements, and facial expressions.

B. THINKING SKILLS

The curriculum of any school includes skills that are used in thinking. Furthermore, many researchers and educators concur that direct instruction on how to think should be given to students,[2] and that learning to think is as valid an educational goal for children who are at risk, disabled, disadvantaged, or limited in speaking English, as it is for those who are gifted and talented.[3] Thinking skills include classifying, comparing, concluding, generalizing, inferring, and others, as exemplified in Figure 11.3 (Section D). Rather than assuming that students have developed these skills, classroom time should be devoted to teaching them directly. As stated by Costa,[4]

We often find a science textbook, for example, which asks students to make a *conclusion* based upon data observed during an experiment. We assume students know how to draw conclusions, yet we seldom teach students that skill. We may hear ourselves or other teachers ask questions that presuppose students' knowing how to perform certain thinking skills: "Who can *summarize* some of the things we've learned about the nomads of the desert?" "Let's *analyze* this problem." . . . While we may assume that students know how to perform the thinking skills implied in the subject matter and the instructional interactions being used in the classroom, we often find they have never learned what it means to perform these basic thinking skills. As a result, students are often dismayed, confused, and handicapped when asked to perform them.

When teaching a thinking skill directly, the subject content becomes the vehicle for thinking. Costa gives these examples: Students can learn the process of *classifying* by using the week's vocabulary list. An elementary school teacher can teach *comparison* during a handwriting lesson in which students learn how to form a "d" and a "b." You can teach students to distinguish *fact* from *opinion* during the study of current events in social studies.

For further insight and specific strategies and the many programs for teaching thinking, see the resources footnoted here and listed in the suggested readings at the end of this chapter. Remember, as presented in Chapter 2, Section E, *you are expected to model the skills that you are teaching your students.*

[2]The academic achievement of students increases when they are taught thinking skills directly. See, for example, Arthur Whimbey, "Test Results from Teaching Thinking." In Arthur L. Costa, ed., *Developing Minds: A Resource Book for Teaching Thinking* (Alexandria, VA: Association for Supervision and Curriculum Development, 1985), pp. 269–271.
[3]Adapted from Arthur L. Costa, *The School as a Home for the Mind* (Palatine, IL: Skylight Publishing, 1991), p. xiii.
[4]Arthur L. Costa, *The School as a Home for the Mind* (Palatine, IL: Skylight Publishing, 1991), pp. 75–76. Reprinted by permission of Arthur L. Costa.

C. DISCUSSIONS

Because of limited resources and materials, and large classes, many teachers use discussions as the dominant mode of instruction. In addition, discussion serves as a goal of education which is, or should be, to guide students to being more mature, self-guided, and interdependent individuals, able to live and work with others cooperatively, productively, and responsibly.[5]

Learning to work cooperatively and productively in groups requires the development of certain social skills. These skills are not innate; they are learned. Consequently, you must have the skills needed to work in groups, and you must have the skills needed to guide your students in their development of those same skills.

Fortunately, there are a variety of techniques for helping students to learn through interactive participation. This section presents some of those techniques, one of which is to consider ways students are grouped for instruction.

Grouping for Instruction

On any given school day, depending on the class and the specific learning activity, a student should experience a succession of group settings for instruction. Teachers should be encouraged to provide both ability grouping and cooperative learning opportunities.[6] Ways of grouping students for instruction are categorized as follows:

Cooperative Learning Group

A cooperative learning group is a heterogeneous (mixed) group of three to six students (most frequently four, but the number of students per group depends on the nature of the learning goals and the specific cooperative learning method being used) who work together in a teacher- or student-directed setting, emphasizing support for one another rather than competition among members of the group.[7] Most often, a cooperative learning group consists of four students of mixed ability, gender, and ethnicity. The group is rewarded on the basis of group achievement, as are individual members within the group. Because peer support must be greater than peer pressure, the teacher must be cautious about any use of group grading. For grading, bonus points can be given to all members of a group, which individuals add to their own scores when everyone in the group has reached preset criteria. The preset criteria must be appropriate for all members of a group. Lower criteria or improvement criteria could be set for students with lower ability so that everyone feels rewarded and successful. To determine each student's quarter and course grades, individual student achievement is measured later through individual student results on tests, as well as the student's performance in groups (see Chapter 14, Section C, "Cooperative Learning and Evaluation").

In cooperative learning groups it is advisable to assign roles to each member (as exemplified in Exercise 10.6, and in the "Sample Unit Plan with One Complete Daily

---

[5]For example, see *What Work Requires of Schools: A SCANS Report for America 2000* (Washington, DC: Secretary of Labor's Commission on Achieving the Necessary Skills, 1991).

[6]Carol J. Mills and William G. Durden, "Cooperative Learning and Ability Grouping: An Issue of Choice," *Gifted Child Quarterly* 36(1):11–16 (Winter 1992).

[7]For a significant research study that reports on group instructional techniques that attain levels of student achievement nearly as high as individual tutoring, see Benjamin S. Bloom, "The Search for Methods of Group Instruction as Effective as One-to-One Tutoring," *Educational Leadership* 41(8):4–17 (May 1984).

Lesson" of Chapter 8), and to rotate roles either during the activity or from one time to the next. Typical roles are (1) *group facilitator,* whose role is to keep the group on task; (2) *materials manager,* whose role is to obtain, maintain, and return materials needed for the group to function; (3) *recorder,* whose role is to record all group activities and processes and perhaps evaluate how the group is doing; and (4) *reporter,* whose role is to report group process and accomplishments to the teacher and to the rest of the class. Group membership can be changed a few times during the year.[8]

Although there are several techniques for using cooperative learning,[9] the primary purpose of each is for the groups to learn, which means if that is to happen, individuals within a group must learn. Group achievement in learning, then, is dependent on the learning of individuals within the group. Rather than competing for rewards for achievement, members of the group cooperate by helping each other learn so that the group reward will be a good one. The theory of cooperative learning is that when small groups of students of mixed backgrounds and capabilities work together toward a common goal, members of the group increase their liking and respect for one another. As a result, there is an increase in each individual's self-esteem and academic achievement.[10]

Dyad

In dyads, students are paired for studying and learning, such as in **peer tutoring** (one classmate tutors another), in **think-pair-share learning** (students are paired to think about and to share what they already know about a topic that is to be studied, and then the pair shares their knowledge with the rest of the class), and in **cross-age coaching** (a student is coached by a student from a higher grade level).

Small Group

Small group discussions are those involving five to eight students in a teacher- or student-directed setting. The use of small groups for instruction, including the cooperative learning group, enhances the opportunities for students to assume greater control over their own learning. Small groups can be formed to serve a number of purposes, such as when students are grouped by (1) learning activity (for example, a reciprocal reading group in which students take turns asking questions, summarizing, making predictions about, and clarifying a book); (2) personality type (for example, a teacher may want to team less assertive children to give them the opportunity for greater management of their own learning); (3) social pattern (for example, it may be

---

[8]Resenting the concept of using groups of students of mixed abilities, parents of students in some schools request that teachers not use *cooperative learning groups.* To avoid controversy, teachers sometimes use an alternate term, such as *collaborative* or *team learning.* However, these terms are not synonymous with cooperative learning. In cooperative learning, there is much more individual student accountability than there is in ordinary collaborative or team learning. Some authorities use the term *collaborative learning* when the teacher is working with students as a partner in learning; *cooperative learning* is used when only students are working together.

[9]Of special interest to many teachers are general methods of cooperative learning, such as Student Team—Achievement Division (STAD) and Teams-Games-Tournaments (TGT), or methods for particular subjects, such as Team Assisted Individualization (TAI) for mathematics, and Cooperative Integrated Reading and Composition (CIRC) for reading and writing. See Robert E. Slavin, *Cooperative Learning: Theory, Research, and Practice* (Englewood Cliffs, NJ: Prentice Hall, 1990).

[10]See, for example, Stephen Balkcom, "Cooperative Learning," *Education Research Consumer Guide* (1), June 1992, and Margaret Hadderman, "Cooperative Learning in Elementary Schools," *Research Roundup* 8(2):5 (Winter 1992).

necessary to break up a group of rowdy friends or desirable to broaden the association among students); (4) common interest; (5) ability in a particular skill; or for (6) the duration of a work project.[11]

Large or Whole Group

Large group discussions are those that involve more than eight students, usually the entire class, and are usually teacher directed.

Student Presentations

You can encourage students to be presenters for discussion of their ideas, opinions, and knowledge gained from their own independent, dyad, and small group study. Adaptable to a variety of subject areas, several techniques encourage the development of certain skills, such as studying and organizing material, discovery, discussion, rebuttal, listening, analysis, suspending judgment, and critical thinking. Forms of discussion involving student presentations are as follows:

1. *Debate.* The debate is an arrangement whereby prepared speeches are made by members of two opposing teams, on topics preassigned and researched, followed by a rebuttal from each team.
2. *Panel.* The panel is a setting in which four to six students, with one designated as chairperson, discuss a topic about which they have studied. A question and answer period involving the entire class then follows. The panel usually begins by each panel member giving a brief opening statement.
3. *Research report.* One student or a team of two or three students gives a report on a topic that they have investigated. This is followed by questions and discussions by the entire class.
4. *Round table.* The round table is a group of four or five students who sit around a table and discuss among themselves (and perhaps with the rest of the class), a problem or issue that they have studied. The rest of the class members make up the round table's audience.
5. *Symposium.* The symposium is an arrangement in which each student participant presents a prepared presentation of his or her position on a preassigned topic researched by the student; after the presentations, questions are accepted from the rest of the class.
6. *Trial.* The trial is a discussion approach in which the class simulates a courtroom, with class members playing the roles of judge, attorneys, jury members, recorder, and so on.

To use such techniques effectively, your students will need your coaching, individually or in whole class sessions, on how and where to gather information; how to take notes, select major points, organize material, present a position succinctly, listen, play roles, and engage in dialogue and debates with one another. Be patient; the results will be worth it.

Now do Exercise 11.1.

[11]The purposes listed were adapted from *Its Elementary* (Sacramento: State Department of Public Instruction, 1992), p. 32.

Exercise 11.1: Investigation of Student Learning and Presentation-Type Techniques

Instructions: The purpose of this exercise is for you and your classmates to investigate techniques of student learning and presentation in elementary teaching. In groups of four, use your university library to research in detail the distinctive characteristics of (1) cooperative learning, (2) student reports, (3) debate, (4) forum, (5) round-table discussion, (6) symposium, and (7) any other type that you find.

Following your research, compile your findings. Then, through your small group discussion, derive examples of appropriate uses for each type of activity, relative to your planned teaching. As a panel of experts, share your findings and examples with the entire class.

Whole Class Discussion

Whole class discussion is another teaching technique frequently used by all teachers. In this section, you are considered to be the expert. Having been a student in formal learning for at least 15 years, you are undoubtedly knowledgeable about advantages and disadvantages of whole class discussions. Explore your own knowledge and experiences by responding to Exercise 11.2a and then to Exercise 11.2b, in which guidelines for the use of the whole class discussion will be generated.

**Exercise 11.2a: Whole Class Discussion as a Teaching Strategy:
What Do I Already Know?**

Instructions: The purpose of this exercise is to explore your knowledge of whole class discussion as a teaching strategy. Answer these questions, then share your responses with other members of your class, perhaps in subject field or grade-level discussion groups. After sharing your responses to this exercise, then, in those small groups, complete Exercise 11.2b.

1. My grade-level interest or subject field is _____

2. For what reasons would I hold a whole class discussion? _____

_____

_____

_____

_____

_____

3. Assuming that my classroom has movable seats, how would I arrange student seating?

_____

_____

_____

_____

_____

_____

4. What would I do differently if student seats were not movable? _____

_____

_____

_____

_____

_____

_____

5. What ground rules would be established before starting the discussion? _____

_____

_____

_____

_____

_____

6. Should student participation be forced? Why? If so, how? _____

_____

_____

_____

_____

_____

7. How would I discourage domination of the discussion by a few students? _____

_____

_____

_____

_____

8. What preparation should the students and I be expected to make before beginning the discussion? _____

_____

_____

_____

_____

_____

9. How would I handle digression from the topic? _____

_____

_____

_____

_____

10. Should I use students as discussion leaders? Why? If so, what training should they receive, if any, and how? _____

_____

_____

_____

_____

_____

11. What different roles are options for me during a class discussion? _____

_____

_____

_____

_____

_____

12. When is each of these roles most appropriate? _____

_____

_____

_____

_____

_____

13. When, if ever, is a "class meeting" appropriate? (A class meeting is for discussing not subject matter but class procedures.) _____

_____

_____

_____

_____

_____

14. Can brainstorming be a form of whole class discussion? Why? _____

_____

_____

_____

_____

15. What follow-up activities would be appropriate after a whole class discussion session? On what basis would I decide to use each? _____

_____

_____

_____

_____

_____

16. What sorts of activities should precede a class discussion? _____

_____

_____

_____

_____

17. Should a discussion be given a set time length? Why? If so, how long? How is the length to be decided? _____

_____

_____

_____

18. Should students be graded for their participation in class discussion? Why? If so, how? On what basis? By whom? _____

_____

_____

_____

_____

19. For effective discussions, 10 to 12 feet is the maximum recommended distance between participants. When a discussion is being led by a teacher, what can a teacher do to keep within this recommended maximum? _____

_____

_____

_____

20. Are there any pitfalls or other points of importance that a teacher should be aware of when planning and implementing a whole class discussion? If so, explain them and tell how to prepare for such contingencies. _____

_____

_____

_____

_____

Exercise 11.2b: Guidelines for Using Whole Class Discussions

Instructions: The purpose of this exercise is to generate a list of guidelines for using whole class discussion as a teaching strategy. When you have shared your responses to Exercise 11.2a with your colleagues, briefly answer the first two questions below, individually. Next, in your small group, using all three questions to guide your discussion, generate a list of five general guidelines for the use of discussion as a strategy in an elementary classroom of your choice. Share your group's guidelines with the entire class. Then, as a whole class, derive a final list of general guidelines.

1. How effective was your small group discussion in sharing Exercise 11.2a? _____

_____

_____

_____

_____

_____

_____

2. What allowed for or inhibited the effectiveness of that small group discussion? _____

_____

_____

_____

_____

_____

_____

_____

3. How effective is this small group discussion? Why? _____

_____

_____

_____

_____

_____

_____

_____

FOR YOUR NOTES

The teacher-led whole-class discussion is an important component of many elementary school classrooms.

Equality in the Classroom

To assure a psychologically safe and effective learning environment for all children, you must attend to all students and try to involve all students equally in all class activities. You must be careful not to fall into the trap of interacting with only the brightest, or the most vocal and assertive, or to have biased expectations about children or to discriminate against them according to their gender or some other personal characteristic. You must avoid the tendency of teachers of all ages and both sexes to discriminate in the classroom. For example, teachers, like the rest of society, tend to have lower expectations for girls than for boys in science and mathematics. They tend to call on and encourage boys more than girls and let boys interrupt girls, but praise girls for being polite and waiting their turn.[12] To avoid being discriminatory may take special proactive effort on your part, regardless of your gender and other personal characteristics.

To guarantee an equality of interaction with students, many teachers (experienced as well as beginning teachers) have found it useful to ask someone secretly to tally classroom interactions between the teacher and children during a class discussion, after which the teacher analyzes the results and arrives at decisions about his or her own attending and facilitating behaviors. That is the purpose of Exercise 11.3.

[12]Betty Vetter, "Ferment: Yes; Progress: Maybe; Change: Slow," *Mosaic* 23(3):34–41 (Fall 1992), p. 34.

You are welcome to make blank copies of that exercise and share it with your teaching colleagues.

In addition to those variables mentioned at the beginning of Exercise 11.3, the exercise can be modified to include responses and their frequencies according to other teacher-student interactions, such as your calling on all students equally for responses to your questions, and calling on children equally to assist you with classroom helping jobs, for their misbehavior, or to assume classroom leadership roles.

Ensuring Equity

Other ways of ensuring that your students are treated fairly in your classroom include the following:

- Maintain high expectations for all children, regardless of their personal characteristics.
- Insist on politeness in the classroom. For example, each child should be shown appreciation, such as with a sincere "thank you" or "I appreciate your contribution," or a whole class applause, and with a genuine smile, for her or his contribution to the learning process.
- Insist that children be allowed to finish what they are saying without being interrupted by others. Be certain you model this behavior yourself.
- Insist that students raise their hands and be called on by you before they are allowed to speak.
- Keep a stopwatch handy to unobtrusively control the wait-time given for each student.
- Use a seating chart attached to a clipboard, and next to each child's name tally each interaction you have with that student.

Exercise 11.3: Teacher Interaction with Students According to Student Gender

Instructions: The purpose of this exercise is to analyze your own interactions with students according to their gender. To become accustomed with the exercise you should do a trial run with it in one of your present college or university classes. Use it again during your student teaching and later, during your first few years of teaching.

The exercise can be modified to include (a) amount of time given for each interaction, (b) response time given by teacher according to student gender, and (c) response time according to other student characteristics, such as ethnicity.

Procedure: Before class select someone to be an observer (this will be yourself during the recommended trial run), such as a colleague, and ask him or her to do the tallying and calculations as follows.

Secret Assignment: During class today, I would like you to quietly tally the interactions between me and individual students in this class. Simply place a tally mark after the name of each student (if you don't know names, use a seating chart) who has any verbal interaction with me from this point on (or whenever you are instructed to begin). Thank you. If you are a student in this class, do not count any of your own interactions, nor yourself in any of the calculations.

Exact time of start = _____

Time end = _____

Total time in minutes = _____

Calculations after tallying:

1. Total number of students present = _____

2a. Number of female students = _____

2b. Number of male students = _____

3a. Percentage of females in class = _____ (= 2a divided by 1)

3b. Percentage of males in class = _____ (= 2b divided by 1)

(3a and 3b check: 3a + 3b should = 100%)

Tallies:

End-of-experiment calculations:

4a. Total females interacting = _____

(This is the number of different female students.)

4b. Total males interacting = _____

5. Percentage of students interacting = _____ (4a + 4b)/1

6a. Total female tallies = _____

6b. Total male tallies = _____

7. Total of all tallies (6a + 6b) = _____

8a. Percentage of tallies female = _____ (6a divided by 7)

8b. Percentage of tallies male = _____ (6b divided by 7)

9a. Most tallies for any one male = _____

9a.1. Percentage of total class tallies = _____ (9a divided by 7)

9b. Most tallies for any one female = _____

9b.1. Percentage of total class tallies = _____ (9b divided by 7)

10. Teacher conclusions as a result of this interaction analysis: _____

_____

_____

_____

_____

_____

_____

_____

_____

_____

_____

_____

_____

_____

_____

_____

_____

_____

_____

_____

_____

_____

_____

_____

	Level I	*Level II*	*Level III*
Problem Identification	By teacher or textbook	By teacher or textbook	By student
Process of Solving the Problem	Decided by teacher or text	Decided by student	Decided by student
Identification of Tentative Solution	Resolved by student	Resolved by student	Resolved by student

Figure 11.1 Levels of inquiry.

D. INQUIRY TEACHING AND DISCOVERY LEARNING

Intrinsic to the effectiveness of both inquiry and discovery is the assumption that students will actively seek knowledge rather than receive it through expository methods (i.e., information delivery, such as by lectures, demonstrations, and textbook reading). Although inquiry and discovery are very important teaching tools, there is sometimes confusion as to exactly what inquiry teaching is and how it differs from discovery learning. In this section the distinctions should become clear as you study the descriptions of these two important tools for teaching and learning.

Inquiry Versus Discovery

Perhaps a major reason that inquiry and discovery are sometimes confused is that, in both, students *are actively engaged in problem solving.* Problem solving is "the ability to define or describe a problem, determine the desired outcome, select possible solutions, choose strategies, test trial solutions, evaluate the outcome, and revise these steps where necessary."[13]

Problem solving is *not* a teaching strategy but a high intellectual behavior that facilitates learning. What a teacher can and should do is to provide opportunities for students to identify and tentatively solve problems. Experiences in inquiry and discovery can offer such opportunities. With the processes involved in inquiry and discovery, teachers can help students develop the skills necessary for effective problem solving. A major difference between discovery and inquiry learning is *who identifies the problem.* Another important difference is *in the decisions that are made by the students.* See Figure 11.1, where three levels of inquiry are described, each defined according to what the student does and decides.

From Figure 11.1, it should be evident that what is called Level I inquiry is actually traditional, didactic, "cookbook" teaching, in which both the problem and the process for resolving it are defined *for* the student. The student then works through the process to its inevitable resolution. If the process is well designed, the result is inevitable, because the student "discovers" what was intended by the writers of the program. This level of inquiry is also called **guided inquiry** or **discovery,** because the students are carefully guided through the investigation to (the predictable) "discovery."

[13]Arthur L. Costa, ed., *Developing Minds: A Resource Book for Teaching Thinking* (Alexandria, VA: ASCD, 1985), p. 312.

Level I inquiry is in reality a strategy within the delivery mode, the advantages of which were described in Chapter 9. As Level I inquiry is highly manageable and the learning outcome is predictable, it is probably best for teaching basic concepts and principles. Students who never experience learning beyond Level I are missing an opportunity to engage their highest mental operations, and they seldom to never get to experience more motivating, real-life problem solving. Furthermore, those students may come away with the false notion that problem solving is a linear process, which it is not. As illustrated in Figure 11.2, true inquiry is cyclic rather than linear. One enters the cycle whenever a discrepancy or problem is observed and recognized, and this can occur at any point in the cycle.

By the time students reach middle grades, they should be provided experiences for true inquiry, which begins with Level II, whereby students actually decide and design the processes for their inquiry. In true inquiry, teachers emphasize the tentative nature of conclusions, which makes the activity more like real-life problem solving, in which decisions are always subject to revision if and when new data so prescribe.

In Level III inquiry, students recognize and identify the problem as well as decide the processes and reach a conclusion. When using individual projects and independent study as instructional strategies, teachers are usually engaging students in this level of inquiry. By the time students enter high school Level III inquiry should be a major instructional strategy.

The Processes

In true inquiry, students generate ideas and then design ways to test those ideas. The various processes used represent the many critical thinking skills. Some of those skills are concerned with generating and organizing data, others are concerned with

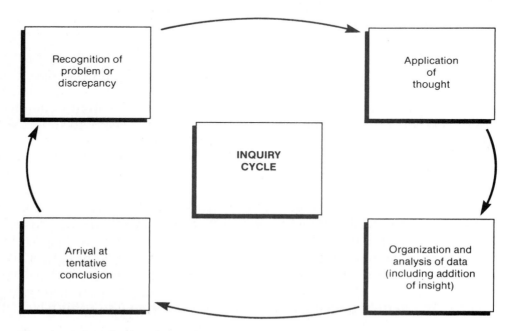

Figure 11.2　The inquiry cycle.

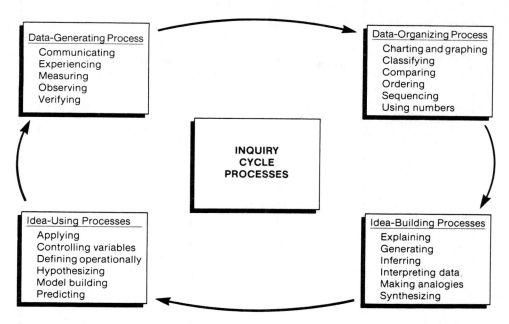

Figure 11.3 Inquiry cycle processes.

building and using ideas. Figure 11.3 presents four main categories of these **thinking processes** and illustrates the place of each within the inquiry cycle.

Some processes in the cycle are discovery processes and others are inquiry processes. Inquiry processes include the more complex mental operations (including all of those in the idea-using category). Children of the middle grades especially, because they are likely to be in the process of developing their higher-level thinking capabilities, should be provided experiences that require these more complex, higher-level inquiry skills.

Inquiry learning is a higher-level mental operation that introduces the concept of the **discrepant event,** that is, an event that establishes **cognitive disequilibrium** (using the element of surprise; discussed in Chapter 2) to help students develop skills in observing and being alert for discrepancies. This strategy provides opportunities for students to investigate their own ideas about explanations. Inquiry, like discovery, depends on skill in problem solving; the difference between the two is in the amount of decision-making responsibility given to students. Experiences in inquiry help students to understand the importance of suspending judgment and the tentativeness of answers and solutions. With those understandings, students eventually are better able to deal with life's ambiguities.

Integrating Strategies for Integrated Learning

In today's exemplary classrooms, teaching strategies are often combined to establish the most effective teaching-learning experience.[14] For example, in an integrated language arts program, teachers are interested in their students' speaking, reading,

[14]See, for example, "SQ3R + What I Know Sheet = One Strong Strategy," *Journal of Reading* 35(1):50–52 (September 1991).

listening, thinking, study, and writing skills. These skills (and not textbooks) form a holistic process that is the primary aspect of integrated language arts.

In the area of speaking skills, oral discourse (discussion) in the classroom has a growing research base that promotes methods of teaching and learning through oral language. These methods include cooperative learning,[15] instructional scaffolding (such as with concept mapping),[16] and inquiry teaching.[17]

In cooperative learning groups, students discuss and use language for learning that benefits both their content learning and skills in social interaction. Working in heterogeneous groups, students participate in their own learning and can extend their knowledge base and cultural awareness with students of different ethnic backgrounds.[18] When children share information and ideas, they are completing difficult learning tasks, using divergent thinking and decision making, and developing their understanding of concepts. As issues are presented and responses are challenged, student thinking is clarified. Students assume the responsibility for planning within the group and for carrying out their assignments. When needed, the teacher models an activity with one group in front of the class, and when integrated with student questions, the modeling can become inquiry teaching. Activities can include the following:

- **Brainstorming.** Members generate ideas related to a key word and record them.
- **Think-pair-share.** A concept is presented by the teacher, and students are paired to discuss the concept. They share what they already know or have experienced about that concept, and then share that information with the rest of the class. This strategy is an excellent technique for discovering student misconceptions (naive theories, as discussed in Chapter 2).
- **Chunking.** Groups of students apply mental organizers by clustering information into chunks for easier manipulation and remembering.
- Use of other **memory strategies.** The teacher and students model the use of acronyms, mnemonics, rhymes, or clustering of information into categories to promote learning.
- **Comparing and contrasting.** Similarities and differences between items are found and recorded.
- **Concept mapping.** Words related to a key word are written in categories around the key word, and the categories are labeled. Linking words are then placed along lines connecting the categories. This gives students a visual comparison of relationships between, and misconceptions about, ideas.
- **Inferring.** For instance, students assume the roles of people (real or fictional) and infer their motives, personalities, and thoughts.
- **Making tests.** Each group creates a test and members of another group take it.
- **Outlining.** Each group completes an outline that contains some of the main ideas but with subtopics omitted.
- **Paraphrasing.** In a brief summary, each student restates a short selection from an author's text.
- **Reciprocal teaching.** In classroom dialogue, students take turns at predicting, questioning, summarizing, and clarifying.

[15]David W. Johnson and R. T. Johnson, *Learning Together and Alone*, 3rd ed. (Boston: Allyn and Bacon, 1991).
[16]Fran Lehr, "Instructional Scaffolding," *Language Arts* 62(1):667–672 (October 1985). See also theme issue "Thinking and Learning Across the Curriculum," *Journal of Reading* 34(7) (April 1991).
[17]George Hillocks, Jr., *Research on Written Composition: New Directions for Teaching* (Urbana, IL: ERIC Clearinghouse on Reading and Communication Skills and the National Conference on Research in English, 1986).
[18]Debbra A. Uttero, "Activating Comprehension Through Cooperative Learning," *The Reading Teacher* 41(4):390–395 (January 1988).

- Using the **SQ4R** or the **SQ3R** study strategies (see Chapter 5).
- Using **Vee mapping**—a kind of road map completed by students, as they learn, showing the route they follow from prior knowledge to new and future knowledge.[19]

For further insight, specific strategies, and the many programs for teaching thinking, see the resources footnoted and listed in the suggested readings at the end of this chapter. Remember, *you are expected to model the skills that you are teaching your students.*

E. DEMONSTRATIONS

Students like demonstrations, especially when they are performed by the teacher. They like them because the teacher is actively engaged in a learning activity rather than merely verbalizing about it. Demonstrations can be used in teaching any subject, at any grade level, and for a variety of purposes. A role-playing demonstration may be used in a social studies class; the mathematics teacher may demonstrate steps in using the Pythagorean theorem; the language arts teacher may demonstrate clustering to students ready for a creative writing assignment; the science teacher may demonstrate the combining of a weak acid and a weak base.

Purposes for a Demonstration

A demonstration can be designed to serve any of the following purposes.

- As a mind-capturing introduction to a lesson or unit of study.
- As a review.
- As an unusual closure to a lesson or unit of study.
- To assist in the recognition of a solution to an existing problem.
- To establish problem recognition.
- To give students opportunity for vicarious participation in active learning.
- To illustrate a particular point of content.
- To model a thinking skill.
- To reduce potential safety hazards (the teacher demonstrates the use of materials too dangerous for students to use).
- To save time and resources (rather than having the entire class doing that which is demonstrated).
- To set up a discrepancy recognition.

Guidelines for Using a Demonstration

When planning a demonstration, you should consider each of the following:

1. *Mode.* Decide which is the most effective way to conduct the demonstration, e.g., as a verbal or a silent demonstration, by a student or by the teacher, by the teacher with a student helper, or to the entire class or to small groups.

[19]For details on how to use Vee maps, see Wolff-Michael Roth and Guennadi Verechaka, "Plotting a Course with Vee Maps," *Science and Children* 30(4):24–27 (January 1993).

2. *Visibility.* Be sure that the demonstration is visible to all students. For this purpose some schools have installed overhead mirrors, or where demonstrations are more frequent and financial resources are available, classrooms use overhead video-cameras with large-screen television monitors.

3. *Practice.* Practice with the materials and procedure before demonstrating to the students.

4. *"Murphy's Law."* Consider what might go wrong, because if anything can, it probably will.

5. *Pacing.* Consider your pacing of the demonstration, allowing for enough wait, see, and think time.

6. *Beginning and ending.* At the start of the demonstration explain its purpose and the learning objectives. Remember the adage: Tell them what you are going to do, show them, and then tell them what they saw. As for any lesson, plan your demonstration closure and allow time for questions and discussion.

7. *Comprehension checks.* During the demonstration, as in other types of teacher talk, use frequent stops to check for student understanding.

8. *Lighting.* Consider the use of special lighting to highlight the demonstration. For example, a slide projector can be used as a spotlight.

9. *Safety considerations.* Be sure that the demonstration table and area are free of unnecessary objects that could distract, be in the way, or pose a hazard. With potentially hazardous demonstrations, such as might occur in teaching science or shop, model proper safety precautions: wear safety goggles; have fire-safety equipment at hand; and place a protective shield between the demonstration table and nearby students.

F. ASSIGNMENTS AND HOMEWORK

Assignments, whether completed at home or at school, can ease student learning in many ways.

Purposes for Assignments

Purposes for giving homework assignments can be any of the following:

- Constructively extending the time that students are engaged in learning.
- Helping students to develop personal learning.
- Helping students to develop their research skills.
- Helping students to develop their study skills.
- Helping students to organize their learning.
- Individualizing the learning.
- Involving parents and guardians in their childrens' learning.
- Providing a mechanism by which students receive constructive feedback from the teacher.
- Providing students with opportunity to review and practice what has been learned.
- Reinforcing classroom experiences.
- Teaching new content.

Guidelines for Using Assignments

In the use of assignments, consider the following guidelines:

1. *Plan ahead.* Plan early the types of assignments you will give (e.g., daily and long-range, minor and major, in class or at home) and prepare assignment specifications. Assignments must correlate with specific instructional objectives and should *never* be given as "busywork" or as punishment.

2. *Parental or guardian permission.* Use caution about giving assignments that could be controversial or that could pose a hazard to the safety of the students. In such cases, especially if you are new to the community, before giving the assignment you may wish to talk it over with members of your teaching team or with the principal. You may also need to have parental or guardian permission for students to do the assignment.

3. *Differentiated assignments.* Provide differentiated assignments, that is, variation in assignments given to students or selected by them on the basis of student interests and abilities. To accomplish the same objective, students can select or be assigned different activities, such as read and discuss, or they can participate with others in a

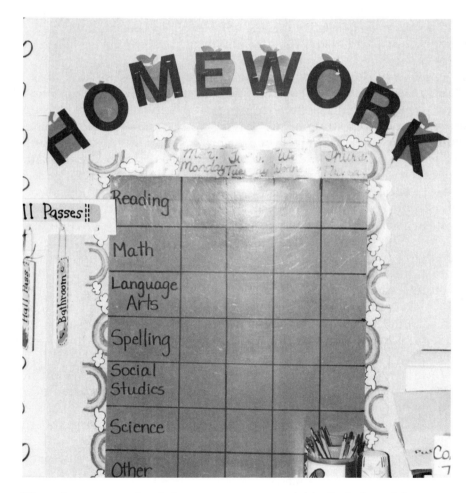

Most elementary school classrooms use a special bulletin board for posting assignments as a reminder to students.

more direct learning experience. Upon completion of their assignments, students share what they have learned.

4. *Time requirement.* The amount of time needed by a student for completing assignments beyond school time will vary according to school policy and grade level. Generally, primary-grade-level students will be given only limited assignments that are fun to do with their parents or guardians, perhaps amounting to only a few minutes a week or night. Intermediate-grade students may be expected to complete assignments that average an hour per day each school day, while middle school students may be expected to spend one to three hours on assignments each day.

5. *Study guide.* Teachers of the upper grades have found it beneficial to prepare individualized study guides with questions to be answered and activities to be done by the student while reading textbook chapters at home. The advantages of a study guide are that it can (1) be individualized for each student, (2) make the reading more than a visual experience, and (3) help organize student learning by (a) accenting instructional objectives, (b) emphasizing important points to be learned, (c) providing a guide for studying for tests, and (d) encouraging the student to read the homework assignment.

6. *Stimulation of thinking.* As a general rule, homework assignments should arouse student curiosity, raise questions for further study, and encourage the self-discipline required for independent study.

7. *Resources availability.* Determine the resources that students will need to complete assignments, and check the availability of these resources. Here, the school librarian is an excellent source of help.

8. *Announcing assignments.* When giving assignments in class, it is best to write them on the board or give them in writing on a ditto (or in the course syllabus, with extra care to be sure that assignment specifications are clear to older students). Never yell out assignments as students are leaving your classroom. Be prepared if a parent complains that you never assign homework. This is another example of how a written syllabus, with assignments, and the use of student portfolios are helpful.

Students should be given sufficient time to complete their assignments. In other words, avoid announcing an assignment that is due the very next day. As a general rule, all assignments should be given at least a week in advance; for major assignments, students should be given a much longer time.

Try to avoid changing assignment specifications after they are given. Especially avoid changing them at the last minute. Changing specifications at the last minute can be very frustrating to students who have already completed the assignment, and it shows little respect for those students.

9. *Due dates.* Maintain assignment due dates, allowing, of course, for legitimate excuses. Consider allowing students to select their due dates from a list of options. Without legitimate reasons, late papers should not be accepted, or accepted only with a severe reduction in grade.

10. *Class time.* Allow time in class for students to begin work on homework assignments, so you can give individual attention (guided or **coached practice**) to students. Your ability to coach students is *the reason* for allowing in-class time to begin assignments. The benefits of coached practice include your being able to (a) monitor student work so that a student does not go too far in a wrong direction, (b) help students to reflect on their thinking, (c) assess the progress of individual students, (d) discover or create a "teachable moment."[20] The latter might occur, for example, when

[20]See John D. Bransford and Nancy J. Vye, "A Perspective on Cognitive Research and Its Implications for Instruction." In L. B. Resnick and L. E. Klopfer, eds., *Toward the Thinking Curriculum: Current Cognitive Research.* 1989 ASCD Yearbook. (Reston, VA: Association for Supervision and Curriculum Development, 1989), pp. 196–198.

the teacher discovers a commonly shared student misconception while observing and monitoring student practice. The teacher then stops and attempts to clarify that misconception.

11. *Timely and meaningful response from teacher.* Timely, constructive, and corrective feedback from the teacher on the homework, and grading of homework, raise the positive contributions of homework dramatically.[21] If it is important for students to do, then you must give your full and immediate attention to the product of their efforts. Read everything that students write. "Students are more willing to do homework when they believe it is useful, when teachers treat it as an integral part of instruction, when it is evaluated by the teacher, and when it counts as part of the grade."[22]

12. *Attention to reading, listening, speaking, and writing skills.* Regardless of grade level or subject taught, each teacher must give attention to the development of students' reading, listening, speaking, and writing skills. Attention to these skills must also be obvious in your assignment specifications and in your assignment grading policy. Reading is crucial to the development of a person's ability to write. For example, to foster high-order thinking, students can be encouraged to write their thoughts about the material they have read.

13. *Teacher comments.* Provide written or verbal feedback about each student's work, and be positive and constructive in your comments. Always think about the written comments that you make, to be relatively certain that they will convey your intended meaning to the student. When writing comments on student papers, consider using a color other than red. To many people, red has a host of negative connotations—blood, hurt, danger, stop.

Proceed now with Exercise 11.4.

Exercise 11.4: Planning Assignments

Instructions: The purpose of this exercise is for you to consider the preceding guidelines in planning assignments. For a unit you intend to teach, plan student assignments. Use the following format, but as space for completion of this exercise is not provided, please use other paper. When completed, share the results of this exercise with your colleagues for their suggestions. Reviewers may need a copy of your unit plan and course syllabus.

1. List all assignments for the unit, oral and written.
2. Correlate these assignments with your course objectives.
3. Identify resources students can use to complete the assignments, and tell where those resources are to be found.
4. Indicate the relative weight (grade) of each assignment, showing its percentage of the total term grade.

---

[21]Herbert J. Walberg, "Productive Teaching and Instruction: Assessing the Knowledge Base," *Phi Delta Kappan* 71(6):470–478 (February 1990), p. 472.
[22]*What Works: Research About Teaching and Learning* (Washington, DC: United States Department of Education, 1986), p. 42.

G. PROJECTS, PAPERS, AND ORAL REPORTS

Regardless of grade level and subject, individual writing and small group projects should be major features of most instruction. *The project is a form of independent or small group study in which students produce something, such as a paper, an investigation, a play, a model, or a report.* The purposes for using this type of instructional strategy are as follows:

- For teaching gifted and talented students.
- For a student to become especially knowledgeable and experienced in one area of subject content or in one process skill, thus adding to the student's knowledge and sense of importance and self-worth.
- For a student to develop skill in communication through sharing this special knowledge and experience with the teacher and with the class.
- For students to learn independently, or to work somewhat independently of the teacher in small groups.
- For students to practice and develop independent learning skills.
- To develop students' skills in writing and in higher-level thinking.

Often, unless students are coached and given guidance, projects can be a frustrating experience for both teacher and students. Students should do a project because they want to and because the project seems important to do. Therefore, students should decide what project to do, and how to do it. The teacher's role is to advise and guide students so they experience success. Remember, the teacher's job is to coach for *success,* not for failure. If a project is laid out in too much detail by the teacher, then it is a procedural assignment rather than a project for learning.

For a project, paper, or oral report to be an educationally helpful experience, the teacher should do the following:

1. *Help students generate ideas.* Stimulate ideas for the independent study by providing lists of things students might do; by mentioning, each time an idea comes up in class, that this would be a good idea for an independent project; by having former students tell about their projects, by showing the results of other students' projects, by suggesting readings that are likely to give students ideas, and by using class discussions to brainstorm ideas.

2. *Provide options, but insist that writing be a part of each student's work.* Allow students to choose whether to do a project, a paper, an oral report, or some combination of these three types of assignments. Regardless of which is selected, and regardless of your subject or grade level, insist that writing be a part of each student's work.

Allow students to choose whether they will work alone or in small groups. If they choose to work in groups, then help them delineate job descriptions for each member of the group. Small groups of no more than three students per group seem to work better than groups of more than three.

3. *Provide coached guidance.* Work with each student or student team in topic selection and in the processes of writing and oral reporting. Allow students to develop their own procedures, but guide their preparation of work outlines and preliminary drafts, giving them constructive feedback along the way. Help students in identifying potential resources and in the techniques of research.

Frequent drafts and progress reports from the students is a must. At each of these stages, provide students with constructive feedback. Provide written guidelines and time lines for outlines, drafts, and completed projects.

4. *Evaluation.* The final project, paper, and oral report should be graded, and the students provided with clear descriptions of how evaluation and grading will be done and informed of the weight of the project grade toward the term grade. Evaluation should include the student's meeting deadlines for drafts and progress reports. The final grade for the study should be based on four criteria: (a) how well it was organized, including promptness in meeting draft deadlines; (b) the quality and quantity of knowledge gained from the experience; (c) the quality of the student's sharing of that learning experience with the rest of the class; and (d) the quality of the student's final written or oral report.

5. *Sharing.* Insist that students share the progress and the results of their study with the rest of the class. The amount of time allowed for such sharing will, of course, depend on many variables. For young children, five minutes might be a reasonable expectation. For middle school students, a longer sharing time will usually be needed. The value of this type of instructional strategy derives not only from individual contributions, but also from the learning that results from the experience and the communication of that experience to others.

Resources on Writing Across the Curriculum

Research examining the links between writing, thinking, and learning has helped to emphasize the importance of writing across the curriculum. Writing is a complex intellectual behavior and process that helps the learner to create and record his or her understanding—to construct meaning. Experimenting with writing should begin as early as kindergarten.[23] In exemplary elementary schools, student writing is encouraged across the curriculum, in all subjects, and at all grade levels.

Resources on writing across the curriculum include the following:

Illinois Writing Project, National Louis University, 2840 Sheridan Road, Evanston, IL 60201.
International Reading Association, 800 Barksdale Road, Newark, DE 19711.
National Center for the Study of Writing and Literature, School of Education, University of California–Berkeley, Berkeley, CA 94720.
National Council of Teachers of English, 1111 Kenyon Road, Urbana, IL 61801.
National Writing Project, 5627 Tolman Hall, University of California–Berkeley, Berkeley, CA 94720.
Whole Language Umbrella, Unit 6-846, Marion Street, Winnipeg, Manitoba, Canada R2J0K4.
Writing to Learn, Council for Basic Education, 725 15th Street, NW, Washington, DC 20005.

To begin your resource file of ideas suitable for student investigations, turn your attention to Exercise 11.5.

---

[23]Joni Lucas, "Teaching Writing," *Curriculum Update* (Alexandria, VA: Association for Supervision and Curriculum Development, January 1993).

FOR YOUR NOTES

Exercise 11.5: Ideas Suitable for Independent or Small Group Investigation

Instructions: The purpose of this exercise is to begin your resource file of ideas suitable for independent or small group investigations. Identify by descriptive title five or more topics that would be suitable for independent or small group assignments for projects, papers, or oral reports, for students at the grade level you are preparing to teach. For each, identify specific potential resources. Questions to keep in mind are, Would the project be valuable for students to do? Is it practical in time, costs, materials, and abilities of the students at this level? Share your list with your colleagues for their feedback.

My subject and/or grade level _____

Idea by Descriptive Title	*Potential Resources*
1.	
2.	
3.	
4.	
5.	
6.	

FOR YOUR NOTES

Type	Characteristics	Examples
*1. Pure game	Promotes laughter and is fun	*New Games*[24] *Cooperation Square Game*[25]
2. Pure contest	Stimulates competition; built-in inefficiency[26]	Political contests, e.g., U.S. presidential race
*3. Pure simulation	Models reality	Toddler play
4. Contest-game	Stimulates competition; fun; built-in inefficiency	Golf; bowling; *Trivial Pursuit*
*5. Simulation-game	Models reality; fun	*Redwood Controversy*[27]
6. Contest-simulation	Competition; models reality; built-in inefficiency	Soapbox Derby of Akron, Ohio
7. Simulation-game-contest	Models reality; fun; competition; inefficiency	*Careers, Life, Monopoly*

Figure 11.4 Classification of educational games.

H. EDUCATIONAL GAMES

Devices that are classified as educational games include a wide variety of types of learning activities, such as simulations, role-play and sociodrama activities, mind games, board games, and sporting games, all of which are fairly low on the Learning Experiences Ladder (presented in Chapter 9); that is, they are experiences that tend to involve several senses and several learning modalities, and to be quite effective as learning tools.

Educational games can play an integral role in interdisciplinary teaching and serve as valuable resources for enriching the effectiveness of children's learning. As with any other instructional strategy, the use of games should follow a clear educational purpose and a careful plan, and be congruent with the instructional objectives.

What are educational games? Seven categories of games fall under the general heading of "educational games." Certain types have greater educational value. Games that do not emphasize the element of competition, that is, that are not "contests," are particularly recommended for use in the academic classroom (those categories marked with an asterisk [*] in Figure 11.4). See Figure 11.4 for the classification and

[24]*New Games* is a collection of published games popular with teachers of preschool and elementary school, and of value to other teachers as well. For information and ordering, contact Animal Town Game Company, P.O. Box 2002, Santa Barbara, CA 93120.

[25]Available in Eugene C. Kim and Richard D. Kellough, *A Resource Guide for Secondary School Teaching: Planning for Competence*, 5th ed. (New York: Macmillan, 1991), pp. 284–285.

[26]This means that rules for accomplishing the game objective make accomplishment of that objective less than efficient; for example, in golf the objective is to get the ball into the hole with the least amount of effort, but to do that, one has to take a peculiarly shaped stick (the club) and hit the ball, find it, and hit it again, continuing that sequence until the ball is in the hole. However, common sense tells us that the best way to get the ball into the hole, with the least amount of effort would be to simply pick up the ball and place it into the hole.

[27]*Redwood Controversy* is a powerful simulation role-play game patterned after the congressional hearings, during President Lyndon Johnson's administration, that were considering enlarging the Redwood National Parks. The game is interdisciplinary, and teachers we know have found it excellent for use in grades 5 and up, especially for social studies, English, science, and interdisciplinary classes. Although published several years ago, the game is still relevant today. The game is inexpensive and includes rules for play, role cards, a transparency, and a wall map. It can be played in approximately two hours, or extended over many days or weeks. Available from Houghton Mifflin.

identification of characteristics and examples of the seven types or categories of games.

Games can be powerful tools for teaching and learning. A game can have one to several functions, as follows:

• To serve as devices by which students learn about issues, such as those concerning the environment (simulation and role-play games).
• To add variety and a change of pace.
• To assist in enhancing student self-esteem.
• To evaluate student learning.
• To motivate learning.
• To provide a time-out from the usual rigors of learning.
• To provide a means for reviewing and reinforcing subject content.
• To provide learning through tactile and kinesthetic modalities.
• To provide opportunity to learn through role-playing real-life situations.
• To provide opportunity to learn through simulation.
• To provide problem-solving situations and experiences.
• To provide skill development in computer usage.
• To provide skill development in inductive thinking.
• To provide skill development in verbal communication and debate.
• To reinforce convergent thinking.
• To socialize students.
• To stimulate critical thinking.
• To stimulate deductive thinking.
• To stimulate divergent and creative thinking.
• To teach content and process.

Sources of Educational Games

There are many sources of commercially available educational games; many have come and gone so quickly that it is impossible to maintain a current list of sources and prices. However, the following is a list of sources with successful histories of marketing useful educational games.

Abt Associates, Inc., 14 Concord Lane, Cambridge, MA 02138.
Carolina Biological Supply Co., 2700 York Road, Burlington, NC 27215.
Dannon Educational Division, 80 Wilson Way, Westwood, MA 02090.
Denoyer Geppert Co., 5215 N. Ravenswood Avenue, Chicago, IL 60640.
Diversified Educational Enterprises, Inc., 725 Main Street, Lafayette, IN 47901.
Edu-Game, P.O. Box 1144, Sun Valley, CA 91352.
Houghton Mifflin, 2 Park Street, Boston, MA 02107.
Hubbard Scientific, P.O. Box 760, Chippewa Falls, WI 54729-0760.
Interact Company, P.O. Box 997, Lakeside, CA 92040.
Krell Software, Flowerfield Building, #7 Suite 1D, St. James, NY 11780.
Marginal Context Ltd., 35 St. Andrew's Road, Cambridge CB4 1DL, England.
New York Zoological Society, Education Department, Bronx, NY 10460.
Nova Scientific Corp., 111 Tucker Street, P.O. Box 500, Burlington, NC 27215.
Simulations Publications, Inc., 44 East 23rd Street, New York, NY 10010.
Social Studies School Service, 10,000 Culver Boulevard, Culver City, CA 90230.
Stasiuk Enterprises, 3150 NE 30th Avenue, P.O. Box 12484, Portland, OR 97212.
Systems Gaming Associates, Triphammer Road, Ithaca, NY 14850.
Teaching Aids Company, 925 South 300 West, Salt Lake City, UT 84101.

I. THE LEARNING ACTIVITY CENTER

One special technique for both integrating and individualizing learning is the use of the special classroom learning station known as the learning activity center (LAC), or learning center. The LAC *is a special station located in the classroom where an individual student (or a group of two, if student interaction is necessary) can quietly work and learn at his or her own pace.* All materials needed are provided at the learning center, including clear instructions for operation of the center. A familiar example is the personal computer station.

The value of learning centers as instructional devices undoubtedly lies with the following two characteristics: while working at the center, the student is giving time and quality attention to the learning task; and, while working at the center, the student is likely to be engaging her or his most effective learning modality, or integrating all learning modalities.

Types of Learning Activity Centers

Learning activity centers are categorized into three types:

1. *Direct-learning center,* where performance expectations for cognitive learning are quite specific.
2. *Open-learning center,* where the goal is to provide opportunity for exploration, enrichment, motivation, and creative discovery.
3. *Skill center,* where the focus is on the development of a particular psychomotor skill, such as the motor coordination needed for the manipulation of blocks.

Purposes for Using a Learning Activity Center

Although in all instances the primary reason for using a learning center is to individualize learning, there are additional reasons for using one in the classroom:

• To provide a mechanism for learning that crosses discipline boundaries.
• To provide a special place for a child with special needs.
• To provide a special place for children to review or to make up work.
• To provide additional opportunity for creativity.
• To provide enrichment experiences.
• To provide multisensory experiences to enhance learning.
• To provide special opportunities for students to learn from learning packages that utilize special equipment or media, of which only one or a limited supply may be available for use in your classroom, such as science materials, a computer, a compact disc or laser videodisc player, or any combination of these.

Guidelines for Setting Up a Learning Activity Center

To set up an LAC you can be as elaborate and as creative as your time and resources allow. Here are guidelines for setting up such a center:

• A center should be attractive, purposeful, and uncluttered.
• A center should *never* be used for punishment.

- Materials to be used at the center should be available and described, and their use easily understood by the student.
- Materials used in the center should be safe for a child to use alone.
- Specific instructional objectives and the instructions for use of the center should be clearly posted and understandable to the child. An audio- or videocassette is sometimes used for this purpose.
- The center should be easily supervised by you or an adult aide.
- The center should contain a variety of activities geared to the varying abilities and interest levels of the students. A choice of two or more activities at each center is one way to provide for this.
- The educational purpose of the center should be clearly understood by the students.
- Topics for the center should be related to the instructional program, as review, reinforcement, remediation, or enrichment.
- When designing a center, consider planning the center's theme in a way that integrates the child's learning by providing activities that cross discipline boundaries.

J. MASTERY LEARNING, QUALITY LEARNING, AND INDIVIDUALIZING YOUR INSTRUCTION

Learning is an individual experience. Teaching, unfortunately, is one of the few professions in which the practitioner is expected to work effectively with "clients" on other than an individual basis—more likely 35 to 1. Much has been written of the importance of individualizing your instruction. We know of the individuality of the learning experience, and that while some children are verbal learners, others are better visual, tactile, or kinesthetic learners. As the teacher, however, you are in the difficult position of simultaneously "treating" 35 students who are separate and individual learners. It seems an impossible expectation, and if occasionally you do succeed, we applaud you. The intent of this final section of this chapter (as, indeed, the intent of this resource guide) is to help you to maximize your efforts and to minimize your failures.

It is aphoristic that student achievement in learning is related to the quality and length of time and attention given to learning tasks. In 1968, Benjamin Bloom,[28] reinforcing a model developed earlier by John Carroll,[29] developed the concept of individualized instruction called **mastery learning,** saying that students need sufficient time-on-task (i.e., engaged time) to master content before moving on to new content. From that concept Fred Keller developed an instructional plan (the Keller Plan or Personalized System of Instruction—PSI) that by the early 1970s enjoyed popular use and success in community colleges and a few four-year colleges. The Keller Plan involves student learning from printed modules of instruction that allow the student greater control over the learning pace. This approach is mastery oriented; that is, the student demonstrates mastery of one module before proceeding to the next. With today's emphasis on mastery of content (quality learning) rather than coverage of content (quantity of learning),[30] the importance of the concept of mastery

---

[28]Benjamin Bloom, *Human Characteristics and School Learning* (New York: McGraw-Hill, 1976).
[29]John Carroll, "A Model of School Learning," *Teachers College Record* 64(8):723–733 (May 1963).
[30]See, for example, Frank N. Dempster, "Exposing Our Students to Less Should Help Them Learn More," *Phi Delta Kappan* 74(6):433–437 (February 1993).

learning has resurfaced. By mastery of content, we mean that the student demonstrates that he or she can use what has been learned. As stated by Horton,[31]

> Mastery learning may be broadly defined as the attainment of adequate levels of performance on tests that measure specific learning tasks. Mastery learning also describes an instructional model whose underlying assumption is that nearly every student can learn everything in the school curriculum at a specified level of competence if the learner's previous knowledge and attitudes about the subject are accounted for, if the instruction is of good quality, and if adequate time on task is allowed to permit mastery.

Assumptions About Mastery and Quality Learning

Mastery and quality learning are based on certain assumptions:[32]

1. Mastery and quality learning are possible for virtually all students.
2. For mastery and quality learning to occur, it is the instruction that must be modified and adapted, not the children. Tracking and ability grouping do not fit into the concept of mastery learning.
3. Although all children can achieve mastery, some may require more time than others. The teacher and the school must provide for this difference in time needed to successfully complete a task.
4. Most learning outcomes can be specified in terms of observable and measurable performance.
5. Most learning is sequential and logical.
6. Mastery learning can ensure that students experience success at each level of the instructional process. Experiencing success at each level provides incentive and motivation for further learning.

Components of a Mastery Learning Model

Any instructional model designed to teach toward mastery will contain certain components:

1. Objectives that are stated in specific behavioral terms, that is, a behavioristic approach to instructional design.
2. Preassessment of the learner's present knowledge.
3. The instructional component with practice, reinforcement, frequent comprehension checks (diagnostic or formative assessment), and corrective instruction at each step of the learning to keep the learner on track.
4. Postassessment to determine the extent of mastery of the objectives.

The section that follows provides instruction and practice in one technique that will absolutely ensure your students' mastery of their learning—the Self-Instructional Package.

---

[31]Lowell Horton, *Mastery Learning,* Fastback 154 (Bloomington, IN: Phi Delta Kappan Educational Foundation, 1981), p. 9.
[32]Adapted from Ibid., pp. 15–18.

The Self-Instructional Package

A modification of PSI, developed at about the same time (early 1970s) and one that is popular with teachers, is the self-instructional technique developed by Rita and Stuart Johnson, called the "self-instructional package" (SIP).[33] The SIP is a learning package specifically designed for an individual student, using small sequential steps, with frequent and immediate learning feedback to the student, and designed to teach a relatively small amount of material at the mastery level, requiring a relatively brief amount of learning time (about 15 minutes for primary-grade children; 30 minutes for upper-grade students). Exercise 11.6 is a self-instructional package designed to instruct you further on how the SIP can be used in your own teaching and to lead you through the process of writing your first SIP. (Exercise 12.2 is another example of a self-instructional package.)

[33]Rita Johnson and Stuart Johnson, *Assuring Learning with Self-Instructional Packages* (Chapel Hill, NC: Self-Instructional Packages, 1971).

Exercise 11.6: Preparing a Self-Instructional Package[34]

Instructions: The purpose of this exercise is to guide you through the process of preparing a self-instructional package for use in your own teaching. The exercise continues for several pages; it is important that you follow it step-by-step, beginning with the following boxed-in "cover page."

Self-Instructional Package Number: *1*
Instructor's Name: Professor Richard D. Kellough
School: California State University, Sacramento
Course: General Methods
Intended Students: Students in Teacher Preparation
Topic: How to Write a Self-Instructional Package
Estimated Working Time: 10 hours

For the challenge of today's classroom . . .

The Self-Instructional Package

You are about to embark upon creating and writing a perfect lesson plan. The result of your hard work will be an instructional module in which you will take a lot of pride. More important, you will have learned a technique of teaching that absolutely assures that learning takes place. For what more could you ask?

Let us get to the essence of what this self-instructional package (SIP) is: this SIP is about "how to write the SIP." The general objective is to guide you gently through the process of preparing and writing your first SIP. Let's begin the experience with background about the history of the SIP.

[34]Copyright 1991 by Richard D. Kellough

A History

Research evidence indicates that student achievement in learning is related to time and to the *quality of attention* being given to the learning task. You knew that already! In 1968, Benjamin Bloom developed a concept of individualized instruction called **mastery learning,** based on the idea that students need sufficient time-on-task to master content before moving on to new content. Did you know that? _____ . (Please read along with a pencil and fill in the blanks as you go.)

Although Bloom is usually given credit for the concept of mastery learning, the idea did not originate with him. He reinforced and made popular a model developed earlier by John Carroll. In 1968, Fred Keller developed a similar model called the Keller Plan, or the Personalized System of Instruction (PSI). The PSI quickly became a popular teaching technique in the community and four-year colleges. In about 1972, enter Johnson and Johnson (not of the Band-Aid family, but Rita and Stuart Johnson), who developed their model of mastery learning and called it the Self-Instructional Package (SIP). Since 1972, I (Richard D. Kellough) have been developing an improved version, which you are now experiencing. As you will learn, *frequent comprehension checks and corrective instruction* are important to the effectiveness of the SIP.

One other thing. There are several devices available to individualize instruction, but the SIP has the flexibility to be adaptable for use at all grade and subject levels, from kindergarten through college. Let me give you what I believe to be the reasons for the popularity of this strategy.

- The SIP allows the teacher to *create an experience that absolutely assures learning.* Creating makes you feel good; when your students learn, you feel good—two reasons for the SIP's popularity.
- The SIP is truly *individualized,* because it is a package written for an individual student, with that student in mind as it is being written.
- Although it takes time to prepare, the SIP *requires little financial expenditure,* a fact important to today's teacher.
- Once you have prepared your first SIP, it is possible that you will see that you have begun a series. Subsequent packages are easier to do, and you may see value in having a series available.
- With today's emphasis on the *basics,* the SIP is particularly helpful for use in remediation.
- When you finish your SIP, you will have completed the content that could be used for a *computer program.*
- With today's *large and mixed-ability classes,* teachers need help! Here is time- and cost-effective help!
- With emphasis today on competency-based instruction, the SIP makes sense.

How are we doing so far? _____ Are your interest and curiosity aroused? _____

Do you have questions? If so, write them down, then continue.

Questions _____

_____

What Is the Self-Instructional Package and Why Use It?

The SIP is a learning package designed for an individual student; it is self-instructional (i.e., if you, the teacher, drop dead—heaven forbid—the student can continue to learn), and *it re-*

quires about 15–50 minutes of learning time. The final package can be recorded on tape, video, or computer disc, or it can be written in booklet form, or it can exist in any combination of these.

Here are ways that teachers have found the SIP to be useful:

- As an *enrichment* activity for an accelerated student.
- As a strategy for make-up for a student who has been absent.
- As a strategy for a student in need of *remediation.*
- As a strategy for introducing basic information to an entire class, freeing the teacher to work with individual students, making the act of teaching more *time-efficient,* a particularly significant value of the SIP.
- As a learning experience especially coordinated with manipulatives, perhaps in connection with a science experiment, library work, a computer, a tape recording, a videotape, a videodisc, or hands-on materials for an activity, or any combination of these.

One other point before we stop and check your comprehension: *The single most important characteristic of the SIP is that it uses small sequential steps followed by immediate and corrective feedback to the learner.* In that respect, the SIP resembles programmed instruction.

 Stop the action!

Let's check your learning with the review questions and instructions that follow.

Comprehension Check 1

Answer the following three questions, then check your responses by reviewing Feedback Check 1. If you answer all three questions correctly, continue the package; otherwise back up and review.

---

1. How would you define an SIP? _____

_____

_____

2. What is the single most important characteristic of the SIP? _____

_____

_____

3. What is one way that the SIP could be used in your own teaching, a way that currently

stands out in your thinking? _____

_____

_____

Feedback Check 1

1. Although we will continue development of the definition, at this point it should resemble this: The SIP is an individualization of learning-teaching strategy that teaches toward mastery learning of one relatively small bit of content by building upon small, sequential steps and providing corrective feedback throughout.
2. Referring to the small, sequential steps, followed by immediate and corrective feedback.
3. Your answer is probably related to one of those listed earlier, but could differ.

How Does the SIP Differ from Other Kinds of "Learning Packages"?

Another characteristic of the SIP is the *amount of learning contained in one package.* Each SIP is designed to teach a relatively small amount of material, but to do it well. *This is a major difference in the SIP from other types of learning activity packages.*

And, in case you have been wondering about what the SIP can be designed to teach, I want to emphasize that it *can be designed:*

- For any topic,
  - At any grade level,
    - In any discipline,
      - For cognitive understanding,
        - For psychomotor development, and
          - For affective learning.

That probably brings to your mind all sorts of thoughts and questions. Hold them for a moment and let's do another comprehension check.

 Stop the action and check your learning.

Comprehension Check 2

Answer the following two questions, then check your responses in the feedback box that follows.

1. How does the SIP differ from other self-contained learning packages? _____

_____

2. Although teachers frequently emphasize learning that falls within the cognitive domain, is it possible for the SIP to be written to include learning in the psychomotor and affective domains? Yes or no? _____

Feedback Check 2

1. Length of learning time is shorter for the SIP, and it is written with an individual student in mind. It is written to teach one thing well, to one student.
2. The SIP *can* be written for any domain, although evaluation is trickier for the affective and for the highest level of the psychomotor.

Perhaps we should now say a word about what we mean when we use the expression *teach one thing well*—that is, to explain what is meant by mastery learning. Theoretically, if the package is being used by an individual student, performance level expectation is 100%. In reality performance level will most likely be between 85 and 95%, particularly if you are using the SIP for a group of students rather than an individual. That 5–15% difference allows for human errors, as can occur in writing and in reading.

Now that you have learned what the SIP is—and how this learning strategy differs from other learning activity packages—it is time to concentrate on development of your SIP. Please continue.

SIP Development

How Do I Develop an SIP?

As with any good lesson plan, it takes time to develop an effective SIP. Indeed, preparation of your first SIP will test your imagination and writing skills! Nevertheless, it will be time well spent; you will be proud of your product. *It is important that you continue following this package, step-by-step; do not skip parts, or we will assume no responsibility for your final product! Understand?* _____ Development of your SIP emphasizes the importance of:

• Writing the learning objectives clearly, precisely, and in behavioral terms.
• Planning the learning activities in small, sequential steps.
• Providing frequent practice and learning comprehension checks.
• Providing immediate feedback, corrective instruction, and assurance to the learner.
• Preparing evaluative questions that measure against the learning objectives.

As you embark on preparing what may be the most perfect lesson plan you have ever prepared, keep in mind the following two points:

1. Prepare your first SIP so it will take no more than

---

15 minutes for primary students
  30 minutes for upper-elementary students

---

2. Use a *conversational tone* in your writing. Write in the second person, as though you are talking directly to the student for whom it is intended. For example, when speaking of the learning objectives, use *You will be able to* rather than *The student will be able to.* Keep in mind that you are communicating to one person rather than to an entire class (even though you may be preparing your package for entire class use). It helps to pretend that you are in a one-on-one situation tutoring the student at the writing board.

 Stop the action, and again check your learning.

Comprehension Check 3

   Answer the following two questions, then check your responses in Feedback Check 3.

1. What maximum learning time duration is recommended? _____

2. What major item of importance has been recommended for you to keep in mind as you write your SIP?_____

_____

Feedback Check 3

1. Fifteen to thirty minutes, depending upon the grade and achievement level.
2. Write in the second person, as if you are speaking directly with the student.

   Now that we have emphasized the *length of learning time, and the personalization of your writing,* here are other important reminders.

3. Make your SIP attractive and stimulating. Consider using cartoons, puns, graphics, scratch-and-sniff stickers, interesting manipulatives. Use your creative imagination! Use both cerebral hemispheres!

Add sketches, diagrams, models, pictures, magazine clippings, humor, and a conversational tone, as students appreciate a departure from the usual textbooks and work sheets.

4. Use colleagues as resource persons, brainstorming ideas as you proceed through each step of package production.

During production, use your best cooperative learning skills.

5. The package should not be read (or heard) like a lecture. It <u>must</u> involve small sequential steps with frequent practice and corrective feedback instruction (as modeled in this package).

". . . and with the course material broken down into small self-instructional units, students can move through at individual rates."

6. The package should contain a variety of activities, preferably involving all three learning modalities—<u>visual, auditory, tactile, and kinesthetic</u>.

7. Vary margins, indentations, fonts, etc.

so the final package does not have the usual textbook or work sheet appearance with which students are so familiar. Build into your package the "Hawthorne Effect."

Note about the cosmetics of your SIP: My own prejudice about the SIP is that it should be spread out more than the usual textbook page or work sheet. Use double-spaced lines, varied margins, etc. Make cosmetic improvements after finishing your final draft. Write, review, sleep on it, write more, revise, add that final touch. This package that you are using has been "toned down" and modified for practical inclusion in this textbook.

8. Your SIP does not have to fit the common $8\frac{1}{2} \times 11''$ size. You are encouraged to be creative in the design of your SIP's shape, size, and format.
9. Like all lesson plans, the SIP is subject to revision and improvement after use. *Write, review, sleep on it, write more, revise, test, revise. . . .*

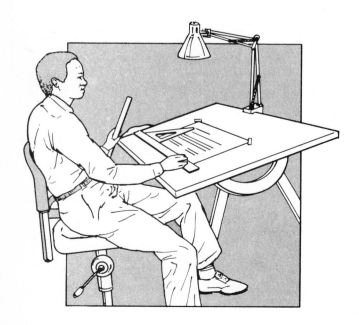

Those are nine points to remember as you prepare your package. Perhaps before proceeding, it would be useful to review them. Remember, too, the well-written package *will assure learning.* Your first SIP will take several hours to produce, but it will be worth it!

Proceed with the steps that follow.

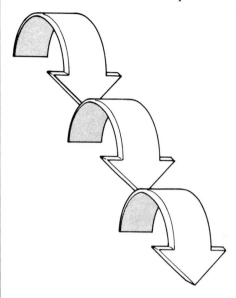

Steps for Developing Your SIP

Instructions: It is important that you proceed through the following package development step-by-step.

One thing you will notice is that immediately after writing your learning objectives you prepare the evaluative test items; both steps precede the preparation of the learning activities. That is not the usual order followed by a teacher when preparing lessons, but it does help to assure that test items match objectives. Now, here we go! *Step-by-step,* please.

Note: From here on, write on separate paper for draft planning.

Step 1. Prepare the cover page. It should include the following items:

- Instructor's name (that is you)
  - School (yours)
    - Class or intended students (whom it's for)
      - Topic (specific but not wordy)
        - Estimated working time

For a sample, refer to the beginning of this package. You can vary the design of the cover page according to your needs.

Step 2. Prepare the instructional objectives. For now, these should be written in specific behavioral terms (as learned in Chapter 7). Later, when writing these into your package introduction, you can phrase them in more general terms.

Recommended is the inclusion of at least one attitudinal (affective) objective, such as "Upon completion of this package you will tell me your feelings about this kind of learning."

Step 3. **Comprehension Check 4**

Share with your colleagues what you have accomplished (with Steps 1 and 2) to solicit their valuable feedback and input.

Step 4. Depending on feedback (from step 3), *modify items 1 and 2,* if necessary. For example, after listing the learning objectives, you may find that you really have more than one package in preparation, and within the list of objectives you may find a natural cutoff between packages "1" and "2." You may discover that you have a *series* of modules begun.

Step 5. Prepare the pretest. If the learner does well on the pretest, there may be no need for the student to continue the package. Some packages (like this one) may not include a pretest, though most will. And if this is your first SIP writing experience, we think you *should* include a pretest.

Suggestion: The pretest need not be as long as the posttest, but it must have a limited sample of questions to determine whether the student already knows the material and need not continue with the package. A pretest also serves to mentally set the student for the SIP.

Step 6. Prepare the posttest. The pretest and posttest could be identical, but usually the pretest is shorter. It is important that both pretest and posttest items actually test against the objectives (of Step 2). Try to keep the items objective (e.g., multiple-choice type), avoiding as much as possible the use of subjective test items (e.g., essay type), but do include at least one item measuring an affective objective (see boxed item in Step 2).

Important reminder: If your package is well-written, the student <u>should</u> achieve 85–100% on the posttest.

Step 7. **Comprehension Check 5**

Share with colleagues your pretest and posttest items (providing a copy of your objectives) for suggested improvement changes before continuing to the next step.

Use the following space to write notes to yourself about ideas you are having and regarding any materials you may need to complete your package.

Dear Self—

Good work so far! Before continuing, take a break.

It is time to stop working for a while . . .   *. . . and go play!*

Step 8. Okay, enough play, it is time to prepare the text of your SIP. This is the "meat" of your package, what goes between the pretest and the posttest. It is the INSTRUCTION. Reminder: For the SIP to be self-instructional, the learner should be able to work through the package with little or no help from you.

An important ingredient in your package is the <u>directions</u>. The package should be self-directed and self-paced therefore, each step of the package should be clear to the learner, making you, the instructor, literally unnecessary. *Everything needed by the learner to complete the package should be provided with the package.*

Use small, sequential steps with frequent practice cycles, followed by comprehension checks and corrective feedback. Make it fun and interesting with a variety of activities for the student, activities that provide for learning in several ways, from writing to reading, from viewing a videotape to drawing, from listening to a tape recording to doing a hands-on activity. And be certain the activities correlate with the learning objectives. The learning cycles should lead to satisfaction of the stated objectives, and the posttest items *must* measure against those objectives.

Step 9. **Comprehension Check 6**

Test your package. Try it out on your colleagues as they look for content errors, spelling and grammar errors, clarity, and offer suggestions for improvement. Duplicate and use the Packet Evaluation Form provided at the end of this exercise.

Stop the Action!
Congratulations on the development of your first SIP!
However, two additional steps need your consideration.

Step 10.   Revise if necessary. Make appropriate changes to your SIP, as a result of the feedback from your colleagues. Then you are ready to give your SIP its first real test—try it out on the student for whom it is intended.

Step 11.   Further revisions. This comes later, after you have used it with the student for whom it was originally intended. Like any other well-prepared lesson or unit plan, it should always be subject to revision and improvement, never "set in concrete."

SIP Evaluation Form

1. Packet identification

   Author _____

   _____

   _____

   Title of SIP _____

   _____

   _____

2. Packet

   Objectives: Do they tell the student

   a. What the student will be able to do? _____

   _____

   _____

   _____

   b. How the student will demonstrate this new knowledge or skill? _____

   _____

   _____

   _____

   Is there a clear statement (overview or introduction) of the importance, telling the learner

   what will be learned by completing the packet? _____

   _____

   _____

   _____

3. Pretest _____

   _____

   _____

   _____

4. Activities (practice cycles)

   Are small sequential steps used? _____

   _____

   _____

   _____

Are there frequent practice cycles, with comprehension checks and corrective feedback to the learner? _____

_____

_____

_____

_____

_____

_____

5. Posttest: Does it test against the objectives? _____

_____

_____

_____

_____

6. Clarity and continuity of expression _____

_____

_____

_____

_____

_____

7. Is the packet informative, attractive, and enjoyable? _____

_____

_____

_____

_____

8. Additional comments useful to the author of this packet _____

_____

_____

_____

_____

_____

SUMMARY

This chapter has continued the development of your repertoire of teaching strategies necessary to becoming an effective teacher. As you know, most children are quite peer-conscious, have relatively short attention spans, and prefer active learning experiences that engage many of their senses. Most children are intensely curious. Cooperative learning, independent study, mastery learning, and teaching strategies that emphasize shared inquiry and discovery within a psychologically safe environment encourage the most positive aspects of thinking and learning. It is important that you select those strategies that encourage students to become independent thinkers and skilled learners who can help in the planning, structuring, regulating, and assessing of their own learning and learning activities. Regardless of your subject and grade-level interest, central to your implementation of any strategy should be a concern to help children with the development of their reading, writing, thinking, and study skills.

Now that you have learned about basic facilitating behaviors (Chapters 3 and 10), about planning (Part II), and about the selection and effective implementation of specific teaching strategies, the next chapter focuses your attention on the many aids and resources available to the classroom teacher, and on how to use them.

QUESTIONS FOR CLASS DISCUSSION

1. While our emphasis is on the elementary school teacher's developing an eclectic model of teaching, authors of other elementary school teaching methods books talk of "teaching models," such as discovery, inquiry, expository, social interaction, and so on. Explain the correlation and the difference between a teaching style and the teacher's choice of strategies. We have talked much of the importance of the teacher being consistent, both in his or her responses and in classroom procedures. Can, and should, a teacher be both eclectic and consistent? Explain.

2. Explain why you would or would not like to teach by inquiry.

3. Are there any cautions teachers need to be aware of when using games for teaching? If so, describe them.

4. Locate and describe research studies on the use of cooperation versus competition in the classroom.

5. Differentiate between "delivery" and "access" strategies. Differentiate between "traditional" and "facilitating" strategies. Describe how the two sets of terms are similar. How are they different?

6. Share with your colleagues good educational games for teaching that you have found. Play the games together.

7. Locate and describe research about strategy choice and achievement in learning with respect to teaching a particular subject at a grade level of your choice.

8. Explain some specific ways that you can help your students develop their skills in reading, writing, thinking, and studying.

9. Describe ways you have learned about how, and to what extent you can and should, individualize learning for your students.

10. Do you have questions about content of this chapter? How might answers be found?

SUGGESTED READINGS FOR CHAPTER 11

Armstrong, J., and Lani, K. "An Integrated Learning Experience." *School Arts* 89(6):38–39 (February 1990).

Artzt, A. F., and Newman, C. M. *How to Use Cooperative Learning in the Mathematics Class.* Reston, VA: National Council of Teachers of Mathematics, 1990.

Brown, R. G. "Schooling and Thoughtfulness." *Journal of Basic Writing.* 10(1):3–15 (Spring 1991).

Carbo, M. "Structuring Whole Language for Students at Risk." *Teaching PreK–8* 22(8):88–89 (May 1992).

Carns, A. W., and Carns, M. R. "Teaching Study Skills, Cognitive Strategies, and Metacognitive Skills Through Self-Diagnosed Learning Styles." *School Counselor* 38(5):341–346 (May 1991).

Carson, L., and Hoyle, S. "Teaching Social Skills: A View from the Classroom." *Educational Leadership* 47(4):31 (December–January 1989–90).

Cooper, H. *Homework: Research on Teaching Monograph.* New York: Longman, 1989.

Davidson, G. "Beyond Direct Instruction: Educational Leadership in the Elementary School Classroom." *Journal of School Leadership* 2(3):180–188 (July 1992).

Elgersma, R. "Discovery Ideas for the Gifted." *Phi Delta Kappan* 72(5):389–393 (January 1991).

Ellis, S. S. "Introducing Cooperative Learning." *Educational Leadership* 47(4):34–37 (December–January 1989–90).

Feder-Feitel, L. "How to Avoid Gender Bias." *Creative Classroom* 7(5):56–63 (March 1993).

Gilmour, S. J. "Reflections on PSI: Good News and Bad." *Journal of Applied Behavior Analysis* 25(1):59–64 (Spring 1992).

Good, T. L., et al. "Using Work-groups in Mathematics Instruction." *Educational Leadership* 47(4):56–62 (December–January 1989–90).

Gray, S. S. "Ideas in Practice: Metacognition and Mathematical Problem Solving." *Journal of Developmental Education* 14(3):24–26, 28 (Spring 1991).

Hagaman, S. "The Community of Inquiry: An Approach to Collaborative Learning." *Studies in Art Education* 31(3):149–157 (Spring 1990).

Harding, L., et al. "Simulation . . . Stimulation?" *Social Studies Journal* 20:44–47 (Spring 1991).

Horton, L. *Mastery Learning.* Fastback 154. Bloomington, IN: Phi Delta Kappan Educational Foundation, 1981.

Johnson, D. W., and Johnson, R. T. "Social Skills for Successful Group Work." *Educational Leadership* 47(4):29–33 (December–January 1989–90).

———. *Learning Together and Alone: Cooperative, Competitive, and Individualistic Learning.* Englewood Cliffs, NJ: Prentice Hall, 1991.

Johnson, D. W., et al. *Circles of Learning: Cooperation in the Classroom.* Edina, MN: Interaction Book Co., 1990.

Kagan, S. "The Structural Approach to Cooperative Learning." *Educational Leadership* 47(4):12–15 (December–January 1989–90).

Kohn, A. "Group Grade Grubbing Versus Cooperative Learning." *Educational Leadership* 48(5):83–87 (February 1991).

Lyman, L., and Foyle, H. C. "The Constitution in Action: A Cooperative Learning Approach." *Georgia Social Science Journal* 21(1):24–34 (Spring 1990).

Margolis, H., et al. "Using Cooperative Learning to Facilitate Mainstreaming in the Social Studies." *Social Education* 54(2):111–114 (February 1990).

Marzano, L. "Connecting Literature with Cooperative Writing." *Reading Teacher* 43(6):429–430 (February 1990).

McClure, M. F. "Collaborative Learning: Teachers' Game or Students' Game?" *English Journal* 79(2):58–61 (February 1990).

McKenzie, F. D. "Equity: A Call to Action." In Gordon Cawelti, ed. 1993 ASCD Yearbook. *Challenges and Achievements of American Education.* Alexandria, VA: Association for Supervision and Curriculum Development, 1993.

Nolan, T. E. "Self-Questioning and Prediction: Combining Metacognitive Strategies." *Journal of Reading* 35(2):132–138 (October 1991).

Noone, E. T., Jr. "A Basketball Simulation." *Arithmetic Teacher* 38(7):36–38 (March 1991).

Novak, J. D. "Concept Maps and Vee Diagrams: Two Metacognitive Tools to Facilitate Meaningful Learning." *Instructional Science* 19(1):29–52 (1990).

Oldfield, B. J. "Games in the Learning of Mathematics." *Mathematics in School* 20(1):41–43 (January 1991).

Ollman, H. E. "Cause and Effect in the Real World." *Journal of Reading* 33(3):224–225 (December 1989).

Prater, D. L., and Terry, C. A. "Effects of Mapping Strategies on Reading Comprehension and Writing Performance." *Reading Psychology* 9(2):101–120 (1988).

Rich, Y. "Ideological Impediments to Instructional Innovation: The Case of Cooperative Learning." *Teaching and Teacher Education* 6(1):81–91 (1990).

Ross, J. A., and Raphael, D. "Communication and Problem Solving Achievement in Cooperative Learning Groups." *Journal of Curriculum Studies* 22(2):149–164 (March–April 1990).

Roth, W. M. "Open-ended Inquiry. How to Beat the Cookbook Blahs." *Science Teacher* 58(4):40–47 (April 1991).

Sapon-Shevin, M., and Schneidewind, N. "Selling Cooperative Learning Without Selling it Short." *Educational Leadership* 47(4):63–65 (December/January 1989–90).

Schultz, J. L. "Cooperative Learning: Refining the Process." *Educational Leadership* 47(4):43–45 (December/January 1989–90).

Schwartz, R. M. "Learning to Learn Vocabulary in Content Area Textbooks." *Journal of Reading* 32(2):108–118 (November 1988).

Slavin, R. E. "Research on Cooperative Learning: Consensus and Controversy." *Educational Leadership* 47(4):52–54 (December/January 1989–90).

———. *Cooperative Learning.* Englewood Cliffs, NJ: Prentice Hall, 1990.

Stahl, A. "Personal and Cultural Factors Interfering with the Effective Use of Individual and Group Learning Methods." *Journal of Educational Through Revue de la Pensee Educative* 26(1):22–32 (April 1992).

Stice, C. F., and Alvarez, M. C. "Hierarchical Concept Mapping in the Early Grades." *Childhood Education* 64(2):86–96 (December 1987).

Tebbutt, M. J. "Simulating Drug or Alcohol Abuse." *School Science Review* 72(261):77–79 (June 1991).

Tiedt, I. M. *Teaching Thinking in K–12 Classrooms: Ideas, Activities, and Resources.* Boston: Allyn and Bacon, 1989.

Totten, S., and Sills, T. M. "Selected Resources for Using Cooperative Learning." *Educational Leadership* 47(4):66 (December–January 1989–90).

Trochim, W. M. K., ed. "Concept Mapping for Evaluation and Planning." *Evaluation and Program Planning* 12(1):special issue 1–111 (1989).

Yachel, E., et al. "Small Group Interactions as a Source of Learning Opportunities in Second-Grade Mathematics." *Journal for Research in Mathematics Education* 22(5):390–408 (November 1991).

Wassermann, S. "A Case for Social Studies." *Phi Delta Kappan* 73(10):793–801 (June 1992).

12

What Aids and Resources Are Available to Me as An Elementary School Classroom Teacher?

You will be delighted to know that there is a vast amount of educational aids and resources from which to draw as you plan your instructional experiences. You might not be so pleased to learn that you will be spending a lot of time reviewing, sorting, selecting, and practicing with the selected materials and tools. Although nobody can make the job easier for you, this chapter will expedite the process by providing guidelines for your use of nonprojected and projected aids, and information about where to obtain additional resources.

Whereas projected aids are those that require electricity to project images onto screens, the first portion of this chapter is about nonprojected materials—printed materials, three-dimensional objects, and flat materials on which to write or display. Historically, of all the nonprojected materials for instruction, the printed textbook has had the most influence on teaching. Use of the student textbook was discussed in Chapters 5 and 11. The following section discusses the use of other nonprojected visual aids.

A. PRINTED MATERIALS

Besides the student textbook and perhaps an accompanying workbook, there are a great many other printed materials available for use in teaching, many of which are available without cost (see Figure 12.1). It is a good idea to immediately begin a file of printed materials and other resources that you can use in your teaching. Exercise 12.3 (at the end of this chapter) is designed to help you begin the process, an activity that will continue throughout your teaching career.

Printed materials include paperback books, workbooks, pamphlets, magazines, brochures, newspapers, professional journals, periodicals, and duplicated materials. When reviewing these materials, be alert to the following:

- Appropriateness of the materials in both content and reading level for the age level of your students.

A Guide to Print and Nonprint Materials Available from Organizations, Industry, Governmental Agencies and Specialized Publishers. New York: Neal Schuman.

Bibliography of Free and Inexpensive Materials for Economic Education. New York: Joint Council on Economic Education.

Civil Aeronautics Administration, *Sources of Free and Low-Cost Materials.* Washington, DC: U.S. Department of Commerce.

Educator's Guide to Free Health, Physical Education, and Recreation Materials. Randolph, WI: Educators Progress Service.

Educator's Guide to Free Science Materials. Randolph, WI: Educators Progress Service.

Educator's Guide to Free Social Studies Materials. Randolph, WI: Educators Progress Service.

Educator's Guide to Free Materials. Randolph, WI: Educators Progress Service.

Educator's Guide to Free Teaching Aids. Randolph, WI: Educators Progress Service.

Free and Inexpensive Learning Materials. Nashville, TN: Division of Surveys and Field Services, George Peabody College for Teachers.

Free Stuff for Kids. Deephaven, MN: Meadowbrook Press.

Index to Multi-Ethnic Teaching Materials and Teaching Resources. Washington, DC: National Education Association.

Materials List for Use by Teachers of Modern Foreign Languages. New York: Modern Foreign Language Association.

Figure 12.1   Resources for free and inexpensive printed materials.

- Articles in newspapers, magazines, and periodicals, related to the content your students will be studying, or to the skills they will be learning.
- Assorted workbooks that emphasize thinking and problem solving rather than rote memorization. With an assortment of workbooks you can have students working on a variety of similar assignments, depending on their interests and abilities—an example of multilevel teaching.
- Pamphlets, brochures, and other duplicated materials that students can read for specific information and viewpoints about particular topics.
- Relatively inexpensive paperback books that would provide multiple reading experiences for your class, and that make it possible for students to read primary sources.

For free and inexpensive printed materials, look for sources in the library of your college or university, in the public library, or in the resource center at a local school district (see Figure 12.1).

Professional Periodicals

Figure 12.2 is a sample listing of the many professional periodicals that can provide useful teaching ideas, and that carry information about instructional materials and how to get them. Most of these periodicals are likely to be in your university or college library. Check there for these and other titles of interest to you according to your grade level and subject interest.

The American Biology Teacher	*The Mathematics Teacher*
The American Music Teacher	*Middle School Journal*
American Teacher	*Modern Language Journal*
The Arithmetic Teacher	*Music Educator's Journal*
The Art Teacher	*Phi Delta Kappan*
Childhood Education	*Physical Education*
The Computing Teacher	*Reading Research Quarterly*
Educational Horizons	*The Reading Teacher*
Educational Leadership	*Reading Today*
The Elementary School Journal	*School Arts*
English Journal	*The School Musician*
English Language Teaching Journal	*School Science and Mathematics*
Hispania	*Science*
Instructor	*Science and Children*
Journal of Elementary Science Education	*Science Scope*
Journal of Home Economics	*Social Education*
Journal of Learning Disabilities	*Social Studies*
Journal of Physical Education and Recreation	*Social Studies and the Young Learner*
Journal of Reading	*Teacher K–8*
Language Arts	*Teacher Magazine*
Language Learning	*Young Children*
Learning	

Figure 12.2 Selected professional periodicals.

The ERIC Information Network: A Resource of Research Studies

The Educational Resources Information Centers (ERIC) system, established by the United States Office of Education, is a widely used network providing access to information and research in education. While there are several clearinghouses providing information on specific subjects, addresses for those of particular interest to elementary school teachers are as follows:

Elementary and Early Childhood Education. University of Illinois, College of Education, 805 W. Pennsylvania Avenue, Urbana, IL 61601.

Handicapped and Gifted Children. Council for Exceptional Children, 1920 Association Drive, Reston, VA 22091.

Languages and Linguistics. Center for Applied Linguistics, 1118 22nd Street NW, Washington, DC 20037-0037.

Reading and Communication Skills. Indiana University, 2606 East 10th Street, Smith Research Center, Suite 150, Bloomington, IN 47408.

Science, Mathematics, and Environmental Education. Ohio State University, 1200 Chambers Road, 3rd Floor, Columbus, OH 43212-1792.

Social Studies/Social Science Education. Indiana University, Social Studies Development Center, 2805 East 10th Street, Bloomington, IN 47405-2373.

Tests, Measurements, and Evaluation. American Institutes for Research, Washington Research Center, 1055 Thomas Jefferson Street NW, Washington, DC 20007-3893.

Copying Printed Materials

In many schools the spirit duplicator (ditto machine) has been replaced with modern dry copiers. Whichever type of copying machine is available at your school, here are important guidelines for its use.

1. You might arrive at the copy room and discover that the copy machine has broken down. If the copy machine has stopped working, be sure you don't! The secret to not being frustrated and incapacitated by a broken copy machine is to plan ahead. Do your copying well in advance.
2. If permissible at your school, learn to operate the copy machine yourself. Some teachers purchase their own home computers, printers, or copy machines, and do their copying at home. That is fine if you have the finances, and is particularly helpful in case of emergency or lack of lead time that may be necessary for school duplication.
3. When using copyrighted materials, cite the appropriate reference (i.e., author, title, date, source, and publisher) and, when necessary, get permission to copy. (See

---

Permitted Uses—You May Make:

1. Single copies of:
   - A chapter of a book.
   - An article from a periodical, magazine, or newspaper.
   - A short story, short essay, or short poem, whether or not from a collected work.
   - A chart, graph, diagram, drawing, or cartoon.
   - An illustration from a book, magazine, or newspaper.
2. Multiple copies for classroom use (not to exceed one copy per student in a course) of:
   - A complete poem if less than 250 words.
   - An excerpt from a longer poem, but not to exceed 250 words.
   - A complete article, story, or essay of less than 2,500 words.
   - An excerpt from a larger printed work, not to exceed 10 percent of the whole or 1,000 words.
   - One chart, graph, diagram, cartoon, or picture per book or magazine issue.

Prohibited Uses—You May *Not:*

1. Copy more than one work or two excerpts from a single author during one class term (semester or year).
2. Copy more than three works from a collective work or periodical volume during one class term.
3. Reproduce more than nine sets of multiple copies for distribution to students in one class term.
4. Copy to create or replace or substitute for anthologies or collective works.
5. Copy "consumable" works, e.g., workbooks, standardized tests, or answer sheets.
6. Copy the same work year after year.

Figure 12.3 Guidelines for copying printed materials.[1]

[1]From section 107 of the 1976 Federal Omnibus Copyright Revision Act.

the guidelines that follow.) When permission is required, there usually is no fee for nonprofit, educational purposes.

4. Use varying colors to highlight printed materials. Ditto masters come in standard blue, as well as in black, red, and green. If not overused, multicolored dittos are interesting and the colors can be meaningful. Dry copy machines are available at commercial copy stores for color duplication, but the cost may be prohibitive for the duplication of class sets of materials. Likewise, for computer printers and computer programs with color commands, the cost of duplicating in several colors may be too high for more than an occasional printing of class sets of materials.

Guidelines for Copying Printed Materials That Are Copyrighted

You must know the laws about the use of copyrighted materials, printed and nonprinted. Although space here prohibits full inclusion of United States legal guidelines, your local school district should be able to provide a copy of current district policies for compliance with copyright laws.

When preparing to make a copy, you must find out whether the copying is permitted by law under the category of "permitted use." If not allowed under "permitted use," then you must get written permission to reproduce the material from the holder of the copyright. You are advised to adhere to the guidelines of Figure 12.3 when using printed materials.

B. THE WRITING BOARD

Can you imagine an elementary school classroom without a writing board? Teacher talk has been discussed in previous chapters; in this section are guidelines for using the classroom writing board as a visual to enhance the verbal communication.

Writing boards used to be slate blackboards. Today's classroom may have either a board of painted plywood (chalkboard); a magnetic chalkboard (plywood with a magnetic backing); or a white or colored (light green and light blue are common) multipurpose board on which you write with special marking pens. **Multipurpose boards** are important for classrooms where chalk dust would create problems—i.e., allergies caused by chalk dust or dust interfering with computer maintenance. In addition to providing a surface on which you can write and draw, the multipurpose board can be used as a projection screen and as a surface to which figures cut from colored transparency film will stick. It may also have a magnetic backing. Whichever the case in your classroom, here are guidelines for using the classroom writing board.

Guidelines for Using the Classroom Writing Board

- At the top of the board frame you may find clips for hanging posters, maps, and charts.
- Avoid blocking students' view of the writing on the board. Learn to write on the board without having to entirely turn your back to students.

- Except for announcements that you place on the board, you should start each class or each day with a clean board, and at the end of each class clean the board, especially if another teacher follows you in that room—simple professional courtesy.
- Maintain a personal supply of chalk (or pens) and an eraser.
- Print instructions on the board, rather than giving them orally.
- Print or write on the board neatly, clearly, and in an orderly fashion, beginning at the far left, and in large enough letters that all students can read them from their positions in the room.
- Use colored chalk (or marking pens) to highlight your "board talk." This is especially helpful for students with learning difficulties.
- Use the writing board to record student contributions.
- When you have a lot of material to put on the board, do it before class and then cover it; or better yet, put the material on transparencies and use the overhead projector rather than the board, or use both.

C. VISUAL DISPLAY MATERIALS

Visual display materials include bulletin boards, charts, graphs, flip charts, magnetic boards, realia (real objects), pictures, and posters. As a new or visiting member of a faculty, one of your first tasks is to find out what visual materials are available for your use and where they are kept. The following are guidelines for their use.

The Bulletin Board

Bulletin boards are used by nearly every elementary classroom teacher, and although sometimes poorly used or not used at all, they can be relatively inexpensively transformed into attractive and valuable instructional tools. Read the following suggestions for effective use of bulletin boards.

Making a C.A.S.E. for Bulletin Boards

How can you effectively use a classroom bulletin board? Your classroom bulletin board will be most effective if you consider your "C.A.S.E.":

C: for colorful constructions and captions.
A: for attractive arrangement.
S: for simple and student prepared.
E: for enrichment and extensions of learning.

C: Colorful Constructions and Captions

Take time to plan the colors you select for your board and, whenever possible, include different materials for the letters and for the background of the board. For letter variety, consider patterns on bright cloth such as denim, felt, and corduroy. Search for special letters: they might be magnetic or ceramic, or precut letters of different sizes. Make unique letters by cutting them from magazines, newspapers, posters, or stencils, or by printing the letters with rubber stamps, sponges, or vegetable prints. You may print the shapes of letters by dabbing colors on ABC shapes with sponges, rubber stamps, or with vegetable slices that leave an imprint.

For the background of your board and the borders, consider gift-wrapping paper, wallpaper samples, shelf paper, remnants of fabric—flowers, polka dots, plaids, solids, or checks. Corrugated cardboard makes sturdy borders: cut out scallops or the shape of a picket fence, or make jagged points for an icicle effect. Other colorful borders can be made with wide braid, wide rickrack, or a contrasting fabric or paper. Constructions for the board may be simple ones made of yarn, ribbon, braid, cardboard pointers, maps, scrolls, banners, pennants, wheels that turn, cardboard doors that open, shuttered windows to peek through, or flaps that pull down or up—to be peered under or over.

If you need more bulletin board space, prepare large, lightweight screens from the cardboard sides of a tall refrigerator carton, available from an appliance store. One creative teacher asked for, and received without charge, several empty gallon ice-cream containers from a local ice-cream shop. The teacher then stacked five of the containers on top of one another, fastened them together with wide masking tape, painted them, and prepared her own bulletin board "totem pole" for display in the corner of the classroom. On that circular display space, the students placed their items about a current unit of study.

A: Attractive Arrangement

Use your imagination to make the board attractive. Ask yourself these questions: Is the arrangement interesting? Did I use texture? Did I consider the shapes of the items selected? Are the colors attractive? Does the caption draw student attention?

S: Simple and Student Prepared

The bulletin board should be simple, emphasize one main idea, concept, topic, or theme, and the captions should be short and concise.

Are your students interested in preparing the bulletin board for your classroom? If so, plan a short class meeting and discuss this with them. The students will have great ideas.

- They can help plan. Why not let them diagram their ideas and share them with each other?
- They can discuss. Is there a more meaningful way to begin to discuss an evaluation of what they see, to discuss the internal criteria that each student brings to class, or to begin to talk about the different values that each student may have?
- They can arrange materials. Why not let them discover the concepts of balance and symmetry?
- They can construct and contribute. Will they feel they are more actively involved and are really participating if it is *their* bulletin board?
- When the bulletin board is finished, your students can get further involved by (1) reviewing the board during a class meeting, (2) discussing the materials used, and (3) discussing the information their bulletin board is emphasizing.

Additional class projects may be planned during this meeting. For instance, do the students want a bulletin board group or committee for their class? Do they want a permanent committee, or a group in which the membership changes from month to month? Do they prefer that existing cooperative learning groups assume bulletin board responsibility, with periodic rotation of that responsibility? Do they want to meet on a regular basis? Can they work quietly and not disturb other students who may still be completing their other learning tasks? Should they prepare the board, or should the committee ask everyone to contribute ideas and items for the weekly or monthly bulletin board? Does the committee want to keep a register, guest book, or guest file of students who contribute to the board? Should there be an honorary list of bulletin board illustrators? Should the authors of selected captions sign their names beneath each caption? Do they want to keep a file binder of all of the different diagrams of proposed bulletin boards? At each class meeting, should they discuss the proposed diagrams with the entire class? Should they ask the class to evaluate which idea would be an appropriate one for a particular study topic? What other records do they want to keep? Should there be a bulletin board medal or a classroom award?

E: Enrichment and Extensions of Learning

Illustrations on the bulletin board can accent learning topics; verbs can vitalize the captions; phrases can punctuate a student's thoughts; and alliteration can announce anything you wish on the board. For example:

Animals can accent! Pandas, panthers, and parrots can help present punctuation symbols; a giant octopus can show students eight rules to remember, eight things to remember when preparing a book report, or eight activities to complete when academic work is finished early. A student can fish for anything—math facts, correctly spelled words, or the meanings of science words. A bear character helps students to "bear down" on errors of any kind. A large pair of shoes helps "stamp out" errors, incomplete work, forgotten school materials, or student misbehavior. Dinosaurs can begin a search for any topic, and pack rats can lead one into phrases, prose, or poetry.

Verbs can vitalize! Someone or something (your choice) can "swing into" any curriculum area. Some of the verbs used most often are *soar, win, buzz, rake, scurry, score, retell,* and *race.*

Phrases point out! Some of the short, concise phrases used as captions may include:

All aboard for ＿＿＿	Grow up with ＿＿＿	Peer into ＿＿＿
Bone up on ＿＿＿	Hop into ＿＿＿	Race into ＿＿＿
Fly high with ＿＿＿	Looking good with ＿＿＿	Roll into ＿＿＿
Get on track with ＿＿＿	Monkey with ＿＿＿	Tune into ＿＿＿

Alliteration announces! Some classroom bulletin boards show Viking ships or Voyages that guide a student to vocabulary words: Monsters monitor Math Madness; other boards present Surprises of Spring, Fantasies of Fall, Wonders of Winter, and Safety in Summer; still other boards send messages about Library Lingo, Dictionary Dynamite, and Thesaurus Treats. For still more ideas, look for *Teaching Off the Wall* by Elaine Prizzi and Jeanne Hoffman (Carthage, IL: Fearon, 1981). For a wide variety of clever patterns for borders, see *Instant Borders* by Anthony Flores (Carthage, IL: Fearon, 1979).

The Story Felt Board

Interacting with figures for a story felt board and retelling stories is an excellent activity for children. This is a language experience that should be encouraged. Specialists in children's literature emphasize that felt boards provide opportunity for children to practice telling stories more easily. Once they have seen their teacher tell a story with felt-board figures, they are eager to do it themselves. In addition to being an attention-getting strategy, another advantage in using a felt board is that the figures can be arranged in sequence and serve as cues for the story. Further, when a storyteller is finished, children can retell the story in their own words. Most children also like to make their own figures and tell their own stories.[2] It is important to carefully select stories that have simple settings, few characters, and fairly uncomplicated plots.[3] Norton emphasizes those stories that lend themselves to felt-board interpretations have only a few major characters and can be told by both adults and children. Norton suggests sharing folktales such as Norway's *The Three Billy Goats Gruff* and England's *The Donkey, the Table, and the Stick.*[4] Traditional and literary folktales that have a sequential accumulation of characters and actions are especially adaptable for flannel-board or felt-board retellings.[5]

The Felt Board: A Felt Board Is T.O.P.S.

Indeed, a felt (or flannel) board may be considered T.O.P.S. in your classroom, since it has many uses and is a flexible teaching tool. With it, you can present lessons from any subject area or stories of any kind. Sometimes the students can follow your presentation on small, individual felt boards, and at other times they may assist you by manipulating the objects on the board. Consider the letters that spell T.O.P.S.:

T: for teacher use.
O: for object variety.
P: for planning, presenting, and plotting.
S: for student use.

T: Teacher Use

For primary students, teachers may use the felt board for (1) presenting stories; (2) presenting rhymes; (3) matching rhyming pictures; (4) presenting objects; (5) listening to beginning sounds, matching them, and classifying object pictures; (6) recognizing colors and color words; (7) selecting pictures showing opposite concepts; (8) arranging objects or pictures in sequence; (9) comparing and contrasting sizes of objects; and (10) creating an individual story with unique combinations of animals, places, and objects.

---

[2]C. S. Huck, S. Hepler, and J. Hickman, *Children's Literature in the Elementary School*, 4th ed. (New York: Holt, Rinehart, and Winston, 1987).
[3]J. I. Glazer and G. Williams III. *Introduction to Children's Literature* (New York: McGraw-Hill, 1979).
[4]D. Norton, *Through the Eyes of a Child: An Introduction to Children's Literature* (Columbus, OH: Merrill/Macmillan, 1991).
[5]B. Cullinan, *Literature and the Child* (San Diego, CA: Harcourt Brace Jovanovich, 1981).

There are felt cutouts for numerals, for arranging members in sets for math; for words, symbols, and punctuation marks for spelling, labeling, and showing quotations in conversations. Commercial bulletin board sets are easily adapted to the felt board and supply ready-made materials for such topics as traffic control symbols, insects, nutrition, the solar system, prehistoric animals, telling time, and the world of money. Primary students can plan balanced meals by selecting colorful food objects, and the life cycle of a plant or insect can be traced by intermediate-grade students; career choice can be a discussion for older students who may display people, props, and labels.

When considering story presentations, you may want to select one of the following:

Primary Students:

Aardema, V. *Borrequita and the Coyote: A Tale from Ayutla, Mexico.* Illustrated by P. Mathers. New York: Knopf, 1991. A crafty little lamb fools a hungry coyote.

Kleven, E. *The Lion and the Little Red Bird.* Illustrated. New York: Dutton, 1992. Two animals don't understand one another's language.

Rounds, G. *Three Little Pigs and the Big Bad Wolf.* Illustrated. New York: Holiday House, 1992. Has capitalized words for reading-aloud activities.

Young, E. *Seven Blind Mice.* Illustrated. New York: Philomel, 1992. Each mouse investigates a strange object until they discover that wisdom is seeing the whole thing.

Middle-Grade Students:

Perrault, C. *Puss in Boots.* Retold by L. Kirstein. Illustrated by Alan Vaes. New York: Little, Brown, 1992. Alliterative prose for reading aloud.

San Souci, R. D. *Sukey and the Mermaid.* Illustrated by B. Pinkney. New York: Four Winds, 1992. An African American girl develops a special friendship with a benevolent mermaid.

Yacowitz, C. *The Jade Stone.* Illustrated by Ju-Yong Chen. New York: Holiday House, 1992. A stone carver carves what he hears in a jade stone and creates three carp.

Your options for including the felt board in a particular lesson are quite varied: (1) you can take the total responsibility of presenting and moving the felt board objects; (2) you can encourage the students to participate and move the objects; (3) you can present the lesson while students follow the story by placing objects from their individual sets on small felt boards at their desks or tables (during a previous activity time, the students would have received ditto copies of characters, cut out the characters, and glued or pasted small bits of flannel or felt to the backs of the characters, in order to prepare their individual sets); (4) you may arrange the students into teams of two, and ask them to tell the lesson or story to one another by moving the board objects; or (5) you may assign one group to a larger board for a group presentation.

O: Object Variety

The variety of objects you may use with a felt board is nearly unlimited. How can you prepare this wide collection of felt board objects?

1. *Consider Pellon objects.* With *permanent* coloring pens, draw directly on white Pellon. (Watercolor from pens will come off on your hands either today or at a future date.) Add facial features, clothing details, or other special items. One teacher adds sequins and small glittering stars. Another adds rickrack or gold glitter. Still another adds beads and tiny buttons to a character's costume. Your artwork as well as that of the students shows up quite well when you draw on Pellon. Pellon is often used for interfacing in clothing, so white Pellon is usually available in a fabric store.

2. *Consider felt, flannel, and sandpaper objects.* Objects may be cut directly from these materials, or the materials may be glued to the back of any object. Students enjoy seeing sandpaper letters, bright felt or flannel cutouts of holiday items—orange pumpkins, green pine trees, red valentine hearts, and shamrocks.

3. *Consider objects from published material.* Save catalogs, magazines, inexpensive books, posters, greeting cards, and discarded textbooks. Cut the objects you need from these materials and back the objects with any of the materials that will adhere to the felt board.

4. *Consider objects from commercial felt-board sets.* Visit your nearest teacher's exchange or write to a school supply company for a current catalog. Look for felt-board sets or bulletin board sets that you can adapt.

5. *Consider objects with a Velcro variation.* Some teachers add a border of Velcro across the top of their felt boards so they can place "real" objects on the board as they tell a story or give a presentation. Other teachers place small pieces of Velcro in strategic spots on the felt board, spots to hold a little bear's small chair, for example, or Mama Bear's bowl and spoon. Remember to back your realia with Velcro also.

6. *Consider objects with a magnet.* Some teachers prepare a felt-board slipcover to slide over a large metal board (such as a large cookie sheet or a piece of sheet metal) in order to use magnets. One teacher prepared a scene for the base of a green felt board to represent grass, flowers, rocks, and trees. Behind each gray felt "rock" was a circular cutout, exposing the metal sheet. This enabled the teacher to remove a felt "rock" at an appropriate time and place a small wooden animal, backed with a magnet, on the board to add interest and a three-dimensional quality to the presentation. Multipurpose writing boards, as discussed earlier in this chapter, usually have a metal backing so they can be used as magnet boards much in the same way as just discussed. Instead of felt materials, you can use various colors of thin plastic film, which will stick to the board when smoothed into place.

7. *Consider a looped-cloth variation.* One fabric, commonly known as looped-cloth, is very useful for a slipcover for your felt board. This cloth has loops in the fabric. Put self-adhesive picture-hanging hooks on the back of the heavier objects and hang these into the loops of the poodle-cloth.

P: Planning, Presenting, and Plotting

Planning, presenting, and plotting are three basics crucial to your felt-board story or lesson. Plan to use familiar objects if possible; present your story or lesson after preparing it thoroughly in a logical, sequential way. Plotting means that you carefully arrange your presentation. You may tell a story with a satisfying ending or share nonfictional information. The information can be facts that portray another point of view or facts about something the students might not have known before. It can be an interesting presentation of the life cycle of an insect, a review of cloud shapes, or a metamorphosis not often illustrated in student texts.

S: Student Use

Get your students involved with felt boards. Individual felt boards are quickly and easily made by pasting 8½ × 11" pieces of felt to the outside of large manila mailing envelopes. (Students may place the objects inside the envelopes to keep them secure.) Students can brace the envelopes against a textbook, at their desks. Extra bits and pieces of felt or other materials that adhere to felt can be placed inside the envelope, and additional objects may be made as needed.

What can a student do with an individual felt board?

- Place objects, along with the teacher, as the story or lesson is told; assist teacher after the lesson by removing the objects in sequence; help to retell the story or summarize the lesson.
- Tell the story to one another in teams of two.
- Place accompanying objects on the board as an audiotape of the story or lesson is heard.
- Create original stories or presentations.
- Create original objects for presentation of information gained from a story or a lesson.

How to Avoid Problems When Using a Felt Board

Problem: The cutouts get mixed up. You may wish to number your cutouts in order of their use in the presentation. Number them on their backs and lay them face down on the table when you are ready to begin. Arrange them in numerical order.

Problem: The cutouts fall off the felt board. Check your board to see whether you need to add another backing of felt. Add more if needed. One teacher uses an old brush to brush up the nap on the back of the cutouts as well as to brush up the nap on the board before each story. Another teacher sprays a light mist of pattern adhesive spray on the felt-board surface before the story. (Pattern spray is available at your nearest fabric store.) Still another teacher periodically replaces the felt on the back of the cutouts. Consider backing your cutouts, not with felt, but with Pellon. If the cutouts fall, prepare to keep your story or lesson moving smoothly by placing a short row of straight pins into the back of your board. When a cutout falls, reach back quickly, select a pin, and again attach the loose character or object. Remember not to crowd your board with too many objects at any one time. Remove objects as your presentation sequence moves along.

Problem: You lose your place in the lesson or story. Rehearse your presentation. If possible, audiotape your presentation in advance, replay the tape, and self-evaluate. How long will the presentation take? Did you practice placing your cutouts on the board? Do you have room for them? Rehearsing with an audiotape will help your presentation flow smoothly as you develop your skill in doing more than one thing at a time. Perhaps you may want to write notes for yourself in large, legible writing and place these notes on the table near the cutouts. One teacher pins large note cards on the back of the board; another prepares a low cardboard screen, about six inches high, to stand in front of the table top. This low screen, cut from three sides of a cardboard box and gaily decorated, conceals the cutouts and the teacher's notes.

Proceed now by doing Exercise 12.1 and optional Exercise 12.2.

Exercise 12.1: Creating a Bulletin Board Display

Instructions: The purpose of this exercise is to give you practical experience in creating an effective bulletin board display. Using the criteria established in the section on use of the bulletin board, work in teams of four (selected according to grade-level interest) to create a bulletin board display around a theme selected by your team, one that could be used in your teaching. After completing your bulletin board, show it and discuss it with the other members of your class for their responses.

Exercise 12.2: Creating a Hand Puppet

Did you ever want to make a puppet? Here is your opportunity to make your own sock hand puppet, which you can use to introduce a story, along with your flannel board, and for any other storytelling time.

Puppet-Making Made Easy: The Sock Hand Puppet*

Materials needed:

1. One sock (any color, large enough to fit over your hand, and clean please!).
2. Two buttons.
3. Needle and thread.
4. Yarn—4 or 5 pieces, 3″ long.
5. Two straight pins.
6. One piece of felt or material 6 × 6″.
7. The pattern for the inside of the mouth.

Follow these simple instructions:

1. Put the sock on your hand and pull it all the way up your arm.

2. Bend your hand so the back of it is looking at your smiling face.
3. Move your hand around and pretend it is talking to you. As you are doing this, decide where you want to put its eyes.

*From a self-instructional package developed by Prudence Taylor. Used by permission.

4. Carefully put the two straight pins into place where you want the eyes.

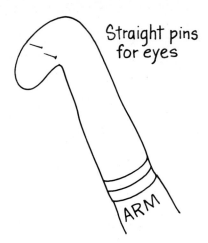

Straight pins for eyes

ARM

5. Take off the puppet sock and sew the buttons into place.

Take a short break!

Buttons for eyes

Talk with your puppet a while
and make friends!

6. Again, put your puppet on your hand. While it is talking, find where you want its mouth to be. Mark this spot with your straight pins. Take the puppet off your hand and cut out the mouth pattern from your material or felt.

Sew mouth on
other side of
sock – eyes
on back

7. Now sew on the mouth piece. This piece goes inside the mouth.

   Your puppet is beginning to take shape!
   Now, put your puppet back on your hand.
   Sew down the corners of the mouth (if you wish).

8. While your puppet is on your hand, take your needle and thread and sew a spot for the nose. (If it is hard for you to do this while your friend is on your hand, mark the spot for the nose, remove the puppet and sew on the nose.

9. Does your puppet need hair?
   If your puppet needs hair, use the yarn and sew it into place with a few stitches. Only you and your puppet can decide where it should be to fit his or her personality.

You may want to unwind the yarn and make it frizzy.

You may want the yarn to be flat and long.

You may want the yarn very short or shaped into a ball.

Remember, the hair can help make the personality.

Wasn't that fun! Your puppet is finished!
Now, after you clean up and put away, play with your newly made friend!

The teacher creates a responsive classroom environment with meaningful and attractive visual displays.

Charts, Posters, and Graphs

Charts, posters, and graphs can be used for displays just as bulletin boards are, but, as a rule, they are better suited for explaining, illustrating, clarifying, and reinforcing specific points in lessons. Charts, posters, and graphs might also be included in a bulletin board display. The previously discussed guidelines for use of the writing board and bulletin board also apply to the use of charts, posters, and graphs. Clarity, simplicity, and attractiveness are essential considerations. Here are additional suggestions for their preparation and use:

- Most students enjoy making charts, posters, and graphs. Involve them in doing so, in finding information, planning how to represent it, and making the chart or poster. Have the author(s) of the chart or poster sign it, and then display it in the classroom. Students should credit their sources on the graphs and charts.
- When making graphs, students may need help in keeping them proportional, and that provides an opportunity to help students develop a thinking skill, the importance of which was discussed in Chapter 11.
- Students also enjoy designing flip charts, a series of charts or posters (may include graphs) to illustrate certain points or a series of related points. To make a large flip

chart, they can use the large pads used by artists for sketching, or small notepads to make mini flip charts to use in dyads.

As should be obvious from the preceding discussion, the preparation and sharing of bulletin board displays, charts, graphs, and posters can be important and integral to interdisciplinary thematic planning and to student learning.

D. PROJECTED AND RECORDED INSTRUCTIONAL AIDS

Continuing with instructional tools that are available for use in teaching, this section focuses on audiovisual aids that depend on electricity to project light and sound and to focus images on screens: projectors of various sorts, computers, sound recorders, video recorders, and laser videodisc players. When using these, it is best to set up the equipment and have it ready to go before students arrive. Such preparation helps avoid the problems in classroom management that can occur when there is a delay (dead time, as discussed in Chapter 4) because equipment was not ready. Of course, delays may be unavoidable when equipment breaks down, or if a videotape breaks.

When Equipment Breaks Down

Remember the "law" that says if anything can go wrong, it will? This is particularly relevant when using the equipment discussed in this section. The professional teacher is prepared for such emergencies. Effectively planning for and responding to this kind of event is part of your system of movement management (as introduced in Chapter 4). That preparation includes the following considerations.

When equipment malfunctions, three principles or rules should be kept in mind: (1) you want to avoid dead time in the classroom; (2) you want to avoid causing permanent damage to equipment; and (3) you want to avoid losing content continuity of a lesson. So what do you do when equipment breaks down? The answer is, *be prepared for the eventuality.*

If a projector bulb goes out, quickly insert another. That means that you have an extra bulb. If a tape breaks, you can do a quick temporary splice with cellophane tape. That means that tape should be readily available. If you must do a temporary splice, do it on the film or videotape that has already run through the machine, rather than on the end yet to go through, so as not to foul the machine or the film. Then, after class or after school, be sure to notify the person in charge of the tape that a temporary splice was made, so that it can be permanently repaired before the next use.

Go to Lesson Plan B

If a fuse blows, or if for some other reason you lose power, or you can see that there is going to be too much dead time before the equipment is working again, it is time to go to your alternate lesson plan. You have probably heard the expression "Go to Plan B." This is a useful phrase, and what it means is that without missing a beat in the lesson, to accomplish your original instructional objective or another objective, you go to an alternative learning activity or activities. This does not mean that you, the beginning teacher, must plan *two* lessons for every one, but that when planning a lesson that utilizes audiovisual equipment, you should plan an alternative activity, just in case. You can then move your students into the planned alternative activity quickly and smoothly.

Projectors

Projection machines today are lighter, more energy efficient, and easier to operate than they were a few years ago. Among the most common and useful to the classroom teacher are the overhead projector, the opaque projector, the slide projector, the filmstrip projector, and, of course, the 16-mm film projector. Because limited space in this resource guide does not allow the luxury of presenting the operating procedures for every model of projector you may come across in classrooms, this presentation is confined to guidelines for their use. Since operations vary little from one projector to the next, this should be no major problem for you. At any school there are teachers who will gladly answer your questions about a specific projector.

The Overhead and Opaque Projectors

The overhead projector is one of the more versatile of teaching tools available today. Along with a bulletin board and a writing board, nearly every classroom has an overhead projector. Yet to find an opaque projector, you may have to look long and hard.

While the overhead projector projects light through objects that are transparent (see Figure 12.4), the opaque projector reflects light from objects that are not transparent, that is, that are opaque (see Figure 12.5). To use the opaque projector, room lights must be turned off, but an overhead projector works quite well in a fully lit room. An opaque projector (especially older models) may be quite large and bulky; the overhead projector is more portable. Truly portable overhead projectors are available, which can be carried from place to place in their compact cases.

Other types of overhead projectors include rear-projection systems that allow the teacher to stand off to the side rather than between students and the screen, and overhead video projectors that use video cameras to send images that are projected by television monitors.

The opaque projector is useful for showing pages of a book, or for showing real objects. *Caution:* Objects placed in older-model opaque projectors may get quite hot; pages will begin to brown as if they were in an oven. Some schools use overhead video camera technology that assumes, and improves upon, the function of the opaque projector, focusing on an object, pages of a book, or a demonstration, while sending a clear image to a video monitor with a screen large enough for an entire class to see clearly.

In some respects, the overhead projector is more practical than the writing board, particularly for a beginning teacher who is nervous. Use of the overhead projector rather than the writing board can help avoid tension by decreasing the need to pace back and forth to the board. Moreover, by using an overhead projector rather than a writing board, you can maintain both eye contact and physical proximity with students. Specific guidelines follow.

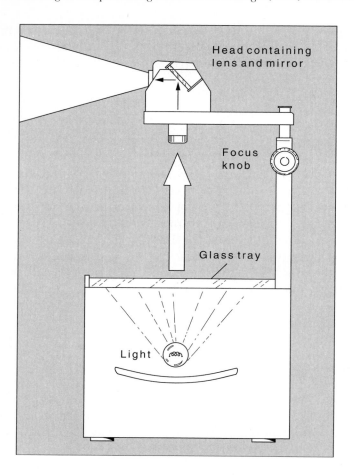

Figure 12.4 The overhead projector, cutaway view. An overhead projector consists of a glass-topped box that contains a light source and a vertical post mounting a head that contains a lens. To use it, place an acetate transparency on the glass top (some overhead projectors are equipped with acetate rolls to use as transparencies), switch on the light, and adjust the focus by moving the head, which contains the lens, up and down. (Courtesy of Robert Heinich et al., *Instructional Media*, 4th ed., New York: Macmillan, 1993, p. 134. By permission of Macmillan Publishing Company.)

Guidelines for Using Overhead and Opaque Projection

- With use of an overhead projector, ordinary felt-tip pens are not satisfactory for writing. Select a transparency marking pen available at an office supply store. These pens have water-soluble ink, so keep the palm of your hand from resting on the transparency or you will have smudges on your transparency and on your hand. Non-water-soluble pens—permanent markers—can be used, but to reuse the transparency it must be cleaned with an alcohol solvent (ditto fluid works but, for safety, be sure there is proper ventilation) or a plastic eraser. With a cleaning solvent you can clean and dry with paper towels or a soft rag. To highlight the writing on a transparency and to organize student learning, use pens in a variety of colors. Transparency pens tend to dry out quickly and are relatively expensive, so the caps must be taken on and off frequently, which is something of a nuisance when working with several colors. Practice writing on a transparency, and also practice making overlays.
- You can use an acetate transparency roll or single sheets of flat transparencies. Flat transparency sheets come in different colors—clear, red, blue, yellow, and green, which can be useful in making overlays.
- Some teachers prefer to prepare an outline of a lesson in advance, on transparencies. This allows more careful preparation of the transparencies, and they are then ready for reuse at another time. Some teachers prefer to use an opaque material,

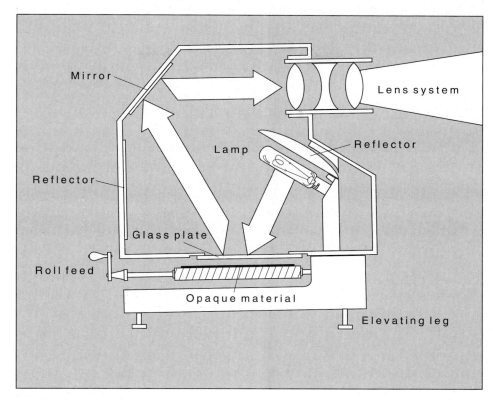

Figure 12.5 The opaque projector, cutaway view. (Courtesy of Robert Heinich et al. *Instructional Media,* 4th ed., New York: Macmillan, 1993, p. 153. By permission of Macmillan Publishing Company.)

such as 3 × 5″ note cards, to block out prewritten material and then uncover it at the moment it is being discussed. For preparation of permanent transparencies you will probably want to use "permanent marker" pens, rather than those that are water soluble and can be easily smudged. Heavy paper frames are available for permanent transparencies; marginal notes can be written on the frames.

• Other transparent materials can be shown on an overhead projector, such as transparent rulers, protractors, Petri dishes, and even objects that are opaque if you simply want to show a silhouette.

• For any projector, find the best location in your classroom. If there is no classroom projection screen, you can hang white paper or a sheet, use a white multipurpose board, or use a white or near-white wall.

• Have you ever attended a presentation by someone using an overhead projector, but not using it properly? It can be frustrating to members of an audience when the image is too small, out of focus, partially off the screen, or partially blocked from view by the presenter. To use this teaching tool, turn on the projector (the switch is probably on the front), place it so that the projected white light covers the entire screen and hits the screen at a 90-degree angle, then focus the image to be projected. *Face your students while using the projector.* The fact that you do not lose eye contact with your students is a major advantage of using the overhead projector, rather than a writing board. What you write, as you face your students, will show up perfectly (unless out of focus, or off the screen). Rather than using your finger to point to detail, or pointing to the screen (thereby turning away from your students), lay a pencil directly on the transparency, with the tip of the pencil pointing to the detail being emphasized.

- Some teachers suggest you turn the overhead projector off when you want student attention to be shifted back to you, or when changing transparencies.
- Thermal processing (copy) machines, probably located in the teachers' workroom or in the school's main office, can be used to make permanent transparencies from magazines, books, and other sources.
- Hand calculators are available specifically for use with the overhead projector, as is a screen that fits onto the platform and is circuited to computers, so that whatever is displayed on the computer monitor is also projected onto the classroom screen.
- Tracing transparent charts or drawings into larger drawings onto paper or onto the writing board is easily done with use of the overhead projector. In the same manner, opaque drawings, as from a textbook, can be projected by the opaque projector. With both, the image projected onto the screen can be made smaller or larger by moving the projector closer or farther away, respectively, and then traced when you have the size you want.
- An overhead projector or a filmstrip projector can be used as a light source (spotlight) to highlight demonstrations by you or by your students.
- Commercial transparencies are available from a variety of school supply houses. For sources, check the catalogs available in your school office or at the audiovisual and resources centers in your school district. See Figure 12.6 for sample sources.

Slides and Filmstrips

Slides and filmstrips are variations of the same medium, and most of what can be said about the use of one is true for the other. In fact, one projector may sometimes serve both functions. Filmstrips are, in effect, a series of slides connected on a roll of film. Slides can be made into filmstrips. Relatively inexpensive technology is now available that allows you to take slides or home movies and convert them into videocassettes. Because of their greater instructional flexibility, low cost, and greater visual impact, videocassettes have virtually replaced films and filmstrips in popularity for school use.

BJ's School Supplies, 1807 19th Street, Bakersfield, CA 93301
Carolina Biological Supply Company, 2700 York Road, Burlington, NC 27215
Denoyer-Geppert Audiovisuals, 5235 Ravenswood Avenue, Chicago, IL 60640
E.M.E., P.O. Box 2805, Danbury, CT 06813-2805
Hammond, Inc., 515 Valley Street, Maplewood, NJ 07040
Lakeshore Curriculum Materials Co., 1144 Montague Avenue, San Leandro, CA 94577
Media Associates, Inc., 7322 Ohms Lane, Minneapolis, MN 55435
MMI Corporation, 2950 Wyman Parkway, P.O. Box 19907, Baltimore, MD 21211
Stasiuk Enterprises, 3150 NE 30th Avenue, P.O. Box 12484, Portland, OR 97212
3M Audio Visual, Building 225-3NE, 3M Center, St. Paul, MN 55144
United Transparencies, P.O. Box 688, Binghamton, NY 13902
Ward's Natural Science, 5100 West Henrietta Road, P.O. Box 92912, Rochester, NY 14692-9012

Figure 12.6 Sources of overhead transparencies.

For teaching purposes, 35-mm slides are still quite useful and are available from school supply houses and, of course, from your own collection and from students and friends. Some schools have equipment for making slides from computer programs.

16-mm Films

As stated earlier, because they are less expensive to make and offer more instructional flexibility, videocassettes and videodiscs have become more popular than 16-mm films. In fact, laser videodiscs may eventually replace traditional textbooks as well.[6] Although there are still some new and effective 16-mm films available for instruction, many others are old and sometimes include dated or incorrect information. As with filmstrips, you need to view films carefully and critically before showing them to your class. Many classic films are now available on videocassette or videodisc.

Videos and Videodiscs

Combined with a television monitor, the VCR (videocassette recorder) is one of the most popular and frequently used pieces of audiovisual equipment in today's classroom.[7] Videotaped programs can do nearly everything that the former 16-mm films could do. In addition, the VCR, combined with a video camera, makes it possible to record and view student activities, practice, projects, and demonstrations, as well as your own teaching. This gives students marvelous opportunity to self-assess as they see and hear themselves in action.

Entire course packages, as well as supplements, are now available on videocassettes or in computer programs. The school where you student teach and the school where you are eventually employed may have collections of such programs. Some teachers make their own.

Laser videodiscs and players for classroom use are reasonably priced, with an ever-increasing variety of disc topics for classroom use. There are two formats of laser videodisc: (1) freeze-frame format (CAV—Constant Angular Velocity, or Standard Play) and (2) non-freeze-frame format (CLV—Constant Linear Velocity, or Extended Play). Both will play on all laser disc players. Laser videodisc players are quite similar to VCRs and just as easy to operate. The discs are visual archives, or visual databases, that contain large amounts of information that can be easily retrieved, reorganized, filed, and controlled by the user with the remote control that accompanies the player. Each side of a double-sided disc stores 54,000 separate still-frames of information— whether pictures, printed text, diagrams, films, or any combination of these. Visuals, both still and motion sequences, can be stored and then selected for showing on a television monitor or programmed onto a computer disc for a special presentation. More than 2,000 videodisc and CD titles are now available for educational use. By the time you are reading these words there may be more than 3,000 titles (see Figure 12.7

---

[6]For example, Random House has a computer program version of its encyclopedia, and the state of Texas, in 1991, became the first state to allow its schools to use state textbook funds to purchase videodisc programs as an alternative to traditional textbooks in science. In 1992, the state of Utah adopted a multimedia system for teaching English as a second language, the first time that state has approved a technology-based product for its textbook adoption list. Other states will most certainly follow these precedents. See Elizabeth Greenfield, "Evolution of the Textbook: From Print to Multimedia," *T.H.E. Journal* 20(10):12, 14, 16, 19 (May 1993).

[7]For example, in a teacher survey conducted by *Instructor,* the videocassette recorder was reported as the most popular technological device used by teachers. See "Teachers Speak Out on Technology in the Classroom," *Instructor* 100(8):71 (April 1991).

Subject	Title	Source
Art	Ansel Adams, Photographer	Image Entertainment
	The Louvre	Voyager
	Michelangelo	Voyager
	National Gallery of Art	Voyager
Earth Science	Earth Science	Systems Impact Inc.
	Fall Brings Spring	Churchill Media
	Gems and Minerals	Smithsonian
	Planet Earth (series)	The Discovery Interactive Library
	Restless Earth	National Geographic
	Science Horizons Earth Science	Silver Burdett and Ginn
	Spring Brings Changes	Churchill Media
English	*David Copperfield*	Pioneer Laserdisc Corporation
	Treasure Island	Pioneer Laserdisc Corporation
Environmental Education	Acid Rain (kit)	National Geographic
	EcoVision	Houghton Mifflin
	Garbage Tale: An Environmental Adventure	Churchill Media
	Solar Energy (kit)	National Geographic
Foreign Languages	Basic French by Video	Pioneer Laserdisc Corporation
	Basic Spanish by Video	Pioneer Laserdisc Corporation
Geography	The Explorers: A Century of Discovery	National Geographic
(See also Social Studies)	Regard for the Planet	Voyager
Health	About Your Body	Churchill Media
	AIDS/HIV: Answers for Young People	Churchill Media
	Communicable Diseases	Churchill Media
	The Body Fights Disease	Churchill Media
History	A Geographic Perspective on American History	National Geographic
	Inventors and the American Industrial Revolution	Churchill Media
Language Arts	Ralph S. Mouse	Churchill Media
Life Science	African Wildlife	National Geographic
	Animal Homes	Churchill Media
	Dinosaurs	Smithsonian
	Encyclopedia of Animals	Pioneer Laserdisc Corporation
	Insects	Smithsonian
	The National Zoo	Smithsonian
	Rain Forest	National Geographic
	Science Horizons Life Science	Silver Burdett and Ginn
	The Planets	National Geographic
	Whales	National Geographic
Mathematics	Adventures in Mathland	Mindscape, Inc.
	Mastering Fractions	Systems Impact, Inc.
Music	University of Delaware Videodisc Music Series	University of Delaware
Physical Education	Jim Fixx on Running	MCA
	Jazz-er-cise	Optical Programming Associates

(continued)

Figure 12.7   Sample videodisc titles and sources.

Physical Science	Energy at Work	Churchill Media
	Flying Machines	Smithsonian
	Physical Science Sides 1–4	Optical Data Corporation
	Science Horizons Physical Science	Silver Burdett and Ginn
Social Studies	America and the World Since WWII	Pioneer Laserdisc Corporation
	Communities	Churchill Media
	The First Ladies	Smithsonian
	In the Holy Land	Optical Data Corporation
	Martin Luther King	Optical Data Corporation
	The Video Encyclopedia of the 20th Century	CEL Educational Resources
	Vietnam: Ten-Thousand Day War	Pioneer Laserdisc Corporation
Space Science	National Air and Space	3M
	Space Archive: Apollo 17	Video Vision

Figure 12.7 *(continued)*

for sample titles). Your school or district audiovisual or curriculum resource center probably has some titles already; for additional titles refer to the latest annual edition of *Videodisc Compendium*.[8]

Carefully selected programs, tapes, discs, films, and slides enhance student learning. For example, laser videodiscs offer quick and efficient accessibility to thousands of visuals, thus providing an appreciated boost to teachers of students with limited language proficiency. In science, with the use of still-frame control, students can visually observe phenomena that previous students only read about. In art, students can be taken on a personal guided tour of an entire art museum.

Resources for Videodisc Titles

Check school supply catalogs for additional titles and sources for videodiscs in your subject and grade level of interest. Here are addresses to which you can send for information about available discs.

Churchill Media, 12210 Nebraska Avenue, Dept. 102, Los Angeles, CA 90025.
Emerging Technology Consultants, Inc., P.O. Box 120444, St. Paul, MN 55112.
Encyclopaedia Britannica Educational Corp., 310 S. Michigan Avenue, 6th floor, Chicago, IL 60604-9839.
GPN, P.O. Box 80660, Lincoln, NE 68501.
Houghton Mifflin, One Beacon Street, Boston, MA 02108.
Hubbard Scientific, 3101 Iris Avenue, Suite 215, Boulder, CO 80503.
IBM Educational Systems, P.O. Box 2150-HO6L1, Atlanta, GA 30301-2150.
Instructional Video, P.O. Box 21, Maumee, OH 43537.
Laser Disc Newsletter, Suite 428, Hudson Street, New York, NY 10014.
Lumivision (Smithsonian Collection), 1490 Lafayette Street, Suite 305, Denver, CO 80218-2193.
MECC, 6160 Summit Drive North, Minneapolis, MN 55430-4003.

[8]Published and sold by Emerging Technology Consultants, Inc., 2819 Hamline Avenue North, St. Paul, MN 55113. Phone (612) 639-3973, Fax (612) 639-0110.

MMI Corporation, 2950 Wyman Parkway, P.O. Box 19907, Baltimore, MD 21211.

Nasco West, Inc., P.O. Box 3837, Modesto, CA 95352.

National Geographic Society, Educational Services Dept. 89, 17th and M Streets NW, Washington, DC 20036.

National Science Programs, Inc., P.O. Box 41, W. Wilson Street, Batavia, IL 60510.

Optical Data Corporation, 30 Technology Drive, Warren, NJ 07059.

Pioneer Electronics, Laserdisc Corporation of America, 5000 Airport Plaza Drive, Long Beach, CA 90801.

Prentice-Hall School Group, 113 Sylvan Avenue, Englewood Cliffs, NJ 07632.

Sargent-Welch Scientific Co., P.O. Box 1026, Skokie, IL 60076-8026.

Silver Burdett & Ginn, 250 James Street, CN 1918, Morristown, NJ 07960-1918.

Tandy Corp./Radio Shack, 1600 One Tandy Center, Forth Worth, TX 76102.

Teaching Technologies, P.O. Box 3808, San Luis Obispo, CA 93403-3808.

The Voyager Company, 1351 Pacific Coast Highway, Santa Monica, CA 90401.

The Computer, Computer Programs, and CD-ROM Programs

As a teacher of the twenty-first century you must understand and be able to use computers as well as you can read and write. To complete your teaching credential, your teacher education program and state teacher licensing commission probably require this at some level of competency.

The computer can be valuable to you in several ways. For example:

- The computer can be used to help in managing instruction by obtaining information, storing and preparing test materials, maintaining attendance and grade records, and preparing programs to aid in the academic development of individual students. This category of uses of the computer is referred to as CMI (computer-managed instruction).
- The computer can be used for instruction, with the use of various instructional software programs. This is called CAI (computer-assisted instruction; see Figure 12.8).
- The computer can be used to teach about computers and to help students develop their skills in computer use.
- With the help of software programs about thinking, the computer can be used to teach about thinking and to help students develop their thinking skills.

For a student, use of the computer is motivating, exciting, and effective as an instructional tool. Consider the following examples.

Computer Programs Can Motivate. For example, one teacher motivated his students to write by sending their writing to another class electronically. That was the beginning of the **kids2kids Writing Circle,** a national electronic writing project.[9]

Computer Programs Can Activate. For example, in Maine, some elementary school students prepare maps of local land and water resources from computer analyses of satellite images of the coastline, analyze the maps, and then advise local authorities on development. Mixing technology and environmental awareness, the students have learned that they can exercise some control over their future.[10]

---

[9]For information on necessary equipment, how to participate, and how to register with the network, see Steven Pinney, "Long Distance Writing," *Instructor* 100(8):69–70 (April 1991).

[10]See Lisa Wolcott, "The New Cartographers: In Maine, Students Are Helping Map the Future," *Teacher Magazine* 2(6):30–31 (March 1991).

Methods	Description	Role of Teacher	Role of Computer	Role of Student	Applications/ Examples
Drill-and-practice	Content already taught. Reviews basic facts and terminology. Variety of questions in varied formats. Question-answer drills repeated as necessary.	Arranges for prior instruction. Selects material. Matches drill to student. Checks progress.	Asks questions. "Evaluates" student response. Provides immediate feedback. Records student progress.	Practices content already taught. Reseponds to questions. Receives confirmation or correction. Chooses content and difficulty level.	Parts of a microscope. Completing balance sheets. Vocabulary building. Math facts. Product knowledge.
Tutorial	Presentation of new information. Teaches concepts and principles. Provides remedial instruction.	Selects material. Adapts instruction. Monitors.	Presents information. Asks questions. Monitors responses. Provides remedial feedback. Summarizes key points. Keeps records.	Interacts with computer. Sees results. Answers questions. Asks questions.	Clerical training. Bank teller training. Science. Medical procedures. Bible study.
Gaming	Competitive. Drill-and-practice in a motivational format. Individual or small group.	Sets limits. Directs process. Monitors results.	Acts as competitor, judge, and score-keeper.	Learns facts, strategies, skills. Evaluates choices. Competes with computer.	Fraction games. Counting games. Spelling games. Typing (arcade-type) games.
Simulation	Approximates real-life situations. Based upon realistic models. Individual or small group.	Introduces subject. Presents background. Guides "debriefing."	Plays role(s). Delivers results of decisions. Maintains the model and its data base.	Practices decision making. Makes choices. Receives results of decisions. Evaluates decisions.	Troubleshooting. History. Medical diagnosis. Simulators (pilot, driver). Business management. Laboratory experiments.
Discovery	Inquiry into data base. Inductive approach. Trial and error. Tests hypotheses.	Presents basic problem. Monitors student progress.	Presents student with source of information. Stores data. Permits search procedures.	Makes hypotheses. Tests guesses. Develops principles or rules.	Social science. Science. Food-intake analysis. Career choices.
Problem solving	Defines problem. States hypothesis. Examines data. Generates solution.	Assigns problems. Assists students. Checks results.	Presents problem. Manipulates data. Maintains data base. Provides feedback.	Defines the problem. Sets up the solution. Manipulates variables. Trial and error.	Business. Creativity. Troubleshooting. Mathematics. Computer programming.

Figure 12.8 Utilization of various CAI methods.[11]

[11]From Heinich, p. 229. By permission of Macmillan Publishing Company.

Computer Programs Can Excite. Particularly exciting to students are computer programs that interact with videodiscs and compact disc technology to create a **multimedia learning environment** that capitalizes on the features of both instructional television and computer-assisted instruction. For example, multimedia kits produced for use in science, kindergarten through grade 6, by *National Geographic Society,* include booklets, activity sheets, teacher's guides, and read-along cassettes.

As another example, introduced at the International Reading Association's annual conference in May 1992, is the *Apple Early Language Connections* program, which provides students in kindergarten through second grade with a multisensory computer-software-based program in reading, writing, listening, and speaking. Central to the program is a package of seven four-week thematic curriculum units. For each unit there are detailed lesson plans covering literature, music, math, and science. Hardware requirements are a *Macintosh LC* with hard disk, plus an *Apple SC CD-ROM* drive, an *Apple OneScanner,* an *ImageWriter II* printer, and *TouchWindows* and *Muppet Learning Keys* keyboards. Also included is a classroom library of more than 350 books from *Scholastic, Inc.,* and story and music audiotapes. Software is available from educational publishers and includes *Kid Works, Reading Magic Library Plus, Muppets on Stage, Reading Maze* and *Word Munchers,* plus four CD-ROM titles from the *Discis Books* series and *Broderbund's Just Grandma and Me CD-ROM Living Book.* Teacher software includes *The Grady Profile—Portfolio Assessment: Early Language Edition* and *The Writing Center.*

The Placement and Use of Computers in Schools

The way you use the classroom computer will be determined by the number of computers you have in your classroom, or where computers are placed in the school, and the software that is available. Considering the placement, here are some possible scenarios and how classroom teachers work within each.

Scenario 1. Many elementary schools have a computer lab which a teacher may schedule to take an entire class, or send a small group of students, for special computer work. In some cases the students' computers are networked to the teacher's computer in the lab, in which case the teacher can control and monitor the computer work of each student.

Scenario 2. Some schools have "Computer" as an elective course. Students in your class who are simultaneously enrolled in the computer course may be given special computer assignments by you, which they can then share with the rest of the class.

Scenario 3. Some classrooms have one computer that is connected to a large-screen video monitor. The teacher, or a student, works the computer, and the monitor screen can be seen by the entire class. As they view the screen, students can verbally respond and interact to what is happening on the computer.

Scenario 4. In your classroom, you may be fortunate enough to have a computer, a videodisc player, an overhead projector that has a light projection from the base, and a LCD (liquid crystal display) projection system. Coupled with the overhead projector, the LCD projection system allows you to project onto your large wall screen (and TV monitor at the same time) any image from computer software or a videodisc. With this system, all students can see and verbally interact with the multimedia instruction.

Scenario 5. Many classrooms have one, or perhaps several, computers. When this is the case in your classroom, then you most likely will have one or two children working at the computer while others are doing other learning activities (an example of multilevel instruction). Computers can be an integral part of a learning activity center within the classroom, and an important aid in your overall effort to individualize instruction within your classroom.

Software Programs

When selecting software programs you and your colleagues need, of course, to choose those that are compatible with your brand of computer(s) and with your instructional objectives. Like laser videodiscs, computer software programs are continually being developed and, with the exception of a few mentioned in Chapter 13, are too many and varied to list in this resource guide. Most school districts and state departments of education provide periodic reviews of software and guidelines for its selection. Check to see whether your local schools have forms for selecting software and whether current software reviews are available. Professional journals, such as the National Science Teachers Association's *Science and Children,* also review software.

For free and inexpensive audiovisual materials, check your college or university library for sources listed in Figure 12.9.

Guidelines for Using Copyrighted Video and Computer Programs

You must be knowledgeable about the laws governing the use of videos and computer software materials that are copyrighted. Although space limitation here prohibits full inclusion of United States legal guidelines (see Figures 12.10 and 12.11), your local school district undoubtedly can provide a copy of current district policies to ensure compliance with all copyright laws. As mentioned earlier in the discussion on the use of printed materials that are copyrighted, when preparing to make any copy you must find out whether copying is permitted by law under the category of "permitted use." If it is not allowed under "permitted use," then you must get written permission to reproduce the material from the holder of the copyright. Here are guidelines for the copying of videotapes and computer software. As of this writing there are no guidelines for fair use of films, filmstrips, and slides.

---

1. Check for sources in professional periodicals and journals for teachers.
2. *An Annotated Bibliography of Audiovisual Materials Related to Understanding and Teaching the Culturally Disadvantaged.* Washington, DC: National Education Association.
3. *Catalog of Audiovisual Materials: A Guide to Government Sources* (ED 198 822). Arlington, VA: ERIC Documents Reproduction Service.
4. *Catalog of Free-Loan Educational Films/Video.* St. Petersburg, FL: Modern Talking Picture Service.
5. From Educator's Progress Service, Randolph, WI.
   Educator's Guide to Free Audio and Video Materials.
   Educator's Guide to Free Films.
   Educator's Guide to Free Filmstrips.
   Guide to Free Computer Materials.

Figure 12.9 Resources for free and inexpensive audiovisual materials.

Permitted Uses—You May:

1. Request your media center or audiovisual coordinator to record a program for you if you cannot or if you lack the equipment.
2. Keep a videotaped copy of a broadcast (including cable transmission) for 45 calendar days, after which the program must be erased.
3. Use the program in class once during the first 10 school days of the 45 calendar days, and a second time if instruction needs to be reinforced.
4. Have professional staff view the program several times for evaluation purposes during the full 45-day period.
5. Make a few copies to meet legitimate needs, but these copies must be erased when the original videotape is erased.
6. Use only a part of the program if instructional needs warrant (but see the next list).
7. Enter into a licensing agreement with the copyright holder to continue use of the program.

Prohibited Uses—You May *Not:*

1. Videotape premium cable services such as HBO without express permission.
2. Alter the original content of the program.
3. Exclude the copyright notice on the program.
4. Videotape before a request for use—the request to record must come from an instructor.
5. Keep the program, and any copies, after 45 days.

Figure 12.10 Copyright law for off-air videotaping.[12]

Permitted Uses—You May:

1. Make a single backup or archival copy of the computer program.
2. Adapt the computer program to another language if the program is unavailable in the target language.
3. Add features to make better use of the computer program.

Prohibited Uses—You May *Not:*

1. Make multiple copies.
2. Make replacement copies from an archival or backup copy.
3. Make copies of copyrighted programs to be sold, leased, loaned, transmitted, or given away.

Figure 12.11 Copyright law for use of computer software.[13]

---

[12]Robert Heinich et al., *Instructional Media*, 4th ed., New York: Macmillan, 1993, p. 436.
[13]From the December 1980 Congressional amendment to the 1976 Copyright Act.

E. THE COMMUNITY AS A RESOURCE

One of the richest resources is the local community, its people, and its places. It will be important for you to build your own file of community resources—speakers, sources for free materials, and field trip locations. Your school may already have a community resource file for your use; however, it may need updating.

A community resource file should contain information about (a) possible field trip locations, (b) community resource people who could serve as guest speakers or mentors, and (c) local agencies that can provide information and instructional materials.

Field trips to community locations can make instruction real, exciting, and educationally valuable for the students, but, when not carefully planned and carried out, a field trip can cause more grief than you can imagine.

Planning for a Field Trip

To prepare for a field trip, there are three important considerations: (1) details of preparation prior to the field trip, (2) planning the details of the trip, and (3) planning follow-up activities. Consider the following guidelines for each.

Before the Field Trip

Today's schools often have very limited funds to support transportation and liability costs for field trips. Some schools have no field trip funds at all. In some instances, parent-teacher organizations and civic organizations help by providing financial resources necessary to ensure that students have these valuable first-hand experiences. When thinking about and planning a particular field trip for your students, you may want to follow these steps:

1. Discuss your idea for a field trip with the school principal or your teaching team, especially when transportation will be needed, *before* you introduce it to your students. There is no cause served by getting children excited about a field trip before you are sure it is feasible. Furthermore, if most of your students have made the same trip during a prior school experience, it may not be worth repeating.
2. Once you have obtained the necessary, but tentative, approval from school officials, take the trip yourself if possible. A pre-visit allows you to determine how to make the field trip most productive and to discover what arrangements will be necessary. If you cannot actually make a pre-visit, you will still need to inquire to get information and to make arrangements for (a) enroute travel directions, (b) scheduling of arrival and departure times, (c) parking, (d) briefing by the host, if there is one, (e) storage of students' personal items, such as coats and lunches, (f) provisions for eating and rest rooms, and (g) fees, if any. If there are fees connected with the field trip, then you need to talk with your principal about who will pay them. If fees are to be paid by students or their parents or guardians, what about those students who may not be able to afford them? Is any student going to say, "I can't afford it"? Or will they all say this? If the trip is worth taking, the school should cover the costs. If that is not possible, then perhaps financial

support can be obtained from the parent-teacher organization or another source. If even that is not possible, then perhaps you should consider an alternative experience that does not involve costs to students. No student should ever be left out of a field trip because of his or her lack of money, or because of the student's race, religion, or ethnicity.

3. Arrange for official permission from the school administrator. It is likely that the school has a form for requesting, planning, and reporting field trips.

4. After permission is obtained, you can now discuss the field trip with your students and arrange for permissions from their parents or guardians. You must realize that although parents or guardians sign official permission forms allowing their children to participate in a field trip, these show only that the parents or adult guardians are aware of exactly what is going on and give their permission. Although the permission form should also include a statement that the parent absolves the teacher and the school from liability should an accident occur, it *does not* lessen the teacher's and school's responsibilities during the field trip if there is negligence by a teacher, driver, or chaperone (see item 11).

5. If relevant, arrange for the children to be excused from their other classes while on the field trip. Using an information form prepared and signed by you, and perhaps by the principal, the students should then assume responsibility for notifying their other teachers of the planned absence from classes, and assure that they make up whatever work is missed because of the field trip. In addition, you will need to make arrangements for your own teaching duties left "uncovered." In some schools, teachers cooperate by covering classes for those who will be gone. In other schools, substitute teachers are hired. Where budgets are extremely limited, a teacher may have to hire his or her own substitute.

6. Arrange for whatever transportation is needed. Your building principal, or the principal's designee, will help you with the details. The use of private automobiles is *not* recommended, because you and the school could be liable for the acts of the drivers.[14]

7. Arrange for collection of money that is needed for fees. If there are out-of-pocket costs to be paid by students, that information needs to be included on the parental permission form.

8. Plan the details for student safety and monitoring of that safety from departure to return. Included should be a first-aid kit and the use of a system of student control, such as a student "buddy system," in which students travel in pairs and must remain paired throughout the trip. The pairs are given numbers that are recorded and kept by the teacher and the chaperones, and then checked at departure time, periodically during the trip, at the time of return to school, and upon return.

9. Plan for adult chaperones to travel with the class field trip. As a rule of thumb, there should be one adult supervisor for every ten students. Your own school or school district may have its own guidelines regarding the ratio of supervisors to students.

10. Plan the complete route and schedule, including all stops along the way. If transportation is being provided, for this consideration you may need to talk with whomever is providing the transportation.

---

[14]Robert L. Monks and Ernest I. Prioux, *Legal Basics for Teachers*, Fastback 235 (Bloomington, IN: Phi Delta Kappa Educational Foundation, 1986), p. 24.

11. Establish and discuss rules of behavior with your students. Included in this discussion should be details of the trip, its purpose, information about where they are going, what they should wear and bring, your academic expectations of them (consider giving each student a study guide), and of the follow-up activities. Also included should be directions about what to do if anything should go awry, for instance, if a student is late for the departure or return, loses a personal possession, gets lost along the way, becomes injured or sick, or misbehaves. *Caution: Never* send a misbehaving student back to school alone. While on a field trip, all students should be under the direct supervision of an adult at all times. Involve the adult chaperones in the pre-visit discussion. All this information should be included on the parental permission form.

12. Plan the follow-up activities. As for any other lesson plan, the field trip lesson is complete when it has not only a proper introduction but also a well-planned closure.

During the Field Trip

If your field trip has been carefully planned according to the preceding guidelines, it should be a valuable and safe experience for all. While at the field trip location, you and the adult chaperones should monitor student behavior and learning just as you do in the classroom. Students may take notes and follow a prepared study guide. You may want to take recorders and cameras so records of the experience can be shared in class upon your return.

After the Field Trip

All sorts of field trip follow-up activities can be planned as an educational wrap-up to this valuable and exciting first-hand experience. For example, a bulletin board committee can plan and prepare an attractive bulletin board display summarizing the experience. Students can write about their experiences in their journals. Small groups can give oral reports to the class about what they experienced and learned. These reports can then serve as springboards for further class discussion. Finally, for your future planning, all who were involved should contribute to an evaluation of the field trip.

Before continuing, do Exercises 12.3, 12.4, and 12.5 to further your understanding of how a teacher procures and uses audiovisual materials and equipment.

Exercise 12.3: Beginning My Professional Materials Resource File

Instructions: The purpose of this exercise is to give you a start in building your own personal file of aids and resources for teaching, an undertaking that will continue throughout your professional career. Begin your file either in a computer data base program or on 3 × 5″ file cards (color coded) listing:

1. Name of resource.
2. How to obtain and when available.
3. How to use.
4. Evaluative comments.

Organize the file in whatever way that makes most sense to you. Cross-reference or color code your system to accommodate the following categories of aids and resources:

1. Articles from magazines, newspapers, journals, and periodicals.
2. Compact discs.
3. Computer software.
4. Examination question items.
5. Games and games sources.
6. Guest speakers and other community resources.
7. Media catalogs.
8. Motivational ideas.
9. Multimedia programs.
10. Pictures, posters, and other stills.
11. Resources to order.
12. Sources of free and inexpensive items.
13. Student work sheets.
14. Supply catalogs.
15. Thematic units.
16. Unit and lesson plan ideas.
17. Completed unit and lesson plans.
18. Videocassette titles and sources.
19. Videodisc titles and sources.
20. Miscellaneous.

Exercise 12.4: Observation of a Classroom Teacher's Use of Media and Equipment

Instructions: The purpose of this exercise is for you to observe the actual use of audiovisual materials and equipment in a classroom. Arrange to visit one classroom for five consecutive days (Monday through Friday). Observe and record the materials and equipment that are used by the teacher, how they are used, and to what extent students are involved in their use. Upon completion, share the results of this exercise with your classmates.

School and class visited _____

Dates of visitation _____

	Materials and Equipment Used	*How Used*	*Student Involvement*
M	_____	_____	_____
	_____	_____	_____
	_____	_____	_____
	_____	_____	_____
	_____	_____	_____
	_____	_____	_____
	_____	_____	_____
T	_____	_____	_____
	_____	_____	_____
	_____	_____	_____
	_____	_____	_____
	_____	_____	_____
	_____	_____	_____
	_____	_____	_____
W	_____	_____	_____
	_____	_____	_____
	_____	_____	_____
	_____	_____	_____
	_____	_____	_____
	_____	_____	_____
	_____	_____	_____

T _____ _____ _____

_____ _____ _____

_____ _____ _____

_____ _____ _____

_____ _____ _____

_____ _____ _____

_____ _____ _____

F _____ _____ _____

_____ _____ _____

_____ _____ _____

_____ _____ _____

_____ _____ _____

_____ _____ _____

_____ _____ _____

1. Give your evaluation of which materials and equipment were most effective, which were least effective, and in each case, why?

Most effective: Why:

_____ _____

_____ _____

_____ _____

_____ _____

_____ _____

_____ _____

_____ _____

_____ _____

_____ _____

_____ _____

_____ _____

_____ _____

Least effective: Why:

_____   _____

_____   _____

_____   _____

_____   _____

_____   _____

_____   _____

_____   _____

_____   _____

_____   _____

_____   _____

2. After sharing and discussing this exercise with your classmates, describe any conclusions that you have drawn, as a group or as an individual.

_____

_____

_____

_____

_____

_____

_____

_____

_____

_____

_____

_____

_____

_____

FOR YOUR NOTES

Exercise 12.5: The Classroom Teacher and the Purchase of Materials and Equipment for Teaching

Instructions: The purpose of this exercise is for you to obtain practical information about how materials and equipment for teaching are procured and the role of the classroom teacher in the process. To complete this exercise, you are to visit a school and talk with teachers about the process. The following questions can be used as a guideline for your interview. After completion of the exercise, share the results with your classmates.

School visited _____

Date of visitation _____

Person(s) interviewed, and their functions, e.g., Mary Quadrangle, sixth-grade math teacher;

Toni Marsalis, second-grade coordinator; Jon Goodfellow, principal. _____

_____

_____

_____

_____

1. In your school, how is it decided what specific equipment and instructional materials will be purchased for classroom use?

_____

_____

_____

_____

_____

_____

_____

_____

_____

_____

_____

_____

_____

_____

_____

2. Does the classroom teacher have money allotted for the purchase of classroom materials during the school year? If so, how much? How is the money obtained and spent by the teacher?

_____

_____

_____

_____

_____

_____

_____

_____

_____

_____

_____

_____

3. What else can you tell me to help me understand the process of obtaining teaching materials, supplies, and equipment?

_____

_____

_____

_____

_____

_____

_____

_____

_____

_____

_____

_____

SUMMARY

You should remain alert to developing educational technologies. Laser videodiscs interfaced with computers (multimedia) offer exciting opportunities for teachers. New instructional technologies are advancing at an increasingly rapid rate. You and your colleagues must be vigilant in regard to new developments, constantly looking for those that can help to make student learning meaningful and interesting, your teaching effective, and that are cost-effective as well.

Using a variety of strategies, resources, and media will help you effectively and efficiently reach more of your students more of the time. It is a huge challenge to teach and to meet the needs of a variety of unique and individual students, all at the same time. We hope that this chapter has helped you to meet that challenge.

The next and final chapter in Part III of this resource guide discusses instructional guidelines, aids, and resources for specific content areas. Then Part IV focuses your attention on how you can determine how well you and your students are meeting the challenge. It deals with the assessment of learning and the assessment of the instruction.

QUESTIONS FOR CLASS DISCUSSION

1. Many schools lack funds to provide modern equipment in the classroom. One suggestion for obtaining equipment is to permit television producers to bring commercials into the schools; in return, equipment would be supplied. Would television with commercials lead students to believe they should be entertained in class? Would this cause a change in a teacher's method of instruction? Are you in favor of such an arrangement for obtaining equipment? Why?

2. The American Psychological Association took the position, in 1985 and reaffirmed in 1992, that there is a link between violence on television programs and aggressive behavior in children. After reviewing hundreds of studies, the association's task force concluded that excessive television viewing by children may be harmful because children might imitate the violent behaviors and attitudes they are exposed to on television. As a teacher, do you support their position? Explain.

3. What do you predict for the future of computers in the classroom? Explain the basis for your prediction.

4. During your visitations to classrooms, to what extent did you see either computers, compact discs, or videodiscs being used?

5. Describe how audiovisual aids help to reduce a reliance on verbalism, and why that is important.

6. In schools in your locale, what is required of the teacher when planning a field trip? Are there field trip funds? If not, do teachers take students on field trips? If so, how are trips financed?

7. In 1991 a school in Stockton, California, was "adopted" by the local Rotary Club, and one of the things the club did was to give $6,000 to that school for field trips. In schools in your locale, what creative ways have teachers found to obtain funds for field trips and other activities? Share your findings with others in your class. As a class, brainstorm and generate a list of possible ways a teacher could find funding for field trips.

8. Historically, changing styles in language and dress have frequently caused good films and filmstrips to lose their educational impact for students. Schools that bought these films and filmstrips may still be stuck with them. Will videocassettes and videodiscs be subject to the same problem? How are tapes, films, and slides discarded by a school or district? On what basis? Who decides? What is the expected life of a videotape? Of a videodisc? Can your class generate a creative list of ways that old films and filmstrips could be recycled?

9. Is there a potential maintenance problem when all of a school's computers are bought at the same time? Is or should purchasing of several items of expensive new equipment, such as computers, be staggered over time? If not, will all of the computers break down at the same time, or do they break down at all? If they do break down, who repairs them? Who maintains them? What is the funding source for repair and maintenance of computers?

10. Should the schoolhouse be a sanctuary from paid advertisement on television? Should programs with television ads in schools (such as Channel 1) expose students to advertisement transmitted by electronic media during the school day? These programs include a 12-minute news show with 2 minutes of paid advertisement for grades 6–12 and are shown to all students every day. In return for showing these programs, a school receives monitors for classrooms, a satellite dish, and a videocassette recorder. One California legislator said, "Excess commercialism pollutes the minds of youth." In what ways do you agree or disagree with that statement?

11. Do you have questions about the content of this chapter? How might answers be found?

SUGGESTED READINGS FOR CHAPTER 12

Beardslee, E. C., and Davis, G. L. *Interactive Videodisc and the Teaching-Learning Process.* Fastback 294. Bloomington, IN: Phi Delta Kappa Educational Foundation, 1989.

Butzin, S. M. "Project CHILD: A New Twist on Integrated Learning Systems." *T.H.E. Journal* 20(2):90–95 (September 1992).

Dalton, D. W. "The Effects of Cooperative Learning Strategies on Achievement and Attitudes During Interactive Video." *Journal of Computer Based Instruction* 17(1):8–16 (Winter 1990).

Dockterman, D. A. "A Teacher's Tools." *Instructor* 100(5):58–61 (January 1991).

Dyer, D. C., et al. "Changes in Teachers' Beliefs and Practices in Technology-Rich Classrooms." *Educational Leadership* 48(8):45–52 (May 1991).

Franklin, S. "Breathing Life into Reluctant Writers: The Seattle Public Schools Laptop Project." *Writing Notebook: Creative Word Processing in the Classroom* 8(4):40–42 (April–May 1991).

Gleason, M., et al. "Cumulative Versus Rapid Introduction of New Information." *Exceptional Children* 57(4):353–358 (February 1991).

Gross, B. "Can Computer-Assisted Instruction Solve the Dropout Problem?" *Educational Leadership* 46(5):49–51 (February 1989).

Hancock, M. K., and Baugh, I. W. "The New Kid Graduates." *Computing Teacher* 18(7):17–19, 21 (April 1991).

Hedley, C. N. "What's New in Software? TESOL Programs for the Bilingual Special Learner." *Journal of Reading, Writing, and Learning Disabilities International* 7(2):165–170 (April–June 1991).

Heinich, R., Molenda, M., and Russell, J. D. *Instructional Media and the New Technologies of Instruction.* 4th ed. New York: Macmillan, 1993.

Hunter, B. "Linking for Learning: Computer-and-Communications Network Support for Nationwide Innovation in Education." *Journal of Science Education and Technology* 1(1):23–34 (March 1992).

Is It Okay for Schools to Copy Software? Washington, DC: Software Publishers Association, 1991.

Johnson, L. N., and Tulley, S. *Interactive Television: Progress and Potential.* Fastback 289. Bloomington, IN: Phi Delta Kappa Educational Foundation, 1989.

Kemeny, J. G. "Software for the Classroom." *Mathematics and Computer Education* 25(1):33–37 (Winter 1991).

Kernan, M., et al. "Making and Using Audiovisuals." *Book Report* 10(2):16–17, 19–21, 23, 25–35 (September–October 1991).

Kolich, E. M. "Effects of Computer-Assisted Vocabulary Training on Word Knowledge." *Journal of Educational Research* 84(3):177–182 (January–February 1991).

Malouf, D. B., et al. "Integrating Computer Software into Effective Instruction." *Teaching Exceptional Children* 23(3):54–56 (Spring 1991).

Marschalek, D. "The National Gallery of Art Laserdisk and Accompanying Database: A Means to Enhance Art Instruction." *Art Education* 44(3):48–53 (May 1991).

Martorella, P. H. "Harnessing New Technologies to the Social Studies Curriculum." *Social Education* 55(1):55–57 (January 1991).

McKenna, M. C. "Computerized Reading Assessment: Its Emerging Potential (Reading Technology)." *Reading Teacher* 44(9):692–693 (May 1991).

Mead, J., et al. "Teaching with Technology." *Teacher Magazine* 2(4):29–57 (January 1991).

Perry, M. *Using Microcomputers with Gifted Students.* Fastback 295. Bloomington, IN: Phi Delta Kappa Educational Foundation, 1989.

Potter, R. L. *Using Microcomputers for Teaching Reading in the Middle School.* Fastback 296. Bloomington, IN: Phi Delta Kappa Educational Foundation, 1989.

Rakow, S. J., and Brandhorst, T. R. *Using Microcomputers for Teaching Science.* Fastback 297. Bloomington, IN: Phi Delta Kappa Educational Foundation, 1989.

Reich, C. F., et al. "Teaching Earth Science Through a Computer Network." *Perspectives in Education and Deafness* 9(5):4–7 (May–June 1991).

Roberts, J. M. "Computers as Tools for Remedial Readers." *Intervention in School and Clinic* 26(5):293–295 (May 1991).

Sayers, D. "Cross-Cultural Exchanges Between Students from the Same Culture: A Portrait of an Emerging Relationship Mediated by Technology." *Canadian Modern Language Review* 47(4):678–696 (June 1991).

Schielack, J. F. "Reaching Young Pupils with Technology." *Arithmetic Teacher* 38(6):51–55 (February 1991).

Snider, R. C. "The Machine in the Classroom." *Phi Delta Kappan* 74(4):316–323 (December 1992).

Tebbutt, M. J. "Simulating Drug or Alcohol Abuse." *School Science Review* 72(261):77–79 (June 1991).

ten Brink, B. "New Frontiers with Science Videodiscs." *Educational Leadership* 50(8):42–43 (May 1993).

Tiene, D. "Channel One: Good or Bad News for Our Schools?" *Educational Leadership* 50(8): 46–51 (May 1993).

Welch, M., and Jensen, J. B. "Write, P.L.E.A.S.E.: A Video-Assisted Strategic Intervention to Improve Written Expression of Inefficient Learners." *Remedial and Special Education* 12(1):37–47 (January–February 1991).

Wishnietsky, D. H. *Hypermedia: The Integrated Learning Environment.* Fastback 339. Bloomington, IN: Phi Delta Kappa Educational Foundation, 1992.

Yeager, E. A., and Pandiscio, E. A. "Newscasts in the Classroom." *Educational Leadership* 50(8):52–53 (May 1993).

13

What Additional Instructional Guidelines, Aids, and Resources Are Available to Me for Specific Content Areas of the Curriculum?

In this chapter the focus is on elementary school curriculum, that is, language arts, mathematics, science, social science, art, music, and physical education. We discuss instructional guidelines and suggest resources we trust you will find useful. In your professional teacher education program, we anticipate that you will receive additional specific instruction in most of these areas.

The areas of the elementary school curriculum that consume a major portion of instructional time are language arts and mathematics. Physical education, foreign language, and the visual and performing arts (art, music, and dance) receive less instructional time. It appears that the efforts of teachers are directed toward the integration of the arts with reading (language and literacy), science, social sciences, and mathematics.

An Opinion: Language Is a Basic Social Skill

We believe that every student should study and learn at least one language other than English, and that this study should begin in kindergarten and continue through all the grades so that upon completion of high school, each student has developed some skills in a language other than English. Language is the most basic of social skills, and children should be introduced to the attitudes, customs, geography, products, traditions, and values of various cultures. "Knowledge of a second language and a second culture enables one to extend his or her view of humanity and to explore other areas of the world. This multifaceted rapport with other peoples is essential to a nation that seeks to enrich its own cultural plurality, to work productively with other countries, and to maintain a respected place in the 'hierarchy of governments.'"[1] We agree with others who maintain that schools in the United States should mandate communicative competence development in a second language. What is your opinion?

[1]California State Department of Education, *Foreign Language Framework for California Public Schools*, 1980, p. 2.

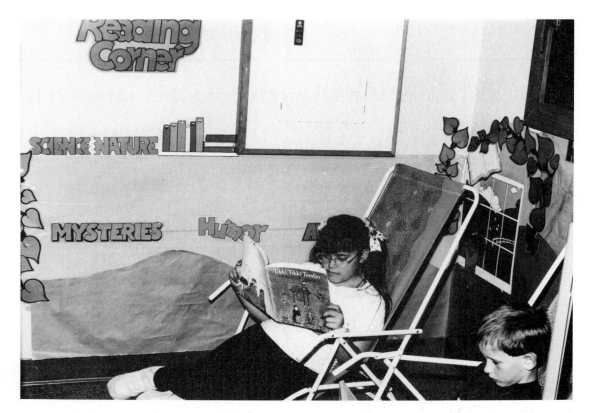

Children engaged in learning activities at a reading corner demonstrate quality on-task behavior.

A. INSTRUCTIONAL GUIDELINES FOR TEACHING INTEGRATED LANGUAGE ARTS

Why Do We Teach Integrated Language Arts?

In an integrated language arts program, you will be interested in the reading, speaking, listening, and writing skills of your students. These skills (not textbooks) form a holistic process that is the primary aspect of literacy in an elementary classroom—and a foundation for integrated and literature-based instruction. Seeing reading as a part of this integrated instruction, *Becoming a Nation of Readers*[2] tells us there is an alternative to the use of basals and skills workbooks—the introduction of whole language instruction. **Whole language** programs for teaching reading introduce students to literacy in the classroom in a natural and holistic manner.[3] In support of this report, some teachers point out that literature-based instruction is receiving increasing attention with a focus on literature study and the use of library books (trade books) in the classroom. Some states and school districts have taken the view that reading goals can reflect the process when literature is suggested for study, and proponents state that teaching with literature will promote the enjoyment of literature for a read-

[2]Richard Anderson et al., *Becoming a Nation of Readers: The Report of the Commission on Reading* (Urbana, IL: Center for the Study of Reading; Washington, DC: National Academy of Education, 1985).
[3]For a useful description of "whole language," see John W. Myers, *Making Sense of Whole Language*, Fastback 346 (Bloomington, IN: Phi Delta Kappa Educational Foundation, 1993).

er's lifetime, stimulate class discussions, motivate writing, and help to teach difficult literary concepts.

Oral Language Through Cooperative Learning, Instructional Scaffolding, and Inquiry

In the area of speaking skills, discussion in the classroom has a growing research base that promotes methods of teaching and learning through oral language. These methods include cooperative learning, instructional scaffolding, and inquiry teaching. In cooperative learning groups, students discuss and use language for learning that has the benefit of providing social meaning—developing students' skills in social interactions. **Instructional scaffolding** means the teacher first provides a verbal structure (scaffold) that gives a foundation for class discussion and then gradually withdraws the structure as the students show they are able to build structures on their own. Inquiry teaching includes student-and-teacher questioning and discussion.

Sometimes teaching is done in a reciprocal way **(reciprocal teaching),** which means the teacher and the students share the teaching responsibility and all are involved in asking questions, clarifying, predicting, and summarizing as they read texts. In this method, students are encouraged to ask thoughtful questions, as well as to respond to questions asked by others.

Cooperative Learning

Cooperative learning can also include instructional scaffolding and inquiry teaching. For example, students work in small groups to accomplish a common goal (when each group has a goal that contributes to the understanding by the whole class of a larger goal or concept, this is a form of cooperative learning known as *jigsaw* learning, like putting together a jigsaw puzzle). As they work, heterogeneous groups of three to four students participate in their own learning, extend their knowledge, and develop their cultural awareness with students of different ethnic backgrounds. When the students give information and ideas to one another, they are completing difficult learning tasks and using divergent thinking, making decisions, and developing concepts related to the content of the study. The girls and boys clarify their thinking when issues are presented and responses are challenged. They take responsibility for planning in a group and for carrying out their assignments. When needed, the teacher may model an activity with one group in front of the class. When integrated with the students' questions, the demonstration can become inquiry teaching.

Writing and the *Writing Report Card*

Writing instruction received attention in the *Writing Report Card: Writing Achievement in American Schools.*[4] This report found that students who use the **process writing** techniques (by which students and teacher focus on the process of writing, rather than on the products of the writing) of planning or rehearsing, drafting, revising, and editing produce superior products. With students of all ability levels, it appears that a teacher's diagnosis and prescription based on actual student errors are superior to sequences in workbooks and front-of-the-room teaching. Also helpful in revising the

[4]Arthur N. Applebee et al., *The Writing Report Card: Writing Achievement in American Schools* (Princeton, NJ: National Assessment of Education Progress, 1986).

writing of students are word processors and computers and accompanying word processing programs. With these tools, a writer can make revisions without copying material by hand. This freedom from hand copying allows a writer to focus on revising, rather than on the labor of recopying. With this freedom, a writer can respond to instruction such as the prewriting of oral language exercises or expository writing, an area of increasing interest in a classroom that includes the study of nonfiction prose as a literary genre.

What Skills in the Integrated Language Arts Do I Need?

Specific guidelines follow for teaching in an integrated and literature-based approach:

1. *Strengthen a young child's language skills to benefit reading progress.* The language and reading connection is supported by research studies that show how language skills benefit a child's reading achievement. Superior language ability correlates with advanced reading ability.[5] Positive influences on reading derive from young children's listening to stories.[6] Improving the oral language skills of Mexican-American children who were beginning readers was found to lead to an improvement in their reading skills.[7]

2. *Strengthen a young child's metalinguistic awareness as it relates to reading to benefit the child's understanding of how language works.* In metalinguistics (thinking about language) awareness, there are three understandings that are related to beginning reading: (1) the functions of print, (2) the forms and structure of print, and (3) the conventions of print. Some children are confused about these concepts that are related to reading. They often do not know what a word is or what the parameters of written words are. Some overgeneralize the ideas the printed symbols stand for; for example, a child may say the word "kitty" for the printed word "cat."

3. *Strengthen a young child's knowledge of the alphabet.* There is a relationship between knowing letter names and success in beginning reading: the students who know the names of letters on entering school may also be those who have the necessary visual perceptions, attention spans, and other skills needed in beginning reading. While it would be an error to think that all children should be taught the names of the letters before learning to read, it seems that young children from various backgrounds come to kindergarten knowing the names of more than half the letters of the alphabet.[8] Children who know most or all of the letters are higher achievers.[9]

4. *Plan reading readiness programs.* For children in preschool and in kindergarten, plan a reading readiness program for all, but focus on those who have little or no knowledge about letters, words, and books. Focus on the interests and abilities of these children during instruction, and they will progress in learning to read.[10]

[5]John Borkowski et al., "Metamemory and Metalinguistic Development: Correlates for Children's Intelligence and Achievement," *Bulletin of the Psychonomic Society* 21(2):393–396 (Winter 1983). See also Catherine Snow, "Literacy and Language Relationships During the Preschool Years," *Harvard Educational Review* 53(1):165–189 (Fall 1983).
[6]Marilyn Cochran-Smith, *The Making of a Reader* (Norwood, NJ: Ablex, 1983).
[7]Eustolia Perez, "Oral Language Competence Improves Reading Skills of Mexican-American Third Graders." *The Reading Teacher* 35(1):24–29 (October 1981).
[8]Dale Johnson and James F. Baumann, "Word Identification," *Handbook of Reading Research*, ed. by P. David Pearson (New York: Longman, 1984).
[9]Jana M. Mason, "When Do Children Begin to Read: An Exploration of Four-Year-Old Children's Letter and Word Reading Competencies," *Reading Research Quarterly* 15(1):203–227 (Fall 1980).
[10]Christine McCormick and Jana Mason, *Intervention Procedure for Increasing Preschool Children's Interest in and Knowledge About Reading* (Cambridge, MA: Bolt, Beranek and Newman, 1984).

5. *Teach phonics to students; those who are taught phonic skills become better readers than those who only memorize sight words.*[11] Systematic instruction in skills in recognizing words leads to better achievement.[12] Beginning readers who learn the sound and symbol associations for consonants first (rather than those for vowels) score significantly higher in reading achievement than students who receive instruction in vowel sounds first.[13]

6. *Teach context clues in context.* This is an aid to word identification, since the clues assist identification of words necessary in reading comprehension. Introducing words in a context helps students to learn the words[14] and also helps them with oral reading since they can evaluate their oral reading scores by referring to the context clues.[15]

7. *Teach a decoding strategy.* When teaching decoding, consider the pattern of development through which children move as they learn to decode. First, children seem to overuse context clues and underuse phonics. Second, they seem to overuse phonics and underuse meaning. Third, children (sometimes as late as grade 6) seem to develop the skill of using phonics and context clues together.[16] Teaching second-grade children with a context-and-phonics approach was found to lead to an instructional level of one-half grade higher for the experimental group than for the control group students who simply read sentences several times.[17]

8. *Teach skills of fast, efficient word identification.* Research studies indicate that one basic difference between good and poor readers is that good readers identify words rapidly and use visual recognition or sound-symbols associations.[18] Students should be encouraged to reread material, and oral rereading should be demonstrated.[19]

9. *Teach reading comprehension.* Teach reading comprehension directly so students can monitor their own comprehension and think about their own thinking (encourage students to use their metacognitive abilities to summarize their understanding of what is learned).[20]

10. *Give instruction in word meanings.* Realize that text difficulty (which includes vocabulary) affects the ability of students to comprehend and retain information; thus, studies show that students who receive instruction in word meanings have greater mastery of those meanings than those who receive no instruction.[21] Teach meaning for some of the difficult words in the selections the students are reading before the students read the selection: this increases comprehension of that selection.[22]

[11]Jeanne Chall, *Learning to Read: The Great Debate* (New York: McGraw Hill, 1967).

[12]Guy L. Bond and Robert Dykstra, "The Cooperative Research Program in First Grade Reading Instruction," *Reading Research Quarterly* 2(1):10–138 (Fall 1967).

[13]Robert L. Hillerich, "Vowel Generalizations and First Grade Reading Achievement," *The Elementary School Journal* 68(2):246–251 (Fall 1967).

[14]Jean Hudson and John Haworth, "Dimensions of Word Recognition," *Reading* 17(2):87–94 (Fall 1983).

[15]Susanna Pflaum and Bryan Ianis, "Oral Reading Research and Learning Disabled Children," *Topics in Learning and Learning Disabilities* 1(1):33–42 (Fall 1982).

[16]Andrew Biemiller, "The Development of the Use of Graphic and Contextual Information as Children Learn to Read," *Reading Research Quarterly* 1(1):75–96 (Fall 1970).

[17]Dixie Lee Spiegel et al., "An Investigation of a Context-Plus-Phonics Strategy for Increasing Second-Grade Students' Use of Context to Aid Word Recognition," *Searches for Meaning in Reading/Language Processing and Instruction*, ed. by Jerome A. Niles and Larry A. Harris (Rochester, NY: National Reading Conference, 1983).

[18]Keith Stanovich, "Toward an Interactive Compensatory Model of Individual Differences in the Development of Reading Fluency," *Reading Research Quarterly* 16(1):32–71 (Fall 1980).

[19]Robert Kann, "The Method of Repeated Readings: Expanding the Neurological Impress Method for Use with Disabled Readers," *Journal of Learning Disabilities* 2(2):90–92 (Winter 1980).

[20]Borkowski, p. 396.

[21]Isabel L. Beck et al., "Effects of Long-Term Vocabulary Instruction on Lexical Access and Reading Comprehension," *Journal of Educational Psychology* 74(3):506–521 (Spring 1982).

[22]Edward K. Kaneenui et al., "Effects of Text Construction and Instructional Procedures for Teaching Word Meanings on Comprehension and Recall," *Reading Research Quarterly* 17(2):367–388 (Winter 1982).

11. *Plan activities before reading a selection.* Prereading activities can activate a student's background knowledge. The relationship between background knowledge and comprehension is positive; the greater the reader's background knowledge that is related to the text, the greater the comprehension of the text material.[23]

12. *Teach the ways that authors arrange stories and informational texts.* This teaching will aid student comprehension of narrative and expository writing styles. When students receive instruction in the structure of texts, their comprehension improves. Understanding of the structure of texts is supported by asking students to predict outcomes, to retell stories, and to discuss causal relationships.[24] Studies of students in grades 4–6 showed that students who had instruction in story grammar improved their comprehension and recall of stories.[25]

13. *Give direct instruction to help students distinguish main ideas in text material.* Direct instruction is needed in assisting students to distinguish main ideas in text material where the ideas appear in different places in the paragraphs, and in assisting students to infer main ideas when the ideas are not stated directly or clearly. In grades 5 and 6, it seems that some students can select main ideas from paragraphs on work sheets but are not able to transfer this skill to finding main ideas in text materials.[26] To encourage transfer of this skill, consider asking students in cooperative learning groups to work at one of the following tasks suitable for their abilities: to select the topic for a paragraph that is taken from an actual text the students are using in one of their content areas; to select the main idea from several choices given; to select the main idea that is located at the beginning, middle, or end of a paragraph taken from a text, or determine that the main idea is not stated and should be inferred from selected paragraphs; or to determine which details from a paragraph support information about the main idea by writing the details on a graphic web, with the main idea recorded in the center and the details recorded on strands that radiate from the center.

In grades 1 and 2, it appears that students can select a stated main idea when it is in the first or the last sentence of a paragraph, but they have difficulty inferring main ideas.[27]

14. *Demonstrate the process of making inferences.* Model the process of inferring in materials on the students' instructional reading levels. The ability to make inferences is one of the skills that differentiate good from poor readers. As part of your direct instruction, you will want to integrate a student's prior knowledge with the text before reading the material and ask questions that call for information inferred by the student.[28]

15. *Teach critical-reading skills to all.* Teach critical-reading skills to all students, including disadvantaged and below-grade-level readers. Intermediate-grade remedial reading students who were taught critical-thinking abilities through listening became significantly better at critical listening and critical reading than a control group.[29] Fur-

[23]R. Scott Baldwin et al., "Effects of Topic Interest and Prior Knowledge on Reading Comprehension," *Reading Research Quarterly* 20(4):497–508 (Spring 1985).
[24]Muriel K. Rand, "Story Schema: Theory, Research and Practice," *The Reading Teacher* 37(4):377–383 (January 1984).
[25]Jill Fitzgerald Whaley, "Story Grammars and Reading Instruction," *The Reading Teacher* 34(7):762–771 (April 1981).
[26]Barbara Taylor et al., "A Comparison of Students' Ability to Read for Main Ideas in Social Studies Textbooks and to Complete Main Idea Worksheets," *Reading World* 24(2):10–15 (Fall 1985).
[27]David W. Moore et al., "Readers' Conceptions of the Main Idea," *Searches for Meaning in Reading Language Processing and Instruction,* ed. by Jerome A. Niles and Larry A. Harris (Rochester, NY: National Reading Conference, 1983).
[28]Betty C. Holmes, "A Confirmation Strategy for Improving Poor Readers' Ability to Answer Inferential Questions," *The Reading Teacher* 37(1):144–148 (October 1983).
[29]Gloria M. Boodt, "Critical Listeners Become Critical Readers in Remedial Reading Class," *The Reading Teacher* 37(4):390–394 (January 1984).

ther, disadvantaged students in grades 4 and 6 and in middle schools were given instruction in critical reading, and after the instruction, were just as capable of reading critically as their advantaged peers.[30]

16. *Encourage the students to make mental images before they read.* Several studies show that visualization training does increase the comprehension of some students. Studies of students in grades 3–6 point out that careful daily instruction in the use of visualization improved student learning from the text.[31]

17. *Ask sequenced questions about the story.* To improve understanding of the story, ask questions in an order that follows the pattern of the story structure and that mention the setting, the initiating event, the reaction of the character, the action, and the consequence of the action.[32]

18. *Teach students to use the survey, question, read, recite, and review approach to study content in materials.* (See SQ4R and SQ3R, Chapter 5.) Research synthesis indicates that these are study habits found in high-achieving students,[33] that questioning before reading (a step in this approach), aids comprehension,[34] and that students using the approach score higher on recall of content material and make gains in content areas.[35]

19. *Plan instruction in outlining and in note taking.* To increase a student's mastery over content material, demonstrate outlining and note taking. Students who outline increase their learning,[36] and those who take notes increase their comprehension and recall of materials.[37]

20. *Give instruction on taking tests.* Take time to teach how to take tests to improve students' performances on tests and to ensure that the results more accurately reflect their learning.[38,39,40] Both low and high achievers can benefit. In one study of both groups, the students who received instruction in test taking increased their grade equivalent scores from three to eight months over a control group.[41]

21. *Demonstrate fluent oral reading.* Instruction in fluent oral reading can be helpful for readers who read with poor expression or phrasing.[42] Read aloud to your students. A program of reading aloud combined with direct teaching was shown to support large gains in academic achievement for third-grade students.[43] Reading aloud facilitates the students' ability to compose stories and improves their narrative writing. Further, children's literature is an important part of the writing context, because it

[30]Barbara K. Clark and Barbara C. Palmer, "Reading and the Disadvantaged: Some Myths and Facts," *Reading World* 21(1):208–212 (Fall 1982).

[31]Robert J. Tierney and Jones W. Cunningham, "Research on Teaching Reading Comprehension." In *Handbook of Reading Research*, ed. by David Pearson (New York: Longman, 1984).

[32]Marilyn W. Sadow, "The Use of Story Grammar in the Design of Questions," *The Reading Teacher* 35(5):518–522 (February 1982).

[33]Thomas H. Estes and Herbert C. Richards, "Habits of Study and Test Performance," *Journal of Reading Behavior* 17(1):1–13 (Fall 1985).

[34]Linda Baker and Ann L. Brown, "Metacognitive Skills in Reading." In *Handbook of Reading Research*, ed. by David Pearson (New York: Longman, 1984).

[35]Abby Adams et al., "Instructional Strategies for Studying Content Area Texts in the Intermediate Grades," *Reading Research Quarterly* 18(1):27–55 (Fall 1981).

[36]Wayne H. Slater, "Teaching Expository Text Structure with Structural Organizers," *Journal of Reading* 28(8):712–718 (May 1985).

[37]Estes and Richards, p. 13.

[38]Melanie Dreisbach and Barbara K. Keogh, "Testwiseness as a Factor in Readiness Test Performance of Young Mexican-American Children," *Journal of Educational Psychology* 74(3):224–229 (December 1982).

[39]Irving P. McPhail, "Why Teach Test Wiseness?" *Journal of Reading* 25(1):22–28 (October 1981).

[40]Debbra A. Uttero, "Activating Comprehension through Cooperative Learning," *The Reading Teacher* 41(4):390–395 (January 1988).

[41]Bob Lange, "Promoting Test Wiseness," *Journal of Reading* 24(8):740–743 (May 1981).

[42]Richard Allington, "Fluency: The Neglected Reading Goal," *The Reading Teacher* 36(6):556–561 (February 1983).

[43]Jose G. Lopez, "The Relative Impact of Oral Reading Combined with Direct Teaching Methodology on Reading Comprehension, Listening, and Vocabulary Achievement of Third-Grade Students," *Dissertation Abstracts International* 47:3974A (1986).

provides authentic experiences for student writers as they borrow and improvise from the literature to create their own texts.

22. *Plan listening instruction.* There is a relationship between reading and listening. One study of fourth-grade students who were reading two and one-half years below grade level were provided 20-minute listening periods daily for 30 days. When compared with the control group, those who had received the listening training performed significantly better on a standardized reading achievement test.[44] In a study of fifth-grade students, the experimental group received instruction with a listening activity and then transferred what had been learned to reading. The control group received instruction in a traditional way. The experimental group made greater gains on a standardized reading achievement test in relationships, interpretation, and appreciation.[45]

23. *Promote a writing and reading interaction in the classroom.* Writing and reading are processes that complement each other. The reading comprehension of good writers is better than that of average writers, and better writers do more free reading than those with lesser abilities.[46] Students in grades 5, 6, and 7, who receive training in writing summaries, have greater comprehension and retention when they apply that skill as they read.[47] Sentence manipulation activities have positive effects on students and their reading and writing ability.

24. *Tell students what they are going to learn, the reasons for learning it, and how the new learning is related to previous learning.* Your direct instruction should include an introduction that tells the students what they are going to learn, the reason for learning it, and how the new learning relates to what they have previously learned. Next, explain the skill and show the students exactly how to use the skill. Then, give some time for guided practice during which you ask the students to use the skill. You may change the context in which the skill is being used and ask students to use it in the new context. Then ask the students to tell what they have learned. More independent practice is suggested as the students use this skill in still another context, perhaps for a homework activity.

25. *Encourage life-long interest in reading.* You can do this by reading to the students and by using the library to provide a wide variety of reading materials. Respond positively to what students read. Use uninterrupted sustained silent reading[48] often to foster interest and positive attitudes toward stories in books. Plan newsletters to parents and guardians to offer ideas for reading aloud to their children, and send home lists of specific books you think the students will enjoy.

Selected Resources for Teaching Integrated Language Arts

For Kindergarten:

How the Turtle Got Its Shell: An African Tale (See-More's Workshop, 1991). Read-along tape introduces Swahili names of characters with African drums as authentic musical background. Side 2 encourages audience participation through dance, songs, and actions.

---

[44]Robert L. Lemons and Samuel C. Moore, "The Effects of Training in Listening on the Development of Reading Skills," *Reading Improvement* 19(2):212–216 (Fall 1982).

[45]Hal W. Seaton and O. Paul Wielan, "A Study of the Effects of Listening/Reading Transfer on Four Measures of Reading Comprehension." In *Comprehension: Process and Product*, ed. by George H. McNinch (Athens, GA: The American Reading Forum, 1981).

[46]Timothy Shanahan, "The Impact of Writing Instruction on Learning to Read," *Reading World* 19(3):357–368 (Spring 1980).

[47]Karen D'Angelo Bromley, "Precise Writing and Outlining Enhance Content Learning," *The Reading Teacher* 38(4):406–411 (January 1985).

[48]Sustained silent reading (SSR) is a period of time when students and their teacher silently and independently read self-selected books.

Muppet Slate: The Word and Picture Processor (Sunburst). This award-winning software program inspires children (grades K–2) to write creatively. Contains 24 language arts lessons. Works with *Muppet Learning Keys* or regular Apple keyboard on the Apple II family of computers.

For First Grade:

Chicka Chicka Boom Boom (Old Tappan, NJ: Simon & Schuster, 1991). Recording of a popular ABC book read by Ray Charles.

Mickey's Magic Reader (Sunburst). In this software program (grades 1 and 2) Mickey Mouse entices beginning readers with rebus sentences, stories, and riddles that build reading comprehension skills. Another award-winning program from Sunburst, it operates with the Apple II family of computers.

For Second Grade:

Flossie and the Fox (Weston Woods, 1991) by Patricia McKissack. Videocassette that shows an appreciation of southern black culture.

1-2-3 Sequence Me (Info Tech Manitoba Educational Technology Program, Canada). This software program (grades K–2) for Macintosh computers is a three-level program that teaches sequencing.

For Third Grade:

Meet Ashley Bryan: Storyteller, Artist, Writer (American School Publications, 1991). Videocassette of Bryan reading *Turtle Knows Your Name*, and some poems, and demonstrating printing.

Podd (Living and Learning, Ltd., England). A computer program (grades K–3) that makes hunting for action verbs fun. Available for the Apple II family of computers.

For Fourth Grade:

Trickster Tales from Around the World (B. G. Schutz-Gruber, 12825 Kimberly, Ann Arbor, MI 48194, 1991). Recording of tales told of groups of school children.

Storybook Theatre (Learningways, Inc.) A series of computer programs (grades 1–4) that encourages children to create animated stories. Available from WINGS for Learning, 1600 Green Hills Road, P.O. Box 660002, Scotts Valley, CA 95067-0002.

For Fifth Grade:

Reading, Writing, and Rhythm (3R's Productions, 1991). Recording presents topics (such as forms of punctuation) with rap and rhyming songs.

Magic Slate II (Sunburst). An award-winning computer program package to teach the writing process (grades 2 and up). For information write to WINGS for Learning, 1600 Green Hills Road, P.O. Box 660002, Scotts Valley, CA 95067-0002.

For Sixth Grade:

Bridge to Terabithia (Public Media Video, 1992). Videocassette based on the Newberry Medal book by Katherine Paterson about the friendship of Jesse and Leslie, fifth-graders from different backgrounds living in rural United States.

What's the Story? (LOGAL). This is a series of nine computer programs for grades 5 and up to help readers compare, predict, and summarize information. Available for IBM, Tandy, and Macintosh computers. For information contact WINGS for Learning, 1600 Green Hills Road, P.O. Box 660002, Scotts Valley, CA 95067-0002.

For Seventh and Eighth Grades:

Ghost Walk: Native American Tales of the Spirit (Lotus Press, 1992). Recording of stories from the Southwest that portray the closeness of the spirit world to the lives of Native Americans.

For Teachers:

Bilingual Education: An Inside View (Berkeley, CA: University of California Extension Media Center). Video of bilingual elementary teachers conducting lessons in first- and second-language acquisition in classrooms.

Hey! Listen to This: Stories to Read Aloud (New York: Penguin, 1992) by Jim Trelease. Anthology of tales to read aloud grouped into subjects such as "Families," "School Days," and "Food for Thought."

The Educated Eye (ALA Video/Library Video Network, 320 York Road, Towson, MD 21204, 1992). Interviews with editors and illustrators to give teachers a sense of the importance of book illustrations.

Wordless/Almost Wordless Picture Books: A Guide (Libraries Unlimited, 1992) by Virginia H. Richey and Katharyn E. Puckett. Information on building thematic approaches.

B. INSTRUCTIONAL GUIDELINES FOR TEACHING MATHEMATICS

A real problem in elementary schools is that many teachers give less attention to mathematics, science, and social science than they give to language arts. Language arts is *not* more important than these other areas and does *not* deserve more extensive treatment, although laws in your state may in fact dictate time requirements that imply the contrary. As discussed previously, many effective teachers combine the teaching of language arts with mathematics, or science, or social science, or with some combination of these, often by using thematic units.

Proceed now to Exercise 13.1.

An effective teacher often combines the teaching of language arts with mathematics, science, and social science.

Exercise 13.1: A Study of Time Devoted to Content Areas in Elementary School Classrooms

Instructions: A study reported in 1985 by the Association for Supervision and Curriculum Development found that, on average, fourth-graders spent 100 minutes per day on language arts, 52 minutes on mathematics, 34 minutes on social studies, and 28 minutes on science. The purpose of this exercise is to survey elementary school classrooms in your area to get an idea of how much time is spent on each content area of the elementary school curriculum. Proceed by following these steps:

1. Select a school and grade level of your choice and, by interviewing one or several teachers at that school, ascertain how much time is spent (average per day) on the various content areas of the curriculum. Identify here the school and grade level taught by teacher or teachers interviewed.

    School _____ Grade _____

2. Record the time (in minutes) spent on average per day at this grade level. *Note:* If the teacher(s) use interdisciplinary thematic teaching or literature-based instruction, it may be very difficult for them to break the time into minutes per discipline. In that case, state here that this is so, and ask the teacher to give a rough estimate. (Major emphasis on use of interdisciplinary units: _____ .)

    Language arts   = _____ minutes.

    　　Reading

    　　Writing

    　　Spelling

    Mathematics   = _____ minutes.

    Social studies   = _____ minutes.

    Science   = _____ minutes.

    Other (identify)

    _____ = _____ minutes.

    _____ = _____ minutes.

    _____ = _____ minutes.

    _____ = _____ minutes.

3. Compare your results with those of others in your class for the same grade level. Obtain an average for the amount of minutes spent per day per content area per grade level. Compare these averages with those indicated in the first paragraph of this exercise.

4. Now, compare your class averages with the elementary school teachers' schedules as found in Figures 1.1 through 1.5 of Chapter 1 in this resource guide.

5. What conclusions does your class arrive at as a result of these comparisons and this exercise?

_____

_____

_____

_____

_____

_____

_____

_____

_____

_____

_____

_____

_____

_____

_____

_____

_____

_____

_____

_____

_____

_____

_____

_____

_____

_____

_____

State or local policy regarding time requirements may be one reason that teachers devote less attention to mathematics, science, and social science. Another reason may be the anxiety of teachers, particularly toward mathematics and science. "Math anxiety" in adults is not a myth, and there is a similar anxiety toward science, particularly in respect to physical science.

Communication, higher problem-solving ability, and scientific and technological literacy are important basic skills that should be learned in mathematics, science, and social science. It is important that the elementary teacher be current in the content and strategies of these curriculum areas, and that he or she resolve any personal anxieties related to these subjects, especially so that similar anxieties, and consequent "turn off" to science or mathematics, are not transmitted to the teacher's students. Workshops, courses, and discussions with other teachers can help improve confidence and attitude about these subject areas and thus reduce anxieties.

Traditional teaching, especially in science and mathematics, has relied heavily on rote memorization, learning governed largely by the left hemisphere of the brain (see Chapter 2). Learning that depends on memorization can produce tension and anxiety in the learner. The right hemisphere is believed to have primary control over the intuitive,[49] creative, and affective intellectual processes. These are the resources that can promote understanding and relaxation. Encouraging the intuitive (right side of the brain) while attending the cognitive (left side) may help us learn and teach more effectively those content areas that traditionally have caused learner anxieties.

Encouraging Right-Brain Learning

There are a number of specific things an elementary teacher can do to encourage right-brain learning:

- Challenge the students with tasks that are within their capabilities.
- Emphasize the positive rather than the negative (e.g., catch students being good, as discussed in Chapter 4).
- Encourage children to think in metaphors (e.g., "All the world's a stage"; the use of mandalas).
- Encourage cooperation rather than competition (e.g., use cooperative learning, as discussed in previous chapters of this resource guide, and educational games that diminish the importance of competition, as discussed in Chapter 11).
- Encourage freedom from prejudice (discussed in several sections later in this chapter).
- Encourage serendipity (the excitement of unexpected discovery).
- Enhance the learning environment (as discussed in Chapter 4).
- Use discovery and inquiry (as discussed in Chapter 11).
- Use lesson and unit plans and learning activities that cross subject boundaries.

---

[49]"Intuition" is knowing without conscious reasoning, and for children not yet in the Piagetian stage of formal operation (and that is *most* children, if not all), it is their primary source of learning.

Two Concerns of Many Teachers

Of major concern to many elementary school teachers is how to find time to teach all of the required content areas. As we have said in previous editions of this resource guide, the answer to that question is integration of the disciplines, which is achieved by using interdisciplinary thematic units.

A second concern of some beginning teachers is stated thus: "How can I know enough about each of the content areas to do a satisfactory job?" We try to answer that question in this chapter, and we also present more ideas for the integration of content areas.

Why Do We Teach Mathematics in the Elementary School?

Mathematics is a basic skill and a major teaching responsibility for many elementary school teachers. What follows are some basic understandings we believe important for those teaching mathematics to children who will be living and working in the twenty-first century.

Knowledge and skill development in mathematics must occur in incremental steps, simultaneously with the development of healthy attitudes about mathematics. The concepts of mathematics become part of our human experiences long before formal schooling begins; therefore, it is important that the program of instruction begin in kindergarten, if not earlier. Earliest experiences are informal and exploratory, such as involving the child in comparing and classifying familiar objects according to size, shape, and color.

The Goals of Elementary School Mathematics

In 1986, the Board of Directors of the National Council of Teachers of Mathematics (NCTM) established the Commission on Standards for School Mathematics in a concerted effort to improve the quality of school mathematics and mathematics instruction. The result of that effort was the 1989 publication of NCTM's *Curriculum and Evaluation Standards for School Mathematics*.[50,51] The NCTM document sets forth the following five general goals of K–12 mathematics education.[52]

1. All students learn to value mathematics.
2. All students become confident in their ability to do mathematics.
3. All students become mathematical problem-solvers.
4. All students learn to communicate mathematically.
5. All students learn to reason mathematically.

---

[50]More than 40 states are using the NCTM standards to guide what and how mathematics is taught and how student progress should be assessed. See the several articles in *Educational Leadership* 50(8):4–18 (May 1993).

[51]In addition to the NCTM standards for mathematics, the National Council on Education Standards and Testing (NCEST) has recommended that education standards be developed for all core subjects—science, history, English, geography, civics/social studies, and the arts. In response, projects for the creation of standards in these subjects are in various stages of development. See Section D of Chapter 5.

[52]Commission on Standards for School Mathematics, *Curriculum and Evaluation Standards for School Mathematics* (Reston, VA: National Council of Teachers of Mathematics, 1989), p. 5.

What Skills in Mathematics Do I Need?

As an elementary school teacher, you need the mathematics skills you will be teaching. The skill level will, of course, vary with grade level, but basic skills have been identified, are addressed in most elementary school programs, and follow eight unifying or integrating strands—functions, algebra, geometry, statistics and probability, discrete mathematics, measurement, number, and logic and language.[53]

In 1983, the National Science Board (NSB) commission identified the following as desirable learning outcomes of K–8 mathematics:[54]

1. Understanding of arithmetic operations and knowledge of when and where specific operations should be made.
2. Development of a thorough understanding of, and facility with, one-digit number facts.
3. Ability to use selective calculators and computers to help develop concepts, as well as to do many of the tedious computations that previously had to be done with paper and pencil.
4. Development of skill in the use of informal mental arithmetic; first, in providing exact answers to simple problems and, later, approximate answers to more complicated problems.
5. Development of skills in estimation and approximation.
6. Development of problem-solving abilities. Methods of trial and error, guessing and estimating, in solving word problems should be actively encouraged at all levels.
7. Understanding of elementary data analysis, elementary statistics, and probability.
8. Knowledge of place value, decimals, percentage, and scientific notation.
9. Understanding of the relationship of numbers to geometry.
10. Understanding of fractions as numbers, comparison of fractions, and conversion to decimals.
11. Development of an intuitive understanding of geometry, and ability to use the mensuration formulas for two- and three-dimensional figures.
12. Ability to use the concepts of sets, and some of the language of sets, where appropriate.
13. Understanding of elementary function concepts, including dynamic models of increasing or decreasing phenomena.
14. Ability to use some algebraic symbolism and techniques, particularly in grades 7 and 8.

The 1989 publication of the NCTM *Curriculum and Evaluation Standards* and the subsequent (1991) publication of its *Professional Standards for Teaching Mathematics* have provided clear and important guidance for the development and improvement of teaching and learning of mathematics in the nation's elementary schools.

---

[53]These eight strands are from the *Mathematics Framework for California Public Schools: K–12* (Sacramento: California Department of Education, 1992), pp. 80–87.
[54]The National Science Board Commission on Precollege Education in Mathematics, Science and Technology, *Educating Americans for the 21st Century* (Washington, DC, September 12, 1983), pp. 93–94.

NCTM Curriculum Assumptions and Standards for Grades K–4

The NCTM standards are based on certain assumptions. For grades K–4 these assumptions are that the mathematics curriculum should:[55]

- Be conceptually oriented.
- Actively involve children in doing mathematics.
- Emphasize the development of children's mathematical thinking and reasoning abilities.
- Emphasize the application of mathematics.
- Include a broad range of content.
- Make appropriate and ongoing use of calculators and computers.

In abbreviation, the 13 NCTM standards for mathematics K–4 are as follows:

Standard 1: Mathematics as Problem Solving

In kindergarten through grade 4, the study of mathematics should emphasize problem solving so that students can:

- Use problem-solving approaches to investigate and understand mathematical content.
- Formulate problems from everyday and mathematical situations.
- Develop and apply strategies to solve a wide variety of problems.
- Verify and interpret results with respect to the original problem.
- Acquire confidence in using mathematics meaningfully.

Standard 2: Mathematics as Communication

In kindergarten through grade 4, the study of mathematics should include numerous opportunities for communication so that students can:

- Relate physical materials, pictures, and diagrams to mathematical ideas.
- Reflect on and clarify their thinking about mathematical ideas and situations.
- Relate their everyday language to mathematical language and symbols.
- Realize that representing, discussing, reading, writing, and listening to mathematics are a vital part of learning and using mathematics.

Standard 3: Mathematics as Reasoning

In kindergarten through grade 4, the study of mathematics should emphasize reasoning so that students can:

- Draw logical conclusions about mathematics.
- Use models, known facts, properties, and relationships to explain their thinking.
- Justify their answers and solution processes.
- Use patterns and relationships to analyze mathematical situations.
- Believe that mathematics makes sense.

[55]*Curriculum and Evaluation Standards for School Mathematics*, pp. 17–19.

Standard 4: Mathematical Connections

In kindergarten through grade 4, the study of mathematics should include opportunities to make connections so that students can:

- Link conceptual and procedural knowledge.
- Relate various representations of concepts or procedures to one another.
- Recognize relationships between different topics in mathematics.
- Use mathematics in other curricular areas.
- Use mathematics in their daily lives.

Standard 5: Estimation

In kindergarten through grade 4, the curriculum should include estimation so that students can:

- Explore estimation strategies.
- Recognize when an estimate is appropriate.
- Determine the reasonableness of results.
- Apply estimation in working with quantities, measurement, computation, and problem solving.

Standard 6: Number Sense and Numeration

In kindergarten through grade 4, the mathematics curriculum should include whole number concepts and skills so that students can:

- Construct number meanings through real-world experiences and the use of physical materials.
- Understand the numeration system by relating counting, grouping, and place-value concepts.
- Develop number sense.
- Interpret the multiple uses of numbers encountered in the real world.

Standard 7: Concepts of Whole Number Operations

In kindergarten through grade 4, the mathematics curriculum should include concepts of addition, subtraction, multiplication, and division of whole numbers so that students can:

- Develop meaning for the operations by modeling and discussing a rich variety of problem situations.
- Relate the mathematical language and symbolism of operations to problems and informal language.
- Recognize that a wide variety of problem structures can be represented by a single operation.
- Develop operation sense.

Standard 8: Whole Number Computation

In kindergarten through grade 4, the mathematics curriculum should develop whole number computation so that students can:

- Model, explain, and develop reasonable proficiency with basic facts and algorithms.
- Use a variety of mental computation and estimation techniques.
- Use calculators in appropriate computational situations.
- Select and use computation techniques appropriate to specific problems and determine whether the results are reasonable.

Standard 9: Geometry and Spatial Sense

In kindergarten through grade 4, the mathematics curriculum should include two-dimensional and three-dimensional geometry so that students can:

- Describe, model, draw, and classify shapes.
- Investigate and predict the results of combining, subdividing, and changing shapes.
- Develop spatial sense.
- Relate geometric ideas to number and measurement ideas.
- Recognize and appreciate geometry in their world.

Standard 10: Measurement

In kindergarten through grade 4, the mathematics curriculum should include measurement so that students can:

- Understand the attributes of length, capacity, weight, area, volume, time, temperature, and angle.
- Develop the process of measuring and concepts related to units of measurement.
- Make and use estimates of measurement.
- Make and use measurements in problem and everyday situations.

Standard 11: Statistics and Probability

In kindergarten through grade 4, the mathematics curriculum should include experiences with data analysis and probability so that students can:

- Collect, organize, and describe data.
- Construct, read, and interpret displays of data.
- Formulate and solve problems that involve collecting and analyzing data.
- Explore concepts of chance.

Standard 12: Fractions and Decimals

In kindergarten through grade 4, the mathematics curriculum should include fractions and decimals so that students can:

- Develop concepts of fractions, mixed numbers, and decimals.
- Develop number sense for fractions and decimals.
- Use models to relate fractions to decimals and to find equivalent fractions.
- Use models to explore operations on fractions and decimals.
- Apply fractions and decimals to problem situations.

Standard 13: Patterns and Relationships

In kindergarten through grade 4, the mathematics curriculum should include the study of patterns and relationships so that the student can:

- Recognize, describe, extend, and create a wide variety of patterns.
- Represent and describe mathematical relationships.
- Explore the use of variables and open sentences to express relationships.

NCTM Curriculum Assumptions and Standards for Grades 5–8

Reflecting the unique characteristics of students of middle school age (see Chapter 1) as "children in transition,"[56] including their ability to begin to think and reason more abstractly, the NCTM standards for grades 5–8 are based on certain assumptions:[57]

- Problem situations should serve as the context for mathematics.
- Communication with and about mathematics and mathematical reasoning should permeate the curriculum.
- A broad range of topics should be taught, including number concepts, computation, estimation, functions, algebra, statistics, probability, geometry, and measurement.
- Connections between these topics should be a prominent feature of the curriculum.
- Technology, including calculators, computers, and videos, should be used when appropriate. Each student should have a calculator; every classroom should have at least one computer.
- Learning activities should incorporate topics and ideas across standards.
- Students should have opportunities to formulate problems and questions that stem from their own interests.
- Learning should engage students both intellectually and physically.
- Classroom activities should provide students the opportunity to work both individually and in small- and large-group arrangements.
- Every classroom should be equipped with ample sets of manipulative materials and supplies (e.g., spinners, cubes, tiles, geoboards, pattern blocks, and so on).

In abbreviation, the 13 NCTM standards for mathematics 5–8 are as follows:

Standard 1: Mathematics as Problem Solving

In grades 5 through 8, the mathematics curriculum should include numerous and varied experiences with problem solving as a method of inquiry and application so that students can:

- Use problem-solving approaches to investigate and understand mathematical content.
- Formulate problems from situations within and outside mathematics.
- Develop and apply a variety of strategies to solve problems, with emphasis on multistep and nonroutine problems.
- Verify and interpret results with respect to the original problem situation.

[56]Ibid., p. 68.
[57]Ibid., pp. 67–68.

• Generalize solutions and strategies to new problem situations.
• Acquire confidence in using mathematics meaningfully.

Standard 2: Mathematics as Communication

In grades 5 through 8, the study of mathematics should include opportunities to communicate so that students can:

• Model situations, using oral, written, concrete, pictorial, graphical, and algebraic methods.
• Reflect on and clarify their own thinking about mathematical ideas and situations.
• Develop common understandings of mathematical ideas, including the role of definitions.
• Use the skills of reading, listening, and viewing to interpret and evaluate mathematical ideas.
• Discuss mathematical ideas and make conjectures and convincing arguments.
• Appreciate the value of mathematical notation and its role in the development of mathematical ideas.

Standard 3: Mathematics as Reasoning

In grades 5 through 8, reasoning should permeate the mathematics curriculum so that students can:

• Recognize and apply deductive and inductive reasoning.
• Understand and apply reasoning processes, with special attention being given to spatial reasoning and reasoning with proportions and graphs.
• Make and evaluate mathematical conjectures and arguments.
• Validate their own thinking.
• Appreciate the pervasive use and power of reasoning as a part of mathematics.

Standard 4: Mathematical Connections

In grades 5 through 8, the mathematics curriculum should include the investigation of mathematical connections so that students can:

• See mathematics as an integrated whole.
• Explore problems and describe results, using graphical, numerical, physical, algebraic, and verbal mathematical models or representations.
• Use a mathematical idea to further their understanding of other mathematical ideas.
• Apply mathematical thinking and modeling to solve problems that arise in other disciplines, such as art, music, psychology, science, and business.
• Value the role of mathematics in our culture and society.

Standard 5: Number and Number Relationships

In grades 5 through 8, the mathematics curriculum should include the continued development of number and number relationships so that students can:

• Understand, represent, and use numbers in a variety of equivalent forms (integer, fraction, decimal, percent, exponential, and scientific notation) in real-world and mathematical problem situations.

- Develop number sense for whole numbers, fractions, decimals, integers, and rational numbers.
- Understand and apply ratios, proportions, and percents in a wide variety of situations.
- Investigate relationships between fractions, decimals, and percents.
- Represent numerical relationships in one-dimensional and two-dimensional graphs.

Standard 6: Number Systems and Number Theory

In grades 5 through 8, the mathematics curriculum should include the study of number systems and number theory so that students can:

- Understand and appreciate the need for numbers beyond the whole numbers.
- Develop and use order relations for whole numbers, fractions, decimals, integers, and rational numbers.
- Extend their understanding of whole number operations to fractions, decimals, integers, and rational numbers.
- Understand how the basic arithmetic operations are related to one another.
- Develop and apply number theory concepts (e.g., primes, factors, and multiples) in real-world and mathematical problem situations.

Standard 7: Computation and Estimation

In grades 5 through 8, the mathematics curriculum should develop the concepts underlying computation and estimation in various contexts so that students can:

- Compute with whole numbers, fractions, decimals, integers, and rational numbers.
- Develop, analyze, and explain procedures for computation and techniques for estimation.
- Develop, analyze, and explain methods for solving proportions.
- Select and use an appropriate method for computing from among mental arithmetic, paper-and-pencil, calculator, and computer methods.
- Use computation, estimation, and proportions to solve problems.
- Use estimation to check the reasonableness of results.

Standard 8: Patterns and Functions

In grades 5 through 8, the mathematics curriculum should include explorations of patterns and functions so that students can:

- Describe, extend, analyze, and create a wide variety of patterns.
- Describe and represent relationships with tables, graphs, and rules.
- Analyze functional relationships to explain how a change in one quantity results in a change in another.
- Use patterns and functions to represent and solve problems.

Standard 9: Algebra

In grades 5 through 8, the mathematics curriculum should include explorations of algebraic concepts and processes so that students can:

- Understand the concepts of variable, expression, and equation.
- Represent situations and number patterns with tables, graphs, verbal rules, and equations and explore the interrelationships of these representations.

- Analyze tables and graphs to identify properties and relationships.
- Develop confidence in solving linear equations, using concrete, informal, and formal methods.
- Investigate inequalities and nonlinear equations informally.
- Apply algebraic methods to solve a variety of real-world and mathematical problems.

Standard 10: Statistics

In grades 5 through 8, the mathematics curriculum should include exploration of statistics in real-world situations so that students can:

- Systematically collect, organize, and describe data.
- Construct, read, and interpret tables, charts, and graphs.
- Make inferences and convincing arguments based on data analysis.
- Evaluate arguments based on data analysis.
- Develop an appreciation for statistical methods as powerful means for decision making.

Standard 11: Probability

In grades 5 through 8, the mathematics curriculum should include explorations of probability in real-world situations so that students can:

- Model situations by devising and carrying out experiments or simulations to determine probabilities.
- Model situations by constructing a sample space to determine probabilities.
- Appreciate the power of using a probability model by comparing experimental results with mathematical expectations.
- Make predictions based on experimental or theoretical probabilities.
- Develop an appreciation for the pervasive use of probability in the real world.

Standard 12: Geometry

In grades 5 through 8, the mathematics curriculum should include the study of the geometry of one, two, and three dimensions in a variety of situations so that students can:

- Identify, describe, compare, and classify, geometric figures.
- Visualize and represent geometric figures, with special attention to developing spatial sense.
- Explore transformations of geometric figures.
- Represent and solve problems using geometric models.
- Understand and apply geometric properties and relationships.
- Develop an appreciation of geometry as a means of describing the physical world.

Standard 13: Measurement

In grades 5 through 8, the mathematics curriculum should include extensive concrete experiences using measurement so that students can:

- Extend their understanding of the process of measurement.
- Estimate, make, and use measurements to describe and compare phenomena.

- Select appropriate units and tools to measure to the degree of accuracy required in a particular situation.
- Understand the structure and use of systems of measurement.
- Extend their understanding of the concepts of perimeter, area, volume, angle measure, capacity, and weight and mass.
- Develop the concepts of rates and other derived and indirect measurements.
- Develop formulas and procedures for determining measures to solve problems.

Many of these skills can be taught while the children are learning science, because many of the skills overlap with the processing skills of science. Teaching mathematics as an extension of sciencing, or of social sciencing, can help to make mathematics learning more meaningful and lasting.

The 1989 NCTM publication of *Curriculum and Evaluation Standards for School Mathematics* was followed by an Addenda Series of 22 supporting books designed to interpret and illustrate how the standards can be translated into classroom practices. These books (available from NCTM for approximately $11 each) discuss not only *what* students should learn but also *how* it should be learned. The themes of problem solving, reasoning, communication, and connections are found as strands throughout the materials, as is the view of assessment as a means of guiding instruction. As an example of the supporting books, the *Kindergarten Book* provides sample lessons, activities that connect models and manipulatives with concepts and mathematical representations, problems that exemplify the use of integration of technology, teaching strategies, approaches to evaluation, and techniques to improve instruction. In the margins of the pages are notes of pedagogical suggestions, such as for grouping students for a learning activity. The book explores four areas: (1) patterns; (2) number sense; (3) making sense of data; and (4) geometry and spatial sense. Covering the same four areas, the *Third-Grade Book* presents 17 activities and the *Fourth-Grade Book* presents 19 activities.

In your own mind, *be assured that there is no gender-linked difference in ability to learn mathematics.* For young children, mathematics is natural and fun. It is up to teachers to make sure that they, the teachers, counter negative comments that children sometimes hear about mathematics, and that they themselves do nothing to create in children a fear of mathematics and a reluctance to engage in mathematical activities. The following practices are encouraged:

- Avoid competitive math games in which winning depends on verbal aggressiveness.
- Be sure your own attitude about mathematics is positive and without bias.
- Call on female students as often as male students, having the same expectations for both. As discussed earlier (see Chapter 11), to ensure such equality you may need to systematize the manner in which you call on students and accept their responses.
- Encourage higher-order thinking and problem-solving skill development in each child, regardless of gender or ethnic background.
- Encourage remediation work in mathematics, just as in reading.
- Give credit for process learning as well as for correct responses.
- Help children understand the usefulness of mathematics.
- In elementary school mathematics instruction girls are generally more motivated by teacher praise and prompting.[58]
- Never use mathematics (or any other subject) as punishment.

---

[58]See E. Fennema and P. L. Peterson, "Effective Teaching for Girls and Boys." In *Talks to Teachers,* ed. by D. C. Berliner and B. Rosenshine (New York: Random House, 1987).

- Provide lessons that depend on hands-on, minds-on, concrete, manipulative activities.
- Spend more than 20 percent of mathematics class time on cooperative, high-level activities.
- Structure your lessons to encourage cooperative problem solving and group work.
- Use a wide variety of teaching strategies and encourage active participation by all students.
- Use diagnostic techniques to individualize the mathematics program.
- When teaching mathematics, use a teaching style that is calm and unhurried.
- Provide real objects for children to manipulate in order to visualize mathematical concepts.[59]

Additional Selected Resources for Teaching Mathematics

For Grades K–3:
Muppet Math (Sunburst). For Apple II; this computer software program integrates children's problem-solving activities.

Number Connections (Prometheus). For Macintosh computers; this software program reinforces student learning of numbers through a variety of ways of looking at numbers.

For Grades 2–5:
Times Table Rap (York 10, 9525 Vassar Avenue, Chatsworth, CA 91311), 1991. Recording of multiplication tables in a rap style and a review in sing-along format.

Bounce! An Introduction to Patterns (WINGS for Learning). Designed for grades K–8 this program (IBM, Apple, Macintosh) reinforces student learning of sequence by using pattern recognition and information gathering.

For Grades 5–8:
Manor House Mystery (Human Relations Media, 175 Tompkins Avenue, Pleasantville, NY 10570), 1992. Videocassette requires knowledge of basic geometry concepts to solve a mystery. To be used with cooperative groups in response to standards of NCTM.

For Teachers:
Teaching Mathematics to Elementary School Children by Douglas E. Cruikshank and Linda Jensen Sheffield (Columbus, OH: Merrill, 1988).

Helping Children Learn Mathematics, 3rd ed., by Robert E. Reys, Marilyn N. Suydam, and Mary Montgomery Lindquist (Needham Heights, MA: Allyn and Bacon, 1992).

Your state framework and the teacher's guides for the curriculum program you will be using are also likely to be a rich source of ideas. In addition, review the resources listed at the end of this chapter.

---

[59]For example, using clay or the new *Crayola® Model Magic™* modeling compound (a lightweight, clean, and non-greasy material that is available in many school supply stores) children can construct their mathematical knowledge as they make three-dimensional models that demonstrate mathematical ideas, e.g., they can develop their understanding of quantities, place objects into sets, and determine size and create objects according to scale.

C. INSTRUCTIONAL GUIDELINES FOR TEACHING SCIENCE

As a revered discipline, science has been struggling since the early 1970s, but there is now a renewed emphasis on the importance of early training in science, on science as a basic discipline. As stated in *Educating Americans for the 21st Century*, "The basics of the twenty-first century are not only reading, writing and arithmetic . . . [but also] include communication and higher problem-solving skills, and scientific and technological literacy."[60] The following are understandings and guidelines that we believe to be important if the elementary school teacher is to teach science effectively to today's children.

Why Do We Teach Science in the Elementary School?

Learning science in school contributes to the broader goals of education by providing children with a scientific understanding of (1) the natural world through knowledge of the basic concepts of science, (2) scientific modes of inquiry, (3) the nature of the scientific enterprise, and (4) the historical, social, and intellectual contexts within which science is practiced. "The ability to apply such scientific knowledge to aspects of one's life is called **scientific literacy**."[61]

Specifically, the reasons for teaching science in the elementary school include the following:

1. *Learning science can build attitudes that are important.* Dogmatic teaching is antagonistic to effective learning in science, whereas freedom of thought enhances a child's natural curiosity. Teach your class of students as if it were a think tank, encouraging guessing and intuitive thought. Healthy skepticism and the ability to suspend judgment are prized behaviors for sciencing.[62] The teacher must model those behaviors too.

Values and attitudes begin forming at an early age, thus there are attitudinal objectives for science learning in the earliest grades—objectives that should be incorporated into the science curriculum begin in kindergarten. The following are examples of sound learning objectives for all grades, beginning in kindergarten:

- The child demonstrates curiosity about the natural world.
- The child demonstrates respect for all living things.
- The child demonstrates conservation practices.

Children learn that science is important to their daily lives and that careers in science and technology are open to all.[63] The elementary school teacher can help dispel fears, misconceptions, myths, superstitions, and stereotypes about science, sciencing, and scientists.

---

[60]The National Science Board Commission on Precollege Education in Mathematics, Science and Technology, *Educating Americans for the 21st Century* (Washington, DC, September 12, 1983), p. v.

[61]These are the goals of school science as presently being developed by the National Committee on Science Education Standards and Assessment of the National Research Council, as reported in "Excerpts from National Science Education Standards: A Sampler," *NSTA Reports* (February/March 1993), p. 6.

[62]*Sciencing* is an acceptable verb and is used to stress the importance of process when talking about what it is a scientist does.

[63]The National Science Education Standards will contain a strong social commitment, defining the level of understanding of science that *all* students should develop, based on the belief that all children can and should learn science.

Through the study of science, children can develop their understanding, appreciation, and respect for life. Children can learn communication skills—skills that improve their ability to get along with each other and to understand the natural world. Our environment is a rich "classroom" in which to teach science to children. We should strive always to leave it a better place than we found it, which means to avoid unnecessary collecting and general "plundering" of the outdoors. We should encourage practices of preservation and enhancement of the environment.

2. *Science and mathematics can build a foundation for understanding.* In mathematics and science—as in integrated language arts—children can practice skills leading to higher-order thinking. For example, kindergarten children can be taught the importance and skill of listening to the ideas of others—a step toward the development of a critical, questioning attitude. They can be taught the skills needed to generate data: observing, recalling, identifying, and measuring. Young children should also be taught how to handle and care for plants, for animals, and for each other.

In science and in mathematics children learn cognitions that should be built upon as they progress from one grade to the next. Kindergarten children learn to *identify* objects with similar characteristics, to *compare* and *match* pictures of animals and their offspring, to *predict* what will happen, given a particular case. These are but a few of the cognitive attainments that lead to the child's developing understanding of the larger conceptual organizations around which the elementary school science and mathematics curriculum programs are built.

Science is taught in the elementary school not only because that is where we must begin laying the foundation for positive attitudes and feelings about science and technology, but because we must stimulate and develop the child's innate curiosity about the natural environment. By learning science in the elementary school children can:

- Develop and apply values that contribute to their affective development.
- Develop positive attitudes toward science and technology.
- Develop an awareness of the relationship between science, technology, and society.
- Develop an awareness of careers in science, mathematics, and technology.
- Develop higher-order thinking skills.
- Develop the knowledge, understandings, and skills that contribute to their cognitive development.
- Develop their psychomotor skills.

What Skills in Science Do I Need?

It is almost impossible for you to have comprehensive knowledge about all areas of science taught in elementary school—astronomy, animals, chemical and physical science, earth science, and weather, to name a few. But you do need a working understanding of the *nature of science* and of *sciencing*. Further, you need knowledge of the importance of assessing children's conceptions (or misconceptions) in science and the importance of building upon those conceptions.

Understanding the Nature of Science

Perhaps there is no better way to discourage childrens' natural interest in science than for a teacher to teach science as if it were "an organized body of knowledge to be learned." That definition of science is grossly inadequate, because it implies that everything about science is already known and all that children need to do is to memorize it. Although science teaching will unavoidably involve students in learning some of the information that has been developed through science, rote memorizing is not science!

Science is an ongoing, cyclic, organic process of observing and looking for order in nature, and it is a human endeavor. The products of this endeavor are human knowledge—facts, which are building blocks, reference points for our understanding of the larger ideas, that is, the principles, generalizations, and concepts. These **products** of learning in science are *tentative* and *accumulative,* an aspect of the nature of science exceedingly important for teachers and children to understand; we refer to this again later in this section.

In elementary school science, equal (if not more) attention must be given to the **processes** of science, as well as the products, while valuing intuitive thought and thoughtful guessing. Guesses are the hypotheses, predictions, and possible explanations to recognized problems and discrepancies. Hypotheses are tested, data are collected and analyzed, and tentative conclusions are drawn. These tentative conclusions (the process is cyclic, not linear) may lead to generalizations that build children's understandings about major scientific themes. Elementary school students accumulate knowledge and build their conceptual understandings by practicing the processes, while learning that they can science and that sciencing is a human activity.

Sciencing is what the scientist does; it is what elementary school students should do when they study science. Historically, children were taught "steps in the scientific method" and were required to memorize those steps. There are problems with that dogmatic approach. First, to ask children to memorize "steps in the scientific method" implies that the process of sciencing is linear—and it is not! It implies that there is a beginning and an end which is final, and that is misleading. It implies to children that, for them, science is a repetition of experiments, of memorizing the facts, and this is dull! By the time students taught in such a dogmatic manner reach intermediate grades or middle school, they will be bored with science. The dogmatic approach also implies that all sciencing is experimental, which it is not. Sciencing can also be descriptive, or it can be a comparative analysis. "Students should learn science by asking appropriate questions and conducting . . . experiments or collecting relative data, not by memorizing dogmatic steps. . . . The strategies used [in sciencing] are as varied as the researchers themselves."[64]

As mentioned earlier, dogmatic teaching of science can destroy a child's natural interest in science. We can all recall teachers who taught us in such a dreary fashion. They taught us to memorize that "Saturn has nine rings." (It has hundreds.) "Roots of plants grow down, and stems grow up." (Some do.) "Green plants produce food." (So do plants that are red and plants that are brown—red algae and kelp of the sea.) "Plants produce oxygen for animals." (Plants need oxygen, too.)

Science as an Ongoing, Cyclic, Organic Process of Observing and Looking for Order in Nature

Rather than being linear, with steps 1, 2, 3, and so on, the process of sciencing is cyclic. One enters the cycle whenever a discrepancy is observed (Piaget's "cognitive disequilibrium," as discussed in Chapter 2). Discrepancy recognition can occur at any point in the cycle. Figure 13.1 illustrates the sciencing cycle.

When a scientist is sciencing, she recognizes a problem or discrepancy, makes a guess as to its explanation, designs an experiment or observation to test the expla-

[64]Richard D. Storey and Jack Carter, "Why THE Scientific Method?" *The Science Teacher* 59(9):19–21 (December 1992), p. 20.

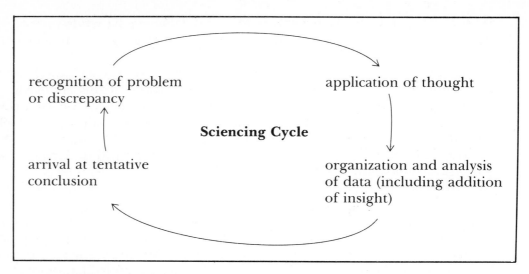

Figure 13.1 Sciencing cycle.

nation, collects and analyzes data, and then arrives at a tentative conclusion. It is important to realize that when a scientist believes that she has arrived at an explanation (either a new explanation for an old phenomenon or an explanation for a newly discovered phenomenon), there is no textbook or instructor to whom she can go to find out whether she is correct. On the basis of her self-confidence in her collection, processing, and analysis of available data, she arrives at her tentative conclusion. At a later date, subsequent data may cause her to revise that conclusion. As another and specific example, when a field botanist believes he has discovered a new species of orchid, he will carefully observe his specimen, checking its anatomical characteristics against those of the written descriptions of previously described species, looking for discrepancies in characteristics that make his specimen unique. When he is satisfied that he has done this thoroughly, and that his specimen is a new species, he draws that conclusion and then communicates the discovery to other botanists. Later, upon further examination of the same or similar specimen, the same or different botanist may substantiate the original conclusion or may draw a different conclusion, such as that the original specimen was not a new species but only a variation of an already-known species of orchid.

In science we do not speak of "absolute" truths. Science supports ideas; it never proves conclusively. Your students, then, will ask questions, generate ideas and explanations, and test them (by experimenting and observing). That is sciencing. The processes involved are varied: some are concerned with generating and organizing data, others with building upon and using ideas. See Figure 13.2 for an illustration of processes in each of these operations.

The Sciencing Cycle

In the sciencing cycle (Figure 13.2) we illustrate those processes that are data generating, data organizing, idea building, and idea using; the processes within each; and the grade levels where each process is most likely to be first introduced. The processes shown are relevant to other disciplines, too, including mathematics and social studies.

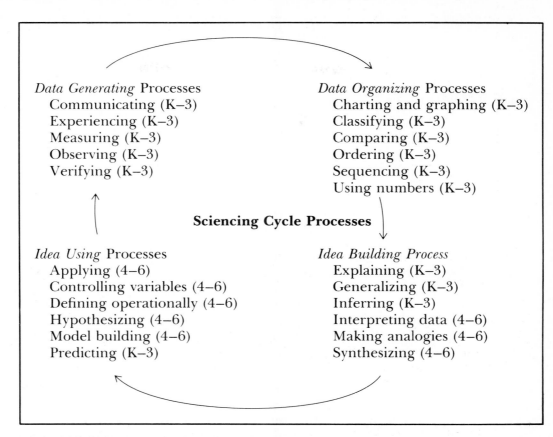

Data Generating Processes
  Communicating (K–3)
  Experiencing (K–3)
  Measuring (K–3)
  Observing (K–3)
  Verifying (K–3)

Data Organizing Processes
  Charting and graphing (K–3)
  Classifying (K–3)
  Comparing (K–3)
  Ordering (K–3)
  Sequencing (K–3)
  Using numbers (K–3)

Sciencing Cycle Processes

Idea Using Processes
  Applying (4–6)
  Controlling variables (4–6)
  Defining operationally (4–6)
  Hypothesizing (4–6)
  Model building (4–6)
  Predicting (K–3)

Idea Building Process
  Explaining (K–3)
  Generalizing (K–3)
  Inferring (K–3)
  Interpreting data (4–6)
  Making analogies (4–6)
  Synthesizing (4–6)

Figure 13.2 Processes in the sciencing cycle.

Discrepancy recognition can occur at any time and at any place within the cycle. While some of the processes in the cycle are discovery processes (see Chapter 9), others are inquiry processes. Inquiry processes are more complex mental operations (for example, all of the processes in the *idea using* category); consequently, early grades usually concentrate on discovery skills. By the time children are adolescents, in the process of developing formal thought, they may be ready for the more complex, higher-level inquiry skills.

Safety Guidelines for the Elementary School Classroom

While all teachers must be constantly alert to potential safety hazards for their students, this is sometimes even more important when doing sciencing. Although your school district or state department of education may be able to provide specific guidelines on safety in your school, a list of general guidelines is presented here:

1. Animal pets should not be handled by students. It is probably best that they not be brought into the classroom.
2. Avoid using flammable materials and alcohol burners; use lighted candles only with extreme caution.
3. Be alert to any child who has the potential for an allergic reaction to plants, animal fur, dust, and so on.
4. Be aware of eye safety precautions. Students should wear safety goggles when appropriate.

5. Before using any electrical equipment, inspect the equipment for frayed cords. If frayed, do not use them.
6. Dead animals should never be brought to the classroom (could be diseased).
7. For no reason should blood or any other body fluids be extracted from students in the classroom.
8. For no reason should children ever be left unattended or unsupervised in the classroom. Every child should be within sight of the teacher or another supervising adult.
9. Have a fully charged ABC-type fire extinguisher available in the classroom.
10. Heavy items should not be stored above the heads of the students.
11. Instruct students in proper classroom conduct, especially during science experimentation.
12. Maintain a neat and orderly classroom, with aisles kept clear and books and coats in designated storage areas.
13. Maintain accurate labels on all drawers, cupboards, and containers.
14. Never allow students to climb or to be in potentially dangerous positions.
15. Never overload an electrical circuit. Avoid the use of extension cords.
16. Plants, animals, chemicals, and apparatus that are poisonous or dangerous should not be allowed in the classroom.
17. Sharp objects and those that could shatter when broken should not be in the classroom without teacher approval and proper supervision.
18. Students should never be permitted to taste unknown substances.
19. Students should not be permitted to overheat or to overexert themselves in the name of a scientific experiment.
20. The teacher and the students should know exactly what to do in case of emergency. Emergency procedures should be posted conspicuously in the classroom.
21. Use caution whenever using mechanical equipment with moving parts.
22. Use proper methods for the disposal of waste materials. Contact your school district to learn the local regulations for disposing of various kinds of wastes.
23. When working with molds, mushrooms, or bacteria, students should be provided with face masks.
24. When you take students on a field trip, solicit adult help, even if only for a short distance from the school (see "Field Trips" in Chapter 11). A reasonable ratio is one adult for every ten children.
25. Whenever you have doubt about whether a science activity or experiment is appropriate for a particular grade level, then it probably is not. In any case, when in doubt discuss the idea with other teachers and the school principal.

Resources for Teaching Science

Resources for teaching science are many and varied. Here we include a sampling of resources that are unique, useful, and interesting.

Audubon, National Audubon Society, 130 Fifth Avenue, New York, NY 10028.
Brown, R. J. *333 Science Tricks and Experiments*. Blue Ridge Summit, PA: TAB, 1984.
Carin, Arthur A. *Guided Discovery Activities for Elementary School Science*. 3rd ed. New York: Macmillan, 1993. Provides more than 200 hands-on, minds-on activities for teaching science to children.

Conservation Report, Conservation News, National Wildlife, and *Ranger Rick's Nature Magazine,* National Wildlife Federation, 1412 Sixteenth Street NW, Washington, DC 20036.

Lowery, Lawrence F. *The Everyday Science Sourcebook.* Dale Seymour Publications, P.O. Box 10888, Palo Alto, CA 94303-0879.

Natural History, The American Museum of Natural History, Central Park W. at 79th Street, New York, NY 10024.

Strongin, Herb. *Science on a Shoestring.* Dale Seymour Publications, P.O. Box 10888, Palo Alto, CA 94303-0879.

Victor, Edward, and Kellough, Richard D. *Science for the Elementary School.* 7th ed. New York: Macmillan, 1993. This resource contains more than 750 activities/experiments with at least one activity for each key science concept. It contains comprehensive coverage of elementary school science content, in outline format, under three general headings: earth and the universe, living things, and matter and energy. In addition, each chapter of Part II provides current listings of appropriate books for children and resources for the teacher.

Zoobooks, Wildlife Education, Ltd., 930 West Washington Street, San Diego, CA 92103.

Bibliographies of interest to elementary and middle school science teachers are:

American Association for the Advancement of Science, "The Science Book List for Children," 1515 Massachusetts Avenue, Washington, DC 20005.

Science and Children, 1742 Connecticut Avenue NW, Washington, DC 20009. A bibliography of outstanding science books for children is published annually in the March issue.

Sample Programs for Teaching Science

For Grades K–2:
Scholastic Science Place (Scholastic, Inc./IPG).

For Grades 3–6:
Britannica Science System (Encyclopaedia Britannica).
Full Option Science Study (Lawrence Hall of Science).

For Grades K–6:
Insights Elementary Science Curriculum (Educational Development Center, Inc.).
Discover the Wonder (Scott, Foresman and Company).

For Grades K–8:
Macmillan/McGraw-Hill Science.

For Grades 6–8:
Prentice-Hall Science Learning System.

For Grade 7:
Science 2000 (Decision Development Corporation).

For Grades 7–8:
Science Plus, Technology and Society (Holt, Rinehart, and Winston, Inc.).

D. INSTRUCTIONAL GUIDELINES FOR TEACHING SOCIAL SCIENCE

Realizing that the children we teach today will be the citizens of the twenty-first century, we want them to have the knowledge and understanding to function within their rights and responsibilities as citizens now and in the future. Knowledge of the social sciences will help prepare them for responsible citizenship. The social sciences include anthropology, economics, geography, history, humanities, political science, psychology, and sociology. With the knowledge acquired from studying these disciplines, our students will be better able to understand our nation's economy, history, ideals, institutions, values, and relations with other nations of the world. Based on a recent state framework in history–social science, the information that follows represents selected instructional guidelines and presents one approach to the teaching of social science: an approach in which history is the center of the study.[65]

1. History can include the political, economic, and social arrangements of a society as well as its beliefs, religions, culture, arts, architecture, law, literature, sciences, and technology. Given this scope, history can become the structure that guides lessons in social sciences.

2. The chronological study of history can become a well-told story and a central focus in the classroom with the use of literature of and about the period being explored. For example, primary-grade children can read, hear, and discuss biographies, myths, fairy tales, and historical stories to understand how the world came to be as it is.

3. Major historical events and time periods can be studied, in an integrated and correlated approach, with language arts, science, and the visual and performing arts.

4. The sequential development of instruction can proceed chronologically through the grades, and a time period in each subsequent grade devoted to a review of previously studied chronological periods.

5. The experiences of many different cultural groups in the United States should be integrated into every grade. Students can become aware of their individual responsibilities and behaviors in society, consider each person's role in its governance, and look at the place of law in society. Good citizenship (civic and democratic values) is encouraged through selecting class leaders, resolving disputes, sportsmanship, fair play, sharing, cooperating, taking turns, and other activities.

6. The fundamental principles in the Constitution of the United States and the Bill of Rights should be studied and discussed. Controversial issues and the role of religion should be presented accurately and within context.

7. Critical, creative, and rational thinking skills may be taught through a variety of content-appropriate methods and materials. Skills include recognizing conclusions based on solid evidence and recognizing illogical thinking, propaganda, and stereotyping, and may be taught with content on laser discs, computer software, and videocassettes that engage students in active learning through cooperative learning groups, debates, drama activities, simulations, and writing.

8. Opportunities for students can be provided so that they may "give something back to their community" and develop a commitment to public service, linking their schools and other community agencies. According to a recent study, six of every

[65]California State Department of Education, *History—Social Science Framework for California Public Schools Kindergarten Through Grade Twelve* (Sacramento, CA: State Department of Education, 1987).

ten United States adolescents between the ages of 12 and 17 participated in at least one volunteer activity in 1991, and the number of young volunteers has been rising about 3 percent per year. About 80 percent of the teen volunteers said that their schools and teachers were the source of their inspiration to join a community activity.[66]

Why Do We Teach Social Sciences in the Elementary School?

Our society needs women and men who understand our political institutions and who will assume the responsibilities of citizenship. Our students can inherit the legacy of our history, our interdependent world, and the common human qualities that make people interdependent. By studying history, students may gain an understanding of individual and social ethics—how people in other times have resolved fundamental questions of justice, personal responsibility, and truth—and then consider how we deal with these issues today. By examining the ideas of others, students can consider the ways in which people have struggled with ethical issues in the past and the consequences we face in the present.

What Skills in Social Sciences Do I Need?

As an elementary school teacher of social sciences you need the following skills:

1. *Ability to develop students' cultural literacy.* This can be done by providing opportunities for students to appreciate the cultures of members of ethnic groups, their economy, educational systems, architecture, literature, technology, and performing arts.
2. *Ability to develop students' ethical literacy.* This can be done by providing opportunities within the curriculum to explore human rights and by examining ways societies have resolved ethical issues. You can show the connection between people's ideas and their actions. You can lead discussions about the universal concern for ethics and human rights.
3. *Ability to develop students' literacy in history and other disciplines of social sciences.* This can be done by giving the students a sense of what it was like to live in a particular time period. You can define a relationship of time and chronology. You can analyze a cause and its effect. You can present reasons for change caused by major events.
4. *Ability to develop students' sociopolitical literacy.* With your students, examine relationships between social and political systems, society and the law, a democratic political system and a nondemocratic system. You can prepare students for a national identity that is pluralistic and multicultural by:
    a. Working toward equity and freedom in the classroom.
    b. Helping students to recognize ways in which minorities, women, and the developmentally different were treated historically.
    c. Demonstrating your own appreciation for newcomers from Asia, the Pacific Islands, the Azores, Latin America, Russia, and other places, who have newly arrived in the United States.
    d. Allowing participation so that students may develop personal, group, and social skills as they confront issues and write commentaries. Students can read origi-

[66]Jim Sanders, *Sacramento Bee* (Sacramento, California, December 3, 1992), pp. A1 and A26.

nal documents and interpret language and meaning, write about events in history and relate them to everyday life. They can define and clarify problems, judge information, suggest resolutions to problems, and draw conclusions.

e. Encouraging use of primary and secondary sources. Students can locate, select, and organize information from written sources. They can analyze information with computers and other media. They can read and interpret maps, globes, models, diagrams, graphs, charts, tables, pictures, and political cartoons. They can organize ideas and express themselves clearly in writing and speaking.

f. Presenting the basic principles of democracy, our nation's constitutional concepts of representative government, separation of powers, and trial by judge or jury. You can demonstrate the responsibilities of a citizen in a democracy—a citizen who is responsible for his or her own ethical behavior.

Selected Resources for Teaching Social Sciences

For Kindergarten:

Learning and Working Now and Long Ago. You may introduce folk literature, nursery rhymes, and stories that show conflicts and values and that help the children to build an awareness of cultural diversity and sensitivity toward others, and to develop a sense of historical empathy. As a resource, you may want to review *Developing Mul-*

Literature-based instruction focuses on literature study and the use of children's literature in the classroom.

ticultural Concepts Through Children's Literature: A Guide for Teachers and Librarians, K–8 (Jefferson, NC: MacFarland, 1992) by Nancy Lee Cecil and Patricia L. Roberts. This book suggests children's stories and includes target activities to accompany the stories.

For Grade 1:

A Child's Place in Time and Space. Young children will continue to develop an awareness of cultural diversity and sensitivity toward others. The girls and boys may listen to fairy tales, folktales, American Indian tales, and stories set in different regions of the United States and other countries. For example, see *City Kids of China,* by Peggy Thomson with photos by Paul Conklin (New York: Harper Collins, 1991).

For Grade 2:

People Who Make a Difference. Children can develop an appreciation of the many people who make a difference, who supply the daily needs of others, and who help make our world a better place. A resource for this topic is *Developing Resiliency Through Children's Literature: A Guide for Teachers and Librarians, K–8* (Jefferson, NC: Mac-Farland, 1992) by Nancy Lee Cecil and Patricia L. Roberts. The resource reviews the research on traits of resiliency in children and suggests children's books in which the major characters demonstrate the resilient traits.

For Grade 3:

Continuity and Change. Students can consider extraordinary people in our nation's history through biographies, stories, folktales, and legends. They can become familiar with features and landforms of their region, build a model terrain, or construct a history of the place where they live today. They can review authentic presentations of American Indians who live in the region and organize a sequence of events in history with time lines and illustrations. They can interview senior citizens and find artifacts and photos of their region in early days. They can compare the past to changes of today and identify immediate issues. They can listen to legends, folktales, tall tales, and hero stories of their community and nation. They can consider some of the stories of our nation's history:

Haley, Gail E. *Jack Jouett's Ride* (New York: Viking Penguin, 1973). The story of Jack Jouett, who warned patriots that the British were coming during the Revolutionary War.

Hancock, Sibly. *Old Blue.* Illustrated by Erick Ingraham (New York: Putnam, 1980). Historical information about a lead steer on a trail drive.

Keats, Ezra Jack. *John Henry: An American Legend* (New York: Knopf, 1987). A tall tale about a baby who grew up to be a steel-driving man.

Lasky, Kathryn. *Beyond the Divide* (New York: Macmillan, 1983). A girl accompanies her father across the continent.

Monjo, F. N. *The Drinking Gourd.* Illustrated by Fred Brenner (New York: Harper & Row, 1970). Historical story about the underground railroad.

Sandin, Joan. *The Long Way to a New Land* (New York: Harper & Row, 1981). A Swedish family emigrates to America in 1868.

Speare, Elizabeth George. *The Sign of the Beaver* (Boston, MA: Houghton Mifflin, 1983). A boy survives in a frontier cabin after an Indian friend teaches him survival techniques.

Tome, Philip. *Pioneer Life: Or Thirty Years a Hunter* (Salem, NH: Ayer, 1989). A story of early settler hunting in Pennsylvania. Frontier history including the dangers faced by settlers.

Wilder, Laura Ingalls. *Little House on the Prairie.* Illustrated by Garth Williams (New York: Harper & Row, 1961). The Ingalls move to Kansas.

For Grade 4:

Our State, A Changing State. Students can learn about the physical setting of their state, early settlements and people, exploration and colonial history, migrations and statehood, periods of rapid population growth, linkage to the rest of the United States, and the modern state and its immigration, technology, and cities. For instance, students can be guided to the books on the following topics:

Early settlements: Discuss the Mayflower by reviewing the full-color cardboard parts—fo'c'sle, main deck, half deck, rudder, masts, sails, and more—with the model in A. G. Smith's *Cut and Assemble the "Mayflower": A Full-Color Model of the Reconstruction at Plymouth Plantation* (Mineola, NY: Dover, 1981). With permission from the publisher to reprint published illustrations on an overhead transparency, a teacher will have black-and-white line drawings with accurate details to back up a discussion of colonial America. See Tom Tierney's *American Family of the Pilgrim Period Paper Dolls in Full Color* (Mineola, NY: Dover, 1982) for an informative text and characters in authentic busks, jerkins, shifts, capes. Review Peter F. Copeland's *Story of the American Revolution Coloring Book* (Mineola, NY: Dover, 1988), with scenes of Paul Revere's ride, Nathan Hale, the Boston Massacre, and others; Copeland's *Early American Trades Coloring Book* (Mineola, NY: Dover, 1988) with scenes of wigmakers, glassblowers, hatters, and other colonial craftsmen, tools, and products; or Copeland's *Everyday Dresses of the American Colonial Period Coloring Book* (Mineola, NY: Dover, 1987) with scenes of farmer, broom seller, wagoner, sailor, and so on.

Colonial history: For authentic detail, see Tom Tierney's *American Family of the Colonial Era Paper Dolls in Full Color* (Mineola, NY: Dover, 1985) with a family of eight in period costumes and researched text.

Our modern state: See Renata Von Tscharner and Ronald Fleming, *New Providence: A Changing Cityscape.* Illustrated by Denis Orloff (San Diego, CA: Harcourt Brace Jovanovich, 1987). This is a look at the development of the downtown area in a fictitious city between 1910 and 1987. American history is revealed through vehicles, architecture, storefronts, and other artifacts. One building is a dry goods store in 1910, a pharmacy in 1955, and a computer store in 1987. Students may collect family photographs (with permission), old maps, and old newspapers to show how history has been recorded over the years in the development of their cities.

For Grade 5:

United States History and Geography: Making a New Nation. Students can learn about the land and people before Columbus, the age of exploration, settling the colonies, the War for Independence, life in the young republic, linking past to present, and people then and now. Students may want to read the following:

Before Columbus: A. G. Smith's *Story of the Viking* coloring book (Mineola, NY: Dover, 1989) has more than 30 detailed illustrations of Viking explorations, raids, ship construction, art, literature, and weapons.

Age of explorers: Carol Greene's, *Christopher Columbus: A Great Explorer* (Chicago, IL: Childrens, 1989). Portrays Columbus as a determined seaman; one of the few texts that discuss Columbus as one who committed some inhumane acts when dealing with his crew and the inhabitants of the islands he landed on. Peter F. Copeland's *Columbus Discovers America* coloring book (Mineola, NY: Dover, 1989) has 41 drawings with captions, showing Columbus with Spanish monarchs, shipboard life, storms at sea, and arrival in the new world.

The colonies: Tom Tierney's *American Family of the Colonial Era Paper Dolls* (Mineola, NY: Dover, 1989) has figures, costumes, and historical background to serve as models for original drawings, friezes, and wall murals.

The War for Independence: See Tom Tierney's *George Washington and His Family Paper Dolls in Full Color* (Mineola, NY: Dover, 1980) to present the figures of Martha, George, and the four Custis grandchildren. Clothing includes black velvet suits and embroidered waistcoats.

Life in the young republic: Review Tom Tierney's *American Family of the Early Republic in Full Color* (Mineola, NY: Dover, 1988) and nine figures with period costumes including cutaways, gingham dresses, pantaloons, and more.

Linking past to present, people then and now: See Patricia L. Gauch, *Thunder at Gettysburg.* Illustrated by Stephen Gammell (New York: Putnam, 1990). Experiences of one person drawn into the battle at Gettysburg.

For Grade 6:

World History and Geography: Ancient Civilizations. Students can learn about early human societies and their development, beginnings of civilization in the Near East and Africa, the foundation of Western ideas, ancient Hebrews and Greeks, West meets East, early civilizations of India and China, East meets West, and Rome.

The following are resources for information on ancient Egypt: *Ancient Egypt* (San Diego, CA: Harcourt Brace Jovanovich, 1989), written by George Hart and illustrated by Stephen Biesty. Through full-color illustrations, historical information, and clear captions, this book covers the time of the building of the great pyramids (2615–2344 B.C.), the rule of King Amenemhet (1991–1962 B.C.), and the rule of King Tut (1361–1352 B.C.). Learn to write hieroglyphics with Stephane Rossini's *Egyptian Hieroglyphics: How to Read and Write Them* (Mineola, NY: Dover, 1989). It has figurative signs and more than 100 key phonetic elements with easy-to-follow instruction. Review *Life in Ancient Egypt Coloring Book* (Mineola, NY: Dover, 1989) illustrations by John Green and text by Stanley Appelbaum. Tells of monuments, art, crafts, Ramses II, and Cleopatra. Consider Ed Sibbett, Jr.'s *Ancient Egyptian Design Coloring Book* (Dover, 1980) to see designs from the eighteenth to the twentieth dynasty. Review the pyramids with charts, tales, photos, and diagrams in J. P. Lepte's *The Egyptian Pyramids: A Comprehensive Illustrated Reference* (Jefferson, NC: MacFarland, 1990).

For Grade 7:

World History and Geography: Medieval and Early Modern Times. Students can learn about connecting with past learnings, the remote past and the fall of Rome, the growth of Islam, African states in the Middle Ages and in early modern times, civilizations of the Americas, China, Japan, medieval societies, Europe and Japan, Europe during the Renaissance, the Reformation, and the scientific revolution, early modern Europe, the age of exploration, the Enlightenment, and linking past to present. Useful resources include the following:

African states in the Middle Ages and early modern times: See John Green's *Life in Ancient Egypt Coloring Book* (Mineola, NY: Dover, 1989) for drawings of monuments, arts and crafts, Ramses II. Ed Sibbett, Jr.'s *Ancient Egyptian Design Coloring Book* (Mineola, NY: Dover, 1989) has authentic pictures based on designs from the eighteenth to the twentieth dynasty. Glossary and captions are included.

Civilizations of the Americas: Consider Matthew Kalmenoff's *Maya Dioramas to Cut and Assemble* (Mineola, NY: Dover, 1989) to show full-color 3-D scenes of Chichen Itza and Tulum with temples, plaza, inhabitants, traders, marketplace, and more.

Civilizations of Japan: See Ming-ju Sun's *Japanese Kimono Paper Dolls in Full Color* (Mineola, NY: Dover, 1986) for examples of Japanese tradition, culture, and art, and the use of floral, geometric, bird, and animal designs.

Medieval societies of Europe and Japan: Review an introduction to European culture in Kathy Albert's *Traditional Folk Costumes of Europe: Paper Dolls in Full Color* (Mineola, NY: Dover, 1983) and see representative figures from Denmark, Poland, Greece, Romania, and other European countries.

Linking past to the present: The Middle Ages (San Diego, CA: Harcourt Brace Jovanovich, 1989) by Catherine Oakes, illustrated by Stephen Biesty, offers the rule of Attila the Hun (445–453), the rule of Charlemagne (768–814), the Magna Carta (1215), the Black Death (1348–1351), and the discovery of America by Columbus (1492).

For Grade 8:

United States History and Geography: Growth and Conflict. Students can learn about connecting with past learnings, our colonial heritage and a new nation, the Constitution of the United States, launching the ship of state, the divergent paths of the American people: 1800–1850, efforts toward a more perfect union: 1850–1879, the rise of industrial America: 1877–1914, and linking past to present.

Tom Tierney's *American Family of the Civil War Era Paper Doll Set* (Mineola, NY: Dover, 1989) has figures, costumes, and historical information to use as models for original illustrations, murals, and friezes.

For grades 5–8, biographies help a student to link the importance of what has been done in the past to our present day. James Bentley's *Albert Schweitzer* (Milwaukee: Gareth Stevens, 1989) and Pam Brown's *Florence Nightingale* (Milwaukee: Gareth Stevens, 1989) both show the achievements of their subjects. See Julia Courtney's *Sir Peter Scott* (Milwaukee: Gareth Stevens, 1989); Michael Nicholson and David Winner's *Raoul Wallenberg* (Milwaukee: Gareth Stevens, 1989) tells of this man's heroism in opposing the cruelty and power of the Nazi forces in Hungary; David Winner's *Desmond Tutu* (Milwaukee: Gareth Stevens, 1989) tells of the physical and emotional toll of apartheid on the people of South Africa. Figures of famous American women and informational notes are presented in Tom Tierney's *Notable American Women Paper Dolls in Full Color* (Mineola, NY: Dover, 1989) and include Mary Cassatt, Jane Addams, Willa Cather, Margaret Mead, Georgia O'Keefe, Lorraine Hansberry, Babe Didrikson Zaharias, and others.

Additional Resources for Teaching Social Sciences

The following are additional resources for teaching social studies in the elementary school classroom.

For Primary Grades:

I Remember Martin Luther King Jr. (Michael Brent, 1986). Cassettes, workbooks, and guide tell King's life through a play accompanied by American black spirituals. Includes musical history and resources for rehearsal and performance; *Indians of America Read Alongs* (Mahwah, NJ: Troll, 1986). Cassettes, paperbacks, and spirit masters about Indian crafts, Indian homes, Indian festivals, Indians of eastern woodlands, Indians of the plains, and Indians of the West.

For Intermediate Grades:

Abraham Lincoln in Song and Story (Eliza Records, 3304 Rittenhouse Street NW, Washington, DC 20015). Cassette includes songs, poetry, and stories to portray Lincoln's life—a way of incorporating music with history for an integrated program; *Indian Legacy* (January Productions, 210 South Avenue, P.O. Box 66, Hawthorne, NJ 07507). Videos and guide, showing the diverse cultural heritage of the American Indian; *Proud to Be Hispanic* (Nystrom/Eyegate). Filmstrip/cassettes include various topics: "Cultural Awareness," "Early Hispanic Americans," and "Hispanic Americans Today."

E. INSTRUCTIONAL GUIDELINES FOR TEACHING ART AND MUSIC

The purposes for teaching elementary school art and music are:

1. Through dance and visual arts, a student can develop aesthetic perceptions and values, creative expression, and a knowledge of historical and cultural heritage.
2. Through drama, a student can experience actions and characterizations, develop skills in storytelling, play making, and play writing.
3. Through music, a student can develop sensitivity to the qualities of music, understand its nature and structure, develop musical skills in singing and in playing instruments. The student becomes aware of styles, idioms, performance media, and purposes of music that are part of our multicultural heritage.
4. Through the study of works of art from various world cultural groups, a student can develop an understanding of the role of visual arts in communicating the beliefs, desires, hopes, rituals, and values of a group of people.
5. Through interdisciplinary relationships, the arts, visual arts, music, dance, and drama can be organized around a topic. For example, a student can learn the significance of dances in different cultures, examine drama of various cultures, compare mask making and its uses in various cultures, and study people's language patterns as well as the patterns of their music or rhythms.

Why Do We Teach Art and Music in the Elementary School?

We teach art and music in the elementary school because they provide enrichment and pleasure. Art and music can be used to send and receive information and emotions and are sources of personal accomplishment and pride. Art and music stimulate thinking and provide a cultural record. As part of a cultural record, the components to consider are dance, drama, and the visual arts. These components have aesthetic, perceptual, creative, and intellectual dimensions for students and can be related to other curriculum areas—language arts, science, mathematics, and social sciences—to make studies of these areas more interesting and meaningful. Art and music, and their various components, foster students' abilities to create, experience, analyze, and reorganize, and encourage intuitive, emotional, and verbal responses from students.

What Skills in Art and Music Do I Need?

As a teacher, you will want to develop knowledge and skills in the following areas:

Art

1. *Assisting students in recognizing selected works of art.*

2. *Assisting students in understanding artists' use of color and line in creating works of art.* Sample activity: To further understand the use of color and line by selected artists in creating their powerful paintings, the students engage in the following:

a. *Note ways colors are used:* Students in a second grade class are shown *The ABC Exhibit* (New York: Macmillan, 1991), by Leonard Everett Fisher. The children are asked to look closely at the illustrations for "Kite" and "Lightning." They are asked to tell which illustration is the night scene. Call attention to the use of colors. Have students place objects from the room in light and in shade to discover how the colors change. Then, based on their observations about color, ask students who chose the painting of the lightning as the night scene to support their selection based on what they have observed.

b. *Note ways horizontal lines are used:* Show students "Hat" and ask them to comment on the appearance of the hats and respond to the question, "Why do the brims look so long?" Point out the use of horizontal lines in the painting. Also draw attention to the extension of the people close to the edge of the painting.

c. Show students "Sailboat" and ask them to comment on the size and the movement of the large boat. Invite students to discuss: "What does the artist tell us about the movement of the huge sail?" "Is it moving quickly or slowly?" "What makes you think so?" "Is it a large sailboat?" "How did the artist make it look so large?" "What did he do to make it look as though it is moving?" Draw attention to the proportion of the sailboat to the total painting. Help the students observe the use of horizontal lines in the horizon, the sky and clouds, and the waves.

d. Remind students of use of horizontal lines, proportion, and use of colors as they draw, paint, and create original artworks such as murals and collage compositions.

3. *Assisting students in developing a knowledge of art history.* Sample activity for grades 2–6: For a further emphasis on the elements of art with explanations of how paintings, sculptures, prints, and drawings are made, students may react to the *Art for Children* series (Philadelphia: Lippincott, 1990) by Ernest Raboff. To discuss works of great artists, students may read *Getting to Know the World's Greatest Artists* series (Chicago: Childrens, 1989) by Mike Venezia. Through this series, students get acquainted with such artists as da Vinci, Picasso, and Rembrandt. The Art Play series (New York: Abrams) offers single-book versions focusing on a single painting or artwork. This series includes *Kandinsky: Sky Blue* (New York: Abrams, 1990) by Max-Henri de Larminat, *Picasso: The Minotaur* (New York: Abrams, 1988) by Daniele Giraudy, and *Delaunay: The Eiffel Tower* (New York: Abrams, 1988).

4. *Assisting students in exploring the characteristics of an artist.* Sample activity: To explore the characteristics of an artist, students, grades 5–6, may listen to excerpts from *Looking at Beasties* (Chicago: Childrens, 1977) by J. Behrens or from *Just Imagine: Ideas in Painting* (New York: Scribner's, 1982) by R. Commings. Girls and boys may view *The Magic Gallery* (EVI) to explore the characteristics of the artist and, later, create art objects in that genre (grades 2–6).

5. *Encouraging students to write scripts, compose music, design sets, and produce artistic productions.* Sample activities for grades 1–3: To see one way a country's customs, costumes, music, and dance come together in an artistic work, invite the students in the primary grades to review a video, *Billy Goat's Bluff* (Beacon Films, 1989). With voices of Vesnyvka Girls Choir adding to the presentation, this Ukranian folktale begins when a father agrees to purchase a frisky goat, Ivan, for son Peter. Ivan is ill-mannered and runs away to Sister Fox's house when faced with punishment. Hungry, Ivan goggles Easter treats and creates havoc in the house. Returning, Sister Fox turns to other animals for help. They want to punish Ivan, but Peter arrives in time to plead for Ivan, using an Easter theme for forgiveness.

6. *Introducing students to symbolic language of dance movements.* Sample activities for grades 3–8: Invite students to see a video, *Songs and Dances of the Nisqually* (Diogenes Foundation), and discuss the explanation of symbolic language in each dance movement shown in a powwow held by the Nisqually.

7. *Encouraging students to identify a good display and to plan an overall design for a classroom bulletin board.* Sample activity: After seeing a video, *Creative Bulletin Boards* (American School Publications), ask students to discuss ways to identify a good display, and plan an overall design by selecting colors and shapes and preparing artwork related to their study. (See also "The Bulletin Board" in Section C, Chapter 12.)

8. *Encouraging students to transfer their knowledge of design to developing a project to present to the class.* Sample activity for grades 4–6: Invite students to look at illustrations by Arnold Lobel in *Dinosaur Time* (New York: Harper & Row, 1974) by Peggy Parish, and the way some pictures break their frames and go right into text. With examples of ways illustrators show dinosaurs in this book and others, engage students in designing projects such as making an informational diorama of a scene with a selected animal whose background has been researched, writing about and drawing a favorite animal, illustrating an original booklet to show their observations, and dramatizing certain events in an animal's life.

9. *Assisting students to understand ways in which artists have been influenced by visual arts and why they became committed to the world of art.* Sample activity for grades 4 and up: Students may select several artists and write to them, inquiring about ways the artists have been influenced by visual arts. To show students how several women artists were influenced by art and became committed to visual art, read aloud excerpts from *Inspirations: Stories About Women Artists* by Leslie Sills (Morton Grove, IL: Albert Whitman, 1989). Artists include Georgia O'Keefe, Freda Kahlo, Alice Neel, Faith Ringold, and others. A biography series, *American Women of Achievement* (New York: Chelsea, 1989), focuses on women whose actions and ideas were crucial in shaping United States history; several are artists: Mary Cassatt, Georgia O'Keefe, Grandma Moses, Louise Nevelson, and Margaret Bourke-White.

10. *Assisting students in recognizing some techniques used by artists.* Sample activity for grade 3 and up: To discuss examples, show students the black-and-white illustrations of the styles of 19 different masters in *Famous Old Masters of Painting* (New York: Dodd, 1951) by Roland McKiney. To focus on one artist, read to students *Meet Edgar Degas* (Philadelphia: Lippincott, 1989) by Anne Newlands, or *Linnea in Monet's Garden* (Old Tappan, NJ: Simon & Schuster, 1987) by Christiana Bjork and Lena Anderson. Reproductions of Monet's paintings are found in Bjork and Anderson's book, and Newland's book includes letters, notebooks, and other materials selected by Degas, discusses his allegorical works of the 1850s, and shows his later scenes of Paris life.

Music

1. *Assisting students in developing theme recognition skills in music.* Sample activity for grades 4–6: After listening to one of the videos in *Adventures in Listening Series* (Merit Audio Visual), entitled *Debussy, Danse Macabre,* or *Peter and the Wolf,* ask the students to discuss the theme in the musical composition. With available rhythm instruments, engage students in working together to compose a brief rhythmic selection and then discuss with others how they tried to keep to their theme.

2. *Assisting students in becoming aware of musical elements.* Sample activities: To become aware of musical elements such as rhythm, melody, harmony, and interpretation, students (grades K–2) may engage in learning about pitch, rhythm, movement, and interpretation by using instruments improvised from pencils and paper towel rolls after hearing *Making Musical Things* (New York: Scribners, 1979) by A. Wiseman or *Musical Adventures* (Musical Munchkins). To further explore these elements, students (grades 4–6) also may observe a video series, *Elements of Music* (SIRS), to become aware of musical elements through analogies between space exploration and music, in regard to rhythm, melody, form, tone color, interpretation, harmony, and dynamics.

3. *Introducing students to different musical instruments.* Sample activity for grades K–2: Introduce musical instruments to students with the video *Peter Ustinov Reads the Orchestra* (Mark Rudin Productions/Alcazar).

4. *Introducing students to information through songs.* Sample activity for all grades: Invite students to begin the school day by singing the message in the "World Pledge Song" from *Barley and Reindeer Milk* (People Records). "World Pledge Song" is based on Peter Spier's book *People* and has a message of caring for earth, sea, and air with peace and justice everywhere.

5. *Developing awareness of people's rhythmic patterns of language and music.* Sample activity for grades 2–5: Invite students to participate in a call-and-answer technique of choral conversations with cassettes in *Beats: Conversations in Rhythm for English as a Second Language* (Educational Activities).

6. *Helping students understand ways in which heritage brings cultural and musical influences to compositions.* Sample activity for grades 5 and up: Invite students to learn of composer Alexina Louie's desire to convey her inner spirit through her work in the video *The Eternal Earth* (Rhombus Media/Bullfrog Films, 1987). From Vancouver's Chinatown, Alexina Louie expresses her East-West sensitivities and integrates traditional Chinese instruments and themes into her symphony about the earth. Alternating between scenes of a street celebration in Chinatown and the Toronto symphony performing her work, Louie intersperses comments and shows her methods of musical notation with use of a ruler and a French curve.

Additional Resources for Teaching Art and Music

Family Folk Festival: A Multicultural Sing-Along (Music for Little People, 1990). Introduces songs by Claudia Gomez, Taj Mahal, and others.

Sing Along with Rosenshontz: Quiet Time (New York: Random House, 1990). Cassette with paperback. Folk music harmony and original music with songs "My Security Blanket," "Going Fishin'," and "It's OK" (nighttime fears). For pre-first grade.

Cole, Joanna, and Calmenson, Stephanie. *The Eentsy, Weentsy, Spider: Finger Plays and Action Rhymes.* Illustrated by Alan Tiegreen (New York: Morrow, 1991). Collection of 38 finger plays with easy-to-follow directions and rhymes that includes "I'm a Little Teapot" and "Two Fat Gentlemen." Musical arrangements are included for some. Black and white drawings. Gives index of first lines and other sources. For preschool to grade 2.

F. INSTRUCTIONAL GUIDELINES FOR TEACHING PHYSICAL EDUCATION

Why Do We Teach Physical Education in the Elementary School?

For each of their school years, girls and boys need a planned program of physical education. Physical education is an integral part of education which contributes to the development of the individual through planned movement or physical activity or exercise. The development of the individual may be centered on the following: (1) *motor skills goal*—to develop efficient and effective motor skills (e.g., dance in the arts curriculum); (2) *physical fitness goal*—to develop and maintain the best possible level of performance, understanding, and appreciation for the importance of physical fitness; (3) *self-image goal*—to develop a positive self-image, which includes awareness and understanding of the performance of one's body; (4) *social behavior goal*—to develop socially desirable behavior in interactions with others; and (5) *recreational interest goal*—

Physical education is an integral part of elementary school education that contributes to the development of the child through planned movement and exercise.

to develop interest and proficiency in using skills essential for successful physical recreational activities.

What Skills in Physical Education Do I Need?

Considering the students and their ages, developmental patterns, and needs, specific kinds of physical activities will be recommended by your own state's curriculum framework for physical education for elementary school children, or by your district's curriculum guide. From one state's framework, highlights of programs for students are reviewed here.[67]

The teacher of physical education in the elementary and middle school should have the ability to plan a daily program that provides for each student opportunities to participate with varying degrees of vigor for short periods of time. There should be a variety of physical activities and alternating periods of rest and relaxation. Parent, student, and medical needs should be considered.

For Kindergarten and Grade 1:

The teacher in kindergarten and grade 1 needs the skills and the ability to:

1. Demonstrate balanced posture in sitting, standing, and moving.
2. Demonstrate gross motor (start-and-stop games), fine motor (batting a ball), eye-body (jumping rope), eye-hand (passing-the-object games), and eye-foot (hopscotch) coordination.
3. Demonstrate bilateral motor development (bear walk) and spatial awareness (walking or running to show shapes of square, circle, or line).
4. Demonstrate solving problems through movement. (How can I move faster or slower?)
5. Develop appreciation of the worth of others (group decision making for rules).
6. Develop leadership and responsibility in self-directing activities (students assume responsibility for care and use of equipment).

For Grades 2 and 3:

The teacher of physical education in grades 2 and 3 needs the skills and the ability to:

1. Demonstrate balanced posture in sitting, standing, and moving.
2. Demonstrate gross motor (start-and-stop games), fine motor (batting a ball), eye-body (jumping rope), eye-hand (passing-the-object games), and eye-foot (hopscotch) coordination.
3. Demonstrate bilateral motor development (bear walk) and spatial awareness (walking or running to show shapes of square, circle, or line).
4. Demonstrate solving problems through movement. (How can I move faster or slower?)
5. Develop appreciation of the worth of others (group decision making for rules).
6. Develop leadership and responsibility in self-directing activities (students assume responsibility for care and use of equipment).

[67]Adapted from the *Physical Education Framework* (Sacramento: California State Department of Education, 1973), pp. 12–24.

For Grade 4:

The teacher of grade 4 needs the skills and the ability to:

1. Demonstrate gross motor (stunts on balance beam), fine motor (playing four-square), eye-body (jumping rope), eye-hand (hitting, throwing, and catching balls), and eye-foot (dancing folk dances) coordination.
2. Organize activities so that students can develop leadership and self-direction (leading a game activity).
3. Develop appreciation of the worth of others (accepting majority decisions).
4. Develop a group feeling in competition activities (team dodge ball).
5. Provide opportunities for each student to develop a positive self-image (each demonstrates or explains a skill or technique that will benefit a group activity.)

For Grade 5–Middle School:

The teacher of grade 5 and up (through middle school) needs the skills and the ability to:

1. Demonstrate gross motor (jumping rope to music), fine motor (bowling), eye-body (soccer), eye-hand (horseshoes), and eye-foot (kick football) coordination.
2. Organize activities that allow for individual differences (game variety for two, four, or more players).
3. Develop appreciation of the worth of others (accepting majority decisions).
4. Provide opportunities for each student to develop a positive self-image (each demonstrates or explains a skill or technique that will benefit a group activity).
5. Provide opportunities for students to think critically (evaluate team plays).
6. Provide opportunities for students to experiment with ideas and to solve problems (create a dance).
7. Provide opportunities that encourage student self-direction, independence, and achievement (each is leader of a team or group).
8. Provide opportunities for acceptable social behavior (demonstrating meaning of team spirit and cooperative sharing of equipment and play areas).

The teacher plans a daily program that provides opportunities for each student to participate in activities that require varying degrees of vigor and strength and that have periods of rest and relaxation. The teacher may want to plan a program for the entire school year, considering the availability of equipment, the weather, indoor and outdoor facilities, and the units of study in other curriculum areas. Dramatic play, guided play, and rhythmical activities have elements in common with social studies, music, and other areas. If desired, physical education activities can follow a social science topic of study. For instance, if young students are studying an American Indian community and view a film about Indian life, they may want to demonstrate some of the ways Indians planted corn and pantomime motions seen in the film (rhythmic activities). The motions could be accompanied by beats of a drum and incorporated into a creative dance in slow motion. Later, research on Indian life may provide examples of the games Indians played, which students can recreate.

As another example, students studying about Mexico may plan a Mexican celebration activity. Girls and boys learn the words to a selected song and dance the steps of a favorite dance. Rhythm instruments can accompany the song and dance. Singing games and dances may be learned and integrated into a music period.

One teacher suggests using sports to involve all students in reading, writing, speaking, and listening.[68] Suggestions include drawing sports scenes, writing short stories, poems, or plays about a favorite sport, and reading quality sports stories. Students may enjoy beginning a class scrapbook about sports, demonstrating techniques of sports they like, or writing to professional athletes. Reading the sports page of the newspaper may be included for current events; creating original jump rope chants may take place indoors on a rainy day in preparation for fair weather; and discussing baseball cards may hold the interest of some. Students may be asked to write about a sport that they do not like, to keep a sports journal or athlete's file, to research the history of a favorite sport or sporting event, or to research one they know little about.

Each day should build on what was taught and learned in an earlier presentation. If a teacher is scheduling a separate physical education period daily (instead of using a three-days-a-week plan), the teacher may want to balance the activities and schedule different types each day. To accomplish this, the teacher should consider scheduling one of the following types of activity each day: apparatus and skill-building activities, rhythmic activities, individual and dyad games, social games for large groups, and relays or team games. In presenting the activities, the teacher will want to act quickly in starting a game, monitor closely for those students who are losing interest and change to a new activity, play with the students, and encourage each to realize his or her contribution to the activity during play.

Your efforts in helping to build a physical education program for your students may be rewarded. For example, two middle school teachers (Judy Hardman and Ken Roberts) created a fitness-based coeducational program that went beyond the traditional instruction in game activities. The key components of their program were physical fitness (including instruction in lifelong fitness), motor skill development, lifetime recreational skills (including an annual snow ski trip for all students), and self-image (promoting a positive self-image through cooperative activities to develop a sense of social responsibility and leadership qualities). In 1988 the teachers' efforts were recognized and they received the Outstanding Middle School Physical Education Program Award by the California Association of Health, Physical Education, Recreation, and Dance (CAHPERD).

Other Related Curriculum Areas

Your state's health instruction framework, if there is one, will be useful since it complements instruction in physical education and other curriculum areas. It may provide information about a state's education code and include sections on instruction. For example, California's *Health Instruction Framework* lists the sections of that state's education code that make recommendations and give requirements in instruction. Among others, the following are selected sections of interest to the elementary school teacher: (1) *Family Life Education*—is recommended and teachers are to receive special training; (2) *Duty Concerning Instruction of Students' Morals, Manners, and Citizenship*—is recommended and teachers are encouraged to instruct students in manners, morals, and principles of free government; (3) *Instruction on Alcohol, Narcotics, and Restricted Dangerous Drugs*—is required; (4) *Courses of Study for Grades 1 through 6*—are mandated and include health instruction; (5) *Excuse from Health Instruction, Family*

[68]Didier Gincig, "Sports and Language Arts: Ideas for Elementary School Teachers," *The California Reader* 22(3):35–37 (March–April, 1989).

Life, and Sex Education, Due to Religious Beliefs—is provided; (6) *Sex Education*—is provided and requires written notification to parents of classes offered, allows for parent review of materials, and allows parents to exclude their children from the instruction; (7) *Personal Beliefs*—are honored and require written permission for administering tests, questionnaires, and surveys about personal beliefs, practices in sex, family life, morality, or religion of students or their families.

Resources for Teaching Physical Education

For any physical education program, supplies and equipment will be needed. At the school, the teacher will be interested in seeing the extent to which the following are available:

For Primary Grades:

Outdoor apparatus (horizontal bars, swings, tether ball set); sandbox and sandbox tools; play equipment (balls for various games, low balance beam, bean bags, jump ropes, tricycles, water-play table, gym mats).

For Grade 4 and Up:

Balls for various games, jump ropes, gym mats, badminton sets, balance beam, tether ball set, checkers, chess, backgammon, rubber horseshoes, hopscotch areas, bowling set, Ping-Pong set, softballs, bats, gloves, masks, and so on.

Additional Resources for Health and Physical Education

A Kid's Guide to Self-Esteem (Irving, TX: Word Inc./Learning Tree, 1992). A book with cartoon-style illustrations that define self-esteem and show why it is important. Grades 1–3.

AIDS by Nigel Hawkes (New York: Glouster Prod/Watts, 1987). A book for grades 5 and up that focuses on AIDS, the research, and some misunderstandings.

Alcohol . . . Drugs . . . and Kids. (Sandler Films/Aims Media, 1988). For grades 4–8, this video addresses the "It can't happen to me" viewpoint as older teens tell of their first experiences with alcohol and drugs and give warnings to viewers.

Be Fair and Take Care (Marshfilm). Filmstrip/cassette about accepting others as they are, valuing friendships, and obeying rules to avoid injury. Grades 1–3.

Building Social Awareness (More Treehouse Series, Part II: Treehouse Communications). Including filmstrips, cassettes and guide, this resource shows real children in real situations making friends, accepting another's point of view, overcoming selfishness, and making peace. See also Part I: *Building Healthy Attitudes*, about self-respect and respect for others. Grades 1–3.

Champion Acrobats of China (VIEW Video, 1992). Two videos show performances of Chinese acrobats and routines dating back to as far as 2500 years ago. Grade 6 and up.

Crack (Educational Activities, 1597 Grand Avenue, Baldwin, NY 11510), 1987. In this video a former addict tells his story, and a teenage girl resists peer pressure to affirm the value of drug-free living. Grade 5 and up.

Drugs and You (Words Inc./Learning Tree, 1983). Topics include the problems of drug use, marijuana, and how to avoid drugs. Five filmstrips/cassettes and guide. Grades 4–8.

Every Dog's Guide to Complete Home Safety (National Film Board of Canada, 1251 Avenue of the Americas, New York, NY 10020), 1987. In this video, Wally, the safety dog, eliminates safety hazards through cartoon illustrations. Grades 1–10.

First Aid with Reddy (Quality Computers, 20200 Nine Mile Road, St. Clair Shores, MI 48080) is a very friendly computer disk (Apple) that uses two characters to teach some first-aid basics. Reddy is a smart character who knows all about first aid, and Mr. Bungle, his friend is always getting into trouble. Primary grades and up.

Drugs (New York: Twenty-first Century Books, 1990), illustrated by David Neuhaus, is a focus series that is factual about drugs. Within the series, look for David Friedman's *Focus on Drugs and the Brain,* which tells how the brain works and how drugs affect it, and about drugs used for medicine and those used for harmful purposes. Catherine O'Neill's *Focus on Alcohol* gives a brief history and tells of alcohol's effects on the body; Robert Perry's *Focus on Nicotine and Caffeine* tells of the effects of these substances on the individual and society; Jeffrey Shukman's *Focus on Cocaine and Crack* states that no amount of cocaine is safe. Paula Kelvan Zeller's *Focus on Marijuana* explains peer pressure and offers techniques to help one say no to drugs. Grades 4–6.

Good Clean Fun (Janet & Judy Records). Cassette includes songs about friends, baseball, and "doing something." Grades K–6.

In Charge: A Complete Handbook for Kids with Working Parents (New York: Knopf, 1983), written by Kathy S. Kyte and illustrated by Susan Detrick. Provides information to help latchkey kids organize their time and tasks and cope with certain crises such as fire, crime, and first aid. Grades 4–8.

Let's Talk About Responsibility (Sunburst Communications, 1988). In this video, four situations give examples of adolescents who show responsible behavior—while babysitting, to an elderly neighbor, to a best friend, and to one's country. Grades 5–9.

Liking Me: Building Self-Esteem (Sunburst, 1986). Students discuss what they can do to like themselves better, and cartoons illustrate low and high self-esteem characteristics. Two filmstrips/cassette and guide. Grades 5–9.

Making Choices (Nystrom/EyeGate, 1988). Topics include accepting responsibility, saying no to drugs, and choosing. Dog characters make the points about refusing drugs. Three filmstrips/cassettes and guide. Grades 1–3.

Me, Myself, and Smoking (Guidance Associates, Box 3000, Mt. Kisco, NY 10549, 1988). A humorous and informative video with Denise and Tom, who present arguments for smoking (that are real to teenagers) as well as the fallacies in the arguments. Grades 5–8.

Nutrition (Benner Productions, 165 Madison Avenue, New York, NY 10016). Topics of these videos include "American Meals" (fast food), "The Consumer and the Supermarket" (shopping for healthy foods), and "You Are What You Eat" (cartoon about what to eat).

Now do Exercise 13.2.

Exercise 13.2: Integrating the Curriculum

Instructions: As discussed or mentioned many times in previous chapters of this resource guide, one way to teach today's students effectively is by integrating the curriculum, rather than by teaching each subject of the curriculum as a separate and unrelated entity. The purpose of this exercise is to plan a thematic unit based on some of what you have learned so far from this guide. Proceed with the following steps.

Step 1. Organize your class into teams of about four members, with each team assigned to one grade level. If there are not enough teams to cover all grades K–6 separately, then teams could be assigned to a combination of grades, e.g., K–1, 2–3, 4–5, 6–7.

Step 2. By brainstorming, either select one instructional and interdisciplinary theme for the entire class, or allow each team to select its own interdisciplinary theme. Your class can make this decision.

Step 3. Using the figure that follows, each team will develop a *content web*. The title of your central theme goes in the center box. Subject content topics related to that theme are to be written in the boxes that represent the individual disciplines of the elementary school curriculum.

Content Web

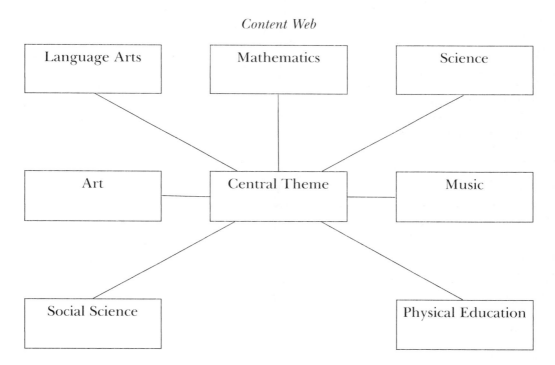

Step 4. Once you have completed your web of content topics related to the central theme, you are ready to develop instructional student-centered activities that will lead to student learning within the content topics—i.e., develop an *activity web*. It is advisable to assign code numbers to each of the content topics of your content web. As activities are identified and written in your activity web, you can assign the content code number to the activity. This helps in the overall organization of your planning.

Activity Web

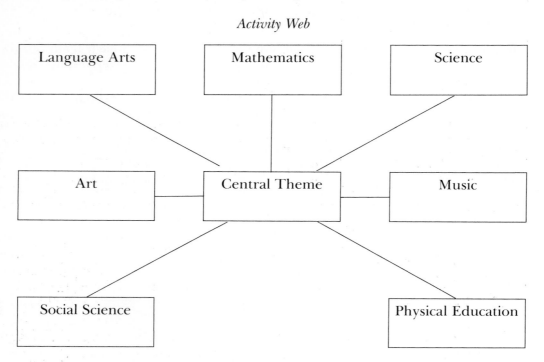

Step 5. You are now ready to sequence the activities and to develop a time line for implementation (refer to Chapter 7).

SUMMARY

Guidelines for teaching in the major areas of the elementary school curriculum have been presented in this chapter in a way that accurately reflects current knowledge of developmental learning and the building of knowledge.

As you know, the guidelines presented here are models and may not exactly represent those you will implement for your school, district, or state.

QUESTIONS FOR CLASS DISCUSSION

1. Consider the following findings. What implications do they hold for your own teaching? In *The Reading Report Card: Progress Toward Excellence in Our Schools* (National Assessment of Educational Progress, 1988), positive trends in education were shown: students, ages 9, 13, and 17, are reading better than in the 1970s; African American and Hispanic students have made sizable improvements in their reading proficiency and have narrowed the gap between minority and majority student performance.

2. In *James Madison Elementary School: A Curriculum for American Students* (Washington, DC: United States Department of Education, 1987), William J. Bennett, former United States secretary of education, provides an extensive list of recommended readings. Considering only a few from the list, express your opinion about the following readings for these grades: For K–3—*The Pied Piper of Hamelin* (Robert Browning), *A Child's Garden of Verses* (Robert Louis Stevenson), and *The Whipping Boy* (Sid Fleischman). For grades 4–6—*Charlie and the Chocolate Factory* (Roald Dahl), *Johnny Tremaine* (Esther Forbes), and *The Merry Adventures of Robin Hood* (Howard Pyle). For grades 7–8—*Alice's Adventures in Wonderland* (Lewis Carroll), *Mutiny on the Bounty* (Charles Nordhoff and J. N. Hall), *The Adventures of Tom Sawyer* (Mark Twain), and *Diary of a Young Girl* (Anne Frank).

3. Censorship often becomes a concern when literature is the base for integrated teaching since there may be attempts to censor books and curricular materials in the schools. You may be interested in reading this brief list of books that have been challenged: *The Adventures of Huckleberry Finn* (Mark Twain), *Deenie* (Judy Blume), *A Light in the Attic* (Shel Silverstein), *Blubber* (Judy Blume), *Go Ask Alice* (Anonymous), *Diary of a Young Girl* (Anne Frank), and *The Chocolate War* (Robert Cormier). Review one of these books and determine how it might be challenged for censorship. Discuss with others in your class.

4. Some researchers have devoted time to studying the effects of reading aloud to children on children's interest in and success with reading. The conclusion: Reading to children makes a difference. In what situations do you plan to read aloud to your students daily in the classroom? What might you say to parents to emphasize the importance of their reading aloud to their children?

5. Elementary school teachers are making greater use of stories and novels in reading programs, and some are asking students to analyze the stories they read. Critics maintain that this will destroy the creativity and spontaneity of children and their pleasure in reading. Do you agree or disagree? Explain.

6. Some children enjoy the poems of Jack Prelutsky because he writes about things they care about (getting into trouble, fights). Prelutsky suggests "doing things"

with a poem, such as adding sound effects, putting a poem to music, reading it dramatically. Poetry collections include *The Random House Book of Poetry* selected by Jack Prelutsky (1983), *All the Colors of the Race* (New York: Lothrop, 1982) by Arnold Adoff with illustrations by John Steptoe, *The Parrot in the Garret and Other Rhymes About Dwellings* (New York: Atheneum, 1982) selected by Lenore Blegvad and illustrated by Erick Blegvad, and *Morning, Noon, and Nighttime, Too* (New York: Harper & Row, 1980) edited by Lee Bennett Hopkins and illustrated by Nancy Hannans. Select a poem and try one of Prelutsky's suggestions. Discuss the results with others in your class.

7. Proponents of integrated language arts (teaching across the curriculum) say integration is needed because classes in the past tended to produce students who could sound out words and memorize facts but were not excited about learning. An integrated approach—using literature as the base—gives students a lifetime interest in literature as they read to learn. With this approach, a story is related to history, geography, social studies, government, current events, and math. A teacher may move from science to social science and back again in a one-hour time period with the students not knowing when the subject changes. However, critics are concerned that without firm scheduling, teachers may not spend the appropriate amount of time on different subjects in the curriculum. What point of view do you support? Explain.

8. What more would you like to know about the teaching of integrated language arts or about interdisciplinary thematic teaching? How might you find the necessary information?

9. Some may believe that boys are better than girls in mathematics because of a sex-linked factor. We stand firm in our belief that there is no sex-linked difference in mathematical ability. We further believe that there is danger to education whenever such difference is hinted at in the media. What do you believe?

10. In *Science Report Card* (National Assessment of Educational Progress, 1989), one finding was a significantly lower level of science achievement among female and minority students. Describe what schools and teachers have done to attempt to correct that situation.

11. What are your views about a history-centered social science program? There are critics who argue against that approach, saying that some strands of information must be suppressed in order to include others, that the priority of topics and the time to be devoted to them has not been determined, and that teachers lack the resources to settle the question of who or what should or should not be included in a history-centered social science program. Explain your viewpoint.

12. In *Cultural Literacy: What Every American Needs to Know*, E. D. Hirsch, Jr., posits that there is a certain base of common background knowledge that people need to know in order to be culturally literate, and that the schools should provide students with this knowledge base. As part of this base and a "national vocabulary of cultural literacy," the book includes an extensive list of nearly 5,000 words, phrases, and names that Hirsch thinks every citizen of this country should know. Hirsch's message has been criticized as being a narrow and test-oriented view. Do you agree or disagree with this criticism?

13. Do you support or not support the idea that elementary schools should provide curriculum specialist teachers in the arts? In physical education? In foreign language? Explain your view.

14. Explain what the following terms have in common: *critical thinking, discovery, inquiry, problem solving, thinking skills.*

15. Do you have questions about the content of this chapter? How might answers be found?

SUGGESTED READINGS FOR CHAPTER 13

Ahlgren, A., and Rutherford, F. J. "Where is Project 2061 Today?" *Educational Leadership* 50(8):19–22 (May 1993).

American Association for the Advancement of Science. *Science for All Americans.* Project 2061. Washington, DC: American Association for the Advancement of Science, 1989.

Baroody, A., and Coslick, R. T. *Problem-Solving, Reasoning, and Communicating, K–8: Helping Children Think Mathematically.* New York: Macmillan, 1993.

Beck, I. L. "Improving Practice Through Understanding Reading." In L. B. Resnick and L. E. Klopfer, eds. *Toward the Thinking Curriculum: Current Cognitive Research.* 1989 ASCD Yearbook. Reston, VA: Association for Supervision and Curriculum Development, 1989.

Chapin, J. R., and Messick, R. G. *Elementary Social Studies: A Practical Guide.* 2nd ed. White Plains, NY: Longman, 1992.

Cobb, P., et al. "Interaction and Learning in Mathematics Classroom Situations." *Educational Studies in Mathematics* 23(1):99–122 (February 1992).

Danielson, K. E. "Literature Groups and Literature Logs: Responding to Literature in a Community of Readers." *Reading Horizons* 32(5):373–382 (June 1992).

Duren, P. E., and Cherrington, A. "The Effects of Cooperative Group Work versus Independent Practice on the Learning of Some Problem-Solving Strategies." *School Science and Mathematics* 92(2):80–83 (February 1992).

Fogarty, R. *How to Integrate the Curriculum.* Palatine, IL: Skylight Publishing, 1991.

Haggerty, D. J., and Wolf, S. E. "Writing in the Middle School Mathematics Classroom." *School Science and Mathematics* 91(6):245–246 (October 1991).

Hill, M. "Writing Summaries Promotes Thinking and Learning Across the Curriculum—But Why Are They So Difficult to Write?" *Journal of Reading* 34(7):536–539 (April 1991).

Hirsch, E. D., Jr., "The Core Knowledge Curriculum—What's Behind Its Success?" *Educational Leadership* 50(8):23–25 (May 1993).

Hull, G. A. "Research on Writing: Building a Cognitive and Social Understanding of Composing." In L. B. Resnick and L. E. Klopfer, eds. *Toward the Thinking Curriculum: Current Cognitive Research.* 1989 ASCD Yearbook. Reston, VA: Association for Supervision and Curriculum Development, 1989.

Jarolimek, J., and Parker, W. C. *Social Studies in Elementary Education.* 9th ed. New York: Macmillan, 1993.

Johns, K. M., and Espinoza, C. *Mainstreaming Language Minority Children in Reading and Writing.* Fastback 340. Bloomington, IN: Phi Delta Kappa Educational Foundation, 1992.

Jones, B. F., et al., eds. *Strategic Teaching and Learning: Cognitive Instruction in the Content Areas.* Elmhurst, IL: North Central Regional Educational Laboratory, 1987.

Kaplan, R. G., Yamamoto, T., and Ginsburg, H. P. "Teaching Mathematics Concepts." In L. B. Resnick and L. E. Klopfer, eds. *Toward the Thinking Curriculum: Current*

Cognitive Research. 1989 ASCD Yearbook. Reston, VA: Association for Supervision and Curriculum Development, 1989.

Maxim, G. W. *Social Studies and the Elementary School Child.* 4th ed. New York: Macmillan, 1991.

Minstrell, J. A. "Teaching Science for Understanding." In L. B. Resnick and L. E. Klopfer, eds. *Toward the Thinking Curriculum: Current Cognitive Research.* 1989 ASCD Yearbook. Reston, VA: Association for Supervision and Curriculum Development, 1989.

National Association for Sport and Physical Education. *Outcomes of Quality Physical Education.* Reston, VA: National Association for Sport and Physical Education, 1992.

Palincsar, A. S., and Brown, A. L. "Instruction for Self-Regulated Reading." In L. B. Resnick and L. E. Klopfer, eds. *Toward the Thinking Curriculum: Current Cognitive Research.* 1989 ASCD Yearbook. Reston, VA: Association for Supervision and Curriculum Development, 1989.

Peterson, P. L., and Knapp, N. F. "Inventing and Reinventing Ideas: Constructivist Teaching and Learning in Mathematics." In Gordon Cawelti, ed. 1993 ASCD Yearbook. *Challenges and Achievements of American Education.* Alexandria, VA: Association for Supervision and Curriculum Development, 1993.

Reys, R. E., et al. *Helping Children Learn Mathematics.* 3rd ed. Needham Heights, MA: Allyn and Bacon, 1992.

Roberts, P. L. *A Green Dinosaur Day: A Guide for Developing Thematic Units in Literature-Based Instruction, K–6.* Boston: Allyn and Bacon, 1993.

———. *Counting Books Are More Than Numbers.* Hamden, CT: Library Professional Publications, 1990.

———. *Alphabet Books as a Key to Language Patterns.* Hamden, CT: Library Professional Publications, 1985.

———. *Alphabet: A Handbook of ABC Books and Activities for the Elementary Classroom.* 2nd ed. Metuchen, NJ: Scarecrow Press, Inc., 1993.

Russell, S. J., and Corwin, R. B. "Talking Mathematics: 'Going Slow and Letting Go.'" *Phi Delta Kappan* 74(7):555–558 (March 1993).

Schoenfield, A. H. "Teaching Mathematical Thinking and Problem Solving." In L. B. Resnick and L. E. Klopfer, eds. *Toward the Thinking Curriculum: Current Cognitive Research.* 1989 ASCD Yearbook. Reston, VA: Association for Supervision and Curriculum Development, 1989.

Sesow, F. W., et al. "Investigating Classroom Cultures." *Social Studies and the Young Learner* 4(3):3–5 (January/February 1992).

Slavin, R. E., et al. "Cooperative Learning Models for the 3Rs." *Educational Leadership* 47(4):22–28 (December/January 1989–90).

Stephens, R. J., et al. "The Effects of Cooperative Learning and Direct Instruction in Reading Comprehension Strategies on Main Idea Identification." *Journal of Educational Psychology* 83(1):8–16 (March 1991).

Stevens, R. J., et al. "The Effects of Cooperative Learning and Direct Instruction in Reading Comprehension Strategies on Main Idea Identification." *Journal of Educational Psychology* 83(1):8–16 (March 1991).

Stice, C. F., and Bertrand, J. E. "What's Going On Here? A Qualitative Examination of Grouping Patterns in an Exemplary Whole Language Classroom." *Reading Horizons* 32(5):383–393 (June 1992).

Sutton, G. O. "Cooperative Learning Works in Mathematics." *Mathematics Teacher* 85(1):63–66 (January 1992).

Victor, E., and Kellough, R. D. *Science for the Elementary School.* 7th ed. New York: Macmillan, 1993.

Willis, S. "Interdisciplinary Learning Movement to Link the Disciplines Gains Momentum." Association for Supervision and Curriculum Development's *Curriculum Update*, November 1992.

PART IV

Assessment and Professional Development

Part IV assists you with:

- Addresses for information on state credential requirements.
- Addresses for professional organizations.
- Guidelines for continuing to be an effective teacher.
- Guidelines for finding a teaching position.
- Guidelines for making your supervisor's visit a good experience.
- Guidelines for meeting and conferring with parents and guardians.
- Knowledge about the student teaching experience.

- Methods of evaluating teacher performance.
- Methods of grading and reporting student achievement.
- Preparing an emergency teaching kit.
- Preparing and administering evaluative instruments.
- Sample grade reporting forms.
- Self-evaluation through micro teaching.
- Tools for assessing student achievement.

When assessing for student achievement, it is important to use procedures that are compatible with the instructional objectives.

For children's continued intellectual and emotional development, your comments about their work should be useful, productive, analytical, diagnostic, and prescriptive.

You must provide opportunities for children to think about what they are learning, how they are learning it, and how far they have progressed in learning it.

Because teaching is both a demanding and stimulating profession, it is not easy to remain energetic and to stay abreast of changes and trends that result from research and practice. You must make a continuous and conscious effort to remain an alert and effective teacher.

14

How Do I Assess and Report Student Achievement?

While preceding parts of this text addressed the *why* (Part I), *what* (Part II), and *how* (Part III) of teaching, Part IV focuses your attention on *how well*—the fourth and final component. This includes how well you are doing and, concomitantly, how well the children are learning. Together, those four components make up the essentials of effective instruction.

Teaching and learning go hand in hand, because they are reciprocal processes that depend on and affect each other. The *how-well* component deals with the assessment of both—how well the students are learning and how well the teacher is teaching.

A. PURPOSES OF THE ASSESSMENT COMPONENT

The *how well* component is the assessment element and serves the following functions:

1. *To evaluate* (assessment is a synonym) *and improve student learning.* To evaluate and improve student learning is the function usually first thought of when speaking of the assessment component, and is the topic of this chapter.
2. *To identify children's strengths and weaknesses.* Identification and assessment of children's strengths and weaknesses are necessary for two purposes: to structure and restructure the learning activities, and to restructure the school curriculum. Concerning the first purpose, for example, data on student strengths and weaknesses of content and process skills are important in planning activities appropriate for both skill development and intellectual development. This is **diagnostic evaluation.** For the second purpose, data on student strengths and weaknesses in content and skills are useful for making appropriate modifications to the curriculum.
3. *To assess the effectiveness of a particular instructional strategy.* It is important for you to know how well a particular strategy helped accomplish a particular goal or objective. Competent teachers continually evaluate their strategy choices, using a number of sources: student achievement as measured by assessment instruments, their own intuition, feedback given by the children, and, sometimes, feedback given by colleagues.

4. *To evaluate and improve the effectiveness of curriculum programs.* Components of the curriculum are continually evaluated by committees of teachers and administrators. The evaluation is done both *while* students are learning (**formative evaluation**), and *after* (**summative evaluation**).

5. *To evaluate and improve teaching effectiveness.* Today's exemplary elementary school teachers are education specialists and are as unique as the clientele they serve. To improve student learning, teachers are evaluated on the basis of (1) their commitment to working with students, (2) their ability to cope with children at a particular age or grade level, and (3) their ability to show mastery of appropriate instructional techniques—techniques that have been articulated throughout this resource guide.

6. *To communicate to and involve parents and guardians in their children's learning.* Parents, communities, and school boards all share in accountability for the effectiveness of the learning of the children. Today's schools are reaching out and engaging parents, guardians, and the community in their children's education. All teachers play an important role in the process of communicating with, reaching out to, and involving parents.

B. GUIDELINES FOR ASSESSMENT

Because the welfare and, indeed, the future of so many people depend on the outcomes of assessment, it is impossible to overemphasize the importance of this component. For a learning endeavor to be successful, the learner must have answers to basic questions: Where am I going? Where am I now? How do I get where I am going? How will I know when I get there? Am I on the right track for getting there? These questions are integral to the assessment component. Of course, in the process of teaching and learning, the answers may be ever-changing, and the teacher continues to assess and adjust plans as appropriate and necessary.

Based on these questions are the following principles that guide the assessment component.

Principles That Guide the Assessment Component

- Teachers need to know how well they are doing.
- Students need to know how well they are doing.
- Evidence and input data for knowing how well the teacher and students are doing should come from a variety of sources.
- Assessment is a continuous process. The selection and implementation of plans and activities require continuing evaluation to check on progress and to change or adopt strategies to promote desired behavior.
- Self-evaluation is an important component of the assessment program. It also involves helping children develop the skills necessary for them to assume increasingly greater ownership of their own learning.
- Much of the assessment process can be systematized. For this purpose, there are computer-managed instructional software packages (CMI), in which learning objec-

tives are set and programmed into a computer system; then specific assessment items are established that reveal when a student has learned those particular skills. These packages also allow individualized learning programs and activities to be prescribed.

- The program of assessment should help teaching effectiveness and contribute to the intellectual and psychological growth of children.
- Evaluation is a reciprocal process, and includes evaluation of teacher performance as well as student achievement. It also involves self-evaluation to guide children in the development of increasingly greater responsibility for their own learning.
- A teacher's responsibility is to facilitate student learning and to assess student progress, and for that, the teacher is, or should be, held accountable.

This chapter is about techniques for evaluating student achievement, as critical as any other aspect of planning. When used inappropriately, evaluation can have long-term damaging results. Evaluating student progress and helping them, especially as they mature, to understand and to take charge of their own learning can consume a large portion of your time. This involves selecting and designing items and instruments, checking and analyzing results, recording, reporting, reading student journals, analyzing their portfolios, and arranging and conducting conferences with children and their parents or guardians. This chapter will make the job of assessment easier for you, although no less significant.

Teaching-learning is a complex human activity, and when evaluating that activity, we can never be absolutely sure of the *validity* and *reliability* of our measures. To help your understanding, we begin by clarifying those and other terms used in this chapter.

Clarification of Terms

When discussing the assessment component, it is easy to be confused with the terminology. The following clarification can help in your reading and understanding.

Measurement and Evaluation

Measurement refers to quantifiable data and relates to specific behavior. Tests and the statistical procedures used to analyze the results are examples. Measurement is a descriptive and objective process; that is, it is relatively free from human value judgments.

Evaluation includes measurement but also other types of information, some of which are more subjective, such as information from anecdotal records and teacher observations and ratings of performance. In addition to the use of objective data (data derived from measurement), evaluation also includes arriving at value judgments on the basis of subjective information.

An example of the use of these terms is as follows: While discussing a particular student with a colleague, a teacher says, "Although Sylvia Lee scored in the 90th percentile on the science section of the state standardized achievement test (a statement of measurement), according to my assessment of her work in my class, she has not been an outstanding science student (a statement of evaluation)."

Validity and Reliability

The degree to which a measuring tool actually measures that which it is intended to measure is called the instrument's **validity.** For example, when we ask whether a test has validity, key questions concerning the test are the following:

- Does the test adequately sample the intended content?
- Does it test the cognitive, affective, and psychomotor skills that are important to the unit of content being tested?
- Does it test for all the instructional objectives of that unit?

For example, if a teacher wants to find out whether the children have learned how the position of the fulcrum in a first-class lever will make a difference in the amount of effort exerted, the teacher should carefully select a test question or performance situation that will clearly indicate that this is what the item is measuring. One way this could be done would be to make a line drawing of a first-class lever, showing a weight at one end of the lever, an effort at the other end, and a fulcrum at a certain position between them. In a performance situation, the teacher would set up an actual, working first-class lever, with weights and the application of force. (The force, in this instance, could be one of the students and that student's known body weight.) The children are then asked to predict the effect of the fulcrum's position on the effort exerted.

The accuracy with which a technique consistently measures that which it does measure is called its **reliability.** If, for example, you know that you weigh 115 pounds and a scale consistently records 115 pounds when you stand on it, then that scale has reliability. Yet if the same scale consistently records 100 pounds when you stand on it, we can still say the scale has reliability. From this example, then, it should be clear to you that an instrument could be reliable (produces similar results when used again and again), although not necessarily valid (in this second instance, the scale is not measuring what it is supposed to measure, so although it is reliable, it is not valid). Although a technique might be reliable but not valid, a technique *must have reliability before it can have validity.*

The need for reliability can be shown clearly with the previous example, that of the effect of the fulcrum's position on the effort exerted in a first-class lever. If the teacher asks the children to predict this effect on the basis of just one position of the fulcrum, the answer will give the teacher no assurance that the children know what will happen. It is necessary to use several positions of the fulcrum and have the children predict what will happen in each case, to be confident that the children know how the fulcrum's position affects the effort exerted. Thus, the greater the number of test items or situations for this problem, the higher the reliability. The higher the reliability, the more consistency there will be in the children's scores measuring their understanding of this particular concept.

C. ASSESSING STUDENT ACHIEVEMENT

There are three general approaches for assessing a student's achievement: (1) *what the student says*—for example, a student's contributions to class discussions; (2) *what the student does*—for example, a student's efforts in independent study or small group projects, which could show how well the student is internalizing the learning; and (3) *what the student writes*—for example, as shown by written tests, homework assignments, and the child's journal writing. Although your own situation and personal philosophy will dictate the levels of importance and weight you give to each approach, you should have a strong rationale if you value and weigh the three categories differently than one-third each.

When assessing for student achievement it is important that you use procedures that are compatible with the instructional objectives. This is referred to as **authentic assessment.**[1] For example, "if students have been actively involved in classifying objects using multiple characteristics, it sends them a confusing message if they are then required to take a paper-and-pencil test that asks them to 'define classification' or recite a memorized list of characteristics of good classifications schemes."[2] An authentic assessment technique would be a performance item that actually involves the children in classifying objects. Another example is a sample question from the "Missouri pilot version of the 4th grade level of Authentic Science Assessment that describes a situation where two individuals are to wash a car with water that is too hot. After proposing hypotheses for cooling the bucket, students are supplied materials to reenact the experiment and generate written results."[3] In other words, to obtain an accurate assessment of a child's understanding of that which the child has been learning, the teacher uses a **performance-based assessment procedure.**

Performance assessment should reflect the elementary school curriculum and instruction, and skills that are stressed in the activities of that program should be included in the assessment. Performance-based assessment should form the basis of assessment in a program using an interdisciplinary approach, that is, one that integrates language arts with other areas of the curriculum.

Evaluating a student's achievement is a three-step process, involving (1) **diagnostic evaluation,** which is an assessment of the student's knowledge and skills *before* the new instruction; (2) **formative evaluation,** the assessment of learning *during* the instruction; and (3) **summative evaluation,** the assessment *after* the instruction, finally represented by the child's term, semester, or year's achievement grade or mark. Grades shown on unit tests, progress reports, deficiency notices, and six-week or quarter grades (in a semester-based program) are examples of *formative evaluation* reports. However, an end-of-chapter test or a unit test is summative if the test represents the absolute end of the student's learning of material of that instructional unit.

Evaluating What a Student Says and Does

When evaluating what a student says, you should (1) **listen** to the student's questions, responses, and interactions with others and (2) **observe** the student's attentiveness, involvement in class activities, and responses to challenges.

Notice that you should *listen and observe.* While listening to what the student is saying, you should also be observing the student's nonverbal behaviors. To do this you can use checklists and rating scales, behavioral-growth record forms, observations of the student's performance in classroom activities, and periodic conferences with the

[1]Other terms used for authentic assessment are *accurate, active, aligned, alternative* and *direct.* Although not all performance assessments are authentic, those that are, are most assuredly performance assessments. See C.A. Meyer, "What's the Difference Between Authentic and Performance Assessment?" *Educational Leadership* 49, 8 (May, 1992):39–41.
[2]Steven J. Rakow, "Assessment: A Driving Force," *Science Scope* 15(6):3 (March 1992), p. 3.
[3]Jeffrey D. Weld, "Measuring a Sense for Science," *Educational Leadership* 50(1):76–77 (September 1992), p. 77.

student. Figure 14.1 illustrates a sample form for recording and evaluating teacher's observations of a student's verbal and nonverbal behaviors.

Please remember that with each technique used, you must proceed from your awareness of expected learning outcomes (the instructional objectives), and you must evaluate a student's progress toward meeting those objectives. This is referred to as **criterion-referenced assessment.**

Guidelines for Evaluating What the Student Says and Does

To evaluate a child's verbal and nonverbal behaviors in the classroom, follow these guidelines:

- Maintain an **anecdotal record book** or **folder** containing a separate section for your records of each student.
- For a specific activity, list the desirable behaviors.
- Check the list against the specific instructional objectives.
- Record your observations as quickly as possible following your observation. Audio or video recordings and, of course, computer software programs can help you check the accuracy of your memory, but if this is inconvenient, you should spend time during school, immediately after, or later that evening, recording your observations while still fresh in your memory.
- Record your professional judgment about the student's progress toward the desired behavior, but think it through before transferring it to a permanent record (see Section D).
- Write comments that are reminders to yourself, such as:
  "Check validity of observation by further testing."
  "Discuss observations with child's parent."
  "Discuss observations with school counselor."
  "Discuss observations with other teachers."

Evaluating What a Student Writes

To evaluate what a student writes you can use work sheets, written homework, student journal writing, student portfolios, and tests. In many schools, portfolios, work sheets, and homework assignments are the usual tools for the formative evaluation of each student's achievement. Tests, too, should be a part of this evaluation, but tests are also used for summative evaluation at the end of a unit, as well as for diagnostic purposes.

Your summative evaluation of a student's achievement, and any other final judgment made by you about a student, can have an impact on the emotional and intellectual development of that child. Special attention is given to this in Section D.

Guidelines for Evaluating What the Student Writes

When evaluating what a student writes, use the following guidelines:

- Work sheets, homework, and test items should correlate with and be compatible with specific instructional objectives.

| Student _____ Grade _____ School _____ |
| Observer _____ Date _____ Period _____ |

| *Objective for time period* | *Desired behavior* | *What student did, said, or wrote* |

Observer's comments

Figure 14.1 Sample form for evaluating and recording student verbal and nonverbal behaviors.

- Read everything a student writes. When a task is important for the student to do, it is equally important that you give your professional attention to the product of the student's efforts.
- Provide written or verbal comments about the student's work, and be positive in those comments. Rather than just writing "good" on a student's paper, briefly state what made it "good." Try to avoid negative comments. Rather than simply saying or pointing out that the child did not do something right, tell or show the student acceptable ways of completing the task. For reinforcement, use appropriate rewards as frequently as possible.
- Think before writing a comment on a student's paper, asking yourself how you think the student (or a parent) will interpret the comment and whether that is the interpretation you intend.
- Avoid writing negative comments or grades in **student journals.** *The purpose of student journals is to encourage children to write, to think about their thinking, and to record their creative thoughts.* In journal writing, students should be encouraged to write about their experiences in school and out of school, experiences related to what is being learned. They should be encouraged to write their feelings about what is being learned, and about how they are learning it. Writing in journals gives them practice in expressing themselves in written form and should provide nonthreatening freedom to do so. Comments and evaluations by teachers might discourage creative and spontaneous expression.
- When reading student journals you can talk individually with students to seek clarification about their expressions. Student journals are useful to the teacher in understanding the students' thought processes and writing skills (diagnostic evaluation), and should *not* be graded.
- When reviewing **student portfolios** you should talk with students individually about the progress in their learning as shown by materials in their portfolios. As with a student journal, the portfolio should *not* be graded or compared in any way with those of other students. Its purpose is to allow student self-assessment and to show progress in learning.

Regardless of avenues chosen, and the relative weights you give them, you must evaluate against the instructional objectives. Any given objective may be checked by more than one method and by using more than one instrument. Subjectivity, inherent in the evaluation process, may be reduced as you check for validity, comparing results of one measuring technique against those of another.

While evaluation of cognitive objectives lends itself to traditional written tests of achievement, the evaluation of the affective and psychomotor domains requires the use of performance checklists for student behaviors observed in action. However, as indicated in the earlier discussion of authentic assessment, for cognitive learning as well, educators today are encouraging the use of **alternative assessment** procedures, as opposed to traditional paper-and-pencil written testing (see, in Section I of this chapter, "Specific Guidelines for Preparing Twelve Types of Assessment Items," for items appropriate for authentic assessment). The advantages claimed for the use of authentic assessment include the direct (performance-based) measurement of what students should know, and an emphasis on higher-order thinking. On the other hand, the disadvantages of authentic assessment include high cost, difficulty in making results consistent and usable, and problems with validity, reliability, and comparability.

Unfortunately for the teacher who may never again see a student after a given school year is over, the effects that teacher has had on a student's values and attitudes may never be observed by that teacher at all. However, in schools where groups or

When students work toward a *common* goal, they increase their liking and respect for one another.

teams of teachers remain with the same cohort of students throughout several years, those teachers often do have opportunity to observe the positive changes in the children's values and attitudes.

Cooperative Learning and Evaluation

As discussed in Chapter 11, Section B, the purpose of a cooperative learning group is for the group to learn, which means that if this is to happen, individuals within the group must learn. Group achievement in learning, then, depends on the learning of individuals within the group. Rather than competing for rewards for achievement, members of the group cooperate by helping each other to learn so that the group reward will be a good one. Theoretically, when small groups of students of mixed backgrounds, skills, and capabilities work together toward a common goal, they increase their liking and respect for one another. As a result, there is an increase in each student's self-esteem and academic achievement.

When recognizing the achievement of a cooperative learning group, group achievement is rewarded, as well as the achievement of individuals within the group. Remembering that peer support should be given greater emphasis than peer pressure, you must be cautious about ever giving group grades.[4] Some teachers give bonus

[4]For an informative review of grading and other aspects of the use of cooperative learning see Dave Ossont, "How I Use Cooperative Learning," *Science Scope* 16(8):28–31 (May 1993).

points to all members of the group to add to their individual scores when *everyone* in the group has reached preset criteria. In establishing preset performance criteria, criteria can be different for individuals within a group, depending on each member's ability and past performance. It is important that each member of a group feel rewarded and successful. Some teachers also give subjective grades to individual students on their role performances within the group. For determination of students' report card grades, individual student achievement is measured later through individual results on tests and other sources of data, and the final grade is based on those as well as on the student's performance in the group.

D. RECORDING TEACHER OBSERVATIONS AND JUDGMENTS

As stated earlier, you must carefully think through any written comments that you intend to make about a student. Children can be very sensitive to what others say about them, and most particularly to negative comments by their teachers.

We have seen anecdotal comments in children's permanent records that said more about the teachers who made the comments than about the recipient students. Comments that have been made carelessly, hurriedly, or thoughtlessly can be detrimental to a child's welfare and progress in school. Teacher comments must be professional; that is, they must be *diagnostically useful to the continued intellectual and psychological development of the child*. This is true for any comment you make or write, whether on a child's paper, in the child's permanent school record, or in a note sent home to a child's parent or guardian.

As an example, consider the following *unprofessional comment* observed in one child's permanent record. A teacher wrote, "John is lazy." Describing John as "lazy" could be done by anyone; it is nonproductive, and it is certainly not a professional diagnosis. How many times do you suppose it takes for John to receive such negative descriptions of his behavior before he begins to believe that he is just that—lazy— and, as a result, acts that way even more often? Written comments like this can also be damaging because they may be read by the teacher who next has John in class; that teacher may simply perpetuate this expectation of John. To say that John is lazy merely describes behavior as judged by the teacher who wrote the comment. More important, and more professional, would be for the teacher to try to analyze *why* John is behaving that way, then to *prescribe* activities that are likely to motivate John to assume a more constructive charge of his own learning behavior.

Entire classes of youngsters have been observed being described in a similarly unprofessional way. In one instance, at the end of the school year, a class of 22 second-graders in a small rural school was described by their teacher as being "unruly and difficult to handle." That one teacher's description preceded that class of youngsters from one year to the next, in effect making it difficult for those children to be anything but "unruly and difficult to handle." Six years later that class, of mostly the same boys and girls who were together in the second grade, graduated with the highest achievement and as the most honored eighth-grade class in the history of the school. It is unlikely that their former second-grade teacher had made any significant contribution toward that outcome.

For students' continued intellectual and emotional development, your comments should be useful, productive, analytical, diagnostic, and prescriptive. The professional teacher makes diagnoses and prepares descriptions; a professional teacher does not label students as "lazy," "vulgar," "slow," "stupid," "difficult," or "dumb." The professional teacher sees the behavior of a child as being goal-directed. Perhaps "lazy" John found that particular behavioral pattern won him attention. John's goal, then, was attention (do we not all need attention?), and John assumed negative, perhaps self-destructive, behavior patterns to reach that goal. The professional task of any teacher is to facilitate the learner's understanding (perception) of a goal, with the identification of acceptable behaviors positively designed to reach that goal.

That which separates the professional teacher from "anyone off the street" is the teacher's ability to go beyond mere description of behavior. Keep this always in mind when you write comments that will be read by students, by their parents or guardians, or by other teachers. Now reinforce this concept by focusing your attention on Exercise 14.1.

Exercise 14.1: A Self-Check Evaluation of Written Teacher Comments

Instructions: The purpose of this exercise is to develop your skill in identifying teacher comments that are helpful and professional. Selected from student records are the following comments written by teachers about their students. Check those you consider to be professionally useful and those that are not. Then compare your responses with the key that follows. Discuss the results with your classmates and instructor.

		Yes	*No*
1.	Sonja performs her writing assignments much better when done in class than when done as homework.	( )	( )
2.	Lucretia was very disruptive in class during our unit on westward expansion.	( )	( )
3.	Aram has a lot of difficulty staying in his seat.	( )	( )
4.	Arthur seems more responsive during science experiments than during my lectures.	( )	( )
5.	Razmik seems to have very little energy, and I have a concern about his health.	( )	( )
6.	Su Chin did very well this year in art activities but seems to have reading difficulties.	( )	( )
7.	Catalina does not get along well with her peers during cooperative group learning activities.	( )	( )
8.	Angela seems unable to understand my verbal instructions.	( )	( )
9.	I am recommending special remediation for José, perhaps through special tutoring.	( )	( )
10.	I do not appreciate Dan's use of vulgarity.	( )	( )

Key to Exercise 14.1

1. This is useful information. Are there distractions at home; less help available?
2. Not useful. There are no helpful specifics. "Disruptive" is merely descriptive, not prescriptive. Moreover, it could cause Lucretia's future teachers to be biased against her.
3. Could be useful to future teachers.
4. Useful.
5. Useful.

6. Useful, although additional specifics would help more.
7. Useful, although additional specifics would help more.
8. Not very useful; it may tell more about the teacher than about Angela.
9. Useful.
10. Not very useful.

Note: It can be argued that those comments identified as not useful, although not prescriptive, could be signals that the student might benefit from a session with the school counselor or that if there had not been, that there should have been a parent-teacher conference.

E. INVOLVING STUDENTS IN SELF-ASSESSMENT

In exemplary elementary school programs, students' continuous self-assessment is an important component of the evaluation process. If children are to progress in their understanding of their own thinking (metacognition), and in their intellectual development, then they must receive instruction and guidance in how to become more responsible for their own learning. During that process they learn to think better of themselves and of their individual capabilities. To achieve such self-understanding requires the experiences afforded by successes, along with guidance in self-understanding.

Student Portfolios

To meet these goals, *teachers should provide opportunities for students to think about what they are learning, how they are learning it, and how far they have progressed.* One procedure is for students to maintain portfolios of their work, using rating scales or checklists periodically to assess their own progress. The student portfolio should be well organized and contain assignment sheets, class work sheets, homework sheets, self-evaluation forms, and other class materials thought important by the students and teacher.[5] (For additional resources on the use of student portfolios, refer to the suggested readings at the end of this chapter.)

While emphasizing the criteria for evaluation, rating scales and checklists provide children with means of expressing their feelings, and give the teacher still another source of input data for use in evaluation. To provide children with reinforcement and guidance in improving their learning and development, teachers meet with individual students to discuss their self-evaluations. Such conferences should provide children with understandable and achievable short-term goals, as well as help them to develop and maintain adequate self-esteem.

Although most any of the instruments used for evaluating student work can be used for student self-evaluation, in some cases it might be better to construct specific instruments for it, instruments constructed by the teacher with the student's understanding of the instrument in mind. Student self-evaluation should be done on a regular and continuing basis, so that comparisons can be made by the child from one

---

[5]To assist teachers in the use of portfolios as a form of assessment is a bulletin, *Portfolio News*, published by Portfolio Assessment Clearinghouse, c/o San Dieguito High School District, 710 Encinitas Boulevard, Encinitas, CA 92024.

time to the next. You will need to help children analyze these comparisons. Comparisons should provide a child with previously unrecognized information about his or her own progress and growth.

Self-Evaluation Checklist

Items on the student's self-evaluation checklist may vary depending on which grade level you teach. Generic items similar to those in Figure 14.2 (pages 505-506) can be used. Checklist items can be used easily by a student to compare with previous self-evaluations, while open-ended questions allow the child to provide additional information, as well as an opportunity to do some expressive writing.

FOR YOUR NOTES

Student Self-Evaluation Checklist*

Student _____ Date _____

Teacher _____ Number _____

Circle one response for each of the first six items.

1. My assignments are turned in:

    a. Always on time.

    b. Always late.

    c. Sometimes late; sometimes on time.

    d. _____

2. Most of my classmates:

    a. Like me.

    b. Don't like me.

    c. Ignore me.

    d. _____

3. I think I am:

    a. Smart.

    b. The smartest in the class.

    c. The slowest in the class.

    d. _____

4. I think I am:

    a. Doing better in _____

    b. Doing worse in _____

    c. Doing about the same in _____

    d. _____

5. In _____ :

    a. I am learning a lot.

    b. I am not learning very much.

    c. _____

6. In _____ :

    a. I am doing the best work I can.

    b. I am not doing as well as I can.

    c. _____

*To be kept in student's portfolio.

Figure 14.2   Student self-evaluation: Sample generic form.

7. Describe what you have learned in _____ since your last self-evaluation and that you have used outside of school. Tell how you used it. (You can refer to your previous self-evaluation.)

8. Describe anything you have learned about yourself since you completed your last self-evaluation. (You can refer to your previous self-evaluation.)

Figure 14.2 *(continued)*

F. MAINTAINING RECORDS OF STUDENT ACHIEVEMENT

You must maintain well-organized and complete records of student achievement. You may do this in a written record book or in an electronic record book (that is, a computer software program, one commercially developed or one you develop yourself, perhaps by using a computer software program spreadsheet as the base). The record book should include tardies and absences, as well as all records of scores on tests, homework, projects, and other assignments.

Record books are often referred to during conferences about students with parents or guardians, counselors, and administrators. The teacher record book, a legal document, is usually turned in to the administration during checkout at the end of each school year. If not turned in, it must be kept in a safe place.

Anecdotal records can be maintained in alphabetical order in a separate binder, a section for each child. Daily interactions and events in the classroom may provide informative data about a child's intellectual, emotional, and physical development. Maintaining a dated record of your observations of these interactions and events can provide important information that might otherwise be forgotten. At the end of a unit, and again at the conclusion of a grading term, you will want to review your records. During the course of the school year your anecdotal records (and those of other members of your teaching team) will provide important information about the intellectual, psychological, and physical development of each child, and ideas about attention that may need to be given to individual students.

G. GRADING AND MARKING STUDENT ACHIEVEMENT

If conditions were ideal (which they are not), and if teachers did their job perfectly well (which many of us do not), then all children would receive top marks (the ultimate in mastery learning) and there would be less need to talk about grading. **Mastery learning** implies that some end point of learning is attainable, but in reality, there probably is no end point. In any case, because conditions are never ideal, and because we are mere humans, let us continue with this topic (of grading) that is undoubtedly of special interest to you, to your students, to their parents, and to the school administration.

Several times in this chapter we have used the term **achievement.** What is achievement? Achievement means accomplishment, but is it the accomplishment of instructional objectives against preset standards, or simply accomplishment? Most teachers probably choose the former understanding, by which the teacher subjectively establishes a standard that must be met in order for a child to receive a certain grade for an assignment, a test, or the course. Achievement, then, is decided by degrees of accomplishment.

Preset standards are usually expressed in percentages (degrees of accomplishment) needed for marks of A, B, C, and so on, or for E (excellent), S (satisfactory), and U (unsatisfactory), as is more common in primary-level grading. If no student achieves the standard required for an A grade, for example, then no student receives that grade. On the other hand, if all students meet the preset standard for the A grade, then all receive A's. Determining student grades on the basis of preset standards is referred to as **criterion-referenced grading.**

Criterion-Referenced Versus Norm-Referenced Grading

As stated in the preceding paragraph, criterion-referenced grading is grading that is based on preset standards. Norm-referenced grading, on the other hand, is based on the relative accomplishment of individuals in the group, by comparing and ranking students, and is commonly known as "grading on a curve."

For determination of grades, norm-referenced grading is *not* recommended, because it encourages competition and discourages cooperative learning. After all, each child is an individual and should not be converted to a statistic on a frequency-distribution curve. For your own information, after several years of teaching, you can produce frequency-distribution studies of grades you have given, but do *not* grade your children on a curve. Grades for student achievement should be tied to performance levels and determined on the basis of each student's achievement toward preset standards.

Determining Grades

For reasons discussed earlier in this chapter, determining final grades or marks for student performance is serious business, for which you must make several important and professional decisions. Although in a few schools, and for certain classes or assignments, only marks such as "E, S, and I" or "pass/no pass" are used, for most intermediate and higher grades, percentages of accomplishment and ABC grades are used.

Guidelines for Determining Grades

For arriving at student marks or grades, consider the following guidelines:

- At the start of the school term, explain your marking and grading policies *first to yourself,* then to your children and to their parents or guardians at back-to-school night, or in an explanation that is sent home, or both.
- When converting your interpretation of a child's accomplishments to a letter grade, be as objective as possible.
- Build your grading policy around accomplishment rather than failure, whereby children proceed from one accomplishment to the next. This is **continuous promotion,** not necessarily from one grade to the next, but within the classroom.
- For the selection of criteria for ABC grades, select a percentage standard, such as 92 percent for an A, 85 percent for a B, 75 percent for a C, and 65 percent for a D. Cutoff percentages used are your decision, although the district, school, or program area may have established guidelines to which you are expected to adhere.
- "Evaluation" and "grading" are *not* synonymous. As you learned earlier in this chapter, evaluation implies the collection of information from a variety of sources, including measurement techniques and subjective observations. These data, then, become the basis for arriving at a final grade, which in effect is a final value judgment. Grades are one aspect of evaluation and are intended to communicate educational progress to both parents and students. For a child's grade to be valid as an

indicator of that progress, you *must* use a variety of sources of data for determination of the final grade.

- In the upper grades,[6] for determination of students' final grades, we recommend using a point system, whereby things that children write, say, and do are given points (but not for journals or portfolios, except, perhaps, simply for whether the student maintains one or not); then the possible point total is the factor for grade determination. For example, if 92 percent is the cutoff for an A, and 500 points are possible, then any student with 460 points or more (500 × .92) has achieved an A. Likewise, for a test or any other assignment, if the value is 100 points, the cutoff for an A is 92 (100 × .92). With a point system and preset standards, the teacher and children, at any time during the year, know the current number of points possible and can easily calculate a child's current grade standing. Then, as far as a current grade is concerned, students always know where they stand in the course.

- Children will be absent and will miss assignments and tests, and it is best that you decide beforehand your policy for makeup work. Your policies for late assignments and missed tests must be clearly communicated to the children and to their parents. For makeup work, consider the following:

  Homework assignments. For homework assignments, our recommendation is that you strictly adhere to due dates, giving *no credit* or *reduced credit* for work that is turned in late. You may think it harsh and rigid, but experience has shown this to be a good policy to which children (and parents) can and should adjust. It reflects the world of work to which they must become accustomed, and is a sensible policy for a teacher who deals with many papers each day. Of course, for this policy to work well, students must be given their assignments long before the due dates.

  Tests. Sometimes children are absent when tests are given. In that case, you have several options. Some teachers allow students to miss or discount one test per grading period. Another technique is to allow each student to substitute a written homework assignment or project for one missed test. Still another option is to give the absent student a choice of either taking a makeup test or having the next test count double. When a makeup test is given, it should be taken within a week of the regular test unless there is a compelling reason (e.g., medical problem or family situation problem) that this cannot happen.

H. TESTING

One source of information used in determining grades is the data obtained from testing for student achievement. Competent planning, preparing, administering, and scoring of tests are important professional skills, in which you will gain valuable practical experience during your student teaching. Here are helpful guidelines that you will want to refer to while you are student teaching, and again, occasionally, during your first few years as a credentialed teacher.

---

[6]Depending on the expected procedures for teachers at a given school, for primary grades a simple checklist system is useful in determination of final marks, which are usually less complicated to determine than ABC grades.

Purposes for Testing

Textbook publishers' tests, test item pools, and standardized tests are available from a variety of sources. Mostly, however, because schools are different, teachers are different, and children are different, you will be designing and preparing many of your tests for your own purposes for your distinct group of children. Tests can be designed for several purposes, and a variety of kinds of tests and test items will keep your testing program interesting, useful, and reliable. As a university student, you are probably most experienced with testing for measuring achievement, but you will use tests for other reasons as well. Purposes for which tests are used include the following:

- To assess and aid in curriculum development.
- To help determine teaching effectiveness.
- To help students develop positive attitudes, appreciations, and values.
- To help students increase their understanding and retention of facts, principles, skills, and concepts.
- To measure student achievement.
- To motivate students.
- To provide diagnostic information for planning individualization of instruction.
- To provide review and drill to enhance teaching and learning.
- To serve as a source of information for children and parents.

After determining the reasons for which you are designing and administering a test, you need to identify the specific instructional objectives the test is being designed to measure. (As you learned in Chapter 6, your written instructional objectives are so specific that you can write test items to measure against those objectives.) So, the **first step** in test construction is to identify the purpose(s) for the test. The **second step** is to identify the objectives to be measured, and the **third step** is to prepare the test items. The best time to prepare draft items is after you have prepared your instructional objectives, that is, while the objectives are fresh in your mind, which means *before the lessons are taught.* After a lesson is taught you will then want to rework your first draft of the test items for that lesson.

When and How Often to Test for Achievement

It is difficult to generalize about how often you should test for achievement, but we believe that tests should be cumulative and frequent; that is, the test items for each test should measure the student's understanding of previously learned material as well as the current unit of study, and by frequent we mean as often as once a week, especially for upper-grade and middle-level students. Advantages of giving cumulative tests include the review, reinforcement, and articulation of old material with the recent. The advantages of frequent testing include a reduction in student anxiety over tests and an increase in the validity of final grades.

Administering Tests

For many students, especially those in the upper grades, test taking can be a time of high anxiety. To measure student achievement more accurately, it is important to take steps to reduce that anxiety. Students demonstrate test anxiety in various ways.

Just before and during testing, some are quiet and thoughtful, while others are noisy and disruptive. To control or reduce student anxieties, consider the following as guidelines when administering tests:

- Since children respond best to familiar routine, plan your program so that tests are given at regular intervals (same day each week) and administered at the same time and in the same way.
- Avoid writing tests that are too long and that will take too much time. Beginning teachers in particular sometimes have unreasonable expectations of children's attention spans during testing. Frequent testing, and frequent sampling of their knowledge, is better than infrequent and long tests that attempt to cover everything.
- Try to arrange your classroom so that it is well ventilated, the temperature is comfortable, and the seats are well spaced. If spacing is a problem, consider the use of alternate forms of the test, whereby students next to one another have different forms of the same test; for example, multiple-choice answer alternatives are arranged in different order.
- Before test time be certain that you have a sufficient number of copies of the test.
- Before distributing the test, explain to students what they are to do upon completion, such as a homework assignment, because not all will finish at the same time. Rather than expecting students to sit quietly after finishing a test, they should have something to do.
- When ready to test, do not drag it out. Distribute tests quickly and efficiently.
- Once testing has begun, avoid interrupting the students. Items of important information can be written on the board or held until all are finished with the test.
- During testing, remain in the room and visually monitor the students.
- If the test is not going to take an entire class period (and most should not), give it at the beginning of the period, if possible, unless you are planning a test review just prior to the test.

Cheating

Cheating on tests does occur, but there are ways to discourage it or to reduce the opportunity and pressure to cheat:

- Space students or, as mentioned earlier, use alternate forms of the test.
- Frequent testing, and not allowing a single test to count too much, reduces text anxiety and the pressure that can cause cheating, and increases student learning by "stimulating greater effort and providing intermittent feedback" to the student.[7]
- Prepare test questions that are clear, that are not ambiguous, thereby reducing the frustration caused by a question or instructions that students do not understand.
- As mentioned earlier, avoid tests that are too long and that will take too much time. During long tests, some students get discouraged and restless, and that is when classroom management problems can occur.
- Consider using open-text and open-notebook tests. When students can use their books and pages of notes, it not only reduces anxiety but helps them with the organization and retention of what has been learned.

[7]Herbert J. Walberg, "Productive Teaching and Instruction: Assessing the Knowledge Base," *Phi Delta Kappan* 71(6):470–478 (February 1990), p. 472.

TABLE 14.1 Time to Allow for Testing as Determined by the Types of Assessment Items

Type of Item	*Time Needed per Item*
Matching	1 minute per matching item
Multiple-choice	1 minute per item
Completion	1 minute per item
Completion drawing	2–3 minutes
Arrangement	2–3 minutes
Identification	2–3 minutes
Short explanation	2–3 minutes
Essay and performance	10 minutes

If you suspect cheating *is* occurring, go and stand in the area of the suspected student. That will usually stop such behavior. When you suspect cheating *has* occurred, you are faced with a dilemma. Unless your suspicion is backed by solid proof you are advised to forget it, but keep a close watch on the student the next time to prevent a recurrence. Your job is not to catch students being dishonest, but to prevent it. If you do have absolute proof, then you are obligated to proceed with school policy on student cheating, which may call for a session with the counselor or the student and the student's parent or guardian.

Time Needed to Take a Test

Again—avoid giving tests that are too long and that will take too much time. Preparing and administering good tests is a skill that you will develop over time. In the meantime, it is best to test frequently and to use tests that *sample* student achievement rather than try for a comprehensive measure of that achievement.

Some students take more time on a given test than others. It is best to avoid giving too much time, or classroom management problems will result. On the other hand, you do not want to cut short the time needed by students who can do well but need more time to think and to write. As a guide, use Table 14.1, showing the time needed for different types of test items. This is only a guide for determining the approximate amount of time to allow students to complete a test. As an example, for a test made up of ten multiple-choice items, five arrangement items, and two short-explanation items, you might plan for about 30 minutes for a group of students to complete the test.

I. PREPARING ASSESSMENT INSTRUMENTS

Preparing good assessment items is yet another professional skill, and to become proficient at it takes study, time, and practice. Because of the recognized importance of a testing program, please assume this professional charge seriously and responsibly. Although poorly prepared test items take no time at all to prepare, they will cause you more trouble than you can imagine. As a professional, you must take time to study the different types of assessment items that can be used, and how best to write them, and then to practice writing them. When writing items, you must be sure that they match and sufficiently cover the instructional objectives. In addition, you must write each item carefully enough to be reasonably assured that each item will be understood by the student in the manner you anticipate.

Classification of Assessment Items

Assessment items can be classified as **verbal** (oral or written words), **visual** (pictures and diagrams), and **manipulative** or **performance** (handling of materials and equipment). Written verbal tests are those traditionally most used in testing. However, visual tests are useful, for example, when working with students who lack fluency with the written word, that is, when testing the knowledge of children with limited proficiency in English.

Performance tests are useful when measuring psychomotor skill development, for example, in performance testing of locomotor skills, such as a child's ability to pick up and carry several blocks, or a student's ability to carry a microscope (gross motor skill), to stack several blocks, or focus a microscope (fine motor skill). Performance testing can also be a part of a wider assessment that includes testing for higher-level affective and cognitive skills and knowledge, as when a student or small group of students are given the task of creating from discarded materials a habitat for an imaginary animal, and then displaying and describing their product to the rest of the class. As mentioned earlier, educators today have rekindled interest in **performance testing** as a means of assessment that is closer to measuring the real thing (that is, **authentic**).

The types of items and tests you use depends on your purpose and objectives. Carefully consider the alternatives within that framework. A good assessment program will likely include items from all three types, to provide validity checks and to account for the individual differences of children.

General Guidelines for Preparing Assessment Instruments

In preparing assessment instruments you should:

- Include several kinds of test items (see types that follow this list).
- Make sure that content coverage is complete, that is, that all objectives are covered.
- Be certain that each item of the test is reliable, that it measures student learning of the intended objective. One way to check item reliability is to have more than one test item measuring for learning for the same objective.
- Be sure that each item is clear and unambiguous.
- Plan the test items to be difficult enough for the poorly prepared student, but easy enough for the student who is well prepared.
- Because it is time-consuming to write good test items, you are advised to maintain a bank of test items, with each item coded according to its matching instructional objective and according to its domain (cognitive, affective, or psychomotor), whether it requires low-level recall, processing, or application, and perhaps according to its level within the hierarchy of the particular domain. Computer software

programs are available for this purpose.[8] When preparing items for your own test bank, use your creative writing skills—prepare items that match your objectives, put them aside, think about them, then work them again.

The test you administer to your students should represent your best professional effort; it should be clean and without spelling or grammatical errors. A quickly and poorly prepared test can cause difficulty for all concerned. One that is obviously prepared in a hurry and fraught with spelling errors will quickly be frowned upon by discerning parents and, if you are a student teacher, will certainly bring about a strong admonishment from your university supervisor, if not your speedy dismissal from the program.

Specific Guidelines for Preparing Twelve Types of Assessment Items

Twelve types of assessment items are presented here, along with their advantages, disadvantages, and guidelines for use. You will notice that some types are appropriate for use in direct or performance assessment **(authentic assessment),** while others are not.

1. Arrangement Type

Description: Terms or real objects (realia) are to be arranged in a specified order.

EXAMPLE 1: From the following list of planets in our solar system, arrange them in order, beginning with the one closest to the sun.

EXAMPLE 2: The assortment of balls on the table represents the planets in our solar system. (*Note:* The balls are of various sizes, such as marbles, golf balls, tennis balls, and basketballs, and are labeled with their appropriate planetary names. A large sphere in the center represents the sun.) Arrange the balls in their proper order around the sun.

Advantages: This type of item tests for knowledge of sequence and order and is good for review, for starting discussions, and for performance assessment. Example 2 is a manipulative (performance) test item. Recommended for use in observing and assessing the skill and intellectual development of children.

Disadvantages: Scoring may be difficult, so be cautious about using this type for grading purposes.

Guidelines for use: Give instructions to children to include the rationale for their arrangement, making it a combined arrangement and short-explanation type, and allow space for explanations on an answer sheet.

---

[8]Ready-made test item banks are available on computer disk, and accompany many programs or textbooks. If you use them, be certain that the items match your course objectives and that they are well written. It does not follow that because they were published they are well written. Some state departments of education have made efforts to develop test banks for teachers. For example, see John A. Willis, "Learning Outcome Testing Program: Standardized Classroom Testing in West Virginia Through Item Banking, Test Generation, and Curricular Management Software," *Educational Measurement: Issues and Practices* 9(2):11–14 (Summer 1990).

2. Drawing-Completion Type

Description: An incomplete drawing is presented, which the student is to complete.

EXAMPLE 1: Connect the following items with arrow lines to show the stages from the planting of cotton to the distribution of wearing apparel to consumers.

EXAMPLE 2: In the following food web, draw arrow lines showing which organisms are consumers and which are producers.

Advantages: This type requires less time than needed for a complete drawing, as may be required in an essay item. Scoring is relatively easy.

Disadvantages: Care needs to be exercised in the instructions so children do not misinterpret the expectation.

Guidelines for use: Use occasionally for diversion, but take care in preparing. Example 1 is typical of this type when used in integrated thematic teaching. This type can be instructive when assessing student thinking. Consider making the item a combined completion-drawing, short-explanation type by having students include their rationales for their drawings. Be sure to allow space for their explanations.

3. Statement-Completion Type

Description: An incomplete sentence is presented, which the student is to complete by filling in the blank space(s).

EXAMPLE 1: The point around which a lever turns is called a _____.

EXAMPLE 2: To test their hypotheses, scientists conduct _____.

Advantages: This type is easy to devise, to take, and to score.

Disadvantages: This type tends to emphasize rote memory. It is difficult to write this type of item to measure for higher levels of cognition. You must be alert for a correct response different from the expected. For example, in Example 2, although the teacher's key has "experiments" as the correct answer, a student might answer the question with "investigations," which is equally correct.

Guidelines for use: Use occasionally for review. Avoid using for grading, unless you can write quality items that extend student thinking beyond that of mere recall. Avoid copying items verbatim from the textbook or workbook. Be sure to provide adequate space for students' answers.

4. Correction Type

Description: Similar to completion type, except that sentences or paragraphs are complete but with italicized or underlined words that must be changed to make the sentence correct.

EXAMPLE: Photosynthesis in *Alabama* is the breakdown of *children* into hydrogen and oxygen, the release of *minerals,* and then the combining of the *arms* with carbon dioxide to make *Legos.*

Advantages: Writing this type can be fun for the teacher (and for children, for review purposes). Students may enjoy this type for the relief of tension afforded by the incorrect absurdities.

Disadvantages: Like the completion type, the correction type tends to measure for low-level recall and rote memory. The underlined incorrect items could be so whimsical that they might cause more classroom disturbance than you want.

Guidelines for use: Use occasionally for diversion. Try to write items that measure for higher-level cognition. Consider making it a combined correction, short-explanation type. Be sure to allow space for student explanations.

5. Essay Type

Description: A question or problem is presented, and the student is to compose a response in the form of sustained prose, using his or her own words, phrases, and ideas, within the limits of the question or problem.

EXAMPLE 1: Explain the major steps in purifying water for drinking in our city. Describe each step, from waste water to potable, explaining its function.

EXAMPLE 2: Describe the relationship and the difference between these two plant flower processes: pollination, fertilization.

Advantages: Measures higher mental processes, such as ability to synthesize material and to express ideas in clear and precise written language. Especially useful in integrated thematic teaching. Provides practice in written expression.

Disadvantages: Essay items require a good deal of time to read and to score. They tend to provide an unreliable sampling of achievement and are vulnerable to teacher subjectivity and unreliable scoring. Furthermore, they tend to punish the student who writes slowly and laboriously, but who may have achieved as well as a student who writes faster. Essay items tend to favor students who have fluency with words, but whose achievement may not be better than others'. In addition, unless the children have been given instruction in their meaning and in how to respond to them, the teacher should not assume that students understand key directive verbs such as *describe* and *explain*, used in the two examples here.

Guidelines for use:

1. When preparing an essay-only type, a test with many questions, each requiring a relatively short prose response (see Type 11), is preferable to a smaller number of questions requiring long prose responses. Briefer answers tend to be more precise, and including many items provides a more reliable sampling of student achievement. When preparing short prose response-type questions, be sure to avoid using word-for-word language from the student textbook or workbook.
2. Be certain that children have adequate test time for a full response.
3. Different qualities of achievement are most likely comparable when all children must answer the same questions, as opposed to their being able to select from a list of essay items to answer.
4. After preparing essay items, you should make a tentative scoring key, deciding the key ideas you expect students to identify, and how many points will be allotted to each.
5. Students should be informed about the relative test value for each essay item. Point values, if different for each item, can be listed in the margin of the test next to each item.
6. When reading student essay responses, read all student papers for one item at a time and, while doing that, make notes to yourself; then reread and score each child's paper for that item. Repeat the process for the next item. While scoring

essay responses, keep in mind the nature of the objective being measured, which may or may not include the qualities of handwriting, grammar, spelling, and neatness.

7. To nullify the "halo effect," some teachers use a number code rather than having students write their names on essay papers, so that while reading the papers the teacher is unaware of whose paper is being read. If you do this, use caution not to confuse the identification codes.

8. While having some understanding of a concept, many children are not yet facile with written expression, so you must remember to be patient, tolerant, positive, and helpful. Mark papers with positive and constructive comments, showing children how they could have explained or responded better.

9. Before using this type of test item, give students instruction and practice in responding to key directive verbs that will be used. For example:

Compare asks for an analysis of similarity and difference, but with a greater emphasis on similarities or likenesses.

Contrast asks for differences more than for similarities.

Criticize asks for the good and bad of an idea or situation.

Define asks the student to express clearly and concisely the meaning of a term, as in the dictionary or in the student's own words.

Diagram asks the student to put quantities or numerical values into the form of a chart, a graph, or a drawing.

Discuss asks the student to explain or argue, presenting various sides of events, ideas, or situations.

Enumerate means to count or list one after another, which is different from "explain briefly" or "tell in a few words."

Evaluate means to express worth, value, and judgment.

Explain means to describe with emphasis on cause and effect.

Illustrate means to describe by means of examples, figures, pictures, or diagrams.

Interpret means to describe or explain a given fact, theory, principle, or doctrine in a specific context.

Justify asks student to show reasons, with an emphasis on the correct, positive, and advantageous.

List means just that, to simply name items in a category or to include them in a list, without much description.

Outline means to give a short summary with headings and subheadings.

Relate means to tell how specified things are connected or brought into some kind of relationship.

Summarize asks the student to recapitulate the main points without examples or illustrations.

Trace asks the student to follow a history or series of events step-by-step by going backward over the evidence.

Prove means to present materials as witnesses and evidence.

6. Grouping Type

Description: Several items are presented, and the student is to select and group those that are related in some way.

EXAMPLE 1: Separate the following pictures of animals into two groups, one that consists of those that are mammals, the other of those that are not mammals.

EXAMPLE 2: Circle the figure that is least like the others (showing a wrench, screwdriver, saw, and swing).

Advantages: This type of item tests knowledge of grouping and can be used to measure for higher levels of cognition. If students manipulate actual items, then it is closer to an authentic assessment type as well. Children like this type of question. It can stimulate discussion. As in Example 2, it can be similar to a multiple-choice-type item.

Disadvantage: You must remain alert for the child who has a valid alternative rationale for grouping.

Guidelines for use: To allow for an alternative correct response, consider making the item a combination grouping, short-explanation type, being certain to allow adequate space for student explanations.

7. Identification Type

Description: Unknown specimens are to be identified by name or some other criterion.

EXAMPLE 1: Identify each of the flowers on the table by its common name.

EXAMPLE 2: Identify by name, and sport in which it is used, each of the balls on the table.

Advantages: Verbalization (that is, the use of abstract symbolization) is less significant, as the student is working with real objects. Should be measuring for higher-level learning than simple recall. An item can also be written to measure for procedural understanding, such as for identification of steps in booting up a computer program. This is another useful type for authentic assessment.

Disadvantages: To be fair, "specimens" used should be equally familiar or unfamiliar to all students. Adequate materials must be provided.

Guidelines for use: If photographs, drawings, photocopies, or copies of recordings are used, rather than actual materials, they must be clear and not confusing to students.

8. Matching Type

Description: Related items in a list of numbered items are to be matched to a list of lettered choices, or those items that are the same or are related are to be connected in some way. Or, to eliminate the paper-and-pencil aspect and make the type more direct, of items on a table, those that are most alike are paired.

EXAMPLE 1: In the blank space next to each word in Column A, put the letter of the best answer from Column B.

Column A	Column B
_____ 1. nutcracker	a. first-class lever
_____ 2. block and tackle	b. inclined plane
_____ 3. knife	c. second-class lever
_____ 4. round door handle	d. screw
_____ 5. ramp	e. pulley
_____ 6. tweezers	f. wedge
	g. wheel and axle
	h. third-class lever

EXAMPLE 2: Match items in Column A (stem column) to those of Column B (answer column) by drawing lines to the matched pairs.

Column A	Column B
snake	worm
eagle	mammal
whale	reptile
praying mantis	insect
	bird

Advantages: Can measure ability to judge relationships and to differentiate between similar ideas, facts, definitions, and concepts. Easy to score. Can test a broad range of content. Reduces guessing, especially if one group contains more items than the other. Interesting to students. Quite adaptable for performance assessment.

Disadvantages: Not easily adapted to measuring for higher cognition. Because all parts must be homogeneous, it is possible that clues will be given, thus reducing item validity. A student might have a legitimate rationale for an "incorrect" response.

Guidelines for use: The number of items in the "answer" column should exceed the number in the stem column. The number of items to be matched should not exceed twelve. Matching sets should have high homogeneity, that is, items in both columns (or groups) should be of the same general category. If "answers" can be used more than once, the directions should so state. Be prepared for the student who can legitimately defend an "incorrect" response.

9. Multiple-Choice Type

Description: Similar to the completion type in that statements are presented, sometimes in incomplete form, but with several options requiring recognition or even higher cognitive processes, rather than mere recall.

EXAMPLE 1: Of the four cylinders, the one that would cause the lowest-pitched sound would be

1. short and thick
2. short and thin
3. long and thick
4. long and thin

EXAMPLE 2: From the following list of planets, the planet in our solar system that is farthest from our sun is _____ .

1. Earth
2. Mercury
3. Pluto
4. Saturn

Advantages: Items can be answered and scored quickly. A wide range of content, and higher levels of cognition can be tested in a relatively short time. Excellent for all testing purposes; motivation, review, and assessment of learning.

Disadvantages: Unfortunately, because multiple-choice items are relatively easy to write, there is a tendency to write items that measure only for low levels of cognition. Multiple-choice items are excellent for major testing, but it takes time to write good questions that measure higher levels of learning.

Guidelines for use:

1. If the item is in the form of an incomplete statement, it should be meaningful in itself and imply a direct question rather than merely lead into a collection of unrelated true-and-false statements.
2. Use a level of language that is easy enough for even the poorest readers to understand, and avoid unnecessary wordiness.
3. If there is much variation in the length of alternatives, arrange the alternatives in order from shortest to longest; that is, first alternative is the shortest, last alternative is the longest.
4. For single-word alternatives, consistent alphabetical arrangement of alternatives is recommended (as in Example 2).
5. Incorrect responses (distracters) should be plausible and related to the same concept as the correct alternative. Although an occasional humorous distracter helps to relieve test anxiety, these, along with absurd distracters, should be avoided. They offer no measuring value.
6. Arrangement of alternatives should be uniform throughout the test and listed in vertical (column) form rather than in horizontal (paragraph) form.
7. Every item should be grammatically consistent; that is, if the stem is in the form of an incomplete sentence, it should be possible to complete the sentence by attaching any of the alternatives to it.
8. It is not necessary to maintain a fixed number of alternatives for every item, but the use of less than three is not recommended. The use of four or five reduces chance responses and guessing, thereby increasing reliability for the item.
9. The item should be expressed in positive form. A negative form presents a psychological disadvantage to students. Negative items are those that ask what is *not* characteristic of something, or what is the *least* useful. Discard the item if you cannot express it in positive terminology.
10. Responses such as "all of these" or "none of these" should be used only when they will contribute more than another plausible distracter. Care must be taken that such responses answer or complete the item. "All of the above" is a poorer alternative than "none of the above" because items that use it as a correct response must have four or five correct answers; moreover, if it is the right answer, knowledge of any two of the distracters will cue it.
11. There must be only one correct or best response. However, this is easier said than achieved (refer to Guideline 19).
12. The stem must mean the same thing to every child.
13. Understanding of definitions is better tested by furnishing the name or word and requiring a choice between alternative definitions, than by presenting the definition and requiring a choice between alternative words.
14. The stem should state a single and specific point.
15. The stem must not include clues that would signal the correct alternative. For example, "A four-sided figure whose opposite sides are parallel is called _____. (a) an octagon, (b) a parallelogram, (c) a trapezoid, (d) a triangle." The use of the word "parallel" indicates the answer.
16. Avoid using alternatives that include absolute terms such as *never* and *always*.

17. Multiple-choice items need not be entirely verbal. Consider the use of realia, charts, diagrams, and other visuals. They will make the test more interesting, especially to students with low verbal abilities or who have limited proficiency in English and, consequently, make the assessment more direct (authentic).

18. Once you have composed a multiple-choice test, tally the position of answers to be sure they are evenly distributed, to avoid the common psychological mistake (when there are four alternatives) of having the correct alternative in the third position.

19. Consider providing space between test items for students to include their rationales for their selections, thus making the test a combination multiple-choice and short-explanation type. This provides for the student who can rationalize an alternative that you had not considered plausible. It also allows measurement of higher levels of cognition and encourages student writing.

20. While scoring, on a blank copy of the test, tally the incorrect responses for each item. Analyze incorrect responses for each item to discover potential errors in your scoring key. If, for example, many children select "B" for an item when your key says "A" is the correct answer, you may have made a mistake in your scoring key or during the lesson.

10. Performance Type

Description: Provided with certain conditions or materials, the student solves a problem or accomplishes some other action.

EXAMPLE 1: Given a class of ten students, you are to prepare and teach an effective 15-minute inquiry lesson. (*Note:* This example is a teacher-education-level question.)

EXAMPLE 2: Show your understanding of diffusion by designing and completing a laboratory experiment using only the chemicals and equipment located at the learning-activity station.

Advantages: Performance tests come closer to direct measurement (authentic assessment) of certain expected outcomes than most other types. However, as indicated in discussion of the preceding types, other types of questions can actually be prepared as performance-type items, that is, those that require the student to actually do what he or she is being tested for. Learning that is difficult to verbalize can be assessed, since little or no verbalization may be necessary. *Students who do poorly on verbal tests may do well on performance tests,* for example, students with learning disabilities.

Disadvantages: Can be difficult and time-consuming to administer to a group of students. Scoring may tend to be subjective.

Guidelines for use: Use your creativity to design and use performance tests, as they tend to measure the most important objectives. To reduce subjectivity in scoring, prepare distinct scoring guidelines, as discussed in scoring essay-type questions.

11. Short-Explanation Type

Description: The short-explanation question is an essay-type item but requires a shorter answer.

EXAMPLE 1: Briefly explain in a paragraph why piano wires are not equal in length.

EXAMPLE 2: Explain what is incorrect or misleading about the following drawing.

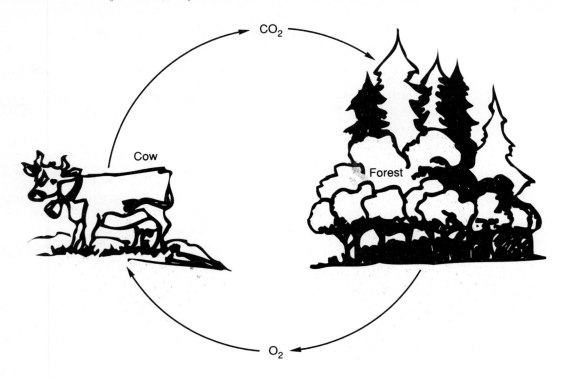

Advantages: As in the essay type, the student's understanding is assessed, but this type takes less time for the teacher to read and to score. In Example 2, for instance, the diagram of the cow and the forest is similar to drawings seen in some science books and represents a **misconception** about our own place in nature. The intent of the makers of such a diagram is to illustrate the interdependence of animals and plants; the lesson frequently learned is that plants use carbon dioxide produced by animals and that animals use oxygen produced by plants. Following such a study, we interviewed teachers and their students and asked, "Do plants use oxygen?" The majority said no. A misconcept was learned: the teachers and their students did not understand that *all* living organisms need oxygen. The focus was too much on what *humans* gain from "interdependence," rather than on the nature of "interdependence." **Artificialism** is the term used by Piaget to represent the tendency to believe that everything here on Earth is for the benefit of humans. Although natural for children in kindergarten and primary grades, this does represent a selfish, prejudiced, nonobjective misconcept that should be corrected and avoided by teachers. As discussed in Chapter 2, teachers have an obligation, and an opportunity, to correct student misconceptions, providing they have a correct understanding of the concept. This type of test item can be useful in assessing conceptual understanding and critical thinking.

By using several questions of this type, a greater amount of content can be covered than with a fewer number of essay questions. This type of question provides good practice for students in learning to express themselves succinctly in writing.

Disadvantages: Many children have difficulty expressing themselves in a limited fashion, or in writing. They need practice and time in doing so.

Guidelines for use: Useful for occasional reviews and quizzes and as an alternative to other types of questions. For scoring, follow the same guidelines as for the essay-type item.

12. True-False Type

Description: A statement is presented that students are to judge as being accurate or not.

EXAMPLE 1: Photosynthesis occurs only in green plants. T or F?

EXAMPLE 2: America was discovered by Christopher Columbus. T or F?

Advantages: Many items can be answered in a relatively short time, making broad content coverage possible. Scoring is quick and simple. True-false items are good for starting discussions, for review, and for diagnostic evaluation (preassessment).

Disadvantages: As illustrated by both examples, it is difficult to write true-false items that are purely true or false, or without qualifying them in such a way that gives away the answer. Much of the content that most easily lends itself to this type of test item is trivial. Students have a 50 percent chance of guessing the correct answer, thus giving this type of item *poor validity and reliability.* Scoring and grading give no clue to why a student missed an item. The disadvantages of true-false items far outweigh the advantages, and true-false items should *never* be used for arriving at grades. For grading purposes, you may use modified true-false items, where space is provided between items for students to write in explanations, thus making the item a combined true-false, short-explanation type. For instance, for Example 2 the student might select "false" and then write his or her explanation as follows:

There were people here before C. Columbus arrived.

or

I selected false because I don't know what is meant by "America." Does the question refer to North America, Central America, Latin America, Canada, or what? If I remember correctly, he landed on some islands somewhere.

Guidelines for use:

1. First write the statement as a true statement, then make it false by changing a word or phrase.
2. Avoid using negative statements since they tend to confuse students.
3. A true-false statement should include only one idea. For more than one reason, Example 1 is a poor item. One reason is that it measures two ideas: that photosynthesis occurs in plants (which is true), and that it does so only in plants that are green in color (which is false).
4. Use close to an equal number of true and false items.
5. Avoid specific determiners, which may signal that the statement is false, for example, "always," "all," or "none."
6. Avoid words that may hint that the statement is true, words such as "often," "probably," and "sometimes."
7. Avoid words that may have different meanings for different students.
8. Avoid using word-for-word language from the student textbook or workbook.
9. Avoid trick items.

10. As stated earlier, for grading purposes you may use modified true-false items, where space is provided between items for students to write their explanations, thus making the item a combined true-false, short-explanation type. Another form of modified true-false item is the use of "sometimes-always-never," in which a third alternative, "sometimes," is introduced to reduce the chance for guessing.

Now do Exercise 14.2.

Exercise 14.2: Preparing Assessment Items

Instructions: The purpose of this exercise is to practice your skill in preparing the different types of assessment items as discussed in Section I. From a course syllabus (Exercise 7.2), or a teaching unit, select *one* specific instructional objective and write assessment items for it. When completed, share this exercise with your colleagues for their feedback.

The objective _____

_____

Grade level and subject area _____

1. Arrangement item _____

_____

_____

_____

2. Drawing-completion item _____

_____

_____

_____

3. Statement-completion item _____

_____

_____

_____

4. Correction item _____

_____

_____

_____

5. Essay item _____

_____

_____

_____

6. Grouping item _____

_____

_____

_____

_____

7. Identification item _____

_____

_____

_____

_____

8. Matching item _____

_____

_____

_____

_____

9. Multiple-choice item _____

_____

_____

_____

_____

10. Performance item _____

_____

_____

_____

_____

11. Short-explanation item _____

_____

_____

_____

_____

12. *Modified* (for use in grading) true-false item _____

_____

_____

_____

_____

J. REPORTING STUDENT ACHIEVEMENT

As a classroom teacher, one of your major responsibilities is to report students' progress in achievement to parents or guardians. In some schools student *progress* and *effort* are reported, as well as achievement. Reporting is accomplished in at least two, and sometimes three, ways. There are two basic formulas for reporting—word comments and symbols. Primary grade-level reporting is usually by teacher comments and/or symbols, which only approximate the number or letter grade system commonly used after the primary grades. As stated earlier, you must decide what achievement is, whether it is progress toward certain set standards, or simply achievement per se. The particular school where you teach undoubtedly has established a philosophy in this regard, a philosophy which is most likely written for you to read and to follow.

The reporting form sent home to parents or guardians will probably separate the social-emotional from the academic behaviors of the child.

The Report Card

About every six to nine weeks a report card is sent home. (Some schools have six marking periods during the year, while others have four or five, and fewer have only two or three.) This grade report represents an achievement grade **(formative assessment)**; the second or third one of the semester is also the semester grade, and for courses that are only one semester long, it also is the final grade **(summative assessment)**. In essence, the first and, sometimes, second reports are progress notices, the semester grade being the one that is transferred to the student's transcript of records. In some schools the traditional report card is marked and sent home either with the student or by mail. In other schools reporting is done by computer printouts, often sent by mail directly to the student's home address. (In some schools, as an effort to involve parents, parents or guardians are expected to come to the school on a given day to pick up the grade report.)

Whichever reporting form is used, you must separate your assessment of a student's social-emotional behaviors (classroom conduct) from the student's academic achievement. Academic achievement (or accomplishment) is represented by a letter (sometimes a number) grade, such as the traditional A through E or F; E (excellent), S (satisfactory), and U (unsatisfactory); O (outstanding), S (satisfactory), N (needs improvement), and U (unsatisfactory); or 1 to 5—sometimes with minuses and pluses. The social-emotional behavior may be indicated by a "satisfactory" or an "unsatisfactory," or by more specific items, or supplemented by teacher-written or computer-generated comments. Sometimes, especially for grade 4 and above, the academic report may include two grades for each subject, one for *achievement* in the subject and one for *effort*. On some report cards there may be a place on the reporting form for the teacher to check whether basic grade-level standards have been met in science, language arts, social studies, and mathematics.

Figures 14.3–14.5 are samples of forms used for reporting student progress in kindergarten, primary, and middle grades. You will notice that in the forms for primary and middle grades, the teacher must indicate whether the student has met "Basic Grade Level Standards," that is, satisfactory achievement of the set basic standards for that grade.

PROGRESS REPORT
Kindergarten

School Year
19 _____ - 19 _____

STUDENT'S NAME: _____ GRADE: _____
TEACHER: _____ SCHOOL: _____

EXPLANATION OF SYMBOLS: S — Satisfactory
N — Needs Improvement

	1	2	3
PHYSICAL DEVELOPMENT			
Shows large muscle control in such activities as:			
Hopping			
Jumping			
Skipping			
Walking on Toes			
Bouncing Ball			
Catching Ball			
Jumping Rope, Assisted			
Walking Balance Board			
Demonstrates small muscle control when:			
Handling crayon, pencil, and scissors			
Tying a shoe			
SOCIAL DEVELOPMENT AND WORK HABITS			
Displays enthusiasm			
Shows reasonable attention span			
Finishes assigned work			
Follows directions			
Shares willingly			
Gets along well with others			
Follows rules			
Works independently			
Listens to directions			
LANGUAGE DEVELOPMENT			
Basic Knowledge:			
Knows full name			
Knows address or bus stop			
Knows telephone number			
Knows days of week			
Knows basic colors			
Knows left from right			
Knows basic shapes			
Knows Pledge of Allegiance			
Knows body parts			
Knows simple nursery rhymes and poems			
Skills and Habits			
Speaks in complete sentences			
Uses adequate vocabulary to express ideas			
Shows interest in books, stories, poetry and pictures			
Writes letters with reasonable skill			
Prints name			
Draws basic shapes			
Letters and Sounds			
Recognizes sound of letters			
Knows names of letters-capital			
Knows names of letters-small			
Knows rhyming words			
COUNTING AND MEASURING			
Recognizes numbers			
Counts by rote			
Writes numbers with reasonable skill			
Counts objects			
Counts backwards, 10-1			
ART			
Demonstrates ability to work with a variety of art media			
MUSIC			
Takes part in rhythmic activities			
Participates in singing			

TEACHER COMMENTS

1st Report _____

2nd Report _____

3rd Report _____

Figure 14.3 Sample progress report for kindergarten.[9]

[9]Reprinted by permission of Vallecito Union School District, Arnold, California, 1983.

PROGRESS REPORT FOR GRADES 1–3

STUDENT'S NAME: _____   GRADE: _____ YEAR: _____

TEACHER: _____   SCHOOL: _____

SYMBOLS: ACHIEVEMENT AND EFFORT
O = Outstanding
G = Good
S = Satisfactory
N = Needs Improvement
U = Unsatisfactory

THIRD GRADE
A = Outstanding
B = Good
C = Satisfactory
D = Unsatisfactory
F = Failing

GRADE LEVEL
A = Above
O = On
B = Below

Quarters	1	2	3	4
READING LEVEL				
Reading				
Effort				
Vocabulary				
Phonics				
Comprehension				
Oral Reading				
Independent Seatwork				
Completes Assignments on Time				
MATH LEVEL				
Mathematics				
Efforts				
Basic Facts Memorized				
Works Accurately				
Understands Concepts				
Completes Assignments on Time				
LANGUAGE				
Effort				
Oral Expression				
Grammar/Punctuation				
Composition				
Handwriting				
Completes Assignments on Time				
SPELLING				
Spelling Lists				
Writing Work				
Effort				

Quarters	1	2	3	4
PARTICIPATES IN (S or N)				
Social Studies				
Science				
Music				
Art				
P.E.				
STUDY HABITS/SOCIAL SKILLS (G S N)				
Listens attentively				
Follows directions first time				
Does neat and careful work				
Attends to task				
Makes good use of time				
Is self-directed				
Does not disturb others at work				
Takes care of materials				
Shows respect for others				
Works well with others				
Works independently				
BEHAVIOR (√)				
Outstanding				
Always exhibits expected behavior without reminders				
Good				
Almost always exhibits behavior without reminders				
Satisfactory				
Usually exhibits expected behavior with occasional reminders				
Unsatisfactory				
Rarely exhibits expected behavior without frequent reminders				

FIRST QUARTER PROGRESS REPORT COMMENTS:
_____
_____

SECOND QUARTER PROGRESS REPORT COMMENTS:
_____
_____

THIRD QUARTER PROGRESS REPORT COMMENTS:
_____
_____

FOURTH QUARTER PROGRESS REPORT COMMENTS:
_____
_____

This Basic Grade Level Standards have been satisfactorily passed in:

Reading ☐   Mathematics ☐   Language ☐

ASSIGNMENT FOR NEXT YEAR:
_____
_____

Figure 14.4   Sample progress report for grades 1–3.[10]

[10]Reprinted by permission of Vallecito Union School District, Arnold, California, 1983.

PROGRESS REPORT FOR GRADES 4–6

STUDENT'S NAME: _____   GRADE: _____ YEAR: _____

TEACHER: _____   SCHOOL: _____

SYMBOLS: ACHIEVEMENT AND EFFORT

A = Outstanding
B = Good
C = Satisfactory
D = Unsatisfactory
F = Failing

HONORS STUDENT:

	1st Qtr.	2nd Qtr.	3rd Qtr.	4th Qtr.
	☐	☐	☐	☐

SUBJECTS	1st Quarter	2nd Quarter	3rd Quarter	4th Quarter
Reading				
Mathematics				
Language				
Social Studies				
Spelling				
Science				

Citizenship				
Physical Education				
Handwriting				
Art				
Music				

O = Outstanding
G = Good
S = Satisfactory
N = Needs Improvement
U = Unsatisfactory

The Basic Grade Level Standards have been satisfactorily passed in:

Reading ☐   Mathematics ☐   Language ☐

FIRST QUARTER PROGRESS REPORT COMMENTS:

SECOND QUARTER PROGRESS REPORT COMMENTS:

THIRD QUARTER PROGRESS REPORT COMMENTS:

FOURTH QUARTER PROGRESS REPORT COMMENTS:

ASSIGNMENT FOR NEXT YEAR: _____

Figure 14.5 Sample progress report for grades 4–6.[11]

[11]Reprinted by permission of Vallecito Union School District, Arnold, California, 1983.

Direct Contact with Parents or Guardians

Although not always obligatory (see section that follows), some teachers make a point to contact parents or guardians by telephone, especially when a child has shown a sudden turn for either the worse or the better in academic achievement or in classroom behavior. That initiative and contact by the teacher is usually welcomed by parents and can lead to private and productive conferences with the teacher. A telephone conversation saves valuable time for both the teacher and the parent.

Another way of contacting parents is by letter. Contacting a parent by letter gives you time to think and to make clear your thoughts and concerns to that parent, and to invite the parent to respond at his or her convenience by letter, by phone, or by arranging to have a conference with you.

K. CONFERENCES WITH PARENTS OR GUARDIANS

You will meet many parents or guardians early in the school year during back-to-school night and throughout the year in individual parent conferences. For the beginning teacher these meetings with parents can be anxious times. Here are guidelines to help you with those experiences.

Guidelines for Meeting Parents (or Guardians)

In many schools, back-to-school night is an evening early in the school year when parents can come to the school and meet their child's teachers. The parents arrive at the child's home base and then proceed through a simulation of their son or daughter's school day, visiting as a group each class and meeting each teacher for a few minutes. Later, in the spring, there is an "open house." At this time parents may have more time to talk individually with teachers, but open house is usually a time for the school and teachers to show off the work and progress of the students for that year. Throughout the school year there will be opportunities for you and parents to meet and talk about the children.

Back-to-School Night

On the evening of back-to-school night, parents are anxious to learn as much as they can about their child's new teachers. You will meet each group of parents for about ten minutes. During that brief meeting you will provide them with a copy of the course syllabus, make some straightforward remarks about yourself, and then briefly discuss your expectations of the students.

Although there will be precious little time for questions from the parents, during your introduction they will be delighted to learn that you (1) have your program well planned, (2) are a "task master," and (3) will communicate with them. The parents and guardians will be pleased to know that you are from the school of the three F's—firm, friendly, and fair.

Specifically, parents will expect to learn about your curriculum—goals and objectives, any long-term projects, when tests will be given and whether they are given on a regular basis, and your grading procedures. They will need to know what you expect of them: will there be homework, and if so, should they help their children with it?

How can they contact you? Try to anticipate other questions. Your principal or colleagues can be of aid in helping you anticipate and prepare for these questions. Of course, you can never prepare for the question that comes from left field. Just stay calm and do not get flustered. Ten minutes will fly by quickly, and parents will be reassured to know you are a person who is in control.

Parent-Teacher Conference

When meeting parents for conferences, you should be as specific as possible when explaining the progress of a child in your class. Be helpful to their understanding, and do not saturate the parent with more information than he or she needs. Resist any tendency to talk too much. Allow time for the parent to ask questions. Keep your answers succinct. Never compare one child with another, or with the rest of the class. If the parent asks a question for which you do not have an answer, say that you will try to find an answer and will phone the parent as quickly as you can. And do so. Have the child's portfolio and other work with you during parent conferences so you can *show* the parent examples of what is being discussed. In addition, have your grade book on hand, or a computer printout of it, but be prepared to protect from the parent the records of the other children.

Sometimes it is helpful to have a three-way conference, including the parent, the child, and you, or the parent, the principal or counselor, and several or all of the child's teachers.

Ideas for Teacher-Parent Collaboration

When a parent asks how she or he may help in the child's learning, here are some suggestions you might want to offer:

- Limit and control the child's television pleasure viewing.
- Set up a regular schedule of reviewing with the child his or her portfolio.
- Consider having students take their portfolios home each Friday to share with their parents, having a place in the portfolio where parents or guardians sign to show they have reviewed their child's work, and then returned the portfolio to class on Monday. The form for the parent's signature could also have a column for teacher and parent comments or notes to each other, to maintain this important line of communication between parent and teacher.
- Set up a regular time each evening for a family discussion about school.
- Ask the child to share with you each day one specific thing learned that day.
- As needed, plan short family meetings *after* dinner, but while you are still seated at the table. Ask for a "tableside" report of "What's happening in the school?" Ask, "How can I help?" When your child expresses a concern, emphasize ways to solve problems. Help the child develop his or her problem-solving skills.
- Helping children become critical thinkers is one of the aims of education and one that parents can help with by reinforcing the strategies being used in the classroom, for example, asking "what if" questions; thinking aloud as a model for your child's thinking development; encouraging the child's own metacognition by asking questions such as, "How did you arrive at that conclusion?" or "How do you feel about your conclusion now?" Ask these questions about the child's everyday social inter-

actions, topics that are important to the child; ask your child to elaborate on his or her ideas; allow your child to make mistakes and encourage the child to learn from them.

- Several books are available for parents to use at home. For example, for parents looking for guidance in reading to their young children, ages 2 to 7, they will find more than 400 useful suggestions in *Read to Me,* published in 1993 by the California State Department of Education. (Order by sending $5.93 to: Publication Sales Office, Department of Education, P.O. Box 271, Sacramento, CA 95812-0271.) John Shefelbine's *Encouraging Your Junior High Student to Read* (Bloomington, IN: International Reading Association, 1991), is a booklet that gives ideas, guidelines, and suggestions to help parents of middle-grade-level students help their children read more and derive more pleasure from reading. At the end of the booklet is a list of resources for parents' reading and of resources for parents from the International Reading Association. The United States government has a variety of booklets available—costing usually less than one dollar and available from Department 587V, Consumer Information Center, Pueblo, CO 81109. Other useful resources are *Helping Your Child Use the Library* (item 465V); *Becoming a Nation of Readers: What Parents Can Do* (item 459V); *Help Your Child Do Better at School* (item 412V). You also can encourage the parent to visit the neighborhood public library and ask for a librarian's help in locating helpful resources. If you and parents are interested in strategies for increasing home-school collaboration, read: *Beyond the Bake Sale: An Educator's Guide to Working with Parents* by Anne T. Henderson, Carl Marburger, and Theodora Ooms (Columbia, MD: National Committee for Citizens in Education, 1985); the special section "Parent Involvement" in *Phi Delta Kappan* (72(5) January 1991); *Communicating with Parents* by Janet Chrispeels, Marcia Boruta, and Mary Daugherty (San Diego: San Diego County Office of Education, 1988); *The Evidence Continues to Grow: Parent Involvement Improves Student Achievement* (Columbia, MD: National Committee for Citizens in Education, 1987); and, *Parenting for Education* by Paula Lowe and Carl Trendler (Seattle: U.S. West Education Foundation, 1989). See also E. Clinchy, "Helping Parents Make the School System Work for Them: Buffalo Public Schools' Parent Center," in *Equity and Choice* 7(2–3): 83–88 (Spring 1991). Parents are guided through their children's classes and take home computers to help in their children's learning.

Dealing with an Angry Parent or Guardian

If a parent or guardian is angry or hostile toward you or the school, here are guidelines for dealing with that hostility:

- Remain calm in your discussion with the parent, allowing the parent to talk out his or her hostility while you say very little. Usually, the less you say the better off you will be. What you do say must be objective and to the point of the child's work in your classroom. The parent may just need to vent frustrations that might have very little to do with you, the school, or even the child.
- Do *not* allow yourself to be intimidated or backed into a corner. If the parent tries to do so by attacking you personally, do not press your defense at this point. Perhaps the parent has made a point that you should take time to consider, and now is a good time to arrange for another conference with the parent for about a week later. In a follow-up conference, if agreed to by the parent, you may want to consider

bringing in a mediator, such as another member of your teaching team, an administrator, or a school counselor.

- You must *not* talk about other children; keep the conversation focused on this parent's child's progress. The parent is *not* your rival, or should not be. You both share a concern for the academic and emotional well-being of the child. Use your best skills in critical thinking and problem solving; focus the discussion by identifying the problem(s), defining it, and then arriving at some mutual decision about how to go about solving it. To this end, you may need to ask for help from a third party. If agreed to by the parent, please take that step.

- Parents do *not* need to hear about how busy you are, or about your personal problems, or about how many other children you are dealing with on a daily basis, unless, of course, a parent asks. Parents expect you to be the capable professional who knows what to do and to be doing it.

Now do Exercise 14.3.

Exercise 14.3: Participating in Role Play: Teacher-Parent Conferences

Instructions: The purpose of this exercise is to prepare your thoughts about what you might do in particular parent-teacher conference situations. Divide into teams of two and select one of the conference situations for a role-playing experience of approximately five minutes. Each situation includes one of the parent behaviors as its main focus. Each five-minute role-play can then serve as a basis for a discussion by your entire class.

Ideas for Role-Playing Teacher-Parent Conferences

1. A fourth-grade girl misses a unit test in history that you administered on Friday. You tell her that she can't make it up during class; however, she can make it up after school. The next morning, the irate mother calls the principal and says that: (1) you are unfair, (2) staying late after school will cause her daughter to miss the bus; and (3) there is no other transportation to the girl's home. The mother asserts that (4) it is unsafe for a girl her age to walk that distance alone; (5) there is no money for a taxi or other transportation; and (6) there is no family car. The mother wants the test given at the lunch hour.

2. A sixth-grade boy is with his friends on the school bus for an environmental education outing. One boy opens his thermos and drinks the liquid. You notice the smell of wine. You take the thermos. After the students leave the bus, you check the other containers. Another thermos holds whiskey. You talk to the boys, verifying possession. Another teacher drives the two boys back to school. The parents are called and a conference is scheduled for four o'clock that afternoon.

3. A fifth-grade girl talks incessantly during class. After several warnings, you call her parents and inform them you will have to give a D in citizenship to the student. The parents ask for a conference. At the conference, the parents suggest you do the following:
   a. Move the student away from the other students who talk.
   b. Move the student to the front of the room so she has more teacher supervision.
   c. Read the student's file (the student has a reading comprehension problem).
   d. Consider the student's past history of grades in citizenship. (The student received all marks of "outstanding" and "satisfactory" the year before.)
   e. Allow the student to bring her books home to complete work not done during class. (The student told her parents she couldn't bring her books home to complete her assignments.)
   f. Become more firm in class. (The student told her parents the other students talked to her, that she didn't begin the conversations in class.)

4. A parent calls to complain about the behavior of one of the third-grade students in your class. This student writes on the back of the other children's T-shirts, wipes paint from a brush onto their jeans, pushes, kicks, and tries to trip others as they walk past him in class and on the playground. This parent wants you to put a stop to this kind of behavior in your classroom and on the playground.

5. Add your own idea for a teacher-parent conference here.

_____

_____

_____

_____

_____

FOR YOUR NOTES

SUMMARY

Preceding parts of this text addressed the *why, what,* and *how* components of teaching, and this chapter focused your attention on the fourth and final component—the *how well* component—and on the first of two aspects of that component. Because teaching and learning work hand in hand, because they are reciprocal processes that depend on and affect each other, the *how well* component deals with the assessment of both—how well the students are learning and how well the teacher is teaching. This chapter addressed the first. In the next and final chapter your attention is directed to techniques designed to help you evaluate how well you are teaching, and to assist your continued development as a professional teacher.

QUESTIONS FOR CLASS DISCUSSION

1. Explain the ways in which "authentic assessment" differs from traditional assessment.
2. Ungraded (continuous promotion; mixed-age) classrooms are making a comeback, as an alternative to retention or holding students in the same grade for another year, in the elementary grades. Research the literature about the pros and cons of this approach and report your findings to your class.
3. Do you believe that a teacher's evaluation of students should be based on their performances according to individual abilities, or on their performances as compared with the rest of the children? Explain.
4. In your school, do children get A's and B's, or do they receive ranks of "Outstanding," "Satisfactory," or "Need Improvement" or an alternative grading method? Advocates of alternative methods say that report cards should be much more detailed than is traditional. For example, instead of a single letter grade for writing, a student can be evaluated on development of ideas, ability to use a variety of writing styles, application of grammar, word usage, and spelling skills. These reports give the kind of information that teachers and parents need. The card then would reduce competition between students and give parents a more detailed evaluation of their child's work—a clearer picture of the strengths and weaknesses of the child. For instance, a child may not write well—perhaps the mechanics need work—but has wonderful ideas and can develop a plot. Under the letter-grade system, the child would perhaps have earned a C or a D. Using the alternative method, the teacher shows where the student is strong. The teacher is diagnosing. The alternative method eliminates the practice of comparing numbers of A's and B's among the children—which often develops in their elementary school years. The alternative method works toward establishing self-esteem, rather than labeling a child. Discuss this with your classmates. Share your opinions about grading systems.
5. Do you consider academic grouping as fair? Some say that because of academic grouping there is a psychic numbing that children in lower tracks experience because of a "dumbed-down" curriculum, a widening gap in achievement between faster and slower groups, and an increased racial isolation of ability groupings. Rather than using academic grouping, it is proposed that schools encourage students of diverse abilities by having capable students tutor others and by team-

ing students of diverse abilities in cooperative projects in which brighter students help slower ones and the students are rewarded according to achievement of the group. Critics of this approach say that this is an injustice, that it harms bright children who are entitled to an education suitable to their abilities. They say that the brighter children are, the more likely it is that receiving group rewards, tutoring others, and teaming with slower students will leave the brighter children unchallenged and their potential unfulfilled. Expecting bright children to spend much of their class time helping slower learners may be a waste of their learning time. Educators should be doing everything they can to find giftedness—especially in youngsters from families that lack the resources to do so themselves—and to nurture it. Educators concerned with slower students need to realize that bright children are due an equivalent share of resources and the teacher's time. Educators should remember that in the future, new solutions to problems in energy, environment, health, housing, and human rights will come from the children in today's elementary schools. Their schools should not hold back their learning. Where do you stand on this question: "Is it fair or unfair to group children by ability?"

6. Do you believe in the use of "therapeutic" grading (rewarding effort rather than achievement)? Explain.

7. As a teacher, what will you say when you meet the parents of your students for the first time at back-to-school night? Try it out on your classmates.

8. At schools you have visited, what standardized achievement tests are administered? What are their purposes? How are their results used?

9. The National Association of School Psychologists (NASP) issued a position statement on retention (*Charlotte Observer,* 1989). According to this statement, it appears that retention is likely to have a negative impact on academic achievement and on a child's self-esteem. Promotion, with remediation, is preferred. Critics maintain that there is no reliable body of studies to clearly support or not support the use of retention. Which promotes achievement—retention or promotion with remediation? What is your opinion? Of what importance is this to the teacher? What is the view of experienced teachers on this issue?

10. Do you believe that teacher certification should be based on teachers' scores on standardized examinations of their knowledge of pedagogy? Explain.

11. Are competency tests administered in schools of your state or local districts? For all subjects? To what grades? How are the results used? Explain the arguments for and against statewide and national competency testing.

12. Do you have questions about the content of this chapter? How might answers be found?

SUGGESTED READINGS FOR CHAPTER 14

Davey, B. "Assessing Comprehension: Selected Interactions of Task and Reader." *Reading Teacher* 42(9):694–697 (May 1989).

Ebel, R. L., and Frisbie, D. A. *Essentials of Educational Measurement.* 5th ed. Needham Heights, MA: Allyn & Bacon, 1991.

Evans, C. S. "When Teachers Look at Student Work." *Educational Leadership* 50(5):71–72 (February 1993).

Feuer, M. J., and Fulton, K. "The Many Faces of Performance Assessment." *Phi Delta Kappan* 74(6):478 (February 1993).

Glazer, S. M. "Assessment in Classroom: Reality and Fantasy." *Teaching PreK–8* 22(8):62–64 (May 1992).

Gomez, M. L., et al. "Reassessing Portfolio Assessment: Rhetoric and Reality." *Language Arts* 68(8):620–628 (December 1991).

Gronlund, N. F., and Linn, R. L. *Measurement and Evaluation in Teaching.* 6th ed. New York: Macmillan, 1990.

Hamm, M., and Adams, D. "Portfolio Assessment." *The Science Teacher* 58(5):18–21 (May 1991).

Hansen, J. "Evaluation: My Portfolio Shows Who I Am." *Quarterly of the National Writing Project and the Center for the Study of Writing and Literacy* 14(1):5–6, 9 (Winter 1992).

Ingalls, B., and Jones, J. "There's a Lot of Things You Can Learn in English That You Can't Really See." *Quarterly of the National Writing Project and the Center for the Study of Writing and Literacy* 14(1):1–4, 9 (Winter 1992).

Jongsma, K. S. "Rethinking Grading Practices (Research to Practice)." *Reading Teacher* 45(4):318–320 (December 1991).

Kohn, A. "Group Grade Grubbing Versus Cooperative Learning." *Educational Leadership* 48(5):83–87 (February 1991).

Krechevsky, M. "Project Spectrum: An Innovative Assessment Alternative." *Educational Leadership* 48(5):43–48 (February 1991).

Kroll, D. L., et al. "Cooperative Problem Solving: But What About Grading?" *Arithmetic Teacher* 39(6):17–23 (February 1992).

Lamme, L. L., and Hysmith, C. "One School's Adventure into Portfolio Assessment." *Language Arts* 68(8):629–640 (December 1991).

Madaus, G. F., and Tan, A. G. A. "The Growth of Assessment." In Gordon Cawelti, ed. 1993 ASCD Yearbook. *Challenges and Achievements of American Education.* Alexandria, VA: Association for Supervision and Curriculum Development, 1993.

Maeroff, G. I. "Assessing Alternative Assessment." *Phi Delta Kappan* 73(4):272–281 (December 1991).

Perrone, V., ed. *Expanding Student Assessment.* Alexandria, VA: Association for Supervision and Curriculum Development, 1991.

Pils, L. J. "Soon Anofe You Tout Me: Evaluation in a First Grade Whole Language Classroom." *Reading Teacher* 45(4):318–320 (September 1991).

Simmons, J. "Portfolio as Large-Scale Assessment." *Language Arts* 67(3):262–268 (March 1990).

Sperling, D. "What's Worth an 'A'?" *Educational Leadership* 50(5):73–75 (February 1993).

Wilson, V. L. "Performance Assessment, Psychometric Theory and Cognitive Learning Theory: Ships Crossing in the Night." *Contemporary Education* 62(4):250–254 (Summer 1991).

Worthen, B. R. "Critical Issues That Will Determine the Future of Alternative Assessment." *Phi Delta Kappan* 74(6):444–454 (February 1993).

15

How Can I Assess My Teaching Effectiveness and Continue My Professional Development?

The bad news is that most of us are not born with innate teaching skills; the good news is that *teaching skills can be learned*. Teachers who wish to improve their teaching can do so, and (in addition to this resource guide) there are many resources that can help.

This chapter addresses the evaluation and development of your effectiveness as a classroom teacher, a process that continues throughout your professional career. Teaching is such an electrifying profession that it is not easy to remain energetic and to stay abreast of changes and trends that result from research and practice. You will need to make a continuous and determined effort to remain an alert and effective teacher.

Whether you are a beginning teacher or an experienced teacher, one way to collect data and to improve your effectiveness is through periodic assessment of your teaching performance, either by an evaluation of your teaching in the real classroom or, if you are in a program of teacher preparation, by a technique called micro peer teaching.

A. PROFESSIONAL DEVELOPMENT THROUGH MICRO PEER TEACHING

Micro peer teaching (MPT) is a useful skill-development strategy, used for professional development by both **preservice** (in training) and **inservice** (employed) teachers. Micro peer teaching is a scaled-down teaching experience involving these factors:

- Limited objective.
- Brief interval for teaching a lesson.
- Lesson taught to a few (8–10) peers as your students.
- Lesson that focuses on the use of one or several instructional strategies.

Micro peer teaching can be a predictor of later teacher effectiveness in a regular classroom, but more important, it provides opportunity to develop and improve specific teaching behaviors. A videotaped MPT allows you to see yourself in action for

Both inservice and preservice teachers evaluate their teaching as part of their on-going progressional development.

self-evaluation and diagnosis. Evaluation of a micro peer teaching session is based on the following:

• The quality of the teacher's preparation and lesson implementation.
• The quality of the planned and implemented student involvement.
• Whether the instructional objective(s) was reached.
• The appropriateness of the cognitive level of the lesson.

Whether a preservice or inservice teacher, you are urged to participate in one or more micro peer teaching experiences. Instructions follow.

Instructions for Micro Peer Teaching—Exercise 15.1

Although not presented in the boxed format of previous exercises, this is Exercise 15.1, the final exercise in this resource guide. For this exercise you prepare and teach a lesson for your peers, at their level of intellectual maturity and understanding, that is, as opposed to teaching the lesson to peers pretending that they are schoolchildren.

This experience has two components:

1. Your preparation and implementation of a demonstration lesson.
2. Your completion of an analysis of the summative peer and self-evaluations, with statements of how you would change the lesson, and your teaching of it, were you to repeat the lesson.

You are to prepare and carry out a 15 to 20-minute lesson to a group of peers. The exact time limit for the lesson is set by your group, based on the size of the group and the amount of time available. (When the time limit has been set, fill "Time Allowed," item 1 of preparation form—Figure 15.2). While some of your peers serve as your students, others will evaluate your teaching. (The process works best when "students" do not evaluate while they are students.) Your teaching should be videotaped for self-evaluation.

For your lesson, identify one concept and develop your content to teach toward an understanding of that concept. Within the time allowed, your lesson should include both teacher talk and hands-on activity for the students. Use Form A (Figure 15.2) for the initial planning of your lesson, then complete a lesson plan, selecting a format as discussed in Chapter 8 (see Exercise 8.2a).

After your presentation, collect your peer evaluations (Form B, Figure 15.3), then review your presentation by viewing the videotape. After viewing the tape, prepare the following:

1. A tabulation and statistical analysis of peer evaluations of your lesson.
2. A self-evaluation based on your analysis of the peer evaluations, your feelings after having taught the lesson, and your feelings after having viewed the videotape.
3. A summary analysis that includes your selection and description of your teaching strengths and weaknesses, as indicated by this peer-teaching experience, and how you would improve were you to repeat the lesson.

Tabulation and Analysis of Peer Evaluations

The procedure for tabulating the completed evaluations received from your peers is as follows:

1. *Use a blank copy of Form B* (Figure 15.3) for tabulating. In the left margin of that copy, to the left of "I. Organization of lesson," place the letters "N" (number) and "Σ" (total) to prepare for two columns of numbers that will fall below each of those letters. On a parallel line and in the far right margin, place the word "Score."
2. *For each item (A through Y) on the peer evaluation form, count the number of evaluators who gave a rating (from 1 to 5) on the item.* Sometimes an evaluator may not rate a particular item, so although there may have been ten peers evaluating your micro peer teaching, the number of evaluators giving you a rating on any one particular item could be less than ten. The number of evaluators rating each item is called "N." Place this number in the "N" column at the far left margin on your copy of Form B, next to the relevant item.
3. Using a calculator, *obtain the sum of the peer ratings for each item.* For example, for item A, "Lesson Preparation," add the numbers given by each evaluator for that item. If there were ten evaluators who gave you a number rating on that item, then your sum for that item will not be more than 50 (5×10). Because individual evaluators will make their X marks differently, you sometimes must estimate an individual evaluator's number rating, that is, rather than a clear rating of "3" or "3.5" on an item you may have to estimate it as "3.2" or "3.9." In the left-hand margin of your blank copy of Form B, in the "Σ" column, place the sum for each item.
4. Now, *obtain a "score" for each item,* A through Y. The score for each item is obtained by dividing "Σ" by "N" and will range between 1 and 5. Write this dividend in the column in the right-hand margin under the word "Score" on a line parallel to the relevant item. This is the number you will use in the analysis phase.

Procedure for Analyzing the Tabulations

Having completed the tabulation of the peer evaluations of your teaching, you are ready to proceed with your analysis of those tabulations.

1. To proceed, you need a blank copy of Form C (Figure 15.4), your self-analysis form.
2. On the blank copy of Form C *there are five items:* "Implementation," "Personal," "Voice," "Materials," and "Strategies."
3. In the far left margin of Form C, place the letter "Σ," for "sum." To its right and parallel with it, place the word "Average." You now have arranged for two columns of five numbers each, a "Σ" column and an "Average" column.
4. *Obtain the total score for each of the five items,* as follows:

    For item 1, "Implementation," add all scores (from the right-hand margin of Form B) for the four items, A, C, X, and Y. The total should be 20 or less (4 × 5). Place this total in the left-hand margin under "Σ" and parallel to "1. Implementation."

    For item 2, "Personal," add all scores (from the right-hand margin of Form B) for the nine items F, G, M, N, O, P, Q, S, and T. The total should be 45 or less (9 × 5). Place this total in the left-hand margin under "Σ" and parallel to "2. Personal."

    For item 3, "Voice," add all scores (from the right-hand margin of Form B) for the three items, H, I, and J. The total should be 15 or less (3 × 5). Place this total in the left-hand margin under "Σ" and parallel to "3. Voice."

    For item 4, "Materials," add all scores (from the right-hand margin of Form B) for item K. The total should be 5 or less (1 × 5). Place this total in the left-hand margin under "Σ" and parallel to "4. Materials."

    For item 5, "Strategies," add all scores (from the right-hand margin of Form B) for the eight items B, D, E, L, R, U, V, and W. The total should be 40 or less (8 × 5). Place this total in the left-hand margin under "Σ" and parallel to "5. Strategies."
5. Now, for each of the five categories, *divide "Σ" by the number of items in the category to get your peer evaluation average score.* For item 1 you will divide by 4; for item 2, by 9; for item 3, by 3; for item 4, by 1; and for item 5, by 8. For each category you should then have a final "average" peer evaluation score of a number *no less than one and no more than five.* If this procedure has been correctly done, you now have average scores for each of the five categories: Implementation, Personal, Voice, Materials, and Strategies. With those scores and evaluators' comments you can prepare your final "summary analysis."

Figure 15.1 illustrates three sample analyses of MPT lessons based *only* on the "scores," that is, without reference to comments made by individual evaluators. However, peer evaluator's comments are important considerations for actual analyses.

	Category/Rating					
Teacher	*1*	*2*	*3*	*4*	*5*	*Possible Strengths and Weaknesses*
A	4.2	2.5	2.8	4.5	4.5	Good lesson, weakened by personal items and voice.
B	4.5	4.6	5.0	5.0	5.0	Excellent teaching; perhaps needing a stronger start.
C	2.5	3.0	3.5	1.0	1.5	Poor strategy choice; lack of student involvement.

Figure 15.1   Sample analyses of MPTs based only on peer evaluation scores.

FOR YOUR NOTES

This form is to be used for initial preparation of your MPT lesson. (For preparation of your lesson, study Form B, Figure 15.3.) After completing this form, proceed with the preparation of your MPT lesson, using a lesson plan format as discussed in Chapter 8 (see Exercise 8.2a). *A copy of the final lesson plan should be presented to the evaluators at the start of your MPT presentation.*

1. Time allowed _____

2. Title or topic of lesson I will teach _____

3. Concept _____

4. Specific instructional objectives for the lesson:

   Cognitive: _____

   _____

   _____

   _____

   _____

   Affective: _____

   _____

   _____

   _____

   Psychomotor: _____

   _____

   _____

   _____

   _____

5. Strategies to be used, including an approximate time plan:

   Set introduction: _____

   _____

   _____

   _____

   _____

   _____

   _____

   _____

Figure 15.2   MPT form A—MPT preparation.

(continued)

Transitions: _____

_____

_____

_____

Closure: _____

_____

_____

_____

Others: _____

_____

_____

_____

6. Student experiences to be provided, i.e., specify for each—visual, verbal, kinesthetic, and tactile experiences. _____

_____

_____

_____

_____

_____

_____

7. Materials, equipment, and resources needed: _____

_____

_____

_____

_____

_____

_____

Figure 15.2   *(continued)*

Evaluators use this form, marking an *X* on each line between "5" and "1." Far left (5) is the highest rating; far right (1) is the lowest. Completed forms are collected and given to the teacher upon completion of that teacher's MPT. These are reviewed by the teacher prior to viewing his or her videotaped lesson.

To evaluators: Comments as well as marks are useful to the teacher.

To teacher: Give one copy of your lesson plan to the evaluators at start of your MPT. (*Note:* It is best if evaluators can be together at a table at the rear of room.)

Teacher _____ Date _____

Topic _____

Concept _____

1. Organization of Lesson	5	4	3	2	1
a. Lesson preparation evident	yes		somewhat		no
b. Lesson beginning effective	yes		somewhat		no
c. Subject-matter knowledge apparent	yes		somewhat		no
d. Strategies selection effective	yes		somewhat		no
e. Closure effective	yes		somewhat		no

Comments

_____

_____

_____

2. Lesson implementation	5	4	3	2	1
f. Eye contact excellent	yes		somewhat		no
g. Enthusiasm evident	yes		somewhat		no
h. Speech delivery	articulate		minor problems		poor
i. Voice inflection, cueing	effective		minor problems		poor

(continued)

Figure 15.3 MPT form B—Peer evaluation.

	5	4	3	2	1
j. Vocabulary use	well chosen		minor problems		poor
k. Aids, props, and materials	effective		okay		none
l. Use of examples and analogies	effective		needs improvement		none
m. Student involvement	effective		okay		none
n. Use of overlapping skills	good		okay		poor
o. Nonverbal communication	effective		a bit confusing		distracting
p. Use of active listening	effective		okay		poor
q. Responses to students	personal and accepting		passive or indifferent		impersonal, antagonistic
r. Use of questions	effective		okay		poor
s. Use of student names	effective		okay		poor
t. Use of humor	effective		okay		poor
u. Directions and refocusing	succinct		a bit vague		confusing
v. Teacher mobility	effective		okay		none
w. Use of transitions	smooth		a bit rough		unclear
x. Motivating presentation	very		somewhat		none
y. Momentum (pacing) of lesson	smooth and brisk		okay		too slow or too fast

Comments

_____

_____

_____

Figure 15.3   *(continued)*

See instructions, "Procedures for Analyzing the Tabulations," for completing this form.

1. Implementation (items a, c, x, y)   5 4 3 2 1
2. Personal (items f, g, m, n, o, p, q, s, t) 5 4 3 2 1
3. Voice (items h, i, j)   5 4 3 2 1
4. Materials (item k)   5 4 3 2 1
5. Strategies (items b, d, e, l, r, u, v, w)   5 4 3 2 1

Total = _____

Comments

_____

_____

_____

_____

_____

_____

_____

_____

_____

_____

_____

_____

_____

_____

_____

_____

_____

_____

_____

_____

_____

_____

_____

_____

Figure 15.4 MPT form C—Teacher's summative peer evaluation.

B. A LOOK AT MY TEACHALOGUE, WITH THIRTY TEACHING SUGGESTIONS

What additional advice can we share with you as a beginning teacher? Can this advice be compacted into some helpful hints, ideas, or secrets? We have summarized them in this "teachalogue," containing 30 teaching suggestions, to help you further evaluate yourself.

Teachalogue Checklist

Before the Lesson:
1. Did you write specific objectives, and will you share them with your students?
2. Did you refer to the established course of study for your grade level and review your state frameworks, the teacher's manuals, and scope and sequence charts?
3. Are your motivational techniques relevant to the lesson, helping students connect their learning to real-world experiences?
4. Are you taking students' interest in a topic for granted, or does your motivational component of the lesson meet the special needs and unique interests of your students?
5. Did you order audiovisual materials pertinent to your lesson, and did you preview these materials?
6. Did you prepare large-size demonstration materials, and will you display them so that all of the children can see them?
7. Have you planned your lesson transitions from one activity to the next, or from one lesson to the next?
8. Do you have the necessary supplies and materials ready for the lesson?
9. Have you mastered manuscript writing so as to provide a model for the primary grades, and mastered cursive writing so as to provide a model in the intermediate and upper grades?
10. Have you established efficient, orderly routines and procedures for your class management tasks, such as collecting homework, taking roll, collecting money, sharpening pencils, distributing and collecting books, obtaining your attention, moving around in the classroom, and dismissing students for recess, for lunch, and at the end of the school day?
11. Have you planned your preassessment strategy, perhaps as an advance organizer for the lesson, to discover what the students already know, or think they know, about the concept of the lesson?
12. Have you built into your lesson plans strategies for student self-assessment of their learning?
13. Have you planned your postassessment strategies, to find out whether the children have, in fact, learned that which you intend them to learn?
14. To the best of your knowledge, do your assessment strategies—preassessment, ongoing assessment, and postassessment—authentically assess the learning objectives?

During the Lesson:
15. Are you clearing the writing board before you begin a new lesson?
16. Are you remembering that sometimes material is clearer to students if they can read it as well as hear it?
17. Are you remembering to write legibly and boldly, with large letters and in an orderly manner, so all can read your writing on the writing board?

18. Are you being gracious and sympathetic to your students, showing that you have confidence in their abilities?
19. Are you allowing your students to participate in discussion (to talk), and be heard, and are you giving each one the individual, private, and specific praise that he or she deserves?
20. Are you setting the mental stage, varying your class activities, and, when possible, building on each student's ideas and contributions during the lesson?
21. Are you making clear all relationships between main ideas and details for your students, and presenting examples of abstract concepts in simple and concrete ways?
22. Are you explaining, discussing, and commenting on any media materials you use in your lesson?
23. When asking questions of students, are you remembering to give students time to review the topic; to hear your frame of reference for your questions; to recognize that your question is on their level of understanding; to use "think time" before they respond to your question?
24. Are you remembering to not answer your own questions?
25. Are you remembering to call on the children and to give them tasks equally according to their gender and other personal characteristics?
26. Are you introducing materials to the children (rulers, protractors, scissors, magnets, media, art supplies, puppets) *before* they are needed in your lesson?
27. Are you evincing enthusiasm in your speech and mannerisms, maintaining a moderate pace in your classroom, and insisting that all children give you their attention when you begin a lesson?
28. Are you varying your use of instructional strategies so that students not only learn subject content but also develop their thinking skills, study skills, social interaction skills, and feelings of self-worth?
29. Are you checking frequently during the lesson to see whether the children are "getting it"; that is, that they understand the content and processes being taught?

After the Lesson:
30. Are you taking time to reflect on how the lesson went, on what might have been "muddy" and what was "clear," and then reteach if necessary?

C. PROFESSIONAL DEVELOPMENT THROUGH CLASSROOM OBSERVATIONS

Teachers who wish to improve their teaching can do so, and, as you are learning in this chapter, there are many resources that can help. If you are already teaching, then certainly one source of information for improvement is student data.

Data from Students

Student data are available throughout the school year, through observing the attentiveness of students in your classroom, from informal discussions with children outside of class, and from the quality of their work on assignments and on achievement tests. Having a colleague, cooperating teacher, or your university or college supervisor review samples of your students' work and discussing with that person your own observations will provide insights for improving your teaching. Through such discussions you probably will discover that your own concerns are not unique to you, and you can learn how other teachers have resolved similar problems.

Comments from Administrators

As an employed teacher, you will receive comments from the principal or the principal's designee. Recommendations for improvement result from administrator evaluations of one or more visits to your class. You may or may not know when administrator visits are going to occur; consequently, the best way to forestall unfortunate events during a visit is to plan each and every day as if you were going to be visited and evaluated. You should be aware that one of the problems that can occur as a result of an administrator's observation (or a college supervisor's observation of a student teacher) is that the evaluator's perceptions of a teacher's effectiveness may be clouded by individual learning modalities (as discussed in Chapter 3).

Classroom Observations

You can also continue your professional development (1) by observing other teachers and (2) by having other professionals observe and evaluate your teaching.

For their self-improvement and for personnel decisions about retention and tenure, teachers are periodically reviewed. Of course, the ultimate purpose of these reviews is to provide the most effective service to students. Essentially, for reemployment, the school district wants to be assured of two things—that, as a classroom teacher, you *can effectively work with and manage youngsters*, and that *you can effectively teach the subject(s)*.

For these reviews, data from several sources are collected, and although from school to school, and even within the same district, forms will vary in wording and in format, there remains a common set of criteria of competencies, which are those that have been presented and discussed in this book.

Data about a teacher's effectiveness are collected from two sources—*teacher self-evaluation* and *evaluations performed by an administrator(s)*, usually the building principal.

Teacher Evaluation: Sample Form

The form shown in Figure 15.5 is a sample that can be used by you to observe and collect data when observing exemplary teachers, by an observer of your teaching, perhaps your mentor. You can also use this form for self-evaluation of a videotape of your own teaching. Although forms vary in wording and in format, there remains a common set of criteria, as shown in the sample.

FOR YOUR NOTES

Teacher _____ Grade _____ Class _____

Date _____ Class size _____ Observer _____

Unit or lesson _____

Section I: General Evaluation
Indicate the extent to which you agree or disagree with each statement concerning the observed teacher: 1 = strongly agree; 2 = agree; 3 = disagree; 4 = strongly disagree; 5 = uncertain or not applicable.

A. Structure and Goals

_____ 1. The teacher clearly conveyed the purpose for each activity of the class period.

_____ 2. The stated purposes were consistently followed throughout the period.

_____ 3. The lesson seemed carefully planned and organized.

_____ 4. The various elements of the class period were effectively integrated.

_____ 5. The lesson built toward one or more basic concepts, processes, or attitudes that the children seemed to understand.

B. Teacher-Student Rapport

_____ 1. The teacher demonstrated fair and equal concern for all children.

_____ 2. The teacher answered student questions in a straightforward and understandable manner.

_____ 3. The teacher encouraged and facilitated quality interaction among the children.

_____ 4. The teacher appeared open to all ideas, suggestions, opinions, and criticisms from the students.

_____ 5. The students seemed genuinely receptive to the ideas of the teacher.

C. Instruction

_____ 1. The teacher conveyed enthusiasm about teaching.

_____ 2. The teacher presented material that was appropriate for this class.

_____ 3. The teacher demonstrated appropriate command of the subject.

_____ 4. The teacher introduced topics in a manner that was stimulating and meaningful to the children.

_____ 5. Transitions between topics and activities were efficiently and effectively implemented.

_____ 6. Major points were effectively reviewed by the teacher.

(continued)

Figure 15.5 Sample form for teacher evaluation by classroom observations.

This teacher evaluation form may be copied and used without the permission of the author or publisher.

_____ 7. The teacher effectively implemented several checks for student comprehension as the lesson unfolded.

_____ 8. The teacher asked questions that required students to express their opinion, prior experiences, knowledge, and thoughts.

_____ 9. The teacher used student responses to encourage or to bring others into the discussion.

_____ 10. Questions were used throughout the lesson.

_____ 11. Students were attentive throughout the lesson.

_____ 12. Audiovisuals and supplementary materials were effectively managed by the teacher.

D. General

_____ 1. I would recommend this class and teacher to children.

_____ 2. I personally found this lesson to be interesting and informative.

_____ 3. I believe that I was able to judge the nature and tenor the teaching-learning process fairly during this observation.

Comments (to clarify or expand any of the preceding ratings) _____

_____

_____

_____

_____

_____

_____

Section II: The Teacher
For each word or phrase listed below, indicate the extent to which it accurately describes the teacher you observed: 1 = this word or phrase does *not* describe this teacher; 2 = this word or phrase partially describes this teacher; 3 = this word or phrase accurately describes this teacher.

_____ 1. Effective use of gestures

_____ 2. Effective use of pauses and silence

_____ 3. Varied pitch and tone of voice

_____ 4. Clear presentations

_____ 5. Use of vocabulary appropriate for the children

_____ 6. Effective use of teacher mobility

(continued)

Figure 15.5 *(continued)*

———— 7. Effective use of eye contact with children

———— 8. Flexible in responses to students

———— 9. Warm and accepting of all children

Comments _____

_____

_____

_____

Section III: Strategies
Read the brief descriptions of each teaching strategy below, and then indicate the extent to which you observed the strategy being employed during this lesson. If possible, also provide concrete examples of how each strategy was used during the observation.

1. *Stage setting:* The teacher mentally prepares the children for the learning that is to follow, often through an analogy, a demonstration, or a leading or thought-provoking question; provides a common frame of reference between the teacher and the children; and increases the interest of the children in the topic to be covered.

———— a. I did not observe stage setting.

———— b. I observed stage setting being used relatively unsuccessfully.

———— c. I observed stage setting being used successfully.

Evidence _____

_____

_____

_____

2. *Variation in the lesson activities:* The teacher uses verbal and nonverbal techniques to vary the mode of the presentation (e.g., variations in types of teacher-student and student-student interaction, movement, planned repetition, audiovisuals, and use of examples, demonstration, and hands-on activities).

———— a. I observed no variation.

———— b. I observed very little variation.

———— c. I observed the effective use of variation.

Evidence _____

_____

_____

(continued)

Figure 15.5 *(continued)*

3. *Encouragement of the children:* In various ways, the teacher encourages student participation (e.g., with a smile, a nod, eye contact, or body position and gestures).

_____ a. I observed no encouragement.

_____ b. I observed a moderate amount of encouragement.

_____ c. I observed the effective use of encouragement.

Evidence _____

_____

_____

4. *Awareness of student attentiveness:* The teacher steadily monitors the class, demonstrating withitness and overlapping behaviors, and redirecting a student whose attention is beginning to wane. The teacher demonstrates this awareness by observing students' facial expressions and their involvement in class activities.

_____ a. The teacher did not demonstrate awareness.

_____ b. The teacher seemed to be moderately aware.

_____ c. The teacher was effectively aware of student attention.

Evidence _____

_____

_____

5. *Clarifying questions:* The teacher responds to superficial or preliminary answers or statements made by students by asking for clarification, which requires them to go beyond a one-word or low-level response. Through the skillful use of probing techniques, the teacher brings more out of students and maintains the level of interest in the discussion.

_____ a. I did not observe the use of clarifying questions.

_____ b. I observed only moderate use of clarifying questions.

_____ c. I observed effective use of clarifying questions.

Evidence _____

_____

_____

6. *Processing questions:* The teacher asks questions that require the children to make sense out of what is being learned, to draw relationships of cause and effect, to synthesize, to analyze, and to compare new information with prior experiences.

_____ a. I did not observe process questioning.

_____ b. I observed moderate use of process questioning.

(continued)

Figure 15.5 (continued)

_____ c. I observed effective use of process questioning.

Evidence _____

_____

_____

7. *Application and evaluation questions:* The teacher asks output-level questions, ones without "correct" answers, which require the children to use both concrete and abstract thinking, to think divergently, and to determine for themselves appropriate responses. Children are urged to explore a problem, to think creatively and hypothetically, to use imagination, to expose their values, and to make judgments.

_____ a. I observed no use of output-level questions.

_____ b. I observed moderate use of output-level questions.

_____ c. I observed effective use of output-level questions.

Evidence _____

_____

_____

_____

8. *Cooperative learning:* The teacher forms small groups of mixed-ability students in which the children work together on problems and tasks, and learning achievement is based on the group's cooperative effort. Each member has and performs a specific function necessary for the successful completion of the group's task.

_____ a. I did not observe the use of cooperative learning.

_____ b. I observed minimal use of cooperative learning.

_____ c. I observed effective use of cooperative learning.

Evidence _____

_____

_____

_____

9. *Closure:* The teacher integrates the major points of a lesson, linking the familiar and the new elements, and providing children with a needed sense of achievement at the end of the lesson.

_____ a. I observed no closure.

_____ b. I observed moderate use of closure.

_____ c. I observed effective use of closure.

(continued)

Figure 15.5 *(continued)*

Evidence _____

_____

_____

_____

10. *Teacher demonstration:* The teacher effectively uses a demonstration to make a point, to grab student attention, to review, or to introduce a concept, process, or discrepant event. The demonstration can last for a few moments or for more than 10 minutes, but the teacher does not drag it out too long, and assures that all children can see, can participate in some way, can question, and are safe from danger. During the demonstration, the teacher stresses process as well as content. When necessary, the teacher models proper safety precautions.

_____ a. I observed an ineffective demonstration or no demonstration.

_____ b. I observed a moderately effective demonstration.

_____ c. I observed an effective demonstration.

Evidence _____

_____

_____

_____

_____

Section IV: Final Comments

1. What part(s) of the class period and lesson seemed to enhance the learning process?

_____

_____

_____

2. What specific suggestions do you have for how this particular class period or lesson could have been improved?

_____

_____

_____

_____

Figure 15.5 *(continued)*

D. PROFESSIONAL DEVELOPMENT THROUGH STUDENT TEACHING

You are excited about the prospect of being assigned as a student teacher to your first elementary school classroom, but you are also concerned. Questions linger in your mind. Will your host (cooperating) teacher like you? Will the two of you get along? Will the students accept you? Will you be assigned to the grade you want? What will the children be like? Will there be many classroom management problems? What about children with special needs? Your questions will be endless.

Indeed, you should be excited and concerned, for this experience—the experience of student teaching—is one of the most significant and important facets of your program of teacher preparation. In some programs, this practical field experience is planned as a coexperience with the college or university theory classes. In other programs, student teaching is the culminating experience. Different sequences are used in different programs. For example, at one college or university the field teaching experience extends over a period of two or three semesters. In other programs, teacher candidates take part in a theory-class-first arrangement, which includes a full second semester of student teaching. Regardless of when and how your student teaching occurs, the experience is a bright and shining opportunity to improve your teaching skills in a real classroom environment. During this experience you will be supported by an experienced college or university supervisor and by carefully selected cooperating teachers, who will share with you their expertise from years of classroom experience. Teacher preparation programs refer to these cooperating teachers by various terms—cooperating teachers, host teachers, master teachers, and mentor teachers.

Everyone concerned in the teacher preparation program—your cooperating teacher, your university instructors, the school principal, and your university supervisor—realize that, for you, this is a practicum in learning how to teach. During your student teaching, you will, no doubt, make some teaching errors, and you will benefit and learn from those errors. Sometimes your fresh approach to motivation, your creative ideas for learning activities, and your energy and enthusiasm make it possible for the cooperating teacher to learn from you. After all, as we have said many times, teaching and learning are most always parts of a reciprocal process. What is of value to both of you on this educational team is that the students who are involved with you in the teaching-learning process will benefit from your role as the teacher-candidate in the classroom.

The following guidelines are offered to help make this practical experience beneficial to everyone involved.

Student Teaching *Is* the Real Thing

Your student teaching is the real thing, because you are teaching active, responsive, young people. You have a classroom setting for improving your teaching skills with real elementary school students. Yet, in one sense, your student teaching is not real, because it is your credentialed cooperating teacher, not you, who has ultimate responsibility (and the final say) for the classroom.

Getting Ready for Student Teaching

To prepare yourself for student teaching you should study, plan, and practice. You should be knowledgeable about your students and their developmental backgrounds. In your theory classes you learned a great deal about students. Go back and review your class notes and textbooks from those courses, or select some readings from those suggested in Part I of this resource guide. Perhaps some of the topics will have more meaning for you now.

Be knowledgeable about your assigned school and the community that surrounds it. Review the subject areas you will be teaching and the content in those areas. Carefully discuss with your cooperating teacher (or teachers, as you may have more than one) and your university supervisor all of the responsibilities that you will be expected to assume.

As a student teacher you may want to run through each lesson verbally, perhaps in front of a mirror the night before teaching your lesson. Some student teachers read through each lesson, audiotaping the lesson, playing it back, and evaluating whether the directions are clear, the sequence is logical, and the lesson closure is concise. Still another student teacher always has a "Plan B" in mind in case "Plan A" turns out to be inappropriate. Yet another student teacher prepares an "emergency teaching kit" (a collection of teaching materials) as a backup for emergencies in the classroom. This emergency kit is carried in a cardboard box in the trunk of the student teacher's car.

What Is in an Emergency Teaching Kit?

In an emergency teaching kit, there can be a wide variety of teaching materials. The materials can support a topic or a theme. Each kit should have a record for singalongs, stories to read aloud, a game to play, poems to read, art activities, riddles to solve, and if possible, some other audiovisual aids. It also might include a science experiment with all the materials needed to carry it out, or a mathematics activity with all necessary manipulative materials needed by children for doing it. See Figures 15.6, 15.7 and 15.8.

---

1. *Recordings.* An appropriate record to guide group singing; an accompanying ditto master that shows words of the songs. Suggestions: *Musical Stories from the Picture Book Parade,* with such songs as "She'll Be Comin' Round the Mountain," "Yankee Doodle," "Clementine," "I Know an Old Lady," and "Waltzing Matilda." Available from Weston Woods, Weston, CT 06883. *I Wish I Was a Dinosaur* (Alcarzar Records, P.O. Box 429, Waterbury, VT 05676). Cassette and lively songs: *Wheels on the Bus* (Crown, 1988) from Raffi's album, *Rise and Shine,* is illustrated by Silvie K. Wickstrom and is a song to read as well as sing. The rickety old bus collects an assortment of passengers and the reader makes the sounds of the bus and the motions of the driver and passengers.

2. *Stories.* Two to four favorite children's books for the teacher to read aloud:
   For Kindergarten Students:
   Bea and Mr. Jones by Amy Schwartz (New York: Bradbury, 1983). A kindergarten girl changes places with an adult.

(continued)

Figure 15.6 Items in a general emergency teaching kit.

Mrs. Pig Gets Cross and Other Stories by Mary Rayner (New York: Dutton, 1991). In this busy Pig household, Father, Mother, and their ten children have adventures: they slip on pancakes, think lettuce is too fat, and all end up in the same bed one night.

Who Said Red? by Mary Serfuzo, illustrated by Keiko Narashi (New York: Macmillan, 1988). Rhyming text as a small boy wants his "very red" kite caught in a bush. Reviews colors.

For Primary Students:

Beans on the Roof by Betsy Byars, illustrated by Melodye Rosales (New York: Delacorte, 1988). Poetic fever for the Bean family as they all write a roof poem.

Merry-go-Round: A Book About Nouns by Ruth Heller, illustrated by the author (New York: Putnam, 1990). Entertaining rhyming text that defines noun forms with realistic illustrations.

For Intermediate Grade Students:

Monster Knock Knocks by William Cole and Mike Thaler, illustrated by Mike Thaler (New York: Archway/Pocket Books, 1982).

101 Monster Jokes by Sam Schultz, illustrated by Joan Hanson (New York: Lerner, 1982). 101 riddles for humorous reading.

The Magic School Bus Inside the Human Body by Joanna Cole, illustrated by Bruce Degen (New York: Scholastic, 1990). Ms. Frizzle shrinks the bus and the class and Arnold swallows them, so the students hear an explanation of the digestive system and the ways blood vessels, nerves, and muscles work.

Buzz Beamer's Radical Sports by Bill Hinds, illustrated by the author (New York: Sports Illustrated/Little, 1990). Buzz reinvents sports with new ideas such as a baseball shaped like a football and jello in a swimming pool. Humorous, easy to read, with cartoons.

Burning Questions of Bingo Brown by Betsy Byars (New York: G.K. Hall, 1989). With some humor, this sixth grader, Bingo Brown, has burning questions about the coming years.

For Middle School Students:

Dragon's Blood by Jane Yolen (New York: Delacorte, 1982). A dragon is trained to be a great fighter in the fighting pits of Auster IV, a fantasy planet.

Celery Stalks at Midnight by James Howe (New York: Macmillan, 1983). A sequel about Bunnicula, the vegetarian vampire.

3. *Games.* Include game instructions; instructions for an inside game for a cold, wet, or windy day; instructions for an outside game when weather conditions permit.

For Primary Students:

Me and My Bean Bag (Kimbo Educational, 10 N. 3rd Avenue, Long Branch, NJ 07740). Cassette and guide to promote listening skills as songs encourage coordination.

For Intermedidate Grade Students:

Play by Play: A Book of Games and Puzzles by Fred Winkowski. (New York: Sports Illustrated/Little, Brown, 1990). Illustrated by the author. Collection of activities, board games, word searches, and trivia questions.

(continued)

Figure 15.6   *(continued)*

For Middle School Students:

Mickey Mantle: The American Dream Comes to Life (Baseball Legend Video Ltd., 120 Montgomery Street, San Francisco, CA 94111). Video shows career highlights and an interview with Mantle, who tells humorous tales of baseball.

4. *Art Activities.* Prepare duplicated sheets for instructions for an art activity, a maze to ponder, or a puzzle to solve.

For Middle School Students:

How to Draw Terrific Cartoons (Educational Dimensions, Box 126, Stamford, CT 06904). Video with guide explains generating ideas, techniques, humor in drawings, and ways to correct mistakes.

5. *Puppets.* Share patterns for making the puppets which accompany a short skit or emphasize the focus of a lesson. For example, the study of predators could be extended with *Predator-Prey Puppets* (Symbiosis Books, 1986) and the accompanying information about habitat and hunting and surviving characteristics of such animals as the frog, rabbit, alligator, and wolf.

6. *Riddles.* Plan a time for a riddle club; share *Wild Pill Hickok: and Other Old West Riddles* by David A. Adler, illustrated by Glen Rounds (New York: Holiday House, 1988).

7. *Poems.* Read poems aloud through the day as you integrate poetry with curriculum areas.

For Kindergarten Students:

Read-Aloud Rhymes for the Very Young by Jack Prelutsky (New York: Knopf, 1986).

For Primary Students:

If You're Not Here, Please Raise Your Hand: Poems About School by Kalli Dakos, illustrated by G. Brian Karas (New York: Four Winds, 1990). Collection of poems about elementary school. Some are very humorous.

For Intermediate Students:

The Place My Words Are Looking For: What Poets Say About and Through Their Work selected by Paul B. Janeczko (New York: Bradbury, 1990). Thirty-nine poets share their writing, personal lives, and thoughts. An anthology of poems about everyday events.

For All Grades:

Oh, the Places You'll Go! by Dr. Seuss, illustrated by the author (New York: Random House, 1990). Humorous verse and illustration about discovering the potential for success.

8. *Listen-Alongs*

For Primary Students:

We Sing America: Songs of Patriots and Pioneers (Price/Stern/Sloan, 410 N. La Cienaga Boulevard, Los Angeles, CA 90048). Cassette of 40 songs and famous quotes about events that led to the creation of some of the music.   *(continued)*

Figure 15.6   *(continued)*

For Intermediate Students:

Pecos Bill (Windham Hill Productions, P.O. Box 9388, Stanford, CA 94309). Cassette plays the tall tale told by Robin Williams.

With a Little of Both (Rainbow Bend Storytelling, 7 Keven Drive, E. Windsor, CT 06088). Cassette and guide for original and adapted stories that include "Rabbit and Tortoise," "Jonny Cake," and "Troll's Dance."

Flying Africans (Earwig Music Co., 1818 N. Pratt Boulevard, Chicago, IL (60626). Cassette with African American heritage in five songs and stories by Alice McGill.

9. *Read-Alongs*

For Primary Students:

A Chair for My Mother (Mulberry Books, 105 Madison Avenue, New York, NY 10016). Cassette and book read by child narrator.

For Intermediate Students:

Mufaro's Beautiful Daughters (Weston Woods, Weston, CT 06883). Cassette and Caldecott Honor book offer the story told by Terry Alexander.

The Titanic Lost . . . and Found (Random House, 400 Hahn Road, Westminster, MD 21157). Cassette and book tell this true story.

10. *Listen Before Reading*

For Middle School Students:

Dinosaurs (California Academic of Science/Kay Productions, Box 1728, Sonoma, CA 95476). Cassette, book, and poster with accurate information.

11. *Favorite Topics.* Perhaps you may want to select a theme that is universally enjoyed by elementary or middle school students. Consider mysteries, adventures, crafts, fairy tales, dinosaurs, and myths as potential topics.

12. *One-Day Unit Approach.* If you wish, prepare all of the previous items to reflect your theme or topic. With your collection of materials, you can respond on a minute's notice and teach a one-day unit centered on your theme.

For example, one student teacher prepared one ditto master for each of the subject areas in a given school day: reading, spelling, writing, mathematics, and so on. Each ditto master reflected one aspect of her selected theme, dinosaurs. Students read about dinosaurs, spelled key words, wrote about them, and measured dinosaur "footprints." Additional materials in the teacher's emergency kit gave her the opportunity to read aloud a dinosaur story, to share a picture book, and to introduce an art project. For young students, a set of teacher-made pictures of dinosaurs were ready to introduce a matching activity; other display cards with sets of dinosaurs gave interest to counting time, if such a time was scheduled. Prepared posters were ready to be placed on a nearby writing board rail, to set the room environment quickly. This student teacher was ready for a teaching emergency!

Figure 15.6   (*continued*)

Here is what one teacher collected in his first emergency kit, using the theme "birthdays."

Books:

Angelina's Birthday Surprise by Katharine Holabird, illustrated by Helen Craig (Southbridge, MA: Potter/Crown, 1989).

Benny Bakes a Cake by Eve Rice (New York: Greenwillow, 1981).

Birthday Moon by Lois Duncan, illustrated by Susan Davis (New York: Viking, 1989).

Birthday Presents by Cynthia Ryland, illustrated by Susie Stevenson (Chicago: Orchard/Watts, 1987).

The Birthday Surprise by Louis Sabin, illustrated by John Magine (Mahwah, NJ: Troll, 1981).

Brave Irene by William Steig (New York: Farrar, Straus & Giroux, 1986).

The Day I Was Born by Marjorie Sharmat, illustrated by Diane Dawson (New York: Dutton, 1980).

Handtalk Birthday: A Number and Storybook in Sign Language by Remy Charlip and Mary B. Miller, illustrated by George Anacona (New York: Macmillan, 1987).

Happy Birthday! by Gail Gibbons (New York: Holiday House, 1986).

Happy Birthday, Grampie by Susan Pearson, illustrated by Ronald Himler (New York: Dial, 1987).

The High Rise Glorious Skittle Skat Roarious Sky Pie Angel Food Cake by Nancy Willard, illustrated by Richard Jesse Watson (San Diego: Harcourt, Brace, Jovanovich, 1990).

Pancake Pie by Sven Nordquist (New York: Morrow, 1985).

What's So Special About Today? by Andrzej Krauze, illustrated by the author (New York: Lothrop, Lee, & Shepard, 1984).

Poems:

The Birthday Door by Eve Merriam, illustrated by Peter J. Thorton (New York: Morrow, 1986).

Birthday Poems by Myra Cohn Livingston, illustrated by Margot Tomes (New York: Holiday House, 1989).

Celebrations by Myra Cohn Livingston, illustrated by Leonard Everett Fisher (New York: Holiday House, 1985).

Recordings:

We All Live Together, Volume III, with guide. Includes "Sing a Happy Song," "If You're Happy and You Know it," "Simon Says," "Rock Round the Mulberry Bush," and other songs. (Youngheart Records, P.O. Box 27784, Los Angeles, CA 90027.)

More resources to support a birthday theme are available from Listening Library, Inc., 1 Park Avenue, Old Greenwich, CT 06870-9990: cassettes include *Babar's Birthday Surprise* by Jean de Brunhoff; *Clifford's Birthday Party* by Norman Bridwell; *Dr. Seuss: Happy Birthday to You* by Dr. Seuss; and *Paddington Bear: A Birthday Treat* by Michael Bond. Cassettes and book sets include *Birthday Presents* by Cynthia Rylant. Filmstrip/cassette sets include *A Birthday for Frances* by Russell Hoban; *Happy Birthday, Henrietta* by Syd Hoff; *Lye and the Birthday Party* by Bernard Waber; *A Letter to Amy* by Ezra Jack Keats; *Mary Betty Lizzie McNutt's Birthday* by Felicia Bond; *Mr. Rabbit and the Lovely Present* by Charlotte Zolotow; and *Party Rhymes* by Marc Brown.

(continued)

Figure 15.7 Birthdays: Emergency teaching kit for primary grades.

Bulletin Boards, Bookmarks, Reward Chart, and Scratch-and-Sniff Stickers:
"Birthday Fun" student-participation bulletin board (21″-high figures, reproducible worksheets, guides); "Super Duper" Ice Cream Class Reward chart, with 36 Scratch-and-Sniff Stickers; "Kids Party" bookmarks (The Peterson System, 2215 Commerce Street, Dallas, TX 75201).

Games:
Literature Games by Karen Van Scoy and Robert Whitehead (Fearon, 1971).
The Second Cooperative Sports & Games Book by Terry Orlick (Pantheon, 1982).

Filmstrip/Cassette Kits:
Friends: How They Help . . . How They Hurt (Storm Products/Sunburst Communications, 39 Washington Avenue, Pleasantville, NY 10570).
Hooper Humperdink . . .? Not Him! by Leo Lesieg, illustrated by Charles E. Martin; and *The Surprise Party* by Annabelle Prager, illustrated by Tomie de Paola (Random House School Division, 400 Hahn Road, Westminster, MD 21157).

Figure 15.7 *(continued)*

Books:
Orp and the Chop Suey Burgers by Suzy Kline (New York: Putnam, 1990).
Peanut Butter and Jelly: A Play Rhyme by Nandine Westcott (Dutton, 1987).

Poems:
Munching: Poems About Eating, edited by Lee Bennett Hopkins, illustrated by Nelle Davis (New York: Little Brown, 1985).

Records:
We All Live Together, Volume II, with guide. Includes "Popcorn" song, along with many others (Youngheart Records, P.O. Box 27784, Los Angeles, CA 90027).

Bulletin Board, Scratch-and-Sniff Stickers:
"The Story Burger" bulletin board (elements of a good story), and Scratch-and-Sniff stickers, with scents of pizza, orange, raspberry, candy cane, pineapple, and pickle (The Peterson System, 2215 Commerce Street, Dallas, TX 75201).

Experiments:
The Random House of 1001 Wonders of Science by Brian Williams and Brenda Williams (New York: Random House, 1990).

Films/Cassette Kits:
Cloudy With a Chance of Meatballs (Live Oak Media, Box 34, Ancramdale, NY 12503).
Edible Encounters (International Cinemedia Center, Stanfield House, Box 3208, Santa Monica, CA 90403).

(continued)

Figure 15.8 Edibles: Emergency teaching kit for intermediate grades.

How to Eat Fried Worms (Reis and Associates/Cheshire Corp., P.O. Box 4544, Englewood, CO 80155).

Stone Soup (Weston Woods, 389 Newton Turnpike, Weston, CT 06883). Video.

The Funny Little Woman by Arlene Mosel, illustrated by Blair Lent; and *Strega Nona*, retold and illustrated by Tomie de Paola. (Weston Woods, Weston, CT 06883).

More resources to support an edibles theme are available from Listening Library, Inc., 1 Park Avenue, Old Greenwich, CT 06870-9990: Book and cassette sets include *Arthur's Christmas Cookies* by Lillian Hoban; Filmstrip/cassette kits include *The Easter Egg Artists* by Adrienne Adams; *This Year's Garden* by Cynthia Rylant.

Figure 15.8   *(continued)*

Student Teaching from the Cooperating Teacher's Point of View

For your consideration, in a question-and-answer format, here is information about student teaching from the viewpoint of a cooperating teacher. You may wish to share this section with your cooperating teacher.

1. *What is my role?* As the cooperating teacher, your role is to assist when necessary: to provide guidance, to review lesson plans *before* they are taught, to facilitate the learning and skill development of your student teacher, and to help your student teacher become and feel like a member of the school faculty and of the profession.

2. *How can I prepare for the experience?* Get to know your student teacher *prior* to the beginning of the experience. Develop a collegial rapport with the student teacher.

3. *Who is my student teacher?* Your student teacher is a person who is making the transition from a previous career, or from being a college student, to being a professional teacher. Your student teacher may be your age, or older, or younger. In any case, your student teacher may be scared to death, anxious, knowledgeable, and, when it comes to elementary school teaching philosophy, somewhere between a romantic idealist and a pragmatic realist. Do not destroy the idealism—help the student teacher with understanding and dealing with the realism of everyday elementary school teaching.

Students in teacher education today have likely had much better preparation and much more pre-student-teaching field experience than you did. For example, many teacher preparation programs today require more than one semester of field experience, perhaps as many as three, including one semester of student teaching in one school or grade level, followed by another semester in a different school or grade level. Learn from your student teacher about the kinds of experiences she or he has had prior to this assignment.

4. *What kind of support, criticism, and supervision should I give?* You will have to decide much of this yourself. However, some teacher preparation programs include seminars for the cooperating teachers, which train them in supervisory techniques for working with student teachers. Today many programs select cooperating teachers *because* of their skill as teachers and their effectiveness in working with other adults. It is possible that you will be working as a member of a team—you, the student teacher, and the university supervisor. It is also possible that your student teacher may have more than one cooperating teacher, who should then also be included as a member of this professional team. Whatever the situation, your student teacher needs support,

helpful suggestions, and productive monitoring. It is unprofessional to place a student teacher into a total "sink-or-swim" situation.

5. *What danger signs should I be alert for?* Your student teacher may be quite different from you, in both appearance and in his or her style of teaching, but may be potentially just as effective a teacher. Be slow and cautious in judging your student teacher's effectiveness. Offer suggestions, but do not make demands.

A student teacher who is not preparing well is likely to be heading for trouble. Be certain to ask for and to receive his or her lesson plans *before* implementation, especially when you feel the student teacher is not preparing well.

Another danger signal is a student teacher's lack of interest in the school and children outside the classroom. The student teacher should be prompt and eager to spend extra time with you, should attend faculty meetings, and should be aware of the necessity of school clerical tasks. If you feel there is a lurking problem, then let the student teacher or the university supervisor know immediately. Trust your intuition. Poor communication between members of the teaching team is another danger signal.

6. *What else should I know?* Your student teacher may be partially employed elsewhere and have other demands on his or her time. Become aware of these other demands, keeping utmost in mind the educational welfare of your students.

Be certain that your student teacher is treated as a member of the faculty, is invited to faculty functions, has a personal mailbox (or is allowed to share yours, with his or her name on it as well), and has a comprehension of school policies, procedures, curriculum documents, and so on.

Once well grounded, the student teacher should be ready to be left alone with the children for increasingly longer periods of time. For a specified period of time, a student teacher's goal is to work toward a competency level that enables him or her to begin the class, teach the entire period, and close the class period—with increasing responsibility for everything. This means that you are nearby and on call in case of an emergency, but out of sight of the children.

Student Teaching from the Principal's Point of View

For your consideration, in a question-and-answer format, here is information about student teaching from the viewpoint of the school principal. You may wish to share this section with the principal.

1. *What is my role?* As the school's chief administrator, we believe you should meet the student teacher when he or she arrives for the first time; give a brief orientation about the school, the community, and important policies; and arrange an introductory tour of the campus. Introduce the student teacher to the grade-level coordinator and to the cooperating teacher. See that the student teacher is encouraged to participate fully in school functions, faculty meetings, activities, and events.

2. *How can I prepare for hosting a student teacher at my school?* Block out some time for the day the student teacher(s) arrives for the first time at your school. It is advisable (and probable) that you have *current* knowledge about the college or university teacher preparation program.

3. *Who is the student teacher?* The student teacher is a person who is making the transition from a previous career, or from being a college student, to being a professional teacher. The student teacher may be your age, or older, or younger. In any case, the student teacher may be scared to death, anxious, knowledgeable, and, when

it comes to elementary or middle school teaching philosophy, somewhere between a romantic idealist and a pragmatic realist. Do not destroy the idealism—help the student teacher with understanding and dealing with the realism of everyday elementary school teaching.

Students in teacher education today have likely had much better preparation and much more pre-student-teaching field experience than when you were in training. For example, many teacher preparation programs today require more than one semester of field experience, perhaps as many as three, including one semester of student teaching in one school or grade level, followed by another semester in a different school or grade level. Learn from your student teacher(s) about the kinds of experiences she or he has had prior to the assignment. Orient the student teacher about how your school is similar to and different from the other schools at which he or she has worked.

4. *Should I give constructive evaluations?* You do not need to be reminded that you are the person responsible for everything that goes on at your school. However, in that role of responsibility we do suggest that you make every effort to visit the student teacher and observe his or her teaching during the assignment at your school. This gives you firsthand information about the competency of this beginning teacher, and how she or he is getting along with your students. It will also give the student teacher insight about the beginning years when evaluation takes place by the chief school administrator.

If your busy schedule permits, it is of value to arrange a brief conference with him or her soon after your observation. Some principals share their district's credentialed-employees evaluation form with the student teacher, using that form as a sort of trial experience for this new teacher. Others mention the strengths they observed and gently indicate any areas that may need attention. Remember, the student teacher may be terrified about all this, because it is likely a "first" for him or her. Your talents can help ease the stress that the student teacher may feel about being evaluated by a principal.

5. *What danger signals should I look for?* Stay in close contact with the cooperating teacher. Listen to what the cooperating teachers and other school personnel are saying when they discuss student teachers. Is the student teacher showing an interest in the school? Is the student teacher reliable, and is she or he punctual each day? Is the student teacher attending the faculty meetings and other school functions? Listen to your intuition. If the verbal and nonverbal signals of your cooperating teachers suggest to you that there is a problem looming, then let the student teacher, cooperating teacher, or university supervisor know your feelings. Keep the channels of communication open between those persons and yourself.

6. *What else should I know?* Does the student teacher commute from a great distance? Does the student teacher have heavy family responsibilities? Is there a financial problem? Is he or she working elsewhere full- or part-time? What is the additional college or university workload? Has there been a severe illness or recent death in the family? A divorce? An engagement called off? As you know, any and all of these can be factors that affect a student teacher's effectiveness in the classroom. It is advisable that you know what is going on.

When the cooperating teacher indicates to you that the student teacher is ready, because he or she appears competent in planning and implementing lessons and in maintaining classroom control, then the student teacher may, with your approval, begin to be left alone with the children for ever-increasing periods of time.

For a specified period of time, a student teacher's goal is to work toward a competency level that enables him or her to gradually take responsibility for entire class periods. This means the cooperating teacher is nearby and on call in case of emergency, but out of sight of the students.

Comments from the University Supervisor

When is the supervisor coming? Is the supervisor going to be here today? Do you see a university or a college supervisor's observation of your student teaching as a pleasant experience or a painful one? Do you realize that classroom observations of your teaching continue during your beginning years of teaching? Being observed and evaluated does not have to be a painful, nerve-racking experience for you. And no—you don't have to become a bundle of raw nerve endings when you realize the supervisor is coming to see you. Whether you are a student teacher being observed by your university supervisor, or a probationary teacher being evaluated by your principal, some professional suggestions may help you turn an evaluating observation into a useful, professionally satisfying experience.

What to Do Before an Observation

"Successful teachers," writes Helen C. Lee, "seem to be able to ameliorate tension and get through an evaluation with skill and tact." Lee suggests that a teacher who is about to be formally evaluated prepare for an evaluator's visit in these ways:

* Decide what you do well in the classroom and plan to demonstrate your best skills.
* Decorate your room and bulletin boards. Display student work.
* Make sure your desk is neat (this shows good organization).[1]
* Select your best skills to discuss first with the evaluator; let your perceived weaknesses be your second targets.

Is your supervisor coming to see you? If so, read the preceding list, and if you decide that the list makes sense, then plan to accomplish every single task on it. As a teacher candidate, you realize that you can present a good, organized appearance, perhaps assume the responsibility of preparing a display table, a chart, or bulletin board in the classroom, and with your host teacher's cooperation, select an academic aspect of the teaching day that demonstrates some of your best teaching skills. If your university supervisor has targeted some of your weak areas, plan to demonstrate growth in those teaching abilities.

What to Do During an Observation

Some supervisors and administrators choose to preannounce their visits. This is certainly true for *clinical supervision* practices. Clinical supervision is supervision that is based on shared decision making between the supervisor and teacher, and focused on improving, rather than evaluating, teaching behaviors.[2] With the use of clinical supervision, you know when the supervisor or administrator is coming, and you will

---

[1]Helen C. Lee, "Evaluation Without Tears," *Educational Horizon* 61(4):200–201 (Summer 1983).
[2]K. A. Acheson and M. D. Gall, *Techniques in the Clinical Supervision of Teachers*, 2nd ed. (New York: Longman, 1987).

probably look forward to the visit because of the rapport that has been established between members of your triad (in student teaching situations, your triad is composed of you, your cooperating teacher, and your university or college supervisor).

Features of effective clinical supervision include a preobservation conference, observation of teaching, and a postobservation conference. In the preobservation conference, the student teacher, cooperating teacher, and the supervisor meet to discuss goals, objectives, teaching strategies, and the evaluation process. During the observation of teaching, the supervisor collects data on the classroom students' performance of objectives and on the student teacher's performance of the teaching strategies. In the postobservation conference, the student teacher, cooperating teacher, and the supervisor discuss the performances. They may compare what happened with what was expected, make inferences about students' achievement of objectives, and discuss relationships between teaching performance and student achievement. The supervisor and cooperating teacher act as educational consultants and may discuss alternative strategies for teaching at this conference or at a later one.

Sometimes your supervisor or administrator may drop in unannounced. When that happens you can take a deep breath, count to ten (quietly), and then proceed with your lesson. You will undoubtedly do just fine if you have been following the guidelines set forth in this resource guide. Additional guidelines for a classroom observation of your teaching follow.

Guidelines for Observation of Your Teaching

- Allow the observer to sit wherever he or she wishes.
- Do not interrupt your lesson to introduce the observer, unless the observer requests it, but *do* prepare your students in advance by letting them know who may be visiting and why.
- Do not put the observer on the spot by suddenly involving him or her in the lesson, but *do* try to discern in advance the level of participation desired by your observer.[3]
- Without "missing a beat" in your lesson, you may walk over and quietly hand the observer a copy of the textbook (or any other materials being used), opened to the appropriate page.
- In some programs the student teacher is expected to maintain a supervisor's binder in the classroom. The binder is kept in a particular location so that the supervisor can pick it up upon entering the classroom and refer to it during the observation. In the binder is the current lesson plan (on top), the current unit plan, previous lessons, tests, assignments, classroom management plan, and a current seating chart with the children's names.

Soon after the observational visit, there should be a conference in which observations are discussed in a *nonjudgmental* atmosphere. It might be necessary for you to make sure that a conference is scheduled. This means that you need to make prior

---

[3]If you have been assigned to a classroom for a student teaching experience, your university supervisor will meet with you and explain some of the tasks you should attend to when the supervisor visits your class. These may vary from the list presented. For instance, some supervisors prefer to walk into a classroom quietly and not interrupt the learning activities. Some prefer not to be introduced to the class or to participate in the activities. Some supervisors are already well known by the students and teaching staff from prior visits to the school. Other supervisors may give you a special form to be completed before he or she arrives for the visit. This form often resembles a lesson plan format and includes space for your objectives, lesson procedures, motivational strategies, related activities, and method of assessing how well the students learned from the lesson. Remember, keep the line of communication open with your supervisor so you have a clear understanding of what is expected of you when she or he visits your classroom to observe your teaching.

arrangements so that you can leave the class, if necessary, for the conference. The purpose of this postobservation conference is for you and the observer(s) to discuss, rather than to evaluate, your teaching and for you to exit the conference with agreements about areas for improvement and *how* to accomplish those improvements.

What to Do During an Observation Conference

Some university supervisors will arrange to have a conference with you to discuss the classroom observation and to begin to resolve any classroom teaching problems. As a teacher or teacher candidate, you should be quite professional during this conference. For instance, one student teacher asks for additional help by requesting resources. Another takes notes and suggests developing a cooperative plan with the supervisor to improve teaching competencies. Still another discusses visiting other classrooms to observe exemplary teachers.

During other conferences, student teachers may ask for assistance in scheduling additional meetings with the supervisor. At such meetings, the teacher (or teacher candidate) views videos of selected teaching styles or methods, listens to audiotapes, or visits an outside educational consultant or nearby resource center.

Almost all supervisors conclude their conferences by leaving something in writing with the teacher or teacher candidate. This written record usually includes (1) a summary of teaching strengths or weaknesses, with a review of classroom management; (2) the supervisor's recommendations; and, perhaps, (3) steps in an overall plan for the teacher's (or student teacher's) continued professional growth and development.

What to Do After the Supervisor Leaves

After your supervisor's visit and conference, you may arrange to observe the classes of other teachers, attend workshops, sign up for conferences, and/or confer with college and university authorities. The following are additional ways to implement your plan for improvement:

- Be sure you debug your lesson plans by walking through them in advance of implementing them in the classroom.
- Do what you and your supervisor-observer have agreed on. Document your activities with a record or diary with dated entries. If you maintain a supervisor's binder, this documentation may be kept in the binder along with the supervisor's written comments.
- If you have a problem with classroom management or organization, review your written classroom management plan and procedures, comparing your plan with the guidelines presented in Chapter 4 of this resource guide. Review your plan and procedures with your cooperating teacher, a trusted teaching colleague, or your university supervisor.
- Obtain help when you need it.
- Send written comments about students' progress to parents or guardians, and leave space for their return messages. Keep positive responses from these adults and share them with your supervisor at your next conference.

E. FINDING A TEACHING POSITION

As your successful student teaching experiences draw to a close, you will embark upon finding your first paid teaching job. The guidelines that follow are provided to help you accomplish that goal.

According to the National Center for Education Statistics, the projected demand for teachers is expected to show a slight drop in 1994, and then gradually increase each year through the remainder of the twentieth century.[4] From that projection it appears that the opportunity for finding a teaching position is good.

Guidelines for Locating a Teaching Position

To prepare for finding the position you want, you should focus on (1) obtaining letters of recommendation from your cooperating teacher(s), your college or university supervisor, and, in some instances, the school principal; (2) your professional preparation as a teacher as evidenced by your letters of recommendation and other items in your professional employability portfolio (discussed next); and (3) your job interviewing skills.

First, consider the recommendations about your teaching that you will receive. At most colleges and universities, there is a career center, typically called a "job (or career) placement center." At that center there is usually a counselor who can advise you how to open your job placement file. That file holds your professional recommendations. It enables prospective personnel directors or district personnel who are ready to employ new teachers to review your recommendations. Sometimes there are special forms for writing these recommendations. It is your responsibility to request letters of recommendation and, when appropriate, to supply the person writing the recommendation with the blank form and an appropriately addressed stamped envelope. Sometimes the job placement files are confidential, so your recommendations will be mailed directly to the placement office. The confidentiality of recommendation letters may be optional, and, when possible, you may want to maintain your own copies of letters of recommendation and include them in your portfolio. Because of the economic depression of the early years of the 1990s, some colleges and universities limited or cut services formerly provided by their job placement centers; if that is the case at your school, then it may be necessary for you to maintain and distribute your own file or a professional employability portfolio.

When requesting letters of recommendation from educators where you did your student teaching, you should ask that the letters include the following information:

- Where you were assigned to do your student teaching.
- The grade levels and subjects you taught.
- Your proven skills in managing children in the classroom.
- Your ability to teach the relevant subject matter.
- Your skills in communicating and interacting with children and adults.

Second, consider your preparation as an elementary teacher. Teachers, as you have learned, represent myriad specialities. Hiring personnel will want to know how you see yourself—for example, as a specialist in elementary core, as a second-grade

---

[4]*Projections of Education Statistics to 2000* (Washington, DC: United States Department of Education, 1989).

teacher, or as an elementary school physical education teacher. Perhaps your interest is in teaching children at any level. Although you are interested in all students, you may indicate a special interest or skill, such as competency in teaching English as a second language. Have you had a rich and varied background of experience so that you will feel comfortable when you are hired and placed in the one assignment in which you were least interested? The hiring personnel who consider your application will be interested in your sincerity and will want to see that you are academically and socially impressive.

Finally, consider your "in-person interview" scheduled with a district official. Sometimes you will find that there will be several interviews scheduled for you or that you will be interviewed simultaneously with other candidates. There may be an initial interview with the district's personnel officer, followed later by an interview with a school principal. Sometimes the principal will ask you to interview with a team of teachers from that school with whom you would be working if you are selected for that teaching position. In all interviews, your verbal and nonverbal behaviors will be observed as you respond to various questions: (1) factual questions about where you participated in student teaching, about that experience, and/or about particular curriculum programs with which you would be expected to work and (2) hypothetical questions, such as "What would you do if . . ." Often these are questions that relate to your philosophy of education, your reasons for wanting to be a teacher, how you would handle a particular classroom situation, and, perhaps, specifically why you want to teach at this particular grade and in this district. See the interview guidelines presented later in this chapter.

The Professional Employability Portfolio (or How to Get Hired by Really Trying)

The concept[5] that follows is one that we have been recommending to our own students for several years, and the feedback about it has been positive. Now, because colleges and universities across the country have experienced severe budget setbacks and, as a result, many have limited the services formerly provided by their career placement centers, this concept of maintaining a personal professional portfolio seems to have even greater significance.

The guidelines set forth here do not ensure that you will be hired for the teaching position that you really want. However, we believe that you may need to be proactive in your job search, and that one way to do this is to create a personal *professional employability portfolio* to be shared with persons who are considering your application for employment.

The portfolio is organized to provide clear evidence of your skills and to make yourself desirable to a hiring committee. We emphasize the word *organized* because the portfolio must be more than simply a collection of your accomplishments randomly tossed into a manila folder. The portfolio must be a deliberate, current, and organized collection of your teaching skills, attributes, and accomplishments.

Because it would be impractical to send a complete portfolio with every application you submit, it might be advisable to have a minimum portfolio (*portfolio A*) that could be sent with each application, in addition to a complete portfolio (*portfolio B*) that you could make available upon request or that you would take with you to an interview. However it is done, the actual contents of the portfolio will vary depending

[5]This concept was first presented in Richard D. Kellough, et al. *Middle School Teaching: Methods and Resources* (New York: Macmillan, 1993), pp. 393–394, and adapted for this resource guide.

on the specific job being sought; you will continually add to and delete materials from your portfolio. The following are suggested categories and subcategories, listed here in the order that we believe they are best presented in portfolios A and B.

1. Table of contents of portfolio (not too lengthy)—portfolio B only.
2. Your professional résumé—both portfolios.
3. Language and communication skills (evidence of your use of the English language and of other languages, including American Sign, if appropriate)—portfolio B. Also state this information briefly in your letter of application (see "The Professional Résumé," which follows later in the chapter).
    *   Your teaching philosophy (written in your own handwriting).
    *   Other evidence to support this category.
4. Teaching skills—portfolio B.
    *   Your ability to plan
        Instructional objectives (see Exercise 6.4).
        A syllabus (see Exercise 7.2).
    *   Your ability to prepare curriculum
        Unit plan (see Exercise 7.4).
    *   Your ability to teach
        A lesson plan (see Exercise 8.2a).
        A video of your actual teaching (see Exercise 15.1).
    *   Your ability to assess
        Personal assessment (see Exercise 15.1).
        Student assessment (see Exercise 14.2).
    *   Letters of recommendation and other documentation to support this category—both portfolios.
5. Other (for example, personal interests related to the position for which you are applying)—portfolio B.

Resources for Locating a Teaching Position

To locate teaching vacancies, you can establish contact with any of the following:

College or university placement office. Establishing a career placement file with your local college or university placement service is an excellent way to begin the process of locating teaching vacancies.

Local school or district personnel office. You can contact school personnel offices to obtain information about teaching vacancies, and sometimes about open job interviews.

County educational agency. Contact local county offices of education about job openings.

State department of education. Some state departments of education maintain information about job openings statewide. See the following list of addresses of those departments.

Independent schools. You can contact non-public-supported schools that interest you, either directly or through educational placement services such as:

IES (Independent Educational Services), 20 Nassau Street, Princeton, NJ 08542.

Commercial placement agencies. Nationwide job listings and placement services are available from such agencies as:

Carney, Sandoe & Associates, 136 Boylston Street, Boston, MA 02116.
National Education Services Center, P.O. Box 1279, Dept. FA, Riverton, WY 82501.

Out-of-country teaching opportunities. Information regarding teaching positions outside the United States can be obtained from:

Department of Defense Dependent Schools, 2461 Eisenhower Avenue, Room 120, Alexandria, VA 22331.
International Schools Service, P.O. Box 5910, Princeton, NJ 08543.

Professional educational journals and other publications. Professional teaching journals often run advertisements of teaching vacancies, as do education newspapers such as *Education Week.* These can be found in your college or university library. For journals specific to your discipline, contact the professional associations listed in Section H of this chapter.

State Sources for Information About Credential Requirements

If you are interested in the credential requirements for other states, check at the appropriate office of your own college or university teacher preparation program to see what information is available about requirements for states of interest to you, and whether the credential that you are about to receive has reciprocity with other states. For example, several states in the Northeast—Connecticut, Maine, Massachusetts, New Hampshire, New York, Rhode Island, and Vermont—share in a regional credential that allows teachers licensed in one state to teach in the others.

Addresses for information about state credentials follow.

Alabama

Teacher Education and
   Certification Section
State Department of
   Education
349 State Office Building
Montgomery, AL 36130
205/261-5060

Alaska

Teacher Education and
   Certification
State Department of
   Education
Pouch F, Alaska Office
   Building
Juneau, AK 99811
907/465-2810

Arizona

Arizona Department of
   Education
Teacher Certification
1535 West Jefferson
P.O. Box 25609
Phoenix, AZ 85007
602/255-4367

Arkansas

Teacher Certification
Room 106-107-B
Arkansas Department
   of Education
Little Rock, AR 72201
501/371-1474

California

Commission on Teacher
   Credentialing
1020 "O" Street
Sacramento, CA
   94244-2700
916/445-7254

Colorado

Teacher Certification
State Office Building
201 East Colfax, 5th Floor
Denver, CO 80203
303/866-6749

Connecticut

Bureau of School Services
State Department of
  Education
P.O. Box 2219
Hartford, CT 06145
203/566-5541

Delaware

Certification and
  Personnel
Department of Public
  Instruction
Townsend Building
Dover, DE 19903
302/736-4688

District of Columbia

Certification and
  Accreditation
District of Columbia
  Public Schools,
  Room 1004
415 12th Street NW
Washington, DC 20004
202/724-4230

Florida

Teacher Certification
Department of Education
Knott Building
Tallahassee, FL 32301
904/488-2317

Georgia

Certification
Georgia Department of
  Education
1452 Twin Towers East
Atlanta, GA 30334
404/656-2406

Hawaii

Office of Personnel
  Services
State Department of
  Education
P.O. Box 2360
Honolulu, HI 96804
808/548-5217

Idaho

Teacher Education and
  Certification
State Department of
  Education
Len B. Jordan Office
  Building
Boise, ID 83720
208/334-3475

Illinois

Teacher Certification
  and Placement
Illinois State Board of
  Education
100 North First Street
Springfield, IL 62777
217/782-2805

Indiana

Division of Teacher
  Certification and
  Placement
State Department of
  Public Instruction
Room 229, State House
Indianapolis, IN 46204
317/232-6636

Iowa

Teacher Education and
  Certification
State Department of
  Public Instruction
Grimes State Office
  Building
Des Moines, IA 50319
515/281-3245

Kansas

Certification Section
State Department of
  Education
120 East 10th Street
Topeka, KS 66612
913/296-2288

Kentucky

Teacher Education and
  Certification
State Department of
  Education
18th Floor, Capital Plaza
  Tower
Frankfort, KY 40601
502/564-4752

Louisiana

Teacher Certification
State Department of
  Education
Baton Rouge, LA 70804
504/342-3490

Maine

Division of Certification,
  Placement, and Teacher
  Education
State House Station 23
Augusta, ME 04333
207/289-5944

Maryland

Certification and
  Accreditation
State Department of
  Education
200 West Baltimore Street
Baltimore, MD 21201
301/659-2141

Massachusetts

Bureau of Teacher
 Preparation,
 Certification and
 Placement
Quincy Center
 Plaza
1385 Hancock
 Street
Quincy, MA 02169
617/770-7517

Michigan

Teacher Preparation
 and Certification
 Services
State Department of
 Education
Ottawa Street Office
 Building
South Tower, Second
 Floor
Lansing, MI 48909
517/373-1924

Minnesota

Personnel Licensing and
 Placement
State Department of
 Education
616 Capitol Square
 Building
550 Cedar Street
St. Paul, MN 55101
612/296-2046

Mississippi

Teacher Certification
State Department of
 Education
P.O. Box 771
Jackson, MS 39205
601/359-3483

Missouri

Teacher Education and
 Certification
State Department of
 Education
Jefferson Building,
 7th Floor
P.O. Box 480
Jefferson City, MO 65102
314/751-3486

Montana

Teacher Certification
Office of Public
 Instruction
Department of Basic
 Instructional Services
1300 Eleventh Avenue
Helena, MT 59620
406/444-3150

Nebraska

Certification and Teacher
 Education
State Department of
 Education
301 Centennial Mall
 South
Box 94987
Lincoln, NE 68509
402/471-2496

Nevada

Teacher Certification
State Department of
 Education
400 West King Street
Carson City, NV 89710
702/885-3116

New Hampshire

Teacher Education and
 Professional Standards
State Department of
 Education
101 Pleasant Street
Concord, NH 03301-3860
603/271-2407

New Jersey

Bureau of Teacher
 Preparation and
 Certification
State Department of
 Education
225 West State Street,
 CN 500
Trenton, NJ 08625-0503
609/984-1216

New Mexico

Teacher Education and
 Certification
State Department of
 Education
DeVargas and Don
 Gasper Street
State Capitol Complex,
 Room 105
Santa Fe, NM 87501-2786
505/827-6581

New York

Teacher Certification
Cultural Education
 Center Room 5A
11 Madison Avenue
Albany, NY 12230
518/474-3901

North Carolina

Division of Certification
State Department of
 Public Instruction
116 West Edenton Street
Raleigh, NC 27603-1712
919/733-4125

North Dakota

Teacher Certification
State Department of
 Public Instruction
State Capital, 9th Floor
Bismarck, ND 58505
701/224-2264

Ohio

Teacher Education and
  Certification
State Department of
  Education
Ohio Department
  Building, Room 1012
Columbus, OH 43215
614/466-3593

Oklahoma

Teacher Education and
  Certification
State Department of
  Education
Hodge Education
  Building
2500 North Lincoln
  Boulevard
Oklahoma City, OK
  73105-4599
405/521-3337

Oregon

Teacher Standards and
  Practices Commission
730 Twelfth Street, SE
Salem, OR 97310
503/378-3586

Pennsylvania

Bureau of Teacher
  Preparation and
  Certification
Department of Education
333 Market Street, 3rd
  Floor
Harrisburg, PA 17126-
  0333
717/787-2967

Rhode Island

Teacher Certification and
  Placement
State Department of
  Education
Roger Williams Building
22 Hayes Street
Providence, RI 02908
401/277-2675

South Carolina

Teacher Certification
State Department of
  Education
1015 Rutledge,
  Room 1004
Columbia, SC 29201
803/758-8527

South Dakota

Office of Teacher
  Education and
  Certification
Division of Elementary
  and Secondary
  Education
Kneip Office Building
700 North Illinois
Pierre, SD 57501
605/773-3553

Tennessee

Teacher Education and
  Certification
State Department of
  Education
125 Cordell Hull Building
Nashville, TN 37219
615/741-1644

Texas

Teacher Certification
Texas Education Agency
William B. Travis State
  Office Building
1701 North Congress
  Avenue
Austin, TX 78701
512/463-8976

Utah

Teacher Certification
Instruction and Support
  Section
Utah State Office of
  Education
250 East 500 South
Salt Lake City, UT 84111
801/533-5965

Vermont

Certification Division
State Department of
  Education
Montpelier, VT 05602
802/828-2445

Virginia

Teacher Education and
  Certification
State Department of
  Education
Box 6Q, James Monroe
  Building
Richmond, VA 23216
804/225-2907

Washington

Certification and
  Licensing
Office of the
  Superintendent of
  Public Instruction
Old Capitol Building
Olympia, WA 98504
206/753-6773

West Virginia	**Wisconsin**	**Wyoming**
Office of Educational Personnel Development	Bureau of Teacher Education and Certification	Certification and Licensing
State Department of Education	State Department of Public Instruction	State Department of Education
Capitol Complex, Room B304, Building 6	125 South Webster Street	Hathaway Building
Charleston, WV 25305	P.O. Box 7841	Cheyenne, WY 82002-0050
304/348-2696	Madison, WI 53707	307/777-6261
	608/266-1027	

The Professional Résumé

How-to books are written about it, computer programs are available for it, and commercial services provide assistance for general résumé preparation, but a teacher's résumé is specific. Although no one can tell you exactly what résumé will work best for you, there are a few guidelines especially helpful for the preparation for a teacher's résumé:

1. The résumé should be no more than *two* pages in length. If it is any longer, it becomes a life history rather than a professional résumé.
2. The presentation should be neat and *uncluttered*.
3. Page size should be standard 8 × 11 inches. Oversized and undersized pages can get lost.
4. Stationery color can be standard white or off-white, but because copies may be made for other members of the hiring committee, be cautious about using bright-colored stationery that may photocopy poorly.
5. Including personal data may make it appear that you are trying to prejudice members of the hiring committee and is simply unprofessional, so do *not* include personal information such as your age, height, weight, marital status, number or names of your children, or a photograph of yourself.
6. Sentences should be clear and concise; avoid educational jargon, awkward phrases, abbreviations, or unfamiliar words.
7. Organize the information carefully, in this order: Your name, address, and telephone number, followed by your education, professional experience, credential status, location of placement file, professional affiliations, and honors.
8. When identifying your experiences—academic, teaching, and life experiences— do so in *reverse chronological order,* listing first your most recent degree or your current position and moving backward chronologically.
9. Take time to develop your résumé; then keep it current. Do not duplicate hundreds of copies; *clean-type it each time you apply for a job.* If you maintain your résumé on a computer disc, then it is easy to print a current copy each time one is needed.
10. Prepare a cover letter to accompany your résumé that is written *specifically* for the position for which you are applying. Address the letter personally but formally to the personnel director. Limit the cover letter to one page, and emphasize yourself, your teaching experiences and interests, and reasons that you are best qual-

ified for the position. Show a familiarity with the particular school or district. Again, if you maintain a generic application letter on a computer disc, you can easily change it to make it specific for each position applied for.

11. Have your résumé and cover letter edited by someone familiar with résumé writing and editing, perhaps an English-teaching friend. A poorly written, poorly typed, or poorly copied résumé fraught with errors in spelling and grammar will guarantee that you will not be considered for the job.

12. Be sure that your application reaches the personnel director by the announced deadline. If for some reason it will be late, telephone the director, explain the circumstances, and request permission to submit your application late.

See the sample résumé in Figure 15.9.

The In-Person Interview

If your application and résumé are attractive to the personnel director during paper screening, then you will be notified and scheduled for a personal or small group interview, although in some instances the hiring interview may precede the request for your personal papers. Whichever the case, during the interview you should be honest, and you should be yourself. Practice your interview ahead of the scheduled time, perhaps with aid of a videocamera and recorder so that you can observe yourself. Ask someone to role-play an interview with you and to ask you some tough questions. Plan your interview wardrobe and get it ready the night before your interview. Leave early for your interview so that you arrive in plenty of time. If possible, long before your scheduled interview, locate someone who works in the school district and discuss curriculum matters, management policies, and popular programs with that person. If you anticipate a professionally embarrassing question during the interview, think of diplomatic ways to respond to avoid harming yourself professionally. This means that you should think of ways to turn your weaknesses into strengths. For instance, if your cooperating teacher has mentioned that you need to continue to develop your room environment skills (meaning that you were sloppy), admit that you realize that you need to be more conscientious about keeping supplies and materials neat and tidy, but mention your concern about the students and the learning, and that you realize you have a tendency to interact with students more than with objects. Assure the interviewer that you will work on this skill, and then remember to do it.

Here are additional specific guidelines for preparing for and handling the in-person interview.

1. When notified, you will be given a specific time, date, and place for the interview. Regardless of your other activities, accept the time, date, and location suggested, rather than trying to manipulate the interviewer(s) around a schedule more convenient for you.

2. Before the interview, you will be told whether the interviewer expects a formal teaching demonstration. If so, sometimes a videotape of your teaching will satisfy that request. Our students have used their MPT tapes or tapes made during their student teaching for this purpose.

3. Dress for success. Regardless of what else you may be doing for living, take the time necessary to make a professional appearance.

Richard Da Teacher
1993 Schoolhouse Drive
Dewey, CA 95818
(916) 278-7020

OBJECTIVE: Seeking an elementary school teaching position

EDUCATION: California Multiple Subject Teaching Credential
California State University, Sacramento—May 1993

Bachelor of Arts Degree in Liberal Studies
California State University, Sacramento—August 1992

RELATED EXPERIENCES: Student Teacher. Foulks Ranch Elementary School,
2/94–5/94 Elk Grove Unified School District, Elk Grove, CA.

Developed and utilized lesson plans in teaching a fourth grade class of 34 ethnically diverse students. Heavy emphasis on cooperative learning and integrated thematic units. Utilized "Bell Works" in teaching math and "San Mateo Series" in language arts. Assisted in CTBS testing.

9/93–12/94 Student Teacher. James McKee Elementary School, Elk Grove Unified School District, Elk Grove, CA.

Planned, developed, and utilized lessons for second- and third-grade students. Year-round scheduling of students was experienced at this school. Planned and taught a literature unit on *The Courage of Sarah Noble* with a multicultural emphasis.

9/92–2/93 Teacher Aide. Premier Day Care Center, Dewey, CA. Worked in teaching and supervisory positions with ethnically diverse children from kindergarten through grade six. Planned weekly thematic activities for all children.

OTHER EXPERIENCES:
- Volunteer at P.A.C.T.S. Science Program, Elk Grove, CA, Spring 1993.
- Volunteer at California Reading Association Conference, Sacramento, CA, Fall 1992.
- Musical Abilities: Have played the saxophone for more than 14 years; can read any type of music. Six years of professional work experience in the music recording industry.
- European travel experiences in Austria, Denmark, Germany, Holland, Luxembourg, Sweden, and Switzerland.

REFERENCES:
- Dr. Don Larson, University Supervisor of Student Teaching, California State University, Sacramento. (916) 278-7020
- Ms. Patricia Roberts, Cooperating Teacher at Foulks Ranch Elementary School, Elk Grove, CA. (916) 778-8900
- Mr. Richard Kellough, Cooperating Teacher at James McKee Elementary School, Elk Grove, CA. (916) 777-2496

Figure 15.9 Sample résumé.

4. Do not arrive at the interview with small children. If necessary, arrange to have them taken care of by someone you trust.

5. After arriving promptly at the designated location, shake hands firmly with members of the committee, and initiate conversation with a friendly comment, based on your personal knowledge, about the school or district.

6. Sometimes school districts will send candidates the questions that will be asked during the interview; in other instances these questions are handed to the candidate upon arrival at the interview. In either case, you need to know that the questions asked are typically identical for each candidate interviewed for the position.

   Questions likely to be asked will cover the following topics:

   • *Your experiences with children of the relevant age.* The committee wants to be reasonably certain that you can effectively manage and teach at the level for which you are applying. You should answer this question by sharing *specific* successes that demonstrate that you are a decisive and competent teacher.

   • *Hobbies and travels.* The committee wants to know more about you as a person to ensure that to the students you will be an interesting and energetic teacher, as well as a congenial member of the faculty.

   • *Extracurricular interests and experiences.* The committee wants to know about all the ways in which you might be helpful in the school, and to know that you will promote the interests and co-curricular activities of students.

   • *Classroom management techniques.* You must convince the committee not only that can you effectively manage children, but that you can do so in a manner commensurate with helping children develop their self-esteem.

   • *Knowledge of the subject taught at the grade level for which you are being considered.* The committee needs to be reasonably certain that you have command of the subject fields, and of knowledge of how it fits with the developmental stages of elementary school students. This is when you should show your knowledge of state and local curriculum documents.

   • *Commitment to teaching at this level.* The committee wants to be assured that you are knowledgeable about and committed to teaching and learning at this level, rather than your wanting this job only until something better comes along.

   • *Your perceived weaknesses.* If you are asked about your weaknesses, you have an opportunity to show that you can effectively self-evaluate, that you can think reflectively and critically, and that you know the value of learning from your own errors. Be prepared for this question by identifying a specific error that you have made, perhaps while student teaching, and explain how you turned that error into a profitable learning experience.

7. Throughout the interview you should maintain eye contact with the interviewer while demonstrating interest, enthusiasm, and self-confidence.

8. When an opportunity arises, ask one or two planned legitimate questions that show your knowledge of and interest in this position and this community and school or district.

9. When the interview has obviously been brought to a close by the interviewer, that is your signal to leave. Do not hang around; this is a sign of lacking confidence.

10. It is important to follow the interview with a thank-you letter addressed to the personnel director or interviewer; even if you do not get the job, you will be better remembered for future reference.

Once you are employed as a teacher, your professional development continues. The sections that follow demonstrate ways in which that can happen.

F. PROFESSIONAL DEVELOPMENT THROUGH MENTORING

Mentoring, one teacher facilitating the learning of another teacher, can aid in professional development. In what is sometimes called peer-coaching, a mentor teacher volunteers or is selected by the teacher who wishes to improve, or is selected by a school administrator, formally or informally. The mentor observes and coaches the teacher to help him or her to improve in teaching. Sometimes the teacher simply wants to learn a new skill. In other instances, the teacher being coached remains with the mentor teacher for an entire school year, developing and improving old and new skills, or learning how to teach with a new program. In many districts, new teachers are automatically assigned to mentor teachers for their first year, as a program of **induction.**

During mentoring, the mentor teacher and the teacher being coached meet in a preobservation conference and discuss the skill or skills to be observed. Then the teacher is observed, and a postobservation conference follows, in which the teacher and mentor discuss the observations and plan for the next observation. The cycle continues until the desired skills have been acquired.

G. PROFESSIONAL DEVELOPMENT THROUGH INSERVICE AND GRADUATE STUDY

Inservice workshops and programs are offered for teachers at the school level, by the district, and by other agencies such as a county office of education, a local agency, or a nearby college or university. Inservice workshops and programs are usually designed for specific purposes, such as to train teachers in new teaching skills, to update their knowledge in content, and to introduce them to new teaching materials or programs. Inservice workshops and programs are often led by veteran teachers, and sometimes by university or college professors.

Inservice programs are offered when teachers are available, which means on minimum days (short school days), in late afternoon or evening, on weekends, and during vacation periods.

University graduate study is yet another way of continuing your professional development. Some teachers pursue master's degrees in an academic teaching field, while many others pursue master's degrees in curriculum and methods of instruction, or in educational administration or counseling. Some universities offer a Master of Arts in Teaching, a program of courses in specific academic fields that are especially designed for teachers. School districts encourage teachers to pursue graduate work by providing pay raises according to units earned and degrees granted.

H. PROFESSIONAL DEVELOPMENT THROUGH PARTICIPATION IN PROFESSIONAL ORGANIZATIONS

There are many professional organizations, often including local teachers' organizations. These are usually discipline-specific, such as, for reading (International Reading Association), mathematics (National Council of Teachers of Mathematics), or science (National Science Teachers Association). In most states there is a statewide organization, probably affiliated with a national organization. In addition, there are the National Education Association (NEA) and the American Federation of Teachers (AFT), which, in a few locales, have joined as the collective bargaining organization for teachers.

Local, district, state, and national organizations have annual meetings that include guest speakers, workshops, and publishers' displays. Professional meetings of teachers are educational, enriching, and fulfilling for those who attend.

In addition, many other professional associations, such as those for reading teachers, supply speakers and publish articles in their journals that are often of interest to teachers other than the target audience.

Professional organizations publish newsletters and journals for their members, and these will likely be found in your college or university library. Sample periodicals were listed in Chapter 12. Additional periodicals of interest to teachers and administrators include *Phi Delta Kappan*, the journal of the Phi Delta Kappa (PDK) professional organization, and *Educational Leadership*, the monthly publication of the Association for Supervision and Curriculum Development (ASCD).

Professional Organizations for Elementary School Teachers

Many professional organizations have special membership prices for teachers who are still college or university students, a courtesy that allows for an inexpensive beginning affiliation with a professional association. For information on special membership prices and association services, write to those of interest to you.

American Alliance for Health, Physical Education, Recreation and Dance, 1900 Association Drive, Reston, VA 22091.
American Association of School Librarians, 50 E. Huron Street, Chicago, IL 60611.
Association for Childhood Education International, 3615 Wisconsin Avenue NW, Washington, DC 20016.
Association for Computers in Mathematics and Science Teaching, P.O. Box 4455, Austin, TX 78765.
Association for Supervision and Curriculum Development, 125 N. West Street, Alexandria, VA 22314.
Council for Exceptional Children, 1920 Association Drive, Reston, VA 22091.
Council for Library Resources, One Dupont Circle, Washington, DC 20036.
Council on Teaching Foreign Languages, Six Executive Plaza, Yonkers, NY 10701.
International Reading Association, 800 Barksdale Road, Newark, DE 19711.
Music Educators National Conference, 1902 Association Drive, Reston, VA 22091.
National Art Education Association, 1916 Association Drive, Reston, VA 22091.
National Association of Biology Teachers, 11250 Roger Bacon Drive, Reston, VA 22090.
National Association for the Education of Young Children, 1834 Connecticut Avenue NW, Washington, DC 20009.
National Association of Geology Teachers, P.O. Box 368, Lawrence, KS 66044.
National Council for the Social Studies, 3501 Newark Street NW, Washington, DC 20016.
National Council of Teachers of English, 1111 Kenyon Road, Urbana, IL 61801.
National Council of Teachers of Mathematics, 1906 Association Drive, Reston, VA 22091.
National Science Teachers Association, 1742 Connecticut Avenue NW, Washington, DC 20009.
Phi Delta Kappa, Eighth Street and Union Avenue, Bloomington, IN 47401.

I. PROFESSIONAL DEVELOPMENT THROUGH COMMUNICATIONS WITH OTHER TEACHERS

One of the valuable experiences that can be gained by visiting teachers at other schools, and by attending inservice workshops, graduate seminars and programs, and meetings of professional organizations, and by sharing with teachers by means of electronic bulletin boards, derives from talking and sharing with teachers from other places. These discussions include a sharing not only of "war stories," but of ideas and descriptions of new programs, books, materials, and techniques that work.

As in other process skills, the teacher practices and models skill in communication, in and out of the classroom. This includes communicating with other teachers to improve one's own repertoire of strategies and knowledge about teaching, and to share one's experiences with others. Teaching other teachers about your own special skills and sharing your experiences are important components of the communication and professional development processes.

J. PROFESSIONAL DEVELOPMENT THROUGH SUMMER AND OFF-TEACHING WORK EXPERIENCE

Whether your school is a year-round school or follows the traditional plan (late August through mid-June), in many areas of the country there are special programs of short-term employment available to interested teachers, especially, although not exclusively, to teachers interested in math and science, offered by private industry, foundations, and research institutes. The interests of these sources include the dissemination of information and the provision of opportunities for teachers to update their skills and knowledge, with an ultimate hope that the teachers will stimulate in more children an interest in science and technology. Participating industries, foundations, and institutes provide on-the-job training with salaries or stipends to teachers who are selected to participate. During the program of employment, teachers, scientists, technicians, and sometimes university educators, meet, usually weekly, to share experiences and discuss what is being learned and its implications for teaching and curriculum development.

There are NSF-sponsored summer programs for teachers. These are field-centered and content-specific programs. For example, one program may concentrate on geology, anthropology, mathematics, or reading, while at another location, the program focus may be on teaching, using a specific new experimental curriculum. These programs are located around the country and may have university affiliation, which means that university credit may be available. Room and board, travel, and a stipend are sometimes granted to participating teachers.

Sources of information about the availability of these programs include professional journals, your local chamber of commerce, and meetings of the local or regional teacher's organization. In areas where there are no organized programs of part-time work experience for teachers, some teachers have had success in initiating their own by establishing contact with management personnel of a local business or company.

SUMMARY

Because teaching and learning go hand in hand, and the effectiveness of one affects the effectiveness of the other, these final two chapters of Part IV of the text have dealt with both aspects of the *how well* component of teacher preparation—how well the students are learning and how well the teacher is teaching. Although you have not been told everything you will ever need to know about the assessment of teaching and learning, it is hoped that these chapters have addressed the essentials necessary to measure and evaluate student achievement and teacher effectiveness. Throughout your teaching career you will continue to improve your knowledge and skills in assessment.

As you arrive at the end of this resource guide, we hope your quest has been enjoyable and profitable, and we wish you well in your new career. Be the very best teacher you can be. The nation and its children need you.

QUESTIONS FOR CLASS DISCUSSION

1. Find out what professional teacher organizations are in your geographical area. Share what you find with others in your class.
2. Attend a regional or national meeting of a professional teachers' association, and report to your class your experience and what you learned about the association.
3. Talk with experienced teachers and find out how they stay current in their teaching fields. Share what you find with others in your class.
4. Invite representatives from AFT and NEA to come to your class and discuss their organizations and the benefits of joining.
5. Find out whether membership in AFT or NEA is obligatory for teachers in your local school districts. Report your findings to your class.
6. Do you believe teachers should ever go on strike? Explain.
7. Must teachers in your local school districts be credentialed in order to be employed?
8. Other than their professional publications, many professional organizations have additional benefits available to members, such as group purchasing power and inexpensive liability insurance coverage. Join with members of your class to investigate the costs and benefits of membership in various professional organizations. Report your findings to your class.
9. In many districts, new teachers are automatically assigned to mentor teachers for their first year, as a program of induction. Find out if your local school districts have such a plan and, if they do, report to your class on how the plan works.
10. Do you have questions about the content of this chapter? How might answers be found?

SUGGESTED READINGS FOR CHAPTER 15

Bullough, R. V., Jr., Knowles, J. G., and Crow, N. *Emerging as a Teacher*. London: Routledge Publishers, 1992.

Darling-Hammond, L., and Goodwin, A. L. "Progress Toward Professionalism in Teaching." In Gordon Cawelti, ed. 1993 ASCD Yearbook. *Challenges and Achievements of American Education*. Alexandria, VA: Association for Supervision and Curriculum Development, 1993.

Farnsworth, B., Debenham, J., and Smith, G. "Designing and Implementing a Successful Merit Pay Program for Teachers." *Phi Delta Kappan* 73(4):320–325 (December 1991).

Merseth, K. K. "First Aid for First-Year Teachers." *Phi Delta Kappan* 73(9):678–683 (May 1992).

Milner, J. O. "Suppositional Style and Teacher Evaluation." *Phi Delta Kappan* 72(6): 464–467 (February 1991).

Petcovic, M. L. "National Certification Won't Help Mobile Educators." *Educational Leadership* 50(8):76–77 (May 1993).

Rabbitt, M. "International Recruitment Centers for International Schools." *Phi Delta Kappan* 73(5):409–410 (January 1992).

Vienne, D. T. "Seasoned Pros Give New Teachers a Helping Hand." *Executive Educator* 13(8):32–33 (August 1991).

Watts, G. D., and Castle, S. "Electronic Networking and the Construction of Professional Knowledge." *Phi Delta Kappan* 73(9):684–689 (May 1992).

APPENDIX

Sample Interdisciplinary Thematic Unit[1]

CRUSTACEANS

CRABS, CRAYFISH, LOBSTERS, & SHRIMP

Grade 3

An Integrated Unit

MEG BATES

LAURIE DURAN

DOREEN HERSH

JOEL SOOBY

INTRODUCTION

The goal of this unit is to familiarize students with the unique characteristics of crustaceans as they exist in the animal kingdom and the role crustaceans play in the man–animal relationship.

To achieve this goal we have created an integrated unit in which we employ several different parts of the curriculum in a variety of different ways. Four different areas have been specifically addressed (science, social studies, language arts, and math), but the lessons in each area also cut across the curriculum to include elements from other subject areas as well.

We have made provisions for students to practice various skills throughout this unit. Specifically students will be honing their skills in observation, measurement, pre-

---

[1] This third-grade thematic unit on crustaceans was provided through the courtesy of Meg Bates, Laurie Duran, Doreen Hersh, and Joel Sooby. Unpublished material.

diction, description, comparing and contrasting, recordkeeping, communicating, and problem solving. Special emphasis has been placed on discovery learning by the students where they will literally take a hands-on approach to investigating crustaceans. Included in the strategies for initiating these processes will be opportunities for students to work in group situations as well as independently. This will provide a helping hand for those less skilled students and the occasion for all students to practice the art of cooperation. Group situations will allow all students to experience some area in which they can be successful.

Finally we have attempted to bring a multicultural element into the language arts portion of the unit by incorporating literature about crustaceans from other cultures. The multicultural issue has been addressed specifically by including lessons on the importance of these animals in past cultures as well as the modern cultures of several countries around the world and even various parts of our own country. The culminating activity has a multicultural flair with a tasty treat of crustaceans prepared in different ways from different cultures.

It is our sincere hope that you enjoy teaching this unit and that your students enjoy learning about crustaceans as much as we enjoyed putting it all together for you!

LESSON PLAN—DAY ONE

Objective. After observing a live crayfish, students will brainstorm other types of animals they think may be crustaceans and what these animals might eat. Students will then predict what type of food the crayfish will like best and test their hypothesis over the next two weeks.

Materials. Aquarium tank or plastic "pen pals" tank; live crayfish; various types of food crayfish might eat (pieces of meat, fish, vegetation); record book; large graph.

Transitional Activities. This is the introductory lesson on crustaceans. Students will tap their prior knowledge through this lesson and begin a unit-long experiment on crayfish.

Purpose. The purpose of this lesson is to introduce the students to crustaceans and to tap their prior knowledge about these animals.

Anticipatory Set. Ask the students to name the animal you have brought into the classroom. Explain that the animal is a member of a special class of animals called crustaceans and that the students will be studying a few members of this class of animals.

Procedure

1. Hold up the crayfish so students can see it. Allow students to go back, group by group, to observe the crayfish for a few minutes. Introduce the crayfish as a member of the class Crustacea.
2. Have students brainstorm some other animals they think might be crustaceans. Write the names of these animals on the blackboard as they will not be used after this lesson. After brainstorming, students will study some of the familiar crustaceans that they named (either on their own or in guided discussion). Inform the students they will be studying lobsters, crayfish, shrimp, and crabs.
3. Next, have the students brainstorm what they think this crayfish might eat. Ask them to consider where it might live and what is available. Write the students' ideas on a piece of chart paper.

4. After the students have come up with some ideas, explain to them that the class will be conducting an experiment over the course of the crustacean unit. They will be trying to discover what crayfish like to eat the best.
5. Have the students list food items in the order they think the crayfish will prefer them, with the first preference as number one and the least desirable as last. Keep the list for the final analysis of the experiment.
6. Explain the experiment.

What I Like Best Experiment

1. Each morning, present the crayfish with a small amount of each type of food item selected. Record on the data sheet how much of each item is given, if the crayfish eats any item immediately, how much of the item is ate, and any other information the students think is relevant. A report will be given to the class each morning on the data collected.
2. Check the crayfish before leaving for the day and record which, if any, items were eaten, how much was eaten, and any other information the students feel is important.
3. Each morning chart the data from the previous day about which items were eaten and the amount on the graph. Repeat steps one and two.
4. Continue collecting data until the ninth day of the unit when the information will be analyzed and the students will see if their hypothesis is correct.

---

7. Students will work in small groups to collect and chart the data. Depending on class size, the groups should be three or four students.
8. Check for understanding. Have the first group of students feed the crayfish and record their data on the data sheets.

Closure Summary. Invite the students to take some time during the day to observe the crayfish. Ask the students to observe one specific thing which is interesting about the crayfish and be ready to tell about it the next day.

Follow-Up/Evaluation. This experiment will continue daily for the duration of the unit. Students will evaluate the data at the end of the unit and test their hypothesis.

SCIENCE LESSON PLAN—DAY ONE

Objectives. After being presented with five types of live creatures, students will, through exploratory learning, be able to verbally or pictorally compare and contrast the animals.

Materials. A science notebook for each student. Separate, numbered tanks or bowls with a crayfish, a lobster, a snail, a crab, and "sea monkeys."

Time Span. One hour.

Set. Say to the students, for example, "Have you ever seen sea monkeys? I have some sea monkeys right here that I got at a toy store. Do you think these little things are monkeys? This is what the box looks like. (Show it.) It shows what sea monkeys might look like if they were bigger. These don't look like pictures of monkeys to me. In fact (hold up fresh or frozen shrimp), *this* is really what a sea monkey would look like if it were larger. I'm not going to tell you what any of these creatures are called yet, but for now, you may call these sea monkeys."

Procedure. Divide the class into five groups. Explain how each creature may be touched (if at all). Explain the procedure to the students, "The groups will observe each creature for four minutes and take notes or draw pictures of that creature regarding its color, size, appearance, and movement patterns. They will then observe each creature again for four minutes and write about how each is similar to, or different from, the others."

Guided Practice. Tell the students, for example, "I noticed that this one, this one, and this one all have pincer-type claws with rubber bands on them. So I would write that down or draw it."

Independent Practice. None.

Closure. "Back to your seats, everybody. Raise your hand if you think you can name at least one of these creatures. Wow! On Wednesday I bet you'll be able to name them all!

SCIENCE LESSON PLAN—DAY TWO

Objectives. After being reminded of the observations that they made on Monday, students will be able to discuss and brainstorm their notes, thoughts, guesses, and pictures regarding similarities and differences between the animals.

Materials. Butcher paper; markers, brainstorm sound effects.

Time Span. 30 minutes.

Anticipatory Set. Indicating the animals in tanks, say to the students, for example, "Who thinks they can name one of these animals?" As correct responses come out, write them on a butcher paper chart.

Procedure. Tell the students, "Now let's brainstorm!" (Play brainstorm sound effects.) "Tell me about number one, a crayfish." "Good, what else? Good, what else? Excellent. Now tell me something about number two, a lobster," etc.... Number five: "Were those monkeys? No! They were shrimp! That's right! Little tiny brine shrimp. Wait a minute. Wait just a minute here. I was trying to trick you! One of these animals does not belong on our chart! I'm trying to trick you, now, so be careful! Which one of these should not be on our chart?" (Hopefully by now the students will have been exposed to enough information that they will know that the snail is out of place. If they don't know it, tell them now.) "That's right!" (With great flourish, cross out or rip off the snail part of the chart.) "Oh, I couldn't trick you because you are too *smart*! You used your brains to think. I didn't trick you at all. Good work everyone!"

Check for Understanding. "Now we're going around the world—everyone will have five seconds—*not six, mind you!*—to tell us what you liked best about these creatures, or to share a note or a picture you drew of these animals. Let's go Aroooooooooooouuuuuunnnnnddd the world!" (Call on someone while looking at your watch and saying, "Good! Next! Yes, yes! Next." etc.)

Closure. "These animals, except the snail, all have one thing in common—an exoskeleton. An exoskeleton is like our skeleton, except it is on the outside and ours is on the inside. They act like a protective covering for the animal. Crabs, shrimps, lobsters, and crayfish only leave their shells when they grow out of them. A snail can go in and out of its shell, but these others with exoskeletons stay inside them until they get too big. That's why the snail did not belong on our chart!"

SCIENCE LESSON PLAN—DAY THREE

Objectives. After being given a fact about a crustacean, students will be able to use critical thinking to pose thoughtful, reasonable, or logical answers to the question, "Why is that?"

Materials. Sound effect instruments; rubber lobsters for all.

Procedure. This is a game called, "Why is that?" Divide the class into two to four teams. A bell/horn/drum is placed where all members of each team can reach their instrument. Facts about crustaceans are read aloud by the teacher, who ends every fact with the question, "Why is that?" Only then can a team sound their bell/horn/drum. The first team to sound their instrument is called on. One response is given. If it is thoughtful, reasonable, or logical, that team scores.

Guided Practice. As an example of what sort of answer you are looking for, you could tell the students, "I might say, 'Lobsters have pincers, or grabbing claws. Why is that?' If you respond first and are called on and say, 'To get food' or 'To hold onto something in the rough ocean waters,' your team would score. If you say, 'To pinch your toes when you go swimming,' you probably would not score." (Answers given for laughs may be discouraged, however, they may be encouraged at the end.)
   Some facts to state before asking "Why is that?" are:

- Shrimp have antennae.
- Crabs have an external skeleton.
- Crayfish have legs that can bend.
- A crayfish has eyes that stick out from its head.
- Lobsters have tails.
- A crayfish can shed its skeleton.
- Lobsters live in sea water.
- Crabs move by walking sideways.
- A shrimp can bury itself in the sand.

   Questions can be repeated, substituting other crustaceans. All of these questions should be repeated to encourage thinking.

Closure. Everyone gets a rubber lobster for participating.

SCIENCE LESSON PLAN—DAY FOUR

Objectives. Students will set up an experiment to judge the value of keeping perishables out of the air.

Materials. Give each pair of students one tomato (quartered); some newspaper; two babyfood jars with lids; water; paper plates.

Time Span. 45 minutes.

Set. Open a can of shrimp and have students note that they are fresh.

Procedure. Split class into dyads. Explain, "We are going to see how to keep food fresh without putting it in the refrigerator. On your paper plate, place one of the tomato slices and leave it there. Wrap the newspaper loosely around another tomato slice. Put another tomato slice in a jar and put the lid on it; put the last slice in the other jar, fill it with water, and put the lid on it."

When everyone is finished, check for their understanding by asking the students to predict what will happen to each piece of tomato. Have them write their predictions in their science notebooks (independent practice).

Closure. "Please put your plate with your group's name on it on the back counter. These are not to be touched for two days."

SCIENCE LESSON PLAN—DAY FIVE

Objectives. After observing changes in their tomato slices, students will be able to identify a way to keep food fresher (to teacher satisfaction).

Materials. Experiment from day four.

Time Span. 30 minutes.

Set. "Boy! I sure am hungry for a tomato! Do you think I could eat any of those?"

Procedure. Have students make notes of the results in their books. Lead a discussion. Ask questions, such as, "Why are shrimp sold in cans of water rather than wrapped in newspaper?" "Would bread be good kept in a jar of water?" "Why not?" "What is in the air that makes food go bad?"

Independent Practice. For homework, assign students the task of writing a list of every food in a can or jar at home.

Closure. "What else would not be good stored in a can of water besides bread? Think about it!"

Science Lessons Resource List

• Lobsters can be purchased live at a supermarket or seafood store.
• Crayfish and crabs can be purchased at a farmer's market or seafood store.
• Snails can be found almost anywhere.

- Sea Monkeys can be purchased at a toy store.
- Brainstorm sound effects can be made by recording two or three people making wind noises close to the microphone.
- Rubber lobsters can be purchased at a novelty or craft shop.
- Tomatoes and canned shrimp can be purchased at a supermarket.
- Start saving those babyfood jars now!

SOCIAL STUDIES LESSON PLAN—DAY ONE

Objective. After performing a survey, students will use the data collected to categorize various ways of earning money and how those jobs may be related to the environment.

Materials. Five surveys per student (see below); five popsicle sticks per student; white paper (4″ × 5″), five per student; construction paper (4½″ × 6″), five per student; crayons or markers; glue sticks; stapler/staples; four boxes with slits cut for posting stick characters (labeled as: community only, community and other cities in state, community and other states, community and other countries); butcher paper.

SURVEY

Name of Employer _____

Job Title _____

Location _____

Do you work in an office?   Y _____   N _____

If no, do you work outside _____ or inside _____ ?

Is your job done in other cities?   Y _____   N _____

Is your job done in other states?   Y _____   N _____

Is your job done in other countries?   Y _____   N _____

Did you have special training/education?   Y _____   N _____

Do you have special tools to do your job?   Y _____   N _____

Surveyor _____

Time Period. Data collection should begin at least one week in advance of the lesson.

Motivation. Survey.

Procedures

1. Students will draw a picture for each of the people in their survey.
2. Pictures are glued to one side of the construction paper and the survey to the other.

3. The popsicle stick will be stapled on as a handle.
4. Each student will raise the stick or sticks that apply as the following categories are mentioned. Helpers may be needed to count and record the answers on butcher paper poster.
    a. People who have special training or education.
    b. People who have special tools to do their job.
    c. People who have jobs that are also done in another country.
    d. People who have jobs that are also done in another state.
    e. People who have jobs that are also done in another city.
    f. People who have jobs only done in our community.
5. Discuss why some jobs are only done in our community. Is the job a unique service or product? Is the job dependent on the topography of the community?

Closure and Evaluation. Students will place stick people/surveys in appropriate holding boxes.

SOCIAL STUDIES LESSON PLAN—DAY TWO

Objective. After listening to the book *Going Lobstering* by Jerry Pallotta (Watertown, MA: Charlesbridge, 1990) and discussing where lobsters can be found, the students will draw a map of the United States and place markers where lobsters can be found.

Materials. Jerry Pallotta, *Going Lobstering*; butcher paper with a large lobster drawn on it; markers (different colors); paper for drawing maps (bond); pencils/crayons.

Motivation

1. Review that jobs can be done in many places and others are dependent on the area where they are located.
2. "Today we will read about a job that is dependent on certain locations." Read *Going Lobstering*.

Procedures

1. Discussion. Teacher records the answers on butcher paper. How did the lobsterman do his job? Why do you think the Lobsterman wanted to catch the lobsters? What do you think happened to the lobsters after the Lobsterman returned to shore? Where can lobsters be found? In all water? Only the Pacific?
2. Point out on map(s) in the classroom where lobsters can be found: the New England Coast, the West Coast, and the Alaskan Coast.

Closure and Evaluation. Students will draw a map of the United States and place markers where lobsters can be found (New England Coast, West Coast, and Alaskan Coast).

SOCIAL STUDIES LESSON PLAN—DAY THREE

Objective. After discussion of the Exxon *Valdez* oil spill and the clean-up efforts, students will understand how jobs may change according to environmental issues and then will write a report about the occupational changes of one of the people they surveyed for day one.

Materials. "Alaska's Big Spill: Can the Wilderness Heal?" *National Geographic* 177(1) January 1990; "Off-the-Shelf Bugs Hungrily Gobble our Nastiest Pollutants," *Smithsonian,* April 1993.

Motivation. Students will brainstorm in cooperative groups as many occupations dealing with water as they can. Reminder: Students need to understand that all answers are acceptable in brainstorming sessions.

Procedures

1. Tell the story of the Exxon *Valdez* oil spill and show pictures from *National Geographic.* Emphasize how the spill damaged the environment, caused people to lose their jobs, and the expense of the clean-up efforts.
2. Questions: What do you think happened to the commercial fishermen? Do you think the jobs disappeared forever? Why? How did their jobs change? Do you think any new jobs came about because of the spill?
3. Summarize the *Smithsonian* article.
4. Due to depletion of available lobsters, lobster farming is now being considered as an option.

Closure. Changes do occur in time with jobs, the way people live, the money they use, and so on. Not all changes result as something tragic happening. Some changes are beneficial for all concerned.

Evaluation. Students will choose one of the people from their survey done on day one and write a report about how their job has changed. The reports will be due in one week and will be evaluated per teacher judgment.

SOCIAL STUDIES LESSON PLAN—DAY FOUR

Objective. After playing and discussing the "Buyers and Sellers" game, students will be able to describe availability of a product and it's effect on prices in a supply and demand market.

Materials. Index cards; lobster bucks; construction paper; timer; butcher paper; sticky dots.

Motivation. "Buyer and Seller" game:

1. Each student receives an index card with a different colored dot on it (blue, green, red, or yellow). The card lists round one through round four and gives necessary information for that round of play. (For all four rounds, sellers begin with two lobsters each; round four, the price of the lobsters is twice as high for the inland people than the coast people.)
2. Each student will receive 15 lobster bucks.
3. The sellers will receive 2″ × 3″ construction paper cards representing the lobsters.
4. Buyers want to buy at a low price. Sellers want to sell at a high price. If Sellers do not sell the lobsters, they are charged one lobster buck for storage costs to be paid to the game leader.
5. Round one—Blue and green are buyers. Red and yellow are sellers. Timer is set for three minutes. Students record their own balances of lobsters and lobster bucks.

6. Round two—Red is seller. Blue, green, and yellow are buyers. Timer is set for three minutes. Students record their own balances.
7. Round three—Yellow, blue, and green are sellers. Red is buyer. Timer is set for three minutes. Students record their own balances.
8. Round four—Blue and yellow go to left side of room. Green and red go to right side of room. The two sides may not interact with each other during this round. Blue and green are sellers. Red and yellow are buyers. In this round, buyers should be given an equitable amount of lobster bucks and instructed to buy as many lobsters as they can.

Procedures

1. After the game, students will use sticky dots to chart on butcher paper graphs what happened in each round.
2. Discuss concepts of supply and demand—short supply makes prices increase, little demand makes prices decrease, and availability of supply effects the price.
3. Discuss why the inland people were not able to buy as many as the coast people.

Closure. Have students describe personal experiences with these economic concepts.

SOCIAL STUDIES LESSON PLAN—DAY FIVE

This is a celebration of cultural diversity and regional differences. It is a tasting feast of various recipes. Use of parent volunteers will be needed. Schedule with adult volunteers dishes they can make and bring in for a tasting tour in the classroom. Such dishes could be: Gumbo, Jambalaya, Shrimp Cocktail, Fried Shrimp, etc.

This activity is strictly meant for fun and to give the students real-life experiences with foods from the crustaceans.

Closure. After tasting the dishes, the students should return to their desks and write a critique of the food (as done in a newspaper column) describing the foods they tasted and where they are found (the tasting buffet will need to be clearly labeled), and which they liked the best and why. The columns can then be posted in a classroom newsletter on butcher paper.

Additional Resources

Economic Education: Curriculum Guide K–12, Rev. Ed., Oklahoma State Department of Education, 1983.
Focus on the Social Studies: A Series of Lessons for Elementary Classrooms Grade Three, Los Angeles Unified School District, 1981.
The Crusty Ones, Solveig Paulson Russel, Henry Z. Walk Inc., New York, 1974.
The Nocturnal World of the Lobster, Joseph J. Cook; Dodd, Mead, and Company, New York, 1972.

LANGUAGE ARTS LESSON PLAN—DAY ONE

Objective. After listening to an oral reading of *The Crab Who Played with the Sea: Just So Stories,* by Rudyard Kipling (New York: Bedrick, 1983), and participation in a directed listening and thinking activity (DLTA) (Figure 1), students in small groups will be able to correctly identify what the author was trying to explain in his pourquoi tale with 90 percent accuracy.

	A		B		C
	What We Know		*What We Wonder*		*What We Learned*
	There is a crab in the story. The crab played with the sea. There are one or two men in the story. There is a child in the story. There are other animals in the story. The crab is very large.		What is the crab's name? Why does he play with the sea? Is he a friend of the people? What are the other animals in the picture doing? Who are the people? Is the child in trouble? What is the story trying to explain?		
	After reading to the second part of the story (p. 156 in my book): The story is set in the beginning of time. It is being told to another person (Best Beloved), probably a child. Continue in this fashion until the entire story is read.		(If some questions are left unanswered, continue looking for the answers as the book is read, as well as developing new questions.) What are the animals playing? Will the girl tell where the crab went? Will Pau Amma be in trouble for playing alone?		The crab is named Pau Amma. The animals are playing. The people are the Eldest Magician, a man, and his little daughter. No, the child is not in trouble.

Figure 1.   DLTA model sheet.

Materials. *The Crab Who Played with the Sea,* Rudyard Kipling; chart paper.

Transitional Activities. The students will be doing a science unit on crustaceans concurrently. The lesson will begin a series of lessons on books involving crabs and crustaceans.

Anticipatory Set. Ask the question, "How many of you have heard of the *Jungle Book*? Can anyone tell me who wrote that story?"

Purpose. The purpose of this lesson is to begin a language arts mini-unit using the theme of crustaceans but going further to explore pourquoi tales of other cultures which have involved these creatures.

Procedure

1. After the questions of the anticipatory set, give the students some background about Kipling with special emphasis on the fact that he was born in India and this provides the setting for many of his stories. Introduce the *Just So Stories.* (Information sheet is included.)

2. Begin the activity by having students list information they know about the story from the title and prior knowledge about Kipling and the pictures before the story is read. (See Figure 1.) List this information on the prepared chart paper under the column "What We Know."
3. Go on to ask the students what they want to know about the story. (See Figure 1.) List this information in the form of questions in the "What We Wonder" column.
4. Begin reading the story to the students. Stop at a number of convenient points in the story and ask students if they are able to answer any of the "We Wonder" questions. If they can, put the answers in the "We Learned" column. Continue reading, stopping, and adding to the "Know," "Wonder," and "Learned" columns throughout the story.
5. If at the end of the story there are unanswered questions, discuss whether the students have enough other information to make a guess at what the answer might be. Discuss whether the information from those questions is really important to understanding the story.

Closure Summary. Ask small groups of students (5–6) to discuss and determine what Kipling was trying to explain in his story based on the information gained through our activity.

Follow-Up/Evaluation. Students should, after discussion in their small groups, be able to state what Kipling was trying to explain in his story with 90 percent accuracy. Students will again be exposed to the story in the next lesson where they will work on sequencing of events.

LANGUAGE ARTS LESSON PLAN—DAY TWO

Objective. After listening to the story, *The Crab Who Played with the Sea,* read aloud and brainstorm the important events of the story. Students, in small groups, will put the events of the story in correct sequence with 100 percent accuracy.

Materials. A time-line made with narrow paper or masking tape across one wall or bulletin board (a spiral sequence); *The Crab Who Played with the Sea,* Rudyard Kipling; 12 sentence strips; pocket chart; construction paper for every two to three students.

Transitional Activities. The previous lesson was an introduction to this story. This lesson will go on through the story to sequence the events. Crustaceans will be studied concurrently so the students may relate ideas and concepts from their science curriculum.

Anticipatory Set. Ask for a student volunteer who can remember the *very first* event of the story. Ask for a volunteer who can remember the *very last* event of the story. Ask how many students can remember all the events in between. Tell them to re-read the story just to be sure everyone can remember the event.

Purpose. The purpose of this lesson is to ensure that the students correctly sequence the events of the story as this is very important to the development of this pourquoi tale and our understanding of it.

Procedure

1. Instruct students to listen closely for the order and sequence of events as the story is re-read.
2. After the story is finished, brainstorm with the students the important events of the story. Write them in complete sentences on sentence strips. (Write two sentences on a strip if necessary to describe the event.) After all events have been written, have the students put the strips in correct order on the pocket chart.
3. Arrange students in groups of two to three students. Have each group select an event from the story. The group should then, in their best writing, copy the sentence(s) describing and illustrating their event on their construction paper.
4. When pictures are done have the students help arrange them on the time-line display.

Closure Summary. Have each group read their sentence(s) in unison from the time-line. This will become a quick class retelling of the story.

Follow-Up/Evaluation. Per teacher evaluation, after listening to the story read a second time, students will be able to list the important events of the story and put them in correct order with 100 percent accuracy.

LANGUAGE ARTS LESSON PLAN—DAY THREE

Objective. After listening to the story, *Why the Crab Has No Head: An African Folktale,* by Barbara Knutson (Minneapolis: Carolrhoda, 1987), and brainstorming some characteristics of other crustaceans that might be interesting to explain, students will write original pourquoi tales explaining one of the listed crustacean characteristics with 90 percent of the students following the plot line of problem and resolution.

Materials. *Why the Crab Has No Head,* Barbara Knutson; chart paper; writing paper; drawing paper for each student.

Transitional Activities. Students have been studying crustaceans in science and should now be aware of the different characteristics of lobsters, shrimp, crabs, and crayfish. They will apply this knowledge in writing a pourquoi tale about one of these characteristics. They will also be experiencing a pourquoi tale from another culture, Africa.

Anticipatory Set. Inform students that they will be hearing a pourquoi tale from a different culture. The tale is still about a crab but the story is from Africa instead of India and has a different twist to the plot. Read the story.

Purpose. The purpose of this lesson is to integrate the knowledge that students have gained throughout their study of crustaceans and their understanding of pourquoi tales.

Procedure

1. After reading the story, discuss with the students the problem in the story, the resolution, and what the author was explaining. Discuss how the author made the students understand what he wanted them to know.

2. Have students list some characteristics of lobsters, shrimp, and crayfish, which they might want to explain. Write the students' ideas on chart paper and display the ideas during the rest of the lesson.
3. Have students select one characteristic and write an original pourquoi tale explaining why (or why not) the animal has this characteristic. Be sure to set the criteria for the stories. *The stories must involve a problem for the crustacean and a resolution to the problem.*

Closure Summary. This lesson may be ended the first day or extended to include an edit, rewrite, and final copy.

Closure for one day lesson: Have students share their stories.

Lesson extension for second day: Have students edit and rewrite their stories. They should

1. Be sure the story has a problem and resolution.
2. Correct for capitalization, punctuation, and spelling.
3. Be sure there are no incomplete sentences.

Closure for day two: Ask for volunteers to state the problem in their stories.

Lesson extension for the third day: Students will rewrite their stories in final copy form and illustrate their stories on the paper provided.

Closure for day three: Students will exchange papers within their groups. Each student will present the story they receive to their group.

Follow-Up/Evaluation. Students will write pourquoi tales about crustaceans of their choice using the problem-resolution plot for the three-day plan, which have correct punctuation, spelling, capitalization, and sentence structure with 80 percent accuracy.

LANGUAGE ARTS LESSON PLAN—DAY FOUR OR SIX

Objective. After reading one act of the book *Sign of the Seahorse,* students will, in small groups, complete a chapter frame of the act with 95 percent accuracy.

Materials. *Sign of the Seahorse,* Graeme Base; one to two copies of the eight acts; chapter frames for each group.

Transitional Activities. As students continue to study crustaceans, the class will explore another type of literature, a play written in verse, in which crustaceans play a prominent part by presenting the work as, "A Novel in an Hour."

Anticipatory Set. Explain that today the class will be continuing with the theme of crustaceans. "We have a wonderful book titled, *Sign of the Seahorse.* This book has wonderful pictures. (Show the book.) There is a puzzle in each picture. There is a tiny shrimp hidden in each one." Tell the students they will get a chance to solve the shrimp puzzle a little later.

Purpose. The purpose of this lesson is to continue our theme of crustaceans through a new kind of literature.

Procedure

1. Read the prologue to the story.
2. Explain to the students that they will do the rest of the story as "A Novel in an Hour." Break the students into eight groups. Give each group copies of one of the acts and a chapter frame. Explain to the students that they are to read the act aloud with each student reading a part and then complete the chapter frame. After all groups are done, they will share the chapter frames. Thus the whole class will get to hear the story.
3. Instruct the students that when they are in the group, they must be very quiet and listen carefully so they can successfully complete the chapter frames. Otherwise the class will become too noisy for the students to work.
4. Instruct the students to begin working. It will take them approximately 30 minutes to read and complete the chapter frames. As groups finish their work, give them one to two minutes to locate the shrimp in the picture that goes with their act.
5. When all groups are finished, have them read their frame. As each group reads their frame, have one member come up and show where the shrimp is hidden in the picture for that act.

Closure Summary. Tell the students that we now know the basic story of *Sign of the Seahorse* by just answering some simple questions about each act. Ask students to name the basic elements of the story (main characters, setting, problem, and resolution).

Follow-Up/Evaluation. Students, in small groups, will complete the chapter frame with 95 percent accuracy.

The teacher will not read the epilogue to the students on day one. Instead she will suggest that they really don't know what happened to the Grouper. Teacher will ask students to think of an appropriate punishment for his crime and be ready to share it the next day.

LANGUAGE ARTS LESSON PLAN—DAY FIVE OR SEVEN

Objective. After reading the epilogue and participating in a discussion about writing in verse, students will write a new ending to the story consisting of two or more stanzas of verse.

Materials. Copies of the epilogue of *The Sign of the Seahorse* for each student; chart paper; writing paper for each student; drawing paper for each student.

Transitional Activities. The students will continue to read and experience crustaceans in literature as well as continue their study of text in verse.

Anticipatory Set. The students are to think of an ending to the story where the Grouper receives a punishment that fits the crime. Having some student volunteers share their endings and relate how they feel their punishment fits the crime Grouper committed.

Purpose. The purpose of this lesson is to experience a new style of writing. The students will have a chance to write in verse as opposed to prose.

Procedure

1. After students have shared some of their endings, read, as a class, the epilogue of the book. Ask the students if they think the Grouper's punishment in the story fits his crime. (Answers will vary.)

2. Next, ask the students what is different about the way this story is written. Guide the discussion to the fact that it is written in verse. Have students identify the characteristics of the stanzas. (For example, the first two lines rhyme and the second two lines rhyme. There are four lines to a stanza (define stanza) and seven beats to each line with two syllables to a beat.) Write the characteristics on the chart paper as the students list them.

3. Instruct students that they will be writing new endings to the story. They are to write their endings in the same type of verse the story is written in. Instruct the students that their endings must be a minimum of two stanzas long. Create a word bank of rhyming words the students might want to use.

4. As students write and come up with rhyming pairs, they may add them to the word bank for others to use.

5. As students finish, have them illustrate their endings.

Closure/Summary. When students have finished, ask for volunteers to read their endings. As students read their endings, have the class silently tap out the beats with their two index fingers. Have the class identify the rhyming pairs of one stanza from the endings.

Follow-Up/Evaluation. Students will write an original ending to the story in verse. There will be at least two stanzas, with ending words rhyming in lines one and two and three and four, with 95 percent accuracy. Eighty percent of the students' endings will have seven beats (14 syllables) in each line.

Extensions to *Sign of the Seahorse*

The use of this story may be extended several more days. Some suggestions follow for additional lessons.

1. Have students pick one of the crustaceans they are studying and write a short story, *in verse,* about an escape from a predator, catching a meal, finding a home, or some other problem/solution situation. Use the writing process to edit, rewrite, and turn out a nice final copy. Publish the stories into a class book about "Crusty Adventures." (Be sure to have students illustrate their stories!) As with all lessons where the writing process is used this may turn into a two- to three-day lesson.

2. Have students draw maps of their characters' travels or of a single crustacean's travels from birth to adulthood. Discuss various types of oceanic topography. (See map on the end pages of *Sign of the Seahorse.*)

3. *Sign of the Seahorse* can easily be adapted to a reader's theater. Have students perform one act or several.

4. As a group of students (or the teacher) reads the story, have other students act the story out in mime.

Bibliography

Kipling, Rudyard. *The Crab Who Played with the Sea: Just So Stories.* New York: Alfred A. Knopf, 1992.

Knutson, Barbara. *Why the Crab Has No Head: An African Folktale.* Minneapolis: Carolrhoda Books, 1982.

Base, Graeme. *Sign of the Seahorse.* New York: Harry H. Abrams.

Sterling, Mary Ellen. *Oceans.* Huntington Beach, CA: Teacher Created Materials, 1990.

Other Books of Interest

Hawes, Judy. *Shrimps.* New York: Thomas Y. Crowell, 1966.

Buck, Margaret Waring. *Along the Seashore.* Nashville: Abingdon Press, 1964.

Stephens, William M., and Stephens, Peggy. *Hermit the Crab Lives in a Shell.* New York: Holiday House, 1969.

Arnov, Boris, Jr., and Mindlin, Helen Mather-Smith. *Wonders of the Ocean Zoo.* New York: Dodd, Mead, and Company, 1957.

MATH LESSON PLAN—DAY ONE

Objective. For students to review addition and subtraction in a nontraditional manner.

Time Frame. 20–30 minutes.

Anticipatory Set. Bring in pictures of crayfish, lobsters, crabs, and shrimp. Place them all over the board (or front of room).

Lesson Plan. Explain to students that they are going to review addition and subtraction in a different way. On the board, overhead, or handout have the following information:

Crayfish	*Lobster*	*Crab*	*Shrimp*
2 eyes	2 eyes	2 eyes	2 eyes
5 pairs of legs	5 pairs of legs	5 pairs of legs	5 pairs of legs
2 large claws	2 large claws	2 large claws	
lays 100 eggs	lives 15 years		

Be sure students understand that five pairs of legs is a total of ten legs. Do examples on the board first. Have students come up front and do problems for the class. Once you feel students understand, pass out handout or have problems on board/overhead.

Examples:

1. Crayfish _____ eyes

    Lobster _____ eyes

    Crab _____ eyes

    Shrimp _____ eyes

    Total = _____

2. Total number of eyes from above _____

    Minus the number of your eyes _____

    Total = _____

3. The number of letters in lobster _____

   Minus the number of letters in crab _____

   Total = _____

4. The number of letters in crayfish _____

   Plus the number of letters in shrimp _____

   Total = _____

5. Number of claws on a lobster _____

   Number of claws on a crab _____

   Number of claws on a shrimp _____

   Total = _____

6. Number of consonants in crayfish, lobster, crab, shrimp _____

   Minus number of vowels in crayfish, lobster, crab, shrimp _____

   Total = _____

7. Number of lobster legs _____

   Number of crab legs _____

   Plus the number of shrimp legs _____

   Total = _____

8. Crayfish lays how many eggs _____

   Minus the number of years a lobster lives _____

   Total = _____

9. Number of crayfish legs _____

   Plus the number of your classmates legs _____

   Total = _____

MATH LESSON PLAN—DAY TWO

Objective. For students to practice measurement using standard and nonstandard methods.

Time Frame. 35–40 minutes.

Anticipatory Set. On the board have an outline of two hands side-by-side.

Lesson Plan. Introduce the words *nonstandard measurement.* Explain that students can learn to use nonstandard measurement by using their hands. However, they will also practice using a ruler for standard measurement. Model measurement using both methods for several examples. Students should work in pairs for this activity.

Examples:

1. Suppose that an average size crab is as big as your two hands spread flat, side-by-side (example on board). How wide and tall is the average crab? (Hint: use a rule and measure your partner's hands, then switch.) Total inches = _____ .

2. How long would five crabs be? _____ inches

3. Using your hands, figure out how many crabs could lay flat on your desk. _____ crabs

4. How many crabs tall is your partner? _____ crabs

5. How many inches tall is your partner? _____ inches

6. Estimate how many crabs you think it would take to fill the garbage can. _____ crabs

7. How many crabs could fit in 100 inches? _____ crabs

8. Choose two objects in your classroom to measure in crabs and inches.

   Object 1 _____ crabs   Object 2 _____ crabs
   _____ inches   _____ inches

MATH LESSON PLAN—DAY THREE

Objective. For students to understand information given to them in word problems and then problem solve the mathematical questions.

Time Frame. 30–35 minutes.

Anticipatory Set. Place shades on one of the crustaceans and then tell the students they are all going on an adventure.

Lesson Plan. Do one or two word problems together as a class. Read through the problem and then go back and write the information down or draw the information on the board. It would be good for students to read the problem, while one student draws and records the information at the board. After doing problems on a group, have the students work in small groups or pairs to continue on their own.

   Examples of word problems: Larry Lobster went for a lovely walk on the beach. Larry walked two miles when he met Sally Shrimp. Together they walked five miles. They stopped for a good game of Marco Polo with friends. After the game they headed back with two other friends, Charlie Crayfish and Cindy Crab. They walked two miles and dropped off Sally and then walked another two miles and dropped off Charlie and Cindy. Larry finished the last mile to his house alone.

1. How many miles did Sally walk?
2. How many miles did Charlie walk?
3. How many total miles were walked?
4. How long did they play Marco Polo?

Charlie Crayfish and Cindy Crab met at Charlie's home. They then drove Charlie's dune buggy three miles to the local store. But Charlie forgot his money, so they had to go back and get it. They got back to the store and bought chips and soda for $2.50. They then drove to pick up Sally who lives four miles from the store. Finally they left to get Larry who lives two miles from Sally's house. They all drove to the local bowling alley, which was three miles away.

1. How many miles did they drive from Sally's house to the bowling alley?
2. How many total miles were driven?
3. How much money did they spend at the grocery store?
4. How many miles was it from the store to Sally's house?
5. How many miles was it from the store to Larry's house?

Larry Lobster and Charlie Crayfish decided to play some one-on-one basketball. Within the first three minutes of the game, Larry had scored five baskets and Charlie had made two baskets. However, as the game continued, Charlie made eight baskets in the next five minutes, while Larry only made two baskets. They were in the last five minutes of the game when Larry twisted his claw, but refused to give up.

1. How many baskets were made in the first three minutes?
2. How many baskets were made in the next five minutes?
3. How many baskets were made altogether?
4. How many points were scored in the next five minutes?
5. How many points were scored by Charlie?
6. How many points were scored by Larry?
7. How many points were scored in the entire game?
8. Who do you think won the game? Why?

MATH LESSON PLAN—DAY FOUR

Objective. For students to work with multiplication and money.

Time Frame. 30–35 minutes.

Anticipatory Set. Explain to the students that they are going to spend money at the store. However, the money is only for lobster, crab, and shrimp.

Lesson Plan. On the overhead, board, or handout, have the following information: 1. Lobster $10.00 per pound; 2. crab $5.00 per pound; 3. shrimp $8.00 per pound; 4. crayfish $8.00 per pound. Do examples on the board showing the students how to multiply the money and pounds desired. Also, model how to figure out how many pounds you can get with so much money. After you feel students understand, have them try problems on their own or with a partner.

Examples:
1. How much money would two pounds of lobster cost?
2. How much money would three pounds of crab cost?
3. How much money would four pounds of shrimp cost?
4. How much money would six pounds of crayfish cost?
5. How much money would one pound of lobster plus four pounds of crayfish cost?
6. How much money would two pounds of shrimp plus two pounds of crab cost?

7. If you had $56.00, how many pounds of shrimp could you get?
8. If you had $60.00, how many pounds of lobster could you get?
9. If you had $80.00, what would you buy and how much of it?

MATH LESSON PLAN—DAY FIVE

Objective. To introduce basic fractions to students.

Time Frame. 25–30 minutes.

Anticipatory Set. Draw a set of crabs (pies) on the board, and explain to the students that you will be giving them pieces of the crab. You might also want to have paper figures for the students to use tactilely.

Lesson Plan. Show students on the board basic fractions such as ½ and ¼. Shade in the appropriate amount. If they have manipulatives at their desk, ask them to show you how much ¼, ½, etc., is. Do several examples before they do it on their own, then give the students a handout for them to color fractions of crabs, shrimp, and lobsters. This would be a fun way to wrap up the week.

Glossary

Accommodation The cognitive process of modifying a schema or creating new schemata.

Accountability Reference to the concept that an individual is responsible for his or her behaviors and should be able to demonstrate publicly the worth of the activities carried out.

Advance organizer Preinstructional cues used to enhance retention of materials to be taught.

Affective domain The area of learning related to interests, attitudes, feelings, values, and personal adjustment.

AFT The American Federation of Teachers, a national professional organization of teachers.

Alternative assessment See *authentic assessment.*

Assignment A statement telling the student what he or she is to accomplish.

Assimilation The cognitive process by which a child integrates new information into an existing schema.

At-risk General term given to students who show high potential for dropping out of school.

Authentic assessment Reference to the use of evaluation procedures that are highly compatible with the instructional objectives. Also referred to as *accurate, active, aligned, alternative,* and *direct.*

Behavioral objective A statement describing what the learner should be able to do upon completion of the instruction, and containing four components: the audience (learner), the behavior, the conditions, and the level or degree of performance.

Behaviorism A theory that equates learning with changes in observable behavior.

Brainstorming A teaching strategy used to create a flow of new ideas, during which the judgments of the ideas of others are forbidden.

CD-ROM (compact disc-read only memory) Digitally encoded information permanently recorded on a compact disc.

Classroom control The process of influencing student behavior in the classroom.

Classroom management The teacher's system of establishing a climate for learning, including techniques for preventing and handling student misbehavior.

Clinical supervision In education, a nonevaluative collegial process of facilitating teaching effectiveness by involving a triad of individuals: in teacher education the triad consists of the student teacher, the cooperating teacher, and the college or university supervisor. Clinical supervision (sometimes known as "effective supervision") will involve: (1) a preobservation conference between the supervisor and the student teacher to specify and agree upon the specific objectives for the observation visit; (2) a data collection observation; and (3) a postobservation conference to analyze the data collected during the observation and to set goals for future observations.

Cognitive domain The area of learning related to intellectual skills, such as retention and assimilation of knowledge.

Cognitive psychology A branch of psychology devoted to the study of how individuals acquire, process, and use information.

Cognitivism A theory that holds that learning entails the construction or reshaping of mental schemata and that mental processes mediate learning.

Compact disc (CD) A 4.72-inch disc on which a laser has recorded digital information.

Competency-based instruction See *performance-based instruction.*

Comprehension A level of cognition that refers to the skill of "understanding."

Computer literacy The ability at some level on a continuum to understand and to use computers.

Computer-assisted instruction (CAI) Instruction received by a student when interacting with lessons programmed into a computer system.

Computer-managed instruction (CMI) The use of a computer system to manage information about learner performance and learning-resources options in order to prescribe and control individual lessons.

Concept map A visual or graphic representation of concepts and their relationships. Words related to a key word are written in categories around the key word, and the categories are labeled.

Constructivism See *cognitivism.*

Convergent thinking Thinking that is directed to a preset conclusion.

Cooperative learning A genre of instructional strategies that use small groups of students working together and helping each other on learning tasks, stressing support for one another rather than competition.

Core curriculum Subject or discipline components of the curriculum considered as absolutely necessary. The core components are English/language arts, mathematics, science, and social science.

Covert behavior A learner behavior that is not outwardly observable.

Criterion-referenced Standards are established and behaviors are judged against the preset standards, rather than against behaviors of others.

Criterion A standard by which behavioral performance is judged.

Critical thinking The ability to recognize and identify problems and discrepancies, to propose and to test solutions, and to arrive at tentative conclusions based on the data collected.

Deductive learning Learning that proceeds from the general to the specific. See also *expository learning.*

Diagnostic assessment See *preassessment.*

Direct intervention Teacher use of verbal reminders or verbal commands to redirect student behavior, as opposed to the use of nonverbal gestures or cues.

Discipline In teaching, the process of controlling student behavior in the classroom. A term that has been largely replaced by the terms *classroom control* or *classroom* *management.* The term *discipline* is also used in reference to the subjects taught, e.g., the disciplines of language arts, science, mathematics, and so on.

Discovery learning Learning that proceeds from identification of a problem, through the development of hypotheses and testing of the hypotheses, to the arrival at a conclusion.

Divergent thinking Thinking that expands beyond original thought.

Eclectic Utilizing the best from a variety of sources.

Emergent literacy A child's early experiences—those that begin to shape the child's view of print, reading, and writing in the natural environment of home, school, and neighborhood.

Empathy The ability to understand the feelings of another person.

Equality Considered to be same in status or competency level.

Equity Fairness and justice, that is, with impartiality.

Evaluation The process of judging the value of results by considering evidence in light of present standards.

Exceptional child A child who deviates from the average in any of the following: mental characteristics, sensory ability, neuromotor or physical characteristics, social behavior, communication ability, or in multiple handicaps.

Expository learning The traditional classroom instructional approach that proceeds as follows: presentation of information, reference to particular examples, application of knowledge to the learner's experiences.

Family See *school-within-a-school.*

Feedback In interpersonal communication, information sent from the receiver to the originator that provides disclosure about the reception of the intended message.

Formative evaluation Evaluation of learning in progress.

Goal, course A broad generalized statement describing the expected outcome of the course.

Goal, educational A desired instructional outcome that is broad in scope.

Goal, instructor A statement telling what the instructor hopes to accomplish.

High school A secondary school that houses grades 9–12 or 10–12.

Holistic learning Learning that incorporates emotions with thinking.

House See *school-within-a-school.*

Inclusion Refers to the commitment to the education of each special-needs learner, to the maximum extent appropriate, in the school and classroom she would otherwise attend.[1] See also *mainstreaming.*

Individualized learning The self-paced process whereby individual students assume responsibility for learning through study, practice, feedback, and reinforcement, with appropriately designed instructional packages or modules.

Inductive learning Learning that proceeds from the specifics to the general. See *discovery learning.*

Inquiry learning Like discovery learning, except that the learner designs the processes to be used in resolving a problem, thereby requiring higher levels of cognition than discovery learning.

---

[1]Source: Joy Rogers, "The Inclusion Revolution," *Phi Delta Kappa Research Bulletin* 11 (May 1993), p. 2

Instruction Planned arrangement of experience(s) to help a learner achieve a desirable change in behavior.

Instructional module Any free-standing instructional unit that includes these components: rationale, objectives, pretest, learning activities, comprehension checks, posttest.

Instructional scaffolding See *concept map.*

Integrated language arts A curriculum that translates the whole language approach of learning through authentic reading and writing situations into classroom practices. Students read, write, and talk about what they read, write, and talk about in content units with themes from social studies, science, math, and the arts.

Intermediate grades Grades 4–6.

Internalization The extent to which an attitude or value becomes a part of the learner. Without the learner's having to think about it, his or her behavior reflects the attitude or value.

Intervention The teacher interrupts to redirect a student's behavior, either by direct intervention (e.g., by a verbal command) or by indirect intervention (e.g., by eye contact or physical proximity).

Intuition Knowing without conscious reasoning.

Junior high school A secondary school that houses grades 7–9 or 7–8 and that has a schedule and program or courses that resemble those of the high school more than those of the elementary school.

Lead teacher The member of a teaching team who is designated to facilitate the work and planning of that team.

Learning A change in behavior resulting from experience. See *behaviorism* and *constructivism* for different interpretations of learning.

Learning modality The way a person receives information—visual modality; auditory modality; kinesthetic modality; tactile modality.

Learning style The way a person learns best in a given situation.

Mainstreaming Placing an "exceptional child" in a regular classroom for all or part of the school day. See also *inclusion.*

Mandala A visual geometric pattern that stimulates right-brain functions.

Mastery learning The concept that a student should master the content of one lesson before moving on to the content of the next.

Measurement The process of collecting and interpreting data.

Mentoring One-on-one coaching or guidance.

Metacognition The ability to plan, monitor, and evaluate one's own thinking.

Metalinguistic Thinking about language.

Micro peer teaching Teaching a limited objective for a brief period of time to a group of eight to ten peers, for the purpose of evaluation and improvement of particular teaching skills.

Middle grades Grades 5–8.

Middle school Schools that have been planned and organized especially for students of ages 10 through 14, generally containing grades 5–8; grades 6–8 is the most popular grade-span organization, although many varied patterns exist. For example, a school might include grades 7 and 8 and still be called a middle school.

Misconception Faulty understanding of a major idea or concept.

Multimedia The combined use of sound, video, and graphics for instruction.

Multicultural education A deliberate educational attempt to help students understand facts, generalizations, attitudes, and behaviors derived from their own ethnic roots as well as others. In this process students should unlearn racism and biases and recognize the interdependent fabric of society, giving due acknowledgment to contributions by its members.

Multilevel teaching See *multitasking.*

Multipurpose board A board with a smooth plastic surface used with special marking pens rather than chalk. Sometimes called "a visual aid panel," the board usually has a steel backing and can be used as a magnetic surface as well as a screen for projecting visuals.

Multitasking In teaching, multitasking occurs when several levels of teaching and learning are going on simultaneously in one classroom.

Naive theory See *misconception.*

NEA The National Education Association, the nation's oldest professional organization of teachers, founded in 1857 as the National Teachers Association and changed in 1879 to the National Education Association.

Norm-referenced Individual performance is judged relative to overall performance of the group.

Overlapping The teacher's ability to attend to more than one matter at a time.

Overt behavior A learner behavior that is outwardly observable.

Paraprofessional An adult who is not a credentialed teacher, but works in the classroom with and under the supervision of a credentialed person.

Performance assessment See *authentic assessment.*

Performance objective See *behavioral objective.*

Performance-based instruction Instruction designed around assessing student achievement against specified and predetermined objectives.

Phrenoblysis The term used to refer to brain growth spurts, times of rapid increase in the mass of the brain followed by periods of stabilization or less growth.

Positive reinforcer A means of encouraging desired student behaviors by rewarding those behaviors when they occur.

Preassessment Referring to diagnostic assessment, that is, assessment of what children know or think they know prior to the instruction.

Primary grades Kindergarten through grade 3.

Probationary teacher An untenured teacher. (After a designated number of years teaching in the same district, upon rehire the probationary teacher receives a tenure contract.)

Procedure A statement telling the student how to accomplish a task.

Psychomotor domain The domain of learning that involves locomotor behaviors.

Realia Real objects used as visual props in teaching, such as political campaign buttons, plants, memorabilia, and so on.

Reciprocal teaching A form of collaborative teaching, whereby the teacher and the students share the teaching responsibility and all are involved in asking questions, clarifying, predicting, and summarizing as they read.

Reflective abstraction See *metacognition*.

Reliability In measurement, the consistency with which an item is measured over time.

Schema A mental construct by which the learner organizes his or her perceptions of the environment. Plural: *schemata*.

School-within-a-school Within a school, and sometimes referred to as a "house," or a "family," a plan whereby one team of teachers is assigned to work each day with the same group of about 125 students for a common block of time, or for the entire school day.

Secondary school Traditionally, any school housing students from grades 7 through 12.

Sequencing Arranging ideas in logical order.

Simulation An abstraction or simplification of a real-life situation.

Special-needs students Students who deviate from the average or norm in one or more of the following: mental characteristics; sensory abilities; neuromotor or physical characteristics; social behavior; communication abilities.

SQ3R A study strategy whereby students survey the reading, create questions, read to answer the questions, recite the answers, and review the original material.

SQ4R Similar to SQ3R; the students survey the reading, ask questions about what was read, read to answer the questions, recite the answers, record important items in their notebooks, then review all work.

Student teaching A field-experience component of teacher preparation, usually the culminating experience, in which the teacher candidate practices teaching children under the supervision of a credentialed teacher and a college or university supervisor.

Summative evaluation Evaluation of learning after instruction is completed.

Teacher leader See *lead teacher*.

Teaching style The way teachers teach, their distinctive mannerisms complemented by their choices of teaching behaviors and strategies.

Teaching team A team of two or more teachers who work together to provide instruction to the same group of students, either alternating the instruction or teaching simultaneously as a team.

Team teaching Teachers working together to provide instruction to a group of students.

Tenured teacher After serving a designated number of years in the same school district as a probationary teacher, upon rehire the teacher receives a tenure contract, which means that the teacher is automatically rehired each year thereafter, unless the contract is revoked by either the district or the teacher and for specific and legal reasons.

Terminal behavior That which has been learned as a direct result of instruction.

Think time See *wait-time*.

Validity In measurement, the degree to which an item or instrument measures that which it is intended to measure.

Village See *school-within-a-school*.

Wait-time In the use of questioning, the period of silence between the time a question is asked and point at which the inquirer does something, such as repeats the question, calls on a particular student, answers the question himself or herself, or asks a different question.

Whole language learning A point of view with a focus on seeking or creating meaning that encourages language production, risk taking, independence in producing language, and the use of a wide variety of print materials in authentic reading and writing situations.

Withitness The teacher's ability to timely intervene and redirect potential student misbehavior.

Children's Literature Index

The author's name follows the book title.

Name Index

Adams, A., 439
Adams, D., 539*n*
Adler, M. J., 31
Ahlgren, A., 483
Albert, K., 470
Aldridge, B. G., 202
Aleman, M. P., 118
Allingron, R., 439
Alvarez, M. C., 65*n*
Alvino, J., 224, 306
Amidon, E., 74*n*
Anderson, C. W., 52*n*
Anderson, L., 473
Anderson, R., 434
Appelbaum, S., 469
Applebee, A. N., 31, 435
Armstrong, T., 72*n*
Arnold, M., 281
Ascher, C., 48
Ausubel, D., 54*n*, 65, 333

Baker, L., 439
Baldwin, R. S., 437
Balkcom, S., 338
Banks, C. B., 83*n*
Barbe, W. B., 70*n*
Baron, E. B., 172
Baroody, A., 485
Bates, M., A-1
Baymann, J. F., 436
Bear, T., 142
Beardslee, E. D., 430
Beck, I. L., 485
Behrens, J., 472
Beilin, H., 83*n*
Bennett, W. J., 293
Benntley, J., 470
Bentley, D., 118
Berenson, E., 34
Berliner, D. C., 455
Bernard, R. G., 189
Berquist, W. H., 75*n*
Bertram, J. E., 486*n*
Biemiller, A., 437
Biesty, S., 469, 470
Bjork, C., 473
Black, J., 13
Blendinger, J., 172

Bloom, B. S., 61*n*, 211, 215, 337, 368
Blythe, T., 72*n*
Boling, A. N., 267
Bommeli, C. L., 267
Bond, G. L., 437
Boodt, G. M., 438
Bordeau, L., 83*n*
Borich, G. D., 118*n*, 128
Borkowski, J., 436, 437
Bormouth, J., 193
Boutte, G. S., 48
Bracy, G. W., 32, 48, 72*n*
Brandhorst, T. R., 431
Brandt, R. S., 21, 202
Bransford, J. D., 83*n*, 358
Braten, I., 57*n*
Briggs, L. J., 211, 224
Brobeck, J. K., 48
Bromley, K. D., 440
Brookfield, S. D., 118*n*, 306
Brophy, J. E., 109*n*, 118*n*, 122, 128, 204
Brown, A. L., 439, 486
Brown, L., 11
Brown, P., 470
Browne, D. B., 83*n*
Bruner, J. S., 54*n*, 62*n*, 63–65, 74, 83*n*, 300
Brutlag, D., 267
Bullough, R. V., Jr., 589*n*
Burrett, K., 219
Butzin, S. M., 430
Bybee, R., 202

Caine, G., 58*n*, 59, 69*n*, 83*n*
Caine, R. N., 58*n*, 59, 69*n*, 83*n*
Calfee, R. C., 48
Callahan, J. F., 193
Calmenson, S., 474
Canter, L., 148, 151
Canter, M., 148, 151
Carin, A. A., 62*n*
Carlsen, W. S., 330, 350
Carnegie Council on Adolescent Development, 49
Carns, A. W., 83*n*
Carns, M. R., 83*n*
Carroll, J., 368

Carter, J., 459
Castaneda, A., 73*n*
Castle, S., 589*n*
Cawelti, G., 49*n*, 84*n*, 589*n*
Cecil, N., 68*n*, 69, 83*n*, 202, 467
Chall, J. S., 58*n*, 437
Chapin, J. R., 485
Charles, C. M., 153
Charney, R. S., 172
Cherrington, A., 485
Cho, J., 85*n*, 172
Clark, B. K., 439
Clark, L. H., 193
Claus, C. K., 207
Clinchy, E., 49
Cobb, P., 485
Cochran-Smith, M., 436
Cole, J., 474
Combs, A. W., 74
Commings, R., 472
Conklin, P., 467
Copeland, P. F., 468
Corwin, R. B., 486*n*
Coslick, R. T., 485
Costa, A. L., 66*n*, 66–68, 83*n*, 88*n*, 89*n*, 108*n*, 118*n*, 306, 308, 310, 311, 327, 336, 351
Courtney, J., 470
Crow, N., 389*n*
Csikszentmihalyi, M., 85*n*
Cullinan, B., 397
Cunningham, J. W., 439
Curry, L., 83*n*

D'Allesandro, J., 147
Dale, E., 300
Dalton, D. W., 430
Danielson, K. E., 485
Darling-Hammond, L., 49, 589*n*
Davey, B., 538*n*
Davis, G. L., 430
Dayton, C., 49
de Bono, E., 67*n*
de Larminat, Max-Henri, 472
DeBello, T. C., 83*n*
Debenham, J., 589*n*
Dempster, F. N., 202, 368
Detrick, S., 480

Subject Index